Pretrial Advocacy

Planning, Analysis, and Strategy

Pretrial Advocacy
Planning, Analysis, and Strategy

MARILYN J. BERGER

Associate Professor of Law
University of Puget Sound
School of Law

JOHN B. MITCHELL

Scholar in Residence
University of Puget Sound
School of Law

RONALD H. CLARK

Adjunct Professor of Law
University of Puget Sound
School of Law
and
Chief Deputy Prosecutor
King County, Washington

LITTLE, BROWN AND COMPANY
Boston   Toronto

Library of Congress Catalog Card No. 87-83339
ISBN 0-316-09162-6

MV

Published simultaneously in Canada
by Little, Brown & Company (Canada) Limited

Printed in the United States of America

This is the last word. . . . Oh wait a minute. I just have one more thing to write. . . . It will just be a minute. . . . What? Fifteen minutes already? Give me a few more minutes. Why don't you go ahead to the park and I will meet you.

What? Back from the park already? It's dinnertime? Just give me a few more minutes. I'm almost finished.

This is it. We are done.

Summary of Contents

Contents

II

Case Theory　17

III

Fact Investigation   53

IV

Client Interviewing   67

V

Witness Interviewing   99

VI

Pleading   **151**

VII

Discovery **189**

VIII
Pretrial Motions   251

IX

Counseling   343

X

Negotiation **385**

XI

Alternative Dispute Resolution   **445**

Pretrial Case Files   **453**

Acknowledgments

This book was made possible by the University of Puget Sound School of Law, both through its commitment to improving legal education and the quality of legal practice, and its consistent generosity in providing financial support for this book through research grants, research assistants, and administrative services. In particular, we acknowledge Fredric C. Tausend, former Dean of the law school, who nurtured and encouraged us in the belief that by "letting a thousand flowers bloom at least one bouquet will be produced." Also, we express our gratitude to the faculty in the law school's comprehensive advocacy program who encouraged us and made many helpful suggestions through the seemingly never-ending drafts and changes: Honorable Rosanne Buckner, Daryl Graves, Marilyn Mauer-Wahlberg, Katrina Pflaumer, Thomas Richardson, and Michael Riggio.

Our thanks to the following University of Puget Sound law students who served as research assistants and proved themselves creative geniuses, assisting us in inventing and breathing life into the numerous State of Major witnesses and mock cases: Margaret Bichl, Gary Boe, Joe Brusic, Andrew Gala, Stephen Hansen, Randall Keyes, Monique Leahy, Robert Lyons, Fran Reichert, and Robert A. Wright. In particular, our gratitude turns to awe when we think about the contributions of Margaret Bichl. With creative wit, artistic style, and computer program in hand, she single-handedly made the jurisdiction of Major come alive with the documents and forms that are the heart of the pretrial case files.

Student photographers who entered into the spirit of capturing our fictitious characters and who brought credence to the State of Major likewise deserve our heartfelt thank-yous: Vince and Wayne Watson; Regina Warren; and Laurie Jones and Tim Guy, video consultants. And we thank those who served as models, making the Summers family more real than we could imagine: Dorian Seawind Berger, Thomas Deming, Jeannie Muckelstone, and Sarah Wescott. Special thanks too to Al Sillstrom, former owner of the Unicorn Tavern, and to Don Waddell, the Unicorn's present owner.

Many experts and academic colleagues willingly met with us and shared their knowledge—trial lawyers, economics professors, law enforcement officials, and others. We thank them all, with special appreciation to John Hoglund, trial lawyer; Bruce Mann, Professor of Economics at the University of Puget Sound; and Jenifer Schramm, Clinical Professor of Law.

Richard Heuser of Little, Brown deserves a special word of appreciation for his vision that made this book better in every respect, and especially for his constant encouragement that every beginning has an end. In addition, a special bravo to Little, Brown manuscript editor Richard Audet, who courageously battled with brackets, semi-colons, and superfluous text, and to our own editorial and manuscript assistant, Hanna Atkins, who made sense of our musings.

We would also like to express our great appreciation to Delilah Johnson for the many thousands of pages of each draft that passed through her copy center.

There remains only the pleasant duty of expressing our appreciation to our legal secretaries, Teri Taylor and Valerie Youngs, for their hard work and persistent good humor as they typed seemingly endless drafts, each with pages covered with microscopic scribbles that purported to be products of our latest round of "final insights." And thanks too to Robin Gwinn for her editorial and typing assistance on the Witness Guide and to everyone else who was there typing when the need arose—Nancy Ammons, Denise Barnett, Laura Brock, Lori Mamone, and Dee Wakefield. Why they didn't throw up their hands and walk out on us we'll never know. But we're glad they didn't. Without them, there wouldn't be any book.

Introduction

This book is intended to provide you with the experience of being a practicing attorney engaged in pretrial activities. Through a series of criminal and civil problems as well as a supportive commentary and case file, the book presents an approach to thinking about, planning, and performing detailed and realistic problems that simulate a wide range of pretrial practice situations and foster the kinds of analytic processes needed to solve these problems.

A discussion of our theory and approach to lawyering in an adversary system is reserved for Chapter I; the object of this introduction is to provide you with a basic understanding of how the book is structured and its intended use.

A. STRUCTURE

This book is divided into eleven chapters. Each chapter covers a separate pretrial subject area—for example, witness interviews, discovery, negotiation—and is composed of text and problems. In each chapter the text, or authors' commentary, elaborates a theoretical approach to the particular pretrial skill that is the subject of that chapter, provides a demonstration of that approach as applied to a hypothetical situation, and offers a series of practical and strategic pointers in the subject area. The examples that we provide in the text are intended to be just that—examples. They are not meant to be exhaustive, but are merely intended to illustrate the point in question. Where possible, the text also includes references to sources that may be of help to you.

In most chapters the text concludes with a series of *general planning questions*. These questions are intended as broad checklists that you may consult when

planning to employ the pretrial skills that are the subject of that chapter.

Following the text and planning questions are both criminal and civil problems. Each problem simulates a different adversarial practice situation (plaintiff's interview with a neutral witness, defendant's interview with an expert witness, defendant making a motion to compel discovery, plaintiff responding to a motion to compel discovery). Most of the problems are based upon a single, but complex, fact pattern that manifests itself in two fictitious cases—a criminal case, *State v. Hard,* and a civil case, *Summers v. Hard.* There are some problems, however, particularly those in the chapter on negotiation, that are totally independent of these principal cases, although they do involve many of the same witnesses as the *Summers v. Hard* case.

The "role" or perspective you assume may shift from one problem assignment to another. Thus in the civil case, your entire approach to a particular problem may vary depending on whether you are a defendant's privately retained attorney or an attorney representing a defendant's insurance company. Again, in *Summers v. Hard* you may be expected in some problems to adopt the perspective of an attorney who is not a counsel in the principal case at all—for example, an attorney who is representing one of the plaintiffs of *Summers v. Hard* in a child custody dispute. Your instructor will clarify each of these roles—and your connection to them—as they appear. Each problem contains a preparation section that refers to the background reading you must do in order to work through the problem. Usually, this reading will include the text from one or more chapters and materials from the case file. There are also references to rules of evidence, civil procedure, and criminal procedure.

Each problem finally offers a series of questions. These questions take you through the planning process that an attorney would use to deal with the situation that is the subject of the problem. ("What information do you want from this witness? Why? What if she tells you that she already gave a statement to the police and doesn't want to discuss the matter any further?") As in practice, these questions include issues of legal interpretation, tactics, factual evaluation, judgment, and ethical matters arising from the particular situation. These questions differ from the general planning questions at the end of the text because they are specifically directed at issues in a given problem. These problem questions thus are intended to alert you to particular areas you might want to think about in your planning and preparation for that problem.

Each problem concludes with a choice of assignments. The choices generally are organized within three categories: (1) pre-class planning and preparation, (2) in-class performance, and (3) post-class analysis. Depending on the problem, the actual choices within these categories may include planning a performance; actually doing a particular pretrial performance (interviewing the client, arguing a motion, negotiating a settlement); writing motions or memos; or drafting a legal document. For each problem, your instructor will choose one or more of the available assignments for you to do.

At the back of the book are the criminal and civil case files for *State v. Hard* and *Summers v. Hard.* These files provide the factual and legal details for the problems. The files include diagrams, documents, expert reports, jury instructions, pleadings, research memoranda, statutes, and witness statements. The research memoranda are a special feature. The memoranda are composed of fictional cases from our fictional jurisdiction, the State of Major. The memos provide all the research you need to deal with the multitude of legal issues in the problems. (Of course, your instructor may prefer that you instead research and use appropriate real cases from your jurisdiction.) The pages in the case file are perforated. This allows you to remove any one element or "Entry" so you can easily work with a document when going through the problems or readily use a document in a classroom simulation (e.g., have a witness mark a diagram during an interview).

Witness Guide: The simulated pretrial skills performances generally involve role-play. Someone in the class must play the client who is being counseled, or the expert economist who is interviewed, or the custodian of records whose deposition is being taken. In order to make these simulations as realistic as possible, your instructor has been provided with a witness guide that contains for distribution all the information each actor requires to make his or her performance realistic—"memorable" background materials detailing the particular witness's personal history, information about the witness's knowledge of the case, and instructions for how the witness is to behave and respond during the particular assignment. Additionally, the witness guide contains confidential instructions that at times will be given to the students who are playing the attorneys (e.g., during negotiation exercises).

B. METHODOLOGY

The book offers a choice of one or more of six learning methodologies from which your instructor will choose:

Reading: The text provides a wealth of information about each skills performance ranging from theory to practice, including illustrations of any given approach so you can understand how the ideas are applied in practice. All of this information will assist you in working through the corresponding problems. The occasional references to other authors' work in the field give you the opportunity for further reading that can broaden your appreciation and understanding of the area.

Planning: The general planning questions and the specific problem questions take you through a planning process that is representative of one an attorney might go through in order to fully and competently prepare for the particular pretrial skills performance. Notice the open space provided on the right side of each page in the problem sections. The open space gives you room to jot down notes and ideas in response to the individual problem questions. Your note-taking will not only provide a handy review of your ideas and assist in your class work, but act as a critical beginning in the process of deepening and clarifying your thoughts for your formal writing exercises. The uninterrupted columns of questions, on the other hand, permit you to view these questions for what they are—not fragmented inquiries, but "patterns" of thinking, many of which recur in various forms and contexts throughout the book. Further, exercises that require you to explain to the instructor how you have planned a particular performance, as well as the planning you inevitably will do for an actual class performance, also provide opportunities for you to learn through planning. In doing so, you will also learn *about* planning. Thus, you may well spend as much time learning how to *think about* witness interviewing, as you will spend actually performing one (although, as you now no doubt sense, the two are totally interdependent).

Explaining and Discussing: As just described, many of the exercises provide opportunities for you to explain a particular plan to your instructor, orally or in a short memo, *before* you begin a performance. Upon completion of the performance, some exercises also require you to explain decisions you would *then* make: Would you use the expert you just interviewed at trial? What investigation will you do next? The problem questions and text, moreover, provide sources for classroom discussions on a range of issues.

Performing: The problems provide the opportunity to learn through simulated performances (interviewing, counseling, arguing motions). The experience of role-playing a witness, or just observing the role-play of fellow law students, will also give valuable insights into the factors that constitute competent attorney performance.

Writing: In addition to the spaces provided for you to write notes and ideas in response to the problem questions, the problem assignments offer a variety of writing opportunities, from planning memos and discovery motions to pleadings and declarations for Constitution-based pretrial motions. As such, many of these involve developing the type of legal analysis you have perfected in law school, translating that analysis into an adversary perspective, and then communicating your position by persuasive writing to the appropriate audience.

Critiquing: Following your performances, you will gain a great deal from the critique of your work by your instructor, and perhaps from fellow class members as well. Furthermore, even as a non-performing class member, learning by example how to critique and what to critique will greatly enhance your ability to evaluate, and thereby improve, your own subsequent planning and performances.

C. YOUR RESPONSIBILITIES

As a class member or as an "attorney" assigned to conduct a particular performance, your own good sense and the directions of your instructor will make your responsibilities clear. Your responsibilities when role-playing a witness, however, are a different matter. The quality of your effort in preparation, and in the subsequent performance of your roles, can make or break the class. Effort put into your role-playing can make an interview come alive by challenging the

planning and performance skills of the student who is playing the attorney. Lack of effort and enthusiasm can result in an unrealistic, fragmented, boring shambles.

As a witness, you have two responsibilities:

1. Preparation. You should prepare for your witness performance by reviewing the assigned problem and readings, the confidential witness information, the pretrial casefile documents listed for the problem for which you are playing the role of a witness, special documents provided by your instructor, and any specific witness instructions for the assigned problem. Be certain to bring to class all your witness information.

2. Innovation. Although we have tried to make the materials as complete as possible, there may be circumstances in which the factual materials furnished to you are insufficient. Therefore, you will have to be somewhat innovative at times. If you are asked questions on matters not covered by the facts you have been furnished, you may add any facts that are consistent with these facts. You may also add details that provide color and reality to your character. You should not add a fact, however, that would be so important that it would determine the outcome of the lawsuit. If in doubt, ask your instructor.

Depending on the actual selection and sequence and performance of the problems in your class, you may encounter gaps in information or may fail to make the acquaintance of some of the witnesses who figure in the principal cases. It has been our experience that such potential gaps in information should not seriously impair your case preparation. If the gaps do present any difficulties, however, consult your instructor.

D. RULES OF THE GAME

1. Jurisdiction; the law; rules of evidence, criminal, and civil procedure; professional rules of responsibility. The two fictitious cases take place in the jurisdiction of the State of Major. The specific setting encompasses the adjoining counties of Jamner and Neva. Jamner and Ruston are cities within the County of Jamner; Neva City is the main city in Neva County. This jurisdiction was chosen for a number of reasons. Its laws reflect, although they are probably not identical with, current law on the various issues raised in this book. Opinions in the jurisdiction of Major are short and to the point, replacing what would be hundreds of pages in other jurisdictions with a small fraction of that volume. The opinions, nevertheless, require careful reading and interpretation. Thus, they provide a good foundation for a series of assignments whose purpose is to teach you how to think about a body of law in an active adversary context, rather than to teach you substantive criminal and civil procedure and doctrine. Do not do *any* outside research unless your instructor tells you to.

The State of Major court rules and rules of criminal and civil procedure are in most instances identical to the Federal Rules of Civil Procedure and the Federal Rules of Criminal Procedure. The Major Evidence Code is identical to the Federal Rules of Evidence. The standards of professional responsibility in the State of Major are based on an amalgam of ABA-inspired texts. Although reflective of thoughts and trends in the area, these ethical standards are not intended to represent any particular jurisdiction at this time. Rather, the rules are merely intended to provide a legal structure against which you can analyze both the particular ethical situations in the problems and evaluate inherent limitations of any code for guiding decisions of professional responsibility. Of course, your instructor may instead ask you to deal with the ethical situations under the current professional responsibility rules in your jurisdiction.

2. Dates: The fictitious incidents take place in the following years—

198X–   Years prior to a central incident
         (198X–2 is two years prior)

198X   Year of the incident (if you like, you
         can fill in the current year)

198X+   Years subsequent to the incident
         (198X+2 is two years later)

3. The civil case and the Fifth Amendment: Whenever you deal with the civil case of *Summers v. Hard,* you should assume that the criminal case has been disposed of in such a manner that the main character, Ed Hard, cannot legitimately resist answering in the civil case by claiming that he will incriminate himself.

E. CONCLUSION

We have just discussed the "rules of the game" for this book, because it *is* a game. No clients will go to prison for life. No one will lose a home or business or be denied access to his or her children. So play, because, ironically, the more you play, the better you will do. But work hard at your play. Your clients are awaiting you in the next few years, and they are completely and totally dependent on you and on your having learned your lessons well.

We hope you enjoy using this book and living with the characters as much as we enjoyed creating it.

Pretrial Advocacy

Planning, Analysis, and Strategy

I
Overview of Pretrial Advocacy

A. INTRODUCTION

In this overview we explain our approach to pretrial and trial practice. In offering our approach, our sole goal is to present you with a systematic way of acquiring a set of professional skills. You will not acquire an attitude, a philosophy, or a methodology for living your life but, simply, a set of skills. Within the professional work arena, these skills potentially can be used for good or ill; accordingly, we presuppose that these skills are being entrusted to those possessed of common sense, perspective, and fundamental human values.

Moreover, in providing this approach to practice, we are mindful of, and in fact embrace, the emerging vision of the attorney as a facilitator rather than a combatant. In light of this, we have included extensive problem sections covering negotiation and counseling, as well as some alternative dispute resolution problems. Yet we also believe that only with a thorough understanding of advocacy in litigation can one appreciate the opportunities and possibilities for alternative methods of dispute resolution. More broadly, whatever vision one might have for the future of the legal profession, that vision must accept as its starting point an attorney who functions as an advocate for a client. That relationship is, after all, at the core of both the theory and reality of our present legal profession.

One or two qualifications are immediately required. Initially, we do not claim that our approach is the only credible one; it is simply one we believe is helpful for reasons that are discussed in some detail later in this overview. Undoubtedly, the ideas of many excellent lawyers would differ from our own in some respects. We do believe, however, that were we to get down to basics, the points of disagreement between us and these attorneys would be few. We would also affirm that the approach offered here does not exist in a vacuum. Accordingly, we discuss the "world" the lawyer inhabits before we delve into this book's approach to acquiring the lawyer's professional skills.

B. THE LAWYER'S WORLD

Our approach to pretrial and trial practice is intended to exist and function in a world where the attorney must deal with human relationships, money and time constraints, ethical responsibilities, and an institutional process that "moves in time."

1. Human Relationships

As an attorney you will be dealing constantly with people, and no approach to practice can ultimately be effective unless you appreciate the full significance of this fact. Your clients may be shy, arrogant, or overtrusting; witnesses may be friendly, hostile, or just unwilling to get involved; opposing attorneys or co-counsel can be pleasant, rude, or even intimidating; judges and court personnel kind and helpful, or cold and indifferent; and jurors will run the spectrum. Whatever the mix of characters and temperaments,

you will have to be able to deal with them all: work closely with some, obtain the cooperation of others, gain the respect of one, find a way to relate to the next.

2. Resource Constraints

Your clients will almost never have a blank check to give you for work on a case. They simply cannot afford the fantasy case where you take every conceivable deposition, research every imaginable legal point as if you were preparing a brief for the Supreme Court, fly witnesses in from Europe, and so on. You may not be given resources to hire private investigators to conduct an investigation, so you and your law clerk may have to do the sleuthing. Similarly, you may not be given resources to hire an expensive expert, so some low-fee local expert or a volunteer interested in the issue may have to be located. Moreover, even if the client has the money to spend, the case simply may not be worth the outlay. Running up $10,000 costs and fees in a $1,500 dispute would quickly bring your sense of judgment into question.

Furthermore, time is itself a resource, unrelated to its price per hour. You only have so much time to devote to a given case. No matter how many hours of your time a client can pay for, you will have other cases and clients. And you will have a life to live, too. You thus have to continually prioritize the allocation of your time among tasks within a single case, among your various cases and clients, and among your personal needs.

Accordingly, when you look at sections of the text such as those covering witness interviews and discovery, read our approach within the context of the realities of the economic and time constraints you are almost certain to face.

3. Ethical Responsibilities

One way to get a sense of the nature and scope of your ethical responsibilities is to comprehend some of the reasons why you have such responsibilities.

You represent a client who usually neither fully comprehends, nor can dispassionately deal with, the legal process. As such, your client is often totally dependent on you for help with his or her problem. Your client thus may be entrusting his future fortunes, his family, or even his life to you. Such *dependence* in itself demands from the attorney an ethical awareness.

In representing this person, however, you must also

Pretrial Advocacy

Planning, Analysis, and Strategy

Pretrial Advocacy
Planning, Analysis, and Strategy

MARILYN J. BERGER
Associate Professor of Law
University of Puget Sound
School of Law

JOHN B. MITCHELL
Scholar in Residence
University of Puget Sound
School of Law

RONALD H. CLARK
Adjunct Professor of Law
University of Puget Sound
School of Law
and
Chief Deputy Prosecutor
King County, Washington

LITTLE, BROWN AND COMPANY
Boston   Toronto

Library of Congress Catalog Card No. 87-83339
ISBN 0-316-09162-6

MV

Published simultaneously in Canada
by Little, Brown & Company (Canada) Limited

Printed in the United States of America

TO OUR FAMILIES
Albert and Dorian
Eva, David, and Sarah
Nancy, Brady, Clancy, and Colby

This is the last word. . . . Oh wait a minute. I just have one more thing to write. . . . It will just be a minute. . . . What? Fifteen minutes already? Give me a few more minutes. Why don't you go ahead to the park and I will meet you.

What? Back from the park already? It's dinnertime? Just give me a few more minutes. I'm almost finished.

This is it. We are done.

Summary of Contents

Contents

I

Overview of Pretrial Advocacy   1

II

Case Theory   17

III
Fact Investigation   53

IV
Client Interviewing   67

V

Witness Interviewing   99

VI

Pleading   **151**

VII

Discovery **189**

VIII
Pretrial Motions   251

IX

Counseling   343

X

Negotiation   **385**

XI

Alternative Dispute Resolution   445

Pretrial Case Files   453

Acknowledgments

This book was made possible by the University of Puget Sound School of Law, both through its commitment to improving legal education and the quality of legal practice, and its consistent generosity in providing financial support for this book through research grants, research assistants, and administrative services. In particular, we acknowledge Fredric C. Tausend, former Dean of the law school, who nurtured and encouraged us in the belief that by "letting a thousand flowers bloom at least one bouquet will be produced." Also, we express our gratitude to the faculty in the law school's comprehensive advocacy program who encouraged us and made many helpful suggestions through the seemingly never-ending drafts and changes: Honorable Rosanne Buckner, Daryl Graves, Marilyn Mauer-Wahlberg, Katrina Pflaumer, Thomas Richardson, and Michael Riggio.

Our thanks to the following University of Puget Sound law students who served as research assistants and proved themselves creative geniuses, assisting us in inventing and breathing life into the numerous State of Major witnesses and mock cases: Margaret Bichl, Gary Boe, Joe Brusic, Andrew Gala, Stephen Hansen, Randall Keyes, Monique Leahy, Robert Lyons, Fran Reichert, and Robert A. Wright. In particular, our gratitude turns to awe when we think about the contributions of Margaret Bichl. With creative wit, artistic style, and computer program in hand, she single-handedly made the jurisdiction of Major come alive with the documents and forms that are the heart of the pretrial case files.

Student photographers who entered into the spirit of capturing our fictitious characters and who brought credence to the State of Major likewise deserve our heartfelt thank-yous: Vince and Wayne Watson; Regina Warren; and Laurie Jones and Tim Guy, video consultants. And we thank those who served as models, making the Summers family more real than we could imagine: Dorian Seawind Berger, Thomas Deming, Jeannie Muckelstone, and Sarah Wescott. Special thanks too to Al Sillstrom, former owner of the Unicorn Tavern, and to Don Waddell, the Unicorn's present owner.

Many experts and academic colleagues willingly met with us and shared their knowledge—trial lawyers, economics professors, law enforcement officials, and others. We thank them all, with special appreciation to John Hoglund, trial lawyer; Bruce Mann, Professor of Economics at the University of Puget Sound; and Jenifer Schramm, Clinical Professor of Law.

Richard Heuser of Little, Brown deserves a special word of appreciation for his vision that made this book better in every respect, and especially for his constant encouragement that every beginning has an end. In addition, a special bravo to Little, Brown manuscript editor Richard Audet, who courageously battled with brackets, semi-colons, and superfluous text, and to our own editorial and manuscript assistant, Hanna Atkins, who made sense of our musings.

We would also like to express our great appreciation to Delilah Johnson for the many thousands of pages of each draft that passed through her copy center.

There remains only the pleasant duty of expressing our appreciation to our legal secretaries, Teri Taylor and Valerie Youngs, for their hard work and persistent good humor as they typed seemingly endless drafts, each with pages covered with microscopic scribbles that purported to be products of our latest round of "final insights." And thanks too to Robin Gwinn for her editorial and typing assistance on the Witness Guide and to everyone else who was there typing when the need arose—Nancy Ammons, Denise Barnett, Laura Brock, Lori Mamone, and Dee Wakefield. Why they didn't throw up their hands and walk out on us we'll never know. But we're glad they didn't. Without them, there wouldn't be any book.

Introduction

This book is intended to provide you with the experience of being a practicing attorney engaged in pretrial activities. Through a series of criminal and civil problems as well as a supportive commentary and case file, the book presents an approach to thinking about, planning, and performing detailed and realistic problems that simulate a wide range of pretrial practice situations and foster the kinds of analytic processes needed to solve these problems.

A discussion of our theory and approach to lawyering in an adversary system is reserved for Chapter I; the object of this introduction is to provide you with a basic understanding of how the book is structured and its intended use.

A. STRUCTURE

This book is divided into eleven chapters. Each chapter covers a separate pretrial subject area—for example, witness interviews, discovery, negotiation—and is composed of text and problems. In each chapter the text, or authors' commentary, elaborates a theoretical approach to the particular pretrial skill that is the subject of that chapter, provides a demonstration of that approach as applied to a hypothetical situation, and offers a series of practical and strategic pointers in the subject area. The examples that we provide in the text are intended to be just that—examples. They are not meant to be exhaustive, but are merely intended to illustrate the point in question. Where possible, the text also includes references to sources that may be of help to you.

In most chapters the text concludes with a series of *general planning questions*. These questions are intended as broad checklists that you may consult when

planning to employ the pretrial skills that are the subject of that chapter.

Following the text and planning questions are both criminal and civil problems. Each problem simulates a different adversarial practice situation (plaintiff's interview with a neutral witness, defendant's interview with an expert witness, defendant making a motion to compel discovery, plaintiff responding to a motion to compel discovery). Most of the problems are based upon a single, but complex, fact pattern that manifests itself in two fictitious cases—a criminal case, *State v. Hard*, and a civil case, *Summers v. Hard*. There are some problems, however, particularly those in the chapter on negotiation, that are totally independent of these principal cases, although they do involve many of the same witnesses as the *Summers v. Hard* case.

The "role" or perspective you assume may shift from one problem assignment to another. Thus in the civil case, your entire approach to a particular problem may vary depending on whether you are a defendant's privately retained attorney or an attorney representing a defendant's insurance company. Again, in *Summers v. Hard* you may be expected in some problems to adopt the perspective of an attorney who is not a counsel in the principal case at all—for example, an attorney who is representing one of the plaintiffs of *Summers v. Hard* in a child custody dispute. Your instructor will clarify each of these roles—and your connection to them—as they appear. Each problem contains a preparation section that refers to the background reading you must do in order to work through the problem. Usually, this reading will include the text from one or more chapters and materials from the case file. There are also references to rules of evidence, civil procedure, and criminal procedure.

Each problem finally offers a series of questions. These questions take you through the planning process that an attorney would use to deal with the situation that is the subject of the problem. ("What information do you want from this witness? Why? What if she tells you that she already gave a statement to the police and doesn't want to discuss the matter any further?") As in practice, these questions include issues of legal interpretation, tactics, factual evaluation, judgment, and ethical matters arising from the particular situation. These questions differ from the general planning questions at the end of the text because they are specifically directed at issues in a given problem. These problem questions thus are intended to alert you to particular areas you might want to think about in your planning and preparation for that problem.

Each problem concludes with a choice of assignments. The choices generally are organized within three categories: (1) pre-class planning and preparation, (2) in-class performance, and (3) post-class analysis. Depending on the problem, the actual choices within these categories may include planning a performance; actually doing a particular pretrial performance (interviewing the client, arguing a motion, negotiating a settlement); writing motions or memos; or drafting a legal document. For each problem, your instructor will choose one or more of the available assignments for you to do.

At the back of the book are the criminal and civil case files for *State v. Hard* and *Summers v. Hard*. These files provide the factual and legal details for the problems. The files include diagrams, documents, expert reports, jury instructions, pleadings, research memoranda, statutes, and witness statements. The research memoranda are a special feature. The memoranda are composed of fictional cases from our fictional jurisdiction, the State of Major. The memos provide all the research you need to deal with the multitude of legal issues in the problems. (Of course, your instructor may prefer that you instead research and use appropriate real cases from your jurisdiction.) The pages in the case file are perforated. This allows you to remove any one element or "Entry" so you can easily work with a document when going through the problems or readily use a document in a classroom simulation (e.g., have a witness mark a diagram during an interview).

Witness Guide: The simulated pretrial skills performances generally involve role-play. Someone in the class must play the client who is being counseled, or the expert economist who is interviewed, or the custodian of records whose deposition is being taken. In order to make these simulations as realistic as possible, your instructor has been provided with a witness guide that contains for distribution all the informa-

tion each actor requires to make his or her performance realistic—"memorable" background materials detailing the particular witness's personal history, information about the witness's knowledge of the case, and instructions for how the witness is to behave and respond during the particular assignment. Additionally, the witness guide contains confidential instructions that at times will be given to the students who are playing the attorneys (e.g., during negotiation exercises).

B. METHODOLOGY

The book offers a choice of one or more of six learning methodologies from which your instructor will choose:

Reading: The text provides a wealth of information about each skills performance ranging from theory to practice, including illustrations of any given approach so you can understand how the ideas are applied in practice. All of this information will assist you in working through the corresponding problems. The occasional references to other authors' work in the field give you the opportunity for further reading that can broaden your appreciation and understanding of the area.

Planning: The general planning questions and the specific problem questions take you through a planning process that is representative of one an attorney might go through in order to fully and competently prepare for the particular pretrial skills performance. Notice the open space provided on the right side of each page in the problem sections. The open space gives you room to jot down notes and ideas in response to the individual problem questions. Your note-taking will not only provide a handy review of your ideas and assist in your class work, but act as a critical beginning in the process of deepening and clarifying your thoughts for your formal writing exercises. The uninterrupted columns of questions, on the other hand, permit you to view these questions for what they are—not fragmented inquiries, but "patterns" of thinking, many of which recur in various forms and contexts throughout the book. Further, exercises that require you to explain to the instructor how you have planned a particular performance, as well as the planning you inevitably will do for an actual class performance, also provide opportunities for you to learn through planning. In doing so, you will also learn *about* planning. Thus, you may well spend as much time learning how to *think about* witness interviewing, as you will spend actually performing one (although, as you now no doubt sense, the two are totally interdependent).

Explaining and Discussing: As just described, many of the exercises provide opportunities for you to explain a particular plan to your instructor, orally or in a short memo, *before* you begin a performance. Upon completion of the performance, some exercises also require you to explain decisions you would *then* make: Would you use the expert you just interviewed at trial? What investigation will you do next? The problem questions and text, moreover, provide sources for classroom discussions on a range of issues.

Performing: The problems provide the opportunity to learn through simulated performances (interviewing, counseling, arguing motions). The experience of role-playing a witness, or just observing the role-play of fellow law students, will also give valuable insights into the factors that constitute competent attorney performance.

Writing: In addition to the spaces provided for you to write notes and ideas in response to the problem questions, the problem assignments offer a variety of writing opportunities, from planning memos and discovery motions to pleadings and declarations for Constitution-based pretrial motions. As such, many of these involve developing the type of legal analysis you have perfected in law school, translating that analysis into an adversary perspective, and then communicating your position by persuasive writing to the appropriate audience.

Critiquing: Following your performances, you will gain a great deal from the critique of your work by your instructor, and perhaps from fellow class members as well. Furthermore, even as a non-performing class member, learning by example how to critique and what to critique will greatly enhance your ability to evaluate, and thereby improve, your own subsequent planning and performances.

C. YOUR RESPONSIBILITIES

As a class member or as an "attorney" assigned to conduct a particular performance, your own good sense and the directions of your instructor will make your responsibilities clear. Your responsibilities when role-playing a witness, however, are a different matter. The quality of your effort in preparation, and in the subsequent performance of your roles, can make or break the class. Effort put into your role-playing can make an interview come alive by challenging the

planning and performance skills of the student who is playing the attorney. Lack of effort and enthusiasm can result in an unrealistic, fragmented, boring shambles.

As a witness, you have two responsibilities:

1. Preparation. You should prepare for your witness performance by reviewing the assigned problem and readings, the confidential witness information, the pretrial casefile documents listed for the problem for which you are playing the role of a witness, special documents provided by your instructor, and any specific witness instructions for the assigned problem. Be certain to bring to class all your witness information.

2. Innovation. Although we have tried to make the materials as complete as possible, there may be circumstances in which the factual materials furnished to you are insufficient. Therefore, you will have to be somewhat innovative at times. If you are asked questions on matters not covered by the facts you have been furnished, you may add any facts that are consistent with these facts. You may also add details that provide color and reality to your character. You should not add a fact, however, that would be so important that it would determine the outcome of the lawsuit. If in doubt, ask your instructor.

Depending on the actual selection and sequence and performance of the problems in your class, you may encounter gaps in information or may fail to make the acquaintance of some of the witnesses who figure in the principal cases. It has been our experience that such potential gaps in information should not seriously impair your case preparation. If the gaps do present any difficulties, however, consult your instructor.

D. RULES OF THE GAME

1. Jurisdiction; the law; rules of evidence, criminal, and civil procedure; professional rules of responsibility. The two fictitious cases take place in the jurisdiction of the State of Major. The specific setting encompasses the adjoining counties of Jamner and Neva. Jamner and Ruston are cities within the County of Jamner; Neva City is the main city in Neva County. This jurisdiction was chosen for a number of reasons. Its laws reflect, although they are probably not identical with, current law on the various issues raised in this book. Opinions in the jurisdiction of Major are short and to the point, replacing what would be hundreds of pages in other jurisdictions with a small fraction of that volume. The opinions, nevertheless, require careful reading and interpretation. Thus, they provide a good foundation for a series of assignments whose purpose is to teach you how to think about a body of law in an active adversary context, rather than to teach you substantive criminal and civil procedure and doctrine. Do not do *any* outside research unless your instructor tells you to.

The State of Major court rules and rules of criminal and civil procedure are in most instances identical to the Federal Rules of Civil Procedure and the Federal Rules of Criminal Procedure. The Major Evidence Code is identical to the Federal Rules of Evidence. The standards of professional responsibility in the State of Major are based on an amalgam of ABA-inspired texts. Although reflective of thoughts and trends in the area, these ethical standards are not intended to represent any particular jurisdiction at this time. Rather, the rules are merely intended to provide a legal structure against which you can analyze both the particular ethical situations in the problems and evaluate inherent limitations of any code for guiding decisions of professional responsibility. Of course, your instructor may instead ask you to deal with the ethical situations under the current professional responsibility rules in your jurisdiction.

2. Dates: The fictitious incidents take place in the following years—

198X–   Years prior to a central incident
         (198X–2 is two years prior)

198X   Year of the incident (if you like, you
         can fill in the current year)

198X+   Years subsequent to the incident
         (198X+2 is two years later)

3. The civil case and the Fifth Amendment: Whenever you deal with the civil case of *Summers v. Hard,* you should assume that the criminal case has been disposed of in such a manner that the main character, Ed Hard, cannot legitimately resist answering in the civil case by claiming that he will incriminate himself.

E. CONCLUSION

We have just discussed the "rules of the game" for this book, because it *is* a game. No clients will go to prison for life. No one will lose a home or business or be denied access to his or her children. So play, because, ironically, the more you play, the better you will do. But work hard at your play. Your clients are awaiting you in the next few years, and they are completely and totally dependent on you and on your having learned your lessons well.

We hope you enjoy using this book and living with the characters as much as we enjoyed creating it.

Pretrial Advocacy

Planning, Analysis, and Strategy

I

Overview of Pretrial Advocacy

A. INTRODUCTION

In this overview we explain our approach to pretrial and trial practice. In offering our approach, our sole goal is to present you with a systematic way of acquiring a set of professional skills. You will not acquire an attitude, a philosophy, or a methodology for living your life but, simply, a set of skills. Within the professional work arena, these skills potentially can be used for good or ill; accordingly, we presuppose that these skills are being entrusted to those possessed of common sense, perspective, and fundamental human values.

Moreover, in providing this approach to practice, we are mindful of, and in fact embrace, the emerging vision of the attorney as a facilitator rather than a combatant. In light of this, we have included extensive problem sections covering negotiation and counseling, as well as some alternative dispute resolution problems. Yet we also believe that only with a thorough understanding of advocacy in litigation can one appreciate the opportunities and possibilities for alternative methods of dispute resolution. More broadly, whatever vision one might have for the future of the legal profession, that vision must accept as its starting point an attorney who functions as an advocate for a client. That relationship is, after all, at the core of both the theory and reality of our present legal profession.

One or two qualifications are immediately required. Initially, we do not claim that our approach is the only credible one; it is simply one we believe is helpful for reasons that are discussed in some detail later in this overview. Undoubtedly, the ideas of many excellent lawyers would differ from our own in some respects. We do believe, however, that were we to get down to basics, the points of disagreement between us and these attorneys would be few. We would also affirm that the approach offered here does not exist in a vacuum. Accordingly, we discuss the "world" the lawyer inhabits before we delve into this book's approach to acquiring the lawyer's professional skills.

B. THE LAWYER'S WORLD

Our approach to pretrial and trial practice is intended to exist and function in a world where the attorney must deal with human relationships, money and time constraints, ethical responsibilities, and an institutional process that "moves in time."

1. Human Relationships

As an attorney you will be dealing constantly with people, and no approach to practice can ultimately be effective unless you appreciate the full significance of this fact. Your clients may be shy, arrogant, or overtrusting; witnesses may be friendly, hostile, or just unwilling to get involved; opposing attorneys or co-counsel can be pleasant, rude, or even intimidating; judges and court personnel kind and helpful, or cold and indifferent; and jurors will run the spectrum. Whatever the mix of characters and temperaments,

you will have to be able to deal with them all: work closely with some, obtain the cooperation of others, gain the respect of one, find a way to relate to the next.

2. Resource Constraints

Your clients will almost never have a blank check to give you for work on a case. They simply cannot afford the fantasy case where you take every conceivable deposition, research every imaginable legal point as if you were preparing a brief for the Supreme Court, fly witnesses in from Europe, and so on. You may not be given resources to hire private investigators to conduct an investigation, so you and your law clerk may have to do the sleuthing. Similarly, you may not be given resources to hire an expensive expert, so some low-fee local expert or a volunteer interested in the issue may have to be located. Moreover, even if the client has the money to spend, the case simply may not be worth the outlay. Running up $10,000 costs and fees in a $1,500 dispute would quickly bring your sense of judgment into question.

Furthermore, time is itself a resource, unrelated to its price per hour. You only have so much time to devote to a given case. No matter how many hours of your time a client can pay for, you will have other cases and clients. And you will have a life to live, too. You thus have to continually prioritize the allocation of your time among tasks within a single case, among your various cases and clients, and among your personal needs.

Accordingly, when you look at sections of the text such as those covering witness interviews and discovery, read our approach within the context of the realities of the economic and time constraints you are almost certain to face.

3. Ethical Responsibilities

One way to get a sense of the nature and scope of your ethical responsibilities is to comprehend some of the reasons why you have such responsibilities.

You represent a client who usually neither fully comprehends, nor can dispassionately deal with, the legal process. As such, your client is often totally dependent on you for help with his or her problem. Your client thus may be entrusting his future fortunes, his family, or even his life to you. Such *dependence* in itself demands from the attorney an ethical awareness.

In representing this person, however, you must also

remain cognizant that you function in a world in which the very words you utter can have an effect upon, and eventually even transform, the reality of the wider society. You may stand in a courtroom and convince a panel of judges that "for purposes of" the Fourth Amendment a motor home is not a home but a "vehicle." Outside of that courtroom, that decision will result in the hundreds of thousands of people whose kitchens and bedrooms are on wheels suddenly finding that, just as Cinderella's coach became a pumpkin, their homes have been reduced to automobiles, and that the police may now rummage through their inner sanctums without need of warrant. Plainly, this is a world in which you tap an enormous reservoir of power. It is not your own power, and no intellectual superiority or special moral goodness on your part accounts for your access to it. It is simply that you know the words, the forms, the incantations that can bring the powerful engine of the legal institution into action. In order to activate this institution, of course, you must always convince a judge or panel of judges. That legal institution, in turn, can be steered to employ its Constitution-based power to close entire state prison systems, throw out volumes of legislation as unconstitutional, stop multimillion-dollar construction projects for environmental concerns, or order a president to turn over documents. Such *power* also demands your ethical awareness.

Moreover, in this world of power you can *actively* influence both the legal and factual nature of the case, and thereby the results. Law students are weaned on appellate opinions where "the facts" are frozen within the borders of a two-dimensional page. In these appellate opinions, if "the blue car ran the red light," then the blue car ran the red light. But, in the attorney's world, facts are fluid, not frozen. No traffic accident will take place in the courtroom. No blue cars will appear; no red lights will be seen. All there will be is the evidence that you as the lawyer will bring into court—evidence that is subject to your influence. The evidence about blue cars and red traffic lights may be information from interviews with a witness who initially has "the impression" that "a blue-greenish vehicle entered the intersection just around the time the light changed from yellow." This evidence will then be filtered through evidence rules governing admissibility and may be challenged by cross-examination pointing out "but, sir, the sun was in your eyes." Finally, this "blue-greenish" car will be the subject of your and your opponent's closing arguments in which you both try to persuade a jury of your respective positions within the context of the applicable burdens. At every stage, therefore, the influence of one or another lawyer contributes to shaping the final nature and impact of this evidence in the case. Similarly, legal issues, so neatly frozen in appellate opinion, are often the final result of some lawyer's choice among various alternatives of how he or she would raise, frame, characterize, focus, and develop a record in support of the client's legal position. Such *influence* demands ethical awareness as well.

What ethical responsibilities then derive from this view of your position relative to the client, the legal institution, and the wider society? Initially, you are responsible for putting effort, skill, and loyalty into achieving the interest of your client. In so doing, you must of course recognize that winning a short-term acrimonious battle will not always serve the client's true interests when the client must maintain an ongoing, cooperative relationship with the other party. Nevertheless, your actions are still guided by the need to represent your client's interests. Whether you will function in a particular instance as facilitator-problem solver, bent on lowering the overall costs of transactions, or as a litigator, prepared to go to the mat, will be determined by those interests.

The reasons why the attorney's actions are determined by the client's interests are not only embedded in the theoretical underpinnings of the adversary system, but are found in the day-to-day reality, touched on earlier, that your clients usually place themselves totally in your protection. Given such trust, the least the client is owed is loyalty and competence. That responsibility accepted, it is still not always easy to know how to proceed, no matter how loyal and competent you may be, when you must counsel your client regarding settlement offers, client decisions, litigation strategies, and so on.

The client poses one focus for your ethical concern and responsibility. In recognition of the world of power which you move in and which you can actively influence, however, you must also display integrity toward the court, your opponent, and the wider society. Much of this area of responsibility is expressed in rules of professional conduct, which do provide some sense of the legitimate parameters of ethical conduct. The latest ABA-inspired rules,[1] however, have moved away from being aspirational and have become more of a statutory scheme for carrying out disciplinary sanctions. As such, the rules often center upon subjective culpability (mens rea). Such a state of mind is rarely easy to prove. This is even more true when applied to a group of people who are specifically trained to develop plausible arguments and jus-

---

1. The latest ABA rules have not been adopted by a majority of jurisdictions.

tifications to legitimize conduct. Violation of ethical rules, such as those dealing with conflicts of interest and possession of confidences from former clients whose interests are adverse to current clients, may also result in a court ordering your removal from a case (including an order that you return all fees) and even a malpractice action against you. Yet, even without these formal rules, there are powerful informal sanctions reserved for an attorney who lacks integrity.

Reputations spread fast, and opponents quickly learn whom they can trust and, therefore, cooperate with, and those to whom they will not give an inch. Judges are also aware of reputations. Since most judicial decisions are entrusted to the court's "sound discretion" (whichever way the court rules will be upheld on appeal), a lawyer whom the court trusts to be thoroughly familiar with the law, to accurately state the facts, and to candidly present his or her positions will consistently be given the benefit of the court's discretion over an attorney with a lesser reputation. Thus, coming full circle, you cannot effectively carry out your responsibility to your client unless your reputation for integrity is positive.

Just as important, and perhaps least subject to clearer articulation, you have the responsibility to exercise your skills as a thoughtful, principled human being.

4. A System "Moving in Time"

Here we are not attempting to provide you with a precise "time line," or to detail typical time requirements dictated by court rules (say, the time allotted between the filing of a complaint and the holding of a deposition). Rather, it is our desire to provide you with a rough sense of the flow of events within a civil and criminal case from inception through trial. Compared to the complex, interrelated, and often fluid nature of the various aspects of the actual process, this presentation may appear mechanical and even a bit misleading. But it is not our intention here to do more than merely provide you with a relative reference point in time and space. As such, it will be helpful to review this section from time to time throughout the course in order to reorient yourself within the litigation process.

a. A Civil Case

A civil case usually begins by a referral or some other contact in which the *potential* client contacts an attorney. There may be a pending matter that needs attention, such as a response to a lawsuit, or the client may wish to commence a lawsuit of his own. Depending on the amount of time available to investigate the client's problem, the amount of information provided at the initial interview, or other circumstances, the attorney decides to take the "potential case" and is retained by the client and a written retainer agreement is signed.

The attorney then begins an *informal* investigation of the facts (interviewing witnesses, reading and obtaining documents from the client, other individuals, public records, and so on) or may hire an investigator to undertake this informal fact-gathering. The attorney also does preliminary legal research to determine the potential legal theories.

After such an investigation, the attorney, if the case is one that needs to be litigated, may decide to contact the opposing party or that party's attorney if the party is represented and make a demand or inquiries about potential settlement.

Generally, these initial settlement attempts are not successful. Therefore, the attorney drafts, serves, and files *pleadings:* a complaint or petition for plaintiff; an answer for a defending party. (In the case of a defending party, the attorney may decide to file preliminary *pretrial motions* attacking the plaintiff's pleadings, such as motions to dismiss, motions for improper venue, improper subject matter jurisdiction, judgment on the pleadings, and so on.) Likewise, upon receipt of responsive pleadings from a defending party, the plaintiff might consider filing motions attacking the responsive pleading.

Depending on the jurisdiction, the court might require a *pretrial* or *discovery case conference* in which the schedule of the case is discussed, including discovery sequence, motions, and a tentative trial date. Substantively the court might limit and direct the discovery that the parties can do and its sequence, and even discuss settlement or other alternatives.

The attorneys then begin *formal discovery*. They might send interrogatories, request production of documents or admissions, take depositions, and so on. Most of the discovery is self-executing, that is, arranged by the attorneys, unless there is a problem. In that case, the attorneys may resort to court to file motions.

More motions may be filed and argued, such as motions compelling discovery or motions for summary judgment. Another pretrial/settlement conference may be held. Some courts use this opportunity to try to settle the case. Other courts generally use the pretrial conference as an opportunity to get the case ready for trial. The judge might review the issues still in contention, discuss witnesses who will testify and exhibits that will be used, rule on motions in limine (which deal primarily with evidentiary matters), and consider proposed jury instructions.

Throughout the pretrial process the attorneys might discuss settlement, but this is especially so when the issues have been refined and the case is in a trial posture. Here the attorneys begin in earnest to *negotiate* for they are influenced by their respective assessments of the risks of going to trial, or by the possible economic (attorney and expert witness fees) and noneconomic (stress on client, publicity) costs of pursuing such a course, or by pressure from a trial judge who makes it clear that he or she believes that "reasonable" attorneys would settle the case and not take up the judge's trial calendar.

As a professional attorney you will find that *counseling* your client, witnesses, and other attorneys involved in a case is a process that occurs throughout the pretrial and trial periods. Your client might not want to file a lawsuit and you will have to explain the advantages and disadvantages of litigating. Or your client might want you to include a bloody photograph to demonstrate her child's injuries and you will have to counsel her about the possible risks: Even should you get by evidentiary objections, which may not be easy, your opponent may turn this evidence on you. For example, your opponent may argue that you are trying to inflame the jury's sympathy and emotions to distract the factfinder from serious weaknesses in the liability portion of the case. In discussing this with your client, moreover, you will also have to consider the proper allocation of decisionmaking responsibility between you and your client in this matter as well as the need to maintain your client's trust and confidence. Counseling can also extend to your co-counsel, who plans to compel discovery as to some portion of a deposition. You feel that this position is not well-founded and will hurt your side's credibility, or that the information sought is trivial, or that it can be obtained another way, or that the overall expense of the motion is too great. Somehow, you must impart your wisdom and perspective to this fellow lawyer who may have some ego invested in his or her stance on this matter.

But let's assume that the negotiation was not successful, the pretrial conference disposed of the motions in limine, and both attorneys submitted their proposed jury instructions. The case will be litigated. The sequence of *trial* events then follows: The sequence begins with jury selection (voir dire); opening statements (although rarely done, the defense can reserve its opening statement until the beginning of the defense case); the plaintiff's case (direct examination) followed by the defense cross-examining plaintiff's witnesses; the defense case (direct examination) followed by the plaintiff's cross-examination of defense witnesses. Both plaintiff and defense can orally make motions for directed verdict after the opponent's opening statements, after an opponent's case in chief, or at the close of either side's case. Assuming that the motion for directed verdict is not granted, the attorneys can submit final proposed jury instructions. The court then informs the attorneys of the court's jury instructions that will be read to the jury; the attorneys can, out of the presence of the jury, oppose the court's determination of instructions and argue their points. Jurisdictions differ in their order of closing argument—some courts instruct the jury and then allow closing argument, other jurisdictions allow closing argument and then instruct the jury. The plaintiff begins closing argument, then the defense argument is heard, and if plaintiff chooses, it may present rebuttal. The jury retires to deliberate—the exhibits, and in some jurisdictions, the jury instructions are given to the jury to take to the jury room. Finally there is a verdict (or hung jury) and post-trial motions (motions for setting aside the verdict or altering the verdict, motions asking for a new trial or appealing, motions for additur, remittitur, bond for appeal).

b.   A Criminal Case

For the defendant, a criminal case begins with an arrest. The arrest may be made on the scene by an observing police officer, or following an investigation that itself may be brief or lengthy, or after the convening of a secret grand jury. The arrest may precede formal filing of charges, or take place at the defendant's voluntary surrender to authorities after charges have been filed. Normally, however, the prosecution will first learn of the case after the police have arrested the defendant and the case is submitted to the prosecution for a charging decision (although police and prosecutor may sometimes consult in the investigation, prearrest, and precharge stages of more serious crimes). The prosecutor will then decide whether and what to charge. If a decision to charge is made (perhaps after the prosecutor's request for further investigation by the police has been met), a charging pleading will be filed with the court. Generally, for misdemeanors, the prosecutor will file a *complaint* in the lower trial court (usually called a district or municipal court) upon which the defendant will face trial. For felonies, the procedure for bringing the charge will vary among jurisdictions. In some, the prosecutor will bring the case before a grand jury, which, if it finds the charges well-founded, will return an *indictment*. In others, the prosecutor will file a charging pleading called an *information* in the upper trial court (generally called the superior court), upon which the defendant will face trial for the felony. In still others, the charge will be stated in a complaint filed in the lower court, which then becomes the focus of a *preliminary hearing* where the prosecutor will put forth evidence to establish "probable cause" to believe the charge is correct. If, after the conclusion of the preliminary hearing, the judge (or magistrate, as the judicial figure at a preliminary hearing is sometimes called) finds probable cause to exist for the charge, the defendant is bound over for trial to the superior court where an information containing the charges found supportable at the preliminary hearing is filed. Many jurisdictions, moreover, have available more than one of these charging procedures.

Generally, it is also near the time of arrest that the defense attorney comes into the case (although sometimes an attorney arranges the initial surrender of a suspect). The first meetings with the client may be in jail, where counsel attempts to arrange bail, or it may take place in counsel's office as the potential client shops around for an attorney to retain.

In or out of jail, however, defense counsel will most often be a public defender or some other form of appointed counsel, and the client indigent.

At this point defendant will be brought into court for the procedure known as an *arraignment*. Technically, it is here that charges are read, a copy of the charging pleading served on the defendant, and defendant's plea (almost always "not guilty") entered on the record. But many other things may occur. Defendant, if not yet represented, will be given a short continuance to obtain counsel prior to entering a plea. The prosecutor, on her own or after discussions with defense counsel, may decide not to file a complaint and the defendant will be released. A motion to reduce bail may have been scheduled to be heard at this time and will therefore be argued. The court may set a date for all pretrial motions to be filed and/or heard. In some jurisdictions, a preliminary hearing (a "probable cause" hearing where witnesses are called and examined by both sides) may be set, and a trial date may even be set within local speedy-trial limits (or defendant may be asked to waive such limits in return for not being rushed to trial).

After arraignment, both the prosecution and defense will be engaged in informal discovery (witness interviews, crime scene investigation, forensic tests by experts). The prosecution's investigation will generally be carried out by the police under direction of an investigating officer, though the prosecutor may assign post-complaint investigation to her own investigator.

If a preliminary hearing has been set in the lower trial court to determine if an accused felon will eventually stand trial in superior court, the hearing will be held within a few weeks after arraignment. If "held to answer" on some or all of the charges, that is, if the magistrate finds probable cause, the defendant will be arraigned again in superior court.

Around this time, formal discovery motions will be filed by the defense (and prosecution where constitutionally permitted) and heard. That discovery permitted by the court will then be turned over and evaluated by the attorneys. In jurisdictions with preliminary hearings, a pre-preliminary hearing motion for discovery may already have been filed and ruled on.

Pretrial motions (suppression, change of venue, and so on) will be filed and set for hearing. The opposing counsel may file a response, and the motions will subsequently be heard and ruled on by the court, often after a full evidentiary hearing with witnesses.

Negotiation may take place, recurrently, all through the process (although defense counsel should first have conducted sufficient investigation and formal discovery to have a good grasp of his client's position). If a disposition is reached, a formal hearing will be set to put the plea on the record and to ensure that the defendant understands the rights she is waiving and the consequences of the conviction. After the plea is entered, the court will usually set a date for sentencing and order a study by the probation department to assist in that task. Actual sentencing will follow.

Counseling the client begins with the first interview ("When we get you out on bail, it would be good if you enroll in that voc-tech program to show the court you're serious about getting your life in order . . .") and continues through trial ("You can put your neighbor on as a character witness, but let me tell you the problem . . .") and beyond ("If we get bail on appeal, you'll be out, but if the appeal is denied a year later you'll probably have to serve the six months' sentence. On the other hand, if you begin serving your time now . . .").

If no settlement or plea decision is reached, trial follows. The sequence of events at trial is fairly universal: motions before the court regarding significant evidentiary issues (in limine motions); jury selection (voir dire); opening statements by the prosecutor, then defense attorney (defense may reserve until the commencement of its case); the prosecution case (direct examination by the prosecutor and cross-examination of witnesses by the defense); the defense case—if any (direct and cross-examination of witnesses); submission of instructions to the judge and arguments over instructions; reading of instructions to the jury (in some jurisdictions, instructions are given after closing argument); closing arguments (prosecution begins, defense follows, prosecution gets rebuttal); verdict (or hung jury); post-trial motions (motion for new trial, bail on appeal, and so on).

C. THE APPROACH

1. An Introduction

There are those who consider advocacy an art where innate talent is the most significant factor. No doubt artistry is at play when watching the work of a fine lawyer, and talent is a factor in every pursuit. Nevertheless, directing almost every competent attorney's work is a basic set of mental processes, or "approaches," guiding that attorney in how to think about and analyze problems. The precise articulation of these approaches, of course, will be expressed in countless variations among different attorneys. Does this mean that every competent advocate will do the same thing in the same situation? Absolutely not. Several lawyers could approach the same negotiation or cross-examination and each might ultimately handle it differently. But most will probably go through a surprisingly similar process of analysis and, as a result, perceive relatively the same set of choices and potential problems before deciding what to do. The actual alternative chosen, however, will be a function of such things as the type of behavior the advocate feels comfortable with, the personality the advocate projects, intuition, and so on.

The basic way in which we have chosen to express our approach is rather simple, though its full articulation is somewhat more complex: Plan every aspect of each skills performance (interviewing, counseling, cross-examination, etc.), keeping in mind your overall objectives.

Behind this relatively simple idea lies a number of separate concepts. To begin with, in thinking about "objectives," we actually have four concepts in mind: the representational strategy; case theory; specific performance-skills objectives; and the basic task at hand.

a. Objectives

(1) Client's Objectives and the Representational Strategy

Initially, there are your client's objectives. What are you trying to achieve for your client in this case? (Damages so she will be able to continue physical

therapy? An equitable division of partnership assets? Acquittal at trial? Avoiding a prison sentence?) This ultimate client objective will be pursued through your representational strategy. Your particular representational strategy (which will always be open to modification, change, or replacement as circumstances indicate) may be to try to negotiate without filing a complaint, or to file a complaint with an eye to a quick settlement, or to force a case to the doorsteps of trial before you will discuss settlement, or to convince the other side of the weaknesses in its case in discovery and then settle, or to take the case to trial unless you are given everything you have requested. This representational strategy, moreover, will be carried out through a strategic mix of three tactically interrelated areas of endeavor—*litigation-directed efforts, negotiation* (and *alternative methods of dispute resolution*), and *counseling*. For example, you may use the pursuit of litigation to force a negotiated settlement (as was implicit in some of the strategies discussed above). Or you may counsel a client whether to file a lawsuit and then when or whether to enter into negotiation. In practice, the line that purports to divide these three areas is not at all a clear one—the threat and risk of litigation plays an important role in negotiation. In litigation, on the other hand, you may negotiate about discovery and may counsel your client concerning the advisability of calling a particular witness. When counseling your client, you will be considering the effect of your advice on litigation or possible negotiation. Moreover, these same three areas that serve your representational strategy are themselves carried out through a variety of skills performances (interviewing, discovery, motions, pleading) and accompanying underlying skills. Thus, at the heart of counseling are interviewing and negotiation skills.

We will refer to this concept of representational strategy throughout the text of this book. As we discuss this concept, however, you must keep in mind that the choice of your representational strategy will be tied to the precise case situation, the particular client, and your own strengths and weaknesses. Therefore, it is difficult to provide a coherent methodology for developing this strategy. Still, there are basic principles for choosing a representational strategy, which you can evolve from experience and common sense. For example, when dealing with a dispute between parties who have an ongoing relationship (say, supplier and dealer in some business enterprise), you probably want to work out some negotiated settlement, and a settlement that both parties can live with, rather than some anger-filled win/lose battle at trial or a settlement that was rammed down one party's throat. This will be especially true if the resolution of the dispute will require further cooperation in compliance with a court order or negotiated agreement (child support, visitation).

(2) Case Theory

The second concept we have in mind in reference to objectives is your overall (tentative) legal-factual plan or case theory. A case theory provides the strategy for your litigation-directed activities, particularly those focused on information-gathering and information-presenting. This is perhaps the principal concept and key idea of this entire book, and is of sufficient significance that we devote a subsequent section of this chapter and all of Chapter II to its articulation.

(3) Specific Objectives of Performance Skills

The third concept refers to the specific objectives one may seek to achieve with a particular performance skill. Let's examine interviewing a witness as an example. As you will come to appreciate later, like all performance skills, interviewing witnesses is but one facet of the strategically directed, goal-oriented enterprise embodied in your case preparation. It should then come as no surprise that planning for a witness interview is likewise goal-directed. Thus, though each witness interview will be as unique as the individual interviewed, you will find it useful to think of the performance of this skill as generally being directed at a specific set of objectives. In this instance, those objectives happen to be gaining information for various uses and establishing rapport for future encounters. Other skills performances will, of course, have their own set of specific objectives. Each chapter in this book articulates such objectives.

(4) Basic Task

The fourth concept we term the "basic task." Each skills performance carries endless levels of possibilities and nuance which a skilled attorney could draw out and accomplish. Yet, in each, we believe there is at least one minimum objective that an attorney must accomplish in order to achieve basic competence. We term this baseline objective the basic task. Generally, this task will involve obtaining information for the case theory (discussed later in this chapter). As an example, imagine the cross-examination of a prosecution witness who has been given a deal (dismissal of charges in another case) in return for his testimony. The defense attorney's basic task in this situation would be to obtain sufficient information about the deal so she could use it to attack the witness's credi-

bility in closing argument. *Once* that basic task is accomplished, counsel could then try to do more—for example, try to emphasize the witness's motive and bias *while* she's examining the witness on the stand:

"You were facing five years on that charge that was dismissed?"

"You just finished serving two years in prison?"

"You didn't like it much, did you?"

"In fact, it was very boring in there?"

"And very frightening?"

"You don't want to go back at all, do you?," and so on.

The point is that, at the least, the attorney must achieve the basic task. Anything beyond that is, of course, all to the good. In most of the chapters that follow, the basic task will be highlighted.

b. Planning

In our formulation the concept of "planning" denotes three concepts. Initially, counsel must in effect plan to plan. This step, which is designated "preparation" in each chapter, consists of assimilating information and creating basic organizational structures for use in the planning process. The second concept in our planning approach we refer to as "content planning." Content planning is the substantive part of a skills performance. The third concept concerns "performance planning"—how you will actually employ the skill. In practice, of course, these latter two concepts may be somewhat interrelated. The content you desire may dictate the performance approach you must employ, available performance techniques may influence the content you may obtain or present, and so on. These two concepts are discussed in some detail later in this overview and appear in each chapter of the text.

2. Rationale Behind the Approach

You may have recognized that our concept of planning is distinct from the actual *doing* of the performance. In contrast, the primary focus of most other advocacy texts seems to be upon this "doing" (although the exercises at the conclusion of each problem in this book do require a set of performances). Why then does our approach so heavily emphasize planning? The rationale is based on a set of four perceptions gained from our own experience and that of many attorneys we know.

a. Anticipate Problems and Responses

First, competent lawyers approach each performance skill with a tentative plan that anticipates problems, including the potential responses of their adversary. In this latter regard, you must keep in mind that you will be functioning in an adversary world. In this adversary world, you are never alone. From first interview to eventual settlement or jury verdict, your client is behind you and your adversary waits in front of you. Your adversary may be kind, cooperative, genuinely desirous of acting as a facilitator. That is all to the good. Yet the fact remains that your opponent, too, represents a client, and to the extent that this client's interests are adverse to those of your client's, this kind, decent person who is your adversary will do everything possible, within the bounds of ethical conduct, to achieve his or her client's interests. In actual litigation, where one side's gain is almost invariably the other's loss, your adversary will simply try to beat you and beat you in every way possible. Impeach your witness. Make evidentiary and procedural objections to keep testimony that is favorable to you from the factfinder. Try to persuade a jury that the logical inferences from evidence that you have claimed favor you, really favor your opponent.

b. Adopt a Goal-Oriented Approach

Second, attorneys take a goal-oriented approach to each task, starting with their overall and immediate objectives and working backwards to develop the means and methods to achieve such objectives (i.e., ends-means thinking). This crucial aspect of attorney-think merits rearticulation. A wise response to "where should I begin?" is "begin at the beginning." In contrast, an attorney generally approaches a task by beginning at the end. The lawyer starts with an eventual goal or objective. This overall objective is determined by the interests of the client and is tempered by what is legally, logically, and factually reasonable. Then from this objective he or she works backwards—employing ends-means thinking—and determines the steps that are necessary to achieve that objective. As an example of ends-means thinking, imagine that you locked yourself out of your house. Now, you could think, "I'm locked out. That means I can't get into the house. I can't get at the food or watch the TV. How could I do this? If I hadn't been distracted by . . ." More likely, after perhaps a brief emotional outburst, you will focus on your end or objective (get into the house) and then search for the means—"Do I have an extra

key? Is a window open? Did I leave an extra key with the neighbor? Should I call a locksmith?" That's end-means thinking.

Accordingly, in this goal-oriented enterprise of advocacy, nothing is done as the result of whim. Nor does an attorney use mechanical thinking ("The rules allow us to file motions, so we better file some motions in this case"). Rather, everything is done for a reason that is ultimately related to the client's objectives and thereby reflects a representational strategy. Such purposeful conduct bespeaks the need for planning.

c. Form an Integrated Plan

Third, competent attorneys approach each aspect of a case in an integrated manner. For example, an interview with a client or witness has a relationship to a subsequent discovery request, an opening statement, a direct examination, and so on. Planning with overall objectives in mind makes this possible.

d. Achieve Competence

Fourth, this approach has seemed to be very helpful for law students and young attorneys. Perhaps this should not be surprising considering the essential connection between planning (preparation) and the above three vital attributes encountered in the many competent attorneys we have known. Employing our general approach, beginning attorneys seem to avoid the usual pitfalls of dealing with each aspect of a case in an ad hoc, fragmented manner, without any sense that what they are doing in one part of a case has any relationship to the others. They also seem both to anticipate potential problems that could arise and to have some plan (albeit vaguely formed) to deal with the problem.

In saying this, we recognize that while emphasizing that mental planning and preparation is vital for competent advocacy, there is a difference between planning and actual performance. For all but a few, initial performances can be scary, even bordering on overwhelming. This will be even more so if an adversary is involved. All their lives (unless they are attempting a second career), students have been "tracked," fifth grade competing with fifth grade, college against college. Now, they may face someone five, ten, twenty years their elder with corresponding additional experience. Moreover, performance requires mastering some skills (giving opening statements, bringing physical evidence before a jury, arguing motions, carrying out negotiations) that simply take time to develop. New attorneys cannot be expected to have ten years' experience in their first three months of practice, nor can they expect it of themselves. In fact, even if by some magic spell they woke up the day after graduation with the talents of an experienced advocate, the court would not give them the same leeway for performance it may extend to their seniors. They have to earn that. Properly focused preparation and planning, however, will generally permit them to competently (though not necessarily smoothly) execute their strategies even with their beginning-level performance skills. Knowing exactly what they want to do and why they want to do it makes up for a whole lot of inexperience. This is particularly so since successful advocates draw upon the same pool of skills that many beginning attorneys have already developed in achieving success in previous arenas in their lives—judgment, understanding of people and their motivations, a sense of tactics, oral and written communication skills, imagination, integrity, hard work, humor, powers of concentration, and on and on.

A final word about our general concept of planning before we get specific: The world is, of course, constantly filled with surprises; no one can plan for every contingency. What then do we envision when we speak of a planning approach? First, the more you plan, the fewer the surprises. Second, the constant process of planning begins to condition you to respond to unforeseen contingencies and new, unanticipated information in a systematic, goal-oriented way, rather than in an emotional or shoot-from-the-hip manner. (This second situation properly can be considered "on-the-spot" planning.)

3. Articulation of the Approach

a. The Plan for Litigation

For us, planning is *thinking* in the context of achieving objectives. In our approach, the lawyer's ultimate objectives are dictated by the needs of the client and are translated into a representational strategy. Those aspects of this strategy that are directed at litigation activities will, in turn, be guided by a separate overall legal-factual plan. This overall plan provides the attorney with a strategic perspective from which to plan each skills performance in the litigation context. Just as a would-be restaurant owner wouldn't go out and independently purchase tableware, plan a menu, design a decor, and pick a location without an overall plan for what the restaurant should be, we don't think that a lawyer should engage in various skills performances without thinking how each of these

skills performances fits into the client's objectives as embodied in the representational strategy and the litigation plan. As noted earlier, we call this litigation plan the case theory.

To briefly illustrate this concept: Imagine you are representing a client who is charged with burglary. The client's interests are clear. Acquittal or dismissal is the overall objective (although this objective may be modified to some extent by plea negotiations and sentencing opportunities as the case progresses). The objective you select will then dictate a series of sub-objectives, each of which will produce its own series of ends-means thought processes.

Look further at the burglary hypothetical. There are two basic defenses to burglary—the client either did the physical act but should nevertheless not be found guilty (because of diminished capacity, insanity, unconsciousness, a mistake that precludes formation of the specific intent) or there is a reasonable doubt that the client is the right person. Imagine that after an interview with your client and initial investigation, you determine that this case falls into the second category—a reasonable doubt that your client is the right person. Assume further that the case against your client is based on eyewitness identification, as opposed to reliance principally on circumstantial evidence (fingerprints, possession of burglary tools). Roughly, you could characterize your case theory as a reasonable doubt of misidentification. This case theory of misidentification will subsequently provide the overall factual and legal strategies for achieving your client's objectives.

Now imagine that you learn through discovery that the prosecution's case revolves around a single eyewitness who claims to have seen your client exit the victim's home and walk near the street where the burglary was committed. In this situation, your opponent's case theory will focus on the correctness of the identification ("beyond a reasonable doubt") and the necessity of establishing every element of the crime of burglary.

To achieve the overall objective of acquittal under your case theory, you immediately know that you will have to achieve the sub-objective of undercutting the credibility of the eyewitness. Further sub-objectives based on your case theory will then emerge (subpoena the prescription for the eyewitness's glasses, make a discovery motion to obtain records of any criminal convictions the eyewitness may have, interview a witness who claims to know some reasons why the eyewitness is biased against the defendant, gain admission of a diagram showing sparse streetlighting, bring out testimony regarding poor lighting).

Just as you are developing information to support your case theory, you will try to anticipate your opponent's moves, moves always made in the context of your opponent's objectives. In the burglary case, your opponent (the prosecutor) wants a conviction. The prosecutor's sub-objective will, therefore, be to ensure that the eyewitness is found credible. Thus, the prosecutor may try to develop information in an interview with the eyewitness that places the defendant close to one of the few streetlights at the moment of identification, make evidence motions to gain admission of weather service documents that indicate there was a full moon that night, establish in direct examination of the eyewitness that the witness was well acquainted with the defendant, and so on. All the prosecutor's moves and countermoves will, of course, be influenced by the presence of a factfinder who must be persuaded.

The point of all this is basic. Litigation-directed performance skills (interviewing, negotiation argumentation, cross-examination) are given their context and direction by this overall factual-legal plan and thus are merely tools for carrying out your litigation objectives. These litigation objectives are, in turn, a function of the client's goals as expressed in the representational strategy. An attorney does not view interviewing, voir dire of a jury, cross-examination, or closing arguments as a series of fragmented performances. Rather, all are thought of as opportunities within a single coherent strategy to achieve his or her objectives. For defense counsel in the burglary case, an interview with the eyewitness can pin down the eyewitness to making the identification of the burglar beyond the area most illuminated by a streetlight. Cross-examination can get this information into evidence. Closing argument can articulate its significance. Voir dire can ensure from the inception of the trial that no one who believes "just because someone is an eyewitness, that person must have perceived accurately" will be on the jury.

Similarly, methods of alternative dispute resolution are considered not for their ideological appeal, but for their possible efficacy in achieving the client's objectives in a particular situation. Client-counseling techniques are likewise utilized principally to achieve the client's legal objectives rather than to afford quasi-therapy. Thus, even when the counseling concerns a personal problem of the client, the advocate's principal objective is how that problem will ultimately affect the client's case.

b. Content Planning

As already discussed, prior to content or performance planning, you must of course do background preparation. This again will include reviewing all the relevant legal and factual material available so you can be as well-informed as possible.

Then, with your representational strategy and an overall (tentative) factual-legal plan (or plans) in mind, you can begin planning for the *content* of each skills performance. Information composes the basic content of each skills performance: What information do you want to obtain (in an interview, discovery, etc.)? What information do you want to present (in a motion, opening statement, examination, etc.)? This central role of "information" is hardly surprising since information, lack of information, and the inferences therefrom compose the basic building blocks of litigation.

When doing an interview, direct or cross-examination, or a closing argument, a lawyer thinks in terms of information and the *inferences* to be drawn from the information. Similarly, cases and statutes contain information from which one can draw inferences about legal issues. Let's look again at the burglary case. Defense counsel knows that the prosecutor will say, "we have an eyewitness identification." But there is no such thing as an eyewitness identification. All that exists is an accumulation of information. The eyewitness will take the stand and, in response to the prosecution's questions on direct examination, will state: "I saw the defendant crawl out the side window of the Smythe home." These particular words by this particular witness will provide some information to the factfinder. But there is more. There will be information that encompasses the witness's perceptual abilities, the physical circumstances of the identification, the witness's motives and biases or lack thereof, and the witness's particular experiences within the process (such as a line-up or a discussion with the police). From this mass of information, each side will press its view of the information. The prosecutor will ask the factfinder to draw the inference that the defendant is the burglar. The defendant's attorney will advocate the inference that there is a reasonable doubt whether the defendant is the burglar.

Looking from another perspective at the attorney's preoccupation with information, it is important to comprehend that, regardless of whether in trial, mediation, or negotiation, both advocates are telling a "story." Each "story" is meant to achieve the attorney's overall objective by legally, logically, and reasonably justifying the result the client desires. The stories are composed solely of information and inferences. Like a children's book that is written with a restricted vocabulary, the attorney's story is limited by the specific information that is available (both factually and as a result of legal rulings regarding admissibility). The significance in the burglary case of a motion to suppress a piece of the victim's jewelry that the police found in the defendant's pocket is not that, if granted, the prosecutor cannot bring the jewelry into court. It is rather that the prosecutor is deprived of that information and can no longer tell, as part of his or her story, ". . . and the victim's locket with her mother's picture was found by Officer Schmeckle right in the defendant's front pants pocket."

In our approach, the case theory generally will directly guide planning for the content of each skills performance in litigation. Your representational strategy generally has more bearing than the case theory on the content of counseling and negotiations, though case theory still plays an important role in these two areas. This is so because the case theory (which is constantly being reanalyzed and revised in light of new factual and legal information) is composed of a factual "story" that the proponent of the theory contends justifies relief under applicable substantive law principles and procedural burdens.

The relationship between "facts" (information), law, skills performance, and case theory is complex. Facts and law focus the advocate on plausible case theories. Plausible case theories focus the attorney on the type of law and facts that must be found and developed in order to support a particular theory. The case theory then provides the structure for directing the attorney's activities, including most skills performances.

Since any "story" is composed of information, absence of information, and the inferences therefrom, planning the content of most skills performances will involve *seeking* information relevant to supporting or altering your or your opponent's case theories or *presenting* information relevant to supporting your case theory or undercutting your opponent's.

Think again about the burglary case. Imagine now that there is a witness in that case who claims that she was drinking with the eyewitness shortly before the time of the alleged identification. You represent the defendant and want this witness to testify for your client on direct examination. How will you plan the content of this examination? You first develop an approach for planning the content of any direct examination of the witness. You then apply your approach to the specific situation in order to plan the actual content. In light of what has already been discussed in this overview, the approach logically should be one that ties your planning to obtaining information for your case theory while, at the same time, reminds you that you are functioning in an adversary system.

Your approach could take the form of a set of considerations specifically applicable to a direct examination: (1) information you will present; (2) evidence concerns; (3) ethical concerns; (4) anticipation of cross-examination. Alternatively, it could consist of a set of general inquiries applicable to almost any information-presenting activity, of which a direct examination is an example. Of course, you could also mix these two forms of approaches. In fact, in presenting our approaches in the text, we encourage you to make additions, alterations, and modifications as your experience leads you.

For the following illustration, assume you've chosen the type of approach that involves a general set of inquiries. This approach would probably take the form of first considering what information you wanted to present in light of your case theory, then considering problems you could anticipate from your opponent, and finally assessing how you might deal with such problems if they arose. As you read through the text, you will no doubt note how similar this approach is to the ones we actually recommend for each pretrial skill. Since each of these steps really constitutes an inquiry, you would find it helpful to think of your approach as taking the form of a pattern or sequence of questions.

Most competent attorneys have so internalized this type of analysis that often the process occurs on an almost subconscious level. If shown such recurrent patterns, in fact, these attorneys might take some moments before they recognized that what they are being shown is what they in fact *do*. As a beginning practitioner, however, consciously considering the questions in such patterned approaches will help you develop a usable structure for approaching and resolving the various problems you may face in practice.

Note, in fact, that the case theory in our burglary hypothetical was itself in effect developed through such a sequence of questions. Implicit in arriving at the defense theory of "misidentification" was the sequence of questions: What are the potential defenses to burglary? Looking at the known information in this case, which defense seems plausible? Why? Now, let's look at the hypothetical and see how a sequence of questions can guide you in using a skills performance to support your case theory:

QUESTION 1
What information do I want to present in this skills performance (i.e., direct examination)? Why, in terms of my case theory?

You probably want your witness to testify that the eyewitness was drinking. This may diminish the credibility of the eyewitness's ability to perceive and will support your theory of a reasonable doubt of misidentification.

QUESTION 2
What problems can I anticipate from my opponent?

Possibly, the prosecutor may attempt to establish that the eyewitness drank very little, or that *your* witness was drunk, or that your witness had a grudge against the eyewitness, or was partial to your client.

QUESTION 3
How will I deal with these potential problems?

There are a variety of possibilities. You would want to clearly bring out whatever, and how much, the eyewitness had been drinking. Even a little alcohol diminishes to some extent the keenness of a witness's perceptual abilities. You would also present a truthful picture of your own witness's sobriety and argue to the jury or other factfinders that, although one who is intoxicated may not be capable of the fine perceptions required for identifying a stranger, such a person certainly is capable of noticing that a companion is also drinking too much. As to grudges, biases, or such, you would already have found out such weaknesses in your witness's testimony when interviewing and preparing your witness. If you decided to use the witness even after you discovered such potential weaknesses, this information would be brought out in your direct examination in a way that would be least harmful. As a general proposition, it is important to realize that virtually any problem can be dealt with to some extent so long as there is enough time to analyze it and plan an approach.

At each step, of course, an attorney must not only think about his or her opponent, but also must consider the factfinder: Who is the factfinder? How does that affect my presentation? What concerns is the factfinder likely to have in accepting my case theory? How can I meet these concerns?

As we said earlier, you also could have approached this planning situation with a list of considerations specifically focused on direct examination. With such an approach, you would then have another specific list for planning the content of cross-examination, another for closing argument, and so on (though each list will contain at least one item that requires you to consider the information you need to bring out in

light of your case theory). This type of approach may be favored by those whose expertise permits them to develop such a specific, finite list for each type of situation. It also may be useful in trial situations where, unlike pretrial practice, the range of situations that are likely to require your attention are somewhat limited and predictable. On the other hand, as the above example demonstrates, a general series of questions applicable to almost any "information-presenting" situation can yield very specific guidance for planning the content of as basic a trial performance skill as direct examination.

In each chapter of the text, we provide an approach to planning for the content of the particular skill involved. We then apply the approach to a hypothetical fact situation like the one we just worked through so you can see both how the approach works and how we would deal with the particular situation. As you review these hypothetical applications of a particular approach, always keep in mind that these are only suggested analyses, offered to provide you with some guidance; they are not intended as gospel. As with all the illustrative analyses that we offer, our actual applications of our approaches combine personal experience (our own and that of others), knowledge, personal choice, and personal perspective. So, when you read through these applications of our approaches, ask yourself: Do you agree with how the situation has been analyzed? What can or would you do differently?

c. Performance Planning

Developing a representational strategy and a case theory and planning the content of each skills performance is necessary, but not sufficient. All is not so simple. Just because you have planned, for example, to obtain certain information (content) from a witness in an interview does not mean that your planning is completed. You must next plan for your *performance:* How will you get the witness to talk with you? How will you record the information? How will you develop a relationship such that the witness will allow you to return for more information? This "planning for performance" is not directly guided by the case theory (which gave a basis both for appreciating why you initially wanted to talk to the witness and for evaluating the information you obtained) or representational strategy. It is, however, directed at concerns that may ultimately determine the overall success of that theory and strategy. In this regard, think back to our restaurateur friend. How the restaurant owner handles a group of employees who are not giving good service to the customer will not vary depending upon whether the restaurant is fast food Polynesian or Mexican salad bar. But the ability to deal with this problem may well determine the ultimate success of the entire enterprise. So too with performance concerns. These concerns require goal-oriented planning that focuses on specific objectives, the means for achieving these objectives, anticipation of potential problems, possible problem solutions, and reevaluation in light of new information.

This system of proceeding from objectives, analyzing alternatives and contingencies, and then engaging in reassessment and reevaluation is not confined to legal advocacy. It is a system of analysis employed by attorneys in non-litigation, or even non-adversarial, situations and even by members of other disciplines. When placed in an adversary situation, however, this system of analysis requires its user to consider the opponent's likely moves and possible countermoves that could be made in response. In this regard, the enterprise of the attorney has aspects that smack of a contest. To think of a lawyer as being involved in a "contest" may initially seem demeaning to the sanctity of such an institution as law. Yet a contest it is. Even those promoting the desirability of resolving disputes without resort to trial litigation, by use of negotiation and other alternative dispute methods, talk about "game theory." Furthermore, to call something a contest does not lessen the seriousness of its consequences. In certain ancient civilizations the entire losing team in a contest would be executed. In law, while the attorney walks away at the end, the client might have lost a child, home, business, decades of freedom, or even a life. Moreover, the laws and principles by which the wider society lives may have been altered as a legal matter proceeds through the appellate process.

The best-thought-out representational strategy and case theory can only be realized through your performance, and that performance is less likely to be successful without careful, thorough planning. Many excellent works have been written that provide theories and practical tips for approaching each of the various performance skills. In each chapter of this text, we will provide you with a list of references that we find representational of the writing in these areas. To these, you can add ideas gained from your instructor, fellow classmates, experiences in analyzing and performing the problems in the book, common sense, and, as your career progresses, from your own experiences and those of fellow attorneys and judges.

What we provide in each chapter of the text is a coherent approach that gives you a structure in which you can effectively utilize all these ideas in planning a particular performance. Similar to what we do when "planning for content," we apply our approach to a hypothetical situation so you can see (and perhaps question) how we would deal with the situation under the approach. Like all our suggested approaches, moreover, we encourage you to gradually alter, modify, and substitute your own ideas within the approach as your subsequent experience, and accompanying understanding, so leads. We also provide you with enough basic information about each of the various skills performances so that, using the approach as a structure, you will be able to carry out a performance that is competent and realistically effective considering your level of experience.

PROBLEM 1

The Role of an Attorney in the Adversary System

You are about to be totally immersed in the world of a practicing attorney. To maximize this experience, these materials will place you in a variety of roles (plaintiff, defense, government and private counsel) and legal arenas (civil and criminal litigation and alternative dispute resolution). But always you will be an advocate.

This environment, however, is more than an amalgam of skills and tactical decisions. It is a human, flesh-and-blood world in which a clear understanding of your role as an attorney is a vital predicate to your effectiveness. But what is your role?

PREPARATION

READ: (1) Pretrial Case File Entry 61; (2) Chapters I and XI. Now think about and answer the following questions:

1. What is the theory behind our adversary system?

2. What is your role as an attorney in this system?

3. How does this role relate to the theory that underlies the adversary system?

4. Consider the statement by Justice Jackson in *Watts v. Indiana,* 338 U.S. 49, 59 (1949) (concurring opinion):

    > To bring in a lawyer means a real peril to solution of the crime, because under our adversary system, he deems that his sole duty is to protect his client—guilty or innocent—and that in such a capacity he owes no duty whatever to help society solve its crime problem. Under this conception of criminal procedure, any lawyer worth his salt will tell the suspect in no uncertain terms to make no statement to police under any circumstances.

    a. According to Justice Jackson, what are the basic principles of representation in an adversary system?

    b. According to Justice Jackson, do prosecutors and defense attorneys have the same general responsibilities in our adversary system? Explain. Should their responsibilities be identical?

5. Does Justice Jackson's view have application in civil litigation?

6. What generally are your obligations to your client?

    a. Should you enter a case thinking "I'm going to get everything I can for the client" or "I'm going to try to reach a disposition that is fair to all parties"?

    b. Are these two attitudes necessarily inconsistent? Explain.

7. Do you have obligations to anyone or anything other than your client? Explain and give examples.

8. Who is your "client" when you are acting as a government attorney?

    a. How does your answer to this question affect how you see your role?

    b. Is the role of a government attorney different from that of an attorney in private practice? How?

9. Is the role of an attorney different in a criminal, as opposed to a civil, arena? How? Why? (Hint: You may get some ideas from your answers to questions 4(b) and 5.)

10. An eminent jurist, Judge Marvin E. Frankel, commented in *Partisan Justice* (1978) that within our adversary system, "Each side is limited and affected throughout by the strategies and choices of the adversary. But the contest by its very nature is not one in which the objective of either side, or of both together, is to expose 'the truth, the whole truth, and nothing but the truth'" (p. 14). He suggests

that such a system does not value candor, mutual respect, and fair dealing.

   a. Do you agree with Judge Frankel's position? Explain.

   b. According to Judge Frankel, what values would he incorporate into a dispute resolution system?

   c. How (if at all) would incorporation of such values change our adversary system?

11. Dispute resolution for some societies is based upon the principle of catharsis. (Catharsis involves a purification or purgation of emotions, thereby leading to a satisfying release from tension.) Litigants air their grievances, freely expressing their aggressions and hostilities. A hallmark of the adversary system is aggressiveness for one's client. The lawyer in the American adversary system has been described as a hired gun. Does aggressiveness in the adversary system perform the same function as the cathartic principle? Explain.

   a. What are the advantages of catharsis as a principle for dispute resolution?

   b. What are the disadvantages of catharsis as a principle of dispute resolution?

   c. How would a cathartic principle operate in the United States? Would it be feasible?

12. The United States system of dispute resolution (court litigation) has been described as a formal system. What makes it formal?

13. Informal systems of dispute resolution, such as mediation and arbitration, are also successfully used by some in our legal process. What characteristics are present to make dispute resolution informal?

14. List the advantages of a formal versus an informal system of dispute resolution.

15. List the disadvantages of a formal versus an informal system of dispute resolution.

16. If you were structuring a dispute resolution system for the United States, would you incorporate any part of a:

   a. Formal system?

   b. Informal system? Explain.

ASSIGNMENT FOR CLASS

Be prepared to discuss the role of an attorney in our adversary legal system.

II

Case Theory

A. INTRODUCTION

In our planning-oriented approach, the case theory comprises the strategic plan for achieving your client's objectives in litigation. You are now about to enter into a case and begin your case preparation. Your representational strategy involves serious pursuit of litigation as one of its components. Beginning here, you will engage in a process that will evolve throughout your representation—a process of developing, refining, revising, even altering, your case theory.

B. OBJECTIVES

The general objective of the case theory is to provide a tactical structure that will serve as the organizing principle for all your pretrial litigation-directed endeavors. Actually your case theory provides direction for every activity from interviewing, pleadings, discovery, and pretrial motions to jury selection, witness examinations, and opening and closing arguments. This case theory, in fact, is literally incorporated in the civil pleadings and in the closing argument to the trier of fact, and constitutes an important component even in the attorney's strategic theory for negotiation.

The specific objective of the case theory in your pretrial litigation activities is to provide a guide for the content of most of your pretrial skills performances.

C. PREPARATION

To talk of background preparation for developing a case theory is somewhat misleading. Throughout the progress of the case, your theory will constantly be subject to change and revision as you review new factual or legal information. In effect, you will therefore be doing background preparation anew each time you recommence this process of modification. Nevertheless, we can speak here of that very early time before your first truly significant thoughts on the case occur. Even at this early point, there is productive work you can do.

Initially, you will want to get a good understanding of the established doctrine and evolving legal concepts in the general area of practice in which the case could arise (from cases, statutes, other attorneys, seminars, law reviews, etc.). Then you want to learn whatever information you can about the case you are about to handle from an initial telephone call or some other direct contact. For example, knowing as defense counsel that the defendant is charged with robbery will lead you to conjure up in your own mind and then research the range of possible theories of defense in that area. Hearing a rumor that some witness has claimed that your client was drunk when arrested at the crime scene will further key you into possible theories of defense (e.g., diminished capacity) and into the possible facts that could bring such legal concepts into play. But, *keep an open mind!* Do not grab a theory early on and subsequently ignore the significance of all factual and legal information that may suggest other, more promising theories.

D. DEVELOPING A CASE THEORY

In order to develop a case theory, you must first understand the selection and development of the *legal theory* and the *factual theory,* the two interdependent components that make up the case theory. While, for clarity, the legal and factual theories are discussed separately, the two concepts are interrelated, linked together through law, information, and the client's objectives. The legal theory is a legal framework developed by a lawyer from interpretation, analysis, and expansion of legal rules and standards (found in cases, statutes, and regulations). It is a framework from which the lawyer posits that, if the facts exist as alleged, the client is legally entitled to the relief sought. Thus, though based on the law, one cannot say that the legal theory "is" the law. It is merely one attorney's interpretation of law. In practice, some legal theories will be beyond dispute (negligence in an automobile accident) while others may encounter quite vigorous opposition (strict liability of handgun manufacturers to those injured by the intentional use of those weapons). In Chapter VI, we refer to these two types of theories respectively as "old shoe" and "cutting edge" (see page 154).

The factual theory is the party's "story" justifying relief under the legal theory and is based on all the information, and logical inferences therefrom, in the case.

1. The Legal Theory

The specific development of the legal theory by a lawyer will vary according to whether one is attorney for the plaintiff or the defendant. The principal difference between civil and criminal legal theories is the legal *source* of the theory. Civil legal theories of both plaintiff and defendant may be founded on common law cases, statutory enactments, administrative regulations, and so on. For criminal plaintiffs (prosecutors), however, there are no common law crimes, only statute-based (legislature-based) ones. Criminal defendants, on the other hand, may base a legal theory on as broad a range of legal sources as his or her civil counterpart.

The advocate must also consider the possibility of multiple or "back-up" theories, which we develop later in this chapter.

a. Civil and Criminal Plaintiffs

For the *civil plaintiff*, the legal theory will correspond to the claim for relief (e.g., negligence, slander, right to possession of land through adverse possession, breach of contract). In setting forth a legal theory, counsel for the civil plaintiff is asserting that he or she can establish (within the required burden of persuasion) every *element* of the civil claim. Thus, to propose a legal theory of "negligence" is to assert that counsel can prove, by a preponderance of the evidence, that (1) defendant had a duty of care to the plaintiff, (2) defendant committed an act that breached that duty, and (3) as a proximate result of that breach, (4) plaintiff suffered compensable harm.

For the *criminal plaintiff* (prosecutor), the legal theory will correspond to the statutory definition (including any interpretation by the courts) of the particular crime involved (e.g., burglary, second-degree theft, arson, conspiracy to import a controlled substance). In setting forth a legal theory, counsel for the criminal plaintiff is asserting that he or she can establish within the required burden of persuasion every *element* of a statutory offense. (The plaintiff's legal theory must also recognize jurisdictional "elements" (e.g., venue) that the plaintiff must establish.) Accordingly, to propose the legal theory of old-fashioned, common law "burglary" is to assert that counsel can prove, beyond a reasonable doubt, that (1) the defendant (2) entered a dwelling (3) at nighttime (4) that belonged to another (5) with the intent to commit theft or another felony.

b. Selecting and Developing Plaintiff's Legal Theory

The potential legal theories for a particular circumstance (an automobile accident, a failed business, a violent death) may be numerous. How then does counsel for plaintiff choose his or her legal theory? This requires a two-part process.

In the *first* part of this process, after considering case law, periodicals, discussions with fellow attorneys, and so on, counsel for the plaintiff will attempt to conceive all the potential legal theories, based on accepted statements of existing law and plausible arguments for expansion and modification of that law, that the available information suggests. When initially developing a legal theory, the lawyer also considers potential information that reasonably may be found during subsequent fact-gathering. To provide a simple illustration of this first part of the process of developing and selecting a plaintiff's legal theory, imagine plaintiff-pedestrian has been hit by a car while on a crosswalk. Through your own knowledge and research, you could immediately think of several possible legal theories for the plaintiff: intentional tort, negligent operation of the car, negligent maintenance of the car (worn brakes), negligent repair of the car by some third party, defective manufacture of the car. Which of these potential theories, however, should you choose as your initial legal theory?

In the *second* part of this process, counsel for plaintiff will answer this question, assessing the strengths and weaknesses of each potential legal theory by *simultaneously* considering the theory:

1. in the abstract
2. in relation to other potential theories
3. in conjunction with the available and potential information in the case

Think again about the automobile accident case. Look at the potential theories (intentional tort, negligent operation) in the abstract. Are any so novel or "cutting edge" as to invite a likely defense attack on their legal propriety? It does not seem so in this case.

While doing this, also look at the practical advantages and disadvantages of each of these potential theories in comparison with each available theory. A theory of defective manufacture may require far more expensive and complex expert testimony than a theory of negligent repair. A theory of intentional tort will require establishing a much greater level of culpability on the part of the defendant than is required for a theory of negligent maintenance. A theory of negligent operation may only require obtaining the evidence of a single neutral eyewitness, or even the evidence of your own client, while a theory of defective manufacture may require gaining court-ordered access to thousands of pages of corporate documents. On the other hand, if the defendant-driver is uninsured and indigent, the manufacturer may be the only source for damages.

At the same time, assess the theories in conjunction with available and potential information. Imagine that through interviewing, investigation, and discovery you obtain information indicating that the brakes are fine and that the car is mechanically perfect. Such information would eliminate defective manufacture, negligent repair, and negligent maintenance as viable legal theories. Imagine further that there exist several witnesses who claim to have seen the defendant-driver looking at a box of tapes for his tape deck at the time of the accident. That information would greatly weaken any theory of intentional tort, but would support "negligent operation" as a good tentative legal theory.

c. Civil and Criminal Defendants

The potential types of legal theories available to a civil or criminal defendant are far more varied than those available to his or her adversary. Plaintiff's case theory, both the legal theory and the factual theory, is literally an attack on the defendant. After all, the plaintiff, through his or her case theory, is accusing the defendant of breaching a contract, stealing property, violating a lease, manufacturing hazardous products, and so on. Defendant can respond to this attack in three ways. One, defendant can focus on weaknesses in plaintiff's case theory, thereby attempting to blunt the attack. Two, defendant can launch a separate counterattack. Three, defendant can decide that negotiation is the most viable alternative. However, even if the representational strategy centers on obtaining some form of settlement, for reasons that will be apparent in the chapter on negotiation, an attorney nevertheless wants to develop the best possible case theory. We will therefore discuss these first two methods of attack, leaving the discussion of negotiation to Chapter X.

(1) Blunting the Attack: Finding Weaknesses in Plaintiff's Case Theory

Defense legal theories that probe weaknesses in the plaintiff's case theory will focus their attack in one or more of four directions:

- Attack the *legality* of plaintiff's case theory. (There is no such legal theory.)
- Attack the *factual sufficiency* of plaintiff's case theory. (Such a legal theory exists, but the party's factual allegations are insufficient as a matter of law to raise the legal theory.)
- Attack the *persuasive sufficiency* of plaintiff's case. (Though such a legal theory exists and suffi-

cient facts have been presented to get by summary judgment motions, motions for a directed verdict, etc., the factfinder should not be persuaded given the applicable burden of persuasion.)
- Attack *procedural* aspects of plaintiff's case theory. (The party is barred because of some procedural rule.)

Additionally, there are defense legal theories that do not specifically attack plaintiff's legal or factual theories, but rather are independent claims in defense. These are termed *affirmative defenses*. Even if plaintiff's legal theory cannot be attacked, defendant should not be liable (or defendant's liability at least should be mitigated) due to some affirmative grounds such as fraud, self-defense, and accord and satisfaction.

Defense legal theories based on attacks on "persuasive sufficiency" and on "affirmative defenses" provide the principal focus for defense litigation strategies in these materials. Yet attacks based on "legality," "factual sufficiency," and "procedural" concerns also constitute legal theories, although some might not initially think of them as such. This may be because these theories are generally directed to the court, which, rather than the jury, will make any factual findings under such theories that are required. (See also discussion of legal and factual theories in Chapter VIII at pages 254-258.) Nevertheless, one must consider and understand these theories in order to be a competent advocate.

(a) Legal Insufficiency

A defense legal theory that attacks the *legality* of plaintiff's case theory focuses on the validity of plaintiff's claim under existing law. This type of attack takes the position that, as a matter of law, plaintiff's legal theory should not be recognized as one for which the court will provide a remedy. In this type of attack, plaintiff has raised all the "elements" of his or her claim, but it is arguable that the claim itself should not be recognized. For example, plaintiff's claim, which attempts to hold a gun manufacturer liable for the intentional use of a handgun by a third party, will be subject to a defense argument that no such claim exists at law. Or a criminal statute may be subject to a defense contention that the criminal statute is unconstitutional on its face, and so forth.

These types of defense legal theories are developed by analyzing plaintiff's legal theory within the context of relevant substantive law. This analysis, of course, is not a neutral inquiry, but takes place from an ends-means perspective. Defense counsel begins with the position that a claim for relief is not stated because current law (statutes, regulations, cases) does not recognize the claim as presented by plaintiff. Counsel then scrutinizes plaintiff's claim and the existing law in an attempt to develop a plausible argument to sustain that position. Naturally, there may not be a plausible argument for this position, and defense counsel then will have to focus on other lines of attack. But discarding inapplicable theories is as much a part of the process of developing a legal theory as locating appropriate ones.

Imagine a civil claim for relief based on "defamation in libel." In raising this legal theory, plaintiff is asserting that he can prove, by a preponderance of the evidence, (1) defendant intentionally or negligently published matter defamatory to some third person; (2) the matter was understood as defamatory of plaintiff; (3) causation; (4) damages. In this case the plaintiff, Albert E. Jones, alleges that a professor of his (now the defendant) wrote in chalk on a small slateboard in the professor's private office: "Reminder—tell Dean that A.E.J. is selling drugs to students." Jones further alleges that several fellow students of Jones's saw the notation when they surreptitiously entered the professor's office to play a prank on the professor. Plaintiff's attorney has pleaded that as a result of this defamation, which plaintiff has alleged is false, Jones suffered significant general damages. Imagine now that plaintiff also tries to sue the chalk manufacturer. If plaintiff claims that principles of strict liability that hold the manufacturer liable for physical harm from its product (e.g., cancer caused by some noxious dust from the chalk) should also apply to emotional harm from its product (here defamation on a blackboard), defense counsel for the manufacturer would argue that, even if plaintiff states all the "elements" of this claim, no such claim for relief can be recognized under existing law.

But note that the line between a problem of legality and one of factual sufficiency is often an inexact one. For example, review the defamation hypothetical. Libel requires only general damages for a claim; slander generally requires an allegation of special damages. While libel is generally considered to pertain to written matter, and slander to oral assertions, one can make a plausible argument under relevant case law that the real difference between the two is the relative permanence or transitory nature of the defamatory remark. Under this analysis, defendant would argue that since chalk on a blackboard is transitory, slander, not libel, is involved. That being so, plaintiff, who has only alleged general damages (thereby failing to allege all "elements" of slander), has arguably failed to state a claim for relief. As such, plaintiff's theory could be attacked on "legality" grounds. At a subsequent point in time, however, the problem will quickly become one of "factual sufficiency": Does plaintiff

possess sufficient information from which he can allege special damages?

(b) Factual Insufficiency

Legal theories based on attacking the factual sufficiency of plaintiff's case theory focus on the lack of a sufficient quantum of evidence to put the case before the trier of fact—that is, plaintiff has failed to make or put forth a prima facie case. A factual sufficiency attack takes the position that even if such a legal theory exists (and the theory is thus not subject to an attack for "legality"), plaintiff's allegations are insufficient "as a matter of law" to permit a reasonable factfinder to find one or more "elements" of that theory. For example, perhaps as a result of successful evidence objections, there is no evidence in a breach of contract suit of *any* consideration. Or, the *only* evidence in a robbery case, due to a successful motion suppressing stolen property found on the defendant's person, is that the defendant was seen within a block of the victim's home.

These defense theories are developed by assessing plaintiff's factual theory in the context of his or her legal theory. Plaintiff's "story" in the defamation hypothetical provides the opportunity for such an attack. In that case, the defamatory matter was revealed to students who surreptitiously entered the professor's office. One element of the legal theory of defamation requires that the matter be published to some third party either intentionally or negligently. Under these circumstances, the attorney for defendant could consider a possible legal theory of factual insufficiency and move for a summary judgment on the grounds that no reasonable factfinder could determine that the publication was the professor-defendant's fault under the facts presented.

Now that we have discussed legal and factual insufficiency, these categories need further comment. While factual insufficiency has been categorized as "factual" for purposes of organization, one could also reasonably have classified it under "legality" inasmuch as it refers to factual insufficiency "as a matter of law." Like most such attempts at categorization, alternative schemes are thus plausible. In fact, defense legal theories could also have been divided according to the decisionmaker given the institutional role of assessing the particular defense legal theory into: (1) those decided by the court (procedural attacks such as venue and lack of personal jurisdiction; failure to state a claim; legally insufficient information to allow claim to be considered by the trier of fact); (2) those decided by the factfinder after the court has determined that there is a prima facie case (affirmative defenses; procedural attacks such as the statute of limitations); and (3) those decided by the factfinder without an initial determination by the court (defense based on persuading the factfinder that plaintiff has not carried its burden as to one or more elements of its legal theory). The categorization employed in these materials, however, was chosen because it facilitates discussing the *development* of the various defense legal theories.

(c) Persuasive Insufficiency

Legal theories based on attacking the "persuasive sufficiency" of plaintiff's case theory focus on plaintiff's inability to convince a trier of fact of his or her position. This type of attack takes the position that even if plaintiff's allegations are sufficient to be heard by a trier of fact, the trier of fact should find that the plaintiff has failed to carry its burden of persuasion as to one or more elements of the civil claim or statutory crime (e.g., expert testimony regarding cause of plaintiff's disability precludes finding of "proximate causation" between car accident and physical injuries; credibility problems in an eyewitness to assault raise "reasonable doubts").

Defense legal theories of this type are developed by comparing the elements of plaintiff's legal theory with all the information defense counsel knows (all of which plaintiff may or may not also know) pertaining to each element. In the defamation hypothetical, plaintiff's legal theory includes the element that the defamatory matter be "understood as defamatory of plaintiff." Reviewing the information known at this point, one notices that the message on the slateboard only referred to "A.E.J." A tentative defense legal theory (subject to subsequent fact-gathering), therefore, would be that plaintiff cannot carry its burden of associating the defamatory matter with the plaintiff "by a preponderance of the evidence."

(d) Procedural Aspects

Defense legal theories that attack procedural aspects of plaintiff's case theory encompass such procedural considerations as failure to obtain personal or subject matter jurisdiction, lack of venue, or a statute of limitations.

Such legal theories are developed by comparing a list of available procedural bars (derived from interpretation of cases, statutes, court rules, and so on, as well as any unique, creative analysis that adds to the list in a particular case) with all information relevant to these procedural postures that exists in the case. Subsequent information, whose significance is appreciated because you have the list of procedural bars and their corresponding elements in mind, may, moreover, add possible procedural grounds as the case progresses.

In the defamation case suppose A.E.J. filed the defamation action in federal court alleging that subject matter jurisdiction is based upon diversity of citizenship. A.E.J. asserts he is a citizen of Maine and defendant-professor is a citizen of Texas. After looking at the college records, defendant learns that A.E.J. signed an affidavit to obtain reduced in-state tuition in which he asserted that he considered himself a citizen of Texas. Defendant would procedurally attack plaintiff's choice of the federal forum.

(2) Mounting a Counterattack: Raising an Affirmative Defense[1]

Defense legal theories do not have to be restricted specifically to attacking plaintiff's legal or factual theory. The defense may put forth an independent claim that, if successful, will preclude (or mitigate) plaintiff's right to relief under its case theory. When asserting this claim, known as an affirmative defense, defense counsel is taking the position that even if plaintiff has established all the elements of its theory, defendant has a legal defense based on case law or statute (e.g., fraud in inducement; latches; insanity). Some affirmative defenses attack the propriety of plaintiff's behavior, accusing the plaintiff, say, of delay or fraud, much as plaintiff's legal theory attacks the defendant; other affirmative defenses merely assert that defendant has done no wrong, claiming privilege, say, or insanity.

As independent claims for relief (seeking to deny or mitigate plaintiff's claim), affirmative defenses are comprised of elements, just as plaintiff's legal theories are. For example, in setting forth an affirmative defense of self-defense in using deadly force, a defendant is asserting that under the applicable burden of proof, which in some jurisdictions is on the defense and in others on the prosecution, (1) defendant reasonably feared he was threatened with death or great bodily injury, (2) the threat was imminent, and (3) the amount of force used in defense was necessary.

It should not be surprising, therefore, that the process for selecting an affirmative defense is analogous to the process of selecting the plaintiff's legal theory. Likewise, *plaintiff's attacks* on a defense case theory founded on an affirmative defense will parallel the types of attacks a defendant generally can make against a plaintiff's legal theory. For instance, the prosecution can argue against a self-defense claim on the theory that the defendant has failed to establish the element of reasonable force.

---

1. In criminal law, some authorities reserve the term "affirmative" defense for a defense in which the proponent carries the burden of proof. When used here, the term does not carry this implication.

In developing an affirmative defense, you must determine the affirmative defenses theoretically possible in the case. This requires examining *plaintiff's* legal theory. Every legal theory carries with it a number of accepted affirmative defenses found in cases, statutes, or court rules, as well as the possibility of new affirmative defenses that evolve out of a creative analysis of case trends. Such new or creative affirmative defenses are also likely to arise through inductive thinking; information in a case can provide a brainstorm for a new affirmative defense theory. You will *then* seek supporting and analogous authority to uphold the theory. See Chapter VI for the "cutting-edge" theories (page 154).

Consider the information that is, and reasonably may be, available in the case. Try to match this information, and the inferences therefrom, with the required elements of each potential affirmative defense. Where appropriate, also consider each affirmative defense in the abstract and in conjunction with one another.

In the defamation hypothetical, your research would reveal a number of potential affirmative defenses to defamation: truth, absolute privilege, consent, and so on. Knowing that not all of these defenses are likely to actually be appropriate to your case, you would next review the known information in your case. From this review, you would realize that the alleged defamation occurred as part of an attempt to warn the dean about drug sales to students. Matching this information to the list of potential affirmative defenses, you would conclude that the conditional "public protection" privilege could offer an affirmative defense and, therefore, a possible legal theory for the defense in the case.

d. Multiple Legal Theories

There are *three* situations in which a party might offer more than one legal theory in a case.

(1) Fact-Gathering

First, counsel may pursue several tentative theories during fact-gathering, which usually takes place at a relatively early stage, but not invariably so. As information is received, these multiple tentative theories generally are eliminated or abandoned because of lack of information to support them, inconsistency, or strategic concerns. Counsel will usually try to select one theory as quickly as is feasible, since the fact-gathering process itself is far more efficient if guided by a single legal theory.

(2) Strategic Sequence

Second, multiple legal theories may be used in strategic sequence. A defendant in a breach of contract case may begin by alleging a procedural bar, then, failing in that, move to dismiss for failure to state a claim for relief, and finally end up arguing the case on the basis that plaintiff's witnesses regarding the "element" of consideration are too biased to be believed. Such use of multiple theories illustrates the concept of the "back-up theory." This concept reflects the necessity that an attorney constantly plan for every conceivable contingency and alternative throughout representation of the client.

(3) Alternatives

Third, a party may present the factfinder, or the adversary in negotiations, with alternative legal theories. The plaintiff in a contract dispute may allege both a breach of contract and the tort of fraud. A criminal prosecutor may charge the same defendant with theft and burglary. At some point, however, the factual theories ("stories") underlying the alternative legal theories may become so divergent, or even inconsistent, that a *choice must be made* prior to negotiation or trial.

Imagine a gas station robbery. Defendant is charged as an accomplice (the "lookout"). Defense counsel has two alternative legal theories: (1) reasonable doubt of misidentification; (2) reasonable doubt regarding the element of intent to aid the robbery. Now, analytically, these two theories are not inconsistent—"There is a doubt my client is the man who was identified pacing back and forth on the corner near the gas station. But even if he is that man, there is certainly a doubt that he had anything to do with the robbery." Fine. But what does defense counsel do when the gas station attendant testifies? Cross-examine to show that the attendant was too preoccupied with, and scared of, the actual gunman to really notice the man on the corner? Or cross-examine to show that the attendant noticed that the client never signaled to the gunman, that the client bent down to help someone who had dropped their groceries, or other such details? If counsel takes only the first line of cross-examination, the factual theory that "he was there, but had nothing to do with the robbery" will severely suffer. If counsel takes the second line, the factual theory that "he is the wrong man" will be devastated. If counsel tries to mix both lines of cross-examination, the factfinders will receive mixed messages. At best, they will be confused; at worst, they will perceive that counsel is desperately groping for anything in order to win, without any regard to what *really* happened.

2. *The Factual Theory*

a. **Civil and Criminal Plaintiffs**

(1) A Story

The factual theory is more than an accumulation of relevant information. To be sure, it is constructed from the mass of information you have (and which you reasonably believe you might subsequently obtain) to support your legal theory. It is, nevertheless, a "story," and you must always think of it that way. (For an excellent discussion of the role of "stories" in jury deliberations, read W. Lance Bennett and Martha S. Feldman, *Reconstructing Reality in the Courtroom* (1981).)

If you represent the *plaintiff,* this story communicates "what happened." Like all stories, it has a plot. This plot will take the form of a set of *central assertions:* (1) the plaintiff bought and paid for the lawnmower; (2) plaintiff took it home and started it up, following the instructions; (3) the mower exploded; (4) the defendant refused to replace it or return the plaintiff's money, wrongly claiming the plaintiff had misused the mower.

These central assertions provide additional functions other than plot structure. They provide a quick focus on where the factual theory is strong and where it is weak. (How do I deal with the "slight" car accident that befell plaintiff as he took the lawnmower home?) They also offer a rough guide for assessing the information that needs to be admitted into evidence in order to make these assertions and, therefore, put forth the factual theory (e.g., what information will show plaintiff "followed instructions"? Is it admissible?).

A plot, however, is only the skeleton for a story. Meat must be put on those bones. Moreover, in constructing this story one must keep in mind that a story has to be conceived both in terms of its genre and audience. Here the story is being presented in an adversary theater to a trier of fact who must be persuaded.

Accordingly, the story (factual theory) must be constructed to withstand three types of defense legal theories and deal with factual assertions (compare attacks on "legality" at page 20):

1. Attacks on *factual sufficiency.* (Plaintiff has failed to state a claim for relief.)
2. Attacks on *persuasive sufficiency.* (Plaintiff has failed to carry its burden as to one or more elements.)
3. Attacks based on *affirmative defenses.*

Your factual theory can withstand the first type of attack, factual insufficiency, by generally being careful to set forth sufficient information to legally fulfill every "element" of the plaintiff's legal theory. For example, even in the heat of a robbery trial, you must not forget to ask, "Where did these events occur?" so as to establish venue. There are some cases, on the other hand, where plaintiff's ability to present a prima facie case in the face of an attack on factual sufficiency is genuinely an issue.

Avoiding the second and third type of defense attacks, however, requires that your story be sufficiently *persuasive* to convince the factfinder that plaintiff has established every element of his or her legal theory within the required burdens of proof, and that plaintiff's factual theory, not defendant's (which may support some affirmative defense), is the correct one. Achieving this persuasiveness in your factual theory is, in turn, a function of (1) *quantity* and (2) *quality* (i.e., "believability," "trustworthiness").[2]

Even if your story contains enough admissible information regarding a particular element of your legal theory to get past a motion for a directed verdict, you will not necessarily have a sufficient *quantity* of information to convince the factfinder that this element exists. Or, looked at from another perspective, the story may not withstand your adversary's attacks on this lack of informational quantity. "Furtive" behavior by a defendant when confronted by police while in possession of stolen property may be sufficient to establish the element of "knowledge of the property's stolen nature" for purposes of a prima facie case of receiving stolen property. Without more, however, even if the jury believes this "furtive" behavior took place, it may not be enough to convince the jury (or other trier of fact) to infer the existence of this same element of "knowledge." Sufficient quantity is lacking. (Compare this with a situation where the factfinder also had information that the goods were purchased for one-third their value, the goods did not come in their original boxes, and defendant had been told the seller was a "fence.")

On the other hand, no matter how much information you have to support your story, it will do you little good if that information or the story itself is not *believable,* that is, suffers "quality" problems. Thus, establishing the believability of your witness and the witness's information is an essential aspect of any story.

---

2. Additionally, making the story *memorable* by giving it a name or central "theme" that captures the crux of your case theory, or adding interesting relevant details that personalize the case for the factfinder, increases its persuasiveness; convincing the factfinder through "images," you offer a bridge between your story and the factfinder's human experience and understanding, and make the story easier to attend to (from the opening statement) and to recall (after closing argument).

But, the story itself must also be believable. It must appear coherent and comport with the factfinder's common sense and everyday experience with human nature. In short, it must "make sense." If a criminal plaintiff's story does not make sense, the factfinders are likely to translate that lack of "quality" into "reasonable doubts." If a civil plaintiff's story does not make sense, the factfinders are likely to give credence to the alternative factual theory that supports the defendant's defense.

(2) An Illustration: A Story About the Sale of a Cow

Imagine a case in which Farmer Green arranged to sell a cow named Bossie to Farmer Brown, who agreed to pay $500 for the cow. Farmer Brown received the cow, but failed to pay. You are counsel for plaintiff, Farmer Green. After an initial client interview, you have selected breach of contract as plaintiff's legal theory. You also have determined that the central assertions of plaintiff's factual theory are: (1) defendant saw and agreed to purchase a cow for $500; (2) the cow was delivered; and (3) defendant never paid, even after repeated requests. Put into story form, your factual theory at this point would be something like the following:

"I'm going to tell you the story of a broken promise and a cow named Bossie. Farmer Green, my client and the plaintiff in this case, owns a farm. The defendant came by my client's farm and inquired if a cow he had seen in the south pasture was for sale. My client indicated that the cow could be purchased for $500, and the defendant agreed. They shook hands and arranged to have Farmer Green bring Bossie to the defendant's ranch, where payment was to be made. The next day, my client brought the cow over to the defendant's barn. When Farmer Green asked for full payment as agreed the day before, the defendant said that, due to a family emergency, he had not had time to go to the bank. He then agreed to deliver the money to my client's farm the next day. Well, that day never came. My client repeatedly requested payment, but the defendant has steadfastly refused, claiming that he had 'miscalculated' the amount of money he had in the bank when he bought the cow and would pay my client, Farmer Green, 'one of these days' when he could."

This story provides sufficient information as to each element of the legal theory of breach of contract to withstand a defense motion for a directed verdict. It contains additional details that place the required elements in a total context that is intended to be meaningful and persuasive to the factfinder. But something is amiss. Though legally sufficient, and not suffering quantity problems, part of the story does not make sense—that is, it has a quality problem. Hearing this story, the factfinder might ponder, "This doesn't add up. Farmer Brown wouldn't just suddenly refuse to pay a neighboring farmer. Something else must be going on that plaintiff isn't telling us." Unless this believability problem is cured, the factfinder will be receptive to a defense factual theory, and accompanying legal theory, which provides a reasonable explanation for this situation: The cow had something wrong with it when delivered, it was the wrong cow, or some other such claim.

As counsel for the plaintiff, what will you do? More information-gathering on plaintiff's behest seems clearly required. You therefore go back to your client and ask the question the jury will ask: Why would Farmer Brown just suddenly refuse to pay for the cow? In the course of this subsequent interview, your client tells you that a few days before the defendant purchased Bossie, Farmer Brown entered into a deal with another farmer to whom he was to sell a piece of very expensive farm equipment. Between the time he bought the cow and the next day when it was delivered, the deal unexpectedly fell through, leaving Farmer Brown without money to pay for the cow. Your subsequent investigation then turns up sufficient admissible corroborating information regarding what your client has told you to allow you to incorporate this failed deal into your story. With the new information about the failed deal, Farmer Green's factual theory now finally makes sense. You might now argue:

"Members of the jury, you've no doubt asked yourselves why Farmer Brown would suddenly just refuse to pay a neighboring farmer. A good question to which we will give a good answer. Farmer Brown thought he had plenty of spare cash until that deal on the piece of farm equipment fell through. Then suddenly, he didn't have the money to pay for the cow, but he wasn't about to give up a cow as special as Bossie either. So, in effect, he asked my client to give him an open-ended, no-interest, no-condition loan on the purchase price of the cow—for eternity perhaps—while he kept Bossie. That, however, just wasn't the deal."

In addition to breach of contract, you might also have other factual theories. The relative persuasiveness of alternative factual theories will often dictate the choice among alternative legal theories. Imagine that instead of breach of contract, you want to raise a legal theory of fraud in the cow case. No direct evidence of fraudulent intent exists. Admission in evidence of a few inconsistent statements by Farmer Brown might get you by a directed verdict motion by the defense focusing on the lack of information to support the element of "intent to deceive." But you are not likely to find success with the factfinder. Now imagine your investigation subsequently finds that three times in the past Farmer Brown "bought" a cow, milked it for days and sold the milk, and then came up with some excuse for not paying. That, as they say, is a "different story" (assuming this information is admissible on the issue of intent).

b. Civil and Criminal Defendants

Defense factual theories, like the range of defense legal theories that they support, are more varied than those of the plaintiff. If you understand how a plaintiff develops a good story, however, you will also understand the process of how a defendant develops one. Though varied, defense factual theories are all guided by one or both of the same two basic aspects that guide the development of plaintiff's factual theories—factual sufficiency and persuasiveness. Factual sufficiency concerns involve convincing the court that you have made a prima facie showing (see Chapter VIII and its discussion of persuading a court at pages 262 and 265); persuasiveness concerns involve convincing the factfinder.

When raising an affirmative defense, the requirements for defendant's story will exactly parallel those of a plaintiff's factual theory. As such, the story underlying an affirmative defense must both establish a prima facie claim (sufficient information as to each element) and be persuasive to the factfinder.

Defense legal theories that attack the legality of plaintiff's theories do not really have stories, although they do incorporate information from the case that is relevant to the particular legal positions underlying the defendant's theories. Those defense legal theories focusing their attack on factual sufficiency highlight within their stories the legally significant inadequacies of the plaintiff's story, although the defendant may provide some of the information in its own case on which this claim of inadequacy is based and move for a directed verdict at the end of all evidence.

Defense legal theories that attack persuasive sufficiency require factual theories that, while not obliged to establish a prima facie case, must themselves be persuasive both as to "quantity" and "quality." This common form of defense factual theory generally provides an alternative view of the information in the case, and thereby of what happened. In a *criminal* system, the Fifth Amendment precludes defendant from being required to testify and requires that the prosecution prove its case "beyond a reasonable doubt." Rather than telling "what happened," therefore, the defense will generally attack portions of the prosecution's story as unreliable or as not making sense ("reasonable doubt") and will suggest alternative stories that "could" have happened ("Isn't it likely my client was innocently walking home after a movie when the victim, hysterical after being robbed, saw him and started screaming 'that's the man' . . . 'that's the man'?"). The defense's attack may be based on the same information presented by the plaintiff, information brought forth by the defense, or a mix of both. Thus, for example, consider a criminal case where the key prosecution witness has been given a deal, but insists in court that her primary motivation in testifying against the defendant is because "he is a dangerous man who must be stopped." The defense may present a perspective on this witness that differs from that of the prosecution: "The prosecutor tells you that the eyewitness, Ms. Flack, was testifying just to be a good citizen. Nonsense. Ms. Flack was facing five years in prison when she agreed to testify in exchange for the prosecutor's promise that . . . ."

Defense factual theories that support procedural attacks vary in their composition depending on the nature of the accompanying defense legal theory. For example, a procedural attack based on a lack of subject matter jurisdiction will, like a defense attack on legality, have no real story. A procedural attack based on a lack of personal jurisdiction may, like an attack on persuasive sufficiency, require a story that itself is persuasive ("Plaintiff claims my client was doing business in his state. Let's look at the facts. Plaintiff speaks of a traveling salesman. But who is this salesman? Is plaintiff speaking of Ernie Smith who accidentally crossed the state line during a fierce storm and . . . ?").

With these ideas regarding defense factual theories in mind, the defendant's story in the tale of the unpaid-for cow could manifest itself in a multitude of possibilities, depending on the available information and whether defendant's legal theory is lack of consideration, fraud, gift, and so on:

- There never was any cow or deal. Plaintiff made it all up because of a grudge he has against my client.

- The cow was payment for a debt plaintiff owed my client.

- My client offered to return the cow, but plaintiff refused, thereby failing to mitigate damages.

- The cow was a gift to Farmer Brown.

- The cow plaintiff delivered was not the same one he showed my client at the farm—and plaintiff knew it.

- My client was promised a good "milker." The cow plaintiff sold was completely dry.

- There was a deal but the cow was never delivered.

- Plaintiff got in an accident on the way over, and the cow died a few days later as a result of injuries suffered in the accident.

3. *The Relationship Between Legal and Factual Theory*

When actually selecting and developing a case theory, you must recognize that the legal and factual theories are interrelated. They are linked together by the client's objectives, the law, and the available information. Tentative case theories start to develop when you are possessed of even minimal information. These hypotheses, à la Sherlock Holmes, arise at an early stage (perhaps even before talking to the client or other witnesses) and are subsequently sifted through as you learn more of your client's objectives, acquire more information, and understand more of the law. Early theorizing is possible because, in each situation, there are generally finite legal theories available, and under each legal theory there is a somewhat foreseeable spectrum of facts (information) that will strengthen or weaken the supporting factual theory.

Perceiving the client's *objectives* (gain an acquittal, obtain damages, avoid damages, receive an injunction), you research the *law* to find authority for a legal theory that can achieve these objectives. Imagine you are representing a client accused of burglary. An acquittal is the client's initial objective, and therefore the initial focus of your representational strategy. Research reveals that the legal theories available to achieve this objective include mental defenses, lack of intent, and misidentification.

Your legal theory, in turn, leads you to seek *information* from which you can develop a factual theory to support the legal theory. In the burglary case, you would look for information that defendant has a history of mental problems, or was intoxicated at the time of the offense, or thought he was entering his own home, or that eyewitnesses were biased, or had perceptual problems, and so on.[3]

The information you obtain will then limit the available legal theories. If defendant in the burglary was caught by police in the home, a reasonable doubt of misidentification will not be a viable legal theory.

Limiting the available legal theories may then alter the client's objectives, bringing you back full circle. If no viable legal theories remain after analysis of the available information in the burglary case, the client's objectives may have to be changed from acquittal to a satisfactory plea bargaining or sentencing resolution.

4. *Adversary Context of Case Theory*

In assessing your case theory, you must always think in an adversary context. You must think how your adversary will respond to the strengths of your theory or exploit its weaknesses. When you develop a novel legal theory, you know that your adversary will attack it on "legality" grounds by filing a motion to dismiss. When you develop a legal theory that is rooted in an accepted interpretation of the relevant case law (an "old-shoe" theory), you know your adversary's focus will shift to your factual theory, looking for any weakness—areas where your story does not make sense, key witnesses whose credibility can be attacked, pivotal information underlying the story that can be targeted for evidence objections that preclude admissibility, and so on. All this has been implicit in the discussions of plaintiff's legal theories and defendant's factual theories. Defense legal theories focused on blunting the plaintiff's attack evolved from various types of perceived *problems* that could be exploited in the plaintiff's legal and factual theories. Plaintiff's factual theories, on the other hand, were developed in *anticipation* of potential defense attacks on "sufficiency" and "believability," and in consideration of possible alternative defense factual theories that could support affirmative defenses.

But what does all this really mean when you're selecting and developing a case theory?

First, *be careful*. Sloppy legal or factual research or

---

3. This process can, of course, flow in the opposite direction. Being first aware of information, you may then look for authority to support the legal theories suggested to you by that information. (Information indicating that your client in the burglary prosecution may have been intoxicated will lead you to consider a legal theory of diminished capacity through intoxication, while a lack of such information will, of course, immediately lead to rejection of that theory because you cannot support it with a plausible factual theory.)

poorly thought-out or incompletely articulated stories will be fodder for your adversary.

Second, *address your weaknesses*. Think as if you were your own adversary, attacking every imaginable aspect of your case theory. Then prepare to shore up or to otherwise deal with any such weaknesses by further fact-gathering or developing an argument for the factfinder that will explain away the weaknesses.

Third, some legal or factual theories available to you are less vulnerable to attack and easier to establish than other available theories. *Avoid difficult proof problems* and accompanying adversary attacks through your choice of legal and factual theories. A legal theory of negligence may be easier to prove than one of intentional tort in a particular case and may yield similar damages. (After all, with the former theory you need only show a failure to meet an objective standard of care, regardless of the best of intentions. With the latter theory, you must actually establish defendant's subjectively "bad" intent.) A factual theory in which you allege that the opposing party was "mistaken" may support the applicable legal theory as persuasively as a story in which you take the more extreme position that the opposing party "lied." At the same time, this factual theory of a "mistaken" opponent may provide an easier story for the factfinder to accept and a more amicable basis for possible settlement.

5. *Relationship Between Case Theory and Pretrial Performance Skills*

The case theory provides a basic perspective from which all pretrial performance skills can be carried out (e.g., interviewing, discovery). In this regard, the case theory functions in two ways.

a. Targets Central Issues

The respective case theories of the litigating parties target each counsel's performance skills toward the central issues in dispute. While counsel must present information to the factfinder establishing every element of the legal theory and supporting persuasively every aspect of the factual theory or "story," nevertheless in most cases there will be critical areas on which the outcome of the case will turn. Such areas are the central issues in dispute.

For example, the real outcome of a traffic accident case might turn on whether the plaintiff-pedestrian's injuries resulted from the accident or a preexisting back injury, that is, on "proximate cause" issues. This, in turn, may depend on whether the jury accepts the

testimony of a single expert witness. During the trial, plaintiff will present evidence of duty, act, breach, and damages. This evidence may come before the trier of fact in a perfunctory way, virtually without opposition from defense counsel. But when that expert takes the stand—fireworks! This happens because both advocates know that the case is really about proximate cause. Moreover, both plaintiff and defense counsel knew that this was the real area of contention all during investigation, discovery, and settlement discussions; they had analyzed each side's case theory so they could recognize and deal with the key issue as the case proceeded.

b. Provides Context for Skills Performance

The case theory also provides a context for a particular skills performance. While that context is not necessarily the only factor guiding your performance, it does substantially contribute to that performance's overall purpose and meaning: You interview your client to obtain information to develop, support, modify, or discard plausible case theories. Witness interviews and formal requests for discovery are both aimed at obtaining information to sift through plausible case theories and to focus on information that will support your existing theories or undercut your opponent's. Affirmative civil pleadings incorporate plaintiff's legal and factual theories; responsive pleadings embody variations of defense legal theories. (Criminal pleadings basically incorporate the prosecutor's legal theory.) Pretrial motions, which are structured by a "motion theory" analogous to a case theory, are commonly used to obtain information helpful to your case theory or to keep out evidence helpful to your opponent. In negotiation, strengths and weaknesses of the respective case theories will be a central factor as you and the opposing party weigh the risk of litigation, attack each side's weaknesses during bargaining, and so forth. Finally, counseling will often involve providing advice bearing on the execution of the case theory either directly (should the client testify in a criminal case?) or indirectly (should you recommend substance-abuse counseling when your client's alcohol problem is getting in the way of her ability to cooperate or even her ability to appear in court?).

c. An Illustration

Imagine a criminal case where the defendant is accused of stealing two seat covers from the victim's car. The plaintiff's legal theory (prescribed by statute) determines that the case is one of petty theft. The elements of this theory are: (1) the defendant took property valued under $500, (2) knowing it to be property of another, (3) with the intent to permanently deprive the owner of such property. The central assertions in the plaintiff's factual theory are: (1) the victim's car was elevated on blocks (with the tires removed) on the street in front of his home; (2) defendant was seen by a witness entering the car and taking the seat covers; (3) the seat covers were subsequently found in the defendant's car. The plaintiff's pleading (complaint), which officially commences legal proceedings, will then basically incorporate this legal theory: "On or about _____, the defendant _____ did take property, to wit, two automobile seat covers valued under $500 belonging to _____, with the intent to permanently deprive the owner of said property in violation of Penal Code Sec. _____. . . ."

Imagine now you are attorney for the defense. Before even conducting your first interview with the client, you are aware that the tentative legal theories that could provide a defense against theft are finite: insanity, wrong person, lack of intent (i.e., mistake, claim of right, diminished capacity), fabrication of the claim by the victim, no asportation, duress. With these theories in mind, early in the client interview you begin the following dialogue with your client:

Attorney: What do you know about these seat covers?

Client: I took them, but I thought it was O.K.

Attorney: Why?

Client: Because I thought the whole car, everything, was trash. Dumped. No one's.

Attorney: Why?

Client: Everyone was stripping it. It had been on blocks for months and no one was working on it. It was junk.

Even at this early point in the case, you can use this bit of your client's story and combine it with your knowledge of the doctrine in the area to form your first tentative defense legal theory—that is, there is a reasonable doubt that defendant did not know that the seat covers were the property of another (and, therefore, there is a failure in the prosecution's proof of this element). The central assertions of your factual theory would then be: (1) the car had been on blocks for over a month without being worked on; (2) it was routinely stripped of various parts by people in the neighborhood; (3) it was reasonable that the defendant would think the vehicle and its contents were abandoned.

Examining the two case theories, the central issue in dispute becomes clear. The case will turn on the

factfinder's perception of the defendant's state of mind. At some point, both advocates will understand this. Even if the prosecutor does not actually know that this defense will be raised, plaintiff's counsel generally will be able to anticipate this possibility from the total fact pattern in the case. This understanding of the requirements of their case theories will guide all of their subsequent pretrial performance activities so long as their basic case theories do not drastically change.

As defense counsel, you will now seek follow-up information from your client in a subsequent client interview to assess whether he was reasonable, and therefore credible, in believing the car was abandoned:

Had anyone told him it was abandoned?

Had he told anyone he thought it was abandoned before taking the seat covers?

Can he prove that the car was on blocks for over a month?

Who else had taken parts from the car?

Which parts? When?

What happened when they did?

Both you and the prosecution (or police) will then conduct informal discovery to find information bearing on your respective case theories by talking to neighborhood residents, eyewitnesses, and the victim about a number of issues, including:

1. Defendant's reasonableness, or lack thereof—
   Did the car look abandoned?
   Had people been taking parts?
   If so, did the victim report these occurrences to the police?
2. Defendant's innocent state of mind, or lack thereof—
   How did defendant act when he took the seat covers?
   What did he say to the arresting officer?
   Was he cooperative?
   Did he act "furtively" in any way when he took the covers?[4]
   Did defendant discuss his taking the seat covers with anyone?

---

4. This seemingly simple line of inquiry could subsequently blossom into an effective cross-examination of the eyewitness, when your pretrial performance, as guided by your case theory, yields results at trial:

My client took these seat covers in broad daylight, didn't he?

Right in the middle of a busy neighborhood?

You were close enough for him to see you looking?

He took his time taking the covers, didn't he?

3. Defendant's prior relationship with the victim—

    Did they know each other?

    Were they close? Would defendant naturally know the victim's state of affairs?

    Was there any bad blood between the two? Were there any unusual incidents that could provide the defendant with a motive to steal from the victim?

Note how different these interviews would be if instead the theory was "misidentification," and the accuracy of the eyewitnesses was the central issue in dispute:

How far away were you standing?

Had you ever seen the defendant before?

Do you wear glasses?

Had you been drinking near that time? If so, how much?

What was the lighting like?

Of course, if you were pursuing both theories at the time of the interview, your interview would include questions directed at uncovering information that supports either theory. Later on in the case, you would (depending on the information you had obtained) select one or the other theory.

Imagine now that in carrying out informal discovery, you interview witnesses in the neighborhood and have located someone who claims to have had a conversation with your client in which the defendant allegedly said, "He [the victim] can afford to lose a few seat covers." Clearly, this hurts your case theory. If the quote was "throw away a few seat covers," or words to that effect, everything would be consistent with your case theory. But "lose" in this context sounds like your client thought of the victim as retaining rights of ownership even when the covers were taken. In response to your further inquiry, this witness acknowledges that he's already told this story to the police. You thus ask how he happened to talk to the police. At this point he begins to seem nervous, becomes evasive, and says, "I don't have any more time for this. I'm not like your client. I earn an honest living." You become suspicious and begin to talk to other neighbors about this witness. Your instincts yield

---

When he removed them, he slowly walked down the street with them?

He didn't run?

He didn't try to conceal the covers?

In fact, he put them in his own car which was parked in front of his house, three doors away?

results. According to the neighbors, the witness has had numerous run-ins with the police, most recently a few weeks ago when he was arrested for a misdemeanor possession of marijuana.

Accordingly, in your formal discovery motion to the prosecution, in addition to seeking evidence showing the reasonableness of your client's belief (e.g., photographs of the car) and his sincerity (any statements made at the time of arrest that you hope will evince an innocent state of mind), you will ask about all deals offered to prosecution witnesses (reduced sentences, dismissed cases in return for testimony) and for all "rap sheets" of prosecution witnesses who will be called at trial. You have to raise a reasonable doubt in the jury's mind that the defendant intended to take another's property. Therefore, any prosecution witnesses who will give information that will enable the jury to infer a culpable intent must be impeached. Witnesses can be impeached with certain criminal convictions that can be used to show lack of truthful character (see, e.g., Fed. R. Evid. 609(a)). They can also be impeached by demonstrating an untruthful motive. A deal struck in exchange for testimony could provide such motive. In light of the circumstances of your conversation with the witness who alleges to have heard the harmful statement, and what you have learned about that witness's criminal involvement from the neighbors, the existence of such a deal seems plausible.

Sure enough, in response to your discovery request, the prosecution reveals that the witness has been promised dismissal of the marijuana possession charges if he testifies consistently with the story he told the police. You can, of course, subsequently use this information for impeachment at trial. But you have more immediate goals in mind. You file a pretrial motion based partly on fragments of case law and partly on your own creative synthesis of those fragments to bar the testimony of the witness on due process grounds: "Your Honor, this deal locks the witness into his story, true or not, when he is under oath. It therefore encourages testimony without regard to its truthfulness." (Don't be too disappointed if you lose, however; the court is unlikely to be willing to rule in your favor, since this practice of deal-making is widespread in the criminal justice system. The court, in fact, will likely distinguish this situation from one in which the deal is conditioned on a conviction, a clear violation of due process.)

Subsequently, in negotiation, you will present the information in your factual theory that would reasonably support your client's belief that the automobile and its contents were abandoned. This weakness in the plaintiff's legal theory (i.e., the element of "knowledge that the seat covers were another's property") will be a strong bargaining point. Finally, in counseling your client whether to accept the prosecutor's offer to plead guilty to theft, with a sentence of probation, you again will have to assess the strength of the respective case theories, your chances of winning or "hanging" the jury, and so on.

The simple point of all this is that throughout your pretrial activities the case theory provided you with a constant guide and frame of reference.

E. PLANNING QUESTIONS

You have considered the various steps, and the rationale for each, in developing a case theory. Following is a series of general questions for developing a case theory. You may want to refer to them (and expand on them) as you develop your own case theories.

I. *Objectives*
1. What are the basic objectives of a case theory?
2. What is the purpose of a legal theory? A factual theory?
3. How does your case theory fit into your representational strategy?

II. *Preparation*
1. How will you prepare to begin planning and developing the case theory in your case?
2. What will you read? With whom will you talk?

III. *Developing A Case Theory*
A. *Legal Theory*
Plaintiffs
1. What possible claims for relief (or statutory criminal offenses) could (theoretically) apply to your situation?
2. Which tentatively seem most applicable? Why?
3. Can your legal theory be attacked on "legality" grounds? If so, how will you respond?
4. What are the "elements" of your legal theory?
5. What information do you have to support each element?
   a. Is this information sufficient to get by a motion to dismiss, summary judgment, directed verdict?
   b. Is it sufficient to persuade a fact-finder?

6. What is the source (witness statement, document, etc.) of the information you have to support each element?
   a. Are there admissibility problems resulting from this source?
   b. Are there credibility problems resulting from this source?
7. What procedural bars could (theoretically) be raised against your legal theory?
   a. Do any of these seem to apply to your case?
   b. How can you avoid or meet any such procedural problems?
8. What affirmative defenses could (theoretically) be raised in response to your legal theory?
   a. Do any seem to apply to your case?
   b. How will you respond to such affirmative defenses (attack its legal basis, attack its factual basis, etc.)?
9. What are the chief weaknesses of your legal theory?
10. How will you deal with these weaknesses if they are raised by your adversary?
11. Do you have a strategic sequence of multiple or back-up legal theories?

Defendants
1. What are possible defenses to plaintiff's legal theory?
   a. Can you attack the "legality" of the claim?
   b. Can you attack the "factual sufficiency" of the claim, arguing that it does not constitute a prima facie case?
   c. Can you attack the "persuasive sufficiency" of the claim, positing it should not persuade a fact-finder?
   d. Can you raise an affirmative defense?
   e. Can you raise a procedural bar?
2. Which defenses will you tentatively choose? Why?
3. If you attack the legality of plaintiff's legal theory and claim that the court should not recognize that theory:
   a. What is the basis of your claim?
   b. What do you expect will be plaintiff's response?
   c. What will be your reply?

4. If you raise the grounds that plaintiff's allegations are insufficient "as a matter of law":
   a. Which parts (elements) of plaintiff's claim will you assert are insufficient? Why?
   b. Why (specifically) can't plaintiff cure this insufficiency through amended pleadings, after discovery, at trial?
5. If you contend that plaintiff cannot carry its burden of persuasion as to one or more elements of its theory:
   a. Which elements?
   b. How will you argue that plaintiff cannot carry its burden as to such elements?
   c. What specific information in the case will you use to support this argument?
   d. What response do you expect from the plaintiff?
6. If you are claiming a procedural bar (statute of limitations, venue, etc.):
   a. What is the legal basis for your contention?
   b. Which facts do you possess to support your contention?
   c. What response do you expect from plaintiff?
   d. What will be your response?
7. If you are considering raising an affirmative defense:
   a. Which possible affirmative defenses could (theoretically) apply?
   b. Which tentatively seem applicable? Why?
   c. Which party has the burden of persuasion as to this defense? What is that burden?
   d. Can this legal theory be attacked on "legality" grounds? If so, how will you respond?
   e. What are the elements of each of these affirmative defenses?
   f. What information do you have to support each element?
      (1) Is this information sufficient to get by a motion for summary judgment, motion to dismiss, motion for directed verdict?
      (2) Is it sufficient to persuade a factfinder?
   g. What is the source of the information you have to support each element?
      (1) Are there admissibility problems resulting from this source?
      (2) Are there credibility problems resulting from this source?
   h. What procedural bars could (theoretically) be raised against your affirmative defense?
      (1) Do any of these seem to apply to your case?
      (2) How can you avoid or meet any such procedural problems?
   i. Could any affirmative defenses (theoretically) be raised in response to your affirmative defense?
      (1) Do any seem to apply to your legal theory?
      (2) How will you respond to this affirmative defense (attack its legal basis, attack its factual basis, etc.)?
   j. What are the chief weaknesses of your affirmative defense as a legal theory?
   k. How will you deal with these weaknesses if they are raised by your adversary?
   l. Do you have a strategic sequence of multiple or back-up legal theories?

B. *Factual Theory*
   1. What is your "story"?
      a. What are the central assertions in your story?
      b. How have you ensured that there will not be sufficiency problems?
      c. How have you ensured that the story will be believable?
      d. What have you done to make the story memorable?
   2. How does your story fit into your legal theory?
      a. Do you have more than one legal theory?
      b. Will your factual theory support each of these theories?
   3. What information do you have that supports your story?

4. What additional information would you like to have? Why?

5. Where (specifically) will you obtain this information (e.g., interviews, depositions, discovery motions)?

6. Looking at all the information that makes up your story:

   a. Where will it come out at trial (e.g., testimony on direct or cross-examination, documents, etc.)?

   b. How will you deal with admissibility issues (e.g., required foundations and foundation witnesses)?

   c. How will you deal with credibility issues?

   d. How will you use this information so it will support your story?

7. Will you present your story in your pleadings? If so, why?

8. Will you present your story in negotiation discussions? If so, how?

9. Taking an overview of your factual theory:

   a. Which are the problem areas your adversary could attack?

   b. How will you respond to such an attack?

C. *Overall Case Theory*

   1. What are the central issues in dispute?

   2. What is your strategy for dealing with such issues?

   3. Reduce your case theory to a simple central "theme" that you can return to in argument, negotiations, and so on. (For example, in the case of Bossie the cow: "This is the case of a defendant whose eyes were bigger than his wallet.")

CRIMINAL PROBLEMS: STATE v. HARD

PROBLEM 2

Prosecutor: Initial Development of a Case Theory
(Non-Fatal Assault)

You are employed in the criminal division of the prosecutor's office for Jamner County, State of Major. It is September 3, 198X. The local police have sent over their reports of a shooting at the Unicorn Tavern for your review. A man named Edward Taylor Hard is being held in custody for shooting Bruno Summers at the Unicorn Tavern. Summers is in intensive care, but, according to the attending physicians you talked to on the telephone, is expected to recover. You have to make a charging decision, which implicitly requires you to begin to develop a case theory.

PREPARATION

READ: (1) Pretrial Case File Entries 4 (read *only* initial "Suspect Information" report and the "Follow-up" report, paragraphs 1-13), 17, 58, 61, 62; (2) Chapters I and II. Now think about and answer the following questions:

1. Let's think broadly about your job as prosecutor.

   a. Is your job to "get a conviction"?

   b. If not, what is your job?

2. Now think generally about the prosecution's charging decision.

   a. What is the appropriate criterion for your charging decision:

      1) The most you can plausibly charge?

2) What you think a typical jury would find?

3) What a "reasonable" jury would find?

4) What you personally think the defendant deserves?

5) The charges that would make the defendant willing to plea bargain?

    b. Under what circumstances should you refuse to charge someone the police have arrested?

3. Next focus on the charging decision in this case.

    a. Focusing on the appropriate statute (and instructions), what offenses could you charge? Why?

    b. What are the "elements" of each offense?

    c. Consulting the police reports, what information appears to support each element of the offense?

    d. As to each element, would you seek any additional information? Which? Why (specifically)?

    e. Where would you look for such additional information?

    f. Do you anticipate having any legal or factual problems with proving any of these elements? Specify.

    g. How do you plan to deal with these problems?

        1) What effect will it have on your case if you cannot solve the problems?

        2) What will you do then?

    h. Do you have any information from which you can infer motive? A theory of motive?

    i. Do you have any reason to believe that the defendant may not have had the opportunity to commit the crime?

    j. Will you allege any enhancements? What will be the effect of such allegation?

    k. Do you anticipate any jurisdictional problems?

4. You've just considered what you could charge. Now you must make a decision. Looking at all the information in your case:

    a. What will you charge? Why?

    b. What are the central assertions in your story?

    c. What (at this point) is your story?

5. Now step back and give yourself some further perspective. This whole situation with Ed Hard sounds like a barroom brawl, where the defense may well raise a claim of self-defense.

    a. How do you know that the defendant didn't act in self-defense?

    b. Should you investigate self-defense as a possibility before you file charges? How?

    c. Are you obligated to investigate possible defenses, or can you rely on the fact that the police arrested Hard?

d. Are there practical reasons to investigate at this point?

e. Are there practical reasons not to investigate?

ASSIGNMENT FOR CLASS

1. Outside of class, assume that you are a deputy attorney in the prosecutor's office. You have been assigned the *State v. Hard* case. You will be meeting with your supervisor about the case. Write a short memorandum discussing possible theories of the case. Include a list of further tasks and investigation to be done at this stage of the case. Hand in a copy of your memorandum to your supervising attorneys.

2. In class, meet with your supervising attorneys in order to brainstorm your theory of the cases and to review further tasks and investigation to be done.

PROBLEM 3 _____

Prosecutor: Initial Development of a Case Theory
(Fatal Assault)

It is now September 7, 198X. You had decided to file a complaint charging Edward Taylor Hard with assault in the first degree for the shooting of Bruno Summers at the Unicorn Tavern. That, however, was before today's telephone message from Detective Kelly. The Edward Hard case has changed: Bruno Summers, who everyone thought was going to recover from his gunshot wound, took a sudden unexpected turn for the worse over the weekend and died this evening at 7:00 P.M. in Mercy Hospital.

You must now consider filing a new complaint. A man is dead as the result of Hard's conduct and a charge of assault no longer reflects this reality. Yet you must think carefully whether the charge should be first-degree, premeditated murder; felony-murder; second-degree murder; voluntary manslaughter; or involuntary manslaughter. The wrong charging theory at the inception could affect the ultimate success of the prosecution.

PREPARATION

READ: (1) Pretrial Case File Entries 4-6, 11, 16, 17, 19, 21, 28, 31, 32, 34, 35, 58, 62, 70; (2) Chapters I and II. Now think about and answer the following questions:

1. Review the applicable statutes and list the "elements" for each possible legal theory on which you could base a homicide charge.

2. If you charge first-degree murder, will you use an "intent to kill-premeditation" theory? Why or why not?

3. Do you foresee any problem in establishing premeditation? Explain.

    a. Which are your strongest facts for claiming premeditation? Which are your weakest?

b. What bearing (if any) does the August 20 incident between Hard and Summers have on this issue?

4. If you have problems establishing premeditation:

   a. Will you deal with them by argument to the jury from existing evidence?

   b. Will you investigate to find (some specific) further evidence? Elaborate.

5. If you rely on a premeditation theory, can the defense use Hard's intoxication? Articulate the legal and factual theory that underlies this use.

6. Could you, as the prosecutor, use Hard's intoxication to aid the premeditation theory? How?

7. Now, think about felony-murder.

   a. If you did charge felony-murder, would the charge be one of first- or second-degree homicide?

   b. Will you encounter any factual problems with your felony-murder theory? Explain.

   c. Will you encounter legal problems with this theory? Explain. You may want to look at *State v. Iman,* 198 Maj. 2d 214 (1960).

   d. Can you develop an argument under *Kern v. Superior Court,* 93 Maj. App. 3d 41 (1974), to meet such legal problems?

   e. Assume the court accepts your argument and rejects the "merger doctrine" for assaultive crimes and felony-murder. Is there any reason not to use felony-murder?

8. Is it possible to charge second-degree murder and forget the problems and complexity of felony-murder and premeditation theories? Explain.

   a. If so, would you use a theory based upon intent to kill without premeditation?

   b. Any problem with basing a second-degree murder charge on "extreme recklessness"?

9. Assuming Hard raises self-defense, could a jury find that the defendant honestly acted in fear for his life and still find him guilty of murder, or, at worst, guilty of some lesser offense—voluntary manslaughter? Explain.

10. Looking at the applicable statutes and instructions with all of the above in mind:

    a. What will you charge? Why?

    b. What are the elements of the offense that you will charge?

    c. At this point, what information tentatively supports each element?

    d. Do you foresee any admissibility (i.e., evidence) problems at this point? Elaborate.

e. Do you foresee any problems with Hard's "opportunity" to commit the crime? Explain.

f. Do you have a theory, and any evidence, of motive? Explain.

g. Do you face any jurisdictional problems? Explain.

11. What is your "story" (including central assertions)?

12. Will you allege an enhancement?

a. Why or why not?

b. How can you ask for a penalty to be added "consecutive to" a life term?

13. Finally, let's give some thought to your representational strategy. Though we've attempted to make these materials as realistic as possible, we cannot really provide you with the complex flow of events and personalities over time in which a strategy evolves and changes. Still, we can give you some feel for the process. *Imagine* that you think your case looks very strong on paper (i.e., on first glance), though it gets shakier as one gets to know your key witnesses better and better. You know that defendant is currently in jail on a high bail he will have difficulty making. Defense counsel appears smart and sincere but far too inexperienced for this type of case. You believe even defense counsel himself senses that he is in over his head. What will be your tentative representational strategy at this point?

ASSIGNMENT FOR CLASS

1. Outside of class, assume that you are a deputy attorney in the prosecutor's office. You have been assigned the *State v. Hard* case. You will be meeting with your supervisor about the case. Write a short memorandum (one page) discussing possible theories of the case. Include a list of further tasks and investigation to be done at this stage of the case. Hand in a copy of your memorandum to your supervising attorneys.

2. In class, meet with your supervising attorneys in order to brainstorm your theory of the case and to determine further tasks and investigation to be done.

PROBLEM 4 _____

Defense Attorney: Initial Development of a Case Theory
(Charge of Assault in the First Degree)

You are employed by a small private firm specializing in criminal defense. It is September 3, 198X. You are about to visit a potential client, Edward Taylor Hard, in the county jail. All you know at this point is that Hard has been charged with assault in the first degree for shooting some man in a tavern. Nevertheless, even with this minimal information, you can start to think about a potential legal theory of defense.

PREPARATION

READ: (1) Pretrial Case File Entries **58, 62**; (2) Chapters I and II. Now think about and answer the following questions:

1. Let's think broadly about your role as defense attorney.

    a. Is your task simply to get your client "off"?

    b. If not, what is your job? Explain.

2. Now think about potential legal theories of defense.

    a. Can you effectively conduct an initial interview with Hard without having tentative legal defenses in mind? Why or why not?

    b. Do you have any tentative legal defenses in mind? What are they?

3. Develop a list of tentative legal defenses. Recognize that you have a finite set of choices. You can either raise a reasonable doubt that Hard is the person who shot the victim, or acknowledge Hard did the shooting and raise some other defense (either attacking some element of the prosecution's legal theory or putting forth some affirmative defense).*

    a. Should Hard raise misidentification (of course, in such a case, he may also have alibi witnesses):

        1) What circumstances are conducive to misidentification?

        2) Did you think about—

            a) physical circumstances affecting perception (lighting, distance, time, obstacles)?

            b) condition of the perceiver (tired, frightened, poor vision, intoxicated)?

            c) suggestion (a suggestive line-up or photo spread, some striking resemblence between your client's clothing, hair, etc., and those of the real assailant)?

        3) Now, what factors would make misidentification less likely?

        4) Next, imagine Hard raises a doubt concerning his identification based on the position that all the eyewitnesses are lying.

            a) What specific factors would make such a defense plausible?

            b) What specific factors would make such a defense less plausible?

    b. If Hard admits the shooting:

        1) What potential defenses to assault in the first degree can you think of? (Of course, each tentative defense must then be researched to determine whether, and in which form, the defense exists in this jurisdiction. A review of the instructions

---

*Assume that you *cannot* base a legal theory in this instance on problems with either the legality or procedural context of the plaintiffs' case theory.

and statutes in Case File Entries 58 and 62 will give you this information in this case.)

2) What type of information would either support or diminish the plausibility of pursuing *each* of these defenses?

ASSIGNMENT FOR CLASS

1. Outside of class, analyze the types of information that you could obtain from your client that could support the following tentative defenses:

   a. insanity

   b. duress

   c. involuntary intoxication

   d. self-defense

   e. voluntary intoxication

2. In class, be prepared to discuss your analysis.

PROBLEM 5

Defense Attorney: Initial Development of a Case Theory
(Charge of Premeditated First-Degree Murder)

It is now September 8th, and the prosecutor has just telephoned you. Bruno Summers died last evening in Mercy Hospital. Your client is no longer facing the original charge of assault in the first degree for shooting Summers in the Unicorn Tavern; instead, in light of the prior history of antagonism between him and Summers, Edward Hard will probably be charged with first-degree murder,* based on premeditation. You must, therefore, begin again to develop a tentative legal and factual theory for the defense.

PREPARATION

READ: (1) Pretrial Case File Entries 1, 4,** 5, 16, 19, 58, 62; (2) Chapters I and II; (3) Notes from client interview if your instructor has already directed you to conduct one. Now think about and answer the following questions:

1. List the complete or partial defenses to the charge of first-degree, premeditated murder that are theoretically possible.

2. What position will Hard be in if you successfully raise the *partial* defenses that you have posited?

---

*At present, Major does not have a death penalty.
**The Jamner County Prosecutor's office has a policy of providing police reports to defense counsel shortly after counsel's entrance into the case without a formal discovery request or motion.

---

3. Refer to your list of complete and partial defenses:

   a. What types of information will make each such defense more or less plausible?

   b. Does any such information appear in the police report? Specify.

4. Does misidentification appear to be a plausible line of defense at this point? Why or why not?

5. At this point, what is your most likely legal theory of defense? Why?

6. What role do the instructions concerning "burden of proof" and "reasonable doubt" play in the development of your legal theory?

7. What is your factual theory or "story" (including central assertions)?

8. What role do the instructions concerning "burden of proof" and "reasonable doubt" play in the development of your factual theory?

9. What part of the prosecution's case, as evidenced in the police reports, seems most problematic to your theory? Why?

10. Do you have tentative ideas about how you will deal with these problems (e.g., a prosecution eyewitness may be biased or have perceptual problems, suppression motions or evidence objections may keep harmful evidence from the factfinder)?

11. Assume for the moment you will raise self-defense:

    a. What are the legal requirements for self-defense?

    b. At this early stage, what appear to be your strengths and weaknesses in meeting each of these requirements?

    c. What if the prosecution argues that Hard "provoked" Bruno and thus is not entitled to raise self-defense?

       1) What fact pattern, plausible in this case, could support such a position?

       2) How would you respond?

12. How would your above analysis differ (if at all) if Hard were charged with (a) second-degree murder based on intent to kill without premeditation; (b) second-degree murder based on extreme recklessness; (c) voluntary manslaughter; (d) involuntary manslaughter?

13. Finally, focus on your representational strategy. For this, imagine the prosecution's evidence is very susceptible to a claim of self-defense. You have determined that your client will have to testify in order to credibly raise this case theory. The problem is that, in your view, your client is totally unbelievable and no amount of working with him is likely to make him otherwise. You do, however, have a number of credible, Constitution-based pretrial suppression motions you could raise, many of which will require full evidentiary hearings with witnesses, cross-examination, objections, and so on. The prosecutor, who is extremely experienced, is currently preparing, in addition to your case, a significant political corruption case that is receiving extensive media coverage. You believe that if successful in the corruption prosecution, the prosecutor plans to run for district

attorney in the next election. What will be your tentative representational strategies?

ASSIGNMENT FOR CLASS

1. Outside of class, assume you are an associate in a law office representing Ed Hard. You have been assigned the *State v. Hard* case. You will be meeting with the senior partners at the firm's weekly session for discussion of cases. Prepare a short memorandum discussing possible theories of the case. Include a list of further tasks and investigation to be done at this stage of the case. Hand in a copy of your memorandum to your senior partner.

2. In class, meet with the senior partners in order to think about and develop theories of the case and to develop a list of further tasks and investigation to be done.

CIVIL PROBLEMS: SUMMERS v. HARD

PROBLEM 6

Plaintiffs' Attorney: Theorizing About Summers v. Hard

You received a telephone call from a law school classmate who told you she referred Deborah Summers to you for consultation. You recall reading about a shooting and death involving Deborah Summers' husband, Bruno. After interviewing Deborah Summers, you also met with Gretchen and Hans Summers (Bruno Summers' surviving parents). Deborah, Gretchen, and Hans Summers have asked you to investigate possibilities for obtaining monetary recovery for themselves and Bruno's minor children, Ronny and Amanda. You obtained signed retainer agreements and consent forms to act on behalf of the Summers family.

You have subpoenaed and received the criminal file, *State v. Hard,* from the prosecutor's office. (As you know, the prosecutor has dismissed the criminal case against Ed Hard and will not be filing it again.) Your law clerk completed a preliminary legal memorandum that you requested. You are now ready to theorize about legal and factual theories for *Summers v. Hard*. Theorizing at this stage of a case is a creative process since you have many potential defendants (Ed Hard; M.C. Davola, the Unicorn Tavern owner, and his employees, Mary Apple and Tom Donaldson; Dr. Brett Day; and others).

PREPARATION

READ: (1) Pretrial Case File Entries 1-35, 59, 60, 63, 90; (2) Chapters II and VI; (3) Notes of interview with Deborah Summers. Now think about and answer the following questions:

1. List your objectives in theorizing about *Summers v. Hard*.

2. Suppose the prosecutor did not dismiss *State v. Hard*. What effect, if

any, would a criminal prosecution of Ed Hard for first-degree murder have on a civil lawsuit for wrongful death?*

3. List the potential parties you want to consider in planning a representational strategy.

   a. Plaintiffs

   b. Defendants

4. What role do the civil jury instructions concerning proximate cause and duty play in the development of your legal theories?

5. What role do the civil jury instructions concerning proximate cause and duty play in the development of your factual theories?

6. The State of Major has wrongful death and survival statutes.

   a. Are these statutes applicable in this case? Explain.

   b. Explain specifically how case law (in the research memoranda) affects the applicability of claims under the statutes.

   c. Can plaintiffs (factually and substantively) base claims on the State of Major wrongful death and survival statutes?

7. List the possible legal theories in this case.

   a. For each theory list the elements.

   b. For each theory list the relevant facts.

8. Is medical malpractice a possible legal claim? Why or why not?

   a. Theoretically, what facts could support a medical malpractice claim?

   b. Specifically, what facts, if any, in *Summers v. Hard* support such a claim in this case?

   c. What facts are problematic in this case?

   d. State a possible factual theory for a medical malpractice claim (i.e., your "story") for *Summers v. Hard*.

9. What defenses, if any, do you foresee defendants could raise if medical malpractice is a claim? Can you overcome them? How?

10. If plaintiffs assert medical malpractice, do you foresee any tactical problems in relying on such a claim? Explain.

11. Do you need additional information in order to determine whether medical malpractice is a possible claim for relief? Explain.

---

*Whenever you deal with the civil case of *Summers v. Hard*, assume that the criminal case has been disposed of in such a manner that Hard cannot legitimately resist answering a plaintiff's complaint, request for documents, interrogatories, and so on, on the grounds that his answers could incriminate him in the murder case. It might, nevertheless, be interesting at this point to imagine for a moment that it were otherwise. What would a plaintiff do if Hard could claim the Fifth Amendment under such circumstances? Move for judgment in the case? Move to have the particular issue upon which Hard took the Fifth Amendment found in plaintiff's favor? How could a plaintiff support such positions? Would such positions be stronger if the party claiming the Fifth Amendment was the plaintiff, who, after all, initiated the suit, rather than the defendant? Would it matter for these purposes if Hard raised the Fifth Amendment in response to plaintiff's inquiries about some affirmative defense Hard had raised? Might plaintiff seek a continuance until the risk of incrimination to Hard no longer pertained? Does this alternative make sense when there is no statute of limitations for first-degree murder?

12. Suppose you rely on (1) medical malpractice, (2) negligent harm (by Ed Hard or by Davola via employees?), and (3) intentional harm by Ed Hard as potential legal theories. Articulate the problems inherent in using these theories together.

13. Suppose both defendants Davola (the Unicorn Tavern owner) and Hard are "judgment-proof." A "novel tort" that fills the gap between indigency and monetary recovery for your clients (if medical malpractice is not viable) may be to claim strict liability against the gun manufacturer for manufacturing and distributing a dangerous weapon, the handgun responsible for killing Bruno Summers.

    a. Will you encounter factual problems with this theory?

    b. Will you encounter legal problems with this theory?

    c. Are there advantages in relying on this theory?

    d. Disadvantages?

    e. State the reasons why you would rely on this legal theory.

    f. If you do not rely on this theory, can you solve the "empty pocket victory"? How?

14. There are two conflicting factual theories: Ed Hard negligently or intentionally shot and killed Bruno Summers.

    a. Can you assert these factual theories, and if so, what effect, if any, will they have on the claims for relief?

    b. How will you deal with these two inconsistent theories if you name Davola and Hard as defendants?

    c. Does it matter if you have two conflicting theories? Explain.

15. What facts seem most problematic (at this stage) to your claims for relief?

16. Explain your tentative ideas of how you will deal with these problems.

17. What factors will you consider in determining which legal theories you will rely on?

18. At this point, what are the most likely legal theories you may rely on?

    a. List the possible plaintiffs for each claim and explain the basis for each plaintiff's claim.

    b. List the possible defendants and the basis for each defendant's liability.

ASSIGNMENT FOR CLASS

1. Outside of class, prepare a short memorandum discussing legal and factual theories and defenses to consider in the Bruno Summers case. In your memorandum, you should focus on who could raise these claims and against whom they could be raised. Give a copy of your memorandum to your senior partner.

2. In class, meet with the senior partners and present the case of the death of Bruno Summers at the law firm's weekly session for discussing cases.

PROBLEM 7 ———————————————————
Attorney for Defendant Hard: Theorizing About Summers v. Hard

Ed Hard received a complaint naming M.C. Davola, Tom Donaldson, Mary Apple, and Ed Hard as defendants in the *Summers v. Hard* lawsuit. You are an associate in a law firm retained by Ed Hard because of the possibility of a judgment in excess of his insurance coverage. (Ed Hard has a homeowner's insurance policy with SAPO Insurance Company.)

You have agreed to represent Ed Hard in the civil law suit brought by Deborah Summers and family. You have explained fully in writing to Ed Hard that he may be entitled to be represented by the SAPO Insurance Company, but that there may be a conflict between SAPO and Hard because of the possibility of a judgment in excess of the insurance policy. The SAPO Insurance Company has indicated to you that it is still evaluating the Hard case. You and Ed Hard have decided that, as Ed's private attorney, you should proceed with Ed's defense while awaiting SAPO's decision.

You have interviewed Ed Hard, researched the law, and your investigator has prepared a report for you. You obtained the *State v. Hard* file from the prosecutor's office.

You plan to discuss the *Summers v. Hard* lawsuit with your partners. The meeting with your partners will be a planning, theorizing, and brainstorming session.

PREPARATION

READ: (1) Pretrial Case File Entries 1-39, 45, 59, 60, 63, 90; (2) Chapters II and VI; (3) Notes of your interview with Ed Hard. Furthermore, in theorizing about Ed Hard's defense to *Summers v. Hard,* refer to the civil complaint (Case File Entry 37) solely for critique purposes. Now think about and answer the following questions:

1. List your objectives (representational strategy) in *Summers v. Hard.*

2. Suppose the prosecutor did not dismiss *State v. Hard.* What effect, if any, would a criminal prosecution of Ed Hard for first-degree murder have on your defense of the *Summers v. Hard* civil lawsuit?*

3. Review plaintiffs' complaint and the documents you possess. List the defenses that defendant Hard could theoretically assert.

4. Refer to your list of possible defenses:

   a. List the facts that support each defense.

   b. List the witnesses and documents that support each defense.

———————————
*Whenever you deal with the civil case of *Summers v. Hard,* assume that the criminal case has been disposed of in such a manner that Hard cannot legitimately resist answering a plaintiff's complaint, request for documents, interrogatories, and so on, on the grounds that his answers could incriminate him in the murder case. It might, nevertheless, be interesting at this

5. When you theorize about your case you should consider, in addition to general denials and affirmative defenses, what action, if any, to take to dismiss or diminish the effectiveness of plaintiffs' claims. Examine plaintiffs' requested damages for Ed Hard's possession of a gun (third claim).

   a. What facts seem most problematic in plaintiffs' third claim? Why?

   b. What facts seem inadequate in plaintiffs' third claim? Why?

   c. Does the third claim seem to be legally inadequate? Why?

   d. Are plaintiffs entitled to punitive damages? Why or why not?

   e. Explain your tentative ideas of how and why you will deal with plaintiffs' third claim (e.g., motions, defenses, discovery).

6. The State of Major has a wrongful death and survival statute.

   a. Are both of these statutes applicable in this case? Explain.

   b. Did plaintiffs properly (factually, legally) allege claims based on the State of Major wrongful death and survival statutes? Explain.

7. Is contributory negligence a possible affirmative defense for Hard? Why or why not?

   a. Factually is this defense supportable?

   b. Will defendant Davola and/or plaintiffs attack this defense? Why?

8. Do you foresee any tactical problems in relying on contributory negligence as a defense? Explain.

9. Do you need additional information in order to determine whether contributory negligence is a possible defense? Explain.

10. Plaintiffs allege that Ed Hard intentionally shot and killed Bruno Summers. Articulate:

    a. The advantages you as Ed Hard's attorney could experience because of plaintiffs' use of this theory.

    b. The disadvantages.

11. Plaintiffs allege two conflicting factual theories: Ed Hard negligently or intentionally shot and killed Bruno Summers.

    a. How will you structure defenses to these two inconsistent theories?

    b. Does it matter if plaintiffs have two conflicting theories? Explain.

    c. What effect does the negligence theory have on Hard's defense?

---

point to imagine for a moment that it were otherwise. What would a plaintiff do if Hard could claim the Fifth Amendment under such circumstances? Move for judgment in the case? Move to have the particular issue upon which Hard took the Fifth Amendment found in plaintiff's favor? How could plaintiff support such positions? Would such positions be stronger if the party claiming the Fifth Amendment was the plaintiff, who, after all, initiated the suit, rather than the defendant? Would it matter for these purposes if Hard raised the Fifth Amendment in response to plaintiff's inquiries about some affirmative defense Hard had raised? Might plaintiff seek a continuance until the risk of incrimination to Hard no longer pertained? Does this alternative make sense when there is no statute of limitations for first-degree murder?

d. Is the negligence theory advantageous for Hard's defense? Why or why not?

12. What factors will you consider to determine which legal defenses you will rely on?

13. At this point, what are the most likely legal theories you may rely on?

14. An opinion letter sets forth an attorney's opinion of a particular question or problem that the attorney has been asked to give advice on. After theorizing about and planning Ed Hard's defense, would it be helpful to send an opinion letter? Why or why not?

15. What allegations of fact in plaintiffs' case, as evidenced so far, seem most problematic to your legal theories? Why?

16. Explain your tentative ideas for how you will deal with these problems (e.g., bias on the part of a witness, perceptual problems).

17. What role do the civil jury instructions concerning proximate cause and duty play in the development of your legal theories?

18. What role do the civil jury instructions concerning proximate cause and duty play in the development of your factual theories?

19. As defendant Hard's attorney you may have a different view of the case than attorney(s) for defendants Davola, Apple, and Donaldson.

    a. List the theories of the case that may be similar to Davola's, Apple's, and Donaldson's.

    b. List the theories of the case that may conflict with Davola's, Apple's, and Donaldson's.

ASSIGNMENT FOR CLASS

1. Outside of class, assume you are an associate in a law office representing Ed Hard in the civil lawsuit, *Summers v. Hard*. You are to present Hard's case at the law firm's weekly meeting for discussing cases. Prepare a memorandum discussing your theories of Hard's case. Give your memorandum to your senior partners.

2. In class, meet with the senior partners.

3. After class, prepare an opinion letter for Mr. Hard concerning representation of him in *Summers v. Hard*.

PROBLEM 8

Attorney for Defendant Davola: Theorizing About Summers v. Hard

M.C. Davola received a complaint naming M.C. Davola, Tom Donaldson, Mary Apple, and Ed Hard as defendants in a lawsuit, *Summers v. Hard*. You are an associate in a law firm on retainer to the EKKO Insurance Company, which is representing Davola, Donaldson, and Apple pursuant to Davola's EKKO insurance policy. Davola also retained a private attorney because of the possibility of a judgment in excess of his insurance coverage. The necessary disclosures in writing were made to Davola concerning possible conflicts of interest.

You interviewed Davola, Donaldson, and Apple, researched the law, and your investigator D. Dapple prepared a report for you. You obtained the *State v. Hard* file from the prosecutor's office.

You plan to discuss the *Summers v. Hard* lawsuit with your partners. The meeting with your partners will be a planning, theorizing, and brainstorming session.

PREPARATION

READ: (1) Pretrial Case File Entries 1-39, 44, 49, 59, 60, 63, 90; (2) Chapters II and VI; (3) Notes of your interview with M.C. Davola, Tom Donaldson, and/or Mary Apple. Furthermore, in theorizing about Davola's defense to *Summers v. Hard,* refer to the civil complaint (Case File Entry 37) solely for critique purposes. Now think about and answer the following questions:

1. List your objectives (representational strategy) in *Summers v. Hard.*

2. Suppose the prosecutor did not dismiss *State v. Hard.* What effect, if any, would a criminal prosecution of Ed Hard for first-degree murder have on your defense of the *Summers v. Hard* civil lawsuit?*

3. Review plaintiffs' complaint and the documents you possess. List the defenses that defendants Davola, Apple, and Donaldson could theoretically assert.

4. Refer to your list of possible defenses:

    a. List the facts that support each defense.

    b. List the witnesses and/or documents that support each defense.

5. When you theorize about your case you should consider, in addition to general denials and affirmative defenses, what action, if any, to take to dismiss or diminish the effectiveness of plaintiffs' claims. Examine plaintiffs' requested damages for Davola's outrageous conduct (see plaintiffs' complaint, fifth claim).

    a. What facts seem most problematic in plaintiffs' fifth claim? Why?

    b. What facts seem inadequate in plaintiffs' fifth claim? Why?

    c. Does the fifth claim seem to be legally inadequate? Why?

    d. Are plaintiffs entitled to punitive damages? Why or why not?

---

*Whenever you deal with the civil case of *Summers v. Hard,* assume that the criminal case has been disposed of in such a manner that Hard cannot legitimately resist answering a plaintiff's complaint, request for documents, interrogatories, and so on, on the grounds that his answers could incriminate him in the murder case. It might, nevertheless, be interesting at this point to imagine for a moment that it were otherwise. What would a plaintiff do if Hard could claim the Fifth Amendment under such circumstances? Move for judgment in the case? Move to have the particular issue upon which Hard took the Fifth Amendment found in plaintiff's favor? How could plaintiff support such positions? Would such positions be stronger if the party claiming the Fifth Amendment was the plaintiff, who, after all, initiated the suit, rather than the defendant? Would it matter for these purposes if Hard raised the Fifth Amendment in response to plaintiff's inquiries about some affirmative defense Hard had raised? Might plaintiff seek a continuance until the risk of incrimination to Hard no longer pertained? Does this alternative make sense when there is no statute of limitations for first-degree murder?

e. Explain your tentative ideas for how and why you will deal with plaintiffs' fifth claim (e.g., motions, defenses, discovery).

6. The State of Major has a wrongful death and survival statute.

   a. Are these statutes applicable in this case? Explain.

   b. Did plaintiffs properly (factually, substantively) allege claims based on the State of Major wrongful death and survival statutes? Explain.

7. Davola may want to assert that the shooting of Bruno Summers was an independent superseding event. What defense can Davola raise? Explain.

   a. Factually is this legal theory supportable?

   b. Will Hard and/or plaintiffs attack a defense based on these facts? Why?

8. Do you foresee any tactical problems in relying on an independent superseding event? Explain.

9. Do you need additional information in order to determine whether an independent superseding event occurred? Explain.

10. Plaintiffs allege two conflicting factual theories: Ed Hard negligently and intentionally shot and killed Bruno Summers.

    a. How will you structure defenses to these two inconsistent theories?

    b. Does it matter if plaintiffs have two conflicting theories? Explain.

    c. Is the negligence theory advantageous for Davola's defenses? Why or why not?

11. Suppose Ed Hard is indigent. You have a well-founded belief that plaintiffs have alleged that defendants Davola and his employees were negligent because the EKKO Insurance Company is "the deep pocket" (filling the gap between Ed Hard's indigency and monetary recovery for plaintiffs).

    a. Will you encounter factual problems defending against this theory?

    b. Will you encounter legal problems with this theory?

    c. Is this "well-founded belief" translatable into a case theory? Explain.

12. Suppose Davola insists that Ed Hard intentionally shot and killed Bruno Summers. Articulate:

    a. The advantages that underlie the use of this theory by EKKO Insurance Company.

    b. The disadvantages.

13. What role do the civil jury instructions concerning proximate cause and duty play in the development of your legal theories?

14. What role do the civil jury instructions concerning proximate cause and duty play in the development of your factual theories?

15. What allegations of fact in plaintiffs' case, as evidenced so far, seem most problematic to your legal theories? Why?

16. Explain your tentative ideas for how you will deal with these problems (e.g., bias on the part of a witness, perceptual problems).

17. What factors will you consider in determining which legal defenses you will rely on?

18. At this point, what are the most likely legal theories you may rely on?

19. As the attorney for Davola, Apple, and Donaldson, you may have a different view of the case than the attorney for Edward Hard.

   a. List the theories of the case that may be similar to Edward Hard's.

   b. List the theories of the case that may conflict with Edward Hard's.

20. An opinion letter sets forth an attorney's opinion of a particular question or problem that the attorney has been asked to give advice on. After theorizing and planning Davola's defense, would it be helpful to send an opinion letter? Why or why not?

ASSIGNMENT FOR CLASS

1. Outside of class, prepare a memorandum discussing your theories of Davola's case. Give your memorandum to your senior partner.

2. In class, meet with the senior partners and discuss *Summers v. Hard*.

3. After class, prepare an opinion letter for Mr. Davola and his employees concerning EKKO Insurance Company's representation in *Summers v. Hard*.

PROBLEM 9

Attorneys for Defendants Hard and Davola: Meeting and Theorizing About Summers v. Hard

Defendants Hard and Davola received a complaint naming M.C. Davola, Tom Donaldson, Mary Apple, and Ed Hard as defendants in the *Summers v. Hard* lawsuit. Ed Hard has a homeowner's insurance policy with SAPO Insurance Company. He retained a private attorney to represent him because of the possibility of a judgment in excess of his insurance coverage.

   The SAPO Insurance Company has indicated that it is still evaluating the Hard case. Ed Hard's private attorney has decided to proceed with Ed's defense while awaiting SAPO's decision.

   Davola is represented by the EKKO Insurance Company. Both Hard's and Davola's attorneys have interviewed their clients, researched the law, and obtained the *State v. Hard* file from the prosecutor's office.

   Ed Hard's attorney has telephoned Davola's attorney to discuss coordinating the defendants' defenses to the *Summers v. Hard* lawsuit. *Before* this meeting, both Davola's attorney and Ed Hard's attorney individually discussed the lawsuit with their partners. (These meetings with partners were planning, theorizing, and brainstorming sessions; see Problems 7 and 8).

Now it is time to think about coordinating the defense case.

PREPARATION

READ: (1) Pretrial Case File Entries 1-39, 44, 45, 59-61, 63, 90; (2) Chapters II and VI; (3) Notes of interviews with respective clients. Now think about and answer the following questions:

1. List your objectives in meeting with the other defendant's attorney concerning *Summers v. Hard*.

2. Will you tell the other defense attorney all you have learned about the case (facts, law)? Explain.

3. Will you discuss your case theories with the other defendant? Explain.

4. Will you share your discovery plan with the other defendant's attorney? Explain.

5. Do you foresee any tactical problems in coordinating defendants' case? Explain.

6. Plaintiffs allege two conflicting factual theories: Ed Hard negligently and intentionally shot and killed Bruno Summers.

    a. Can defendants structure consistent defenses to these two inconsistent theories?

    b. Does it matter to both defendants if plaintiffs rely on two conflicting theories? Explain.

    c. What effect does the intentional theory have on Hard's defense?

    d. What effect does the intentional theory have on Davola's defense? Why?

7. When planning and theorizing about *Summers v. Hard*, defendants should consider what coordinated action, if any, to take in order to dismiss or diminish the effectiveness of plaintiffs' claims. Analyze plaintiffs' claims in terms of coordinating defense actions.

    a. What facts seem most problematic in plaintiffs' claims? Why?

    b. What facts seem inadequate in plaintiffs' claims? Why?

    c. Do any of the claims seem to be legally inadequate? Why?

    d. Explain defendants' tentative ideas of how and why defendants plan to deal with plaintiffs' claims (e.g., motions, defenses, discovery).

8. At this point, what are the most likely consistent legal theories defendants can rely on?

ASSIGNMENT FOR CLASS

1. Outside of class:

   a. Davola's and Hard's attorneys arrange to meet, discuss, and plan strategies for defending the *Summers v. Hard* lawsuit.

   b. After the meeting, give your senior partner a short memorandum detailing your meeting.

2. In class, discuss your memoranda.

III

Fact Investigation

A. GENERALLY

This chapter is meant to serve as an overview to the material on information-gathering in Chapters IV, V, and VII—client interviewing (which you probably have already done), witness interviewing, and discovery. While each of those chapters focuses on the theory and practice of fact-gathering in terms of a particular skill, none highlights the interrelationship between one information-gathering skill and another in the total fact-gathering process. Describing that interrelationship is one purpose of this chapter. The other is to provide you with a helpful organizational tool that we call a fact-gathering chart. As such, our brief discussion is not intended as an exhaustive treatment of the theory and practice of fact investigation. An excellent book that does provide such a treatment is David A. Binder and Paul Bergman, *Fact Investigation: From Hypothesis to Proof* (1984).

From the first moments you hear of the case through the first client interview, you are engaged in some process of shaping factual theories that might support the legal theories you are sifting through. This inevitably leads you to a hunt for information, since the factual theory evolves through gain of information, lack of same, and the inferences therefrom. See Chapter I at page 11. In this hunt for supporting information, you must also be open to finding information that will modify, or even change, your factual theory to such an extent that alteration of your legal theory is required in turn. Early in the case, moreover, this search for information will aid you in selecting among competing legal theories. (Of course, your representational strategy will have a bearing on how you go about this task. Thus you may want a quick settlement before much information-gathering occurs if you believe that the more the other side knows, the weaker your position will appear. Or you may pursue extensive formal discovery because it will help your negotiation—the more information that is known, the weaker the opponent's case will appear.)

As an illustration of the concept, imagine you are representing a civil plaintiff who has filed a negligence suit after she was injured when the bleachers at a minor league ballpark collapsed. Having identified the appropriate defendant, your legal theory will include the negligence elements: duty of care, breach of duty, proximate causation, and injury. For this example, think only about the element of injury. What are the assertions in your factual theory or "story" that support this particular element? Such a story might contain assertions such as, "For a month the plaintiff was in excruciating pain, trapped in a nightmare of machines and tubes in an intensive care unit." These assertions, however, can only be made if they are supported by information (e.g., photographs, the plaintiff's version of the events). Information, in turn, will be located through some form of fact investigation.

There are many different methods for carrying out this hunt which we refer to here as information-gathering or fact investigation: hiring a consultant/expert to investigate the scene; scientific testing by experts or laboratories; client interviewing; witness interviewing; formal discovery. You may even consider using special federal and state statutes that give you access to information (Freedom of Information Acts.) Thus in your quest for information to support the factual assertions underlying the element of damages in the negligence case described above, you may interview a hospital nurse and find out your client was writhing in pain day in and day out, conduct a follow-up client interview and obtain a dramatic recita-

tion of plaintiff's agony, visit your client's room in intensive care and videotape the claustrophobic surroundings in which she was confined, and take the deposition of an expert witness who can explain why painkillers would not work in plaintiff's situation.

The chapters of this book dealing with case theory, client interviews, witness interviews, and discovery provide detailed perspectives from which to approach your planning for fact-gathering. We would like, however, to provide you with two additional approaches to fact investigation. First, we want you to appreciate how to select and use an expert in your fact investigation to help you prepare your case and develop your case theory. Accordingly, an extensive treatment of this topic follows. Second, we want to introduce you briefly to organizing an overview of your fact-gathering by the use of a diagram.

B. SELECTING AN EXPERT

At some point in your preparation, you may decide that your case probably needs a particular type of expert to testify as a consultant or as a witness at the trial, and then you will select a particular person to be that expert. But how do you initially determine that an expert should be involved in the case? And how do you select the particular *type* of expert (i.e., odontologist, engineer, doctor)? Finally, what criteria guide you in selecting a particular individual to be the expert?

1. Developing Your Case Theory

In discussing these issues that govern the selection of an expert, we rely on the following hypothetical.

Imagine you represent plaintiff, a 42-year-old woman. She has told you that she decided to wash the windows of her three-story home. She rented an aluminum ladder and began washing the windows. Near the end of the day's work, she placed the fully extended ladder against the house, climbed to the third floor from the top rung of the ladder, and stretched forward to wash a bedroom window. The rung bent slightly, the ladder slid out to the side, and plaintiff fell three stories. She is now permanently disabled. You examined the ladder and found a sticker on a leg of the ladder that, in one-sixteenth-inch print, states, "Do not climb above the fourth rung from top of ladder. Remain vertical on ladder; do not lean out."

Do you need to involve an expert in this case? Ask yourself two questions: (1) Can I develop my case theory without one? (2) Even if I can, am I able to support that theory or meet my opponent's theory without one? If the answer to either question is "no" (or even "I'm not sure"), you should consider seeking an expert. Analyze the hypothetical. What is your legal theory? Did the manufacturer produce an unsafe design and provide unsafe warnings? Was the ladder damaged through negligent handling by the shipper when it left the manufacturer? Did the retail rental store fail to adequately maintain the ladder? If you ask yourself the first of the two key questions—Can I develop a theory without an expert?—you will quickly realize that, without an expert, you will likely not even know *who* the responsible parties are in this case, let alone *which* theory makes them responsible (although both factors are interrelated in practice.)

2. *Using an Expert*

Imagine now that after investigation (which, as we will discuss later, itself required consultation with an expert), you have determined that you wish to bring suit against the manufacturer on a strict liability legal theory. Elements of this strict liability legal theory require you to prove: (1) the condition was unreasonably dangerous (not safe for a use to which it would likely be put); (2) the condition existed when it left defendant's manufacturing company; (3) injury was caused by the defective condition; and (4) the injury resulted in general and special damages. Focus only on the first element, "unreasonably dangerous condition," and ask yourself the second of our key questions—Am I able to establish this without an expert? While theoretically possible, appeals to common sense may not be an effective strategy for convincing a jury that the design of a product is flawed so as to be *unreasonably* dangerous. Without the use of an expert how, for example, will you establish the existence of safer alternative structural designs that the manufacturer could have used? What can a lay witness say about what is or isn't a sufficient warning?

So you now know you want an expert, but what kind? The general topics may narrow the range. Concern about the design of the ladder may lead you to seek some type of products engineer. There may be experts on ladder safety standards who could assess the adequacy of the written warning. Also keep in mind that one expert may lead to another.

You may in fact need an expert to find the right expert or additional experts. The more technical the case is, the more likely you will need an expert as a consultant. A consultant/expert may assist you in identifying areas requiring expert investigation if you are to ascertain substantive information to support your case theory. For instance, an expert on ladder manufacturing and design process might suggest to you that you employ a metallurgist in order to investigate and (you hope) find that the aluminum in the rung was bad, thereby constituting an unsafe condition. (The consulting expert may also provide you with ideas for matters you should seek in discovery.)

Also, as you become familiar with a particular area of practice (or with someone who is), you will begin to become familiar with the usual range of expert fields that apply to the area. Take criminal law as an example. Imagine you are the prosecutor trying to build a case around a weak identification. You could engage in a process analogous to one we suggest in our discussion of discovery in Chapter VII and first list every area of expertise that could help. Then you would match these areas to what you know about your case. Begin, therefore, by asking yourself, "What possible fields of expertise could theoretically connect a defendant to the crime, crime scene, or the victim, and what investigation needs to be conducted?" Quite a list should follow, but just consider one potential category on that list, "trace" evidence.

A *trace evidence theory* holds that every criminal leaves something (e.g., a fingerprint) at the crime scene and takes something with him or her (e.g., the victim's blood, hair); an exchange always occurs. For example, trace evidence that a suspect could leave behind and that could be used by various experts in the forensic sciences to connect the suspect with the victim and the crime scene include the following:

Hair: The suspect may have shed some hair and if it were found either at the crime scene or on the victim, and compared to known hair (i.e., hair taken from the suspect), a criminalist might determine the hairs are similar in characteristics.

Fiber: Fibers from the suspect's clothing could have been left either on or near the victim, and an analysis of the fiber left at the scene and fiber from the suspect's clothing might show they have similar properties.

Fingerprints: The suspect might have left fingerprints on an object found at the scene, and a comparison of latent prints with known prints belonging to the suspect might conclusively establish the suspect left latent fingerprints on the object.

Biochemical evidence: If the suspect left blood at the scene of the crime, it could be compared with a sample of the suspect's blood to determine not only whether it matches the suspect's blood type, but also whether other characteristics of the blood (red cell antigens or enzymes) match. Approximately 80 percent of the population are secretors; they secrete blood factors (A, B, O, and enzymes) in bodily fluids (i.e., semen, vaginal secretions, and saliva). If any one of these body fluids was left at the crime scene in sufficient quantity, it could be compared with biochemical evidence taken from the suspect.

Bite mark: An odontologist might be able to compare marks left on a victim's body with suspect's teeth to determine whether or not the suspect bit the victim.

With this list, you can look to your case. Were there hairs on the suspect's clothing matching the general character of the victim's? Find an expert in hair matches. (Of course, an expert may have been employed to seek out the hairs in the first place. Analogous to the interrelationship between the legal and factual theories, knowing the experts that are available leads you to look for the raw data these experts can use, while finding certain raw data leads you to think of certain types of experts.) Were there cloth fibers under the suspect's fingernails? Locate an expert in fiber comparisons, and so on.

But there is a caveat. While this suggested mental process is a powerful tool, for it results in a concentration of efforts on accomplishing a particular result (i.e., finding the appropriate expert), it can trap you in tunnel vision. You can be ensnared in at least two ways. First, the analysis of what type of expert investigation or testimony is needed is premised on your tentative case theory and what that theory requires. If the theory is wrong or if a better one exists, you may miss the significance of substantive information that might lead to other conclusions: a better case theory or a different way of proving the theory. For instance, in the products liability case, you premised your selection of an expert on your tentative decision to follow a strict liability case theory. But this is not the only potential case theory under the fact pattern; another possible legal theory is negligence. Under that theory, the contention might be that the defendant was negligent in failing to do what an ordinary prudent ladder manufacturer would do. A tunnel vision approach that focuses exclusively on the elements of a strict liability theory (e.g., product defect, inadequate instruction) might result in counsel not considering, or not giving sufficient attention to, a negligence theory based on defendant's omissions (e.g., failure to employ a safety engineer). Second, advancements in scientific technology, or a novel application of an existing one, may have created new means of proof outside the usual ones, and these other scientific techniques might be missed. Therefore, you must always keep your mind open to every possible way expert investigation and testimony might be used. The more you know about scientific techniques, the more possibilities you can explore as means to build an effective case theory or to undermine your opponent's theory.

C. THE PROCESS OF ELIMINATION

You have now determined that, in light of your case theories, you can use an expert and have even focused on the field of expertise required. All that, however, does not mean that you will in fact use an expert. There is much more to the selection process. The next stage in this process is one that may be characterized as a process of elimination. Matters coming into play at this stage include, among others, economic factors; the lack of any available scientific technique; an absence of evidence; and the existence of a better approach.

1. Economic Factors

Expert witnesses can be expensive, and the cost may be prohibitive. While the prosecutor in a homicide case may be able to obtain the services of publicly funded crime laboratory experts, private counsel, such as plaintiff's counsel in the products liability case, generally has no such advantage. Private counsel must consider expense funds at every stage beginning with case development, when an expert may provide valuable advice and technical information on such matters as understanding technical aspects of the case, case theory development, and complaint drafting, right through expert investigation (i.e., scientific testing) and, ultimately, direct testimony.

You need to consider whether you can justify the expense of employing an expert's services. You may decide not to use an expert because in your judgment (perhaps after consultation with an expert or after self-education on the technical aspects) the expert is not likely to produce the results you want, and it's just not worth the expense. For instance, as plaintiff's counsel you might decide only to employ an engineer with an expertise in ladder design as a consultant during early case development. While at this early stage you might consider hiring a metallurgist to test the ladder rung, you may decide to spare the expense, at least for the time being, until the engineer has concluded the investigation and been able to advise you about whether or not it is necessary to employ a metallurgist. On the other hand, the nature of the problem may not be one of weighing cost against need; rather, your expense fund simply may not be able to cover the cost of the scientific testing or the expert's fee.

2. *Scientific Techniques Unavailable*

Another factor that can help determine if you will use an expert in a case investigation is whether any scientific technique that could produce useful information in fact exists. For instance, assume in a criminal case that spots were found on the victim's clothing, and you as the prosecutor speculate they may be blood spots from the suspect's scratched hand. If you explored this possibility, the blood spots might be tested to determine whether or not the blood is of the same type and has similar enzyme properties as the suspect's blood. On the other hand, you might learn there is insufficient current technology to test such a small quantity of blood as was found on the victim's clothes. Therefore, science might dictate that you cannot hire an expert.

3. *Absence of Evidence*

The absence of any evidence to be tested would also block expert investigation and testimony. For example, in a homicide case, you might ask the criminalists to explore the possibility that hair evidence was left on the victim's clothes. Criminalists could carefully inspect the victim's clothing for hairs, only to find none. Moreover, the absence of evidence might be the result of a failure to recognize it where it does exist. For instance, it is estimated only a small percentage of bite-mark evidence is recognized by investigators in homicide cases.

4. *A Better Approach*

You may decide that using other evidence (i.e., lay testimony, exhibits) or even argument in lieu of expert testimony is tactically a better approach. For example, the testimony of an expert on eyewitness identification may be limited in impact by the expert's very background ("All of your articles were based on studies of pilots in Korea responding to information on their navigation panels, or on staged crimes in schoolrooms. None were based on actual crimes, were they?"). In argument, counsel will have no such lim-

itation, however, in discussing fundamental problems of eyewitness identification ("All of us have experience identifying and being identified, and from that experience we've all learned a few basic things."). Argument that directs the jury to its common experience may simply be a better approach than using the expert. As another example, a jury may be more convinced that a defendant suffers mental problems from the testimony of friends, neighbors, and associates who really knew him than from the opinion of a *second* defense psychiatrist. (Many courts require some expert psychiatric testimony before they will give an insanity or diminished capacity instruction, so you will likely need at least one psychiatric expert.)

D. A MODEL FOR THE SELECTION PROCESS

Assuming that after this process of elimination you still want an expert from a particular field, you have arrived at the point during case preparation when you will need to choose a specific expert. Initially, you should be aware that an expert may be selected for you without your direct involvement. For example, in a criminal homicide case, the medical examiner might enlist the services of an odontologist when, during the autopsy, the medical examiner observes what appear to be bite marks on the victim's shoulder. Without your involvement, the odontologist would then have examined the body, photographed the marks and taken impressions, compared photographs and impressions of the suspect's teeth with the photographs and impressions of the marks, and finally reached conclusions. Similarly, in a personal injury case, the plaintiff's treating physician may, in effect, have been chosen by circumstances (i.e., that your client went to see this doctor and not some other) as your expert on the extent of injury.

In the usual situation, however, you will have to select the expert yourself. We propose a model decisionmaking process for the selection of a specific expert, which involves an analysis of the person in the light of these considerations:

1. the likelihood the expert will reach conclusions compatible with your case theory;
2. the person's skills as an investigator, a witness, and an expert; and
3. practical considerations, such as the number of experts available, their accessibility, and your ability to pay an expert.

1. Conclusions Compatible with Your Case Theory

Analysis of whether or not to choose a particular person as the expert begins at the beginning—your case theory. Underpinning your decision to select the person as your expert is the premise that the expert will provide testimony helpful in proving your case theory or in attacking your opponent's case theory. Therefore, a primary consideration might be whether the person would make investigative findings and render helpful testimony.

As an illustration, consider from the prosecutor's perspective the homicide case where bite marks appeared on the victim. The prosecutor wants to establish that the suspect committed the crime. In deciding whether or not to use a particular odontologist, the prosecutor might want a person who is likely to investigate and come to the conclusion the suspect's teeth made the bite marks. The prosecutor must recognize the realistic possibility that scientific investigation may lead to findings that are either inconclusive or exclude the suspect as the person who left the marks. In the latter situation, the scientific investigation would produce exculpatory evidence that either would justly lead to the release of an innocent man or, if the prosecution believed under the circumstances that there still existed sufficient evidence of guilt, would have to be disclosed to the defense.

If the prosecutor's only obligation was to prove the case, and not to seek justice as it is, the prosecutor would think only about finding a bite-mark expert who would tell the prosecutor what the prosecutor wished to hear. Such a viewpoint certainly may be offensive to all those who would hope that scientific testing and expert opinion would be objective and not subject to outside influences such as who hired the expert. Realistically, however, some experts may be influenced. Also, science is not cut-and-dry. Reasonable people can differ, situations can be ambiguous, and, especially in "soft" sciences like those studying human behavior, an expert who routinely works with attorneys, and who adopts an ends-means perspective, can plausibly support a position that is 180 degrees from that of an opponent's expert. Consequently, if the prosecutor wants to find an expert likely to tell the prosecutor what she wants to hear, what might the prosecutor consider in analyzing potential experts? The prosecutor could look to prior performance. Is the person one who has repeatedly testified for the prosecuting authority? Has the expert usually rendered an opinion favorable to the party who employed him? Does the witness harbor a pro-prosecution bias? (You will, of course, want to know if this expert has been persuasive in this prior testi-

mony, as discussed in the next section.) Does it appear the expert is seeking notoriety by testifying in newsworthy cases?

Now stand back from what we've been doing. While the prosecutor may want to find the expert who will make favorable findings, blind attachment to such an approach has intrinsic perils. Paramount is the danger such an expert is merely a hired gun, who will distort any factual situation to reach the result desired by the party who employed him. This carries two problems. A talented forensic faker can demean the justice system as well as the legal profession, no matter what the verdict might be. On a more practical level, the distortion may be exposed at trial. In fact, any evidence during the trial that the expert's work has been influenced by an excessive fee arrangement, bias toward a party, or personal inclination may greatly diminish the expert's testimony and possibly damage the proponent's entire case.

The prosecutor in our hypothetical, of course, has an ethical obligation that should override any tendency the prosecutor might have to select a biased expert. The prosecutor's duty is to do justice, not just to convict. Mindful of this principle, the prosecutor should decide to choose the expert based on the person's expertise in the field, as well as the person's investigative and forensic skills.

But now consider the decisionmaking processes of defense counsel in the same criminal case. Defense counsel's responsibility is to ensure that a criminal defendant, who is constitutionally guaranteed competent representation, receives the best defense ethically possible. That does not involve responsibility to seek potentially damaging information. Therefore, defense counsel would want to choose the expert who would render a favorable finding. For example, in the criminal homicide, counsel would want an expert who would be likely to find that the marks on the body were either not bite marks, or if they were bite marks, that the marks either excluded the suspect or were inconclusive. Defense counsel could consider the prior performance and other factors (the expert has customarily testified for the defense) in deciding whether to employ the person.

However, like the prosecutor, defense counsel would be concerned about hiring a person who might be vulnerable to being exposed as having a bias or interest. Also, even the defense attorney must consider both the risks involved if the expert reaches conclusions damaging to the defense case, and the likelihood such a damaging conclusion will be reached. The prosecution may, for example, learn that the defense consulted the expert and, finding the expert will not be called, might bring this information before the jury, asking the jury to draw the appropriate inferences. (Analogously, in a civil case, although counsel is *generally* not required to make an expert witness who has been informally consulted available for discovery, opposing counsel might learn the expert had been employed and under certain circumstances could obtain the expert's findings. If the results were damaging, opposing counsel might be able to use the person as his or her witness.) Consequently, after having considered all these possibilities, the defense attorney might decide not to use the person because the expert might make adverse findings, or because even if the expert's findings are favorable, the expert will appear biased, or because the expert can't be trusted to proceed forthrightly and honestly.

2. *Skills of the Expert*

One approach to choosing a specific expert is to evaluate the characteristics of the possible experts against a profile of the ideal expert witness. While you may not find the perfect expert witness, the profile will allow you to weigh the strengths and weaknesses of potential experts. Think about the characteristics of the ideal expert witness. Commonly, an expert will perform essentially two functions—one as *investigator* and another as *witness*—and the person's abilities in these areas should be major considerations.

a. The Expert as Investigator

An ideal expert would be a highly competent investigator. Preferably, the investigation would personally involve the expert in evidence-gathering. An expert would carefully examine all evidence, perform appropriate scientific tests, and prepare or suggest for preparation demonstrative evidence that would be helpful in illustrating the expert's testimony (e.g., photographs, models). Implicitly, this means that the expert should be someone with whom you can work.

b. The Expert as Witness

Now consider the profile of the ideal expert witness from the perspective of the expert's role as a witness. In order to be a successful forensic expert, the person must have an ability to effectively communicate findings and conclusions to the jury. This key factor may lead you to choose a particular expert over more experienced experts with better technical qualifications. Factors to consider include: how the person will pre-sent himself or herself to the jury; how the person communicates (i.e., does she speak in comprehensible lay terms and explain both the findings and opinions in common-sense language that the jury can understand?); and the expert's track record (i.e., to the extent you can determine, how persuasive did previous attorneys who employed the expert find her and how did jurors react?).

c. Impartiality and Objectivity

The ideal expert would also be a person the jury would perceive as impartial and objective. Information about the expert, which you might consider in deciding whether or not the person probably will project these qualities, include: whether the witness testified more often for one side in a lawsuit than the other (the witness is a defense expert witness); whether the person has a financial interest in the case; whether the expert usually finds the same facts or comes to the same conclusions (after examining the bite marks, the expert invariably finds the bite marks were not those of the defendant); whether an employment bias exists (expert testifies in favor of the party who has hired her); whether personal or professional bias is a factor (adheres to a particular theory over which there is a dispute). Naturally, an expert's qualifications are important, especially if they are particularly impressive or better than the qualifications of an expert called by the opposing party. The expert's qualifications will also determine the permissible scope of his or her testimony. For example, a police officer who, because of training and experience, qualifies to give an opinion about an accident from skid-marks evidence may not be qualified to estimate speeds by applying principles of physics to car damage.

3. *Practical Problems*

Two frequently encountered practical problems facing you are how to locate a suitable expert and how to compensate the expert.

a. Locating Experts

A reliable way to find a suitable expert who most closely matches the expert witness profile is to consult with others whose judgment is trusted (other attorneys, experts) and who have firsthand knowledge of the expert's ability. In addition, you may resort to directories of forensic evidence experts, such as *The*

Forensic Science Directory (National Forensic Center) or *The New Directory of Experts in Attorney Services* (California Trial Lawyers' Association).

b. Compensation

You also need to be concerned about compensation of the expert witness. As previously mentioned, government attorneys may be provided with no-cost services from a publicly funded state or local crime laboratory or be able to call upon the services of the Federal Bureau of Investigation Crime Laboratory for assistance. Beyond that, both a prosecutor and an indigent defendant may be able to request a court-appointed expert and have the court order payment from either a state or local budget. In civil cases, such as a products liability case, economics plays a key role in hiring an expert, since rarely will courts appoint experts in such cases.

If an expert made observations and reached conclusions (say, as a treating physician) before becoming a court-appointed expert, local law may provide that the person may be subpoenaed and required to testify for only the usual fee paid to a lay witness. While compelling testimony without an expert fee might be economical, you may well be faced with a recalcitrant witness.

4. *Number of Experts*

Finally, you must decide on the number of expert witnesses to employ. First, while you may want to call several experts to speak on a single issue so that each, in effect, corroborates the other and the jury does not get the sense that only one person's opinion is being heard, there are some possible problems with this tactic that you should consider. The risk is that multiple expert witnesses in the same field might ren-

der contradictory or somewhat inconsistent findings or opinions, or rely on different bases for their opinions, and therefore might undermine each other's credibility. Second, you must view your case as a whole. How many areas of your case really require expert testimony? Is such testimony necessary to present the foundation for exhibits that the expert developed (e.g., models) or the source for information found in the expert's investigation (hair, fibers)? Or to prove some aspect of your case theory—liability, source of injury, medical damages, projected economic loss? Or to blunt something raised in your opponent's case, including information provided by your opponent's experts? Although your case may require multiple experts, again you should be aware of the potential risks involved in their use. While experts testifying about *different* issues are generally not going to contradict each other, there still remain concerns. A case inundated with expert witnesses, techniques, and jargon may become confusing for the jurors. Also, to the extent your case appears to center on expert testimony, you may lose the genuine underlying emotions and equities in your case, replacing them with a series of academic questions answered by experts, and may precipitate a "battle of experts" in which the jurors will flip a coin between your experts and your opponent's. Third, the expense of hiring multiple experts may also be a determinative factor regarding how many experts you will use.

E. ORGANIZING FACT INVESTIGATION: A DIAGRAM

The chapters of this book dealing with case theory, client interviews, witness interviews, and discovery provide detailed perspectives from which to approach

Plaintiff's legal theory (divide into elements) or *Defendant's legal theory* (divide into elements of plaintiff's legal theory that are subject to attack; also list separately each element of any affirmative defenses)	Principal factual assertions supporting each element	Information that could attack or support the factual assertions underlying each element	Evidentiary concerns with this information (and the specific information for any evidentiary foundations required to meet such concerns)	Sources of information	Investigative method

your planning for fact-gathering. In such planning, however, you might also find it helpful to create a diagram, which helps you maintain a rough overview of the information you seek and the methods you will use in this process. We suggest a fact-gathering chart that will help you organize your factual investigation. (In Chapter VII we provide an analogous organization in the form of a chart that reflects a discovery plan.) This chart thus might be organized by focusing on the factual assertions you want to support or attack, thinking about the types of information or lack of information (whether helpful or harmful to you) that might be relevant to that assertion (including related evidentiary concerns), positing the source of the information (witnesses, documents) and then identifying the methods appropriate to the task (e.g., witness interview, discovery).

CRIMINAL PROBLEMS: STATE v. HARD

PROBLEM 10
Prosecutor and Defense Attorney: Fact Investigation Overview

You have developed tentative legal and factual theories regarding the current charge of first-degree murder against Edward Taylor Hard. Those theories, when placed in the context of your representational strategy, will serve as guides for your factual investigation. Conversely, the results of your factual investigation may lead you to alter your current case theory. You have many methods available to you to obtain information. At this point, you should think broadly about their use.

PREPARATION*

READ: (1) Pretrial Case File Entries 4, 5, 7, 11, 16, 17, 19, 21, 28, 31, 32, 58, 62, 74; (2) Chapters I, IV, V, and VII. Now think about and answer the following questions:

1. What specific information will you seek?

2. Why (in terms of your theory) do you want this information?

3. List all the methods (theoretically) available to you in a criminal case for obtaining information. Indicate if the method is *only* available to either the prosecution or defense.

4. What are the advantages and disadvantages of each method?

5. Which methods will you use? Why?

6. Match the information you are seeking (question 1, supra) with the methods you have chosen to obtain this information (question 5). Explain your choices.

7. Do you anticipate problems in obtaining any of the information you seek, regardless of the method available?

   a. Explain.

   b. If so, how do you propose to deal with these problems?

---

*Defense Attorney: For this problem assume that the *only* information you have received from the pretrial case file at this point is the police reports.

---

8. Later on, you will do interviews with your client (if you are the defense**) and with other witnesses, and engage in discovery (motions and subpoenas). At this point, however, focus on two other methods of obtaining information—investigation of the relevant physical scene(s) and scientific tests.

    a. Investigation of the relevant physical scene(s):

        1) Which scene(s) will you investigate? Why?

        2) Explain in detail what you will be looking for. Why (in terms of your theory of the case)?

        3) How will you record any information you find (photographs, notes, diagrams)? Why?

    b. Scientific tests:

        1) Which tests (if any) would you have done? Why (specifically)?

        2) Are there reasons not to do such tests? Explain.

        3) If, in *State v. Hard*, the prosecution *fails* to do tests that could potentially provide exculpatory as well as inculpatory evidence as to the defendant (e.g., finger-printing), can the defense make use of this fact at trial?

            a) How?

            b) Does the prosecution have a response?

            c) Would the same analysis apply if it was the *defense* that failed to do the test and the prosecution that wanted to take advantage of that failure? Explain.

        4) If you have an expert perform a test, does the other side have the right to your expert's report? (See *Nibbles v. State*, 202 Maj. 2d 791 (1962).)

            a) Does the answer depend on whether you are the prosecution or the defense?

            b) Explain.

        5) Will you hire expert witnesses at this point? Why?

            a) What will be their field of expertise?

            b) What role will they play?

ASSIGNMENT FOR CLASS

1. Outside of class, the prosecutor and the defense attorney develop a fact investigation plan. Give a written copy of this plan (no more than two typed pages) to your supervisor.

2. In class, be prepared to discuss your plan.

****Defense Attorney:** You may have already conducted an interview with your client.

PROBLEM 11

Prosecutor and Defense Attorney: Planning and Doing On-Site Discovery

You should prepare to go to the scene of the shooting. You have seen photographs and diagrams of the Unicorn Tavern, but actually going there provides an entirely different feeling and perspective.

PREPARATION

READ: (1) Pretrial Case File Entries 4, 16, 17, 19, 28, 31, 32; (2) Chapters I, II, IV, V, and VII. View a videotape of the Unicorn Tavern.* Now think about and answer the following questions:

Before **Visiting the Unicorn Tavern . . .**

1. What will you do to prepare for a view of the scene? Why?

2. What specifically will you be looking for? Explain.

After **Viewing the Unicorn Tavern . . .**

1. What did you see?

2. How did the reality compare with your mental image of the tavern?

3. Did what you see help your case? Hurt? Require revision of your theory? Explain.

4. Is there any follow-up fact investigation you want to do? Why?

5. If the case goes to trial, would you want to take the jury to see the Unicorn Tavern? Explain. (Consider: What can you gain? What are the risks?)

6. If you'd want the jury to view the scene, how would you argue that the court should exercise its discretion to permit a view of the scene?

7. If your opponent wants the jury to view the scene but you do not, how would you argue that the court should exercise its discretion to deny such a view?

ASSIGNMENT FOR CLASS

1. Outside of class, sketch a diagram of the Unicorn Tavern marking where (based on the police reports, witness statements, photographs, and such) you believe all the central players and witnesses were located (a) at the time of the fight on August 20, 198X and (b) at the time of the shooting on September 3, 198X.

2. Having watched the videotape of the Unicorn Tavern scene, be prepared to discuss in class the Unicorn Tavern scene and its bearing on your case theory.

---

*Alternatively, your instructor may direct you to visit a tavern that will be designated as your "Unicorn Tavern" for purposes of this problem.

CIVIL PROBLEMS: SUMMERS v. HARD

PROBLEM 12

Plaintiffs' and Defendants' Attorneys: Fact Investigation Overview

You have developed tentative legal and factual theories regarding *Summers v. Hard*. Those theories, when placed in the context of your tentative representational strategies, will serve as guides for your factual investigation. Conversely, the results of your factual investigation may lead you to alter your current case theory. You have many methods available to you to obtain information. At this point, you should think broadly about their use.

PREPARATION

READ: (1) Pretrial Case File Entries 1-35, 58, 60, 62, 90; (2) Chapters II and III. Now think about and answer the following questions:

1. What specific information will you seek?

2. Why (in terms of your theory) do you want this information?

3. List all the methods (theoretically) available to you in a criminal case for obtaining information.

4. What are the advantages and disadvantages of each method?

5. Which methods will you use? Why?

6. Match the information you are seeking (question 1, supra) with the methods you have chosen to obtain this information (question 5). Explain your choices.

7. Do you anticipate problems in obtaining any of the information you seek, regardless of the method available?

    a. Explain.

    b. If so, how do you propose to deal with these problems?

8. Later on, you will do interviews with your client (if you have not done so already) and with other witnesses, and engage in formal discovery (e.g., interrogatories, depositions, requests for admission). At this point, however, focus on two other methods of obtaining information—investigation of the relevant physical scene(s) and consultation with experts.

    a. Think about investigation of the relevant physical scene(s):

        1) Which scene(s) will you investigate? Why?

        2) Explain in detail what you will be looking for. Why (in terms of your theory of the case)?

        3) How will you record any information you find (photos, notes, diagrams)? Why?

    b. Now think about hiring and consulting experts:

1) Will you consult with expert witnesses at this time? Why (specifically)?

2) What will be their field of expertise? Explain.

3) What role will they have (at this time)?

4) If you consult with an expert, does the other side have the right to your expert's report? Explain.

ASSIGNMENT FOR CLASS

1. Outside of class, plaintiffs' and defendants' attorneys develop a fact investigation plan. Give a written copy of this plan to your supervisor.

2. In class, be prepared to discuss your plan.

PROBLEM 13
Plaintiffs' and Defendants' Attorneys: Planning and Doing On-Site Discovery

You should prepare to go to the scene of the shooting. You have seen photographs and diagrams of the Unicorn Tavern, but actually going there provides an entirely different feeling and perspective.

PREPARATION

READ: (1) Pretrial Case File Entries 1-35, 59, 60, 63, 90; (2) Chapters II and III; (3) Fed. R. Civ. P. 34. View a videotape of the Unicorn Tavern.* Now think about and answer the following questions:

Before **Visiting the Unicorn Tavern . . .**

1. What will you do to prepare for a view of the scene? Why?

2. What specifically will you be looking for? Explain.

After **Viewing the Unicorn Tavern . . .**

1. What did you see?

2. How did the reality compare with your mental image of the tavern?

3. Did what you see help your case? Hurt? Require revision of your theory? Explain.

4. Is there any follow-up fact investigation you want to do? Why?

5. Would you want to take the jury to see the Unicorn Tavern? Explain.

6. If so, how would you argue that the court should exercise its discretion to permit a view of the scene?

7. How would you argue that the court should exercise its discretion to deny such a view?

---

*Alternatively, your instructor may direct you to visit a tavern that will be designated as your "Unicorn Tavern" for purposes of this problem.

ASSIGNMENT FOR CLASS

Having watched the videotape of the Unicorn Tavern scene, be prepared to discuss in class the Unicorn Tavern scene and its bearing on your case theory.

IV
Client Interviewing

A. BEGINNING THE CLIENT INTERVIEW
   1. Setting Objectives
   2. Organizing the Interview: The "Funnel" Approach
B. PREPARING FOR YOUR PLAN
C. PLANNING THE CONTENT OF A CLIENT INTERVIEW
   1. A Suggested Approach
   2. Applying the Approach
   Question 1. What tentative case theories are indicated by the information you are currently aware of?
   Question 2. What areas of information could the client possess that are relevant to the tentative case theories?
   Question 3. Which areas will you focus on at this point?
   Question 4. What further information will you seek in such areas in light of your tentative case theories?
   Question 5. What information did you obtain?
   Question 6. What is the significance of this information?
   Question 7. What further information will you now seek?
D. PERFORMANCE PLANNING
   1. A Suggested Approach
   2. Applying the Approach
   Question 1. What is the range of possible practical/strategic considerations and situations that could arise in a client interview?
      Area One. Developing and maintaining the "three relationships" (legal, economic, and cooperative) with the client
         The Legal Relationship
         The Economic Relationship
         The Cooperative Relationship
      Area Two. Deciding whether to take the case
      Area Three. "Factoring in" the setting for the interview
      Area Four. Organizing the interview structure
      Area Five. Obtaining information for legal measures you might take
      Area Six. Getting accurate and complete information
      Area Seven. Preserving information
      Area Eight. Imparting information
      Area Nine. Dealing with a prejudiced client
   Question 2. Which of these practical/strategic situations will you deal with at this point?
   Question 3. What are your objectives in this situation?
   Question 4. How will you achieve your objectives?
   Question 5. What problems do you anticipate?
   Question 6. How will you meet such problems?
   Question 7. If you can't solve the problems, what will you do?
   Question 8. What ethical concerns do you face in attempting to achieve your objectives?
E. PLANNING QUESTIONS

A. BEGINNING THE CLIENT INTERVIEW

1. Setting Objectives

You are about to meet with your client, or with a prospective client if you have not yet been retained. This is your initial client interview, though others will follow. You may have obtained a sketchy idea about the case from a telephone conversation with the person who set the appointment and, from this minimal information, you may already be developing a range of loosely articulated case theories. Or you may know almost nothing about your client and his or her needs and be going into the interview cold. In any of these events, what will you do?

A client interview is too important to be approached haphazardly, relying solely on your intuition or your powers of perception to come through for you. You do need a plan. Whatever the precise form of your plan, it will be developed in the context of three basic objectives. Although this chapter concentrates on the initial interview, these same three objectives will repeat themselves in subsequent interviews and contacts with your client throughout the case. Your specific objectives for a particular interview may be narrower than the full list of objectives suggested here—for example, in a criminal case where the client is in custody, the only objectives of the initial interview might be to meet the client, get information for a motion to reduce bail, and to then set up the next interview. Nevertheless, the following objectives will at some level inform your initial interview with each new client:

1. Developing and evaluating information for your legal representation, including:
   a. information relevant to developing your case theory (such as your client's story, whereabouts of potential witnesses, existence of documents) and your overall representational strategy;
   b. information about client's background (e.g., address, nearest relatives);
   c. information that presents a picture of the client as a person (e.g., how the client speaks or dresses, the client's occupation or hobbies);
   d. information necessary for various motions and legal emergencies (e.g., the realization that the statute of limitations is about to run);
   e. information necessary for counseling the client (should the client bring a lawsuit? should the client try to settle the case before answering the complaint?);[1]
   f. information necessary for negotiation (the relative importance to the client of settling quickly, the client's desire to preserve an ongoing relationship with the opposing party).[2]
2. Imparting information to the client (explaining the legal process, your fee policy, how you will work with the client).
3. Developing and maintaining a special relationship (of course, the interview could also convince you not to take the case).

---

1. Counseling the client—that is, giving advice, helping the client make various decisions—is an integral part of the attorney-client relationship and is often an element in the interviewing process. For clarity of focus, however, counseling will be discussed in detail in Chapter IX.

2. See the discussion of negotiation in Chapter X.

While you are likely to possess some feeling for the concepts involved in the first two objectives—developing, evaluating, and imparting information—the third objective, the notion of developing a special relationship, merits some further expansion. The special relationship between an attorney and a client is really composed of three concurrent relationships, and, although we will neither discuss nor present examples of all three facets of the attorney-client relationship, you will have to consider that relationship and develop it throughout your representation. Each attorney-client relationship can be understood in the following three ways:

It is a *legal* relationship. The formation of this legal relationship is less a matter of tactical choice than a product of the substantive law of the controlling jurisdiction. Nevertheless, it will affect your overall relationship with a client in a number of respects. This legal relationship commits you to a particular set of duties (e.g., confidentiality, loyalty), subjects you to professional discipline for breaching those duties, opens you to civil liability (malpractice action for missing a statute of limitations), locks you into a relationship from which you may need court approval to withdraw, often adds a Constitutional dimension to your activities (e.g., in a criminal case where the attorney's duties and obligations are circumscribed by the Sixth Amendment), and provides a basis on which to build a cooperative relationship (more on this below), as your professionally required duties of confidentiality, loyalty, and zeal help instill client trust.

It is an *economic* relationship. At its most basic, this generally involves obtaining a fee for your representation. Developing an equitable economic relationship is plainly important. A perception by the client at any point in your representation that the fee arrangement is unfair will have a negative impact on the formation of a good cooperative relationship. Without fair fees (from enough of your cases), you in turn will not have the economic resources to competently carry out representation in those cases in which you have been retained. Moreover, for attorneys appointed to represent indigent clients, economics can play a more subtle role in the relationship between the attorney and client. Raised in a market economy where the byword is you get what you pay for, some indigent clients may initially distrust their attorney's abilities. Or aware that the attorney is being paid by the government, some indigent clients may initially think that the attorney is part of "the system" and, therefore, not have trust in the attorney's loyalty to their cause.

It is a *cooperative* relationship, one where the client's trust in the attorney's abilities and motives is given in return for the attorney's commitment to give the client his or her loyalty (expressed as zeal for the client's interests or respect for the client's confidence), and to employ his or her competence and diligence in the client's cause. The importance of developing such a relationship should be apparent. Without it, you will find difficulty in getting the full information from the client that is needed to develop your case theory, and will lack the client cooperation that is required to put the theory into practice. Where a good working partnership is missing, the client seemingly listens dutifully to your advice and then does what he pleases—destroys business records against your advice, goes to the home of his estranged spouse in violation of a restraining order, and so on. In contrast to the economic relationship, which is usually established around the time of the first interview, the cooperative relationship is constantly evolving. Nevertheless, the initial interview may well set the tone for the future growth of this cooperative relationship.

2. Organizing the Interview: The "Funnel" Approach

Never having actually seen a client interview, however, you may be having some difficulty putting all these concepts into a coherent picture. What then does a client interview look like? We can perhaps best portray the interview by focusing on its overall organizational structure. Although different attorneys will approach such interviews with a variety of organizational structures, we have found the widely used four-step "funnel" organization (so termed because it starts broadly, then begins to narrow its focus) to be useful in achieving the basic objectives of this skills performance—that is, *if* it is perceived as a general, flexible guide and not a rigid, mathematical formula. After all, not every attorney and client will impart information and develop a relationship in exactly the same manner and sequence. An interview conforming to the funnel model would follow these four steps:

Establishing an open-ended inquiry, where, after introducing yourself and putting the client at ease, you begin to develop a rapport with the client and to gain information by using non-leading questions (e.g., "So, tell me, what can I do for you?"). This sort of inquiry allows the client to vent emotions, builds rapport by indicating the attorney's interest in the client's story, avoids "coaching" of the client, and permits you to hear what the client really wants.

Placing the information into a clear chronology, where you go back over the information and begin to take control of the interview as you gradually shift away from the open-ended phase of the interview ("Let me get this straight. You woke up Monday to find your neighbor had parked on your lawn."). This puts information in a form that an attorney can use and begins a transition in the interview from rather free-flowing storytelling to a point where you start to take charge and begin to organize the information. Further, in summarizing the client's information in order to form this chronological structure, you are also impressing on the client that you are paying attention.

Verifying facts, where you begin focusing your questions on specific points you perceive as important. Of course, you may be doing some of this throughout the interview ("Exactly where on your lawn was he parked?" "Had you ever told him he could park there?"). At this point you confirm and clarify specific information, questioning the client about further areas and details that seem appropriate. It is at this step that you begin sifting through tentative case theories.

The closing, where you've arrived at the end of the interview and now must make plans with the client for the next steps that will be taken ("We need to meet again. Are you free Wednesday morning at . . ."). Here, as attorney, you set the course for the next stage—arrive at a date for the next appointment, resolve fee issues, instruct the client to drop by certain documents, confirm a court date, and so on.

B. PREPARING FOR YOUR PLAN

What is this preparation we have in mind? Specifically, we are referring to your need to gather information. You will need information to effectively carry out an adopted plan, or to structure a plan, or even to be alert to a specific situation that may require a plan. How do you know what specific information to focus on in this preparation? Your objectives should provide your initial focus: After all, the only reason you want the information is to plan for your objectives. Also, your experience, common sense, intuition, as well as ideas from other attorneys, will assist you in this endeavor. In this latter regard, as in Chapter II, we will continue to suggest possible sources of information we feel relevant to your preparation.

Let's put all these ideas about preparation into play. You want a functioning cooperative relationship with the client. Therefore, the client must have confidence in your ability. One way to achieve this is to appear

well prepared by being conversant with the client's situation from the start. You cannot be conversant, however, and thus cannot carry out your plan, unless you first know something about the legal and factual aspects of the prospective client's case. To do so you must first gather all reasonably available information about the potential client's situation. Often you will find out something about this situation from the telephone conversation during which the initial appointment was arranged, or from a copy of a complaint or other document that the client has dropped by your office. You can also obtain information by drawing inferences from observational data. In that regard, your office staff may be an excellent resource if you plan accordingly. The receptionist who makes the appointments with a prospective client might have information about the client's emotional state or personality traits. For instance, you can instruct the receptionist to ask questions about the matter that the client wishes to consult you about or to observe the client's demeanor. Or you can have a form for each prospective client to fill out before your meeting.

Obtaining information by using these types of sources has advantages and disadvantages that you should consider. For example, using a client form for information-gathering may not be equally appropriate in each situation. Consider such things as your personal style; the type of client you generally represent (unschooled or elderly people may have difficulty with written forms); the type of cases you may handle (tax, family, corporate). Nevertheless, even with minimal information, you can get a sense of the general legal areas involved in a prospective client's case and begin to familiarize yourself with the applicable body of law pertaining to those areas. At some point in your career, especially if you specialize, you will be able to perceive a wide range of potential legal issues and theories with the most bare-bones information.

You also want to achieve the objective of obtaining information. Your early consideration of potentially applicable bodies of law can present you with a sense of the spectrum of legal theories reasonably available and therefore the basis for a fact-gathering plan. (Of course, the best solution for the client may not be one that leads to litigation: In a domestic relations case, reconciliation (along with counseling) may be far more beneficial for the client than dissolution litigation pursued under a brilliant case theory.) An awareness of the spectrum of available legal theories, in turn, cues you to the range of potential information from the client that could be relevant to these legal theories, so you can appreciate the significance of this information if it emerges or seek it if it doesn't. If you know the client was injured in an automobile accident, and your initial research reveals that you are in a "contributory negligence" jurisdiction, any information about seat belts will be of particular interest to you.

You also want to be able to deal with difficult, interpersonal matters that may arise with the client in such a manner as to effectively resolve the matter, instill confidence in your ability to deal with difficult situations, and appear concerned with the client's welfare as an individual. This is most likely if you have already anticipated the potential situation by paying careful attention to the tenor of early contacts with the client or have listened for hints in conversations with relatives and acquaintances, and, therefore, have been exposed to information that alerted you to the need for a plan. You may have found out that the client does not trust lawyers, the client is frightened of authority figures, the client does not speak English, the client couldn't afford the lawyer he really wants and is "settling" for you. With this information gleaned in your background preparation, you can then devise a tentative plan (perhaps using our approach to performance planning discussed later in this chapter) to deal with such interpersonal matters. You may decide to concentrate on being very straightforward with the client who does not trust attorneys, ensure the presence of a good interpreter for the non-English-speaking client, and so on. Preparation and resultant planning might also increase the likelihood that you will be initially retained on the case, thereby forming an economic relationship.

C. PLANNING THE CONTENT OF A CLIENT INTERVIEW

1. A Suggested Approach

Planning the content of your client interview will focus your attention on obtaining information for developing, supporting, or revising your case theory or on undercutting your opponent's. The case theory focuses your efforts, but it should not constitute a constraint upon the breadth of your information-gathering activity. Remember that you are still dealing with tentative case theories and want to obtain all the information you can during this information-gathering phase.

The initial interviews with the client will generally take place when your analysis of the case is in its early stages. Later, of course, you will gain far more sophistication as your knowledge of the client and case

increases. At this point, however, there might not even be a case to consider. The client may want your advice on how to avoid being sued or on whether to file a complaint; the client may need you to write a letter or make a telephone call; or the client may simply want to just drop the whole matter by the day of the interview. So, although your case theory may always be in some process of development and refinement throughout the case, it is not unlikely that your initial case theory or potential theories will not even begin to crystallize until after you've begun talking to the client. In this regard, the client will generally, although not always, have his or her version of what happened. Often your client's story will provide the basis for the factual theory and subsequent fact-gathering. As such, it may both limit and suggest possible legal theories.

The approach we have developed for determining the content of a client interview consists of seven questions that focus on gathering and evaluating information for your case theory. We have found this approach helpful for ourselves and our students and believe it will be similarly helpful for you. It is one possible approach, not the only one. We offer it in that spirit, encouraging you to add to it or modify it in ways that your experience teaches you are helpful. The questions composing the approach are:

1. What tentative case theories are indicated by the information you are currently aware of?
2. What areas of information could the client possess that are relevant to the tentative case theories?
3. Which areas will you focus on at this point?
4. What further information will you seek in such areas in light of your tentative case theories?
5. What information did you obtain?
6. What is the significance of this information? (Does it support, revise, undermine your tentative case theories?)
7. What further information will you now seek?

> **BASIC TASK: Obtain information from which you can develop a case theory and, if appropriate, potential settlement positions.**

2. Applying the Approach

Imagine you are interviewing your client, a criminal defendant who has been charged with petty theft. You are nearing the end of the stage of open-ended questions, and are now about to focus on specific aspects of the client's information:

Attorney: Do you know why you were arrested?

Client: I think so. The store security guard told the police she had seen me pick up a pack of cigarettes, wander around the store, then walk outside without paying. . . . She took the cigarettes from me when she stopped me outside the store.

What should be the content of the next phase of this client interview? Begin applying our approach:

QUESTION 1
What tentative case theories are indicated by the information you are currently aware of?

From this fragment of information you can begin to sift through tentative case theories, which will form your defense. Given the client's remarks, you will probably not try to argue that there is a reasonable doubt that defendant is the right person or that he never took any cigarettes or that the cigarettes were his. Your client's information suggests that it is unlikely that you will be able to build a defense based on the elements either of "identification" or "taking another's property." Rather, whether the client's exit from the store with the cigarettes was intentional or inadvertent will likely be the central issue in dispute. Your legal theory, therefore, will likely focus on attacking the element of "intent to deprive another of his property," and your factual theory will present a story displaying the possibility that walking out of the store was an innocent mistake. (Assuming no evidence of mental illness or intoxication appears, lack of capacity to form the intent does not seem a viable theory.) With this theory, your entire case will focus on attacking the element of intent in the prosecution's case by raising the spectre of mistake ("We've all walked out, or almost walked out, of a store with some unpaid-for article in our hand").

QUESTION 2
What areas of information could the client possess that are relevant to the tentative case theories?

It has been our experience and that of other attorneys we have known that the client will likely possess a broader spectrum of information integral to your case theories than most witnesses you will interview. This information, moreover, will often be embedded in a wide range of subject areas. For your guidance, therefore, we have developed six subject areas that we feel may be ripe with information pertinent to your case theory analysis and that should be kept in mind during your client interview.

These subject areas come with three cautions. First, they are certainly not all-inclusive or static, but provide a method for thinking about all the diverse information your client might possess. As is the case with all such classifications, you should feel free to make up your own subject areas if helpful. Second, though listed separately for clarity, in practice the subject areas will merge and fragment again and again throughout the interview, information from one area spilling into the other, and will not necessarily arise in any particular sequence. Third, the information in these areas will be useful for reasons beyond the development and evaluation of a case theory. Background information may help you in contacting the client, prove useful for a bail motion, play a part in negotiations, assist in determining your fee arrangement, and so on. Similarly, information about the client as a person can help you determine whether to take the case, or guide how you will work with the client if you do take the case, or help in determining whether you need to refer the client to counseling.

Our six suggested subject areas are as follows. Consider:

- the client as a person;
- the client's "story";
- the client's awareness of supporting evidence (e.g., potentially favorable witnesses, documents);
- the client's background;
- the "other side's" case (in the criminal defense area, your entire case theory may consist of keeping your client from testifying and attacking the persuasive sufficiency of an element of the other side's (here the government's) case (i.e., raising reasonable doubts));
- legal motions and matters.

QUESTION 3
Which areas will you focus on at this point?

You have just learned something about the other side's case through your client's version of the statement allegedly made by the arresting security guard. Already you have digested this information and have considered its import on your tentative case theories. At this point, you might want to focus back on the client's story regarding these events. Presumably, various portions of the client's story have already come out in the initial, open-ended stage of the interview unless you specifically told the client not to tell his story or consciously directed the interview to a similar end. Some attorneys avoid hearing the client's story in the initial interviews because they want fuller information about the case, uninfluenced by the client's story, before they hear the client's version. Their legitimate concern is that, without fuller information, they risk not getting accurate information from the client because they will not know what questions to ask, what areas to probe, and so on. The client then, having innocently provided inaccurate information, may subsequently feel locked in to this initial inaccurate position even though it is to his or her legal detriment. The reality of this risk will likely vary with different levels of client sophistication and case complexity, and must be balanced against the likely time frame that is involved before one must obtain further information. (Hours? Days? Weeks?)

QUESTION 4
What further information will you seek in such areas in light of your tentative case theories?

You will want to obtain information that will raise the *inference* that your client wandered out of the store without realizing that he wasn't paying (e.g., he had plenty of money to pay, he was holding the pack in his hands when he left the store and had not secreted it in an inner coat pocket).[3] So you might ask your client:

Attorney: Could you have paid for the cigarettes?
Client: Yes.
Attorney: How?
Client: I had about $40 cash and a bunch of credit cards.

---

3. Note that when seeking information to support your case theory, you may instead come across information that weakens the theory (e.g., witnesses may claim that the defendant fled from the security guard). This is, nevertheless, important information. Among a broad variety of possible responses to this new information, you may then decide to explain this information ("My client panicked when, for the first time, he realized he had the cigarettes"), bring in new information (the security guard was not in uniform and was running at your client "like a madman"), or even settle the case (plea bargain for no jail time). Again, you want to know the bad as well as the good.

QUESTION 5
What information did you obtain?

The client had $40 in cash. The client also had various credit cards. Knowing this information about the client's economic resources, you must now evaluate its significance.

QUESTION 6
What is the significance of this information?

This sixth question in the approach really involves three interrelated categories of inquiry: logical probativeness, credibility, and admissibility.

You must initially consider the logical probativeness of the information you receive, analyzing how it fits into your overall case theory. Note that such information tends to anticipate or support a legal theory based on an attack for lack of persuasive sufficiency. You must ask yourself, Does the information "help"? Does it "hurt"? Additionally, you must assess the credibility of the information and its source. Note that this information, too, can anticipate or support a legal theory attacking persuasive sufficiency. You must evaluate the credibility of the client in general (e.g., prior convictions, reputation for honesty, appearance, education, manner of speech), the credibility of the client in this particular case (bias or lack thereof, ability to perceive, consistent or inconsistent statements), and the credibility of the client information (internal consistency, consistency with other information in the case, accuracy of the particular process that produced the information, such as a computer print-out ultimately derived from data that was not systematically checked for accuracy). An additional word, however, seems in order regarding information pertaining to client credibility. Your entire case at trial may turn on how the client appears as a witness. Many cases have "key" non-client witnesses. Few, however, will give testimony with impact equal to that of the client. While the factfinder will have difficulty finding for a party it perceives as unsympathetic, it will find it all but impossible holding for a party it does not find credible.

Finally, you must assess the admissibility of the information. Successfully denying admission of an opponent's information through an evidence objection will obviously assist in attacking the persuasive sufficiency of an opponent's case. After all, denial of any significant information can seriously weaken the persuasiveness of the opponent's position, both as to "quantity" and "quality." (See Chapter II at pages 24-25.) Elimination of a central piece of information (e.g., one establishing a necessary element of proof) may even support an attack on factual sufficiency. In the criminal area, constitutional criminal procedure will also provide potential grounds for the exclusion of information.

Now, with these concepts in mind, consider our hypothetical shoplifting case and the information about the money and credit cards. The information is *logically probative,* and in a way that "helps." It supports a lack of intent ("My client had no reason to steal these cigarettes. He had plenty of money to pay for them. And, although there are people who shoplift out of illness rather than need, there is no evidence that my client is other than mentally healthy. Certainly there is a reasonable doubt that this taking was totally unintentional"). On the other hand, at this point, you must be aware that this information is totally dependent on your client's word, which leaves you with *credibility* concerns.

Admissibility, however, should be no problem. Here you have circumstantial evidence that bears directly on an element of the prosecution's proof—that is, intent to steal.

QUESTION 7
What further information will you now seek?

In this seventh question in our approach, the word "now" is intended to refer to two separate points in time. One of these points occurs when the interview is completed. At this point you will assess the overall interview and make plans for seeking such further information as you find appropriate in light of available tentative case theories. Such "further information" may be sought from a variety of sources, including subsequent client interviews, discovery, and witness interviews.

The other point in time or, more accurately, points in time, take place throughout the course of the interview itself. A client (or any witness for that matter) will provide a constant flow of information in response to your questions. With each new piece of information, you must quickly assess what the significance might be of the information you have just received, analyzing it in terms of logical probativeness, credibility, and admissibility. Having made this rapid assessment of significance, you will then use follow-up questions to uncover further information.

Follow-up questions may even be necessary in or-

der to determine whether a piece of information is helpful or not. For example, an accused in a robbery case is stopped by the police one block from the crime scene. Does this information help or hurt the prosecution? Although superficially it seems to help, more inquiry is necessary. When was he stopped? If it was 30 minutes after the crime, this information has little or no probative value. Which direction was he walking? If he was walking back toward the crime scene, the information might actually lead to inferences helpful to the defense.

This quest for further information, however, is not aimless. Rather, your follow-up questions are once more informed by the same three categories you considered in assessing the information's significance—logical probativeness, credibility, and admissibility. (Of course, you will be likely to gather information from sources other than the interview that will also aid in achieving these objectives.) With your focus on these three categories, your follow-up questions will follow a predictable pattern. You will try to find information that adds to the logical probativeness of helpful information while seeking that which weakens the logical probativeness of harmful information. You will seek information to emphasize credibility strengths and try to find that which will deal with credibility weaknesses. (If dealing with a witness, you will engage in the former if the witness is helpful, but attempt the opposite if the witness's information is harmful.) You will seek information to gain admissibility of helpful information and look for that which will bar admissibility of harmful information.

When a client or any other witness provides a piece of information at an interview, your mind, in a manner akin to a physical reflex, must respond with the question, "Is it admissible?" This question, in turn, should trigger companion questions: "What are the possible evidence theories that could apply to this information (e.g., hearsay and its exceptions, expert opinion testimony)?" and, where applicable, "What are the required evidentiary foundations under these theories (e.g., foundations for expert testimony, lay opinion, business records and authentication, demonstrative and physical evidence, various exceptions to the hearsay rule, best-evidence rule)?" The entire thrust of an interview may in fact be directed solely at finding information that, say, a business record that hurts your case was not kept in the "normal course of business," from which you can argue at trial that the record is not admissible under the business records exception to the hearsay rule. Of course, even if the records are ruled admissible, this same information can be used to diminish the evidentiary weight of the record.

This cycle of receiving information from your client in response to inquiries, assessing the significance of that information, and then seeking further information through follow-up questions will, of course, repeat itself over and over again throughout the course of the interview.

Back to our hypothetical interview of the defendant in the shoplifting case: You might seek information that would corroborate his story about having money and credit cards. This could blunt any attacks on his credibility regarding this issue. This same information could also prove useful as an independent source from which to establish the point that the defendant had plenty of money to pay for the cigarettes, should you make the tactical decision to keep your client off the stand, and argue reasonable doubts about his intent. Therefore, you might ask your client:

Attorney: Does anyone besides you know about this money?

Client: Sure. The officer who booked me into the jail. She marked it down on a list. I kept saying to her "don't forget those two twenties . . . don't forget." I don't think anyone else knew—wife, friends, bank teller. No. No one else knew.

RETURN TO QUESTION 5
What information did you obtain?

The officer who booked the client into the jail wrote down his assets. The client kept reminding the officer of his money.

RETURN TO QUESTION 6
What is the significance of this information?

In regard to *logical probativeness,* this all seems very helpful. The booking list should solidify that portion of your client's factual theory that he had $40 plus credit cards. His statement seems consistent with a man who had, and knew he had, the money. Further, as regards *credibility,* you have found out about two potential sources of corroboration—the officer (who may be more likely to remember your client because of his statement) and the booking sheet. But there may be *admissibility* problems. What if the booking officer is no longer available, or does not recollect the incident, or denies it? You will have to find the booking list and qualify it as a business record over hearsay

objections. Moreover, if the booking officer is available and you ask her on the stand, "What did my client say?," you are sure to get a hearsay objection.

RETURN TO QUESTION 7
What further information will you now seek (from your client)?

The *credibility* questions about your client's having the money could potentially be resolved by witnesses or documents. Your client has already told you that there was a booking officer and a booking sheet. Accordingly, you may ask him if he can provide you with the name or a description of the booking officer or other witnesses who might remember he had the money or remember his statement, and whether he has a copy of a receipt from the jail showing his assets.

As to the *evidentiary* issues, the matter is a bit more complex, as it is the substantive law of evidence that will key your inquiries in this regard. Although your client's information will not likely be determinative on the evidentiary issues, his information can still help. He may be able to give you information regarding how the booking list was prepared (was it on a form? did the officer file it? was there a copy? did the client sign it?). Supplied with such details, you will be better able to pinpoint the information about the jail's property records and recordkeeping that you may seek in investigation and discovery for use in establishing the evidentiary foundation for a business record or past recollection recorded. But what about the client's statement to the booking officer? It may be difficult to characterize the circumstances of this booking process in such a way that you could meet the foundation for an "excited utterance" exception to the hearsay rule. After all, how startling was the event? On the other hand, a "state of mind" exception (whether characterized as an exception to the hearsay rule or merely circumstantial evidence of that state of mind) might work. With this evidentiary theory in mind, you could question your client about all the reasons why he thought he had two twenties ("When did you last look in your wallet prior to arrest? Why?"). The statement to the booking officer could then be coupled with this information to corroborate the sincerity of his belief that he had $40 ("The question isn't whether my client had the money, but whether he believed he did and, so believing, would have no reason to steal. Therefore, this statement is not being brought in for the truth of the matter asserted (i.e., that he actually had the money) but for his state of mind (i.e., that he *believed* he had the money) and the probative inferences therefrom").

RETURN TO QUESTION 7
What further information would you now seek (from any available source after conclusion of the interview)?

Your initial client interview may now move in many possible directions; for the present, however, you have completed your inquiries concerning the money and credit cards. After the client leaves, you can pursue other possible sources of information concerning these assets. For example, you may want to talk to the person who booked your client about the $40 and the jail's recordkeeping; request a copy of the jail booking records through discovery; and then get back to your client on this matter if new information so dictates.

However, note that this analysis was not intended to portray a complete client interview. It merely dealt with a portion of your client's story—that is, his assets at the time of arrest. Recognize that, even as to the matter of his intent, many other subjects would have been pursued in a full interview—whether there were witnesses who could testify whether or not he was acting "furtively" when walking through the store; whether he was holding the pack openly in his hands when he walked out of the store; whether he was "totally cooperative" when told to stop.

D. PERFORMANCE PLANNING

Having planned for the content is half the battle, but you still must be prepared to actually do the client interview. Planning to perform a given skill requires you to think about a wide and divergent range of practical/strategic considerations as well as situations that may arise. Some of these situations may superficially appear to pose practical nuts-and-bolts issues, ones where you must simply make some decision; however, strategic concerns may well lie beneath the surface. For example, you must decide whether to take notes, use a tape recorder, or use other means to collect information. Your choice, however, may determine whether the witness will even participate ("I won't talk while you play that tape"), how effectively you subsequently can use what the witness said for impeachment (your investigator's scribbled notes will

not have the certainty of the witness's voice on tape), and such. At other times you will be aware of possible problem situations, which may require you to call on certain technical skills should the problems indeed arise. For example, you learn your client has a poor understanding of English. Whatever characterization you use in describing these myriad contingencies and tactical decisions when they arise in the performance of a client interview, you will find yourself dealing with them constantly.

Therefore, prior to performing the actual interview, you want to develop a basic approach to help you deal with these potential practical/strategic situations—an approach that allows you to generate a tentative plan for dealing with each such situation as it appears ("tentative" because "the best laid plans of mice and men . . ."). As you do more client interviews, you will begin to develop a catalog of approaches you can use (with appropriate modification) when considerations similar to those in the past arise. The same is true of the other performance skills in this text. At this point, you have no such experience, however, and so we do not leave you on your own. We offer you an approach that is intended to assist you in planning for any practical/strategic decision or contingency in the area of client interviewing. Even relatively early in the case, when your knowledge of case and client is limited, this approach will generally yield an acceptable plan for a not-too-complex situation. As your own knowledge of the facts, law, and players progresses over time, the approach will produce far more sophisticated and subtle planning and will help you in approaching increasingly complex situations.

1. A Suggested Approach

The approach we propose for developing a plan to deal with the myriad considerations and situations that can emerge in a client interview consists of nine questions. The following references may help you analyze these questions by providing practical and theoretical ideas supplementing those provided in this section of the text: D. Binder and S. Price, *Legal Interviewing and Counseling* (1977); A. Watson, *The Lawyer in the Interviewing and Counseling Process* (1976); D.E. Rosenthal, *Lawyer and Client: Who's in Charge?* (1974).

The questions in this approach are:

1. What is the range of possible practical/strategic considerations and situations that could arise in a client interview?
2. Which of these practical/strategic situations will you deal with at this point?

3. What are your objectives in this situation?

4. How will you achieve your objectives? (If alternatives exist, assess the strengths and weaknesses of each alternative and make the best choice you can.)

5. What problems do you anticipate?

6. How will you meet such problems?

7. If you can't solve the problems, what will you do? (If you can, what will your next steps be?)

8. What ethical concerns do you face in attempting to achieve your objectives?

The genesis of the first question is obvious: You can't make a plan until you know what you are planning for. Thus, the first step in any plan is to recognize the potential situations for which you must plan. The second question flows naturally from the first, while the remaining questions indicate that, in conducting a client interview (as in all skills performances), you are involved in a goal-oriented enterprise. Questions 3 through 8 thus follow a progression fashioned from common experience and common sense.

2. Applying the Approach

Imagine that you are interviewing your client, the defendant in an automobile accident in which defendant allegedly rear-ended plaintiff on the highway. Your client has told you that he was suddenly "cut off" by the plaintiff and therefore unable to avoid the collision. You quickly develop a tentative case theory centered on a legal theory that plaintiff's negligence, not defendant's, was the proximate cause of the accident and a factual theory based on defendant's "cut-off" story. Your tentative case theory suggests that you will need to find information to further support defendant's story (and to anticipate an attack on that story by the plaintiff). One of the subjects you might inquire about is defendant's state of mind shortly before the accident. You might ask the following questions to find out about his state of mind:

Attorney: How were you feeling?
Client: Just fine.
Attorney: This was the morning commute?
Client: Uh huh.
Attorney: Were you on time for work?
Client: Sure. I was in no hurry at all. He just cut me off, that's all.

Satisfied about the information you obtained, you then explore other topics. At the end of the interview, you arrange a follow-up interview at your office next week.

Later that day, defendant's sister calls to discuss some aspect of the fee arrangement. During the course of this conversation, she mentions that she is worried about your client's job. Without his car (which was badly damaged in the accident) he is having trouble getting to work on time and "he was already warned about losing his job for frequently being late just two days before the accident." Initially, you are concerned because it seems that this information could be harmful to your client's case in two possible ways. It could help impeach his credibility if he testifies he was not in a hurry (since this case looks like a credibility contest between defendant and plaintiff). Opposing counsel could then cross-examine (and subsequently argue, in closing, from the information she received in cross-examination) along these lines:

Plaintiff's Counsel: You were in no particular hurry to get to work?
Defendant: Yes.
Plaintiff's Counsel: Just an average commute?
Defendant: Yes.
Plaintiff's Counsel: If you were on time, fine; if a few minutes late, no big deal?
Defendant: Yes.
Plaintiff's Counsel: You had a little talk with your boss a few days before the accident, didn't you?
Defendant: Uh . . . Yes.

The information you have learned from defendant's sister could also allow the factfinder to infer that because defendant had a motive to be in a hurry, he might have acted on that motive; if he acted on that motive, he might have been careless; and if he had been careless, he would have been more likely to have just run into plaintiff as plaintiff claims. You are equally concerned that your client may not be giving you accurate information. What will you do?

Begin applying the approach:

QUESTION 1
What is the range of possible practical/strategic considerations and situations that could arise in a client interview?

In order to assist in this first step, we draw on our experience and suggest nine areas where key practical and strategic concerns seem likely to emerge.[4] By

---

4. Preparing your client to be a witness at trial is not dealt with in these materials, though some of the same concerns are noted in the discussion in Chapter VII of preparing the client for a deposition.

thinking about any or all of these areas in advance of the client interview, you will be able to prepare an approach for those situations that might arise during your performance and thereby anticipate how to handle potential problems. However, whether you use our nine suggested areas, embellish them, or draft areas of your own, the important thing is that you consider some such catalog of key areas of concern before you commence planning the interview.

Each of the nine areas, in turn, suggests an endless number of specific situations that could arise under it. We have, therefore, indicated a number of such tactical considerations and contingencies in the commentary accompanying each area, in addition to some select pointers we have chosen to provide. These situations and pointers, like the areas themselves, are not intended to be all-encompassing. Instead they are intended to give you a sense of the range and type of decisions you must consider in your planning.

As you can see, our catalog of key areas (and accompanying examples and illustrations) goes on for several columns. Since in all those pages of detail you might lose the flow of the application of our basic approach to the present hypothetical, you may want to quickly glance through Areas One to Nine at this point, read through the remainder of our analysis of the approach to performance planning, and then go back and review the catalog at leisure.

Area One
Developing and maintaining the "three relationships" (legal, economic, and cooperative) with the client

Although already discussed, this area of consideration is so significant that it justifies further contemplation.

The Legal Relationship

What will you do if the client's sister wants to come to a meeting with the client, potentially jeopardizing the application of the attorney-client privilege? If you have a potential conflict of interest, are there circumstances where you would explain the conflict and the attempt to obtain a waiver?

Consider the following as an example of this latter concern: Two men come into your office, accused of robbing a liquor store. According to police, one went into the store and one sat out in the car as a lookout. Can you represent both? There is a potential conflict of interest. The one in the car could say the other one

was robbing the store and that he was sitting in the car in something akin to a state of shock, confused and frightened by his companion's sudden, unexpected criminal behavior. Moreover, each man could, depending on the eyewitness testimony, claim he was the one in the car and the other the one in the store. If the latter is the theory behind the defense of either man, you cannot represent both interests. But what if they both tell you, "We were together at a party on the other side of town at the time this robbery was supposed to have taken place"? Now, the defenses are not conflicting and, if neither client's interests would be diminished by joint representation, you can explain potential conflicts to both men and receive their assent to joint representation. See generally ABA Model Rule 1.7. If you decide on joint representation, write a memo for your files confirming, in detail, what you told the men and describing their assent. Preferably, also incorporate all this into a written agreement covering the various aspects of your representation and have both men sign it. Many lawyers, however, would not take this case, fearing problems may emerge down the line that would require one to immediately withdraw from representing both clients—for example, factual conflicts (one man's alibi turns out to be far weaker than the other's and will likely taint the latter alibi by being put forward in conjunction with it) or strategic conflicts (the attorney will be forced into strategies meant to accommodate both men but not necessarily in the interest of both, such as not calling a character witness for one defendant because the other has no character witness to call).

The Economic Relationship

How will you set your fee? Will you hand out fee information? Will you use a standardized fee agreement?

There are general ethical guidelines for fee arrangements (see ABA Model Rule 1.5), but as far as the practicality of setting a fee, you can ask fellow attorneys for a range of appropriate fees. Your fee will generally be set at an hourly rate (unless contingent). It will principally reflect your level of experience, your overhead, and at times, the potential severity of consequences involved, that is, the magnitude of the responsibility you are accepting (e.g., defense of a death penalty case). If you bill against a retainer, you will need a separate trust account. Whatever billing format you use, keep exact records, documenting all your activities on your client's behalf, even if the activity took only a few minutes (".1 hours: discussed resetting Furman deposition with opposing counsel"). Clients are happier if they can see what they are paying for. Also, clients like clear fee information. Put all fee policies in writing and generally have the client sign a fee agreement. Get the business aspects of lawyering settled and out of the way so you can totally focus yourself on representation.

The Cooperative Relationship

How will you develop rapport? What if the client is shy, distrustful, hysterical, slow-witted? Will you have a legal worker with a background in psychology do an initial screening interview for you? Will you explain the process to the client? How will you get information so you can keep in touch with the client over the course of the case? What will you do to keep the client informed throughout the case?

Several examples of methods for developing a relationship with the client are found at page 71.

Area Two
Deciding whether to take the case

Do you have current economic constraints? Time constraints? Are there personality problems that preclude effective representation of the client?

A potential client walks into your office. She has fallen down what she believes was an unsafe staircase in a department store. Her side was sore for a week, but she feels fine now and, according to her doctor, will suffer no lasting damage from the fall. She also incurred $500 in out-of-pocket medical expenses, her employer's insurance plan having covered the remainder. Should you take this case? First, you know "slip-and-fall" cases are generally difficult to win. Juries tend to believe people trip because they weren't watching what they were doing. So you will have to put much effort into preparation if you are going to come up with a convincing claim. Second, there will be real expenses in pursuing the case. You will probably have to take depositions, and you will need an expert to testify about the structural unsoundness of the staircase. Based on verdicts in these types of cases in your jurisdiction, the most you believe a jury would award is a few thousand dollars, and you would bill $125 an hour or a 40 percent contingency fee after the client pays costs out of her share. This case is simply not worth the time and expense to you or the client, unless you find something about it that would make you want to take it pro bono (ABA Model Rule 6.1) or you can get the department store to enter into some method of alternative dispute (e.g., mediation

or arbitration) that could quickly resolve the case. (However, if parties have a prior agreement to use such methods, they might not accede to alternative dispute resolution unless a suit has been filed and some discovery completed).

Area Three
"Factoring in" the setting for the interview

How will you arrange an interview in a jail where there may be problems with noise, restrictive visitation hours, privacy concerns, and the inability to physically hand the client documents or diagrams? In an office setting, will you see the client in the intimacy of a small office or in a more imposing conference room?

Let's examine an interview in a jail. You first will call to find the hours when you can visit (jails are generally closed to legal visits during meals and during "the count") and to make an appointment if necessary. There may be one or two visiting rooms for private attorneys (which, unlike what is often the case with regular visiting areas, are not monitored) and you can then reserve one. You can usually bring in a tablet and pen, but rarely such items as tape or video recorders. For such items, you generally will have to learn any applicable regulations for making arrangements with jail personnel. If, after going through this process, they still refuse to let you bring in a tape or video recorder, and you believe you need this equipment for the interview, you will have to seek a court order through a motion arguing that the policy behind forbidding the recorder can be met through less restrictive means or is comparatively minor compared to the interests of the attorney-client relationship (and those of the Sixth Amendment in criminal cases). If your client is in an isolation room behind glass and you must speak with her over a telephone, and you thus cannot hand her documents to read or sign, or diagrams to review or mark, you will have to go through a similar process to that discussed regarding the tape recorder if you need "contact" visits.

Area Four
Organizing the interview structure

Where will you start? How will you finish? Will the interview be free-form or structured?

The funnel organization discussed near the beginning of this chapter at page 69 provides a good approach to organization. Nevertheless, even though you might use the funnel approach or a variant, you still may find that you will need a more specific structure to deal with the particular information that you wish to obtain from your client, as well as the information that your client might actually give you throughout the interview. We suggest that in planning your interview you might outline the topics or subject areas you want to ask about, and then arrange your questions as to each individual subject area using the funnel method. Such an outline will thus ensure that you have worked out a structure that you can use to organize your interview and to respond to information that your client provides.

Area Five
Obtaining information for legal measures you might take

Will you have a checklist of emergency and other pretrial matters that commonly arise (e.g., a temporary restraining order to stop spousal abuse, statute of limitations about to run)?

A reading of Chapter VIII will provide a basis for dealing with this area.

Area Six
Getting accurate and complete information

When will you use leading or non-leading questions? How can you make your questions clear? Will you have the client mark diagrams? Read and sign his/her statement? Will you test the client's credibility? How? Will you show the client statements of opposing witnesses before you get the client's story? Do you want a criminal defendant's story before you know the prosecution's case?

Obtaining complete and accurate information is, of course, a critical issue; another issue of significant ethical concern and debate is whether, before obtaining your client's story, you should reveal all the legal and factual information you already know about the case. Note the complexity of this issue. You do not want to, and legally and ethically cannot, assist the client in developing false information. You do, however, want the client to give you the full and accurate information necessary for carrying out effective representation. If before getting the client's story, you show the client relevant documents or the statement

of some witness (favorable or unfavorable), or tell the client about the other side's case or about the applicable law, you run a risk. The client may consciously tailor his story to fit the facts or the law or, perhaps, may have his story subtly changed by suggestion, sometimes to the client's detriment. If you do not give this information to the client prior to obtaining the client's story, you also run a risk.[5] Daily life is filled with a mass of data, only a minute fraction of which is relevant to a particular lawsuit. Without the focus offered by first showing the client some witness statements, the client may not be able to recollect significant details or provide full and accurate information. When a client goes to a tax lawyer who asks "do you have any other business expenses?," it would not be surprising if the client responded, "what other categories of things can constitute a business expense?" It is not that the client is trying to cheat; she simply does not know what information among all the work-related data in her mind is legally significant.

Which risk then are you going to take? Will you risk fabricated testimony to get a complete story? On the other hand, must you presume that, given any opportunity, your client will cheat and lie (especially in the criminal area where the client is constitutionally presumed innocent)? Is there a genuine risk that, without some initial direction, the client may give inaccurate information and then become committed to this inaccuracy to his or her detriment? These again are complex issues on which there is a wide disparity of opinion.

Some believe that in the criminal arena the entire system is directed at giving the benefit of the doubt to the defendant, thereby willingly risking the acquittal of guilty people to ensure that the innocent are not convicted. As such, they reason, the decision as to which of the above risks to take has already been resolved by the central philosophy of the criminal justice system itself. Others strongly disagree, positing that the ethical issues involved cannot be resolved by reference to the existence of Constitutional procedural concepts such as reasonable doubt. Whatever your view, if you have a client who your instincts tell you might be trying to use your expertise to create a false story, you can try to diplomatically obviate the problem. For instance, you might state: "I really need to hear your story first, and then I can figure out what law may be involved. . . . I wouldn't speculate about the law here until I know what's going on." If this strategy is not successful and you continue to feel wary

---

5. Notice the congruence between the analysis above and the issue of whether to obtain a client's story at an initial interview. See page 73.

of your client's story, you can refuse the representation (ABA Model Rules 1.2(d)(e) and 1.16) or withdraw if you have already been retained (ABA Model Rule 1.16).

Area Seven
Preserving information

Will you take notes, tape record, videotape, have a witness, such as an investigator, attend the interview? How can you preserve this information so as to protect its confidential nature?

Confidentiality is a central feature of the attorney-client relationship. Accordingly, be certain that every tangible piece of information given you by your client is clearly marked something like "CONFIDENTIAL: ATTORNEY-CLIENT AND WORK PRODUCT MATERIAL." Then don't let "non-essential" persons, those not falling under the attorney-client privilege as agents or associates, near the information. Finally, store this information in such a manner that you can argue you took all reasonable steps to ensure its confidentiality. Although reading of the information by non-essential persons would generally not waive the privilege, since it is not your privilege to waive, the law in many jurisdictions has permitted third-party eavesdroppers to testify about the fruits of their snooping into privileged information. This seems to be changing somewhat; some courts will now preclude even the testimony of eavesdroppers if "reasonable" precautions to preserve confidentiality were taken.

Area Eight
Imparting information

Will you have written materials explaining the legal process for the client? Will a paralegal describe the process before the client meets with you? What information will you impart?

Often, parts of the initial interviews are used to give information to the client. This information usually consists of what the client can expect from the attorney, what the attorney expects in turn from the client, and what the client can expect from the process he or she is about to face. As such, this discussion may range from clarifying the fee arrangement, articulating the client's duties regarding keeping appointments, and detailing how the client will have to assist with interrogatories, to explaining what to expect at an arraignment, what an answer to a complaint is, the

nature of attorney's duty of confidentiality, the lawyer's role at a deposition noticed by the adversary, and so on. By clarifying these various sets of expectations, you can accomplish a number of objectives: The attorney-client relationship is enhanced when the expectations between the two parties are clear from the start; the client can better play a more effective, contributing role in the overall strategy when he or she understands the nature of the process; and the client is likely to feel less stress if expectations are clear and the process less mysterious.

Area Nine
Dealing with a prejudiced client

Suppose you are an associate in a law firm and have been working on the Clever Corporation litigation for the past year, but never met directly with the president of the corporation, Mr. Slivermon. You are scheduled to meet with Mr. Slivermon to prepare a response to a complaint filed against the company. When you greet Mr. Slivermon, he acts surprised that you are the same man he has talked to on the telephone for the past few months. At the meeting, he expresses some reluctance to work with you. You suspect that this is because you are black. Later, he tells your senior partner that he would like someone he can "relate to better." Will you confront the client with his alleged racial prejudice? Ignore the attitude of the client and do the best job possible? Or will you try to convince him of your expertise? Should the senior partner ignore the client's request? Or should the senior partner try to convince him of your abilities? Should another lawyer in the firm represent the company? Or should the law firm tell the client that unless he is represented by you, that the firm no longer wants his business? (Women, and at times men, can face analogous problems with a client due to gender. Or one might encounter religious or ethnic prejudice in a client. Be prepared in the event such an unfortunate situation should occur and plan your response, leaving flexibility for actual circumstances.)

QUESTION 2
Which of these practical/strategic situations will you deal with at this point?

In the rear-end collision hypothetical, your client may not be telling you the whole truth. In this situation you must reconcile a possible conflict between your desire to get complete and accurate information from your client (see Area Six) with your desire to maintain a good cooperative relationship with the client (Area One).

QUESTION 3
What are your objectives in this situation?

Your theory is that your client did not cause the accident. Instead, you allege that the plaintiff caused it when he suddenly cut off your client, leaving your client no opportunity to avoid the collision. Evidence that your client was speeding would damage your story (factual theory), to a degree likely irreparable. As discussed, the information about your client's tardiness at his job provides a motive for speeding, and a jury can infer that he was, in fact, driving in a hurry and there is a basis for impeachment if he says he wasn't. Also, regardless of the potential significance of this information at trial, it appears your client may not be truthful with you. You, therefore, want to obtain accurate, complete information about your client's state of mind the morning of the accident and to impress upon the client that, in the future, he must always give you accurate and complete information to the extent possible.

QUESTION 4
How will you achieve your objectives?

You could do nothing, let the matter pass, and hope this lapse in candor does not happen again. The problems with this alternative are many. You may then be basing your case theory on incomplete or even false information. You may face damaging contradiction at trial where opposing counsel impeaches your client's version. You may become enmeshed in ethical concerns (discussed later in this section). You may set a pattern in your relationship with the client where you continue to receive inaccurate and incomplete information. In contrast, you could lessen these risks inherent in doing nothing by pursuing some method of confronting your client. The problem with this alternative is that you risk losing future client trust and cooperation in the process. Given the choices, how-

ever, we do not believe that you can passively accept an attorney-client relationship bereft of candor. That being so, what techniques are available to you to confront the client?

There are a number of ways you can delve deeper into your client's story to test it. The method you actually choose will vary with your personal style and assessment of the client and the situation. For example, you can ask him about his sister's information (without necessarily revealing the source). Of course, at this point, your client may convince you that the sister's story is not correct. Or you can point out aspects that make his story seem improbable ("Weren't you at the county line around 7:45 when this accident took place? When were you due at work? 8:00 A.M.? How far is the county line from work? So you had eight miles of commute traffic and you also had to find a parking space and get to your work place?"). At the same time, you can impress on him the importance of giving you accurate information ("Look, I can deal with the bad as well as the good if I just know about it. But, if you don't give me accurate and complete information, and we present the court or jury with inaccurate information about even a minor detail, we risk losing our credibility in the entire case"). Simultaneously, you may want to emphasize to the client that you are bound by ethical obligations to maintain his confidences, and that he should therefore feel free to tell you the whole story, knowing it will go no further.

QUESTION 5
What problems do you anticipate?

On the one hand, you need accurate information so you can perform competently. You also have an ethical obligation not to present false information in a case. On the other hand, while part of the cooperative relationship requires that the client assist you by providing accurate information, underlying the whole relationship is the necessity for trust and the corresponding ethical obligation of loyalty to the client. The relationship will obviously be jeopardized if your client thinks, "you're calling me a liar." In this regard, keep in mind that even if the sister's story is accurate, you should not assume that your client is lying to you. Clients do not always give accurate information, not because they lie, but because they are emotionally biased and recall events consistent with that bias, or because (like many witnesses) they are inaccurate perceivers.

QUESTION 6
How will you meet such problems?

Notice that as in most practical/strategic situations, the approach taken here evolves from common sense and human experience. Some of the best "how to" reference materials are, in actuality, systematizations of how some attorney with good common sense and understanding of human experience functioned. With this perspective in mind, consider two suggestions for how to deal with this problem. First, you can ask how the client would explain "to the jury" why, "assuming this story about your work situation is accurate, you still wouldn't be in a hurry?" This at least communicates that, while his prior work situation may be a problem in the case, you are neither discounting the client's story nor calling him a liar. He may have an explanation: "Oh. We worked that out the next day. I come in a half-hour later and work a half-hour later."

Second, you can couple the types of "truth-testing" techniques already discussed with good judgment about how to deal with the individual client. Some clients you may need to get tough with, vividly showing them how their story will crumble once cross-examined and telling them to stop the nonsense. With others, you might want to be more diplomatic, prefacing questions with "now let's anticipate what the opponent will ask," or "I'm a little concerned about how this will look to the jury."

Keep in mind that your overall objective is to assist the client in achieving his reasonable goals. The effectiveness of any approach you take towards establishing your relationship with a client must, therefore, be judged by its tendency to promote or impede this goal. Thus, unlike the relationships of friends, social companions, and family members, these relationships between attorneys and clients are means, not ends in themselves, and the methods chosen to establish them must be judged accordingly.

QUESTION 7
If you can't solve the problems, what will you do?

What is your back-up strategy? The hypothetical, as described, would be an extreme situation and might call for extreme measures. You might engage in more aggressive truth-testing ("Why don't we talk to your sister?"; "I'd better check this out with your boss.").

Or you could even withdraw (perhaps with the necessity of obtaining the court's permission) on the grounds that if your client is not truthful, you cannot work together and thereby you cannot provide effective representation. ABA Model Rule 1.16.

QUESTION 8
What ethical concerns do you face in attempting to achieve your objectives?

If you believe the client's whole story is false, pleading it in a response would be a "frivolous" action, barred by ethical and court rules. ABA Model Rule 3.1; Fed. R. Civ. P. 11. If you merely have a substantial basis to believe this one statement is false, you may pursue the client's defense, but may not permit your client to repeat the false information under oath. In a civil case, you must try to dissuade the client and, if that fails, withdraw and report the client's intent to the court. In a criminal case, you must also try to dissuade the client, but after that, the actions that defense counsel may take and still comport with the Sixth Amendment are completely unclear and in wide debate. You might want to research these points further: See Note, "Professional Ethics of Criminal Defense Attorneys: Is There a Single Solution to the Issue Raised by a Perjuring Client?," 16 Meph. St. U.L. Rev. 531 (1986); cf. *Nix v. Whiteside*, 475 U.S. 157 (1986).

E.   PLANNING QUESTIONS

You have considered the various factors, and the rationale for each, involved in preparing for a client interview. Following is a series of general questions for preparing client interviews. Also look at the planning questions for witness interviews in Chapter V at page 105. You may want not only to refer to the following questions and the questions in Chapter V but to expand on them in planning your client interviews.

   I.   *Objectives*
      1. What are the possible objectives of a client interview?
      2. What are the specific objectives of this interview?
      3. What is your "basic task"?

II. *Preparation*
1. How will you prepare for this interview?
2. At this point, what do you know about:
    a. the client?
    b. the client's case (situation)?
    c. the law in the applicable area (if the area is known)?
3. What more do you want to know about these three areas prior to this interview?

III. *Content Planning*
A. *Obtaining Substantive Information*
1. What are your tentative legal theories (if any)?
2. What types of information will make each of these tentative theories more or less viable?
3. What specific information do you want from this client about the case?
    a. What might this client know about the "other side's" case?
    b. What types of pretrial motions might you (theoretically) be able to raise in this case?
        (1) Are any indicated?
        (2) What information might the client have that bears on such motions?
    c. How will you determine if the client knows of, or possesses, potentially favorable evidence?
    d. Will you elicit the client's story? If so, how?
4. What information do you want concerning possible immediate needs and emergencies?
    a. Which such immediate needs could reasonably arise in this type of case (situation)?
    b. Do any appear to be specifically indicated?
5. What background information will you seek?

B. *Reassessment and Reevaluation (After Completion of Interview)*
1. What potential representational strategies seem appropriate after the interview?
2. What potential legal theories seem viable now after the interview?
3. What information did you obtain that could be used in developing possible supporting factual theories?
    a. Are there any problems with this helpful information?

b. Do you have concerns with either the credibility or admissibility of the information?
4. What information that you obtained seems potentially harmful?
5. How will you deal with this harmful information?
6. Based on the interview, what other information will you seek?
    a. Where will you look for this information?
    b. Are you seeking any of this information to corroborate your client's information?
7. Evaluating the client:
    a. What kind of witness would the client make?
        (1) Are there problems?
        (2) If so, how do you propose to deal with such problems?
    b. How will the client be to work with (cooperative relationship)?
        (1) Are there any problems?
        (2) If so, how do you propose to deal with such problems?

IV. *Performance Planning*
A. *The Relationship Between Attorney and Client*
1. The *legal* relationship:
    a. When does the attorney-client relationship form?
    b. What are the legal consequences of this relationship?
    c. What steps can you take to avoid having a person with whom you've talked mistakenly believe that you represent him or her? What can you tell the person?
2. The *cooperative* (or working) relationship:
    a. What constitutes an ideal relationship with a client for you?
    b. What are your responsibilities to the client?
    c. What are the client's responsibilities to you?
    d. How can you gain the client's trust and confidence?
        (1) What methods are (theoretically) available?
        (2) Which will you use in this case?
        (3) Do you anticipate any particular problems in obtaining the client's trust in this case?

(4) How will you deal with such problems?
    (a) What will you do if the client is hysterical?
    (b) What will you do if the client is hostile?

(5) Do you face different problems if the client is indigent, as opposed to a paying client?

(6) What client personality traits will you look for?
    (a) What would make an ideal client in this case?
    (b) Is there a type of client personality that would make you seriously consider turning down the case?

(7) How will you gain the trust of an indigent client?

3. The *economic* relationship:
  a. How will you convince the client to retain you?
  b. Considering your fee:
    (1) How will you set your fee?
    (2) How will you explain it?
    (3) Will you insist on the money "up front"? On "security"?

B. *Imparting Information*
1. What information will you give to the client?
2. What can the client expect from you in the course of your representation?
3. What do you expect from your client?
4. What (if anything) will you tell the client about:
  a. the process?
  b. the attorney-client relationship?
  c. confidentiality and the attorney-client privilege?
5. If you do discuss any of these concepts, how will you explain them?

C. *Technical Interviewing Skills*
1. What techniques will you employ to ensure that you will receive information effectively?
2. Are some of these techniques better for some types of clients than others? If so, what type of client are you dealing with?
3. How will you organize your interview?
  a. Will you use a "funnel" approach?
  b. Some other organization?

4. Will you engage in "truth-testing"? If so, how will you do so in this case?

D. *"Nuts-and-Bolts" Matters*
1. What mechanical matters must you consider in this interview (e.g., what forms to have available, how to arrange the setting)?
2. Will you give the client a standardized form to fill out?
  a. If so, what will the form contain?
  b. When will the client fill it out?
  c. When will you review it?
  d. How will you use the form?
3. Will you have a standardized fee agreement?
  a. What purpose could such an agreement serve?
  b. What would it contain?
  c. Will you also provide a written explanation of your fee structure?

E. *Ethical Considerations*
1. What are your ethical responsibilities as to:
  a. confidences?
  b. setting fees?
  c. conflicts of interest?
  d. diligence and competence?
2. Will you show the client statements of favorable and adverse witnesses, tell the applicable law, etc., *before* you hear his or her story?
  a. What if you ask, "What happened?" and the client responds, "What do the witnesses say happened?"
  b. What if the client responds, "It's a bit fuzzy. Let me refresh my memory with the witness statements"?
  c. What if the client asks to first be told the applicable law?
    (1) What if you answer, "Why don't you tell me your version first" and the client replies, "No. I want to know the law first"?
    (2) What if the client then adds, "Look. You're a lawyer. Your business is to know the law. That's why I'm paying you all this money. Now tell me the law"?
    (3) Will you try to find out a criminal defendant's "story" in the initial interview(s)?

(a) Is there any reason you would not want the story at this point?

(b) Would you ever instruct the client not to give his or her story at this juncture?

CRIMINAL PROBLEMS: STATE v. HARD

PROBLEM 14

Defense Attorney: Interviewing Ed Hard Regarding a Non-Fatal Assault
(The Formation of an Attorney-Client Relationship)

It is September 3, 198X, 11:30 P.M. You were home comfortably watching your favorite television show when you received a call that some man named Edward Taylor Hard is in county jail on $15,000 bail for assault in the first degree. According to the caller, who is a relative of Hard's, Hard wants to see you tonight about representing him and getting him out of jail. Off with the television, on with your lawyer outfit, and you instinctively begin to prepare for your first interview with Edward Hard. The interview will take place in the small, institutional-green, "attorney interview" room of the jail.

PREPARATION

READ: (1) Pretrial Case File Entries 58, 61, 62; (2) Chapters II, IV. Now think about and answer the following questions:

1. What are your overall and specific objectives for this interview?

2. How specifically will you prepare for this interview?

   a. What legal information do you want in order to conduct this initial interview?

   b. What factual information do you want? Why?

3. Assuming you want Hard to trust and have confidence in you:

   a. How will you accomplish this?

   b. Must you "take charge" in order to accomplish this goal? Explain.

   c. What do you think Hard expects of you?

4. Now think about the information you want from Hard:

   a. What information do you want about the case?

      1) Will you ask his "story"? Why or why not?

      2) How would it affect your decision (if at all) to get his story if you will not have the police reports for two days? Two weeks? Explain.

      3) Will you try to learn what the "other side" (police and prosecution) knows? Why?

      4) What could Hard know about the other side's case?

  b. Do you want to ask Hard about his prior knowledge of, and encounters with, Bruno Summers? Why?

  c. What do you want to know from Hard in addition to information about the current criminal charges?

5. What potential problems could you face in this interview?

  a. Are there special problems interviewing a person in a jail? How will you deal with such problems?

  b. To what extent would you face an additional set of concerns in this initial interview if Hard were indigent and you were an appointed attorney from the private bar? A public defender?

6. Finally, for some business realities:

  a. Since you are a private attorney and probably want to take Hard's case, you will have to convince him that he should retain you? How will you accomplish this?

  b. How will you set your fee?

  c. What agreements should you make to ensure that you will collect your fee?

  d. Suppose Hard can only raise part of the fee? Do you, nevertheless, have an obligation to take his case?

ASSIGNMENT FOR CLASS

1. Outside of class, plan your interview with Ed Hard.

2. In class, conduct your initial interview with Edward Taylor Hard in his jail cell. Be certain to obtain information about Hard's background and to delve into areas related to your potential defenses to the substantive changes. (Do *not* discuss bail. See Problem 15.)

3. After class, write a short memoranda evaluating your interview with Hard by answering the following questions:

  a. What tentative defenses are now possible?

  b. At this point, what are the strengths of the theories of defense? (Evaluate both legal and factual theories and their interrelationship.)

  c. What appear to be the weaknesses of the theories of defense?

  d. Do you have any representational strategies in mind?

  e. Are there points regarding Hard's personality or background that appear important? Why?

  f. What further information do you want? Why?

  g. Where will you look for this information?

  h. Is there any other information that you wish you had obtained in the interview? Explain.

PROBLEM 15

Defense Attorney: Interviewing Ed Hard for a Bail Reduction Motion
(Charge of Assault in the First Degree)

Remember that your new client, Ed Hard, is languishing in jail on $15,000 bail.

During your interview with Hard you will therefore need to obtain information for a motion to reduce bail. You know a bondsperson who will take 10 percent in cash ($1,500) plus some security (Hard has only $5,000 equity in his home; his mother has over $45,000 equity in her home). Hard can only come up with $750 cash.

PREPARATION

READ: (1) Pretrial Case File Entries 61, 65; (2) Chapter IV.
Now think about and answer the following questions:

1. What is the importance of obtaining bail for Hard?

2. What are the legal standards for bail?

3. What information should you seek from Hard in preparing a bail motion? Why?

4. What bearing (if any) does the defendant's prior criminal record have on a bail motion?

5. What will you do if Hard says, "Just get me out on bail and I'll be in South America in 24 hours"?

ASSIGNMENT FOR CLASS

1. Outside of class, plan for obtaining information relevant to bail. Write a short memorandum summarizing your planning, preparation, and analysis, and give a copy to your supervisor.

2. In class, obtain the necessary information for your bail reduction motion from Hard.

3. After your interview with Hard, evaluate the results of your interview by answering the following questions:

   a. What information did you obtain in the interview that will aid the bail motion?

   b. Is there some information that you must follow up? Confirm?

PROBLEM 16

Defense Attorney: Interviewing Ed Hard Regarding a Fatal Assault
(The Formation of an Attorney-Client Relationship)

It is mid-morning, September 8th. Things have been moving fast since your initial interview with Edward Taylor Hard a few days ago in the county jail where he retained you to represent him. At that time Hard was only charged with assault in the first degree, as the result of his alleged shooting of Bruno Summers in a tavern. Since then, Summers has died, and Hard now faces a charge of premeditated, first-degree murder. You are now on your way to county jail for an extensive interview with Hard in light of these new charges.

PREPARATION

READ: (1) Pretrial Case File Entries 3-7, 11, 16, 17, 19, 21, 58, 61, 62; (2) Chapter IV. Now think about and answer the following questions:

1. What are your overall and specific objectives for this interview?

2. What preparation will you do?

3. What reaction do you expect from Hard when you tell him about the new charge in the case?

   a. Will this affect this second interview?

   b. How?

4. Think about the information you will seek:

   a. What will be the factual focus of this interview? Why?

   b. Does Summers' death and the new charge really change your legal theory and the information you want from Hard?

5. Imagine now that you have in your possession reports, witness statements, and other documents.* You have a choice of asking Hard about the subject matter covered by those documents before or after showing him each document.

   a. What is the problem with showing him the document first?

   b. What is the problem with not showing him the document first?

   c. Look at Hard's alleged statement contained in Detective Kelly's police report (Case File Entry 4):

      1) In Hard's statement to Detective Kelly, is Hard saying that the gun went off "accidentally" *as* he was going to aim away from Summers (i.e., at the wall), or *after* Hard thought he had aimed at the wall? Or is he saying something else? What difference does this make both legally and factually in your defense?

      2) Will you ask Hard about this statement to Kelly?

      3) Will you show him Kelly's report first?

         a) If so, will you point out the ambiguity?

         b) What will you answer if he asks you to explain the significance of each of the plausible meanings for his case?

         c) What will you do if you ask Hard about this ambiguity and he responds by saying: "I'm innocent. I acted in self-

---

*In real life, you may not have obtained all the reports at this early date.

defense. Which version is most likely to get me off, because that's the one I want to tell"?

d) To what extent (generally) should you "test" the truthfulness of your client's story? Explain.

e) What methods can you use to engage in such testing?

ASSIGNMENT FOR CLASS

1. Outside of class, plan your interview with Ed Hard. Write a short memorandum summarizing your planning, preparation, and analysis, and give a copy to your supervisor.

2. In class, interview Edward Taylor Hard. This time either (1) assume he is indigent and imagine you are a public defender; (2) assume he has money and you are retained private counsel.** (Do *not* discuss bail during this interview.)

PROBLEM 17 _____

Defense Attorney: Interviewing Ed Hard for a Bail Reduction Motion
(*Charge of First-Degree Murder*)

Your client has been sitting in jail on a $15,000 bail that he can't make. That bail was set when Bruno Summers was still alive and Hard was facing charges of assault in the first degree. Your client is now facing a first-degree murder charge. You still want to try to reduce bail (or at least limit the amount it may be raised in light of the new charges), and thus you will need to obtain information for a bail reduction motion.

PREPARATION

READ: (1) Pretrial Case File Entry 65; (2) Chapter IV.

ASSIGNMENT FOR CLASS

1. If you did *not* do Problem 15:

   a. Outside of class, plan for obtaining information relevant to bail. Write a short memorandum summarizing your planning, preparation, and analysis, and give a copy to your supervisor.

   b. In class, be prepared to meet with Hard and obtain the necessary information for your bail reduction motion.

2. If you did Problem 15:

   a. Outside of class, analyze what further information you would now seek from Hard regarding bail (if any). Write a short memorandum summarizing your planning, preparation, and analysis, and give a copy to your supervisor.

   b. In class, be prepared to discuss if you would seek additional information in light of the current murder charge.

_____
**Your instructor will tell you which option to choose.

CIVIL PROBLEMS: SUMMERS v. HARD

PROBLEM 18 _____

Plaintiffs' Attorney: Interview of Deborah Summers

You are an associate attorney in a law firm. Deborah Summers was referred to you by your law school classmate Casper Jones, an assistant prosecutor. The receptionist has scheduled an appointment for you to meet with Ms. Summers. When making the appointment, Ms. Summers stated: "I need help in obtaining money owed to my late husband, Bruno Summers, from his employer."

You have heard and read about Bruno Summers being shot and killed by Edward Taylor Hard. You are also aware that the prosecutor has decided not to prosecute Ed Hard for the shooting. The criminal case, *State v. Hard,* has been dismissed.

PREPARATION

READ: (1) Pretrial Case File Entries 1, 2, 59 (§§11 & 12); (2) Chapter IV. Now think about and answer the following questions:

1. Explain what you did (if anything) to prepare for your interview with Deborah Summers (including "nuts and bolts," legal research, etc.).

2. Will the statement made by Deborah Summers, "I need help in obtaining money owed to my late husband, Bruno Summers, from his employer," have an effect on this interview? Explain.

3. Does the criminal matter against Edward Hard have any effect on this interview with Deborah Summers? Explain.

4. Bruno Summers allegedly died after he was shot by a third person. Does that incident have any effect on this interview? Explain.

5. Suppose Deborah Summers is shy and withdrawn. How will that influence your relationship with her if she becomes your client?

6. Suppose Deborah Summers has an aggressive personality. How will that influence your relationship if she becomes your client?

7. Suppose Deborah Summers begins to cry uncontrollably during the interview. What will you do?

8. You will probably want to write a memorandum for your file detailing the interview with Deborah Summers (entitled "Memorandum to file: Client interview—Deborah Summers (date)"). The memorandum could include the facts you obtained, your observations about the potential client and the case, and whatever follow-up seems needed.

    a. How will you ensure that you will recall the details of the interview in order to write a memo for the file?

    b. Will your method interfere with your interviewing? Explain.

9. Will you discuss your fee arrangement? Explain.

ASSIGNMENT FOR CLASS

1. In class, be prepared to interview Deborah Summers.

2. After class, write a memorandum for the file about the client interview. Give a copy to your senior partner. In your memo evaluate your interview with Deborah Summers by answering the following questions:

   a. What tentative claims are now possible?

   b. At this point, what are the strengths of each of the claims? (Evaluate both legal and factual theories and their interrelationship.)

   c. What appear to be the weaknesses of the claims?

   d. Are there additional people you wish to talk with? Who? Why?

   e. What further information do you want? Why?

   f. Where will you look for this information?

   g. Is there any other information that you wish you had obtained in the interview? Explain.

PROBLEM 19 _____
Plaintiffs' Attorney: Follow-up to Deborah Summers Interview

You have just finished your first interview with Deborah Summers. The matter appears to be much more complex than Deborah's original statement to your receptionist indicated. In fact, major issues need resolution.

Follow-up to the initial client interview takes two forms: planning the legal research and planning what additional factual information you need to assess the problem. Therefore, it is an ideal time to formulate a plan for research and fact-gathering.

PREPARATION

READ: (1) Pretrial Case File Entries 1, 2, 59 (§§11 & 12); (2) Chapters II-IV; (3) Your notes of interview with Deborah Summers. Now think about and answer the following questions:

1. Will you research the law at this stage of the Summers case? Why?

2. What is the relationship between the law and the facts at this stage of the case?

3. Follow-up factual investigation is basically informal discovery, interviewing witnesses who will talk with you and obtaining accessible documents. (Later on you will be engaged in formal discovery where you can obtain information from your adversary.) Think about the informal discovery you will do after your interview with Deborah Summers.

a. Will you contact particular persons? If so, whom will you contact?

   b. How will you contact them?

   c. Which facts will you obtain from these persons? Why?

4. After interviewing Deborah Summers, are there documents that you would like to obtain?

   a. Which documents?

   b. From whom?

   c. Why?

5. Are the documents important to obtain *now*? Why?

6. Do you anticipate problems with obtaining any of the information you seek?

   a. Explain.

   b. If so, how do you propose to deal with these problems?

7. Is Deborah Summers your only client in this matter?

   a. If there are additional potential clients, list who they are.

   b. What action will you take as to other potential clients? Explain.

8. Do you have a tentative representational strategy? Explain.

ASSIGNMENT FOR CLASS

1. Outside of class, draft a memorandum explaining the legal research and investigation you need at this stage and explain why. Do not worry about the format. Your memorandum can be entitled: "Memorandum for the file: Plan of Action after initial client interview." Give a copy of your memorandum to your senior partner.

2. In class, be prepared to discuss your plan.

PROBLEM 20
*Plaintiffs' Attorney: Interview of Ronny Summers**

A few weeks have passed since Bruno Summers' death. Deborah, Gretchen, and Hans Summers have retained you as their attorney. You are considering whether to file a wrongful death lawsuit. As plaintiffs' attorney, you have wanted to interview Ronny (age 8), because Ronny is one of Bruno Summers' minor children. You refrained from interviewing Ronny because of the emotional trauma Ronny may have experienced upon his father's death.

Ronny has been living with his grandparents, Gretchen and Hans

---

*Note, however, that this problem can be assigned at any time, whether before or after a lawsuit has been filed. If assigned after the lawsuit is filed, your reading should include Case File Entries 1-37, 40-41, 48, 59, 60, 63, 90, and Chapters II-IV.

Summers, since September 4, 198X. Gretchen Summers, although not happy with your request to interview Ronny, has reluctantly agreed.

Gretchen Summers and Ronny will be at your office at 4:00 P.M.

PREPARATION

READ: (1) Pretrial Case File Entries 1-35, 59, 60, 63, 90; (2) Chapters II-IV. Now think about and answer the following questions:

1. What are your objectives for the interview with Ronny?

2. Explain the legal theory that you will use to structure the interview with Ronny.

3. How can the civil jury instructions help you in structuring the content of your interview? Explain.

4. Will you interview Ronny the same way you would an adult witness? If not, explain the differences in your approach to the child witness.

5. Is it preferable to interview Ronny with his grandmother present? Alone? Explain.

ASSIGNMENT FOR CLASS

1. Outside of class, prepare a memorandum explaining your objectives and what you plan to ask Ronny Summers when you interview him. Hand in a copy of your memorandum to your senior partner.

2. In class, conduct the interview of Ronny Summers.

PROBLEM 21 _____

Attorney for Defendant Hard: Client Interview

Ed Hard has told your receptionist he would like to talk to a lawyer about a civil lawsuit brought against him for shooting and killing someone at the Unicorn Tavern. You are quite familiar with the shooting incident referred to by Hard from reading newspaper articles, and an attorney friend represented Hard in the criminal case. Ed Hard has left the complaint for *Summers v. Hard* and his SAPO insurance policy with your receptionist. An appointment has been scheduled with Ed Hard for later in the week at 9:00 A.M.

PREPARATION

READ: (1) Pretrial Case File Entries 1, 2, 36, 37, 45, 59-61, 83, 90; (2) Chapter IV. Now think about and answer the following questions:

1. What will you do to prepare for your interview with Ed Hard?

   a. In the "nuts-and-bolts" category?

   b. Substantively?

2. Are your objectives in interviewing Ed Hard in the civil case the same or different from those in the *State v. Hard* criminal case? Explain.

3. Ed Hard may be indigent. If he is, what will you do?

4. What relevance, if any, does Hard's SAPO insurance have on the *Summers v. Hard* case?

   a. What are your obligations as a private attorney concerning Hard's defense?

   b. What are SAPO's obligations concerning Hard's defense?

5. The criminal case, *State v. Hard,* was dismissed. What relevance does it have to the civil lawsuit, *Summers v. Hard?*

6. What questions will you ask Hard after reviewing the summons and complaint in *Summers v. Hard* (Case File Entries 36 and 37)? Why?

7. Suppose the story Ed Hard tells you appears to be inconsistent? Will you confront him? Explain.

8. Suppose Ed Hard tells you the following story: "Bruno Summers was pulling a knife out of his pocket. I shot him to stop him from stabbing me." Ed's story appears to be inconsistent with plaintiffs' complaint. Will you confront Ed Hard with the inconsistency? Explain.

9. Suppose Ed Hard tells you he has enough assets to pay you a fee, but is going to dispose of the rest so "Bruno's brats don't get anything if they win." What will you say?

10. Suppose Hard begins the interview by stating: "Tell me what the defenses are to this lawsuit, then I'll talk." What will you do?

11. What will you do at the end of the interview with Ed Hard? (Make another appointment? Talk to his two friends, Gooding and Karr, who were at the Unicorn Tavern with Ed Hard on the night of the shooting, September 3? Something else?) Why?

12. Do you have a tentative representational strategy? Explain.

ASSIGNMENT FOR CLASS

1. Outside of class, prepare a memorandum explaining your interview objectives and what you plan to ask Ed Hard. Hand in a copy to your senior partner.

2. In class, interview Ed Hard.

3. After class, write a short memorandum evaluating your interview with Hard by answering the following questions. Give a copy to your senior partner.

   a. What tentative defenses are now possible?

   b. At this point, what are the strengths of the theories of defense? (Evaluate both legal and factual theories and their interrelationship.)

   c. What appear to be the weaknesses of the theories of defense?

d. Are there points regarding Hard's personality or background that appear important? Why?

e. What further information do you want? Why?

f. Where will you look for this information?

g. Is there any other information that you wish you had obtained in the interview? Explain.

PROBLEM 22

Attorney for Defendant Davola: Client Interview

M.C. Davola has told your receptionist he would like to talk to a lawyer about a lawsuit brought against him as the owner of the Unicorn Tavern. He has left the *Summers v. Hard* complaint with your receptionist. He also muttered something about "slashed seats in his tavern."

Mr. Davola has been scheduled for an appointment later in the week at 9:00 A.M.

PREPARATION

READ: (1) Pretrial Case File Entries 1, 2, 36, 37, 59-61, 90; (2) Chapter IV. Now think about and answer the following questions:

1. What can you do to prepare for your meeting with Davola ("nuts-and-bolts" matters, research, etc.)?

2. Do you have any tentative theories about Davola's defense? Explain.

3. Davola is a defendant in a lawsuit, *Summers v. Hard et al.* Will that fact affect the interview? Explain.

4. Suppose Mr. Davola insists that you "countersue" the plaintiffs. Will that position influence the interview? Explain.

5. If M.C. Davola has liability insurance on the Unicorn Tavern, will that have any effect on the interview? Explain.

6. Are there potential problems that you may have to address because of Davola's insurance? What are they and how will you address them?

7. Suppose Mr. Davola is very angry about the lawsuit. How will that attitude affect the interview? Explain.

8. Suppose Mr. Davola is shy and withdrawn. How will that influence your relationship with him if he becomes your client?

9. Suppose Mr. Davola has an aggressive personality. How will that influence your relationship if he becomes your client?

ASSIGNMENT FOR CLASS

1. Outside of class, prepare a short memorandum explaining your objectives and what you plan to ask Mr. Davola. Hand in a copy to your senior partner.

2. In class, interview M.C. Davola.

3. After class, write a short memorandum evaluating your interview with Davola by answering the following questions. Give a copy to your senior partner.

    a. What tentative defenses are now possible?

    b. At this point, what are the strengths of the theories of defense?

    c. What appear to be the weaknesses of the theories of defense?

    d. Are there points regarding Davola's personality or background that appear important? Why?

    e. What further information do you want? Why?

    f. Where will you look for this information?

    g. Is there any other information that you wish you had obtained in the interview? Explain.

PROBLEM 23
Attorney for Defendant Davola: Interview of Mary Apple

You have interviewed M.C. Davola and read the criminal file that you obtained from the prosecutor's office. You are interviewing clients and witnesses before drafting a response to the plaintiffs' complaint in *Summers v. Hard*. You have arranged to interview Mary Apple, who has been named as a defendant in the lawsuit filed by the Summers family.

    You have heard that a patron in the tavern, Bert Kain, claims he overheard Mary Apple say: "Oh God, I shouldn't have served them." Be sure you obtain the facts about the circumstances surrounding this statement directly from Ms. Apple.

PREPARATION

READ: (1) Pretrial Case File Entries 1-37, 44, 59-61, 90; (2) Chapter IV; (3) Notes of interview with M.C. Davola. Now think about and answer the following questions:

1. What are your objectives for the interview with Mary Apple?

2. Suppose Mary Apple gives inconsistent responses to your questions. What will you do? Why?

3. Would your interview with Mary Apple differ if she were a witness instead of a client? Explain.

4. Will you confront Ms. Apple with the statement that Bert Kain, an eyewitness, claims he heard Apple say: "Oh my God, I shouldn't have served them"? Explain.

5. Suppose Mary Apple becomes hostile during the interview. What will you do?

6. Where will you interview Mary Apple? Why?

7. If Davola has insurance, should Davola's insurance company represent Mary Apple, Davola, and Donaldson? Explain the benefits and risks.

ASSIGNMENT FOR CLASS

1. Outside of class, prepare a memorandum of the areas in which you may question Mary Apple. Hand in this outline to your senior partner.

2. In class, along with your investigator, interview Mary Apple.

V

Witness Interviewing

A. FIRST PERSPECTIVES
B. DETERMINING THE CONTENT OF A WITNESS INTERVIEW
    Question 1. What tentative case theories are indicated by the information you are currently aware of?
    Question 2. What areas of information could this witness possess that are relevant to the tentative case theories?
    Question 3. What areas will you focus on at this point?
    Question 4. What further information will you seek in such areas in light of your tentative case theories?
    Question 5. What information did you obtain?
    Question 6. What is the significance of this information?
    Question 7. What further information will you now seek?
C. DEVELOPING A PLAN FOR PERFORMING THE INTERVIEW OF A POTENTIALLY DIFFICULT WITNESS
    Question 1. What is the range of possible practical/strategic considerations and situations that could arise in a witness interview?
    Area One. Establishing a rapport
    Area Two. Deciding whom to interview
    Area Three. Deciding when to interview
    Area Four. Organizing the interview
    Area Five. Conducting the interview
    Area Six. Circumstances and setting
    Area Seven. Getting clear and accurate information
    Area Eight. Preserving the information
    Area Nine. Retaining the ability to subsequently refresh the witness's recollection or impeach the witness
    Area Ten. Ensuring the witness's appearance in court
    Area Eleven. Dealing with gender-related problems
    Question 2. Which of these practical/strategic situations will you deal with at this point?
    Question 3. What are your objectives in this situation?
    Question 4. How will you achieve your objectives?
    Question 5. What problems do you anticipate?
    Question 6. How will you meet such problems?
    Question 7. If you can't solve the problems, what will you do?
    Question 8. What ethical concerns do you face in attempting to achieve your objectives?
D. PLANNING QUESTIONS

CRIMINAL PROBLEMS: *State v. Hard*
    Problem 24. Prosecutor: Interview of Dr. L.H. Jackson, Medical Examiner
    Problem 25. Prosecutor: Interview of Peter Dean
    Problem 26. Prosecutor: Interview of Fred Faye
    Problem 27. Prosecutor: Interview of Jack Waters
    Problem 28. Prosecutor: Interview of Detective Kelly (Investigating Officer for the Case)
    Problem 29. Prosecutor: Interview of Detective Kelly (Witness for a Suppression Motion)
    Problem 30. Prosecutor: Interview of Officer Yale (Witness for a Suppression Motion)
    Problem 31. Prosecutor: Interview of Dr. T.A. Loopman, Pharmacologist (Witness for a Suppression Motion)
    Problem 32. Prosecutor: Reevaluating and Synthesizing the Information from Witness Interviews

A. FIRST PERSPECTIVES

You have begun to develop a tentative case theory and now you are about to plan for a witness interview. How should you begin? Start with thinking about the specific objectives towards which you want to direct your planning efforts. Remember that planning always takes place in the context of objectives:

(1) Develop rapport with the witness so the witness will cooperate during the interview, allow you to conduct subsequent interviews, if necessary, and not fight you when examined by you at a deposition, evidentiary hearing, or trial.

(2) Obtain information—that is, (a) information that supports, undercuts, or alters your legal or factual theories (and will, therefore, also influence your overall representational strategy as well as the content of your pleadings, your future fact-gathering, and your strategy if you eventually go to trial); (b) information that bears on the credibility of the witness (which will also affect your case theory); and (c) information that is relevant to negotiations. Later in the case, you will also interview witnesses in order to help them prepare to present their information through testimony.

With these objectives in mind, you can begin background preparation for your interviews by reviewing your case theory and all the factual and legal information you have obtained, and then factoring in any information you can find about the particular witness. If you are dealing with an expert witness, you may also want to obtain a copy of the expert's vitae, read technical articles and texts to familiarize yourself with the general vocabulary in the area of expertise, review works written by the expert, and even prepare yourself by talking to other experts. (A discussion of the process of selecting an expert appears in Chapter III.)

You should also familiarize yourself with applicable jury instructions. As an example, imagine you are representing plaintiff in a wrongful death case. You know that damages are one element of your legal theory, and that part of your witness interviewing should be directed at finding information regarding this element. However, if you look at the instruction the jury will receive for wrongful death damages, you will see that damages contain sub-elements. One factor, the instruction reads, that "should be considered to measure damages for wrongful death" is "[w]hat the decedent could reasonably have been expected to contribute to his [survivor, children, dependent mother and father] in the way of support, love, care, guidance, training, instruction and protection."

You will find jury instructions can provide precise focus for your interview, and will alert you to seek information that directly corresponds to the very categories (or sub-elements) of damages that the jury will consider in its deliberations. For example, suppose you want to interview a neighbor who knows the survivors and knew the decedent. Using the jury instruction, you might explore the various sub-elements within the instruction when interviewing the neighbor and plan to ask: "Can you tell me about Donald's relationship with his children? Was he actively involved with them in sports? Hobbies? So, he taught Kathy how to play the piano. How often were they involved in this activity together?"

What will the witness interview look like? Organizationally, the interview could take a form similar to the funnel approach we discussed in Chapter IV (pages 69-70), except that the range of information at each stage is likely to be narrower and more focused when talking to a witness than to a client. As a result, a major portion of this chapter will concern developing primary questions and follow-up questions as you progressively probe these relatively focused areas in which the witness may possess relevant information.

B. DETERMINING THE CONTENT OF A WITNESS INTERVIEW

Witness interviews provide one of the main sources of information for evolving, supporting, or modifying your own case theory and for probing the strengths and weaknesses of your opponent's theory. However, the caution we offered for client interviewing also applies here: The case theory provides a focus, but it should not constitute a constraint on the breadth of your information-gathering. A witness's information can suggest or limit legal theories, as well as support assertions for your "story" (factual theory). It may only be a small piece of information or a significant one; it may support your case theory or weaken it; it may do a little of both—no matter. The important thing is that you know both the good and the bad in advance so you can deal with it. A good attorney can and must deal with virtually every potential negative that arises, but it's far better if these negatives do not come packaged as last-second surprises.

We will develop our approach to planning the content of a witness interview within the framework of a hypothetical case. Imagine that you are the attorney for the defendant in an attempted burglary case. You are about to interview the only eyewitness. According to the signed statement the eyewitness gave the police, he saw your client "near the house, not climbing out of it or anything, just near it." What should be the content of this witness interview?

The approach we would apply for determining the content of the interview in this situation is based on the same seven questions, and the underlying rationale for each, that we developed in detail in Chapter IV. This should be no surprise. Both client and witness interviews are essentially information-gathering activities:

1. What tentative case theories are indicated by the information you are currently aware of?
2. What areas of information could this witness possess that are relevant to the tentative case theories?
3. What areas will you focus on at this point?
4. What further information will you seek in such areas in light of your tentative case theories?
5. What information did you obtain?
6. What is the significance of this information? (Does it support, revise, undermine your tentative case theories?)
7. What further information will you now seek?

BASIC TASK: Obtain information to further develop, support, modify, or alter your case theory, including information that will allow you to assess the witness's credibility.

Begin applying the approach:

QUESTION 1
What tentative case theories are indicated by the information you are currently aware of?

You begin by referring to your tentative case theories as structures on which to build your search for information. At this point, you have two tentative case theories you are sifting through while you interview this witness: (1) a reasonable doubt based on the theory that defendant, though near the house, was there innocently, and therefore did not have the intent for attempted burglary (of course, the prosecution will also have to prove the actus of attempted burglary by establishing that the defendant went beyond "mere planning and preparation," and this will also be in your mind during the interview); (2) a reasonable doubt based on the theory that the eyewitness incorrectly identified the defendant as the man who was near the house. (Remember that in criminal defense, you may keep the defendant off the stand and raise reasonable doubts in the prosecution case upon any available theory.[1])

QUESTION 2
What areas of information could this witness possess that are relevant to the tentative case theories?

This man is an eyewitness. He could reasonably have information about:

- the circumstances of his observation
- his conduct prior to the observation (no sleep? drinking?)
- any identification procedures (line-up, photo spread, montage)
- any descriptions he gave
- his perceptual abilities (age, glasses)
- the suspect's conduct (precisely what did he see the suspect doing?)

You no doubt can think of other areas.

QUESTION 3
What areas will you focus on at this point?

Imagine that you decide to start with the circumstances of the identification, then filter in what the witness saw the suspect doing, because you feel this strategy would provide a natural lead-in to information bearing on either case theory.

QUESTION 4
What further information will you seek in such areas in light of your tentative case theories?

For your first theory (no intent), you would probably want any information about what the suspect was doing that would negate any inference of criminal in-

tent—lack of furtive behavior, no sight of burglary tools, no sight of the suspect touching windows, and so on. For your second theory (misidentification), you would probably seek information about the circumstances of the identification that would draw the identification itself into question—time of the incident, distance, light, and so on. (Of course, you will also be alert to information that weakens one or both of these tentative theories.)

QUESTION 5
What information did you obtain?

You would probably have received a great deal of information. Let's focus on a small portion. Imagine that when you asked the eyewitness, "Where did you first see the man you've identified as my client?," the witness said, "Like I told the police, I saw the man I described near the house."

QUESTION 6
What is the significance of this information?

How does this little piece of information fit into your first case theory (no intent)? From a first impression, this information hurts because it appears to support the prosecution theory by providing information from which criminal intent could be inferred: Defendant was "near the house" late at night; all of us know that strangers generally do not invite us to linger about their homes and would view such action as a serious threat to their safety if done late at night; people thus do not normally place themselves in close proximity to the private dwellings of strangers late in the evening unless they are up to no good; defendant was likely up to no good.

QUESTION 7
What further information will you now seek?

Follow-up questions, conceived with your case theories in mind, are necessary, however, to test the strength of this seemingly harmful inference to your no-intent theory (i.e., the inference your client had an "opportunity" to commit the crime). If "near" means "where the driveway meets the public sidewalk," the

---

1. But one commentator has voiced disagreement with this view. See Subin, "The Criminal Lawyer's 'Different Mission': Reflection on the 'Right' to Present a False Case," 1 Geo. Jour. Legal Ethics 125 (1987); see also Mitchell, "Reasonable Doubts Are Where You Find Them: A Response to Professor Subin's Position on the Criminal Lawyer's 'Different Mission,'" 1 Geo. Jour. Legal Ethics 339 (1987).

harmful inference from this information is not nearly as strong as the inference would be should "near" mean "next to the window that was shattered." So you might ask, "Where exactly was the man standing?" Suppose the witness responds, "Less than two feet away from a window that looked open, holding a crowbar which he dropped when he looked in my direction and ran."

In the domain of logical probativeness, this information from the eyewitness really hurts. The suspect has not only been placed next to the house away from areas of public ingress and egress, but holding a tool (and you have learned the window was pried open by some metal device), and then fleeing when spooked, thereby demonstrating consciousness of guilt.

But what about the witness's credibility? Besides delving into the same perceptual areas that you might explore when attacking the witness's identification in your misidentification theory, you may also be able to use the witness's statement to the police to question his credibility in this particular case. After all, the eyewitness apparently never mentioned anything about the crowbar or flight in that statement. Accordingly, you may want to ensure its use for impeachment:

Attorney: You gave a statement to the police?
Witness: Yes.
Attorney: That was within an hour after you saw the man?
Witness: About that.
Attorney: Things were fresh in your mind then?
Witness: I was pretty upset, but yeah—I guess so.
Attorney: You tried to tell everything important?
Witness: Yes. But they left out the crowbar.
Attorney: Could you explain that?
Witness: I looked at that statement last week. The crowbar's not in there. They must not have heard me.
Attorney: Where were you?
Witness: In Detective Broud's office.
Attorney: Was it noisy?
Witness: No. He had the door closed.

Now you have to think about admissibility. Can you keep this new story about the crowbar and flight out of evidence? Almost certainly not. What can you do?

You want to discredit this story. First, you want to bring out information enabling the jury to believe that the witness never mentioned the crowbar or flight when he gave his statement to the police. You could do this directly by introducing the testimony of Detective Broud (assuming Broud will deny that the witness had ever mentioned the crowbar or flight at the interview), or circumstantially through the witness's written statement that does not include mention of

the crowbar or flight (perhaps introducing it through Detective Broud who will explain why it is important to take accurate statements, how he is trained to record all important information, and so on). Is this information indicating that the witness did not mention the crowbar or flight at the initial interview admissible? Yes. It is relevant, permitting the following chain of inference: At the time of the statement, events were fresh in the witness's mind; the witness must have known that his information was being used to apprehend a possible criminal; in this circumstance, the significance of the crowbar and flight must have been obvious to the witness; thus, if he'd really seen the crowbar and flight, he would have mentioned these matters to Detective Broud. (Additional inferences harmful to the prosecution's case can be drawn by the jury if it believes that the witness not only did not mention these events in the initial interview, but is now lying in claiming he did.) Detective Broud's testimony or the written statement (once authenticated) would serve as impeachment on this very material issue in the case. If Broud could directly contradict the witness, the written statement would then serve as circumstantial evidence to corroborate Broud's testimony that the witness never gave the information. If Broud cannot contradict the witness ("I can't recall"), then the statement could be identified by Broud or the witness and be characterized for evidentiary purposes either as a prior inconsistent statement or as circumstantial evidence from which the jury can infer that the absence of mention of the crowbar and flight in the statement call into question whether the witness ever saw those things.

Second, you may want to bring out the witness's seemingly weak explanation for the omissions in the statement. You would thus ask about the "noise," why he didn't notice the omissions when he read over his statement before signing, and so forth. (Keep in mind, however, that the witness is likely to present his explanation for the omission on direct examination in its most credible form in anticipation of your attack.)

RETURN TO QUESTION 6
What is the significance of this information (for your second case theory)?

Now, consider your second case theory (misidentification). Look at all the information the witness has given about "near the house," the crowbar, and flight. How does the information fit into your case theory? Notice that under this identification theory, the "near-the-house" information may have a very different impact than it did for the first theory (no intent). Specifically, if you are concerned with a mistaken identification theory, you may be glad to find that the suspected burglar *was* near the window and, therefore, further from both the eyewitness and the good lighting along the sidewalk. Surely you will have little interest in the "opportunity" of the person seen "near" the victim's home, or in the crowbar, if your defense theory is that there is a reasonable doubt that the defendant is that person. Note that if your opponent interviewed this witness, he or she would similarly conduct follow-up questions concerning the meaning of "near." These questions, however, will be determined by your adversary's own case theory.

RETURN TO QUESTION 7
What further information will you now seek?

Your misidentification theory naturally leads you to ponder. What about credibility? You might focus on the witness's statement and his story about the crowbar and argue "this witness has such a personal stake in this case—that of playing the part of the state's star witness to the hilt—that he keeps embellishing his story to make it appear stronger." Or you could probe the witness's credibility in this particular case by probing the perceptual components of his identification (e.g., eyesight, lighting, fear) and any possibility for "suggestion":

Attorney: Did you go to a line-up or view a photo spread?
Witness: Photo spread.
Attorney: Did you pick anyone out?
Witness: You bet. Your client.
Attorney: How do you know?
Witness: Detective Broud told me afterward.

Does this strengthen or weaken the witness credibility? It depends. If the photograph display and accompanying procedures seem fair to the factfinder, the witness's credibility will be increased. If not, his in-court identification may be undercut. You need to ask more questions:

What were you told before you viewed the photographs?

How many photographs were there?

How long did you look at them?

Is the information admissible? If the photo spread and the procedure are arguably suggestive, you can get this information before the jury and argue, "The eyewitness is not identifying my client from the house; he's identifying him from the photo spread." If the photo spread and the procedures were extremely suggestive, you may be able to bring a motion based on due process grounds to exclude both the in-court and photo-spread identifications. It is likely this approach would leave the prosecution vulnerable to an attack for factual sufficiency.

RETURN TO QUESTIONS 6 AND 7
What is the significance of the information you have now received (at the conclusion of the interview)? What further information will you seek?

After completion of the interview, what is the significance of the information you have obtained and what further information will you seek? At this point, your first theory (no intent) seems troublesome. It will be hard to argue that the witness is mistaken about the house, the crowbar, and so on. It is one thing to misidentify the person you see. It is quite another to be mistaken as to someone being next to the house, holding a crowbar, and running away. This theory will likely require that you raise doubts that the witness is lying. But how can you raise a reasonable doubt that he is lying? Look for information about the person in general (e.g., a felony record) and in relation to this case (is he having his own charges dismissed in another criminal case in return for testimony in this one?). Check with Detective Broud about taking the witness's statement in light of the witness's explanation for the omissions. Was the statement tape-recorded? How long did this take? Was the witness told to carefully read the statement before signing?

The second theory (misidentification) looks better, although subsequent information could change that. Under this theory you do not have to call the witness a liar; he could simply be mistaken. Also, the positioning of the suspect near the house (and away from the light) is helpful and so might be the photo spread. What other information will you seek? You might seek additional information about the witness's perceptual abilities. Do neighbors ever see the witness wearing glasses? Did anyone see the eyewitness drinking that evening? You will have to gather more information about the photograph identification (e.g., talk to Detective Broud, review reports, seek photos used in the photo display).

C. DEVELOPING A PLAN FOR PERFORMING THE INTERVIEW OF A POTENTIALLY DIFFICULT WITNESS

Imagine you are the attorney for the defendant in the hypothetical rear-end highway collision described in Chapter IV at page 77. You are about to interview the tow-truck driver who, you learned, says that your client was intoxicated at the time of the accident. According to your client, he was not intoxicated and was never closer than ten to fifteen feet to the tow-truck driver. You anticipate that, if he believes your client was drunk, the tow-truck driver may be hostile to your client and his position. What will you do?

You could plan for this situation by using the same eight-question performance planning approach we developed in Chapter IV:

1. What is the range of possible practical/strategic considerations and situations that could arise in a witness interview?
2. Which of these practical/strategic situations will you deal with at this point?
3. What are your objectives in this situation?
4. How will you achieve your objectives?
5. What problems do you anticipate?
6. How will you meet such problems?
7. If you can't solve the problems, what will you do?
8. What ethical concerns do you face in attempting to achieve your objectives?

In developing your answers as you work through the approach, you may also wish to review the references included in Chapter IV. See page 76. Now, using our approach, develop a plan for the interview of the tow-truck driver:

QUESTION 1
What is the range of possible practical/strategic considerations and situations that could arise in a witness interview?

To help you in your investigation of this question, we suggest eleven areas where the most likely practical and strategic concerns may emerge. Within each area we suggest the kinds of considerations or situations you might face and provide some pointers. Once again, you may wish to glance quickly through these areas, read through the remaining questions in our analysis of performance planning, and then return and review the eleven areas at leisure.

Area One
Establishing a rapport

How can you anticipate a witness's likely attitude? What strategies do you have for dealing with witnesses who are shy (or evasive or hostile or biased in your favor)? For dealing with expert witnesses? Police witnesses? How will you leave open the possibility to return for subsequent interviews?

The present illustration deals with this very area—developing rapport with a potentially hostile witness. Let's try another illustration, one that involves a "reluctant" witness. Dr. James is the treating physician for your client who was injured in an automobile accident. She makes her living treating people, not by testifying as a medical expert in court. She has been brought into this case only because of the coincidence that her patient happens to be bringing a lawsuit. She does not think that much of lawyers and does not want to become involved in a lawsuit. What can you do? You can try to tie her cooperation in the lawsuit to her interest in her patient ("This will help your patient get all those years of treatment she will need; remember, that insurance company is offering her almost nothing").

Area Two
Deciding whom to interview

What factual reasons could lead you to decide not to interview an otherwise important witness? Can you ever interview represented or unrepresented persons who are potential parties? Can you question a person who may have Fifth Amendment concerns without pointing out the nature of those concerns and accompanying rights to that person?

There are reasons why you may not want to interview a witness: The witness may be too far away geographically to visit without great expense; he may already have given a statement to some agency or to the police that tells you all you need to know; you may know that he will refuse to speak with you, you cannot reach him on the phone, and the impeachment value of this refusal at trial is not worth the time and expense of tracking him down at his home or workplace; you might not want to give him a sense of how you will approach him at an upcoming deposition or trial and you are concerned that the interview could provide him with some such information that he could use to prepare for you. Of course, in an interview you could also get a sense of the witness and pin him down on helpful points for your subsequent examination of him under oath. But you might already have planned to take his deposition anyway and feel there is little advantage to doing a prior interview. If you decide you do want to interview the witness and he is represented, you cannot do so ethically without first obtaining his attorney's permission. ABA Model Rule 4.2. If the witness is unrepresented and reasonably facing potential liability in the matter you are investigating, you must make the interests you are representing clear to him. ABA Model Rule 4.3.

Area Three
Deciding when to interview

When you first get into the case? Before formal discovery? Before you take the witness's deposition?

There are advantages to talking to witnesses early in a case—in fact, this is particularly so before a complaint is filed and battlelines clearly drawn. The witness may not yet appreciate the full significance of his information or even have thought through his story in advance. Accordingly, he may be less selective in the information he provides and how he characterizes it. Also, details will be fresher in his mind and he will not be as likely to have begun the process of "filling-in." (We like our stories to be complete and coherent. Thus, over time, details that do not neatly fit together and gaps in our story will gradually be "filled in" by our minds, without conscious realization, as we retell our tale.) On the other hand, without a real sense of what the case may be about, you may have difficulty in the interview knowing what information to pursue as it emerges, where to focus your questions, and so on. This could be a real problem if you are likely to get only one crack at this witness for an interview.

Area Four
Organizing the interview

How will you begin? How will you end?

The "funnel" organization described at pages 69-70 should provide you with guidance in this area.

Area Five
Conducting the interview

Will you conduct the interview alone? With an investigator (or paralegal or legal worker) taking notes? Will an investigator conduct the interview with you taking notes? Or will your investigator handle it alone?

The distribution of tasks between you and the persons accompanying you on an interview will be a function of the group dynamic, individual style, and that of the witness (e.g., certain witnesses will be more open with persons of the same sex and age, while others will be more at ease with someone older or the opposite sex). Your investigator (or legal worker) can do the interview alone, but then you will not have a first-hand impression of how the witness is likely to appear to a judge or jury. Some witnesses, in fact, may not be comfortable talking openly if they know that an attorney is standing there. But, if at all possible, avoid doing an interview by yourself. If the witness testifies at variance to what she has told you in an interview (and, as is likely, you do not have the statement taped or in writing), you face a real problem. How are you going to impeach the witness? Through your testimony? Generally, ethical rules forbid an attorney from testifying in the same case she is trying. ABA Model Rule 3.7.

Area Six
Circumstances and setting

Will you conduct your interview at your office? At the witness's home? The witness's workplace? Will you call ahead? Show up at dinner time?

Note initially that this same idea of setting was discussed in assessing a jail interview as a factor in client interviewing. In contrast, consider here an interview in a private home. A witness will likely be confident and at ease at home. Further, the witness will generally lack the sense of hurry and self-consciousness that often accompanies meetings at the workplace, where the time clock ticks and fellow workers pass by and stare. However, if you just appear at someone's home without prior invitation, you risk resentment and perhaps refusal to allow any interview, because of your unannounced intrusion into someone's sanctum. On the other hand, if you call ahead, the witness may also refuse, or initially agree but then back out when he's "had time to think about it" or to talk to the opposing party (with whom his sympathies align) and not be home at the time of the appointment. This becomes a matter of judgment, of choosing between the alternatives. Getting the witness to come to your office, on the other hand, has a number of advantages. You don't have to take time traveling out of the office and you have access to a variety of helpful resources—secretaries and devices for taking statements, extensive case files and legal materials, duplicating equipment, your own telephone, and so on. If the meeting is to be held in your office, you may wish to plan the desired mood. Comfortable, with the witness and you facing each other in padded armchairs? Exuding authority, with you sitting behind a large desk and the witness positioned at a distance?

Area Seven
Getting clear and accurate information

How will you frame your questions? When will you employ leading or non-leading questions? Will you have the witness draw diagrams? Will you bring photographs or diagrams for the witness to mark? Will you tell the witness about other information in the case that bears on her testimony?

If you and the witness have a number of relatively similar events to deal with (telephone calls, meetings), or you and the witness must review a sequence of events over time, you need to develop a way to designate each of these events so you know the one to which the witness's information applies and the witness is clear what is being sought ("Let's call the time period in which you had seen the blueprint, but *before* you received any money, the 'first period' when we discuss this." . . . "Now, we're talking about the second phone call, the one where he asked you to put the proposal into writing"). Also, review the techniques suggested in Chapter IV at pages 80-81.

Area Eight
Preserving the information

Will you take notes? Tape-record? Take a statement? If you take a statement, what will you put in or leave out? Can you protect the statement as confidential or as work product?

First, before you take a witness's statement, be aware that eventually it is likely to be seen by the opposing party. For example, even if the work-product privilege is held to apply to mere witness statements unaccompanied by any of your analysis (which is a legal position that is not certain to prevail), the privilege may not be applicable at trial, or if the opponent can show special need, or if the witness reviews the statement for a deposition. Second, if you do decide that you want to pin down the witness with a recorded statement, you might have to use some diplomacy in getting the witness to cooperate ("I want to accurately record your statement. This is for your protection as well as mine. With this no one will be able to say that you said anything but what is recorded here"). Third, to be useful for impeachment, the witness must adopt the statement. Make her read it over *carefully* before she signs it. Have her write in any corrections if you have had the statement typed. The point is that you do not want the witness to be able to claim later while testifying that the statement is incorrect as to some crucial point. In fact, some attorneys deliberately put minor "typos" and mistakes in the statement that the witness then finds and corrects by hand. This is to raise the inference that the witness reviewed the statement carefully in order to undercut any subsequent claim that she "never really read it." Some attorneys we know, however, would view this as a sharp practice that does not reflect the level of candor and integrity that counsel should exhibit.

Area Nine
Retaining the ability to subsequently refresh the witness's recollection or impeach the witness

Will you take along a third party to witness your interview? Who? Will you ask the person you are interviewing to read and sign his or her statement? How can you ask questions so as to pin down important points in such a way that the witness's story in these areas cannot easily be changed? These concerns are covered by Areas Five, Seven, and Eight.

Area Ten
Ensuring the witness's appearance in court

Will you carry blank subpoenas with you? If you desire the witness's appearance, will you serve the witness after the interview even if the witness has already been subpoenaed by your opponent? Even if the witness is friendly and gives her word that she will appear? How will you explain to the witness your decision nevertheless to subpoena her in these circumstances?

Some witnesses are offended if you try to subpoena them. They take it as a statement that you don't trust them and that you are now going to force them to cooperate. But, if the witness is ill or has to temporarily leave the court's venue at the time of trial, and you seek a continuance to obtain the witness's testimony without having subpoenaed the witness, many courts will refuse the motion on the grounds that you did not do all that was reasonably possible to initially secure the witness's attendance at trial. So explain, "This protects my client if you are sick. . . . It's a formality. I have to do it for the court. I totally trust you and know you'll show up. In fact, why don't we have my paralegal, Bill, pick you up the day you're going to testify so you won't have to find a parking space downtown."

Area Eleven
Dealing with gender-related problems

Suppose the attorney is a woman and the witness states, "I would feel much better if I spoke to a man about these matters. This type of thing shouldn't be for a woman to hear. It is too obscene." Will you, as a female attorney, agree with the witness and get a man to do the interview? Or will you try to convince the witness that you have sufficient professional expertise to hear the matter? If so, will you tell the witness about similar cases you worked on? Will you insist that the witness explain his position and argue with him about your capabilities? Will you be jeopardizing the case if you insist on interviewing this witness? What reaction do you expect from the witness? Hostility? Understanding? A change in his opinion? If he proves hostile, will you tell him he is a "male chauvinist pig"? If you have an emotional outburst, will you be able to obtain the information you need? Will other members of your firm subsequently be impeded from obtaining this information if you have such an outburst? Will you tell anyone else about the witness's attitude? Will that depend on such factors as the witness's age, background, importance to the case? Men can also face gender-related problems in an interview. A woman who is a sexual assault victim may feel uncomfortable or even be

completely unwilling to discuss her situation with a male attorney. Query: To what extent does this situation lend itself to the analysis discussed in reference to the female attorney?

QUESTION 2
Which of these practical/strategic situations will you deal with at this point?

Of course, you want to get clear, accurate information (Area Seven). To accomplish this in this situation, however, you will need to find a way to develop rapport so that you can gain the cooperation of a potentially hostile witness (Area One).

QUESTION 3
What are your objectives in this situation?

As you recall from Chapter IV (page 77), the defendant in this case is claiming that plaintiff "proximately caused" the accident by suddenly swerving into defendant's lane and cutting him off. Plaintiff claims he was driving along when, suddenly, defendant rear-ended him. If the jury was presented with information that raised inferences that defendant was intoxicated at the time of the accident, plaintiff's factual theory would be overwhelming ("But, of course, my client had no way of knowing as he calmly drove to work, that mere yards to his rear loomed the most dangerous weapon in our nation—a drunk driver—a man without normal perceptions, reflexes, and judgment"). One objective in this interview is to find out if, in fact, the tow driver will say that your client was intoxicated. If he sticks to a story that your client was intoxicated, a second objective emerges: You want to find the basis of his opinion and then try to find other information to weaken that basis. You may even be able to attack such an opinion by just knowing its basis, without obtaining any additional information. For example, if the basis of the tow driver's opinion is that your client was "unsteady and weaving," you can easily argue to the factfinder that this was likely the result of the accident or even argue to the court that the driver's opinion lacks sufficient foundation to be admissible as lay opinion.

QUESTION 4
How will you achieve your objectives?

You will need to arrange an interview with the tow driver (assuming, of course, that you can locate him). You will ask if he believes your client was drunk, and, if he does, you will inquire into the basis of his opinion ("How far were you from my client? What were you doing? It was raining hard, wasn't it? Could you smell alcohol? What did you see my client do?").

You will take an investigator or other witness with you to ensure you have a witness who can impeach the driver at trial if he gives you helpful information in the interview, but tells a different story on the stand.

QUESTION 5
What problems do you anticipate?

One concern is that the tow driver may be hostile toward anyone he believes is intoxicated while driving and toward anyone representing such a person, since he has likely seen with his own eyes the ravages of drunk drivers on our highways. As a result, he may be curt in the interview, giving little information, or refuse to cooperate completely.

QUESTION 6
How will you meet such problems?

To deal with the tow driver's possible hostility, you have a variety of choices. You can begin the interview with *small talk* about your experiences with a tow driver ("so Dad had this service station and this old tow truck"). *Empathize* with the driver's position ("I agree. Drunk drivers are the worst. See, that's what I've got to find out. I've got to find out the kind of man I'm really representing"). *Articulate your duty* ("All I'm trying to do is find out what really happened from a neutral witness like you. See, if after learning about this case I feel my client was wrong, that other guy who got banged up in the accident is going to get paid"). However, how will you choose among these and other options? Probably it will be best to enter the interview with several options in mind, making your choice dependent on the actual situation

(after all, the tow driver may not be hostile). This may even involve using several options over a single session.

QUESTION 7
If you can't solve the problems, what will you do?

You have tried small talk, empathy, articulating your duty, but not one of these strategies has borne fruit. The tow driver is hostile and is not answering your questions. You still have some further tools available to obtain the tow driver's information. You can take the tow driver's deposition but this involves a serious tactical decision because the opposing party may not know about the tow driver's allegation of intoxication. Or, at trial, you could dig into the basis of the driver's opinion on cross-examination. You could also bring out his refusal to cooperate on cross-examination and then argue the driver's obvious bias to the jury. This trial strategy, however, will not allow you discovery from which you can thoroughly prepare your case on this crucial issue of intoxication before the actual moment of confrontation.

QUESTION 8
What ethical concerns do you face in attempting to achieve your objectives?

You cannot make false statements or misleading statements of material fact. Thus, you could not claim that you represent the plaintiff in this case. However, what about feigning emotions, offering sympathy to the witness even if you have none, or conjuring up homey stories of "Daddy's garage and old tow truck" when, in fact, your father was a doctor in New York who only went into a gas station when the taxicab he was riding in pulled in to refuel? Our personal moral sense and judgment, however, preclude such deception as the latter tactic, and we advise against it and its ilk. By misleading a witness in this manner you not only may lessen your personal sense of self-worth, but risk your professional reputation and credibility as others learn of your tactics (and sooner or later they usually learn). In those tough circumstances when your personal moral sense seriously conflicts with your ability to get information helpful to your client, you may have to seriously contemplate withdrawal from the case.

D. PLANNING QUESTIONS

You have considered the various factors, and the rationale for each, involved in preparing for a witness interview. Following is a series of general questions for preparing witness interviews. You may wish to refer to them and expand on them in planning your witness interviews.

I. *Objectives*
1. What are the possible objectives of a witness interview?
2. What are your objectives with this witness? Why?
3. What is your "basic task"?

II. *Preparation*
1. How will you prepare for the interview?
2. What reports, statements, documents, etc. will you review? Why?
3. Are there other people you would wish to speak with? Who?
4. Will you visit the scene?

III. *Content Planning*
A. *Obtaining Information*
1. What information will you seek?
   a. Why (in terms of your case theory) will you seek this information?
   b. Why do you think that the witness may have this information?
2. What specific questions will you ask?
3. At this point:
   a. What is the significance of the witness to the case?
   b. Does the witness help? Hurt? Explain.
4. Now think about the credibility of the witness. What factors affect a witness's credibility?
   a. Which seem to apply to this witness?
   b. If you want to *support* the credibility of this witness, what will you look for?
      (1) What problems do you anticipate?
      (2) How will you deal with such problems?

c. If you want to *undermine* the credibility of this witness, what will you look for?
5. Regarding the credibility of information itself: How does it fit (consistent? inconsistent?) with other information in the case of which you are aware?
6. Generally, what kind of admissibility problems can arise concerning a piece of information?
   a. Are any of these potential problems likely to arise with this witness's information?
   b. How specifically will this affect the information you will seek in this interview?
   c. If you want to get the information into evidence, where will you focus this aspect of your interview?
   d. If you want to keep it out, where will you focus this aspect of your interview?

B. *Reassessment and Reevaluation (After the Interview)*
1. What information did you obtain?
2. How did it affect your case theory? Why?
   a. Will it lead to other investigation? Specify.
   b. Does it require you to consider altering your legal or factual theories? Explain.
3. How did it affect your representational strategy?
4. What was your overall impression of the witness (e.g., appearance, credibility)?
5. What kind of impression do you think this witness will make on a jury?
6. Would you call this witness at trial? Why or why not?
7. Does the witness's information present admissibility problems? Specify.
   a. If you want to keep the information out, how will you accomplish this?
   b. If you want it admitted, what will you do?
8. What is the overall significance of this information in the case?
   a. How does it relate to other information in the case?
   b. If it is admitted, how will you use

it or deal with it in closing argument? How will your adversary?

IV. *Performance Planning*
   A. *Technical Interviewing Skills*
     1. What techniques can you use to build rapport?
       a. Why are you concerned with establishing rapport?
       b. How would your approach to gaining the cooperation of the witness vary if the witness is (1) a hostile witness; (2) a friendly witness; (3) a neutral witness?
       c. How would you keep open the possibility of a follow-up interview should you desire one?
     2. Would you approach an expert in a different manner than a lay witness? Explain.
       a. What difference would it make if the expert was yours, your opponent's, or the court's?
       b. Would it matter if you are interviewing a true expert (e.g., an economist who will testify concerning "net worth" in a dissolution) or a quasi-expert (e.g., a narcotics officer who will testify about street slang for drugs)?
     3. Thinking about the *form* of questioning (i.e., "leading" or "non-leading"):
       a. What will be the likely effect of using one or the other form of questioning in an interview?
       b. Why would you use one form as opposed to another?
       c. When during the interview are you likely to use (1) non-leading or (2) leading questions? Explain.
     4. As to vocabulary (i.e., the specific types of words you will choose in asking your questions—the implications of saying "before the car bumped into you" versus "before the car smashed into you"):
       a. How would you adopt this strategy (if at all) in your interview? Why?
       b. Which word would you use to ask about Hard's initiation of the August 20 fight ("scuffle"? "incident"? "assault"?) if you were the *prosecutor*? Why?
       c. What vocabulary would you employ to ask about Summers' physical response to Hard on August 20 if you were the *defense attorney*? Why?

   B. *"Nuts-and-Bolts" Matters*
     1. What considerations will determine if you will call in advance for an appointment, or just show up at the witness's home or place of work?
     2. Would you prefer to hold interviews in your office? Why or why not?
     3. Will you do the interviews yourself? If so, why?
     4. Will you take someone with you? Why? Who would you take?
     5. Will you bring a tape recorder? Video recorder?
     6. Will you take notes?
     7. Will you show the witness a diagram? Will you have the witness mark it?
     8. Will you bring applicable photographs? How will you use them?
     9. Will you try to have the witness sign a written statement? Why?
     10. What will you do if the witness does not want to sign?
     11. Do you always want a written statement if you can get it? Explain.
     12. How will you be certain that you can again locate the witness if you should need to do so in the future?

   C. *Ethics*
     1. Are there any limits to the techniques that you can use to gain the cooperation of a witness?
       a. Can you misrepresent who you are? What you want?
       b. Can you pay a non-expert witness money?
       c. Are there problems in the prosecution offering a witness a deal (e.g., dismissal of criminal charges in exchange for testimony)?
       d. Are there problems in a civil lawyer offering to pay a witness's expenses (e.g., child care, lunch, transportation, lost wages)?
     2. Are there ethical limits to the techniques you can use to gain the information you desire?
       a. Careful use of vocabulary? (I.e., trying to shape a witness's answer by the way you phrase questions.)
       b. Letting the witness know in ad-

---

vance what information would be
helpful?

c. Gaining a witness's sympathy for
your client or creating antipathy
for your opponent's client?

d. Impressing upon a witness any
personal obligation the witness
may have to your client?

3. Notice that in a case theory approach

you know in advance what information will be helpful to your case and
what will be harmful.

a. How does this fact itself raise the
specter of potential ethical difficulties?

b. Why are these difficulties likely to
be greatest with a friendly witness who is biased in your favor?

CRIMINAL PROBLEMS: STATE v. HARD

PROBLEM 24

Prosecutor: Interview of Dr. L.H. Jackson, Medical Examiner

You have filed a first-degree murder charge in *State v. Hard*. You still have
some questions, however, about Summers' death. After all, one minute
Summers was supposed to be fine; the next, he was dead. You have an
appointment with the medical examiner who did the autopsy and wrote
the coroner's report, Dr. L.H. Jackson.

PREPARATION

READ: (1) Pretrial Case File Entries 4, 7, 9, 20, 24, 58, 62; (2) Chapter
V; (3) Fed. R. Evid. 701-705; (4) Notes from all the interviews you have
seen and done in class. Now think about and answer the following
questions:

1. What are your objectives for this interview?

2. How will you prepare for this meeting?

3. What questions do you want to ask? Why?

4. What specific legal concept provides the basis for your inquiries?

5. Is the medical examiner an expert on "proximate causation"?*

    a. Isn't "proximate cause" a legal, not medical, concept?

    b. If "proximate cause" is a legal concept, what can the coroner tell
    you about "proximate cause" in this case?

6. If the medical examiner tells you that cause of death for Bruno
Summers was respiratory distress secondary to pneumonia, do you
foresee any problems with the case? Explain.

7. Are there any other witnesses with whom you would want to discuss
the "proximate cause" issue? Explain.

8. If "proximate cause" does seem to be a problem, will you reconsider
your representational strategy? How?

---

*Within the term "proximate causation," your supervisor is incorporating both "but for"
and "legal" cause.

ASSIGNMENT FOR CLASS

1. Outside of class, plan the interview of the medical examiner. Write a short memorandum summarizing your planning, preparation, and analysis, and give a copy to your supervisor.

2. In class, meet with the medical examiner. In particular, you should discuss and assess with the medical examiner:

   a. whether you have problems with "proximate causation" in the case;

   b. if so, how you can deal with such problems at trial.

PROBLEM 25

Prosecutor: Interview of Peter Dean

You should prepare for an interview with Peter Dean in the *State v. Hard* murder case. Mr. Dean was a close friend of the deceased, Bruno Summers. He was with Summers at the Unicorn on September 3, and at Summers' parents' home on August 26 when Hard allegedly telephoned and threatened Bruno.

PREPARATION

READ: (1) Pretrial Case File Entries 4, 16, 17, 28, 31, 32, 61; (2) Chapter V; (3) Fed. R. Evid. 803(2), 901; (4) Notes from all the interviews you have seen and done in class. Now think about and answer the following questions:

1. What information can Peter Dean provide in the context of your theory?

2. Does his information help (support) your case theory? Hurt? A little of each? Explain.

3. What are your objectives in this interview?

4. How will you achieve these objectives?

5. What specific information do you want to know regarding Dean's credibility (e.g., ability to perceive, bias)? Why?

6. You may face some strenuous evidence objections when you try to present evidence of the telephone call to the jury.

   a. What will be the objections?

   b. What information could Dean give you that could assist you in meeting these objections?

7. How will you prepare for this interview? Why?

8. Assume you decide to bring photographs of the Unicorn Tavern with you. How specifically will you use the photographs?

9. Are there potential problems with the fact that Peter Dean was Bruno's friend? Explain.

10. What will you do if Dean begins the interview with: "I want to do anything I can to help you fry the guy who murdered my pal"?

11. What if Dean asks: "What do you want me to say?" How will you respond?

12. Are there other problems you anticipate in this interview?

    a. List them.

    b. How do you plan to deal with these problems?

13. What type of personality characteristics (appearance, manner of speech, cooperation) will you be looking for in this potential witness? Why?

14. Suppose you decide that your investigator will accompany you to interview Peter Dean.

    a. How will you allocate responsibilities between you and your investigator for this interview?

    b. Does the allocation of responsibilities between you and your investigator reflect the difference in your roles in the legal system, or pragmatic considerations, or both? Explain.

ASSIGNMENT FOR CLASS

1. Outside of class, plan the interview of Peter Dean. Write a short memorandum summarizing your planning, preparation, and analysis, and give a copy to your supervisor.

2. In class, you and your investigator interview Peter Dean. You may bring the diagram and/or photographs of the Unicorn Tavern (Case File Entries 28, 31, 32) with you to the interview.

PROBLEM 26

Prosecutor: Interview of Fred Faye

You are going to interview Fred Faye in the *State v. Hard* murder case. Faye is the gun store owner who allegedly sold Hard the murder weapon. Faye also has copies of the two registration applications for the gun, and a photocopy of the check that was used to pay for the weapon. The date that the check was received is file-stamped on the photocopy.

PREPARATION

READ: (1) Pretrial Case File Entries 4, 6, 19; (2) Chapter V; (3) Fed. R. Evid. 801(d)(2), 803(6), 901, 1101-1104; (4) Notes from all the interviews you have seen and done in class. Now think about and answer the following questions:

1. What information can Faye provide to support your theory of the case?

2. What specific information do you want from Faye? Why?

3. Will you ask Faye to come to your office or meet him at his shop? Explain.

4. Are there any potential problems you anticipate in the interview?

   a. List them.

   b. How do you propose to deal with such problems if they arise?

5. Ideally, you would like Faye to be able to identify Hard as the man who purchased the fatal weapon.

   a. How will you determine if Faye can identify Hard?

   b. What effect will it have on your case if Faye cannot identify Ed Hard?

   c. Will you show Faye a photograph of Hard? Why or why not?

   d. Could showing Faye a photograph potentially lead to problems at trial? Explain.

   e. If you choose to show Faye photographs and he cannot identify Hard, must you report this fact to the defense under *Branty v. State,* 201 Maj. 2d 86 (1962), and *State v. Augie,* 228 Maj. 2d 118 (1968)? (See Case File Entry 75.)

6. Even if you can show Hard purchased a gun from Faye, how will you establish that it is the same gun that shot Bruno?

7. What significance would it have for your case theory if you could establish that the gun Hard purchased from Faye was the one that killed Summers?

8. Is the date of the purchase important? Why in terms of your case theory?

9. If the date is important, how will you establish it?

10. Generally, what do you want to know about the process of purchasing a handgun?

    a. Why?

    b. Is this information relevant in a civil case for the wrongful death of Bruno Summers?

11. In *this* case, what do you want to know about the certificate of gun registration? Why?

12. Generally, what do you want to know about Faye's recordkeeping? Why?

13. Suppose you ask Faye if he keeps file-stamped photocopies of the checks he receives for handguns and he answers, "Why do you ask?" What will you say?

14. If you already have the two certificates of gun registration, why do you need the photocopy of the check for your case?

15. Are you looking for any particular personality characteristics in this witness? Specify.

ASSIGNMENT FOR CLASS

1. Outside of class, think about the information you want from Fred Faye. Write a short memorandum summarizing your planning, preparation, and analysis, and give a copy to your supervisor.

2. In class, you and your investigator plan the interview of Fred Faye. If you wish, you may "create" a photograph of Ed Hard that you may then take with you to the interview. Then perform the interview.

PROBLEM 27 _____
Prosecutor: Interview of Jack Waters

You are about to interview Jack Waters as part of your pretrial investigation for the *State v. Hard* murder case. Waters, who has a significant criminal history, is currently in jail on charges of receiving stolen property.

Waters came to your attention through a somewhat circuitous route. Waters contacted police officers a few days ago while in jail, claiming he had valuable information in the Hard case. The police brought him to you, where Waters asked for full immunity in return for his information. You refused. After further negotiations, however, you agreed to ask for leniency from the sentencing judge in Waters' current case (after Waters pleads guilty) in return for Waters' information and testimony in Hard's case.*

Waters claims that he was at the Unicorn on September 3, 198X and that, just before the shooting, he heard Hard tell Summers, "You asked for it and now you're going to get it." To which Summers allegedly responded, "Don't do it. I'm not armed."

PREPARATION

READ: (1) Pretrial Case File Entries 4, 11, 16-18, 61; (2) Chapter V; (3) Fed. R. Evid. 801(d)(2), 803(2)(3); (4) Notes from all the interviews you have seen and done in class. Now think about and answer the following questions:

1. First, think about Waters' evidence:

    a. How exactly does it help your case?

    b. How do you expect the defense to respond to Waters' information in its closing argument to the jury?

    c. Assume a hearsay objection is made to each statement Waters claims he overheard. How will you respond?

2. Now focus on the deal you have given Waters in exchange for his testimony.

    a. Is it ethical making such a deal in exchange for his testimony?

---

*If you have already made a deal under Problem 127, assume that that deal applies in this problem instead of the deal outlined above.

b. Could the defense promise benefits (e.g., money) to its non-expert witnesses?

c. Ethics aside, what will be the practical results of this deal when you present Waters' testimony to the jury?

d. How will this concern affect your interview?

e. Will you encourage Waters to conclude his own criminal case *before* he testifies in the Hard case? Why or why not?

f. Regardless of when the deal is fulfilled, are you obligated to inform the defense of its existence under *Branty v. State,* 201 Maj. 2d 86 (1962), and *State v. Augie,* 228 Maj. 2d 118 (1968)? (See Case File Entry 75.)

3. Now think about the interview. What information do you want from Waters? Why? (Remember: You want to know both the good and the bad.)

a. What will you ask Waters that bears on the credibility of his perceptions that evening?

b. What will you ask him about his criminal record? Why?

c. What will you ask about the circumstances and nature of the deal you made with him?

d. Will you want to know about his past relationship with (1) Summers; (2) Hard; (3) Tom Donaldson? Why?

4. Will you try to check out all the details of Waters' story? Why?

5. How will you be certain he was not in jail on September 3?

6. Will you generally try to check out the stories of your witnesses? Explain.

ASSIGNMENT FOR CLASS

1. Outside of class, plan the interview of Jack Waters. Write a short memorandum summarizing your planning, preparation, and analysis, and give a copy to your supervisor.

2. In class, you and your investigator interview Jack Waters.

PROBLEM 28

Prosecutor: Interview of Detective Kelly
(Investigating Officer for the Case)

Detective Kelly is sitting in the waiting room outside of your office. Detective Kelly is directing the investigation in the *State v. Hard* murder case, and thus will sit by you at the counsel table during trial as your investigating officer. At *this* point, you are *only* interested that Detective Kelly:

1. directed the taking of photographs at the scene of the shooting on September 3;

---

2. took measurements at the scene and made a rough sketch;

3. supervised the preparation of a detailed diagram of the scene;

4. authored the initial suspect information report and the follow-up report;

5. took the statement of Deborah Summers the day after the shooting; and

6. took the statement of Tom Donaldson on the night of the shooting.*

PREPARATION

READ: (1) Pretrial Case File Entries 4, 5, 16, 17, 19, 28, 31, 32; (2) Chapter V; (3) Fed. R. Evid. 401, 801(d)(1); (4) Notes from all the interviews you have seen and done in class. Now think about and answer the following questions:

1. Initially, think about this meeting (you have already had a number of brief conversations with Detective Kelly, but this is the first extensive interview you will have).

   a. What (institutionally) is the appropriate relationship between you as prosecutor and the police?

   b. What do you see as the nature of Detective Kelly's and your respective roles in this forthcoming meeting?

   c. How is this affected by the fact that Kelly will be the investigating officer in this case and, undoubtedly, many cases in the future?

2. What are your objectives in this meeting?

3. How do you intend to achieve these objectives?

4. What specific information will you seek from Detective Kelly regarding the overall investigation of the Hard case?

5. Besides reviewing the police reports, what other preparation (if any) should you do for this meeting? Why?

6. Now focus on the photographs and diagrams.

   a. Will you use these in your case? How?

   b. What are the requirements for their use and/or admissibility at trial?

   c. In light of these evidentiary considerations, what information will you seek from Detective Kelly regarding the admissibility of the photographs and diagrams?

   d. If you represented plaintiff Summers in a civil wrongful death case, would you use these photographs and diagrams? Why or why not?

---

*Kelly *also* had initial contact with Jack Waters and was present when the prosecutor made a deal for Waters' testimony; took the defendant's statement; and referred Hard to Officer Yale for a breathalyzer test. For this problem, however, you should only be concerned with the above six areas, unless your instructor has directed otherwise.

7. Do you have any questions concerning these items unrelated to admissibility concerns? Specify.

8. Finally, think about the suspect information report. In this report Detective Kelly notes that Tom Donaldson saw Hard shoot Summers. In Donaldson's statement, however, Donaldson denies witnessing the shooting.

   a. Will you ask Kelly about this?

   b. What could account for the inconsistency between Kelly's report and Donaldson's statement?

   c. Imagine Kelly insists that Donaldson told him that he had seen Hard shoot Summers, but Donaldson continues to deny making this statement. What will you do?

      1) Would you want to get Kelly's version into evidence?

         a) How would it advance your case theory?

         b) Any reason not to bring Kelly's contradiction of Donaldson?

      2) Assuming you want to get Kelly's version into evidence, how will you do so?

ASSIGNMENT FOR CLASS

1. Outside of class, plan your meeting with Detective Kelly. Write a short memorandum summarizing your planning, preparation, and analysis, and give a copy to your supervisor.

2. In class, meet with Detective Kelly, your investigating officer on the Hard case. Unless your instructor directs you otherwise, interview Kelly regarding the *six* areas noted.

PROBLEM 29
Prosecutor: Interview of Detective Kelly
(Witness for a Suppression Motion)

You have already met with Detective Kelly regarding his initial photographing and measuring of the crime scene and other matters in the *State v. Hard* murder case. At that meeting, you did not have time to discuss the statement he took from Hard shortly after the defendant's arrest. That statement seems helpful to your case, and is almost certain to be the subject of an eventual defense suppression motion (i.e., a motion that will keep you from using the statement at trial).

You now want to interview Kelly solely in regard to Hard's statement to him and this anticipated suppression motion. In approaching this interview, keep in mind that Hard's grounds for suppression will likely be:

1. that he was too intoxicated to either *voluntarily* give a statement or to *knowingly* waive his constitutional rights; and/or

2. that his *Mintz* (identical to *Miranda*) rights were not respected.

PREPARATION

READ: (1) Pretrial Case File Entries 4, 5, 17, 73; (2) Chapters V, VIII; (3) Fed. R. Evid. 801(d)(2), 701-705, 1101; (4) Notes from all the interviews you have seen and done in class. Now think about and answer the following questions:

1. Why would the defense want to suppress Hard's statement?

2. Why do you want to oppose suppression?

3. Assuming it is not suppressed, what will you respond at trial if the defense makes a hearsay objection to your attempt to elicit the statement from Kelly?

4. Now, thinking about Hard's possible intoxication:

    a. What will you ask Detective Kelly about this potential defense contention? Why?

    b. Give examples of the type of information that could defeat such a defense claim.

    c. Will the court let Kelly give his "opinion" that Hard was not intoxicated over a defense objection that a lay witness cannot give an opinion?

    d. What foundation do you need for such a lay opinion?

    e. Can you qualify Kelly as an expert on recognizing intoxication? Any problem?

    f. Do the Rules of Evidence ever apply at a suppression hearing?

    g. Even if admissible, is such a conclusory opinion the best way to make your point at the hearing on the suppression motion? Explain.

5. Does Hard's intoxication have a bearing on any areas of your case other than a possible suppression motion? Explain.

6. Now, as to the possible defense claim that Hard's *Mintz* rights were not scrupulously respected:

    a. What information do you want to know from Detective Kelly?

    b. Why?

ASSIGNMENT FOR CLASS

1. Outside of class, plan your interview with Detective Kelly. Write a short memorandum summarizing your planning, preparation, and analysis, and give a copy to your supervisor.

2. In class, meet with Detective Kelly, your investigating officer for the Hard case. Find out about *every* aspect of the statement (e.g., content, legality).

PROBLEM 30

Prosecutor: Interview of Officer Yale
(Witness for a Suppression Motion)

You are now preparing to meet a suppression motion filed by the defense in the *State v. Hard* murder case. The motion seeks (among other objectives) to keep the murder weapon and Hard's false statement to Officer Yale ("I was home all night") out of evidence. Yale's testimony is central to this particular part of the motion. As such, you have visited the police department to interview him.*

PREPARATION

READ: (1) Pretrial Case File Entries 21, 22, 30, 34, 73, 76, 77; (2) Chapters V, VIII; (3) Notes from all the interviews you have seen and done in class. Now think about and answer the following questions:

1. Officer Yale has already made a written report.

    a. Why do you need to interview him further?

    b. How will you use the report in your interview? Why?

2. The defense is claiming that the gun is inadmissible because the police should have had an arrest warrant when they arrived at Hard's home. (See Case File Entry 76.)

    a. Looking at the cases, what sort of facts would make it more likely a court would find such a warrant required?

    b. What sort of facts would lead a court to dispense with the need for an arrest warrant?

    c. How will your answers to questions 2(a) and 2(b) provide a guide for the information you will seek from Yale? Explain.

    d. Are there ethical concerns that arise when you conduct an interview knowing in advance what information you would like?

    e. Does the fact that a police officer may tend to see a suppression motion as a technicality, unrelated to guilt or innocence, increase your concerns? Explain.

    f. How can you conduct the interview so as to minimize such ethical concerns?

3. One response you are contemplating making to the defense's claim of the absence of an arrest warrant is that Hard "consented" to the police entry. You know that Hard's attorney will, in turn, counter your position by claiming that Hard did not consent, but merely "submitted to authority."

    a. What does "submission to authority" really mean?

---

*Officer Yale also gave Hard a breathalyzer test and wrote down a statement Hard made in response to a question on the "Alcohol Influence Report" (Case File Entry 5). Neither of these activities is intended to be the subject of this interview, unless your instructor directs you otherwise.

b. In light of your understanding of the legal phrase "submission to authority," what sort of facts will you seek from Officer Yale regarding the circumstances of his entry? Why?

4. As for Hard's false statement that he was "home all night," Hard is claiming it is inadmissible because he was not first given his *Mintz* rights. (See Case File Entry 73.)

   a. You want to argue that *State v. Rhodes* is determinative on the *Mintz* issue. (See Case File Entry 73.) In this regard, list the specific questions you will ask Yale.

   b. You also want to argue that *State v. Moth* is determinative on the *Mintz* issue. (See Case File Entry 73.) In this regard, list the specific questions you will ask Yale.

ASSIGNMENT FOR CLASS

1. Outside of class, plan the interview of Officer Yale. Write a short memorandum summarizing your planning, preparation, and analysis, and give a copy to your supervisor.

2. In class, interview Officer Yale in preparation for opposing the defendant's motion to suppress the gun and the false statement ("I was home").

PROBLEM 31

Prosecutor: Interview of Dr. T.A. Loopman, Pharmacologist
(Witness for a Suppression Motion)

As you know, shortly after his arrest Edward Hard gave a statement to Detective Kelly in which Hard admitted shooting Summers. The statement is important to your murder charge in *State v. Hard* because it includes a number of arguably contradictory statements that you could use to Hard's detriment at trial. Hard's attorney, however, has filed a motion to suppress this statement so it cannot be brought in at trial. Among the grounds that defense counsel has raised is that Hard was too intoxicated (Hard had a 1.6 breathalyzer after arrest) to either "voluntarily" make the statement or to waive his *Mintz* rights. You do not want to lose the suppression motion.

Your supervisor has suggested that you may get some assistance from a pharmacologist—a person who specializes in the effects of drugs or other chemical substances on living organisms. You do not know if such an expert will help to combat the position raised in the defense motion, but you have made an appointment with Dr. Loopman. At this point your only concern in this interview is the use of this area of expertise (and perhaps this particular expert) at the motion to suppress. You have obtained a copy of Dr. Loopman's resume prior to the interview.

PREPARATION

READ: (1) Pretrial Case File Entries 4, 5, 17, 26, 73-75; (2) Chapters V, VIII; (3) Fed. R. Evid. 701-705; (4) Notes from all the interviews you have seen and done in class. Now think about and answer the following questions:

1. How can a pharmacologist help you?

   a. Isn't "voluntariness" a legal, not a medical, issue?

   b. Are there tactical advantages in directing the issue in the defense suppression motion into the realm of expert discourse?

   c. What if the defense uses a pharmacologist at the suppression motion who takes the opposite position of your expert (i.e., that Hard's intoxication made him incapable of "voluntarily" giving a statement or waiving his *Mintz* rights)?

   d. Can Dr. Loopman help you even if you don't actually call him as a witness at the hearing? How?

2. Think about preparation for this interview:

   a. How will you prepare?

   b. What (if anything) will you try to find out about Dr. Loopman and pharmacology prior to the interview?

   c. Why would you want this information?

   d. Where will you look for this information?

3. Explain your specific objectives for this initial interview.

4. You have made a list of all the questions you will ask Dr. Loopman. Now you must prioritize them. After all, Dr. Loopman may well be rushed for time, so you want to make certain you get answers to your highest priority questions.

   a. List up to five questions that you would consider high priority.

   b. List up to five questions that you would rank lower in priority.

5. Why (in terms of the theories of the defense motion, rules of evidence of expert testimony, and so on) did you designate these as higher and lower priority questions?

6. If the information from Dr. Loopman hurts your position on the motion to suppress, must you give it to the defense as exculpatory evidence under cases dealing with the prosecution's duty to provide the defense with exculpatory evidence?

7. If the situation was reversed and a defense expert had prepared a report with information helpful to you, would you automatically be barred from seeing the report by *Nibbles v. State,* 202 Maj. 2d 791 (1962)? (See Case File Entry 74.)

8. Assume you want to argue at trial that Hard's intoxication would be likely to make him belligerent and less likely to be reasonable in employing self-defense. Isn't the evidence you are seeking from Dr. Loopman for this suppression motion inconsistent with the position you want to take at trial regarding Hard's intoxication? Explain.

ASSIGNMENT FOR CLASS

1. Outside of class, plan the interview of Dr. Loopman. Write a short memorandum summarizing your planning, preparation, and analysis, and give a copy to your supervisor.

2. In class, interview Dr. Loopman.

3. Afterwards, evaluate: (a) the use of pharmacology in opposition to the defense's suppression motion; (b) the use of Dr. Loopman as your expert.

PROBLEM 32

Prosecutor: Reevaluating and Synthesizing the Information from Witness Interviews

You have interviewed a number of witnesses for trial in the *State v. Hard* murder case.* In this context, you should evaluate the results of your interviews.

PREPARATION

READ: (1) Pretrial Case File Entries 4-7, 16, 17, 19, 21, 28, 31, 32, 75; (2) Chapters II, V; (3) Notes from all the interviews you have seen and done in class. Now think about and answer the following questions:

1. How does the additional information you received from these witnesses affect your theory of the case?

   a. Did you discover information helpful to the *defense?*

   b. How will you deal with this pro-defense information if it is presented at trial?

2. Do the cases of *Branty v. State,* 201 Maj. 2d 86 (1962), and *State v. Augie,* 228 Maj. 2d 118 (1968), require you to provide the defense with this helpful information? Explain. (See Case File Entry 75.)

3. How (if at all) does this additional information affect your tentative representational strategies?

4. At this point, would you use any of these people you interviewed as witnesses at trial? Explain.

5. What problems, if any, would you have in presenting any of these people as credible witnesses (e.g., faulty memory, bad appearance)?

6. How do you propose to deal with these problems?

ASSIGNMENT FOR CLASS

1. Outside of class, analyze the significance of all the information that you, the police, and your experts have obtained to date. Include in

---

*Review your list of witness interviews that your instructor has assigned.

your assessment how the information affects your representational strategy; how it affects your case theories; what you will do with the information; whether there are potential evidence problems; and whether there is other information you will need. Draw up a list of future tasks. Be certain to look at each piece of evidence individually and in its relationship to the other pieces of evidence. Write a short memorandum summarizing your planning, preparation, and analysis, and give a copy to your supervisor.

2. In class, be prepared to discuss your evaluation of the information.

PROBLEM 33

Defense Attorney: Interview of Tom Donaldson

You are about to interview Tom Donaldson, the bartender at the Unicorn Tavern, for the *State v. Hard* murder case. Donaldson gave a statement to the police on the night of the shooting in which he identified your client as the aggressor in the August 20 incident, without giving any indication that Bruno was excessive in his response. In the same statement Donaldson also maintained that on September 3, Hard and his friends had several rounds of drinks and that at some point Hard said, "That Nazi had better not come near me again."

In addition to this information in his initial statement, Donaldson has subsequently given an oral statement to the police in which he places a man named Jack Waters in the area around the back of the tavern at the time of the shooting. This is significant because Waters claims that he overheard an extremely incriminating conversation between Hard and Summers immediately prior to the shooting. As far as you know, no other witness even remembers seeing Waters in the Unicorn on September 3, let alone next to the fatal action.

PREPARATION

READ: (1) Pretrial Case File Entries 4, 5, 16, 17, 19, 28, 31, 32; (2) Chapter V; (3) Notes from all the interviews you have seen and done in class. Now think about and answer the following questions:

1. Donaldson has already given a statement.

   a. Why do you need to interview him?

   b. How will you employ Donaldson's statement in planning, organizing, and conducting his interview?

   c. As you review Donaldson's statement, does the information it contains help your theory of the case? Hurt your theory? Explain.

   d. What information could Donaldson plausibly have, other than the information in his statement, that could help or hurt you in terms of your case theory?

2. Do you anticipate any problems in getting Donaldson to cooperate with you?

a. What if he says, "My boss doesn't want me to discuss the case. There may be some civil problems here"?

b. What if he says, "I already gave a statement to the police. Look at that. I'm busy now"?

c. What if he says, "Your client is scum. Leave me alone"?

3. What are your specific objectives in this interview?

4. Assuming you believe that the information in Donaldson's statement really hurts you:

a. What information will you look for in this interview that could weaken his credibility?

b. As to the August 20 incident, what information could you obtain from him that could diminish the weight of his testimony?

c. As to the September 3 incident:

1) What type of information would be likely to make Donaldson's assertion about your client's alleged statement concerning "that Nazi, etc." less credible? (E.g., Donaldson was very busy, the place was noisy, there was a juke box, Donaldson is hard of hearing.)

2) What could undermine his placing of Jack Waters near the back of the Unicorn Tavern at the time of the shooting?

a) What factors could affect the accuracy of Donaldson's perception as to where Waters was standing?

b) Donaldson provided the police with the information about Waters' location in the tavern when police visited him at the Unicorn several weeks after the shooting. What would you want to know about this police interview?

d. Overall, would you want to know about Donaldson's relationship with the various people involved in the case (Hard, Bruno, Deborah, Waters, Hard's friends, Summers' friends)?

1) Why?

2) What specifically would you want to know about his relationship with (a) Hard, (b) Bruno? Why?

ASSIGNMENT FOR CLASS

1. Outside of class, plan the Tom Donaldson interview. Write a short memorandum summarizing your planning, preparation, and analysis, and give a copy to your supervisor.

2. In class, you and your investigator interview Tom Donaldson.

PROBLEM 34

Defense Attorney: Interview of John Gooding

You plan to seek discovery from the prosecution as part of your fact-gathering for the *State v. Hard* murder case. At the same time, you must continue your own investigation. You and your investigator are therefore about to interview John Gooding.

Mr. Gooding is a friend of the defendant who was with Hard (1) at the Unicorn on August 20 and (2) at the Unicorn again on September 3. Further, according to your client, Mr. Gooding is also willing to speak about Hard's good, non-violent character and Summers' bad character.

PREPARATION

READ: (1) Pretrial Case File Entries 4, 5, 16, 17, 19, 28, 31, 32, 61; (2) Chapter V; (3) Fed. R. Evid. 404, 405, 608; (4) Notes from all the interviews you have seen and done in class. Now think about and answer the following questions:

1. What are your overall objectives in this interview?

2. How do you intend to prepare for the interview?

3. What information can Mr. Gooding provide to support your case theory?

4. What specific information do you want from him? Why?

5. Upon which witness credibility factors (e.g., appearance, ability to communicate) will you focus? Why?

6. What will you want to know about Gooding's proposed character testimony? Why?

   a. What are the evidentiary requirements for the admission of such testimony?

      1) When can you bring such testimony into evidence?

      2) What is the foundation for its admission?

   b. How will this evidentiary perspective affect your interview?

7. Do you anticipate any problems in this interview?

   a. List any problems you can think of.

   b. How will you deal with such problems?

8. Suppose you ask Mr. Gooding about the August 20 incident and he states, "It's very important in this case that I saw Bruno threaten Ed, isn't it?" How will you respond?

9. Suppose Mr. Gooding states in regard to the August 20 incident, "My memory is a bit vague about that." How will you respond?

10. Will you ask Mr. Gooding if he has already spoken with the prosecution and the police?

    a. Why do you care?

    b. If he says yes, what (if anything) will you then ask him? Why?

ASSIGNMENT FOR CLASS

1. Outside of class, plan the John Gooding interview. Write a short memorandum summarizing your planning, preparation, and analysis, and give a copy to your supervisor.

2. In class, you and your investigator interview John Gooding. Take notes. Be sure to assess Mr. Gooding as a character witness for Hard and against Summers.

PROBLEM 35

Defense Attorney: Interview of Cindy Rigg

As part of your investigation in the *State v. Hard* murder case, it is now time to plan your interview with Cindy Rigg. Ms. Rigg is an eyewitness to the August 20 fight between Hard and Summers at the Unicorn Tavern. She does not seem to be friends with either Summers or Hard.

PREPARATION

READ: (1) Pretrial Case File Entries 4, 16, 19, 28, 31, 32, 61; (2) Chapter V; (3) Notes from all the interviews you have seen and done in class. Now think about and answer the following questions:

1. What could reasonably be the emotional range of Ms. Rigg's attitude toward you as Hard's attorney?

2. How will this factor affect your approach to the interview?

3. As you prepare for the interview, does Cindy Rigg appear to be a favorable witness for your side? Explain.

4. Could her testimony be unfavorable to you in any way? How?

5. What are your objectives in this interview?

6. How do you intend to achieve these objectives?

7. What will you ask Cindy Rigg about? Why?

8. Will you bring photographs or a diagram of the Unicorn Tavern to the interview? Why or why not?

   a. How would you use a diagram in the interview?

   b. How would you use photographs?

9. What witness credibility factors (e.g., appearance, ability to communicate) will you focus on? Why?

10. Will you call her in advance for an interview appointment, or just show up at her door? Explain.

11. Suppose you just show up and tell her that you want to discuss the shooting at the Unicorn Tavern with her, and she states, "I don't really want to get involved, but you're the government so I guess I have to talk to you."

a. How will you respond?

b. Are your responsibilities in this situation different from those of your investigator if he were unaccompanied by you? Explain.

c. What would be the appropriate conduct of the *prosecutor* if told the same thing by Ms. Rigg in seeking an interview?

ASSIGNMENT FOR CLASS

1. Outside of class, plan the Cindy Rigg interview. Write a short memorandum summarizing your planning, preparation, and analysis, and give a copy to your supervisor.

2. In class, be prepared to discuss your objectives and strategies for your interview and any ethical concerns you may have. Then, you and your investigator do the interview.

PROBLEM 36 _____
Defense Attorney: Interview of Betty Frank, Nurse

Your investigator has just come back from talking to Betty Frank, a nurse at Mercy Hospital, as part of the investigation in the *State v. Hard* murder case. Nurse Frank watched over Bruno Summers in the intensive care unit when he was admitted to Mercy shortly after the shooting at the Unicorn.

In a previous visit to the hospital, your investigator reviewed portions of Summers' hospital records in order to evaluate the alleged cause of death and had seen a hospital record in which a statement was recorded that was attributed by Nurse Frank to Summers: "I should have left when I saw him."

Your investigator discussed the statement with Nurse Frank. She remembers that Bruno said something about the shooting, which she related to Dr. Day, but she cannot now remember what Bruno said. Even showing her the hospital record did not refresh her recollection. Your investigator went on to obtain detailed information bearing on Nurse Frank's ability to hear the statement (e.g., her position in the room when she heard the statement, noise from machines, hearing ability), but did not, however, consider evidence issues concerning admissibility of the statement in the records.

PREPARATION

READ: (1) Pretrial Case File Entries 4, 7; (2) Chapter V; (3) Fed. R. Evid. 803(2)(6), 804(b)(2)(3), 901; (4) Notes from all the interviews you have seen and done in class. Now think about and answer the following questions:

1. What specific bearing does Nurse Frank's information have on your case theory?

a. Would you want to use such a statement at trial?

b. Explain.

2. How would you use the statement in an argument to a jury?

3. What response would you expect from the prosecution?

4. Now think about admissibility:

   a. What evidentiary problems do you face?

   b. What theories of admissibility do you have?

   c. What problems with such theories?

   d. How will you deal with such problems?

   e. What is the specific foundation for satisfying each theory of admissibility?

   f. Might you need some witnesses in addition to Nurse Frank? Additional records? Explain.

5. Imagine you subpoena the records and the hospital resists, claiming the physician-patient privilege.

   a. What will you respond?

   b. What bearing (if any) in the fact that a medical records clerk had previously permitted your investigator to review the records?

ASSIGNMENT FOR CLASS

1. Outside of class, write a short memorandum summarizing your planning, preparation, and analysis, and give a copy to your supervisor.

2. In class, you and your investigator meet with Nurse Frank and obtain the information that you believe necessary for an evidentiary foundation to obtain admission of the statement in the hospital record.

PROBLEM 37
Defense Attorney: Evaluating Refusal of Witness to Cooperate with Interview

One of your investigators in the *State v. Hard* murder case has contacted Deborah Summers. Deborah made it clear that she has no intention of providing any assistance to the defense and she practically slammed the door in the investigator's face. You, of course, must fully evaluate this encounter as part of your preparation for the case.

PREPARATION

READ: (1) Pretrial Case File Entries 4, 19; (2) Chapter V; (3) Notes from all the interviews you have seen and done in class. Now think about and answer the following questions:

1. How would you have tried to get Deborah to talk with you?

2. Did your investigator waste her time, or did she still obtain information that is helpful for the trial? Explain.

3. What specifically will you ask your investigator about the circumstances of this "interview"? Why?

ASSIGNMENT FOR CLASS

1. Outside of class, evaluate the significance of Deborah's refusal to discuss the case. Be prepared to discuss this with your supervisor. Write a short memorandum summarizing your planning, preparation, and analysis, and give a copy to your supervisor.

2. In class, you and your investigator go back to Deborah Summers and try to get her to talk with you. (Note: Your objective in this assignment is to get her to talk, not to conduct a full interview.*)

PROBLEM 38

Defense Attorney: Interview of Marty Saunders
(Witness for a Suppression Motion)

Within a few hours after the shooting of Bruno Summers at the Unicorn, police (led by Officer Yale) went to Hard's home. According to the police, Hard agreed to let the police into his home, where the fatal gun was found and seized. In planning a suppression motion (a motion to keep the gun out of evidence), you have been developing a twofold legal attack.

First, you are prepared to argue that the police needed an arrest warrant to enter Hard's home prior to seizing the gun.

Second, you will take the position that there existed neither exigency nor valid consent as could obviate the need for an arrest warrant (because, among other grounds, Hard's "consent" was a "mere submission to authority").

A discussion with your client this morning has added a totally new dimension to this search issue. According to Hard, the police report is "A bunch of nonsense! Consent nothing! They just kicked my door in, and I had a guest there who was a witness—Marty Saunders."

Hard's story is legally significant in two respects:

(1) With or without a warrant, police can generally not force in a door without first giving "knock-notice."

(2) Such an action by the police would also undermine any government attempt to use "consent" as a theory that could circumvent the need for an arrest warrant.

You have made plans to meet with Marty Saunders.

PREPARATION

READ: (1) Pretrial Case File Entries 21, 22, 30, 72, 76, 77; (2) Chapters V, VIII; (3) Notes from all the interviews you have seen and done in class. Now think about and answer the following questions:

---

*Your instructor, of course, may decide that you should conduct a full interview of Deborah *if* you can convince her to talk.

1. When you first meet with Saunders, will you tell him what Hard has told you? Why or why not?

2. How will you find out what Saunders knows?

3. What information will you seek from him? Why?

4. If you use Saunders at the suppression hearing, won't you be calling the police liars?

   a. What problems may this cause you with the judge?

   b. How will you deal with such problems?

5. Who is the court likely to believe, Hard's friend or the police? Explain.

6. What kind of information could make Saunders appear more credible? Less credible?

7. Think about information, not personal to Saunders, that, nevertheless, affects the credibility of his story:

   a. How can you explain that he was not mentioned in the police report?

   b. Will you go to Hard's house and inspect Hard's front door? What if it does not seem to be broken?

   c. Do you want to determine Hard's opportunities to communicate with Saunders (visits, phone calls, messages) between the time of his arrest and now? Why?

8. Assume the prosecution has the burden of persuasion (by a "preponderance of the evidence") both for establishing consent and for justifying a failure to give "knock-notice." Can you use this burden to try to avoid calling the police liars? How?

9. Even if the court believes Saunders' story, it may still find (a) that exigent circumstances obviated the need for an arrest warrant to enter Hard's home (making consent irrelevant) and (b) that compliance with the "knock-notice" rule was excused in this case. (Of course, there is no way to project how the court's belief that the police have lied would affect the whole dynamic of the hearing on the motion.)

   a. List the sort of facts that (1) could excuse the need for an arrest warrant and (2) could excuse compliance with "knock-notice."

   b. How specifically will this list affect your interview with Saunders?

ASSIGNMENT FOR CLASS

1. Outside of class, plan the interview of Marty Saunders. Write a short memorandum summarizing your planning, preparation, and analysis, and give a copy to your supervisor.

2. In class, you and your investigator interview Marty Saunders.

3. Afterwards, provide your supervisor with a short, written evaluation explaining (a) why you would or wouldn't use Saunders at the suppression hearing and (b) what points you would present in his testimony if you did use him.

PROBLEM 39

Defense Attorney: Interview of Police Officer Monroe
(Witness for a Suppression Motion)

Shortly after the shooting at the Unicorn Tavern, Officer Yale and numerous others went to Hard's home. The officers entered without an arrest warrant, arrested Hard, and seized the fatal weapon. You are preparing a motion to suppress the gun. In anticipation of the eventual hearing on the motion, you are going to interview one of the officers who conducted the arrest and seizure of the gun—Officer Monroe. Your potential defense theories for suppression of the gun are:

(1) The police had no arrest warrant when they entered, which makes the entry illegal and taints the subsequent seizure of the gun.

(2) Consent cannot obviate the need for a warrant because (a) the "consent" was a "mere submission to authority" and (b) Hard was too intoxicated to voluntarily consent.

(3) The police version of the facts is not true. The police forced in the front door making valid consent impossible and violating the requirement of "knock-notice."

Keep these in mind as you approach the interview.

PREPARATION

READ: (1) Pretrial Case File Entries 21, 22, 30, 72, 76, 77; (2) Chapters V, VIII; (3) Notes from all the interviews you have seen and done in class. Now think about and answer the following questions:

Interviewing Police Officers in General

1. What kinds of problems do you imagine might arise when trying to interview a police officer?

2. What (if anything) makes an officer different from the average lay witness?

3. In addition to reviewing the reports and documents in the case file, do you want to know about local police procedures (e.g., acting in the field, making reports, communicating with headquarters)? Why?

4. How do you locate a police officer whom you want to interview?

5. Do you call and make an appointment? Should you just show up at the station between shifts?

6. Will you take someone with you? Why or why not?

7. What sort of attitude do you expect from an officer who was involved in your client's arrest?

8. What if the officer doesn't want to talk with you?

   a. What approaches could you take to convince him or her to cooperate?

   b. Could you use the officer's refusal to cooperate at a suppression motion? How?

c. Is any of this information relevant for defendant Hard if he is a defendant in a civil case for damages for the wrongful death of Bruno Summers?

Interviewing Officer Monroe

9. Will you ask Officer Monroe about her background, education, experience? Why?

10. Think about the potential defense theories for suppression of the gun.

   a. As to *each* of these theories, what information will you seek? Why? (Do you care how the officers at the door were dressed? Whether they had weapons? Details about Hard's behavior?)

   b. What specific questions will you ask to get this information?

   c. What will you ask about the other police at the scene? Why?

   d. Do you want to know what information Officer Monroe possessed about the case *before* she arrived at Hard's home?

11. You have already talked to Marty Saunders, who claims to have been a guest in Hard's home at the time of the search. It is Saunders' information that forms the basis for your potential theory that the police just forced in Hard's front door.

   a. What (if anything) will you ask Monroe about Saunders? Explain.

   b. How does it bear on your motion if Monroe remembers Saunders and says he was "very polite"? If she says Saunders was "calling us pigs"?

12. Imagine that you determine Officer Monroe will be a good witness to call at the hearing. You go to serve her with a subpoena and she says, "Don't do that. I'll just have to come to court and spend the day sitting outside the courtroom waiting to be called. Instead, call the station when you're ready for me. I'm right next door to the courthouse, and I can be over in two minutes." What do you do?

ASSIGNMENT FOR CLASS

1. Outside of class, plan the Officer Monroe interview. Write a short memorandum summarizing your planning, preparation, and analysis, and give a copy to your supervisor.

2. In class, interview Officer Monroe. (In advance of class, inform your supervisor whether you will bring your investigator.)

3. After the interview be prepared to discuss with your supervisor (a) what bearing Officer Monroe's information has on your suppression motion and (b) whether you might call Officer Monroe as a witness.

Defense Attorney: Interview of Elizabeth F. Lift, Psychologist
(Feasibility of Survey of Community Attitudes to Support a Motion to Change Venue)

The *State v. Hard* murder case has received a great deal of adverse pretrial publicity. As a result, you are in the process of preparing a motion for a change of venue. A colleague has suggested that a survey of community attitudes toward Hard might be helpful for this motion. At this point, however, you don't know a thing about the nature, value, feasibility, or cost of such a survey. You hope that your upcoming interview with Dr. Lift, a psychologist who is an expert in conducting such surveys, will clarify these points. Prior to the interview, you have obtained a copy of Dr. Lift's resume and a sample survey.

PREPARATION

READ: (1) Pretrial Case File Entries 1, 2, 13, 25, 66; (2) Chapters V, VIII; (3) Fed. R. Evid. 701-705; (4) Notes from all the interviews you have seen and done in class. Now think about and answer the following questions:

1. How, generally, can such a survey help your motion to change venue?

2. Is the answer to question 1 part of what you must learn in the interview?

3. Imagine that, as you begin the interview, Dr. Lift asks, "What do you want me to do?" What will you respond?

4. Why (if at all) do you want to know about:

    a. Dr. Lift?

    b. The doctor's discipline?

    c. The theory and methodology of such surveys?

    d. The doctor's experience with such surveys? The limits and problems of such surveys?

    e. The survey that would be conducted in *this* case?

5. What else (if anything) do you want to know? Why?

6. What will you say if, after the interview, Dr. Lift asks, "What do you want me to do now"?

7. Overall, how will you prepare for this interview?

8. If Hard is a defendant in a civil wrongful death action brought by plaintiffs, can he use this information to support a change of venue?

ASSIGNMENT FOR CLASS

1. Outside of class, plan the Dr. Lift interview. Write a short memorandum summarizing your planning, preparation, and analysis, and give a copy to your supervisor.

---

2. In class, interview Dr. Lift.

3. Afterwards, assume you want to do the survey. Hard, however, does not have the money to pay for one. Thus, you must make a motion to the court to get money in order to do the survey. (Remember that the survey is intended to support your ultimate venue motion.) Your motion to get money will include your sworn statement (by declaration or affidavit) laying out the factual allegations in your motion. Write (no longer than two typewritten pages) the portion of this "Declaration in Support of a Motion for Money for a Survey" that explains the nature and value of such a survey for your venue motion. (Note: The court is not about to give you money unless it is convinced that this survey has real value.)

PROBLEM 41 ─────────────────────

Defense Attorney: Interview of James Raven, Polygrapher

Your client has consistently maintained his innocence to the first-degree murder charge in *State v. Hard*. You are now considering giving Hard a polygraph. As such, you have set up a meeting with polygrapher James Raven. You have obtained Mr. Raven's resume prior to the interview.

PREPARATION

READ: (1) Pretrial Case File Entries 5, 17, 19, 27, 75; (2) Chapters V, VIII; (3) Fed. R. Evid. 701-705; (4) Notes from all the interviews you have seen and done in class. Now think about and answer the following questions:

1. Assume the results of a polygraph are inadmissible in court. List all the reasons you might still want to give a client a polygraph. Are any of these reasons persuasive in this case?

2. What specific preparation will you do for this interview?

3. What are you looking for in a polygraph operator? Why?

4. As to the polygraph itself:

   a. What generally do you want to know?

   b. What do you want to know about the procedure and technique?

   c. Do you want to know what it can show about Hard? The risks of inaccuracy? The variables that affect accuracy?

   d. *State v. Fream*, 212 Maj. 2d 413, 416 (1963), states: "For a novel scientific process or test to be admitted into evidence, the proponent of the scientific innovation must either establish that the test or process is 'generally accepted as reliable in the relevant scientific community' [cit. omitted] or establish for the trial court that the particular test or process is reliable." How (if at all) will *Fream* affect your interview with Raven?

5. Hard is claiming that he should be excused because his actions were "necessary" and "reasonable" in light of that necessity. Polygraphs

deal with "true" and "false." What true/false inquiries are possible in Hard's case?

6. If Hard takes the polygraph and fails, do you have to tell the prosecutor? Explain.

7. If a prosecution witness took a polygraph and failed, could you argue that the prosecutor has a duty to disclose this information under the cases of *Branty v. State*, 201 Maj. 2d 86 (1962), and *State v. Augie*, 228 Maj. 2d 118 (1968)? (See Case File Entry 75.)

8. Could you argue that this duty to disclose under *Branty* and *Augie* would still apply even if polygraph evidence is not admissible? Explain. What will be the prosecutor's response?

9. Would Hard's "failure" of a polygraph affect how you would subsequently pursue his case? Explain.

10. Is the information that Hard took and passed a polygraph test relevant in a civil wrongful death case? Explain.

ASSIGNMENT FOR CLASS

1. Outside of class, plan the James Raven interview. Write a short memorandum summarizing your planning, preparation, and analysis, and give a copy to your supervisor.

2. In class, interview James Raven. Be prepared to discuss with your supervisor whether Hard should take a polygraph.

PROBLEM 42

Defense Attorney: Reevaluating and Synthesizing the Information from Witness Interviews

You have interviewed a number of witnesses for trial in the *State v. Hard* murder case. Review the witness interviews your instructor has assigned. Each time you obtain information you must think how it affects your theory of the case. In this context, you should evaluate the results of these witness interviews along with the police reports, interviews with Ed Hard, and all documentary evidence.

PREPARATION

READ: (1) Pretrial Case File Entries 4, 16, 17, 19, 28, 31, 32; (2) Chapters II, V; (3) Notes from previous interviews. Now think about and answer the following questions:

1. Does the information you obtained from these witnesses lead you to seek other information? Explain.

2. Did you discover any information that may be helpful to the *prosecution?*

3. How will you deal with pro-prosecution information if it is presented at trial?

4. At this point, do you think that you would use any of these witnesses at trial? Explain.

5. What problems (if any) would a party have in presenting any of the persons you interviewed as credible witnesses at trial?

6. How would you deal with these problems if you were the party vouching for their testimony?

ASSIGNMENT FOR CLASS

1. Outside of class, analyze the significance of all the information obtained to date in investigation and discovery. Accordingly, your assessment should include how this information affects your representational strategies; how it affects your case theories; what you will do with the information; whether there are potential evidence problems; and whether there is other information you will need. Draw up a list of future tasks. Be sure to look at each piece of evidence individually and in its relationship to the other pieces of evidence. Write a short memorandum summarizing your planning, preparation, and analysis, and give a copy to your supervisor.

2. In class, be prepared to discuss your evaluation of the information.

CIVIL PROBLEMS: SUMMERS v. HARD

PROBLEM 43

Plaintiffs' Attorney: Interview of Tom Donaldson

You have interviewed Deborah Summers, reviewed the criminal file that you obtained from the prosecutor's office, and researched the law. Deborah, Gretchen, and Hans Summers have retained you as their attorney concerning the death of Bruno Summers. You plan to informally investigate the incidents at the Unicorn Tavern and Ed Hard's role in the shooting in order to assess whether to file a lawsuit.

Peter Nye, your investigator, has contacted Tom Donaldson. Mr. Donaldson has agreed to speak with you, albeit reluctantly. He told Nye: "Yeah, I have nothing to hide; I said it all in my police report." Mr. Donaldson will meet with you at the Unicorn Tavern at 4:00 P.M.

PREPARATION

READ: (1) Pretrial Case File Entries 1-35, 59-61, 63, 90; (2) Chapter V. Now think about and answer the following questions:

1. Tom Donaldson is 5'7" tall and weighs approximately 155 pounds. Will his physical appearance suggest specific subject areas you may want to discuss with him? Why?

2. Tom Donaldson was interviewed by the police and signed a written statement. What additional information do you seek that was not contained in his statement? Why?

3. Donaldson is potentially an adverse witness. Why?

4. If Donaldson is reluctant or hostile when you meet with him, how will you obtain his cooperation in this interview?

5. How will you assess whether the information Donaldson gives you is reliable?

6. Peter Nye, your investigator, made an appointment to see Donaldson at the Unicorn Tavern. Is the Tavern a good place to interview Donaldson? Why?

7. Tom Donaldson is a potential defendant in any lawsuit you may file against Ed Hard. Is it ethical for you to interview Tom Donaldson? Discuss.

8. In a criminal case, if Donaldson is a potential defendant, the police would have to caution Donaldson about his rights to remain silent and to have a lawyer, and that anything that he may say may be used as evidence against him. Do you have to caution Donaldson if he is a potential defendant in a civil case? Discuss.

ASSIGNMENT FOR CLASS

1. Outside of class, prepare a memorandum explaining your objectives and what you plan to ask Tom Donaldson. Give a copy to your senior partner.

2. In class, conduct the interview of Tom Donaldson.

PROBLEM 44

Plaintiffs' Attorney: Interview of Peter Dean

You have interviewed Deborah Summers, reviewed the criminal file that you obtained from the prosecutor's office, and researched the law. Deborah, Gretchen, and Hans Summers have retained you as their attorney concerning the death of Bruno Summers. You plan to investigate the incidents at the Unicorn Tavern and Ed Hard's role in the shooting in order to assess whether to file a lawsuit. Peter Nye, your investigator, has arranged for Peter Dean, a friend of Deborah and Bruno Summers, to be interviewed. He will be at your office at 9:00 A.M.

PREPARATION

READ: (1) Pretrial Case File Entries 1-35, 59-61, 63, 90; (2) Chapter V. Now think about and answer the following questions:

1. During your interview with Deborah Summers, she told you about the shooting on September 3. Will you tell Peter Dean what Deborah told you? Explain.

2. Bruno had a knife in his pocket on the night of the shooting. Suppose Detective Kelly told you it appeared that Summers was going to knife Hard.

   a. Would you ask Dean a question such as: "Bruno didn't say anything to you about knifing Hard, did he?"

   b. What are the advantages or disadvantages of asking this type of question?

3. Should Peter Dean sign a statement? Explain.

4. Suppose Peter Dean states: "I want to help Deborah." How will you respond?

ASSIGNMENT FOR CLASS

1. Outside of class, prepare a memorandum explaining your objectives and what you plan to ask Peter Dean. Give a copy to your senior partner.

2. In class, conduct the interview of Peter Dean.

PROBLEM 45
Plaintiffs' Attorney: Interview of Bert Kain

You have interviewed Deborah Summers, reviewed the criminal file that you obtained from the prosecutor's office, and researched the law. Deborah, Gretchen, and Hans Summers have retained you as their attorney concerning the death of Bruno Summers. You plan to informally investigate the incidents at the Unicorn Tavern and Ed Hard's role in the shooting in order to assess whether to file a lawsuit.

Peter Nye, your investigator, has located three potential eyewitnesses to the August 20 incident and the September 3 shooting—Bert Kain, Tom Donaldson, and Peter Dean. Bert Kain has agreed to be interviewed by you and Peter Nye at your office at 9:00 A.M.

PREPARATION

READ: (1) Pretrial Case File Entries 1-35, 59-61, 63, 90; (2) Chapter V. Now think about and answer the following questions:

1. What are your objectives for the interview with Bert Kain? Why?

2. Should the law affect your interview?

3. What information will you seek from Bert Kain to support your theory of the case?

4. Is there a difference between the attorney and investigator roles in interviewing?

5. Bert Kain appears to be a "neutral" eyewitness. Does that make the information he tells you reliable? Explain.

6. Does Bert Kain's neutrality as a potential eyewitness make him a credible witness? (Can you assume he is telling the truth?)

7. Suppose Bert Kain is hesitant or confused about what he heard or saw at the Unicorn Tavern. Will you try to pin him down to one story? Explain.

8. Are there fundamental differences between interviewing Bert Kain (eyewitness), Tom Donaldson (bartender at the Unicorn Tavern), and Peter Dean (friend of Bruno Summers)? Explain.

ASSIGNMENT FOR CLASS

1. Outside of class, prepare a memorandum explaining your objectives and what you plan to ask Bert Kain. Give a copy to your senior partner.

2. In class, conduct the interview of Bert Kain.

PROBLEM 46

Plaintiffs' Attorney: Interview of Dr. Brett Day

You have interviewed Deborah Summers, reviewed the criminal file that you obtained from the prosecutor's office, researched the law, and obtained Bruno Summers' hospital records. Deborah, Gretchen, and Hans Summers have retained you as their attorney concerning the death of Bruno Summers. You plan to informally investigate the incidents at the Unicorn Tavern and Ed Hard's role in the shooting in order to assess whether to file a lawsuit.

According to Peter Nye, your investigator, Dr. Brett Day was the surgeon who operated on Bruno Summers the night of the shooting and attended Bruno until he died. Dr. Day has agreed to see you at his office at 5:30 P.M.

PREPARATION

READ: (1) Pretrial Case File Entries 1, 2, 4, 5, 7, 9, 12, 23, 24, 35, 40, 41, 59-61, 63, 64, 90; (2) Chapter V; (3) Fed. R. Civ. P. 26(b)(4), 35; (4) Fed. R. Evid. 702-705. Now think about and answer the following questions:

1. In the criminal matter against Edward Hard, the prosecutor would have interviewed the medical examiner and explored the issue of proximate cause of death. When you interview Dr. Day you will most likely also be interested in the issue of proximate cause. Compare how you would explore the issue in both the civil and criminal context.

2. Federal Rule of Civil Procedure 26(b)(4) provides that facts or opinions held by expert witnesses who will not testify as expert witnesses at trial are *generally* not discoverable except upon a showing of exceptional circumstances. Will this discovery rule have an effect on the interview of Dr. Day? Explain.

3. Federal Rule of Evidence 702 will permit Dr. Day, if qualified by "knowledge, skill, experience, training or education," to testify at trial as an expert witness. Will this rule of evidence have any effect on your interview? Explain.

4. Dr. Day is a potential expert witness, as opposed to a lay witness. How will that affect preparation for your interview?

5. Should documents already in your possession be read before speaking with Dr. Day? Why?

6. Will you question Dr. Day about any particulars in the:

   a. hospital records?

   b. death certificate?

   c. medical examiner report?

7. Potentially, Dr. Day could be friendly, neutral, or hostile toward your case. Can you explain what would cause him to adopt any one of these attitudes?

8. How will you approach Dr. Day if he is hostile?

9. Doctors are notoriously busy. Are there any particular things you can do to alleviate Dr. Day's anxiety before, during, or after the interview because of time pressures? List them.

ASSIGNMENT FOR CLASS

1. Outside of class, prepare a memorandum explaining your objectives and what you plan to ask Dr. Day. Hand in a copy to your senior partner.

2. In class, conduct the interview of Dr. Day.

PROBLEM 47

Private Attorney for Deborah Summers: Interview of Karen Sway
(Deborah Summers' Child Custody Case)*

A few months have passed since the shooting and death of Bruno Summers. You are an attorney who has been consulted by Deborah Summers concerning a child custody matter and now have been retained by Ms. Summers to represent her in this matter. (The child custody dispute is separate and distinct from the lawsuit concerning Bruno Summers' death.)

It seems that Bruno Summers' parents, Gretchen and Hans Summers, have filed for legal custody of Ronny and Amanda, Bruno's children by an earlier marriage. Deborah Summers has also expressed interest in the children and may want to contest the petition filed by Gretchen and Hans Summers.**

You have decided to interview Karen Sway, a close friend of Deborah's, concerning the child custody matter. The attorney who is representing Deborah Summers and Bruno's parents and children concerning Bruno's

---

*Deborah Summers' attorney is not the same attorney who is representing the Summers family in *Summers v. Hard*.

**See Problem 118 for factual background in the child custody dispute.

death has spoken to Karen Sway by telephone but has not interviewed Ms. Sway in person. Ms. Sway will be at your office at 9:00 A.M.

PREPARATION

READ: (1) Pretrial Case File Entries 1, 2, 40, 41, 61, 63, 64, 79, 90; (2) Chapter V. Now think about and answer the following questions:

1. Why do you want to interview Karen Sway?

2. Will the *Summers v. Hard* lawsuit concerning Bruno Summers' death and Karen Sway's role in that case have any effect on your interview with Karen Sway? Explain.

3. Karen Sway spoke to Deborah Summers' attorney by telephone in the wrongful death case. Can you ask Karen Sway what she said? Discuss.

4. Suppose Karen Sway has forgotten what she said in that telephone call with Deborah's attorney in the wrongful death case. Should you ask that attorney for information as to what Karen Sway said about Deborah's emotional condition? Explain.

ASSIGNMENT FOR CLASS

1. Outside of class, prepare a memorandum explaining your objectives and what you plan to ask Karen Sway when you interview her. Hand in a copy of your memorandum to your senior partner.

2. In class, conduct the interview of Karen Sway.

PROBLEM 48 _____

Plaintiffs' Attorney: Interview of Karen Sway

Deborah, Gretchen, and Hans Summers have retained you as their attorney concerning the death of Bruno Summers. It is a few months since the shooting and death of Bruno Summers, and Deborah still appears to be upset about Bruno Summers' death. You would like to explore Deborah's emotional condition more fully.

You have just received a telephone call from Deborah Summers. She has told you that she has retained an attorney to represent her in a child custody matter. It seems that Bruno Summers' parents have filed for legal custody of Ronny and Amanda, Bruno's children by his prior marriage. Deborah may contest the petition filed by Gretchen and Hans Summers. Deborah's child custody attorney has interviewed Karen Sway, who is a close friend of Deborah's.

A few months ago, you spoke with Karen Sway by telephone to confirm her willingness to be a potential witness in a wrongful death case. Karen Sway has agreed to be interviewed by you and Peter Nye, your investigator. She will be at your office at 9:00 A.M.

PREPARATION

READ: (1) Pretrial Case File Entries 1-35, 40, 41, 59, 61, 63, 64, 79, 90; (2) Chapter V. Now think about and answer the following questions:

1. What are your objectives in interviewing Karen Sway?

2. Explain how Civil Jury Instruction 4 can provide guidance in planning the content of this witness interview.

3. Will the child custody matter and Karen Sway's role in that case influence your interview of Karen Sway? Explain.

4. Suppose Karen Sway is reluctant to talk to you. What will you do?

    a. Is that helpful for Deborah's emotional distress claim?

    b. Harmful? Explain.

5. Will you ask Karen Sway to tell you what she has already told Deborah Summers' child custody attorney? Explain.

6. Should you instruct Karen Sway that she should tell Deborah Summers' child custody attorney the same information she has related to you in this interview? Discuss.

ASSIGNMENT FOR CLASS

1. Outside of class, prepare a memorandum explaining your objectives and what you plan to ask Karen Sway when you interview her. Hand in a copy of your memorandum to your senior partner.

2. In class, conduct the interview of Karen Sway.

PROBLEM 49

Attorney for Defendant Hard: Interview of Alan Long

You have interviewed Ed Hard, reviewed Ed Hard's homeowner's insurance policy with SAPO Insurance Company, read the criminal file that you obtained from the prosecutor's office, and researched the law. Ed Hard's "rich cousin" has paid your fee. You have agreed to represent Ed Hard in the *Summers v. Hard* lawsuit.

Before responding to plaintiffs' complaint in *Summers v. Hard*, you want to seek additional information concerning the Bruno Summers-Edward Hard incidents.

Ed has told you a brother from the "pen," Alan Long, was a patron at the Unicorn Tavern on August 20 and September 3, 198X. Ed said, "Long will give you the scoop. Just tell him what we need and he will do the rest."

Alan Long agreed to be interviewed by you and your investigator. He will be at your office at 6:00 P.M.

PREPARATION

READ: (1) Pretrial Case File Entries 1-37, 59-61, 63, 90; (2) Chapter V; (3) Fed. R. Evid. 404, 405, 609. Now think about and answer the following questions:

1. Ed Hard has told you Mr. Long may be a convicted felon. Will that information have any effect on your interview with Mr. Long? Explain.

2. Suppose Mr. Long was at the Unicorn Tavern on August 20, 198X. He denies being at the tavern on September 3, 198X. Is any information concerning August 20 relevant to Ed Hard's defense in *Summers v. Hard?* Explain.

3. Will you ask Mr. Long if he has a criminal record? Explain.

4. Suppose Mr. Long admits he has a criminal record. What effect will that have on the interview?

5. Suppose Mr. Long denies being a "fellow pen-pal" of Ed Hard's.

   a. Are there other ways to find out if Long has a criminal record? Explain.

   b. Suppose you have written proof that Long has a criminal record. What effect will that have on the interview?

6. Should you tell Mr. Long: "Ed said, 'Long will give you the scoop. Just tell him what we need . . .' "? Explain.

ASSIGNMENT FOR CLASS

1. Outside of class, prepare a memorandum explaining your objectives and what you plan to ask Alan Long when you interview him. Hand in a copy of your memorandum to your senior partner.

2. In class, conduct the interview of Alan Long.

PROBLEM 50 _____

Attorney for Defendant Hard: Interview of Rebecca Karr

You have interviewed Ed Hard, reviewed Ed Hard's homeowner's insurance policy with SAPO Insurance Company, read the criminal file that you obtained from the prosecutor's office, and researched the law. Ed Hard's "rich cousin" has paid your fee. You have agreed to represent Ed Hard in the *Summers v. Hard* lawsuit.

Ed Hard went to the Unicorn Tavern on August 20 and September 3, 198X with John Gooding and Rebecca Karr. During the past few weeks, Ed has asked you, as his attorney, to speak with Rebecca. On three occasions, you had appointments with Rebecca, but each time she did not call or appear for her appointment. You have not told Ed that Rebecca has not been a cooperative witness.

You have scheduled one last appointment to speak with Rebecca concerning the Bruno Summers-Edward Hard incidents.

Rebecca has agreed to be interviewed by you and your investigator. She will be at your law office at 2:00 P.M.

PREPARATION

READ: (1) Pretrial Case File Entries 1-37, 59-61, 63, 90; (2) Chapter V. Now think about and answer the following questions:

1. Rebecca Karr was acquainted with Bruno Summers and is, according to Ed Hard, a good friend of Ed's. Suppose Karr begins the interview by stating, "Ed was my friend until he committed cold-blooded murder."

    a. Will you ask Rebecca to explain what she means by her statement? Explain.

    b. Should you try to convince Rebecca that Hard did not commit cold-blooded murder? Explain.

    c. Should you tell Rebecca that Ed said he acted in self-defense? Explain.

2. Should you confront Ms. Karr about the three appointments she failed to keep? Why?

3. You have heard a rumor that Rebecca attended a neo-Nazi survivalist meeting. Will you ask her about her experience? Why?

4. Are there any circumstances under which you should preserve the interview with Ms. Karr? Explain.

    a. How can you preserve the interview? Discuss.

    b. If you preserve the interview and Rebecca Karr is no longer available as a witness, will you have to give defendant Davola and plaintiffs access to your witness interview (statement, tape)? Explain.

ASSIGNMENT FOR CLASS

1. Outside of class, prepare a memorandum explaining your objectives and what you plan to ask Rebecca Karr when you interview her. Hand in a copy of your memorandum to your senior partner.

2. In class, conduct the interview with Rebecca Karr.

PROBLEM 51

EKKO Attorney for Defendant Davola: Interview of Roberta Montbank

Before responding to the Summers' complaint, you plan to informally investigate the incidents alleged.

The EKKO insurance investigator located another patron, Roberta

Montbank, who claims to have been at the Unicorn Tavern on September 3. (It seems that the police had inadvertently written down Robin Luntlebunk as being a patron at the Unicorn Tavern instead of Roberta Montbank. Therefore, the police never located her for the criminal case, *State v. Hard*.) As Davola's insurance company attorney, you have arranged to interview Ms. Montbank at the Stillwater Retirement Home on October 26, 198X.

PREPARATION

READ: (1) Pretrial Case File Entries 1-37, 44, 59-61, 63, 90; (2) Chapter V; (3) Fed. R. Evid. 601, 612. Now think about and answer the following questions:

1. Roberta Montbank was not interviewed, nor did she give a statement to the police after the shooting. She was discovered by the investigator for the EKKO Insurance Company.

    a. How do these facts affect your interview?

    b. If Ed Hard were being prosecuted, how would these facts affect your case as prosecutor? Defense attorney?

2. Ms. Montbank is 78 years of age. She appears to be slightly hard of hearing. Will this factor have any influence on the interview? Explain.

3. Would a diagram of the Unicorn Tavern be helpful to you in conducting the interview of Roberta Montbank? Why or why not?

4. Suppose Ms. Montbank provides helpful information for Ed Hard's defense. What will you do after the interview?

ASSIGNMENT FOR CLASS

1. Outside of class, prepare a memorandum explaining your objectives and what you plan to ask Ms. Montbank. Hand in a copy to your senior partner.

2. In class, along with the EKKO investigator, interview Roberta Montbank.

PROBLEM 52 _____
Attorney for Defendant Davola: Interview of Antje Lenz

M.C. Davola received plaintiffs' complaint in *Summers v. Hard*. You have interviewed M.C. Davola, read the criminal file that you obtained from the prosecutor's office, and researched the law. You have agreed to represent M.C. Davola and will be coordinating your defense with EKKO Insurance Company attorneys. Before responding to the complaint, you want to obtain additional information concerning the Bruno Summers-Edward Hard incidents.

Antje Lenz was one of the patrons at the Unicorn Tavern on September 3, 198X. You contacted Antje Lenz and he has agreed to be interviewed by you and your investigator. He will be at your office at 9:00 A.M.

PREPARATION

READ: (1) Pretrial Case File Entries 1-37, 44, 59-61, 63, 90; (2) Chapter V; (3) Fed. R. Evid. 701. Now think about and answer the following questions:

1. Antje Lenz was not interviewed by the police in the criminal case, *State v. Hard.* Will that have any effect on your interview with Mr. Lenz? Explain.

2. Suppose that during the interview Mr. Lenz tells you that he observed Hard and Bruno Summers all night, and Hard was not intoxicated.

   a. Is Lenz's information helpful for Davola's case? Explain.

   b. But suppose also that Lenz tells you that he had a few shots of straight tequila that very night. Is Lenz a helpful witness? Harmful witness? Why?

ASSIGNMENT FOR CLASS

1. Outside of class, prepare a memorandum explaining your objectives and what you plan to ask Antje Lenz when you interview him. Hand in a copy of your memorandum to your senior partner.

2. In class, conduct the interview of Antje Lenz.

PROBLEM 53 _____

Attorney for Defendant Davola: Interview of Officer M. Yale

You have interviewed M.C. Davola, read the criminal file that you obtained from the prosecutor's office, and researched the law. You are interviewing clients and witnesses before drafting a response to the *Summers v. Hard* complaint.

Officer Yale investigated the shooting at the Unicorn Tavern and talked to Ed Hard after the shooting. Officer Yale has agreed to be interviewed by you. The interview will take place at 9:00 A.M. at the police department.

PREPARATION

READ: (1) Pretrial Case File Entries 1-37, 59-61, 63, 90; (2) Chapter V; (3) Fed. R. Evid. 702-705. Now think about and answer the following questions:

1. What are your objectives for this interview? Explain.

2. Is Officer Yale a potential witness in the civil case? Explain.

3. If Officer Yale is a potential witness in the civil trial, will his testimony present evidence admissibility problems? How will these potential problems affect this interview?

4. Officer Yale conducted a breathalyzer test on Edward Hard. How will you prepare before interviewing Officer Yale about the breathalyzer test?

   a. Is there any background reading you would do? Explain.

   b. Documents you will examine?

   c. Generally, are breathalyzer test results admissible in a civil case to prove that a party or witness was intoxicated?

   d. Is the breathalyzer test result relevant in *Summers v. Hard*? Explain.

5. Would it be better for Hard's attorney, rather than you, Davola's attorney, to interview Officer Yale? Why?

6. Should Hard's attorney accompany you to the interview of Officer Yale? Why?

7. Should you be accompanied to the interview by an investigator? Explain.

8. Should your investigator obtain a witness statement from Officer Yale?

ASSIGNMENT FOR CLASS

1. Outside of class, prepare a memorandum of your objectives and what you plan to ask Officer Yale. Hand in a copy to your senior partner.

2. In class, along with your investigator, interview Officer Yale at the police department office.

VI

Pleading

A. PLEADING IN THE CONTEXT OF A REPRESENTATIONAL STRATEGY

Pleading, like other parts of the pretrial process, uses a goal-oriented approach—specifically, ends-means thinking. Using ends-means thinking to plead means that any pleading you draft will be guided by a representational strategy. As you may recall from Chapter I, representational strategy refers to the overall objectives that you want to achieve in your case (e.g., an early settlement, a large amount of money). In addition to reflecting a representational strategy, pleading also serves specific functions within the legal system. Therefore, your pleading will need to reflect and accomplish interrelated goals. We refer to these interrelated goals as pleading objectives:

- to formally invoke the court's jurisdiction by asserting a claim you allege is within its jurisdictional competence
- to give notice of claims or defenses (to your adversary, trier of fact, the public)
- to narrow issues in controversy
- to frame issues for discovery
- to persuade and educate your adversary with the aim of resolving the dispute (judgment on the pleadings, summary judgment, settlement, or, as a defending party, dismissal)

At the same time, even where your pleading objectives and representational strategy goals are not congruent, your representational strategy will directly affect the emphases that you make within the content of your pleading and how you express those emphases in your pleading. For instance, factual investigation and pleading have a symbiotic relationship. Federal Rule of Civil Procedure 11 requires a reasonable factual and legal investigation before a pleading is filed. Therefore, your factual investigation should be planned in part with regard to the information you will need to draft a pleading. Since fact investigation is broader than just obtaining information to support the existing assertions in your pleadings, you might obtain information that will expand or modify the assertions in your pleading.

Of course, your case theory will also provide a framework for determining the actual content of your pleading. Later in this chapter, we explore how your case theory guides your choice of claims, parties, and relief within the pleading.

Formal discovery and pleading are inextricably tied together. Discovery allows you to obtain the broadest amount of information that will support your case, refute your adversary's case, and develop other potential issues. Since pleading is based on specific legal theories, the inclusion of claims, parties, and relief within the pleading helps to crystallize the issues. Yet, to ensure full discovery, pleading should be inclusive of all potential case theories supported by law and fact. For example, in an automobile rear-end collision, if you do not plead a claim that the car was defective, you could potentially be precluded from discovery of relevant facts that might support a products liability claim because your pleading did not cover that issue.

Finally, pleading and negotiation are also interrelated. For instance, if you plead and then negotiate, you need to consider how the pleading content will affect negotiation. Is your pleading a persuasive tool? Then perhaps your pleading, because it is persuasive, will entice your adversary into negotiation. Is your pleading vituperative? This may hinder your negotiation efforts.

This chapter presents our approach for drafting affirmative and responsive pleading. We emphasize that the drafting of a pleading is an endeavor that must be carried out in the context of your representational strategy and with an appreciation of its impact on other pretrial tasks—case theory, factual investigation, the scope of discovery, negotiation. We believe that pleading is a tool that allows the advocate to accomplish a representational strategy. To illustrate our approach, this chapter includes two examples of pleading, both based on the Federal Rules of Civil Procedure (see pages 172-179). We are mindful that there are differing pleading styles, philosophies, and requirements (such as code and notice pleading) that can affect drafting. Nevertheless, we believe that by including these examples we can best show you a framework that you can adapt for your drafting style and jurisdictional requirements.

B. PLEADING TERMINOLOGY

To begin your preparation, you should review the basic terminology of pleadings. These terms will appear throughout this chapter and refer to types of pleadings as well as to the internal structure of pleadings. For civil cases, there are two types of pleadings: affirmative and responsive pleadings. An *affirmative pleading* describes a legal claim upon which the substantive law provides a remedy.[1] A *responsive pleading* is a defendant's response to plaintiff's allegations.[2] Both affirmative and responsive pleadings consist of four parts: the *caption* (providing information about the court, the parties, and the type of pleading); the *body* (a description of the event, including claims, defenses, and the parties involved); the *remedy* (or request for relief);[3] and the *signature*. We will refer to these four parts again when discussing how to organize information for your pleading.

In the civil arena, there are, theoretically, two styles of pleading, *code pleading* and *notice pleading*. Notice pleading requires a "short and plain statement of the claim showing that the pleader is entitled to relief" (Fed. R. Civ. P. 8(a)). Typical code pleading rules require a "statement of the facts constituting the cause of action, in ordinary and concise language" (Cal. Civ. Proc. Code §425.10 (1988)). Some commentators find practical differences between notice and code pleading: They suggest that code pleading requires strict adherence to pleading the elements of the substantive law and that notice pleading merely requires setting forth facts. Other commentators argue that only philosophical differences exist, and any practical distinctions that might result are insignificant where drafting is concerned. They base their position on the fact that both code and notice pleading require legal and factual sufficiency. They argue that, even in notice pleading, facts must have legal relevance in describing how the event occurred, who was involved, why the client is entitled to relief, and what relief is sought. In this text, we take the position that a pleading must be legally and factually sufficient (i.e., be able to withstand defense legal theories attacking legality and factual sufficiency). We have not made distinctions in drafting because of code or notice pleading rules. Later in this chapter, we discuss how, if at all, code and notice pleading distinctions might affect a pleading.

In the criminal arena, the only pleading is the charging document, which relates the criminal offenses the defendant is facing.[4]

---

1. Affirmative pleadings include a complaint (also referred to as a petition, bill, or writ), a counterclaim, a cross-claim, and a third-party complaint. See note 2.

2. Responsive pleadings include answers and replies filed by a defending party. In many jurisdictions, a defendant can file an answer (also referred to as a response or reply) and/or a motion. Under the Federal Rules a defending party can respond by an answer and a motion simultaneously, or by an answer or motion solely. This chapter discusses answers. For a full discussion of motions, see Chapter VIII.

A defendant can answer plaintiff's complaint in any or all of three ways. Federal Rule of Civil Procedure 8(b) provides that a defending party "state in short and plain terms [the party's] defenses to each claim asserted and shall admit or deny the averments upon which the adverse party relies. If a party is without knowledge or information sufficient to form a belief as to the truth of an averment, the party shall so state and this has the effect of a denial."

First, defendant can assert that plaintiff is not entitled to the relief requested by directly responding to each of plaintiff's contentions (admitting or denying plaintiff's allegations).

Second, defendant, in addition to responding to plaintiff's allegations, can assert an affirmative defense. An *affirmative defense* does not deny the truth of the plaintiff's contentions but instead asserts that, even if plaintiff's contentions are true, other facts prevent the plaintiff from obtaining relief from the defendant. For example, if plaintiff alleged that defendant owed plaintiff money, but defendant did not owe the plaintiff money because he already paid it, defendant could respond by denying plaintiff's allegations. Additionally, defendant could plead an affirmative defense asserting, "I admit, I owed plaintiff the money; but I already paid her." That raises an affirmative defense (accord and satisfaction).

Affirmative relief is not granted to the defendant by either responding to plaintiff's allegations or pleading an affirmative defense.

Third, if a defendant wants to request affirmative relief from the plaintiff, defendant can assert a counterclaim or cross-claim in the answer. A *counterclaim* asserts defendant's claim and request for relief against plaintiff. A *cross-claim* asserts defendant's claim against another defendant that plaintiff has named in plaintiff's complaint and requests relief from that defendant. Defendant's counterclaim and cross-claim are pleaded in defendant's answer. But sometimes plaintiff has not named as a party a person who defendant believes is responsible for plaintiff's or defendant's claim. In such a situation, defendant can file a *third-party complaint* (a separate and different pleading from the answer) joining that person as a party (the new defendant is referred to as a third-party defendant.) A third-party complaint asserts defendant's claims against the third-party defendant.

3. A request for relief includes such things as dismissal, damages, injunction, declaratory relief, restitution, and specific performance. There are two types of relief—equitable and legal. Certain claims and remedies historically are considered to be equitable, others legal. If you request a remedy that historically is classified as equitable (e.g., injunctions, specific performance, restitution), your selection of a remedy may determine whether you have a jury as the factfinder. (A purely equitable request for relief—such as a request for injunctive relief—may preclude your client's right to a jury trial.)

4. Generally, the charging document is referred to by three names (although terminology may vary somewhat among jurisdictions.) When filed at the inception of a case in the lower trial court by the prosecutor, it is called a *complaint;* when filed by the prosecutor in the superior court or when embodying the probable cause determination of a court after a preliminary hearing, an *information;* when incorporating the findings of a grand jury, an *indictment.* (See Chapter I, pages 5-6.)

These charging documents can be significant to advocates in a number of ways. First, defense counsel may, depending on the jurisdiction, be able to demurrer to the charging pleading on the grounds that the statutory offense pleaded is unconstitutional, the pleading does not charge a crime, the pleading reveals some defense (e.g., statute of limitations) on its face, or the pleading does not give sufficient information for the accused to prepare a defense. (Note that this last ground may be used as a means for discovery when accompanied by a request for a bill of particulars.)

Second, since to one preparing a defense the charging pleading expresses the plaintiff's legal theory, due process considerations of fair notice will limit the variance permitted between this pleading and subsequent proof at trial. It is hard to imagine that a court would let a plaintiff who has charged a June 1984 burglary prove at trial that the burglary really happened in June 1985. Whether

---

C. PREPARATION

1. Obtaining Information

As we noted earlier in this chapter and in Chapter III, before filing a pleading you have an ethical duty to make a reasonable investigation and inquiry of law and fact under the circumstances. This section discusses the preparation you need to undertake before you are ready to draft a pleading. This lengthy preparatory process is in fact your first step in actually drafting a pleading.

a. Legal Theory as a Basis for Pleading

You may recall from our discussion of the development of a case theory that only events, things, or occurrences that are legally significant (cognizable by substantive law) result in a remedy. Likewise, in pleading, only occurrences that are legally significant can form the basis of your pleading. Thus, the substance of your pleading also must be based on a legal theory.

Our discussion of case theory also treated legal and factual sufficiency. These two concepts are of particular importance in drafting a pleading since you must draft a pleading that will be sufficient and not subject to attack. In this section we will focus on legal sufficiency. Legal sufficiency means that your claim will state a basis for relief and thereby withstand an attack on legality. Under Federal Rule of Civil Procedure 8(a), legal sufficiency means:

> A pleading which sets forth a claim for relief, whether an original claim, counterclaim, cross-claim, or third-party claim, shall contain . . . (2) a short and plain statement of the claim showing that the pleader is entitled to relief, and (3) a demand for judgment for the relief to which he deems himself entitled.

The remedy for insufficiency under Federal Rule of Civil Procedure 12(b)(6) is that a motion to dismiss will be granted for "failure to state a claim upon which relief can be granted." There are two types of legal theories that affect the legal sufficiency of a pleading, "old-shoe" and "cutting-edge" theories. Generally, a

pleading based on old-shoe legal theories will be legally sufficient. Old-shoe legal theories are grounded in legal precedent, custom, and statutes. Thus, when planning your pleading, you will review case law, statutes, and jury instructions and adopt old-shoe claims or defenses, parties, and relief for inclusion in your pleading.

Cutting-edge legal theories are just that, the cutting edge of established law. These legal theories are problematic. As we discussed in developing a cutting-edge legal case theory, if you plead based on a cutting-edge legal theory, you may subject your pleading to attack by a motion to dismiss, judgment on the pleading, or summary judgment. Yet, there may be circumstances in which, because of your representational strategy, you want to plead based on a cutting-edge legal theory because such a theory potentially expands the scope of a lawsuit by adding new claims, parties, or remedies. You are, in effect, creating new law. As an example, in recent years we have seen the emergence of the new legal theory of tortious breach of contract, which allows recovery of punitive damages, a remedy not available in contract. Likewise, strict liability for dangerous products has been extended to the manufacturer, thus expanding the parties who could be joined in a lawsuit. As in developing your case theory, to plead a cutting-edge theory (whether it relates to claims, parties, or relief), you search for clues in case law—footnotes, dicta, or dissenting opinions—or in law review articles, legal periodicals, or specialized legal journals.

Cutting-edge legal theories can also be developed by your own factual theorizing. Some facts that you possess may not suggest any of the accepted legal theories. Instead, these novel facts may suggest a new legal theory to fit them. More than likely, however, you will try to plead novel facts within an established claim rather than through the proposal of a novel one: Your pleading will be less likely subject to attack for old-shoe claims and relief than for cutting-edge claims and relief. For instance, right to recovery for breach of an employment contract might be less likely to be attacked than the assertion of a novel tort such as wrongful discharge.

b. Factual Theory in Pleading

In addition to legal sufficiency, your pleading must resist attacks on factual sufficiency. Factual sufficiency under Federal Rule of Civil Procedure 8(a) requires "a short and plain statement of the claim showing the pleader is entitled to relief." Factual sufficiency means that your pleading must contain facts to describe the

---

the court would allow amendment of the pleadings to conform with the proof for a one- or two-day variance, on the other hand, would vary with the specific circumstances of the case.

Third, the charging pleading in a prior case may have a bearing on a claim that the defendant is facing double jeopardy in a current case.

elements of the legal theory. Therefore, your pleading must describe factually, and not in the abstract, the event that gives rise to your client's injury, the person who caused it, and the remedy you seek—that is, the claim, the party, and the relief. But pleading your factual theory must be done in a legally significant manner. The elements of your legal theory will provide the structure for pleading your story of what occurred. Essentially, this story is your factual theory.

To determine which facts to plead, whether for an old-shoe or cutting-edge legal theory, you might examine cases for guidance. You may find, however, that some facts that are essential for an element of a claim or defense are missing (e.g., the exact date of the incident, specific location of the event); however, if you reasonably believe in good faith that these missing facts may be obtainable, you can file the claim (or defense) alleging the facts upon information and belief.

c. Procedural Rules

Critical to the content and technical drafting of your pleading are such procedural rules as (1) who has the burden to plead the claim or defense; (2) whether your pleading must contain specific or particular allegations; (3) which claims or defenses can be joined; (4) who can and should be named as a party; and (5) which format requirements prevail.

(1) Burden of Pleading

Burden of pleading is generally determined by procedural rule, although sometimes it is determined by statute, case law, or established custom. The burden of pleading is particularly important in determining the content of your pleading—that is, in determining whether something must be pleaded as a claim or defense. For example, in most jurisdictions, procedural rules establish that a plaintiff in an affirmative pleading has the burden of pleading a defendant's negligence but is not required to plead the absence of his or her own negligence. Thus, a plaintiff does not have to plead, "I was wearing a seat belt at the time of the crash." Instead, the procedural rule establishes that a plaintiff's negligence is an affirmative defense which the defendant has the burden of pleading. Yet some jurisdictions have the opposite procedural rule and place the burden on the plaintiff to plead the absence of negligence by plaintiff. You need to be aware of how the particular rules within your jurisdiction deal with allocating burdens of pleading.

(2) Specific Allegations

You also need to be aware of procedural rules that require specific factual allegations. For example, the Federal Civil Procedure Rules require factual allegations establishing subject matter jurisdiction; specific allegations if fraud, mistake, or special damages are pleaded; and descriptions of the capacity of parties (e.g., the suit involves a minor, a corporation, a partnership, a class action). Procedural rules in other jurisdictions might not require or might even prohibit certain allegations from being pleaded (e.g., specific monetary amounts for general damages).

(3) Joinder of Claims or Defenses

You need to consider how procedural rules can affect which claims or defenses you can join in your pleading. Some procedural rules allow and even encourage that all claims and defenses be joined in one lawsuit. For example, a plaintiff can plead unrelated claims of negligence and contract against a defendant. Procedural rules established by case law such as res judicata, collateral estoppel, and statutes of limitation might influence you to join claims because the consequence of failure to plead a claim or defense may preclude you from raising the claim or defense in a subsequent lawsuit. Therefore, you might plead, in the same lawsuit, two claims or defenses that you may not have wanted to join (a medical malpractice claim against the treating doctor and a claim for common law negligence against the driver of the automobile). Or you might join two affirmative defenses (accord and satisfaction and fraud).

You also need to be aware of other procedural rules that can limit defenses that may be joined. For example, a defending party can plead only affirmative defenses related to the claim or transaction alleged by plaintiff.

(4) Joinder of Parties

Procedural rules, case law, and statutes can affect your representational strategy by defining whom you can and must name as a party, and how you technically describe a party. For instance, you may want to selectively name a party in order to pursue a particular strategy. Suppose your strategy in a products liability case is to assert a claim against only the manufacturer. Nevertheless, a procedural rule for joinder of parties may require that you join the retailer as a party because the rules define the retailer as an essential party.

On the other hand, you may want to join a party but different procedural rules or substantive law governing personal jurisdiction, subject matter jurisdiction, venue, or service of process may prohibit you. For instance, you might want to join defendants in a class action, but procedural rules requiring you to give notice to defendant class members may prohibit you from pleading a class action if you cannot comply (for economic or logistic reasons) with this personal jurisdiction requirement.

(5) Technical Format

All pleadings must conform to particular formats. Generally, procedural rules specify such requirements as paper size, paragraph divisions, topical headings, and so on. You will need to be familiar with the particular format that is appropriate or required.

d. References

Throughout this text, we have stressed the need for consulting everything from reference texts to other attorneys and court personnel. This is a special necessity in pleading because requirements unique to particular jurisdictions are often a matter of custom in such jurisdictions. Additionally, we suggest you might want to consult the following references for their ideas and views on pleading: Alterman, "Plain and Accurate Style in Lawsuit Papers," 2 Cooley L. Rev. 243 (1984); J. Glannon, *A Student's Guide to Understanding Civil Procedure* (1987); R. Haydock, D. Herr & J. Stempel, *Fundamentals of Pretrial Litigation* (1985); R. Keeton, *Trial Tactics and Methods* (1973). A word of caution is in order about particular pleading sources such as form books. Such books contain both approved court forms and forms that are generally used by attorneys in a particular jurisdiction. Generally, sources such as form books, and even some experienced and highly competent attorneys, might approach pleading in a technical and highly stylized manner. You might be advised, "This is the customary way to plead," when another approach would more effectively achieve your overall objectives. Or you might even be given poorly drafted examples. Just as we continue to caution you in using our approach, we also want to add a caveat about other references. Use these resources as a source of ideas, but also use your own judgment when pleading.

2. *Organizing Information*

A major aspect of our planning approach to pretrial advocacy involves organizing information. This is of particular importance in pleading. You will be gathering, or already have gathered, a vast amount of legal and factual information, and pleading requires that this information be presented in a highly structured manner. We have found it helpful to organize information by following the actual structure of a pleading as described at page 153: the caption, the body, the remedy or request for relief, and the signature. We include four charts that will help you organize the type of information you potentially might use for drafting affirmative and responsive pleadings based on the Federal Rules of Civil Procedure.

The charts are broadly designed, allowing you to include all kinds of information that potentially might be of benefit in preparing your representational strategy. As with all our suggestions, feel free to adopt or modify these charts to reflect your organizational needs.

In order to observe how these charts organize information, we will be referring to a hypothetical set of facts. Later in this chapter, these hypothetical facts will be used again in our illustrations and in our pleading examples to demonstrate our approach to drafting a pleading (see pages 172-177). Let's assume the attorneys for Alby, the plaintiff, and Brady, the defendant, have obtained the following information:

Albert Alby lives in California and has a summer home in Oregon. He owns and operates a bakery. Clark Brady lives in Texas and is a registered nurse. On June 15, 198X, Alby and Brady were driving on Interstate Highway 5 in the State of Major. Brady crashed into the rear of Alby's 198X red sports car. The week before the crash, Alby made an appointment to have his gas pedal adjusted. At the scene, Alby told the police that his car abruptly slowed down. Both Alby and Brady suffered personal injuries and property damage. Alby was hospitalized and incurred hospital and medical bills of $5,000; two weeks of lost profits to his business, $5,000; property damage of $10,000; and general personal injuries set at $50,000.

Brady was not injured, but had $8,000 property damage. Brady was given a breathalyzer test at the scene and registered a .25 blood-alcohol level. The state highway police issued a citation to Brady for violation of State of Major motor vehicle code section 14.0, which provides "It is unlawful to operate a motor vehicle while intoxicated. . . . Presumption of intoxication is .1." The Major State Supreme Court in *Susanah v. David*, 182 Maj. 3d 118, 236, firmly establishes common law negligence and negligence per se, allowing only compensatory damages. In addition, footnote 2 states in part:

> A level of intoxication which exceeds the presumptive .1 intoxication level is outrageous [and] people driving while so intoxicated should be punished.

CHART I

Party Description

Jurisdictional Requirements	*Parties*	
	Plaintiff (Alby)	Defendant (Brady)
1. Subject matter jurisdiction (elements)		
a. Diversity of citizenship (28 U.S.C. §1332(a)		
(1) individuals from different states	California	Texas
(2) $10,000 in dispute	$50,000 personal injuries; $ 5,000 lost profits; $ 5,000 medical expenses; $10,000 property damage	$8,000 property damage
b. Federal question	none	none
2. Venue (elements for diversity jurisdiction, 28 U.S.C. §1391)		
a. Place where the cause of action arose	Accident in State of Major	Accident in State of Major
b. Corporation's residence*	not applicable	not applicable
c. Individual's residence**	resides in California; summer home in Oregon	resides in Texas
3. Appropriate court and preferences for venue***		
a. State court	States of Major, California, and Oregon	State of Texas
b. Federal court	United States District Courts in Major, California, and Oregon	United States District Court in Texas

*Venue for a corporation is based on a corporation's residence, which is defined by 28 U.S.C. §1391(c) as the location where the corporation has its principal place of business, the places where it is licensed to do or does business, and its places of incorporation.

**Venue for an individual for diversity jurisdiction is based on an individual's place of residence. Venue is appropriate either where all plaintiffs reside or all defendants reside.

***Selecting an appropriate state or federal court takes into consideration personal jurisdiction, venue, and subject matter jurisdiction criteria. Strategy decisions as to which court to select reflect such issues as geographical convenience of client and attorney, choice of law to be applied, and selection of decisionmaker.

A recent law review article by Professor Waldman, "Excessive Intoxication—The Case for a New Tort," 3 Maj. L. Rev. 1 (198X), argues a new legal tort theory based on excessive intoxication while driving—"reckless endangerment."

Chart I organizes information for drafting the caption and the first paragraph of the body of a complaint. This opening paragraph describes the parties and subject matter jurisdiction according to Federal Rule of Civil Procedure 10. The chart may also be of help to a defendant in raising a procedural attack on the pleading.

The legal elements for party description and subject matter jurisdiction provide the structure for the factual allegations. Chart I also includes a framework for listing information relevant to personal jurisdiction and venue, even though the Federal Rules of Civil Procedure do not require a plaintiff to affirmatively plead jurisdiction and venue. Including these legal elements in the chart will help Alby's attorney to draft the pleading properly, and can also prepare a defendant for raising issues of improper personal jurisdiction or venue.

Chart II organizes information for a plaintiff to draft the remainder of the body (including the claim, the party, and the injury) and the relief portion of an affirmative pleading. This chart can also help the defendant in determining whether there are legal and factual deficiencies in plaintiff's pleading. Chart II also provides a framework for including a factual theory, legal theory, and documents. By including this framework, the chart can be used either to formulate this information for the pleading or response, or to plan a representational strategy.

Chart III (page 160) is based on a response to the sample complaint included at the end of this chapter. This chart can help organize an answer to a plaintiff's allegations. The structure of the chart is based on the four ways one can respond to plaintiff's allegations: (1) admit; (2) partially admit and partially deny;[5] (3) deny; (4) deny with a reason (upon information and belief).[6]

Chart III can help a responding party list each of plaintiff's allegations or compare plaintiff's allegations with the facts that defendant knows to exist or in good faith believes to exist. Defendant's response to each plaintiff allegation can then be recorded under the appropriate category. A plaintiff can use the chart to determine the facts and issues in controversy.

Chart IV (page 161) is similar to Chart II in that it organizes information according to the legal elements within an affirmative defense, counterclaim, cross-claim, or third-party complaint. Some commentators maintain that affirmative defenses do not have to factually plead legal elements. But since affirmative defenses are subject to motions as to their legal and factual sufficiency, the better view is to plead defenses according to the requirements of legal elements.

This chart provides a framework for including legal and factual theories and documents. Using Chart IV

for organizing an affirmative defense can help organize information that is relevant to a counterclaim against plaintiff or to cross-claims against other defendants. Additionally, it can help you focus on whether a third-party complaint is necessary in the event a defendant was not joined as a party by plaintiff. A plaintiff, in turn, can use this chart to determine the legal and factual sufficiency of a defendant's response claims.

D. PLANNING THE CONTENT OF A PLEADING: AN APPROACH AND ILLUSTRATION

> **BASIC TASK: Selecting claims, party, and relief to draft a pleading that is legally and factually sufficient and carries out your representational strategy.**

Your representational strategy, pleading objectives, and case theory provide a framework for determining the content of your pleading. In this section, we propose eight questions to help you plan the substantive content of a pleading. Some of the issues represented by separate questions are in fact interrelated and require simultaneous analysis; however, the questions are listed separately to help isolate and clarify particular areas you might want to consider.

In addition to explaining our approach through these eight questions, we provide two pleading examples at pages 172-177 to illustrate how our approach translates into an actual pleading. Note that our approach to planning the content and (in the next section) to technically drafting a pleading refers to plaintiff's complaint. The same approach and thought processes, however, are applicable to drafting Brady's answer, with the exception that defendant's answer must respond to allegations in plaintiff's complaint. To see how our approach is applied to a responsive pleading, see the annotations to Brady's answer at pages 180-181. Our eight-question approach follows:

1. What is your representational strategy and pleading objectives?
2. How can your pleading achieve your representational strategy?
3. What claims (or defenses) will you plead?
4. What parties will you plead?

---

5. Partially admit and partially deny means that, in the paragraph you are responding to, some of the facts are true and some may not be true or even known. For example, suppose plaintiff pleads in Paragraph 5 that Defendant Brady, the owner of a blue sedan, was proceeding south. A potential response by Defendant Brady might be: Defendant admits part of Paragraph 5. He *is* the owner of a blue sedan, but he denies the rest of the paragraph. He was proceeding east, not south.

6. When a responding party lacks knowledge of the actual facts, the defending party can assert lack of information and can deny the allegation.

CHART II

Claim, Party, Relief

Legal Theory	Factual Theory	Legal Claim	Legal Elements of the Claim	Facts to Plead	Documents	Parties	Remedy
Negligence	Intoxication (Brady) Failure to keep a careful lookout	Common law negligence	Duty owed	Event occurred on 6/15/8X		Plaintiff: Alby (owner, driver). Defendant: Brady (owner, driver).	
				Alby driving car on public highway	Alby's car registration		
				Brady driving car on public highway	Brady's car registration		
			Breach of duty	Brady: .25 blood-alcohol level while driving	Police report, breathalyzer test, state police citation		
			Proximate cause of injury	Brady crashed into Alby	Three witness statements under oath		
			Injury and relief	$10,000 property damage; pain and suffering	Bills for car repair and car rental		General damages, $10,000; pain and suffering
				$5,000 doctor and hospital expenses; $5,000 lost profits	Doctor and hospital bills; Bakery financial books and records		Special damages, $10,000
Negligence Per Se	Brady was presumptively intoxicated (above a .1 blood-alcohol level) and was driving while intoxicated, which is in violation of State of Major motor vehicle code §14.0	Negligence Per Se	Duty	State of Major vehicle statute protects Alby, a driver, from Brady, who was driving while intoxicated on a public highway on 6/15/8X	Statute; police citation	Plaintiff: Alby (injured driver). Defendant: Brady (owner, driver).	
			Breach of duty	Brady had a .25 blood-alcohol level (tested by the police shortly after the crash). A blood-alcohol level of .1 is presumption of intoxication.			
			Proximate cause of injury	Brady crashed into Alby	Three witness statements under oath		
			Injury and relief	$10,000 property damages; pain and suffering	Bills for car repair and car rental		General damages, $10,000; pain and suffering
				$5,000 doctor and medical bills; $5,000 lost profits	Doctor and hospital bills; Bakery financial books and records		Special damages, $10,000

CHART III

*Responding to Allegations**

Plaintiff's Allegations (corresponding to the numbered paragraphs in plaintiff's complaint)	Admit	Partially Admit/ Partially Deny	Denial	Denial Because of Lack of Information Sufficient to Form a Belief
1. Subject matter jurisdiction is based on diversity jurisdiction.				1 (Don't know if Brady is truly a citizen of Texas)
2. Plaintiff Alby is a citizen of California.				2 (Same as allegation 1)
3. Defendant Brady is a citizen of Texas.	3			
4. The matter in controversy exceeds $10,000.				4
5. On 6/15/8X Alby and Brady driving south on Highway 5 in Jamner, Major.	5			
6. Defendant Brady negligently crashed into Alby.			6 (Brady was not negligent; Plaintiff might have a defective gas pedal)	
7. Brady proximate cause of injuries to Alby. Property and personal damages; loss of income.				7 (Don't know all the facts)
8. Alby incurred medical and hospital expenses, loss of profits, loss of wages.				8
17. Special damages, $10,000.			17	
18. General damages according to proof at trial			18	
19. Punitive damages, $500,000			19	
20. Costs, interests, and other relief			20	

*Chart III is based on the sample pleading at pages 172-177. The plaintiff's allegations correspond to the *Alby v. Brady* complaint, paragraphs 1 through 8 (including the first claim for relief) and paragraphs 17 through 20 (pertaining to general relief requested for negligence). The numbers in the remaining four columns also correspond to the paragraphs in plaintiff's complaint.

5. What relief will you plead?
6. How much information will you plead?
7. Are there ethical issues you should consider?
8. What reaction to your pleading do you anticipate?

To apply our approach, imagine that you represent the plaintiff-driver, Albert J. Alby, in the automobile accident we previously described and that you wish to draft a complaint. Imagine that you have obtained all the information that is set forth in the four organizing charts included in this chapter. As Alby's attorney you wish to consider how your representational strategy can be implemented by your pleading.

CHART IV — *Affirmative Defense, Counterclaim, Third-Party Complaint*[*]

Legal Theory	Possible Factual Theories	Legal Elements of the Defense	Facts	Documents	Parties Named in the Lawsuit — Plaintiff	Parties Named in the Lawsuit — Defendant	People Not in the Lawsuit but Potentially to be Joined as Defendants	Remedy	Potential Pleading to Be Filed	Miscellaneous Things to Do
Contributory negligence (also referred to as comparative fault and negligence)	Duty to keep car in good repair if it is driven on a public highway	Duty	Alby and Brady were driving their cars on a public highway on 6/15/8X in the State of Major.		Alby	Brady				Investigation as to road construction and other obstacles on highway proves negative. Obtain repair documents for Alby's car.
		Breach of duty	Alby's car abruptly slowed down on the highway. Alby may have had a faulty gas pedal that needed repair. OR	Police report	Alby				Counterclaim in Brady's answer.	Investigation: contact private investigator, other attorneys specializing in products liability. Obtain repair records from automobile repair shop. Think about third-party complaint by Brady against repair shop.
			Alby's car abruptly slowed down on the highway. Alby had an appointment to have his gas pedal repaired one week prior to the crash. Alby either did not get the repair done or did not see to it that it was done properly and continued to drive with a faulty gas pedal.	Police report; Alby's statement to the police at the scene	Alby					
		Proximate cause of injury	Alby's abrupt slowing down on the highway because his gas pedal may not have been working properly caused Brady to unavoidably crash into Alby.		Alby					
		Injury	$8,000 property damage to Brady's car.	Car repair bills	Alby			$8,000 and according to proof at trial	Counterclaim and/or motion dismissing plaintiff's complaint. Think about third-party complaint.	

[*]As you will note, this chart illustrates one theory for contributory negligence. There may be additional factual theories that Brady could assert for contributory negligence, such as negligent repair of the gas pedal by the car repair shop; defectively manufactured gas pedal; or defect occurring because of negligence in shipping of the car. If these other factual theories were to be included in the chart, they would require the same application of the listed legal elements with the relevant facts, documents, parties, and so on to be filled in in the appropriate places.

QUESTION 1
What are your representational strategy and pleading objectives?

Let's develop your representational strategy. As Alby's attorney you believe liability against Brady is strong and damages are easily provable. Your beliefs are based on documentary proof of Brady's intoxication and proof of damage. You have multiple case strategies— to settle the case at the earliest possible time, obtain maximum compensation for your client, and prepare yourself for litigation if the case does not settle. Your pleading should reflect these representational strategies by making a persuasive case on liability and damages, and by drafting it in such a way that it is sufficient to give notice, narrow the issues in controversy, and frame issues for discovery. (Be mindful that, although you have multiple representational strategies and pleading objectives, some might be more important than others.)

QUESTION 2
How can your pleading achieve your representational strategy?

In Alby's case, your primary objective is to make your pleading persuasive and give sufficient notice of Alby's claims. How can your pleading accomplish these particular representational strategies? That requires selecting persuasive legal claims, parties, and relief that are consistent with your client's objectives.

QUESTION 3
What claims (or defenses) will you plead?

Now you need to consider which claims Alby should plead. As preparation for drafting your pleading, you focused your efforts on selecting a legal theory, which will be the basis for the claims or defenses, parties, and relief you will plead. You engaged in this process when you researched old-shoe and cutting-edge law and examined the facts in your client's case. Keep in mind that pleading consists of the two parts of your case theory, both legal and factual. Your legal theory is the underlying legal basis for your claim or defense. Your factual theory, to the extent that it is pleaded, is the specific factual description of your claim or de-fense, developed according to an applicable legal theory.

You developed three plausible legal theories. Two legal theories are based on old-shoe negligence law in the State of Major: common law negligence based on Brady's intoxication, and negligence per se (breach of State of Major statute for intoxication.) The third legal theory is based on a plausible interpretation of the State of Major Supreme Court case, *Susanah v. David,* which in a footnote stated, "[e]xcessive intoxication might recklessly endanger others." A law review article by an eminent professor also suggests that driving while excessively intoxicated might potentially be considered a "new tort."

What claims are suggested by these three legal theories? Two claims, common law negligence and negligence per se, are suggested by the old-shoe legal theories. There are facts to support both old-shoe claims as indicated by the police report—Brady's intoxication while driving, and breach of a State of Major statute by being intoxicated while driving. Imagine as Alby's attorney that you assert a claim for common law negligence. The facts you allege will be structured by the elements of the legal theory—duty, breach, cause, injury.

Duty:	1. On June 15, 198X, Alby and Brady were driving on a public highway in the State of Major.
Breach of Duty:	2. Brady negligently drove his car into Alby,
Cause:	causing Alby to suffer injuries that hospitalized him.
Injury:	3. Alby had medical expenses totaling $5,000 and personal injuries of $50,000.

Note that some commentators believe that you need not plead separate and distinct claims that are derived from identical substantive law but raise different factual or legal theories of negligence. Others disagree. But if you plead only one claim for negligence, you must be careful that the statement of the claim is sufficiently broad to include all legal and factual theories of recovery.

The third legal theory is at the cutting edge of the law because it is potentially expanding negligence law by suggesting a new tort claim, reckless endangerment, based on a new legal theory. A claim such as reckless endangerment is essentially just a more expansive use of facts and relief for a negligence claim (outrageous conduct instead of negligent conduct; punitive damages instead of compensatory damages).

Therefore, the same elements used in the established negligence claim could constitute the reckless endangerment claim. The facts in Alby's case fit a reckless endangerment interpretation. Brady's .25 blood-alcohol level is well beyond the blood-alcohol level for negligence. But suppose instead of .25, Brady's blood-alcohol level was .12. If most negligence claims of driving while intoxicated are based on a blood-alcohol level between .1 and .15, Alby's facts would be weak for attempting to assert a cutting-edge claim for reckless endangerment.

Now stand back and consider: Do these claims help achieve your representational strategies? Since a motivating force in determining which claims to plead will be your representational strategies, you must decide what you want to achieve and how this pleading can help in that goal. Let's suppose, for illustration, that your representational strategy is to try to settle the case for the greatest amount possible. In order to achieve this strategy, the pleading should be legally sufficient, factually sufficient, and convince your adversary to settle for a maximum amount of compensation for Alby.

Both claims based on negligence will be sufficient and persuasive (if sufficient facts are pleaded) because they are established by present law. But your objective of maximizing damages might not be achieved by pleading only the two negligence claims. Relief under a negligence theory is limited to compensatory damages and would not maximize compensation for Alby since damages for negligence under State of Major case law do not include punitive or treble damages.

Maximizing damages might be better achieved by the reckless endangerment claim, which suggests the potential for punitive or treble damages. But there are two serious drawbacks to a reckless endangerment claim. First, since a reckless endangerment claim is at the cutting edge of the law, it is not established, thereby subjecting it to an attack because of legal insufficiency. Second, a claim for reckless endangerment might not be as persuasive to your opponent because it is a novel claim.

As Alby's attorney you will have to decide which claims will best achieve your representational strategy. Does that mean you plead only those claims that are strongest, such as the old-shoe claims? Or do you include your cutting-edge claim even though it is legally problematic? There are two philosophies. The view that suggests you only plead your strongest, non-problematic claims is based on practical considerations of avoiding costly and time-consuming attacks on your pleading. The other view is that you plead all plausible claims, including claims that are inconsistent, as long as they have a reasonable basis in law and fact. This position views pleading as a potential

negotiation tool. Thus the third claim might provide leverage in negotiating. It can also educate as to a potential expansion of negligence law. Any problems with the third claim can eventually be resolved by dismissing the cutting-edge claim, but why do that now? Adopting this view, you tentatively plan to plead all three claims and to eventually sort out the claims or defenses that are the most likely to be proved at trial.

QUESTION 4
What parties will you plead?

Important strategy questions for all parties are at issue here. Is the plaintiff a proper party? Is the defendant? Should defendant file a cross-claim against a co-defendant? If plaintiff has not joined a defendant, should you, as responding party, file a third-party complaint? For clarity of analysis, we have posed discrete questions for determining claims, parties, and relief. But in actuality the approach to party determination is part of a concurrent analysis similar to that for determining claims or defenses.

As in determining which claims or defenses to plead, the decision as to what parties to include is determined by the legal theory that supports the claim or defense you are relying on. In order to name a party, either as a plaintiff or a defendant, the party must have a causal connection to the event as defined by the legal theory. For example, suppose a bystander witnesses a bloody accident and suffers emotional distress by witnessing the impact. The bystander wants to file an action for emotional distress against the defendant-driver. Is the bystander a proper party plaintiff? If the law is that no duty is owed to unrelated bystanders who suffer emotional distress as a result of witnessing a bloody accident, the bystander is an improper party because the bystander is not causally connected to the event under the present law of negligence.

Or suppose a plaintiff is injured by a driver who became intoxicated while attending a party. Plaintiff wants to bring an action for damages based on negligence, naming as a defendant the host who served intoxicating liquor and then permitted the intoxicated guest to drive home from the party. Is the host a proper defendant? If the law is that social hosts have a duty under present law to protect a third party from injury by not permitting their inebriated guest to leave their house in an intoxicated state and to drive a car, the social host is causally connected to the event and is a proper party defendant.

Analyze next whether there are sufficient facts to

connect the potential party to the legal claim. In our hypothetical, for example, Brady is a proper party because he is causally connected to the accident under negligence law. He owed a duty to Alby to exercise reasonable care. He breached that duty by crashing into Alby's car and was the proximate cause of the accident. Factually, Brady is connected to the event since he is the owner and driver of the automobile that crashed into Alby.

Finally, consider your representational strategy. Analyze how joining a party would help or hurt your case. Will it burden your financial and time resources? Complicate or confuse the issues? How is your strategy affected by naming just Brady as a defendant? Your case is a simple negligence rear-end collision case. But suppose Brady's intoxication was caused by drinking too much at his company's annual employee picnic. Should we name Brady's employer as a defendant? What effect does that have on your representational strategy? Does the additional defendant complicate the issue of liability? Of damages? How much more will it cost to litigate the case? How much more time will you spend on the case? What resources will the employer devote to the case compared to what would happen if you just named Brady as a defendant? Is there a possibility of the employer's insurance company being involved? Who will be the attorneys representing the employer? If you join the employer as a defendant, will Brady file a cross-claim? If you do not join the employer, is your pleading subject to attack for failure to join an essential party? (A responding party can file a motion under Federal Rule of Civil Procedure 12(b)(7) to dismiss for failure to join a party.) Or will Brady file a third-party complaint?

QUESTION 5
What relief will you plead?

Suppose Alby's representational strategy is to try to settle the case and obtain the most compensation. What relief will you plead?

In determining the relief to plead, you will apply an analysis similar to the one you used to determine the claims and parties to plead. Alby's relief will be based on the same legal theory that is the basis for the claim. If Alby requests punitive damages or treble damages as a remedy for negligence, then Alby's request for relief in all probability will be challenged as legally insufficient (subjecting the remedy section of your pleading to a motion to dismiss) because State of Major does not permit punitive damages for negligence. But if Alby pleads the cutting-edge claim, reckless endangerment, there is a potential for punitive relief suggested by dicta in *Susanah v. David* and the Waldman tort article.

Do the facts support punitive relief? The facts in Alby's case certainly suggest outrageous conduct, an intoxication level of .25 that is well beyond the presumptive level for intoxication. Alby's attorney could argue that punitive damages are appropriate to punish the wrongdoer and compensate plaintiff for conduct that is far more egregious than negligence.

Does the request for punitive relief accomplish your representational strategy? Pleading treble or punitive damages would be on the cutting edge, and although the pleading would appear to accomplish your objective for recovery, the claim and relief probably would be subject to a motion to dismiss for legal insufficiency. Consider: If the relief can be attacked for legal insufficiency, does the requested relief achieve your representational strategy? If an objective of the pleading is to plausibly raise the stakes for negotiation, then, in all likelihood, your representational strategy might be well implemented. Defendant Brady now knows that if he moves to attack the legality of the reckless endangerment claim in court and loses—and, with the language in *Susanah v. David* and the general sentiment about drunk drivers, he could—the cost of settling the case at that point will increase.

QUESTION 6
How much information will you plead?

Examine how much information you should include in pleading a claim for common law negligence. There are two types of pleading methods. We have nicknamed them "bare-bones" and "fully-dressed." Bare-bones pleading means that you include just enough information to give notice of your claims. Many attorneys plead by the bare-bones method; preference for bare-bones pleading is partially due to the belief that the function of pleading is to give notice of claims, and that formal discovery is the process for providing specific facts.

The fully-dressed pleading method allows you to tell your story as to what occurred legally and factually. The fully-dressed method of pleading might describe legal and factual theories; document in detail the relief requested; anticipate your opponent's position and affirmatively justify your own (even though burden of pleading may not require such justification); discard weak theories; and so on. The rationale for pleading by this mode is that pleading should persuade, obtain publicity for your case, and educate the public, the court, and your adversary. Depending on the amount of information you include, this type of pleading might be highly controversial because it does not merely give notice or state the facts constituting the claim for relief, but uses pleading as an advocacy tool. It also provides much early discovery to the opposition. Pleading in the fully-dressed method might mean that your pleading will not conform to procedural rules. Your opponent might even file a motion to strike evidentiary facts. For example, procedural rules only require sufficient information to state a valid claim for relief. That means that you do not have to plead evidentiary facts or witnesses. Yet you may, by using the fully-dressed method, include evidentiary facts if your objective is to persuade your adversary.

Suppose you plead Alby's negligence claim by using the fully-dressed method of pleading:

> "Three eyewitnesses—a minister and two teachers—saw defendant Brady act erratically and drive negligently through the intersection when the light was red. Brady, who had a .25 blood-alcohol level, was intoxicated. Because of his intoxication, he negligently lost control of his car, crashing into plaintiff. Brady was the proximate cause of the injuries to Alby."

You could also attach exhibits such as a breathalyzer report or a police report.

The bare-bones method might be as follows:

> "Defendant Brady negligently and carelessly crashed his automobile into plaintiff Alby's automobile."

Which method of pleading should you use? First, consider legal and factual sufficiency. Recall that the type and amount of information is determined by the legal theory that is the basis for your claim or defense. Both pleading illustrations include sufficient information according to the legal elements of a negligence theory. Generally, pleading according to the elements of the legal theory you are relying on will be legally and factually sufficient for both code and notice pleading requirements. (If you want to merely give notice and do not want to plead according to legal theory, you will need to consult references in your particular jurisdiction in order to determine whether you can plead fewer facts than your legal theory suggests.)

Second, consider the effect of bare-bones and fully-dressed pleading methods on your representational strategy and pleading objectives. Your representational strategy is to try to settle the case for the highest amount possible. By pleading persuasively, you may promote settlement with your adversary or resolution of the dispute by summary judgment. Fully-dressed pleading will likely be more convincing than a mere bare-bones statement of negligence because it contains specific evidence that supports your factual theory. But fully-dressed pleading might also be detrimental to achieving your objectives. By explicitly including evidentiary facts, you might limit the development of other potential case theories. For instance, if you plead a factual theory of "intoxication," you might later be precluded from obtaining discovery or presentation of witnesses at trial based on a factual theory of "inattentiveness" for Alby's common law negligence claim. Of course, you can amend your pleading throughout pretrial and even at trial. Nevertheless, there may be occasions when you might be precluded because of statutes of limitations, procedural rules, or unfairness to your adversary. Therefore, a fully-dressed pleading method should also be broad enough to encompass as many potential legal and factual theories as possible.

Now examine bare-bones pleading. Does that help you to achieve your objectives? "Defendant Brady negligently and carelessly crashed his automobile into plaintiff Alby's automobile" has as its primary objective giving notice of plaintiff's claims. Such pleading, although not persuasive, is factually sufficient. If the philosophy of your pleading is that it is merely a stepping stone to discovery, then bare-bones pleading is a more flexible strategy for carrying out that objective.

Finally, consider local custom. What is acceptable in your jurisdiction? If bare-bones pleading is the customary method of pleading and you plead using the fully-dressed method, you should be prepared for the ramifications of your break with tradition. Although ignoring local custom should not result in a motion for insufficiency, you might be perceived as failing to plead properly. And although your pleading theoretically is persuasive, your pleading might be viewed by others as weak because it is presented in an unfamiliar manner.

QUESTION 7
Are there ethical issues you should consider?

Federal Rule of Civil Procedure 11 provides a specific ethical duty that requires you as the attorney preparing a pleading to certify by signing it that you have read the pleading and made a reasonable inquiry that it is well grounded in fact, warranted by existing law, and not filed for purpose of harassment. Although Rule 11 includes specific ethical requirements, it only provides broad parameters that caution against egregious ethical breaches (filing frivolous lawsuits or dilatory motions, total failure to investigate). Determining specific ethical boundaries remains a matter of judgment since Rule 11, professional codes of conduct, and substantive law prohibit dishonest conduct or conduct prejudicial to the administration of justice. Many ethical problems, however, do not involve clear acts of dishonesty.

In our hypothetical case, you will have to consider such ethical issues as how extensive an investigation you should do before pleading Alby's complaint. As a responding party, can you deny an allegation or must you investigate? How much of a reasonable inquiry must you engage in when responding to a plaintiff's allegations? For instance, do you have a duty to investigate the citizenship of Alby and Brady or can you allege citizenship of the parties upon information and belief? Do you need proof that the gas pedal was defective before alleging it was? Can you include *inconsistent* facts: Brady caused the accident because of his intoxicated state and Alby's gas pedal was defective, causing the accident? Can you assert a cutting-edge claim for reckless endangerment based on the Waldman law review article?

Ethical questions such as these remain issues of reasonableness and good faith according to circumstances at the time of pleading—reasonable factual investigation, reasonable interpretation of present law, reasonable basis for filing the pleading. As with these or other ethical issues, rules, although specific in nature, are difficult to apply. Rather, striving to maintain a good reputation within the legal profession while vigorously, but ethically, representing your client will ensure ethical judgment in pleading.

QUESTION 8
What reaction do you anticipate?

While drafting your pleading, you should try to anticipate the reaction to your pleading from your adversary, the court, and others. By considering potential reactions, you might decide to reconsider the content of your pleading to avoid problems. For instance, is your pleading subject to any motions (motions to dismiss, judgment on the pleading, summary judgment, failure or misjoinder of parties)? You then need to

think about the basis of these attacks—factual and/or legal insufficiency; failure to join parties or claims; and so on. You might wish to make a list of potential problems that can and might occur.

To illustrate, let's consider your pleading in Alby's case. Suppose your first claim is based on the legal theory of common law negligence. First, consider whether the pleading is subject to an attack for factual insufficiency. Can you avoid factual insufficiency? If you fail to include acts describing one of the legal elements, such as Alby's injury, you should anticipate that your negligence claim is factually insufficient, since you failed to allege facts showing you are entitled to relief. If you plead the cutting-edge claim, reckless endangerment, which requires reckless or outrageous conduct, and you fail to describe that Brady's conduct was reckless or outrageous, your pleading might be factually insufficient. Or if your pleading is so barebones that it is deficient in giving notice of your claim—"Brady negligently crashed into Brady, breaching State of Major statutes"—such pleading might be factually deficient. On the other hand, if your pleading reads like a trial transcript, your pleading might be attacked for including irrelevant matter.

Second, consider whether your pleading will be attacked for legal insufficiency. If you plead the cutting-edge reckless endangerment claim, your pleading will probably be attacked as legally insufficient. Or if you request treble or punitive damages, you can also expect an attack on the type of relief you request because that relief is not established by law.

Any of these potential problems should alert you to redraft your pleading content to avoid costly and time-consuming motion preparation. Thus, at the very least, draft your claim—for example, reckless endangerment—so as to have the strongest possible record when it is attacked and you must go to court.

E. DRAFTING TECHNIQUES

A major objective when pleading is to draft a technically sufficient pleading that will accomplish your pleading objectives and representational strategy. The following five questions suggest an approach for dealing with technical drafting aspects of your pleading:

1. What are your technical pleading objectives?
2. What technical problems might occur?
3. What drafting techniques can you use?
4. What is an appropriate pleading?
5. What follow-up will you do?

> **BASIC TASKS: Draft a pleading technically correct and not subject to attack for defects; use pleading techniques to achieve your representational strategy.**

Suppose we draft Alby's complaint in the hypothetical rear-end automobile collision.

QUESTION 1
What are your technical pleading objectives?

You will have two major technical objectives. First, you want to avoid an attack on your pleading because of technical insufficiency. Although technical insufficiency will not result in an attack dismissing your pleading, it is nevertheless a costly and time-consuming process to amend a pleading because of technical insufficiency. (Note, however, that a pleading technically sufficient in one jurisdiction may be insufficient in another.) Second, the technical format and writing style of the pleading should assist you in achieving your representational strategy.

QUESTION 2
What technical problems might occur?

We include four areas of practical considerations that you might want to think about and, within this context, we raise some of the issues that affect pleading. We will consider two more practical concerns, format and writing style, when we consider drafting techniques in Question 3. There we discuss how these concerns can affect your representational strategy and subject your pleading to attack because of technical insufficiency.

Area One
Forum choice

Will you choose federal or state court? Which geographical location within the forum? What will your decision be based on? Procedural or evidentiary differences? Quality of judges? Different composition of juries? Time delays in hearing the case? Availability of appellate review? Cost of review? Familiarity with court procedures? Litigation cost difference?

Area Two
When to file

Will you file a pleading before or after negotiation? Are there prerequisites before you can file? Do you have to file a claim with an agency? Exhaust administrative remedies? Examples: Before filing a complaint against a government body, it might be necessary to file an administrative claim within a certain period of time or you might be precluded by a statute of limitations from further court action; employment discrimination cases filed in federal court require exhaustion of administrative remedies with the Equal Employment Opportunity Commission prior to pleading in federal court.

Area Three
How to file and serve a pleading

Who will serve process? Do you need to serve by a marshal? Registered process agent? When should you serve the pleading? (Note that service of process in some jurisdictions begins the action, while failure to serve process means that the statute of limitations is not tolled.) Who does it have to be served upon? Are there requirements for proof of service such as affidavits? Declarations? If you join a government body as a defendant, are there any special requirements to fulfill? (Filing a pleading that names the United States or a federal agency might require service on the Attorney General's office as well as the federal agency.)

Area Four
How a defendant should respond

Should a defendant answer or file a motion? For instance, according to the Federal Rules, a defendant can include in an answer all the matters that could be the subject of a motion, such as improper venue, process, joinder of parties, and so forth. When should either be filed? Are there time limits that create waivers? (Failure to file a motion alleging defective service of process before answering can result in waiver of the process issue. But other issues can be raised at any time either by motion or answer—e.g., lack of subject matter jurisdiction, misjoinder of parties.)

QUESTION 3
Which drafting techniques can you employ?

Although there are a multitude of drafting techniques to consider under this question, we will highlight two practical areas—format and writing style. Both areas can be used to help achieve your representational strategy through pleading and to avoid technical insufficiency.

Area One
Format

Does your pleading have to be on a specific paper? Generally, most courts require what is referred to as pleading paper, with numbers from top to bottom along the left-hand margin. Does the caption have to appear in a certain format? Do you need topical headings? Are there specific paragraph structure rules? Do the factual allegations need to be numbered? The answer to the last question is yes—most jurisdictions require that each factual allegation be separately stated and numbered. The numbering system will vary with jurisdictions, although it will always be the rule that your numbering system must be logical. As such, use consecutive numbers that are not duplicative.

By following prescribed requirements you can avoid an attack for technical insufficiency because of incorrect format. General and local court rules, sample pleadings in form books, and experienced attorneys and court personnel (clerks, bailiffs) can help you use the proper format. You may also want to look at the examples in the appendix to this chapter.

In addition to avoiding problems, you can use the format to make your pleading more persuasive and understandable. You might use topical headings to help educate your reader and to focus issues. If you plead three claims for relief, by using a topical heading identifying each claim, your pleading might be more understandable for adversary, court, and client. For example, one of your topical headings might read, "First claim for relief: Common law negligence."

Area Two
Writing style

A simple and clear writing style can transform your pleading from being just adequate to being a piece of work that distinguishes you as a formidable advocate who can accomplish a client's objectives. For instance, one of the difficulties generally with pleadings is that legalistic words and phrases often make a pleading difficult to understand and get in the way of the advocate's "story." Many pleadings contain meaningless, ritualistic legal jargon such as, "Hear Ye: Cometh the plaintiff, before this Honorable Court, to plead a complaint herein," "herein, heretofore, wherefore, attached hereto, hereby, move for leave, aforesaid," and other such words and phrases. Instead of the pleading impressing people by its validity, the pleading is unintelligible. Yet clarity is particularly important as a communication tool if the pleading is given to your client, or if it is read to the jury (as required by court rules), or disseminated to a public audience. Use plain English instead of legal jargon to make your pleading understandable and persuasive. Eliminate such expressions as "on or about," which can easily be stated as "approximately." Or, instead of "wherefore" or "plaintiff prays for," plead "Plaintiff Alby requests the following remedy." Your pleadings should include legal jargon only when it communicates a specific legal concept. For instance, it is easier to use the legal jargon "upon information and belief" than to explain in your pleadings: "I believe in good faith that I will discover or be able to prove that . . . ." When in doubt always assume that your pleading will be more understandable and persuasive if you use plain English. An excellent reference is R. Wydick, *Plain English for Lawyers* (1979).

Using vocabulary that is too descriptive, emotional, or flamboyant can subject your pleading to attack. Suppose you describe Brady as "a homicidal maniac" because he was driving while intoxicated. While perhaps satisfying to your client Alby, your pleading may be attacked by Brady's attorney with a motion to strike offensive and slanderous language. Your vocabulary should specifically achieve your representational strategy and your pleading objectives. If you have to amend your pleading or defend against the motion, you need to consider whether these options, both time-consuming and costly for you and your client, are consistent with your representational strategy. Also, as discussed later, slanderous language is usually not conducive to building an atmosphere for rational negotiations.

Think about using your pleading to tell your client's story, including those facts that are essential to the flow of the story. Consider applying to pleading the storytelling techniques suggested by W.L. Bennett and M.S. Feldman, *Reconstructing Reality in a Courtroom* (1981). By constructing your pleading according to a story, it might be more readable and ultimately more persuasive.

QUESTION 4
What is an appropriate pleading?

You now have a tentative plan for the substance of your pleading and its technical requirements. You have a list of potential problems that might occur, ranging from motions to dismiss because of failure to state a claim for relief (legal and factual insufficiency) to attacks for technically failing to state and number factual allegations separately.

It is now time to consider finalizing your pleading. Each pleading you file should be appropriate for the particular circumstance. In making this determination you might want to consider the appropriateness of the pleading by analyzing your representational strategy and applying factors such as the economic and non-economic risks and benefits to your client. This sort of analysis is one that we have referred to and apply throughout this text in evaluating our decisions.

To illustrate, let's examine Alby's draft pleading. Suppose you have included a claim for reckless endangerment, a novel cutting-edge claim. This novel claim might potentially award Alby treble or punitive damages, and maximizing potential recovery might be an important representational strategy. But, in all likelihood, such a claim will subject your pleading to a motion to dismiss for failure to state a claim and you must consider the effects on time and cost. If you plead the reckless endangerment claim as part of a negotiation strategy to settle the case at the pleading stage, does pleading a cutting-edge claim increase the persuasiveness of your position? Or does it make your case less persuasive? What risks might you face if your negotiation strategy is not successful? Is an appeal likely to reverse the trial court decision dismissing the claim? Can Alby afford such an appeal? Is establishing and potentially obtaining treble damages necessary for Alby's particular circumstance? On the other hand, if you proceed with old-shoe claims such as negligence and negligence per se, you might successfully be awarded compensatory damages. Is it therefore necessary to subject your pleading to attack?

Applying the same analysis, you can also evaluate whether the pleading techniques you have used help achieve your client's representational strategy. Technically, is it beneficial to describe Brady as a "homicidal maniac"? Does that help Alby's representational strategy of settlement? On the other hand, if Alby wants publicity for his case, describing the defendant in such colorful terms might accomplish that purpose.

For each part of your pleading you will need to consider its effect on your representational strategy and analyze its effect on you and your client in terms of time, costs, and emotions. This analysis is similar to that in the negotiation arena where you assess the effect of incentives on settlement (see Chapter IX). After you analyze such factors, you will have a considered basis for exercising your judgment as to the appropriate pleading to file.

QUESTION 5
What follow-up will you do?

Drafting a pleading is a continually evolving process, one that begins and continues throughout your case. You will be thinking about drafting and redrafting (amending) pleadings every step of the way, from your initial client interview through your research of the law and your informal investigation of the facts, through the development of your case theory and your counseling sessions where you advise the client whether to pursue litigation or other alternatives, through formal discovery, and finally even during trial. As your view of the case evolves, and as you learn new information, you might want to think about amending your pleading to add to or change claims, parties, or relief. But at all times you need to keep in mind your representational strategy, pleading objectives, and the technical procedural rules (e.g., statutes of limitations) that can control when and how you plead.

F. PLEADING EXAMPLES

The pleadings in the appendix to this chapter at pages 172-177 illustrate a specific style and philosophy of pleading based on the approach we have discussed in this and other chapters. These examples reflect our interpretation of federal rules and general custom and our concept of representational strategy. Some lawyers might differ with our drafting content and style. Some of their disagreement might stem from different procedural rules, drafting customs, or philosophies about the function of pleadings. Instead of dwelling on these differences, we suggest that you look at the annotations describing some of the *choices* that we made in formulating these drafts; you might later consider these choices when drafting your own pleadings. Keep in mind that the pleading examples are not designed to meet the requirements of a particular district; they are intended to be a guide to help you think about many of the technical and strategic issues that might confront you when drafting a pleading. We urge you to supplement the Alby and Brady complaint and answer by examining applicable procedural rules, substantive law, and other lawyers' pleadings used in your jurisdiction. Then you should form and adapt your own pleading style to the particular strategy that you want your pleadings to accomplish.

G. GENERAL PLANNING QUESTIONS

Following is a series of general planning questions for drafting pleadings. You may want to refer to them, and expand on them, in drafting your affirmative and responsive pleadings.

I. *Preparation*
 1. Generally, explain the steps you have taken so far that have helped you to prepare a pleading.
    a. What informal investigation have you done?
    b. What reports, documents, or materials are relevant to your pleading?
    c. Are there any facts that you have not obtained that you need? Why?
 2. Specifically, what legal research have you done (e.g., cases, jury instructions, periodicals, form books)?
    a. Describe the "old-shoe" legal theories that might be applicable.
    b. Describe the "cutting-edge" legal theories that might be applicable.
 3. Do the facts support any legal theory? Explain.
 4. Do you have facts to plead each legal theory? Explain.
 5. What procedural rules have you consulted (e.g., state court rules, federal or state civil procedure rules)?
 6. How will you organize the information for your pleading? (Charts? Diagrams?)

II. *Content Planning*
 1. What is your representational strategy?
 2. What are the general objectives in pleading?
    a. Do you have special objectives to accomplish with your pleading? What are they?
    b. Explain how your representational strategy might influence your pleading.
    c. Will you plead your legal theory?
    d. Will you plead your factual theory?
    e. Will you attach documents to your pleading? Explain.
 3. Which claims are "old-shoe"? Why?
 4. Which claims are "cutting-edge" claims? What makes them cutting-edge? (Facts? Law?)
 5. How will you plead the old-shoe claim/defense?
    a. What legal theory supports your claim/defense?
    b. What are the legal elements of the claim/defense?
    c. What factual theory supports your claim/defense?
    d. What are the facts that you will plead for each element of the claim/defense?
    e. Are there any facts that you are unsure of? Explain.
 6. How will you plead the cutting-edge claim/defense?
    a. What legal theory supports your claim/defense?
    b. What are the legal elements of the claim/defense?
    c. What factual theory supports your claim/defense?
    d. What are the facts that you will plead for each element of the claim/defense?
    e. Are there any facts that you are unsure of? Explain.
 7. Will you plead all potential claims or defenses? (Strong ones? Weak ones?) Explain.
 8. Will you plead potentially inconsistent claims or defenses?
 9. Do your old-shoe claims help you achieve your representational strategy? Explain.
 10. Do your cutting-edge claims help you achieve your representational strategy? Explain.
 11. Potentially, what claims/defenses do you plan to plead?
 12. List each person or entity who is a potential party, both plaintiffs and defendants.
    a. What is the legal basis to name the person or entity as a party?
    b. What is the factual basis to name the person or entity as a party?
    c. How will you describe the legal capacity of the party (e.g., minor, corporate)?
    d. If you name each person or entity you listed, how does that affect your case

strategy? (Any risks? Benefits?) Consider such factors as:

    (1) economic factors (litigation costs)

    (2) the issues in the case

    (3) resources (attorney, client)

   e. Will there be any problems if you do not name each person or entity you listed (e.g., an attack on your pleading)?

13. What relief will you request?

   a. Explain the legal basis (legal theory) that supports your request.

   b. Explain the factual basis that supports your request.

   c. Is the relief you seek old-shoe relief? Explain.

   d. Is the relief you seek cutting-edge relief? Explain.

   e. Explain how the relief you request affects your case strategy.

14. How much information will you plead?

   a. Will you plead using the "bare-bones" or "fully-dressed" method? Explain.

   b. How much information will you include to describe claims/defenses?

    (1) Evidentiary facts?

    (2) Factual theory?

    (3) Legal theory?

    (4) Will you include information to minimize potential defenses?

    (5) Will you include exhibits?

    (6) Do you have to include specific or particular information?

   c. How much information will you include to describe parties?

    (1) Evidentiary facts?

    (2) Factual theory?

    (3) Legal theory?

    (4) Will you include information to minimize potential defenses?

    (5) Will you include exhibits?

   d. How much information will you include to describe your request for relief?

    (1) Evidentiary facts?

    (2) Factual theory?

    (3) Legal theory?

    (4) Will you include information to minimize potential defenses?

    (5) Will you include exhibits?

   e. Is the information enough to plead a factually sufficient claim/defense? Party? Relief?

   f. Does the amount of information you plead help achieve your case objectives? Explain.

15. List any potential ethical problem your pleading might encounter as to:

   a. Federal Rule of Civil Procedure 11 (inclusion or exclusion of information).

   b. Professional codes of conduct.

   c. Criminal and civil law.

   d. Your reputation as an ethical attorney.

16. What reaction (potential problems) do you anticipate as to:

   a. Factual insufficiency (claims, parties, relief)?

   b. Legal insufficiency (claims, parties, relief)?

   c. Improper parties? Why?

   d. Improper relief? Why?

17. Will these problems be raised by motion or responsive pleading?

18. Can you avoid any of these problems?

III. *Responding to Pleadings*

1. Does the pleading state sufficient facts for a claim/defense?

2. Does the pleading state a legal basis for relief under the substantive law? Explain.

3. Are the proper parties in the pleading?

   a. Is there a factual basis connecting the named parties to the claims?

   b. Is there a legal basis connecting the named parties to the claims?

4. Are all the essential persons named as parties? Explain.

5. Do you anticipate joining parties who are not named in the pleading?

6. What are the determining factors for deciding which allegations should be admitted?

   a. Which allegations will you admit?

   b. Which allegations will you admit in part?

7. What are the determining factors for deciding which allegations should be denied?

   a. Which allegations will you deny?

   b. Upon what basis will you deny?

8. Will you include in your pleading any affirmative defenses?

   a. Are you legally required to assert all your affirmative defenses (e.g., res judicata, collateral estoppel, statute of limitations)?

   b. List the affirmative defenses you will plead, if any.

c. Explain the legal theory you will rely on for each affirmative defense.

d. Explain the factual theory you will rely on for each affirmative defense.

e. What are the legal elements of your defense?

f. What facts will you assert for your defense?

g. How does the affirmative defense help achieve your case strategy?

9. Will you assert any cross-claims?

a. List the cross-claims you will assert, if any.

b. Explain the legal theory for each cross-claim.

c. Explain the factual theory for each cross-claim.

d. How does the cross-claim help achieve your case strategy?

10. Will you assert a third-party complaint?

a. List the parties you will name in your third-party complaint.

b. List the claims you will assert, if any.

c. Explain the legal theory for each claim.

d. Explain the factual theory for each claim.

e. What relief will you request? Explain.

f. How does the third-party complaint help achieve your case strategy?

IV. *Performance Planning*

1. What are your technical drafting objectives?

2. List the potential technical issues or problems that might occur.

3. Is the pleading format correct?

a. Paper size?

b. Caption information (e.g., court number, name of court)?

c. Paragraph structure?

d. Each allegation numbered?

e. Place for signature, address, telephone number?

f. Does the format help you achieve your case objectives?

4. Does the pleading use a good writing style?

a. Does the legal jargon communicate important concepts?

b. Is the pleading drafted in plain English?

c. Is the vocabulary appropriate?

d. Does the writing style help you achieve your case objectives?

5. Do you anticipate any motions being filed objecting to the pleading technically?

a. Which motions?

b. Are the motions timely, objecting to technical requirements?

c. What is the legal and factual basis for the motions?

d. Can you avoid these motions? How?

e. If the pleading is lacking in form, can you alter your pleading? Explain.

6. What follow-up will you do?

a. Will you amend your pleading? Explain.

b. If you will amend your pleading, when will you amend?

APPENDIX. SAMPLE COMPLAINT AND ANSWER

[Caption] UNITED STATES DISTRICT COURT
MIDDLE DISTRICT OF MAJOR[1]

ALBERT J. ALBY, Plaintiff,	Civil Action, File Number 1743
v.	Plaintiff's Complaint for Negligence;
CLARK BRADY, Defendant[2]	Negligence Per Se; Reckless Endangerment

Subject Matter Jurisdiction[3] and Parties

[Subject Matter Jurisdiction]

1. Subject matter jurisdiction is founded on diversity of citizenship, 28 U.S.C. §1332.[4]

[Citizenship of Plaintiff and Description of Party]	2. Plaintiff Albert J. Alby, an individual, is a citizen of California.
[Citizenship of Defendant and Description of Party]	3. Defendant Clark Brady, an individual, is a citizen of Texas.[5]
[$10,000 in Controversy]	4. The matter in controversy exceeds, exclusive of interest and costs, the sum of ten thousand dollars ($10,000).

Claim I:[6] Common Law Negligence[7]

[Duty]	5. On June 15, 198X, Plaintiff Alby and Defendant Brady were driving south on Interstate 5 in Jamner, Major.
[Breach of Duty]	6. Defendant Brady negligently crashed his automobile into Plaintiff Alby's automobile.[8]
[Proximate Cause; Injury]	7. As a result of the collision, Plaintiff suffered damage to his property and person. He suffered physical and mental pain. His injuries prevented him from continuing his business.[9]
	8. Plaintiff incurred medical and hospital expenses in the sum of $5,000, $5,000 loss of profits, and loss of wages.[10]

Claim II: Negligence Per Se[11]

	9. Plaintiff adopts by reference paragraphs 1-8.[12]
[Duty]	10. Defendant has a duty under State of Major statutes to refrain from drinking intoxicating beverages while driving and to drive his automobile while sober.[13]
[Breach]	11. Upon information and belief, Defendant, while driving, was drinking intoxicating beverages and was intoxicated while driving.
[Proximate Cause; Injury]	12. Defendant's conduct, which violates State of Major statutes, was a proximate cause of Plaintiff's injuries.

Claim III: Reckless Endangerment[14]

[Duty]	13.	Plaintiff adopts by reference paragraphs 1-12.
[Breach Described by Evidentiary Facts]	14.	Defendant Brady, without regard for the safety and welfare of other drivers, intentionally and with malice recklessly consumed alcohol until he was so intoxicated that he had a blood-alcohol level of .25. (Presumption of intoxication under a State of Major Statute is .10.)
[Document Attached]	15.	Defendant Brady was cited by the State of Major Highway Patrol for driving while intoxicated. A copy of the State of Major Highway Patrol breathalyzer report for Defendant Brady is attached as Exhibit A.[15]
[Proximate Cause]	16.	Defendant's conduct outrageously and recklessly endangered Plaintiff's safety.[16]

Plaintiff requests relief as follows:[17]

[Remedy]	17.	Special damages in the sum of $10,000.
	18.	General damages, pain and suffering, loss of wages, according to proof at trial.[18]
	19.	Punitive damages in the sum of $500,000.
	20.	Costs, interest, and any other relief the Court or Jury finds appropriate.

Date: January 7, 198X

NICKELS, DIMES, AND
DOLLARS

[Signature]   by _____[19]

Rob Coyne
Penny Sent

1800 International Bank Building
Second Street
Jamner, Major

(206) 383-0000

Attorneys for Plaintiff

[Jury Trial Request]   PLAINTIFF ALBY REQUESTS A
TRIAL JURY[20]

UNITED STATES DISTRICT COURT
MIDDLE DISTRICT OF MAJOR

ALBERT J. ALBY,
    Plaintiff,

v.

CLARK BRADY,
    Defendant

Civil Action, File Number 1743

A.J. Brady's Answer, Counterclaim,
and Cross-Claim[21]

Defendant Brady answers Plaintiff Alby's complaint:[22]

**[Answering Each of
Plaintiff's Allegations]**

1. Admits paragraphs 3 and 5.[23]

2. Denies paragraphs 6, 11, 12, 14, 16-20.

3. Admits paragraph 15, that he was cited by the State of Major Highway Patrol, except denies knowledge or information sufficient to form a belief as to the truth of the citation and Exhibit A.[24]

4. Is without knowledge or information sufficient to form a belief as to the truth of the allegations in paragraphs 1, 2, 4, 7, 8-10, and 13, and therefore denies those paragraphs.

FIRST AFFIRMATIVE DEFENSE: Failure to State a Claim[25]

**[Affirmative Defense
or Motion]**

5. Plaintiff's complaint fails to state a claim against Defendant upon which relief can be granted.

SECOND AFFIRMATIVE DEFENSE: Contributory Fault[26]

[Duty]

6. Plaintiff Alby has a duty to keep his automobile in good repair.[27]

[Breach]

7. Plaintiff Alby negligently failed to keep his automobile in good repair.

[Proximate Cause]

8. As a result of Plaintiff Alby's negligence, Alby's automobile abruptly began to slow down,

Defendant unavoidably crashed into
Plaintiff Alby's automobile.

COUNTERCLAIM: Negligence[28]

[Duty, Breach,
Proximate Cause]

9. Defendant adopts by reference
paragraphs 6-8 of Defendant Brady's
Second Affirmative Defense.

[Injury]

10. Plaintiff Alby was responsible for
causing his own injuries and is
responsible for causing Defendant to
suffer property damage, totaling
$8,000.

CROSS-CLAIM Against Defendant Manufacturer[29]

[Assumes
Manufacturer was
Named as a Defendant
by Plaintiff]

11. Defendant Brady adopts by reference
paragraphs 6-8 of Defendant's
Second Affirmative Defense.[30]

12. Upon information and belief,
defendant manufacturer was
negligent in manufacturing,
installing, and/or shipping an
automobile to Plaintiff Alby with a
defective gas pedal.

13. Upon information and belief,
defendant manufacturer's negligence
was a proximate cause of Plaintiff's
and Defendant's injuries.

Defendant requests relief as follows:[31]

14. Dismissal of Plaintiff Alby's
complaint;

15. General damages against Plaintiff
Alby and defendants according to
proof at trial;

16. Costs, interest on any judgment, and
any other relief the Court or Jury
finds appropriate.

Date: February 1, 198X

GETT AND GRABB

[Signature]   by _____

Norman Gett
Leon Grabb

43 The Major State Bank Building
Jamner, Major

Telephone: (206) 383-1212

Attorneys for Defendant Brady

Annotations to Appendix

1. **Format.** Alby's complaint and Brady's answer generally follow the format requirements specified in the Federal Rules of Civil Procedure: the division of each factual allegation into separate paragraphs, each with its own number, the identification of claims and defenses, and so on.

Alby's complaint illustrates two technical format concerns. First, when should one place facts in separate paragraphs? For example, should you allege subject matter in one paragraph or four separate paragraphs? Your decision might be guided by procedural rules (Federal Rule 10 provides that each factual allegation of the circumstance or occurrence be described in a separate paragraph), the custom in the particular jurisdiction, concern for clarity, or simply by personal taste. In Alby's complaint, as far as subject matter jurisdiction is concerned, the decision to draft one or four paragraphs is of little critical importance. For example, if the allegations were in one paragraph, one's understanding of the pleading would not seriously be affected since the subject matter jurisdiction allegations are preceded by a topical heading and are themselves concise and clear. But often such a decision can be critical for the response to the pleading. If you have put the facts describing subject matter jurisdiction in one paragraph instead of four, responding might be more difficult.

Second, should one use specific topic headings? The rules require that you identify claims and defenses, but do not require you to specify a claim or defense by labeling it with your legal theory. Both Alby's and Brady's pleadings use specific topic headings to identify by name different parts of the pleading (subject matter jurisdiction, individual claims and defenses). Generally, topic headings are not required and using specific headings is a matter of personal taste and strategy. In this instance, specific headings are used to enhance understanding and to provide information to the reader. Some attorneys would argue that specific labeling might limit you to advocating only those theories you have identified and give too much information to your adversary.

2. **Caption format.** The captions in Alby's complaint and Brady's answer follow the format in Federal Rule of Civil Procedure 10. The caption includes the name of the court; the title of the action; the names of the parties; the court file number (generally assigned by the clerk of the court when the pleading is filed); and the specific name of the pleading (Plaintiff's Complaint; Defendant Brady's Answer, Counterclaim, and Cross-Claim).

3. **Burden of pleading.** Federal case law establishes that a plaintiff has the affirmative burden of pleading subject matter jurisdiction.

4. **Factual sufficiency.** Paragraphs 1-4 illustrate how you determine which facts to plead for subject matter jurisdiction.

Subject matter jurisdiction in the Alby-Brady case is based on diversity jurisdiction, codified in 28 U.S.C. §1332 and interpreted by case law. To determine the facts to plead for diversity jurisdiction, Alby relies on procedural rules, the elements of the diversity statute, and case law as the framework for the factual allegations. By including factual allegations for all the elements of diversity, the pleading is factually sufficient.

Procedural rule and case law specify that you inform the court as to the basis of subject matter jurisdiction. Paragraph 1 states that the basis of subject matter jurisdiction is diversity of citizenship.

The first element of the diversity statute (also required by case law) is complete diverse citizenship of both adverse parties. Paragraphs 2 and 3 factually describe citizenship of the parties in relation to that legal element (complete diversity between the states of the parties). Paragraph 2 states plaintiff Alby's citizenship is in California. Paragraph 3 factually asserts defendant Brady's citizenship is in Texas.

A second element of diversity jurisdiction, according to the statute, is that more than $10,000 be in dispute. Paragraph 4 factually describes that the amount in controversy exceeds $10,000.

The allegations of subject matter jurisdiction would be factually insufficient if Alby did not plead either paragraph 2 or 3, the citizenship of Alby and Brady. The pleading would also be insufficient if Alby only pleaded "Alby and Brady are diverse citizens"—a legal conclusion. A pleading must consist of facts. Citizenship in California and Texas is a fact, not a legal conclusion.

5. **Description of parties.** Two requirements—legal capacity and causal connection—guide the factual description of parties in a pleading. Capacity, according to procedural rule, requires that a pleading identify a party by legal status (individual, corporation, association, class action). Paragraph 3 describes Brady's legal capacity—that is, Brady is "an individual." If Brady were a corporation, Alby would have pleaded: "Brady is a Texas corporation having its principal place of business in Texas and is incorporated in Texas." Note that the facts describing a corporation are based on the elements from diversity jurisdiction and venue statutes.

You must also plead the party's causal connection—that is, that the party is legally responsible according to substantive law. Paragraphs 5, 6, and 7 in Alby's common law negligence claim illustrate causal connection to the event by stating that Brady breached his duty and caused Alby's injury. Common law negligence establishes that Brady is responsible for negligent actions that cause injury.

6. **"Old-shoe" and "cutting-edge" claims.** In Alby's complaint, Claims I, II, and III illustrate both old-shoe and cutting-edge claims based on the substantive law of negligence. Claims I and II are old-shoe claims established by the substantive law of the State of Major. Claim III, reckless endangerment, is a cutting-edge claim, plausibly an expansion of negligence and suggesting a new tort.

7. **Legal and factual sufficiency.** Paragraphs 5 through 8 illustrate legal and factual sufficiency for Claim I. A claim is legally sufficient when the claim, party, and relief are established by substantive law. Claim I is based on common law negligence. The substantive law of negligence is firmly established. (The law of negligence establishes an old-shoe claim. Brady owed Alby a duty to exercise reasonable care and breached that duty, which caused the injury to Alby.) The substantive law of negligence establishes that Brady is a proper party because he is causally connected and there is a right to the relief Alby requested, damages.

Paragraphs 5-8 also illustrate that the claim is factually sufficient. Alby includes facts according to the elements of substantive law. The legal elements of common law negligence, duty (paragraph 5), breach (6), cause (7), and injury (8), are the framework for Alby's factual description. Since the legal theory for the claim, common law negligence, is established, and facts are alleged for each element of negligence, Alby's common law negligence claim is legally and factually sufficient. But note, if the legal theory was not established as in the case of Claim III, the claim would be legally insufficient. Or if Alby failed to allege causation by Brady (paragraph 7), Claim I would have been factually insufficient. If a claim is legally or factually insufficient, it will be subject to a motion to dismiss, Fed. R. Civ. P. 12(b)(6).

8. **Number of facts pleaded: "bare-bones" or "fully-dressed."** Paragraphs 5 through 8 illustrate bare-bones pleading. Just enough information is included to give Brady notice of the claim and relief requested. The facts allege negligence, but do not specify a particular factual theory: "Defendant Brady negligently crashed his automobile into Plaintiff Alby's automobile."

Was it Brady's intoxication that caused him to be inattentive and careless? Or did Alby's car abruptly slow down on the highway? But suppose that Alby's strategy is to plead his negligence claim in a compelling and persuasive manner.

Let's compare the bare-bones pleading in paragraph 6 with how paragraph 6 would read using the fully-dressed pleading method:

> "Driver Brady, while intoxicated with a .25 blood-alcohol level, drove his car erratically, without any regard for the safety of plaintiff or others. Because of his intoxication, he negligently crashed into plaintiff Alby."

Note how the fully-dressed pleading method, by pleading Alby's factual theory and some of the evidence he will probably rely on, presents a more compelling picture of negligence. If Alby views his pleading as an advocacy tool to accomplish an objective, such as a settlement, he might adopt this pleading strategy. But be aware that some attorneys reject the fully-dressed style of pleading. They believe pleadings should *never* contain factual theories or evidentiary facts. They argue the only function for pleading is to give notice.

9. **Burden of pleading: exclusion of information.** Paragraphs 5 to 8 of Claim I illustrate how the burden of pleading affects your decision to exclude allegations from your pleading. Federal Rule 8(c) puts the burden of pleading plaintiff's negligence on defendant Brady. Plaintiff Alby need not plead freedom from contributory negligence (e.g., car was in good repair, attentiveness to driving, sober driver). Rather, Brady's answer, paragraphs 6 to 8, alleges plaintiff Alby's contributory negligence as defendant's second affirmative defense.

10. **Burden of pleading: inclusion of information.** Paragraph 8 illustrates how a specific pleading burden, type of damages (special and general damages), affects inclusion of facts. Loss of profit is considered special damage and, therefore, Alby specifically pleaded the loss of $5,000 profit.

11. **When to separate claims.** A question that troubles many pleaders is determining when to plead separate claims. The three claims included in Alby's complaint illustrate some of the choices in this area. You may have to look to many sources—procedural rules, substantive statutes, custom in your jurisdiction, personal judgment—to make your decision. Ultimately, your decision might rest on a combination of your desire for clarity of presentation, your judgment, and your case strategy. In deciding to plead three claims in Alby's complaint, we found some guidance in Federal Rule 10: "Each claim founded upon a separate transaction or occurrence and each defense other than denials shall be stated in a separate count (or defense) whenever a separation facilitates the clear presentation of the matters set forth." We interpreted Rule 10 to mean that, even though the three claims stem from the same legal theory of negligence, they are based on different factual theories (carelessness, breach of a statute, and reckless conduct) and therefore we chose to plead them as separate claims for the sake of clarity.

Some commentators would differ and plead one claim for negligence that would encompass common law and negligence per se. (They might be guided by a different interpretation of Rule 10, personal judgment, or perhaps custom.) They would argue that you should not separately plead claims that rely on different factual theories of negligence. On the other hand, these same commentators might, were they to plead our hypothetical reckless endangerment claim, separately state that claim even though it is a derivative of negligence. In this instance their desire for clarity would control (pleading the recklessness and outrageousness of Brady's behavior and requesting punitive damages might confuse the negligence claim).

Whichever position you follow, you will encounter advantages and disadvantages. There is an obvious advantage that if you plead negligence and negligence per se as two separate claims, you can better educate your adversary as to your specific case theory and potentially increase the chance of early settlement in the case. On the other hand, if you plead two separate claims, you might discover later on that your theory was incorrect and you or your adversary will ask for dismissal of the claim. However, if you adopt the position to plead only one claim for negligence, and do not state your factual theories separately, you must be careful that your factual allegations are sufficiently broad to include all of your potential legal theories.

12. **Writing style: plain English.** Paragraph 9 and the topic heading for paragraphs 17 to 20 use plain English, which makes this pleading more understandable, especially to people without legal training. Compare the legal jargon that is generally used in form books with the plain English used in paragraph 9:

Legal jargon: "Plaintiff realleges and incorporates herein by reference each and every allegation contained in paragraph 1 of plaintiff's first claim for relief as if fully set forth in full."

Plain English (paragraph 9): "Plaintiff adopts by reference paragraphs 1-8."

Or compare the customary legal phrase, "Wherefore," which traditionally has been used to introduce the remedy requested, with the topic heading for paragraphs 17-20, which describes plaintiff's remedy this way: "Plaintiff requests relief as follows."

On the other hand, Alby's and Brady's pleading also retains some legal jargon where to do so helpfully communicates legal concepts. For example, the pleading uses "upon information and belief" because it is easier to state than, "I believe, in good faith, that I will discover or be able to prove that . . . ."

The use of plain English or legal jargon is mainly an issue of personal style, but nevertheless an important one in making Alby's and Brady's pleading more understandable.

13. **Specific allegations: pleading a statute.** Paragraph 10 illustrates the bare-bones method to plead the violation of a statute. Note that the description does not cite or quote the text of the statute. Although the Federal Rules might not require any more specificity than what is contained in paragraph 10, you might want to cite or quote the text of a statute if you believe it would be helpful to accomplish your advocacy objective. (Also note that some jurisdictions require more specificity when pleading violation of a statute.)

14. **"Cutting-edge" claim for relief.** Claim III, reckless endangerment (a hypothetical claim based on hypothetical law), illustrates pleading based on the cutting edge of the law. Paragraphs 14, 15, and 16 factually describe Brady's intoxication as not just a negligent act, but an intentional, malicious, outrageous, and reckless act. Note that the decision to factually describe Brady's intoxication in this manner is based on the dicta in *Susanah v. David:* "A level of intoxication which exceeds the presumptive .1 intoxication level is outrageous [and] people driving while so intoxicated should be punished." The facts in Alby-Brady support such a claim—Brady's .25 blood-alcohol level exceeds the presumptive intoxication level. Drinking while driving could be considered outrageous conduct, not just negligent conduct.

Why did Alby plead a cutting-edge claim?

One reason might be that Alby's attorney cannot accomplish his client's objectives by pleading just negligence. Alby wants Brady to be punished for his wrongdoing by paying punitive damages. Negligence claims, however, are limited by the scope of negligence law. The relief that can be awarded based on negligence is limited to general and special damages. The State of Major might not recognize culpability.

The major benefit for Alby's attorney in pleading a cutting-edge claim, reckless endangerment, is that Alby could plead punitive damages in addition to compensatory damages ("People driving while so intoxicated should be punished for conduct as egregious as Brady's"). Alby's attorney could increase the potential damage recovery. He could also, by increasing the value of the case, increase his leverage in negotiation.

You might ask whether there are any reasons why Alby should not plead this new claim. Cutting-edge pleading, although creative, is problematic. Assume that Brady will challenge the legal sufficiency of Alby's reckless endangerment claim ("failure to state a claim upon which relief can be granted," Fed. R. Civ. P. 12(B)(6)). Therefore, Alby's attorney should consider the time, cost, and obligations to his client before asserting such a novel claim in his pleading.

15. **Amount of information: attaching exhibits.** Generally, documents are not attached to pleadings, except in those few instances where legal precedent, rule, or custom mandate attaching documents. In this instance, Alby's attorney might believe that attaching documents will be a strategic help in accomplishing an advocacy objective. For instance, it might prove quite educational for Alby's adversary or the judge, or promote settlement with Brady to attach documents showing Brady's intoxication (e.g., police report, breathalyzer report, State of Major Highway Patrol citation to Brady.) But note that, in some lawyers' judgment, if you do attach documents you are using pleadings inappropriately to "litigate your case."

16. **Writing style: choice of vocabulary.** Paragraph 16 describes Brady's excessive intoxication as having "outrageous and recklessly endangered Plaintiff's safety." Note that if Alby describes Brady by using more vivid language, such as "Brady, a confirmed alcoholic," Alby might subject the pleading to a motion to strike offensive or slanderous language.

17. **"Old-shoe" and "cutting-edge" relief.** Paragraphs 17 through 20 illustrate two types of relief, "old-shoe" and "cutting-edge." Paragraphs 17, 18, and 20 request old-shoe relief—general and special damages, costs, and interest—firmly established by negligence law.

Paragraph 19 illustrates cutting-edge relief, which is based on the dictum in *Susanah v. David*, ". . . people driving while so intoxicated should be punished."

18. **Specific allegations: damages.** Paragraph 18 illustrates when to include or exclude specific information in your pleading. Alby did not plead a specific amount of general damages in paragraph 18. This illustrates the view that a specific damage amount should not be included if it is based on guesswork and not fact. Indeed, some jurisdictions by statute or rule prohibit pleading specific figures for monetary damage. However, as a matter of strategy, you might (if not prohibited in your jurisdiction) request general damages based on your best estimate if this is helpful in achieving your case strategy.

19. **Ethical considerations: Federal Rule of Civil Procedure 11.** Every pleading must be signed by the attorney of record, Fed. R. Civ. P. 11. The signature represents that the pleading was read, drafted after reasonable inquiry, is well grounded in fact, and warranted by existing law or a good faith interpretation of existing law. Before drafting Alby's complaint, does Alby's attorney have to know with certainty that Brady was intoxicated while driving? Paragraph 11 illustrates that all that is required is a reasonable inquiry before pleading. Alby can allege intoxication while driving upon information and belief. Suppose that you found out that Alby's gas pedal was defective. Could you assert claims against the manufacturer of the gas pedal and against Brady for intoxication? Inconsistent claims are permissible as long as either is a likely possibility suggested by the facts.

Although Alby's and Brady's pleadings are not verified or accompanied by an affidavit, the rules specify that some pleadings, such as fraud, must be verified.

20. **Request for jury trial.** Federal Rule 38(b) allows either party to request a jury trial in its pleading. In Alby's case the type of relief requested and the nature of the claim were legal, entitling him to a jury trial. But in some instances, if the remedy or the nature of the claim is equitable (e.g., injunctions, specific performance, restitution), a jury might be precluded as factfinder.

21. The same format principles for drafting a complaint apply to drafting an answer. See the annotations to Alby's complaint.

22. **Responding to allegations.** Paragraphs 1 through 4 illustrate the following ways defendant Brady can answer plaintiff Alby's allegations: admit; partially admit and partially deny; deny; deny with a reason, including lack of sufficient information.

You also need to be aware of ethical obligations in responding; see annotation 19.

23. **Answer: admitting allegations.** Paragraphs 3 and 5 in the complaint are the only allegations defendant Brady has direct knowledge of; therefore, he admits those allegations. If Brady has any doubt, or lacks *direct* knowledge, he will deny the allegations.

24. **Answer: admitting and denying.** Paragraph 3 illustrates a partial admission and denial. Brady denies everything that he does not have personal knowledge of and could not obtain the knowledge of with reasonable inquiry, including subject matter jurisdiction.

25. **Affirmative defense.** Paragraph 5, Brady's first affirmative defense, illustrates the choice that the Federal Rules provide a defending party as to when to raise defenses. A defending party can simultaneously raise certain matters by responding in an answer or by motion. (Under the Federal Rules, some matters that must be timely raised include venue, personal jurisdiction, and service of process.)

In paragraph 5, Brady is attacking the legal sufficiency of plaintiff's third claim, reckless endangerment, by pleading an affirmative defense in his answer. Brady could instead have filed a motion. The choice is based on strategy. A motion must be heard on a certain date and be accompanied by a brief (points and authorities). Raising the matter in Brady's answer does not require a presentation on a certain date nor a brief. Hence, raising the matter in the answer might provide more time to prepare for the defense.

26. **"Old-shoe" affirmative defense.** Paragraphs 6-8, covering Brady's second affirmative defense of contributory negligence, illustrate an old-shoe affirmative defense. See Fed. R. Civ. P. 8(c), which lists most old-shoe defenses.

27. **Affirmative defense: amount of information to include.** Paragraphs 6 through 8 illustrate our interpretation of how to plead an affirmative defense. This approach is based on our interpretation of Federal Rule of Civil Procedure 8(b): A defending party should "state in short and plain terms his defenses to each claim asserted." Our interpretation of the rule is that a defendant's defense, just like a plaintiff's claim, should be legally and factually sufficient. Paragraphs 6-8 illustrate the same approach used by plaintiff in pleading a claim for relief; see Annotations 7 and 8.

On the other hand, some commentators urge that affirmative defenses should be pleaded in a general way, such as "Plaintiff's negligence caused Plaintiff's own injuries." Resolving this dilemma is similar to plaintiff deciding which facts to plead. Ultimately, your interpretation of the rules and your strategy will determine your choice. Pleading Brady's affirmative defense by including specific facts represents a strategy to make the defense as persuasive as possible, rather than just giving notice of the defense.

28. Counterclaim. Paragraphs 9 and 10 illustrate the difference between an affirmative defense and a counterclaim. Brady asserts a counterclaim, negligence, based on the same facts that support Brady's second affirmative defense. Brady's claim for $8,000 property damage against plaintiff cannot be asserted in his affirmative defense of contributory negligence. (Affirmative relief cannot be granted in an affirmative defense.) Brady had a choice of pleading his counterclaim in his answer or beginning a lawsuit for his damages. His determination to plead a counterclaim is based on federal rules, case law, and strategy. Briefly stated, federal rules and case law generally provide that if a counterclaim is compulsory (arises out of the same transaction or occurrence), it should be pleaded or it may be barred. All other counterclaims are permissive and need not be pleaded. (But if a defendant chooses to plead a permissive counterclaim, it must be supported by its own subject matter jurisdiction in federal court).

29. Cross-claim and third-party complaint. Paragraphs 11 through 13 illustrate how to plead a cross-claim. But note that although paragraphs 11-13 plead a cross-claim, they are technically incorrect because plaintiff Alby did not join the manufacturer as a defendant.

A cross-claim asserts defendant's claim (which arises out of the same transaction or occurrence as stated by plaintiff) against other defendants that plaintiff has joined and requests relief from those defendants. Generally, cross-claims,

like counterclaims, are included in a defendant's answer, although they could be pleaded separately.

If Brady wants to assert a claim against the manufacturer, or any other defendant who is not joined by plaintiff, Brady must file a third-party complaint. A third-party complaint is a separate pleading from defendant's answer. The third-party complaint would assert defendant Brady's claims against the third-party defendant manufacturer. A third-party complaint is identical in form to plaintiff's complaint, except it uses different terminology when referring to the parties. If Brady filed a third-party complaint against the manufacturer, he would be the third-party plaintiff and the manufacturer would be referred to as the third-party defendant.

Note that, in alleging a cross-claim or third-party complaint, defendant Brady has used bare-bones pleading instead of fully-dressed pleading. That choice is, as it was for plaintiff, a question of strategy. See Annotation 8.

30. Cross-referencing. Note that some of the same facts might be applicable for differing defenses (or claims). Federal Rule of Civil Procedure 10 provides that, instead of repeating the same allegations, you can adopt them by reference in a different part of the same pleading.

31. Relief. Since Brady is pleading a counterclaim and cross-claim, he could, if victorious, obtain affirmative relief of $8,000 damages. The same would have been true had he filed a third-party complaint.

CRIMINAL PROBLEM: STATE v. HARD

PROBLEM 54
Prosecutor: Drafting a Criminal Pleading

You have already filed a charging pleading (a criminal complaint) accusing Ed Hard of first-degree premeditated murder in *State v. Hard*. Your pleading embodied your legal theory and formed a part of your representational strategy. That pleading also began the formal criminal judicial process, and constituted the charge to which Hard pleaded not guilty. Your supervisor has now asked you to draft three additional complaints—one charging Hard with unpremeditated, intentional second-degree murder; one charging second-degree extreme recklessness murder; and one charging voluntary manslaughter. "We need these on hand in the event of a possible plea bargain," your supervisor said. "The deal would be that we'd file the new charge we agreed on (if any) with defense counsel, and the defendant would plead to the new charge. Then we'd dismiss the first-degree murder charge."

PREPARATION

READ: (1) Pretrial Case File Entries 3, 4, 58, 62; (2) Chapter VI. Now think about and answer the following questions:

Questions 1-5 focus on criminal pleadings in general:

1. Generally, what should you put in a complaint?

2. Where will you get this information?

3. Will you just "track" the language of the applicable statute? Why or why not?

4. Does it matter if you include the exact date of the crime? Is "on or about" a certain date good enough? Explain.

5. Does it matter if you allege the name of the victim (if the particular crime has a victim)? Why or why not?

Questions 6-8 focus specifically on *State v. Hard:*

6. Imagine your investigation indicated that Hard was trying to rob Summers when he shot him. Any problem with filing a new felony-murder complaint at trial? The month before?

7. Is this different than asking for a "lesser included" instruction of second-degree unpremeditated murder at the close of a trial where Hard has been charged with first-degree premeditated murder?

8. What if the complaint mistakenly said that Summers died on September 13, 198X? Could you move at trial to "amend the pleading to conform with the proof at trial"?

   a. What response would you expect from defense counsel?

   b. How would you expect the judge to rule? Why?

ASSIGNMENT FOR CLASS

Draft a *separate* complaint charging Hard with *each* of the following:

1. Second-degree unpremeditated intentional murder.

2. Second-degree extreme reckless murder.

3. Voluntary manslaughter.

CIVIL PROBLEMS: SUMMERS v. HARD

PROBLEM 55

Plaintiffs' Attorney: Planning and Drafting Pleadings

You have interviewed the Summers family (Deborah, Gretchen, Hans, and the children, Amanda and Ronny); reviewed the criminal file you obtained from the prosecutor's office; obtained medical records, bills, and other documents; researched the law; theorized about the case; and interviewed some witnesses.

The Summers family has requested that you represent them. They requested that you contact the potential defendants in the case to see if the defendants will settle. You have done so but were not successful in settling the case. The Summers family has requested that you pursue litigation; that means you should draft a complaint.

PREPARATION

READ: (1) Pretrial Case File Entries 1-35, 40, 41, 47, 48, 59-61, 63, 83, 90; (2) Chapter VI; (3) Fed. R. Civ. P. 7-21.

Your instructor will inform you whether to answer Questions 1 through 8 based on the sample complaint, *Summers v. Hard* (Case File Entry 37), or a complaint prepared by students in your class.

1. Are the plaintiffs who are named in the complaint correct parties? Why?

    a. Explain the substantive basis (substantive law, procedural rules) that allows joinder of these parties as plaintiffs.

    b. Explain the factual basis (relationship, causation alleged) that allows joinder of the parties as plaintiffs.

2. Are the defendants who are named in the complaint correct parties?

    a. Explain the substantive basis (substantive law, procedural rules) that allows joinder of the parties as defendants.

    b. Explain the factual basis (relationship, causation alleged) that allows joinder of these parties as defendants.

3. Are there any defendants that you believe should have been joined by plaintiffs but were not? Explain.

4. Should plaintiffs' attorney have included more factual information as to plaintiffs' claims? Explain.

5. Should plaintiffs' attorney have included any references to the law? Explain.

6. Does plaintiffs' complaint inform as to their legal or factual theories of the case? Should it? Explain.

7. Would defendants be successful if they filed any of the following motions? Explain.

    a. Motion to dismiss.

    b. Motion to strike.

    c. Lack of specificity.

    d. Summary judgment.

8. Lawyers are accused of using legal jargon in order to obfuscate and complicate the simplest of concepts.

    a. What legal jargon would you eliminate from the *Summers v. Hard* complaint?

    b. Would you retain any legal jargon? Explain.

As to the complaint you will draft, consider the following:

9. Explain the steps you have taken in preparation for drafting a complaint.

10. What are your pleading objectives?

11. What are your representational strategies?

12. Explain how your pleading will affect your pleading objectives and representational strategies.

13. Whom will you join as plaintiffs?

   a. Explain the substantive basis (substantive law, procedural rules) for joining the parties.

   b. Explain the factual basis (relationship, causation) for joining the parties.

14. Whom will you join as defendants?

   a. Explain the legal basis (substantive law, procedural rules, evidentiary concerns).

   b. Explain the factual basis.

15. In naming the parties you plan to include in the lawsuit, did you base your decision on any other matters (e.g., wealth, cooperation)? Explain.

16. What claims for relief will you state? Against whom?

17. Are there additional facts that you will plead in your complaint that were not included in the sample complaint? List the facts and explain them.

18. Would you plead any law in your complaint? Explain.

19. Will you include in your complaint material that anticipates potential defenses? Explain.

20. Will you plead your theories of the case in the complaint? Why or why not?

21. Will you verify the complaint? Will your clients? Explain.

22. Suppose you verify the complaint in the Summers case and later find out that a critical fact in the complaint is incorrect. What will you do? Why?

ASSIGNMENT FOR CLASS

1. Outside of class, draft a complaint seeking redress for Bruno Summers' death. Your instructor will discuss the format to follow in preparing your complaint. Hand it in to your senior partner.

2. In class, be prepared to discuss your pleading.

PROBLEM 56
Defendants' Attorneys: Planning and Drafting Responsive Pleadings

You have reviewed the summons and complaint in *Summers v. Hard;* interviewed your respective clients (Ed Hard, M.C. Davola, Mary Apple, and Tom Donaldson); reviewed the criminal file you obtained from the prosecutor's office; obtained some of the relevant documents (medical records of Bruno Summers); researched the law; informally interviewed some witnesses; and theorized about defenses to the lawsuit.

Informal discovery has concluded. Of course there are additional witnesses and documents to examine, but you have enough information to respond to the *Summers v. Hard* complaint.

A major problem that is still unsettled is whether the SAPO Insurance Company lawyer or Ed Hard's own lawyer will be representing Ed Hard. Ed Hard's insurance company has agreed that it will draft the appropriate responsive pleadings invoking its reservation of rights clause in the insurance contract in order to protect the issue of "duty to defend." M.C. Davola and his employees, Mary Apple and Tom Donaldson, are represented by both EKKO Insurance Company and a private lawyer.

PREPARATION

READ: (1) Pretrial Case File Entries 1-39, 44, 45, 59-61, 63, 83, 90; (2) Chapter VI.

Your instructor will inform you whether to answer Questions 1 through 14 based on the sample *Summers v. Hard* complaint and answers in the case file, or a complaint prepared by students in your class.

Looking at the sample *Summers v. Hard* complaint (Case File Entry 37) or one prepared by students in your class, think about the following:

1. Is the Summers' complaint technically correct in form?

2. If the complaint is lacking in form, will you file a motion?

    a. What motions will you file?

    b. Why?

3. Does the Summers' complaint state sufficient facts to state claims for relief? Explain.

4. Does the Summers' complaint state a basis for relief under the substantive law? Explain.

5. Would defendants be successful in a summary judgment motion against the plaintiffs' complaint in *Summers v. Hard?* Explain.

6. Suppose plaintiffs' complaint did not name Tom Donaldson and Mary Apple as defendants. Should they be joined in the lawsuit as defendants?

    a. Explain the procedural basis for defendants to join Donaldson and Apple.

    b. Explain the factual and legal basis for defendants to join Donaldson and Apple.

    c. Would Davola want to join Donaldson and Apple? Explain.

    d. Would Hard want to join Donaldson and Apple? Explain.

    e. Tactically, what is the consequence for plaintiffs if Donaldson and Apple are joined?

7. Are there any other parties that should be joined by defendants? Explain.

Now look at the *Summers v. Hard* complaint (the case file sample or one by students in your class) as to the allegations:

8. Which allegations in the complaint will you admit? Why?

9. Which allegations in the complaint will you deny? Why?

10. Are there allegations in the complaint to which you are not sure how to respond? Explain.

Now turn to the answers of defendants Hard and Davola (Case File Entries 38 and 39):

11. As to defendant Hard's affirmative defenses: Referring to the sample *Summers v. Hard* answer by Ed Hard, respond to the questions as to the second affirmative defense—

    a. Should defendant Hard have pleaded additional facts in support of his affirmative defense? Why or why not?

    b. Is it necessary to plead the law? Should he plead law? Explain.

    c. What is the case theory for the affirmative defense?

12. As to defendants Davola, Apple, and Donaldson's affirmative defense and cross-claim: Referring to the sample *Summers v. Hard* answer by Davola, respond to the questions for the affirmative defense and cross-claim—

    a. Does the affirmative defense allege enough facts to support it? Explain.

    b. What is the case theory for the affirmative defense?

    c. Is the cross-claim pleading sufficient (legally and actually)?

    d. What is the case theory for the cross-claim?

Now look at the *Summers v. Hard* complaint (the case file sample or the one by students in your class) and examine the language. Most pleadings contain legal jargon. If you were drafting the complaint:

13. Would you retain any legal jargon? Explain.

14. Would you eliminate any legal jargon?

As to the answer you will draft, consider the following:

15. Explain the steps you have taken to prepare you to draft an answer.

16. What are your pleading objectives in your answer? Explain.

17. What are your representational strategies?

18. Explain how your pleading will affect your pleading objectives and representational strategies?

19. What are the determining factors for deciding which allegations in the Summers' complaint you will admit?

20. What are the determining factors for deciding which allegations in the Summers' complaint you will deny?

21. How does Federal Rule of Civil Procedure 11 influence your decision to admit or deny allegations in plaintiffs' complaint?

22. Suppose you verify a responsive pleading and later find that a critical fact in the pleading is incorrect. What will you do?

23. Suppose Deborah pleads in the complaint that Amanda and Ronny are Bruno's children.

    a. Will you admit those allegations? Why?

    b. Will you deny those allegations? Why?

24. Suppose the other defendants' attorney informs you that Amanda and Ronny are Bruno's children. Will you admit the allegation in plaintiff's complaint? Explain.

25. Suppose Deborah pleads she was lawfully married to Bruno Summers and is now his widow.

    a. Will you deny that allegation? Explain.

    b. What are the consequences of denying that Deborah was lawfully married to Bruno Summers? Explain.

26. Will you include in your pleading any affirmative defenses?

    a. List the affirmative defenses you will plead, if any.

    b. Explain the legal theory you are relying on for each affirmative defense.

    c. Explain the factual theory you are relying on for each affirmative defense.

27. Will you assert any cross-claims?

    a. List the cross-claims you will assert, if any.

    b. Explain the legal theory you are relying on for each cross-claim.

    c. Explain the factual theory you are relying on for each cross-claim.

28. Explain the procedural steps you will take to assert cross-claims.

29. Will you plead your legal and factual theories of the case in your responsive pleadings? Explain.

30. If you represent defendant Hard, could you ethically plead two inconsistent defenses: that he shot Bruno Summers accidentally; and in self-defense? Explain.

31. Will you send a draft copy of your responsive pleading to the other named defendants before filing it? Explain.

ASSIGNMENT FOR CLASS

1. Outside of class, draft an answer to the complaint and/or appropriate motions. Hand in the original pleadings to your senior partner.

2. In class, be prepared to discuss your responsive pleading.

VII

Discovery

A. FORMAL INFORMATION-GATHERING IN SERVICE OF STRATEGIC OBJECTIVES
B. PREPARATION
    1. Procedural and Substantive Rules
    2. Types of Discovery Devices
        a. Interrogatories
        b. Requests for Documents and Other Physical Items
        c. Depositions
        d. Physical and Mental Examinations
        e. Requests for Admission
    3. Developing a Discovery Plan
    4. Relationship of Case Theory to Discovery
C. PLANNING THE CONTENT OF YOUR DISCOVERY
    1. A Suggested Approach
    2. Applying the Approach
        Question 1. What tentative case theories are indicated by the existing information that you are aware of?
        Question 2. What new information will you seek through formal discovery?
        Question 3. What information did you obtain?
        Question 4. What is the significance of this information?
        Question 5. What further information will you now seek?
D. PLANNING YOUR SKILLS PERFORMANCE
        Question 1. What is the range of possible practical/strategic considerations and situations that could arise in seeking discovery?
          Area One. Determining which discovery device to employ in a civil case
          Area Two. Determining which discovery device to employ in a criminal case
          Area Three. Determining the timing and sequence of formal discovery
          Area Four. Drafting discovery requests
          Area Five. Representing a lay client or friendly non-party witness at a deposition; Taking the deposition of an adverse lay party or non-party witness
          Area Six. Representing an expert witness at a deposition; Taking the deposition of an expert
          Area Seven. Determining whom to serve with a discovery request
          Area Eight. Anticipating objections to your discovery request
          Area Nine. Determining when to make a motion to compel discovery
          Area Ten. Making a sufficient record of your discovery request
          Area Eleven. Drafting a motion to compel discovery
          Area Twelve. Determining the appropriate manner for responding to an opponent's discovery request
          Area Thirteen. Storing and indexing the discovery you have received
        Question 2. Which of these practical/strategic situations will you deal with at this point?
        Question 3. What are your objectives in this situation?
        Question 4. How will you achieve your objectives?
        Question 5. What problems do you anticipate?
        Question 6. How will you meet such problems?

A. FORMAL INFORMATION-GATHERING IN SERVICE OF STRATEGIC OBJECTIVES

Discovery is a skills performance that is dedicated to information-gathering. You can call upon it to require the opposing party to show all of her non-privileged playing cards—that is, all non-privileged information that may have a bearing on the case. She in turn can use discovery to see your cards. You both can use discovery to demand information from third parties and entities. Like all pretrial skills, discovery serves your representational strategy. If summary judgment is the aim of your representational strategy, discovery will be directed toward obtaining sufficient undisputed facts upon which to bring that motion. If litigation is to be the ultimate tool of that strategy, the information generated through discovery will be sought for a variety of uses. This information can provide support, demand modification, or even require abandonment of your case theory; it might suggest new case theories. It might reveal the opposing party's case theories, including the basis, strengths, and weaknesses of such theories. It might lead to more

investigation, further interviews with your client, and further discovery. If settlement is the goal of the representational strategy, discovery plays a complex role. It may support litigation, which in turn becomes a goad to negotiation. It may reveal strengths in your case theory or weaknesses in the opposition's that will affect the "top" and "bottom" of the opponent's "bargaining range" (discussed in Chapter X). It may reveal information directly applicable to your negotiation (e.g., that the opposing party has cash-flow problems, so a settlement offer that requires little cash flow may be enticing). The very pressure and projected cost from legitimate discovery may encourage settlement and influence the amount of settlement.

In this chapter, we discuss both civil and criminal discovery. For concrete examples of formal discovery devices, see the criminal discovery motion in the appendix to this chapter (page 214), the deposition excerpt in Case File Entry 56, and the excerpt from a set of interrogatories in the appendix to Chapter VIII (pages 277-279). You will note as you read through this chapter that most of our discussions of discovery take place in the context of the litigation-directed case theory. There are two reasons for this. First, as we will discuss later, we believe that there should be a reasonable focus within discovery, rather than an attempt to use discovery to obtain everything imaginable. Second, as will also be discussed later, discovery itself exists in a legal rule-bound context, and in using the case theory during discovery, one should be mindful of those rules. You should always be aware, however, that every part of this discovery process ultimately is directed toward achieving the objectives of the representational strategy. Accordingly, if your final objectives can best be achieved by settlement, and you are engaged in productive and cooperative negotiation sessions to that end, serving 300 interrogatories on opposing counsel may serve the case theory's hunger for information, but might severely harm your representational strategy by escalating the litigation aspect of the case.

The list of objectives for formal discovery is dominated by a search for information:

1. obtaining information, both good and bad, that is relevant to developing your case theory and motions, and that can provide you with a basis for realistically assessing your overall position for possible settlement;
2. "creating" information (e.g., obtaining a court order to conduct a scientific test);
3. influencing your adversary to change his or her position (e.g., an agreement to negotiate or settle, or to change the grounds for settlement) by seeking relevant, but sensitive, information that the opponent does not want to release (e.g., the identity of a police informant, details of a store's security system), and by making it clear to the adversary that you are serious about the case and mean to work diligently in your client's behalf.[1]

This last objective should be clearly distinguished from the practice of using discovery as a means of grinding a less affluent opponent into submission, unreasonably delaying cases, artificially raising the costs to the opponent of non-capitulation, and so forth. Such practices are, to say the least, of questionable ethical propriety. Unfortunately, however, these practices are not totally uncommon and an advocate must be prepared to anticipate and deal with such tactics.

Before you proceed to actually prepare and plan for discovery, you should appreciate that discovery is characterized as "formal" information-gathering. This is so for two reasons. First, discovery is associated with a range of formal discovery devices (depositions,

interrogatories) that contrast with the less structured tools of informal information-gathering (witness interviews, informal inspection of the accident scene). Second, the roots of discovery's very existence and legitimacy are formal. Discovery is legislatively or judicially sanctioned access to information that is in the control of your opponent or some third party. Significantly, this access is backed up by potential enforcement—a court order. Lest you get the wrong impression, however, you should be aware that most formal civil discovery is self-executing.[2] The majority of parties resort to court only in cases where information considered essential is refused, or compliance with discovery requests has been subject to extreme delay, or where there have been disputes over discoverability or privilege.

B. PREPARATION

Preparation is tied to your general philosophy of discovery and the specific case you are involved in. There are competent lawyers who see discovery as directed at getting everything imaginable. While we encourage a broad view of discovery—after all, you do not want to miss the piece of information that will suggest a new case theory or that disastrous piece of information that suggests the futility of not settling—we believe discovery should be *focused*. In our view, the current realities of the average attorney's time resources do not suggest a philosophy of discovery that results in counsel being inundated by mounds of useless data.[3] Furthermore, the courts seem to be impatient with unfocused, "shot-gun" discovery requests that bog down the courts with endless hearings on the scope of discovery, vagueness, overbroadness, burdensomeness, and so forth. (Note that the focus in federal courts is to institutionalize a discovery conference and plan, Fed. R. Civ. P. 26(f)).

In this section, we deal with two types of knowledge you must obtain as groundwork before you begin

---

1. This aim may be central to a representational strategy that seeks eventual dismissal of a civil suit or criminal charges or, at least, a favorable disposition.

2. In practice, this formal-informal distinction is also far from clear in the criminal area. You may need a court order to interview a witness (e.g., a police informant) or to inspect the premises of a private business. On the other hand, opposing counsel may turn over documents without formal request as a cooperative gesture.

3. This may be less likely to happen in the average criminal than civil case. In a criminal case, commonly only a single, isolated event is involved; the information sought by the defense is generally that which was specifically gathered by the police in investigating that event. The criminal defendant's defense can also be based on a *lack* of evidence in the prosecution's case, a lack that may be revealed by knowing all that the prosecution has.

your planning. The first is procedural and organizational information—procedural rules, discovery techniques available, and discovery plans. The second involves a mental perspective—an appreciation of the relationship between case theory and discovery.

1. *Procedural and Substantive Rules*

Legal rules, standards, and doctrine circumscribe formal discovery. They dictate both the procedural requirements for obtaining discovery and the scope and limits of discovery itself. Accordingly, when planning for discovery, review appropriate rules such as the Federal Rules of Civil Procedure (Fed. R. Civ. P.), Federal Rules of Criminal Procedure (Fed. R. Crim. P.), local court rules, and state statutes. You should also review applicable cases, as well as determine the "custom and usage" of particular courts and judges (gleaned from personal observation and discussions with other attorneys and court personnel). With this background information, you will be able to intelligently contemplate an array of procedural matters, such as appropriate devices for discovery, discovery conferences, time requirements, omnibus hearings, required forms for discovery requests, protective orders, and procedures for compelling responses to your discovery requests when your opponent fails to comply. This information will also help you determine what you may request and what may be requested of you. As such, your research will reveal the permissible scope and standards for discovery, case doctrine that deals with the appropriateness or inappropriateness of requesting certain items or types of items of information, and the grounds upon which an objection to a request for discovery can be made.

You will, of course, be looking for information to help you develop, support, and modify your tentative case theories and refute your adversary's. Accordingly, you will review your own and your adversary's tentative case theories and the information you have obtained from informal discovery, so you can begin to think about what you want. You also will research likely sources of information for your particular type of case so you can have an idea where to look once you decide the type of information you want to request. (What kinds of files, records, and memos does the kind of business you are suing generally keep? What is likely to be in those records?)

In a civil case, before planning for discovery you should be familiar with the discovery devices available for obtaining various types of information—interrogatories, requests for production of documents and inspection of things, depositions, physical and mental examinations, requests for admissions, subpoenas. (We discuss the much narrower range of available criminal discovery devices later in this chapter when dealing with strategic considerations. See page 200. Note, however, that some discovery in criminal cases is often obtained as a side product of some evidentiary hearing—bail suppression, severance of defendants.) Each of these civil devices has a particular use depending on the information that you want. Therefore, we will review the general types of civil discovery devices and discuss how they can be used.

2. *Types of Discovery Devices*

a. **Interrogatories**

Interrogatories are written questions that must be responded to under oath. They can be sent only by parties to the lawsuit to other parties to the lawsuit. They are most useful for obtaining and locating information (names and addresses of witnesses; documents that may exist) or determining the basis for a party's legal and factual position. One type of interrogatory, known as a contentious interrogatory, allows you to inquire into the legal and factual basis of a party's allegations or defenses in a pleading. ("What is the basis for your claim of comparative fault?" "What is the basis for your statement, 'He was intoxicated,' in paragraph 8 of your answer?")

The advantage of using interrogatories is that they are inexpensive, basically limited to the cost of preparing, copying, and mailing them. Attorneys in this technological age generally have computers with interrogatory banks. As your law practice progresses, you may be aided by reference to your own interrogatory bank, which contains previously drafted interrogatories used in similar cases. However, you should use such interrogatory banks cautiously. Use of such banks has led to abuse by attorneys who send hundreds of interrogatory bank questions that are often irrelevant and that frequently ask for cumulative information. In response, many jurisdictions by local or judge-made rule have limited the number of interrogatories and also assess sanctions for the clear use of irrelevant and cumulative bank-like interrogatories (e.g., a sanction might cover the cost of 400 interrogatories in a dissolution case in which only $10,000 in property must be allocated between the warring spouses). Therefore, when using your interrogatory bank, be certain to adapt your interrogatories for your particular case and circumstance.

b. Requests for Documents and Other Physical Items

This discovery device is much like an interrogatory. It is a written request that can be sent only to parties to the case and allows one to inspect, view, and (where feasible) copy writings, documents, photographs, and other physical items, including property. The request must be specific in what it requests. A general request for "everything that you have concerning the automobile crash" is not specific enough; "All repair bills from June 1966 through the present for your 1965 Chevy Impala, license no. CRAZY" is a specific request. The items that you request must be in the possession or control of the party to whom you send the request. This can include the party's agents—for example, attorneys or investigators. The request is inexpensive to prepare, but like an interrogatory, must be tailored to the specific dispute.

c. Depositions

Depositions are the most widely used discovery device because they can be addressed to anyone. They are usually oral examinations of witnesses under oath and are much like a "mini-trial" because you can ask questions, follow up on questions, and observe the demeanor of the witness. (There are also written depositions that function much like interrogatories.) Depositions are more expensive than the written discovery devices—court reporter fees and transcript orders must be considered. On the other hand, depositions are much more useful. They allow you to develop and follow up on areas of inquiry, assess the credibility of witnesses, and preserve testimony. At trial, they present an excellent written device for impeachment, serving as prior inconsistent statements if the witness's trial testimony is at variance with that in the deposition.

d. Physical and Mental Examinations

This discovery device can only be used in civil cases by parties against parties when the physical or mental condition of a party is at issue. (With a strong showing to the court, witnesses may be examined in criminal cases.) Generally, to use the device in a civil case one needs a court order, although most attorneys agree among themselves to allow an examination. This device gives an adversary the opportunity to have an examination (physical or mental) of the other party,

which, in most cases, will be the allegedly injured plaintiff. This allows the adversary to confirm or refute the medical condition of the injured party.

e. Requests for Admission

Again, these can be addressed only to parties. They are written, must be answered under oath, and allow the requesting party to find out the basis for the responding party's denials of material relevant facts that are in dispute (in particular, the identification and admissibility of documents). A request for admission is an inexpensive device that a party can use, for example, to find out if any particular documents will be contested and why. As with interrogatories, some courts limit the number of requests for admission.

3. Developing a Discovery Plan

To coordinate all this legal and factual information, you need to develop a "discovery plan" (see Chapter VIII for a discussion of the analogous idea of a "motion plan"). Such a plan ensures that you will deal with discovery as a coordinated enterprise directed toward achieving your representational strategy and case theory, rather than as a fragmented series of sorties pursued without overall goals and with neither a sense of how they relate to one another nor how they will be accomplished. Your discovery plan is a comprehensive overview of all the information you will seek and whom you will seek it from, and is the basis of your legal rationale for each request. This rationale generally will emerge naturally from your analysis of what you want. The plan will also include the specific discovery devices you will use in seeking each piece of information, and some consideration of likely objections you can anticipate from opposing counsel to your individual requests, as well as a sense of your possible responses to these objections. Finally, all this will be placed in the context of a time line, ordering the use of each discovery device (interrogatories, requests for admissions, depositions) in the sequence you feel desirable, and scheduling these devices at specific points in time, determined both by court and statutory rules and by the pace you feel is desirable and feasible in light of the interests of the case and your other commitments. Many jurisdictions require such a discovery plan. In federal court, for example, discovery planning is specifically structured by the rules.

A chart may be helpful in working out your plan:

Claim/ Defense	Element	Facts to prove claim/ defense	Information/ Source	Discovery device	Sequence	Problems/ Evidence concerns	Date for scheduling

This chart includes: (1) A statement of your claim or defense; (2) each element of the claim or defense that embodies your legal theory (or the elements you will attack for lack of factual or persuasive sufficiency); (3) the assertions of your factual theory supporting each element; (4) the information you will request pertaining to each assertion and the source of the information (e.g., a witness, documents under control of a custodian of records); (5) the discovery device you will employ to get this information; (6) the sequence of this device relative to other devices you will use; (7) problems/evidence concerns you may face in making your request, which include developing rationales for each request, and anticipating objections or requests for protective orders; and (8) specific dates for employing each device (when you will file interrogatories, set a deposition, and so on).

4. Relationship of Case Theory to Discovery

Part of your preparation is mental. Specifically, you must conceptualize the role of the case theory in relation to discovery. The formal discovery process and the concept of case theory are intimately related. First, formal discovery is a significant method for obtaining information to support, modify, or adopt new case theories and to learn about your opponent's theories. The case theory will thus provide a guide in determining the information you will seek through your discovery requests, just as it did in determining the information you sought in the interviewing process. Second, case theory is generally central to objections to discovery (e.g., overbroad requests, privileged information). If the refusing party's objections are successful, the requesting party is denied information. The less information you have, however, the fewer potential "stories" and accompanying legal theories you can rely on, and the weaker those stories will tend to be. Therefore, by limiting available information, objections to discovery either tend to strengthen the refusing party's legal theories by focusing on a lack of factual/persuasive sufficiency in the requesting party's story, or keep information from the requesting party that could be used to attack the factual/persuasive sufficiency of the refusing party's story. Third, the case theory bears a relationship to the legal standards circumscribing discovery. In a practical sense, the case

theory guides not only what you will request, but also what you are legally entitled to request and the actual form your request must take. This third relationship between case theory and discovery requires further elaboration.

Unlike informal methods of fact-gathering, such as interviewing, where the power of the court is generally not involved, discovery operates within a legal structure. Civil discovery is generally guided by standards provided in rules (which are then interpreted by case law), such as the Federal Rules of Civil Procedure:

> *In General. Parties may obtain discovery regarding any matter, not privileged, which is relevant to the subject matter involved in the pending action,* whether it relates to the claim or defense of the party seeking discovery or to the claim or defense of any other party, including the existence, description, nature, custody, condition and location of any books, documents, or other tangible things and the identity and location of persons having knowledge of any discoverable matter. *It is not ground for objection that the information sought will be inadmissible at the trial if the information sought appears reasonably calculated to lead to the discovery of admissible evidence.* [Fed. R. Civ. P. 26(a)(1) (emphasis added).]

Criminal discovery, which is generally a product of judicial opinions, although guided by statutory or court rules in some jurisdictions, is somewhat different. It evolved slowly. Concerned with defendant perjury should the prosecution's case be known in advance, courts slowly progressed from denying all discovery to eventually requiring a stringent "good cause" showing for production of even the few items of discovery that courts would then permit defendants to obtain (e.g., the defendant's own statement to police). (Good cause also used to be the standard for civil discovery prior to the Federal Rules.) As criminal discovery broadened, courts in effect found good cause to apply as a matter of law to a wider and wider variety of items. Thus, current criminal discovery characteristically encompasses a set, although often limited, catalog of items that might be available to the parties.

In many jurisdictions, criminal discovery is the realm of the defense. With the exception of some "notice of alibi" statutes, the Fifth Amendment has traditionally stood as a bar to obtaining a wide range of information from the defense. However, there are some recent statutory schemes that implicitly give less weight to such Fifth Amendment concerns. Some provide the prosecution with some carefully delineated discovery from the defense that goes beyond notice of alibi. Others seem to limit the scope of the Fifth Amendment to information directly from the defendant and view all other discovery as a two-way street. On the other hand, while the plaintiff in a criminal case is generally severely limited in court-ordered discovery by the Fifth Amendment, the government can do a great deal analogous to discovery through its powers of search and seizure, arrest, police interrogation, and grand jury investigation.

Criminal discovery is generally regulated by case law, or articulated in statutes such as the Federal Rules of Criminal Procedure, or listed in local court rules, or accepted in the custom and usage of a particular court. The type of discoverable information varies from jurisdiction to jurisdiction. But generally the defense can discover such items as police reports and physical evidence. A good cause showing, however, is still required for anything not in the prescribed catalog. In most instances, criminal discovery will be accomplished by a formal, written motion to the court, though a great deal of informal provision of information by the prosecution takes place in some jurisdictions and court systems. The sample discovery motion in the appendix to this chapter (page 214) provides a spectrum of items that a defendant may reasonably try to obtain, although the defendant cannot expect that this reasonable try will invariably be successful.

Where does case theory fit into the legal discovery structure? In both the civil and criminal areas, the discovery process is limited in scope by a legal structure that envisions that information will be provided only if there is a "reasonable possibility" (civil) or "good cause" (criminal) that the information could bear on your case (including attacks on your adversary's case). "Reasonable possibility" and "good cause," however, are both members of the "relevance" family (in fact, Rule 26(a) specifically uses the term "relevant"), and relevance is always a function of case theory. The defendant's knowledge at the time of shooting the victim that the victim had committed prior violent acts will be relevant to a self-defense theory as bearing on the reasonableness of defendant's fear, but not be relevant to a misidentification theory. Thus, whether or not an item bears on your case will be determined by how you and your adversary articulate your case theories. However, you should not and do not have to bind yourself to one specific case theory in discovery. After all, one objective of discovery is to assist you in sifting through plausible alternative theories. Rather, you could say, "this information could lead to information that would be admissible in support of a defense of . . . ."

Your case theory, therefore, not only guides you in determining what to ask for, but provides the frame of reference for legally justifying your request under the applicable legal structure. You focus on information for discovery because it has some potential relevance to your case theories. This same type of "relevance" is implied in the legal standards for discovery. Thus, in practice, the same process from which you determined the information that you would seek in discovery will also provide the basic legal rationale for justifying the request because of the above-described relationship between the doctrinal standards and case theory. In addition to general standards for discovery found in statutory schemes and cases, *specific* items of information may be discussed in opinions and legislative histories in such a manner as to provide guidance for your request for such items of information (e.g., cases concerning the prosecution's duty to provide exculpatory evidence articulate the specificity with which the criminal defendant must request such information).

In this regard, imagine that you represent the defendant in a negligence suit in which you are defending against a slip-and-fall claim. Plaintiff claims to have fallen because of a wet spot on the floor of defendant's store. You believe you can successfully defeat plaintiff's claim if you can show that plaintiff's injuries (or at least their magnitude) were not caused by the fall or that plaintiff is fabricating the whole incident. You have determined that you want information concerning any of plaintiff's prior injuries and prior similar lawsuits. Prior injuries bear on a possible attack of the elements of "causation" and "damages" in plaintiff's legal theory. Prior similar suits could provide the basis for a credibility attack on plaintiff's factual theory. How can you justify obtaining this information about prior injuries and lawsuits under applicable legal standards? Look to your case theory. Your discovery request, if attacked as not meeting the legal standards for discovery, can be defended as follows:

> "This information about plaintiff's prior injuries that we've requested is reasonably calculated to lead to information that would show that plaintiff's injuries are not a result of the fall or that, if injured, the resulting damage is only slightly incremental to preexisting injuries. The information about prior similar suits could lead to information showing this is all part of an ongoing fraudulent scheme."

C. PLANNING THE CONTENT OF YOUR DISCOVERY

1. A Suggested Approach

In our experience, there is generally a finite number of categories of information that could be available in discovery:

- identities of witnesses
- information possessed by particular witnesses (obtained in discovery through such devices as depositions, interrogatories, or requests for admissions; this category of information is also available informally through witness interviews)
- pieces of paper and recorded information (documents, records, memos, charts, policy statements, witness statements, specifications, cassette tapes, videotapes, computer programs)
- physical and demonstrative evidence (fingerprints, guns, broken camshafts, photographs, diagrams)
- opportunities to create information (e.g., court order to permit your defense expert to perform a firearms comparison on weapon the prosecution claims was used in assault)

Of course, you'd like to ask the opposition and third parties to hand over everything; that request, however, may be found a bit overbroad and vague. So how do you determine the *specific* information among these categories that you should request in your particular case? For that task, we have provided you with a model approach.

Since discovery is an information-gathering task, our five-question approach is similar to the approaches in other information-gathering skills performances, such as witness or client interviewing and the information-gathering aspect of motion making:

1. What tentative case theories are indicated by the existing information that you are aware of?[4]
2. What new information will you seek through formal discovery?[5]

---

4. As we have said in earlier chapters, your case theory should provide a focus, but it should not act as a constraint on the breadth of your information-gathering activity. Remember that you are dealing with tentative case theories and want to obtain all the information that you can during this information-gathering phase.

5. Note that in a formal discovery, you must think about the person or entity in charge of a source of information (e.g., a party, a custodian of corporate records), as well as the source in which the sought-after information is contained (e.g., witness testimony, document, piece of physical evidence).

3. What information did you obtain?
4. What is the significance of this information?
5. What further information will you now seek?

> BASIC TASK: Request information that bears on (supports, modifies, undercuts) your and your opponent's case theories.

---

2. Applying the Approach

You are the attorney for plaintiff in a civil fraud case. The core of your legal theory is that the defendant automobile garage intended to defraud your client. This legal theory is based on a "story," the central assertion of which is that defendant, who was to fix all four of plaintiff's brakes, fixed only plaintiff's front brakes, while charging for repairing both front and rear brakes. Defendant acknowledges that it fixed only plaintiff's front brakes, while charging for both front and back. Defendant's "story," however, is that this was the result of a mistake when two work orders were inadvertently switched on a very busy day. This assertion of an inadvertent mistake supports a legal theory attacking the element of intent to defraud in your legal theory.

You are beginning to plan formal discovery and want to determine what information to seek. (You will then determine which discovery devices to employ, the sequence of the devices, and so forth.) How will you reason through this task?

Begin applying the approach:

QUESTION 1
What tentative case theories are indicated by the existing information that you are aware of?

You have a tentative case theory: Civil fraud based on the garage having intentionally charged plaintiff for repairing both front and rear brakes while knowing that it had repaired only the front brakes. Also, after studying defendant's responsive pleading, you believe that the defendant will rely on the defense of "mistake" due to an "inadvertent mix-up" in repair work orders.

QUESTION 2
What new information will you seek through formal discovery?

This question in our approach has particular meaning in the area of discovery. Just as in witness and client interviewing, you will be seeking information in this request that will be relevant to supporting, developing, modifying, or refuting your and your adversary's tentative case theories. Specifically, your case theory will focus on those areas wherein you will need to obtain information. Begin with your legal theory (or theories, since you will often be seeking discovery in part to choose among alternative tentative theories), and those theories you suspect the opposing counsel is entertaining. Plaintiff will be concerned with establishing every element of its theory, defendant with the possibility of attacking each element. (If defendant raises an affirmative defense, the positions will be reversed.) Each element of these legal theories will thus provide a separate area to focus on for discovery.

Then look at the respective factual theories. You need information to support, or must become aware of information that weakens, the existing assertions in your factual theory (especially the central assertions), or you need to find information that will allow you to add assertions to fill gaps in your story. Recall the discussion of the story of Bossie, the unpaid-for cow, in Chapter II (see page 25). As always, you want to know the bad as well as the good. Aware of such negative information, you may be able to deal with it within the context of your theory, or by modifying or changing your theory, or by seeking an acceptable settlement. Without such an awareness, disaster awaits. You also need information to undercut your opponent's story. Every assertion in your and your opponent's factual theories thus provides a potential area for discovery.

But recognizing an area as a focus for seeking information that will help or hurt your case theory does not tell you the *specific* information that you should seek in that area. For that, we employ a two-step process that we have developed from personal experience.

The first step requires common sense and imagination (akin to the brainstorming you used to develop tentative case theories). This step involves a "chicken-egg" process in which you simultaneously consider both what you want and what the party from whom you might seek discovery is likely to have. For clarity, however, this step can be considered as involving two separate but related processes. In Process

A, you start with what you want for your case theory or what you need to undercut your opponent's theory and then look for likely sources for this information. In Process B, you start with likely sources (certain witnesses, types of records a person or entity is likely to keep), and assess what information these sources could contain that bears on the respective case theories. Each process, of course, yields ideas that trigger its companion process as your mind moves back and forth between the two.

The second step requires thoroughness combined with imagination. You will have already used your case theories to provide your areas of focus, and used the two interrelated processes to determine the information you want within the areas. In this second step, you conceive of *all* the sources that could contain this information, although you might have already identified one or more sources in the first step.

Now we are ready to apply this analysis to our hypothetical automobile-repair fraud case. In this hypothetical case, the areas indicated by analysis of your legal theory ("intent to defraud") and the defendant's factual theory ("mistake" due to an inadvertent switching of work orders) are fairly congruent. You want to focus on the question of "mistake." But what specific information will you seek? Begin the two-step process.

Step One, Process A: What do you want? You want information from which you can argue that the over-billing was not a mistake, but was indeed intentional (or at least you want to learn that such information does not exist, or that there is contrary information). What type of information could undercut this defense claim of "mistake"? Who might possess such information? Use your imagination. You are unlikely to have anyone tell you, "Yes, that repair job was a fraud all right." But information that the defendant's story is unlikely under current procedures ("They might have switched work orders, but then he would have been billed under the wrong order, too, and only been charged for the front brakes"), or that employees are telling materially contradictory stories in this matter (or obviously "pat" stories) would help you in arguing that the jury should infer that this incident did not occur because of a mistake.

Who or what could be the source of this information? Clearly, various employees. Thus, you need to know how to locate all potential employee witnesses (through interrogatories asking for names, addresses, and telephone numbers of all employees working at the time) so you can seek such information in a deposition. If you were to use a deposition to obtain the specific information, you can employ the information-gathering methods for witness interviews described in

Chapter V. Similarly, evidence indicating that defendant has done this same thing in the past (modus operandi) might help. Business records of the defendant (whose existence and location you have determined through interrogatories) or of some state licensing agency may contain the names of prior customers who have made such complaints. However, note that only because of this brainstorming, guided by your case theory, did you even think of seeking customer names. Simultaneously, you may also be pursuing informal fact-gathering (e.g., talking to people at the Better Business Bureau). Information gained from this informal process, moreover, can be used to provide legal cause (see page 195) for subsequent formal discovery. You also want to find any information that *supports* defendant's assertion of "mistake" so you can deal with it. The same documents and witnesses already discussed will also aid in this enterprise.

Now embark on *Step One, Process B: What sources of information might the person or entity from whom you are seeking discovery be likely to have?* You must think about the types of information these sources could provide, and which among these types of information could have a bearing on the focus areas for your discovery that you derived from analyzing your and your opponent's case theories. What sources of information could defendant possess? The defendant probably has written documents such as a work order, written procedures for each job, policy manuals, and such, all of which could be obtained in a request for production of documents. What types of information could these sources contain? Work orders will show what was to have been done on a particular job. Procedures and policy manuals could provide how work orders are to be handled, jobs completed and billed, and so forth. Which among these types of information could concern the area of "mistakenly" failing to repair the brakes? If your client's work order clearly indicates that it was his car (make, color, license) upon which all four brakes were to be repaired, then a mistake may seem less likely. On the other hand, the work order may be so vague as to make a mistake believable. It may even describe plaintiff's car incorrectly. Written procedures and policy manuals may caution on the necessity of not mixing up work orders, or may describe a system under which such a mix-up would be improbable. Again, however, the manuals may support your opponent.

Generally, a helpful technique for fully appreciating the significance of the information you are seeking in discovery for your case theory is to imagine how you or opposing counsel could use the information in closing argument. After all, the closing argument is the final embodiment of your case theory: "Ladies and Gentlemen of the jury, as you can see, no one could have looked at that work order and thought anything but that all four brakes were to be repaired. Defendant concedes this point, as it must. Instead, defendant now claims that the orders were inadvertently switched. But, if you examine Policy Manual #6 and Procedures Section 15, you can see that it was virtually impossible for this to happen."

Now you move to *Step Two: Theorize about all the sources that could contain the information you are seeking.* A policy manual might emphasize the importance of not confusing work orders. This could be useful to the plaintiff, assuming the manual was widely read and there was a work order. This information would show a state of mind on the part of defendant's employees inconsistent with any "mistake." (Of course, the defense can argue that the very fact these concerns are even in the policy manual is itself a recognition that such confusion is a common fact of day-to-day life in the repair business.) There are, however, other sources that could also contain analogous information bearing on the central issue of "mistake" (memos, training manuals, and materials from refresher courses on general maintenance). As the civil plaintiff's counsel, you would want to be certain that you request all these sources.

QUESTION 3
What information did you obtain?

Imagine that among all the information your discovery requests yielded, you received the work orders of your client and the other person whose order defendant claims to have mistakenly switched with that of your client. Let's focus only on these two products of your discovery, the two work orders.

QUESTION 4
What is the significance of this information?

On the negative side, defendant has produced what is allegedly the other customer's order. This removes your ability to argue, for example, "How interesting that defendant cannot locate this other order, and does not even know whose car it was. Of course the reason that it cannot find the order is that it never existed. One more fraud in a seemingly endless series of deceptions." On the positive side, it provides you with a potentially powerful witness, the other customer, whom you can now interview, subpoena to a deposition, and so on.

QUESTION 5
What further information will you now seek?

You will want to find out the other customer's story. Were his front and back brakes repaired, even though he requested only that the front brakes be fixed? Was the garage busy that day as defendants maintain? Were the other customer's keys clipped to his work order, making switching unlikely? When did the other customer bring his car in and when did he pick it up? (Think of the significance if he picked his car up and paid for the work at 10 A.M. and your client did not even come in until 11 A.M.) Who is the other customer? (If he supports defendant's story, and is the owner's son-in-law, his support of defendant may be to your advantage.) How you will actually obtain this information is a matter of strategy—assessing the risks and benefits of informal investigation versus further formal discovery.

D. PLANNING YOUR SKILLS PERFORMANCE

You are the attorney for plaintiff in the same rear-end automobile collision you dealt with in both witness and client interviewing (see pages 77-105). A few days ago, you reviewed defendant's statement to the police, which he made at the hospital on the evening of the accident. You have also reviewed the report of the officer who first came to the scene. (You obtained these at the police station, paying the duplicating charge.) The police report notes there was a "SLOW DOWN CONSTRUCTION" sign 100 yards before the point of the accident. Defendant never mentions this sign in his statement although his statement is rather detailed and fact-specific as to how he "was driving along and plaintiff just suddenly cut [him] off." You are pleased with discovering the discrepancy between the police statement and defendant's statement. You reason that if defendant had mentioned seeing the sign, it would reinforce that his state of mind was one consistent with that of a prudent and cautious driver, and he would not have been likely to just ram into your client's rear bumper.

Yesterday, however, an informal source overheard a conversation in a restaurant in which the defendant was loudly discussing his side of the case. Your source had the "impression" that defendant's tale included something to do with his being careful because of the road construction sign he had just seen. You want more information on the matter and are considering some form of formal discovery. How will you proceed?

You could use the same eight-question performance planning approach we offered in Chapters IV and V (see pages 76-77; 105). You may first want to look at the following references for useful theoretical and practical advice: A.G. Amsterdam, *Trial Manual for the Defense of Criminal Cases* (4th ed. 1984); 11 M. Bender, *Bender's Forms of Discovery*, ch. 1 (1963); 15 M. Bender, *Bender's Forms of Discovery*, ch. 12 (1967); Bureau of National Affairs, Inc., *Civil Trial Manual*, ch. 31 (1987); Bureau of National Affairs, Inc., *Criminal Practice Manual*, ch. 41 (1987); R.S. Haydock and D.F. Herr, *Discovery Practice* (1982); 1 F. Lane, *Goldstein Trial Technique*, ch. 6 (3d. ed. 1984).

Apply the performance planning approach to this hypothetical.

QUESTION 1
What is the range of possible practical/strategic considerations and situations that could arise in seeking discovery?

Based on our experience, we have arrived at thirteen areas, each of which includes a range of possible considerations and situations that could arise within that area and some select pointers relevant to the area:

Area One
Determining which discovery device to employ in a civil case

When will you use depositions, interrogatories, requests for documents, requests for admissions, requests for inspection, requests for physical examination? What are the general advantages and disadvantages of each device? In this specific case? Which will serve best for use in subsequent impeachment? Which will aid in preparing for settlement?

How will cost affect your choice of a particular device, or of the number of such devices you will use?

Information about this area is presented at pages 209-210.

Area Two
Determining which discovery device to employ in a criminal case

Will you file a formal discovery request? Will you subpoena third parties to provide documents? Can you ask for a deposition in your jurisdiction? When will you seek a bill of particulars?

Answers to these questions will generally be determined by the type of information you need, and the source of the information you are seeking. You will make a formal motion for discovery[6] if the government (or defense) will not informally provide all information you desire or if you want a continuing court order to the effect that all new discoverable information that the government obtains must be provided to you (partly so if this new information suddenly appears at trial without your prior knowledge of it, you will have the basis for a remedy, such as continuance or exclusion). If the information is in tangible form, and in the hands of a third person who is not under the opponent's control, you will need to serve the person with a subpoena duces tecum. Additionally, the circumstances may call for two less common criminal discovery devices: the deposition and the bill of particulars. Depositions in criminal cases are generally limited to the rare instance when the witness is likely to be unavailable for trial (e.g., terminal illness, a move to Europe), though a few jurisdictions permit deposing material witnesses who refuse to cooperate in an interview (which gives you some clout when a witness does not want to cooperate in informal discovery). In those jurisdictions in which it is recognized, a bill of particulars is a device that technically is a response to the prosecution's charging pleading (e.g., information, complaint) and that asks for clarification of the pleading in terms of dates, means of committing the offense, and other such facts that directly underlie the elements of the charge ("Your Honor, the information alleges only that my client possessed 'a controlled substance.' By this bill of particulars we seek to learn what specific substance my client is to have possessed. Without that information,

he does not know the true nature of the charges he is facing, and accordingly can neither enter a plea nor begin to prepare an effective defense").

Area Three
Determining the timing and sequence of formal discovery

Will you commence formal discovery before, during, or after you have begun (completed?) informal discovery? Will you complete discovery through interrogatories and requests for admissions prior to noticing depositions? How will you decide whether to set an early deposition of a party, thereby enhancing the possibility of an early settlement, or to wait until later when you know more about the case and can therefore obtain more information? Will you schedule a deposition even before you file a lawsuit (by court order to obtain information so that you can file a lawsuit or to preserve information)?

Strategically, you want to consider when you will use your discovery devices. As with the substance of what you seek, you should consider obtaining information in a sequence that will help you in terms of your objectives—locating more information, settlement, preservation of information, and so on. For example, it is helpful at the beginning of discovery to use interrogatories to identify whether information exists and where it is. In that way you can decide whom to depose, whether certain documents exist and, if so, where you might find them. Additionally, you may want to inspect and copy documents before taking the deposition of a witness whom you might want to question about a particular document or about information that you learned from a document. But you may not be able to wait—you might have to consider such things as the health of the potential witness. (Should I depose the 90-year-old man? Do I want to preserve his testimony?) You may even want to schedule depositions before you file a lawsuit (by court order to obtain information so you can file a lawsuit, or to preserve information that may otherwise be lost before you can file suit and commence discovery). Or you may want to wait until shortly before trial to have the injured plaintiff examined since it is possible that the plaintiff's medical condition may have improved substantially. On the other hand, perhaps an early examination will help you settle the case before the plaintiff begins deteriorating. You may decide—again, strategically—to send requests for admission late in

---

6. See the sample criminal discovery motion in the appendix to this chapter at page 214.

your discovery because there is a greater chance that your adversary will be able to answer them. And so on and so on. Each scheduling decision is a strategic one.

Area Four
Drafting discovery requests

What level of precision is necessary in your requests if you are to have a reasonable likelihood of obtaining the information you are seeking? Will you ask many separate questions in interrogatories or fewer questions, each with sub-parts?

Your interrogatories, requests for admission, and requests for production of documents are the basic written devices enabling you to obtain predicate information for depositions (telling which person to depose, which documents he possesses) and for focusing your subsequent use of written requests. In drafting these types of discovery devices, you must keep two matters in mind—relevance and adoption of a technique employed within ethical boundaries. Relevance is the starting point. Any request that you make must meet the basic, relevance-related legal standard for discovery. As you already know, case theory will provide the reference point for your relevance concerns. Technique is manifested by a variety of principles, four of which you should focus on in particular: employ a combination of broad and narrow questions; pose questions that are unambiguous; ensure that the information you receive will be clearly identified (and identifiable); and carefully compose a detailed "preamble" to your requests.

First, use a combination of broad and narrow questions. Though guided by your and your opponent's tentative case theories, discovery must have a broad sweep. After all, your theories are only tentative at this relatively early stage of the process and you do not want to so narrow the focus of your discovery that you fail to obtain information that would indicate the possibility of other more applicable case theories. Also, you do not want information bearing on the case theories you currently have in mind to fall through the cracks because it is not specifically addressed by any particular inquiry. Broadly phrased questions fulfill the function of providing this broad scope to your discovery. These broad questions can be placed at the beginning of a series of individual specific questions (or sub-parts) as "lead-in" questions (Example A), or at the end of such a series of questions as "catch-alls" (Example B):

Example A

Interrogatory 15

In paragraph xiii of your complaint, you ask for special damages. Detail all the special damages you are claiming and why you are entitled to each.

[Broad Lead-in Question]

   a. What is the amount of each such special damage claim?

[Narrowly Focused Specific Questions]

   b. State the method you used to compute such amount.

   c. Have you received any medical treatment in conjunction with any of those damage claims?

   d. If so, please provide.

Example B

Interrogatory 16

Is there anything you should add to the answers you provided to questions 12-15 regarding expenses attributable to the injuries you allege you received as the result of a fall from a forklift on 5/17/8X?

[Broad Catch-all Question]

Use of specific questions, like the ones appearing in sub-parts a through d in Example A, allows you to focus on precise information for your case theory analysis. These specific questions also force specific information from the responding party. They are thus unlike the broad questions that at times can generate vague, and, accordingly, not very helpful responses. An interesting variation on the use of narrow, directed questions involves a strategy that combines the use of contentious interrogatories (which are briefly discussed at page 192) with requests for admission. As you recall, contentious interrogatories focus on specific factual allegations in the opposing party's pleadings and seek the basis for the allegation. For example:

Interrogatory 24

In paragraph xi of your complaint you state "and plaintiff thereby suffered extreme emotional distress."

   a. State all the facts upon which you base this claim.

   b. Provide the names of all witnesses who you contend support any or all of these facts.

c. For each such witness, provide legal name or name known by, last known address, and phone number.
d. Describe each document, including the person or persons who are in possession of and/or have control of each such document and its location, which you contend supports this claim.

After you file such contentious interrogatory, you can then follow it up with a request for admission. This will be particularly helpful if you get an incomplete response to your interrogatory or have left out of your interrogatories an area you wish you had covered. (For example, you may have failed to specifically inquire whether the emotional distress claim involves any physical injury as either a cause or result of the emotional distress. This would be significant in a jurisdiction where the right to recover for emotional distress without some associated physical injuries is not clear.) Thus, if you receive an incomplete response to your contentious Interrogatory 24, you can follow up with:

Request for Admission 3
Admit or deny: You suffered no emotional injuries as a result of . . .

If you inadvertently omitted the important issue of associated physical injury:

Request for Admission 4
Admit or deny: Your claim of emotional distress is not associated with any physical injury.

These requests for admission, following on the heels of your contentious interrogatories, are particularly valuable as tools for obtaining specific information, because if a party *denies* the allegation that is the basis of the request, she must then provide the factual basis (document, specific fact) that justifies the denial.

Second, be certain that your questions have a clear, specific meaning—that is, be sure that they are unambiguous. Note that even narrow questions can be ambiguous.

Interrogatory 9
Name all property, real and personal, which was given you as a gift by plaintiff between April and July 198X.
a. Name all vehicles you received, providing identification numbers.

The request for "all vehicles" is certainly narrow when compared with "all property," but it is ambiguous. What constitutes a "vehicle"? Car, bicycle, horse,

skateboard? Only motorized transportation? Are airplanes and boats included? Such ambiguity carries two problems. For those whose discovery philosophy is to find every excuse possible not to give information, such a question plays right into their strategy. ("Defendant can not answer plaintiff's Interrogatory 9, that question being too vague and ambiguous to permit a response.") For those whose discovery philosophy is to provide all information to which the other party is reasonably entitled, this question does not give sufficient guidance for providing the information.

Third, make certain that any information about persons or documents you do receive in response to your requests is sufficiently identified so you will be able to later locate it. Note the information that is requested concerning witnesses (addresses, phone numbers) and documents (location, custodian) back in Interrogatory 24, sub-parts c and d.

Fourth, you will have to create a "preamble" to open your written requests. This provides your personal, customized rules of the game that the opposing party must follow in answering. The preamble, which can be several pages in length, can include the particular party (spouse, corporation, partnership) to which the request is directed, the time for answering, definitions ("When using the term 'writing,' plaintiff means 'any transcription including film, video, tape recording'"), mechanics ("Answer within the space provided. If you need more space . . ."), and instructions concerning the information that is expected to be provided ("When a witness is provided, also include last known address and telephone number. If you cannot provide full information in response to a particular question, explain why you can't provide the information and when you plan to come in possession of such information"). Ideas for your preamble can come from form books, other attorneys' discovery papers, and your own previous preambles. But the precise preamble must be tailored to the individual needs of the particular case.

For a preamble to an interrogatory, see the interrogatory exhibit that is part of the civil pretrial protective order motion (pages 277-279). A deposition preamble is included in Dr. Croup's deposition excerpts (Case File Entry 56).

Ethically, an attorney is obligated to expedite litigation and not make frivolous discovery requests. ABA Model Rules 3.2 and 3.4(d). Grinding down the other side by submitting hundreds of generic questions from your interrogatory bank would seem to run afoul of these ethical guidelines. However, if a jurisdiction does not limit the number of interrogatories permitted (many jurisdictions do have a numerical limit, and some even count sub-parts as individual questions) and your questions are tailored to the particular case, there will be little practical chance of someone attacking your efforts on ethical grounds, no matter how voluminous your request. (You can even allege that, by providing thorough interrogatories, you are attempting to avoid the expense of depositions.) However, although it is unlikely you will be subject to formal sanctions for unethical behavior, what have you done to the overall mood of the case? You have probably turned it into a war of paper, with the other side responding in kind and your client paying the bills for the endless skirmishes and battles that will ensue.

Area Five
Representing a lay client or friendly non-party witness at a deposition; Taking the deposition of an adverse lay party or non-party witness

How do you prepare your client, or a witness who is friendly to your case, for a deposition by the opposing party? Should you meet with the deponent? For how long? What information for the deposition will you discuss with the deponent? What objections can you make? Which must you make? How do you plan to take the deposition of an adverse lay client or a non-party witness?

Let's start by considering a deposition where you are representing the deponent (at least during the deposition) and opposing counsel is taking the deposition. Preparing a deponent client or witness has two parts—preparing a deponent for the mechanics of a deposition and preparing the deponent for the substantive content of the deposition. In this section, we concentrate primarily on the mechanical aspects and provide you with a list of practical tips, although we do add a few thoughts on content too.

You should assume that most lay persons are not very familiar with the deposition process. So begin by explaining what a deposition is. Many attorneys do this by sending a letter that outlines all the information the deponent needs to know about his deposition. The letter might also include documents, diagrams, prior statements, or depositions that you want the deponent to be familiar with. Many attorneys in this electronic age also prepare a short (10-15 minute) videotape, which shows how a deposition looks. However, even with a prepared letter and a videotape, you will still want to meet with the deponent. You will want to discuss again most of the nuts-

and-bolts topics because the more the deponent hears about the mechanics, which can be presented in a number of different ways, the more familiar, and perhaps less intimidating, the deposition process might appear.

In your discussion you will want to provide a general description of a deposition including information about the ways a deposition can be used (admissions, impeachment, substantive evidence); travel routes to the deposition location (specific directions, map); appropriate dress (suggested or mandated by you); the persons who will be present (parties, attorneys, court reporter) and their roles; the oath; opening remarks of counsel (what they consist of and why they are made); objections to questions (how and when they are made, deponent's role when they are made); and finally your role at the deposition. (Generally your role will be passive. But there are some instances when you may find it essential to examine your client or friendly witness at the deposition: You might want to clarify misleading information lest the deponent's deposition be used at trial or for a particular purpose such as summary judgment; as such you will want to be certain that the deposition is correct and contains the information you need for your motion.)

You will want to give specific advice about the manner in which questions might be asked and how the deponent might respond. For instance, you might want to discuss the following with the deponent: the identity and function of the attorney who will be asking questions; the anticipated manner of opposing counsel (brusque? nice?); general strategies for responding to questions (listen carefully to the question, think, do not speculate, pause before answering); the purpose of objections; and the necessity that the deponent should listen to your directions as to how he should respond if you do object. You might want to provide the deponent with some caveats such as: do not guess in answering a question; do not argue with nor be lulled into friendship with the attorney; always consult with you when in doubt; answer the question asked without volunteering information; answer truthfully. (For a related discussion concerning counseling for a deposition, see Chapter IX at pages 352-354.)

Preparation for the content should in most cases include rehearsing the deposition with the deponent. You can do this with another attorney or a paralegal assistant playing the role of opposing counsel. You will want to religiously and painstakingly review prior statements, explanations for any potential inconsistencies in the deposition testimony, or any documents and diagrams that might be used. You should assume that your opponent has evaluated the content of his or her deposition strategy in the manner suggested at pages 196-199.

Finally, you will have to be prepared to make objections to opposing counsel's questions.

In most jurisdictions, you will need to object to errors or irregularities in the form of the question or answers. Unless a timely objection is made at the deposition, objections to the irregular form of the question will be deemed waived. That means you must object to questions that might be ambiguous, unintelligible, compound, too general, calling for a narrative answer, asked and answered, misquoting a witness, leading, argumentative, assuming fact not in evidence, or calling for speculation. Answers that are non-responsive also must be objected to or you may likewise waive the right to strike the answer if you make that request at trial. However, you do not need to object to evidentiary problems in the substantive content of the question or in testimony such as hearsay or inadmissible parol evidence. Those types of objections are preserved for trial and can be raised in that forum without first making a record at the deposition.

One important caveat is in order. These are two types of questions to which you should both object and instruct the witness not to answer—questions calling for information you believe irrelevant, and questions asking for information that is protected by some privilege (the most common examples we have encountered in litigation involve such privileges as attorney-client, work product, Fifth Amendment self-incrimination, and trade secrets). The reasons for this should be clear to you. If you reveal irrelevant information, you provide the very information you wanted to deny your opponent; if you provide possibly privileged information, you not only provide the information, but likely waive the privilege as well.

Now let's concentrate on how you prepare to take a deposition of an adverse lay client or a non-party witness. The preparation process is of critical importance; you cannot approach the deposition process aimlessly and wait until the time of the deposition to decide how you will proceed mechanically. Often, your objectives and the content and the mechanical aspects of taking a deposition are related. Your basic content planning (structured around topics in a manner analogous to the methods you used in interviewing) should be conducted using the types of analytic processes suggested earlier in this chapter at pages 196-199.

Alan E. Morrill, in section 12.5 of *Trial Diplomacy* (2d ed. 1972), recounts that there are 14 reasons for taking a deposition: impeachment; obtaining admissions; preserving evidence; appraising the opposition and its witnesses; calculating the issues; acquiring unknown facts and evidence; narrowing facts and the controversy; establishing support for summary judgment; expediting settlement; refreshing a witness's memory; exposing fraudulent claims; preparing for cross-examination; determining if all necessary parties have been joined; and committing the deponent to a definite version of the facts. Your purposes will dictate some of the nuts and bolts—when you will take the deposition (early or later in the litigation); the manner and thoroughness of your preparation; your elected demeanor.

Preparation includes *total familiarity with all the information* in your case file that pertains to the issues and the deponent (witness statements, prior testimony, documents).

Since you will be taking the deposition, you will need to set the time and place for the deposition. You need to notify all parties within the time frame specified by the rules. You need to decide whether to subpoena the deponent or send a notice (which depends on factors such as your relationship with opposing counsel and the witness's dependability). If you will need documents or particular exhibits when examining the deponent, you should obtain those before the deposition so you have time to study them. (Consider obtaining the materials you think you might need by sending a subpoena if the materials are held by non-parties or a request to produce if the materials are in the possession of a party.)

You must make arrangements with a reliable court reporting service—confirm by letter as to time, date, place, travel directions, set the approximate length or hours for the deposition, and anticipate specific needs such as a date for the transcribed transcript, fees, and so forth.

As preparation for the deposition, you will want to think about stipulations you will agree to or refuse to agree to, such as waiver of signatures or a specific time period for review of the deposition, as well as formalities you want to observe, such as having an oath given to a deponent or filing the deposition with the court. Therefore, be aware of the attorney who might try to sandbag you by beginning the deposition with, "Usual stipulations, counsel?" Find out what they might be! For example, one stipulation you should avoid is waiver of the deponent's reading and signing of the deposition once it is transcribed, because you might need to rely on using the deposition in circumstances where the signature is important to show that the deponent has verified the accuracy of the deposition. (A deponent has the right to read and correct a deposition and you want this done before trial, not while you are cross-examining; avoid the possibility of the deponent/witness declaring, "No. That's not what I said. . . . No. I've never read this deposition before.")

Before the deposition, try to anticipate objections. If opposing counsel does object, unless the objection concerns privilege or relevance, you should proceed and tell the deponent to respond to your question. Try to avoid being intimidated by opposing counsel and resulting interruptions.

If you are using exhibits, make sure well before the deposition that you have legible, facsimile copies (unmarked) that you can provide the deponent and opposing counsel while you are questioning. This will save time at the deposition. You will also need to give the court reporter a copy for inclusion with the transcript. When using a document, you will mark it as an exhibit and refer to it specifically so the transcript is clear and understandable.

At the deposition, there are a few mechanical practice tips that may help you. Opening remarks at the deposition are of prime importance. Be sure that you have the witness given an oath and that you deliver a complete preamble specifying the rules of the deposition (see Entry 57 in the case file for the preamble included in Dr. Croup's deposition excerpts). Be sure that confidential files and documents are left in your office. Any papers, documents, or notes that you do bring should be taken with you if you leave the room unattended. Think about your demeanor at the deposition. A friendly demeanor might help you obtain information if that is your purpose. On the other hand, some attorneys believe that hostility and belligerence might help the flow of information by provoking the deponent to reveal information.

Closing remarks are equally important as opening remarks. Consider an effective wrap-up question: "Is there anything you would like to add to any of your responses? Or do you want to correct anything you stated?"

Area Six
Representing an expert witness at a deposition; Taking the deposition of an expert

What if opposing counsel asks to stipulate to take your expert's deposition; should you agree? How will you prepare your expert witness for a deposition by opposing counsel? How will you prepare to take opposing party expert witness depositions? Can you question about everything?

This section discusses some of the issues you must consider in preparing your expert for a deposition to be taken by opposing counsel and in your own preparation for taking opposing party expert witness depositions. Many of the nuts-and-bolts aspects of lay depositions also apply to expert witness depositions. We encourage you to reread Area Five as one preparation for considering expert witness depositions.

The first issue you must consider is procedural. Are all your experts subject to being deposed by opposing counsel? Recall that experts are treated separately according to Federal Rule of Civil Procedure 26(b)(4). Commonly, only those experts who will be testifying at trial are subject to discovery and then discovery is generally limited to sending a limited type of interrogatory to opposing counsel. Depositions are only available if the court issues a court order or if the parties stipulate. If an expert will not be testifying at trial, that expert may not be subject to discovery unless exigent circumstances exist. And some experts who are "informally" consulted (the question of what is an informal consultation is subject to analysis) are never subject to discovery.

You must next focus on the actual preparation of your expert witness for his or her deposition. You should explain, just as you did with lay deponents, the deposition process as a whole (if the expert has never been deposed) and review the substantive content for the deposition.

One important nuts-and-bolts issue to consider when dealing with an expert is scheduling. You should inform opposing counsel of the scheduling needs of your expert and communicate the date for the deposition to your expert. The more each counsel cooperates on technical points, the easier the process is on everyone.

Prior to the deposition, have your expert assemble her full file on the case—that is, all the information the expert relied on in rendering an opinion. You should work with your expert to ensure that the file is complete and so you can maintain in good faith that only those items that you will claim are privileged have been removed. The necessity for this preparation becomes clear as you proceed to prepare your expert for the content of the deposition—the anticipated subject matter of the questions.

Topics that will be the subject of the deposition will generally include all those areas that are ripe for cross-examination. Generally, these areas include the possibility of bias (compensation, time spent on case, prior history of consultations and for whom); qualifications (to testify, particular expertise); reliability of scientific area (treatises, procedures or tests, instruments used, acceptability by others); underlying factual data and investigation used in rendering the opinion (time spent, data given to the expert, data developed through testing and investigation by the expert, data relied on that is acceptable in the field); and the expert's opinion (consistency with treatises, the factual data, other opinions by your expert).

You should review all of these areas with your expert. In particular, your expert should understand and be familiar with the assignment and the limit of the opinion that you requested. You should have your expert review prior opinions, data, and cases testified about in order to ensure consistency in the expert's factual basis and opinion. Some caveats are in particular order. Caution your expert about being too talkative, going to extremes in his or her opinion, speculating, or wandering far from his or her expertise.

Now we want to shift gears and discuss taking an opposing party expert witness deposition. This is a very difficult task, but clearly one you can master by following certain rules, all of which require your utmost concentration on planning and preparation. As always, think about your objectives—look back to the list of 14 reasons to take a deposition discussed in Area Five (page 204). Primarily, you will be concerned about obtaining admissions to help your case theory and information to prepare for cross-examination to blunt your opponent's case theory.

The easiest way to prepare is to work with your own expert as a consultant to help you review the five areas that might be fruitful for cross-examination: bias; qualifications; scientific area; factual data; the opinion. Your expert can help you formulate questions that will expose any weaknesses and can also help you prepare to ask questions that pin down areas of agreement.

You must also become something of a "mini-expert" in the field. Ask your expert to recommend treatises, then read them, talk to other attorneys who have handled similar cases, and meet with your expert so you understand all aspects of the expert's field. Research and read everything that the adverse expert has written, try to obtain transcripts of other cases in which he or she has testified, talk to attorneys who have been involved with or who are knowledgeable about the adverse expert. Have your expert talk to her colleagues to find out about the adverse expert's standing in the field, personality, and work habits. In other words, both you and your expert will immerse yourselves in the adverse expert and his field. Clearly, however, the extent to which this advice can be carried out must always be weighed against economic and time constraints.

Before the deposition, you should obtain the adverse expert witness's file and have your expert review it. Unfortunately, this might not be possible. If you do not receive the file until the deposition, do not despair. Ask your expert to be in your office or at a place near where the deposition is proceeding so your expert can review the adverse expert's file and help you formulate specific questions. And remember that you can continue the deposition, although that is an expensive, time-consuming, and irritating option for everyone. (Perhaps suggesting that this option might be necessary can convince your adversary to aid you in obtaining the adverse expert's file well before the day of the deposition.)

Depending on your objectives, your questions should allow the expert to "talk" with you, giving you information as to all aspects and ideas that the expert has about your case. Ask as many questions as it requires to fully understand all aspects of the expert's opinion. This means developing the full scope of each topic you examine. (Unless, of course, the deposition is a substitute for trial testimony, then it will follow the conventions of a standard cross-examination at trial.)

This Area simply highlights the issues that you should think about when considering expert witness depositions. You may wish to consult specialized texts that can give you clear examples for questioning particular types of witnesses. See Am. Jur. 2d, Proof of Facts (1984) (an encyclopedia source that contains checklists, examples, and trial transcripts for all types of expert witnesses).

Area Seven
Determining whom to serve with a discovery request

Will you use interrogatories to try to determine who is in possession of the information you are seeking? How will you get jurisdiction over non-parties? Custodians of documents? Federal agents in a state case? In a criminal case, will you serve discovery requests on both the prosecution and the police?

As already discussed, interrogatories and depositions can be used to discover the identities and locations of non-party witnesses in a civil case. Non-parties can then be subpoenaed into a deposition. Once so subpoenaed, they can also be asked to bring documents and records with them (subpoena duces tecum). In a criminal case, the names of witnesses may be found in police reports, through a formal request for a witness list, or (if the particular jurisdiction permits or requires) through testimony at a preliminary hearing. However, the police are not third parties. While in many jurisdictions they exist administratively as totally separate agencies from the prosecution, they are part of the same executive branch of government as the prosecution and, even after arrest, they often have the principle responsibility for investigation in the case. (Some prosecutors' offices have their own investigative arms.) Nevertheless, the police will commonly have their own investigative files for a case that frequently contain information that is not in the prosecution's file. While arguments can be raised that serving the prosecution with a discovery request should be deemed to be equally a request to the investigating police, and some jurisdictions' court rules or customs specifically require disclosure of all information in the hands of "law enforcement," it is safest to also serve a copy of your request on the police. This avoids the possibility of a moment at trial when the prosecution brings information you have never seen before, but was covered by the court's discovery order: "I'd never seen this information before myself until this morning when Officer Smith showed me the police investigative file in this matter. I guess I just never got a copy of this document from the police."

Area Eight
Anticipating objections to your discovery request

Will you make your requests less broad? Will you break up your requests into smaller, more specific parts? Will you try to lay a foundation to overcome an anticipated claim of privilege?

This latter concern is, of course, a central focus of the hypothetical beginning at page 199.

Area Nine
Determining when to make a motion to compel discovery

What weight will you give to the significance of the information you are seeking? To your time and other tasks to be done in this (and perhaps other) cases? To the overall behavior of your adversary in discovery? What bearing will the cost to your client have on your decision?

In both criminal and civil cases, it is common practice that the party seeking discovery initially files a request for discovery with the opposing party, resorting to the court with a motion for discovery (criminal) or motion to compel discovery (civil) if some or all of the requested information is not forthcoming. (In the criminal area, the request and the motion are often filed at the same time, with the areas the parties can agree on being settled prior to the hearing on the motion. As already noted, however, there are jurisdictions where the plaintiff voluntarily "opens its files" to the defendant, obviating these formal processes in most cases.) Whether or not to bring a motion to compel will be determined by at least two types of considerations beyond the plausibility of your position—the importance of the information that is being withheld and the general behavior of the opposing party in discovery. In this latter regard, you may seek to compel the discovery of even relatively minor information (although you are likely to include it in a single motion to compel with more significant information that has also been withheld); if the opponent has been unreasonable throughout discovery, this instance will expose that unreasonableness, and you want this behavior to be seen by the court. Your hope is that the court, seeing this unreasonable behavior, will get involved and assist you in the future in obtaining reasonable access to information in your opponent's possession. Also, by bringing the motion, you show your opponent that you are willing to go to the trouble of filing a motion and to argue in court in order to obtain that to which you are entitled. This may give the opponent second thoughts before refusing any particular requests for discovery in the future.

Area Ten
Making a sufficient record of your discovery request

Will you make a list of all discovery voluntarily provided by your adversary? Will you file this list with the court? Will you detail on the record the justification for a request that has been objected to in a deposition? Will you file detailed declarations in support of subpoenas duces tecum? Will you articulate your case theory in a motion to compel? In what detail?

All of these questions contain good suggestions for this Area. The point is that in your record you want to (1) detail what you are requesting; (2) articulate all the reasonable steps you took to obtain the discovery from your opponent before you were forced to resort to a formal motion; and (3) explain clearly why, under applicable legal standards, you are entitled to the information.

Area Eleven
Drafting a motion to compel discovery

What will your motion contain? What form will it take? Under court rules and statutes, must you first meet with your opponent in an attempt to resolve your discovery dispute before bringing such a motion? If so, must the results of this meeting appear in a written affidavit or declaration in support of your motion? What else will you put in your affidavit or declaration? Will you seek the costs involved in bringing your motion from the opposing party?

To give you a general sense of the form of the motion, a model pretrial civil motion for a protective order appears at page 274. Though not a motion to compel, the format of this motion will prove instructive for you. Similarly, a criminal pretrial discovery motion (see page 214) can give you a feeling for the appropriate form and structure. You also can consult Chapter VIII and the suggested motion format at page 263.

You can find information specifically pertaining to a motion to compel discovery in court rules, from local attorneys and court clerks, and from the types of sources detailed earlier in this chapter at page 192. In many jurisdictions, a motion to compel in a civil case may be accompanied by a request for costs (i.e., your attorney fees attendant to bringing the motion) and sanctions (a fine). In civil cases, costs may be awarded even if the opposing party acted in good faith in refusing discovery. Sanctions require a finding of bad faith or, at least, unreasonableness. As a practical matter, sanctions are rarely imposed unless there is a history established in the case that reveals a pattern of dilatory behavior on the part of your opponent. Courts simply do not like to call either party "bad." On the other hand, courts currently are becoming far less tolerant of the extensive delays occasioned by the parties' behavior in discovery and, in fact, are beginning to see this as a major problem in the system. Increased use of sanctions may therefore be forthcoming.

Area Twelve
Determining the appropriate manner for responding to an opponent's discovery request

What must you answer under statutory rules (e.g., the Federal Rules of Civil Procedure or case law)? Will you read the requests technically (narrowly, literally) so as to give as little information as possible? Will you jeopardize your credibility with the court if you are too technical or literal? Will you raise any objections to the discovery requests? Will you raise any claims of privilege? Will you seek protective orders? What are the ethical limits of opposing discovery?

Begin your response by reading the instructions provided by the preamble. If anything is unclear, do not guess at the meaning. You always should have a clear idea of what the other party is seeking before answering. Assuming that you are not sure what is being requested, however, what will you do? For attorneys whose philosophy of discovery is to withhold as much as possible (one technique of which is to deny information if any word in the request is ambiguous), this will provide the opportunity to return the request a month or so later indicating that, due to the particular lack of clarity, they could not provide any response. Attorneys whose philosophy of discovery is that each side should provide all requested information to which a party is reasonably entitled, will call or write opposing counsel indicating their desire to respond, and will request any clarification that is required to accomplish this end. We fall into this latter group. This decision has a sufficient practical basis that we do not need to emphasize the ethical dimension. (It is unethical to "fail to make reasonably diligent efforts to comply with a legally proper discovery request," ABA Model Rule Rules 3, 4(d).) Like the example of oppressive interrogatories discussed under Area Four, two can play at the find-an-excuse-not-to-answer game. If you respond in this way, a response in kind is not unlikely. And so the case, and not improbably your client's resources, will go. (Or, maybe worse, the other side will play it straight, and bring home your contrasting approaches regarding "the truth" and willingness to be forthcoming with information to the judge.)

Also consistent with this position is our belief that you should attempt to assess the reasonable meanings of discovery requests and then try to provide complete, unambiguous responses (by giving an answer, referring to a document also available to the other party, or attaching a copy of the document). Of course, you should be certain that in providing answers you are not giving away privileged information or opening the door for a possible claim that you have waived a privilege. Before you file your response, therefore, comb through its text with a checklist of possible privileges in mind (attorney-client; work product; physician-patient). If you do feel that some request delves into privileged terrain, you can raise an objection to that request as your answer. ("Defendant objects to Request for Production of Documents, number 6 as asking for privileged Attorney-Client information.") Before you raise such a claim, however, be certain that it is well-founded. If such a refusal to provide information is brought before the court by your opponent on a motion to compel and you lose, even if you are clearly in good faith, courts will often assess the opponent's costs (attorney's fees, travel) to your client. Also, if the court does not regard your objection as well-conceived, you may lose credibility on subsequent legal positions you take in discovery.

Area Thirteen
Storing and indexing the discovery you have received

Will you index the discovery by witness, elements of the offense, or cause of action to which it pertains? Will you keep it in files? Trial binders?

What you will do will depend largely on personal preference and the extent of information involved. In a small criminal case, you may keep all your information in a single file folder. In a complex antitrust suit, you may have a warehouse full of documents that are cross-indexed on a computer. In any event, you do need some system that permits both quick retrieval of information and fast correlation of the information to those aspects of your case theory or negotiations to which the information is relevant.

QUESTION 2
Which of these practical/strategic situations will you deal with at this point?

Initially, in our hypothetical about the rear-end collision and the road sign (page 199), you must determine whether you will pursue formal or informal information-gathering and, if formal, which specific discovery devices you will employ (Area One).

QUESTION 3
What are your objectives in this situation?

You want information about the defendant and the road sign and must choose a means for obtaining it. In choosing the best method for obtaining that information, you will probably have a number of factors in mind. You need a method from which you can clearly determine what defendant will say about the road construction sign. Your informal contact may have been mistaken, and defendant may never have claimed to have seen the sign. Or he might qualify his statement—"Thinking back over it all, I have an impression that there was some kind of temporary sign." You also want the flexibility to pursue defendant's responses if he now claims to have seen the sign, probe the basis of his claim, judge his credibility, and "set up" possible impeachment for trial.

QUESTION 4
How will you achieve your objectives?

You have to select an information-gathering device that will fit the situation. But which one? Informal information-gathering does not seem to be a viable choice. Since defendant is represented, it would be unethical for you or your agent to talk to him without first contacting his attorney, and defense counsel is extremely unlikely to sanction such an interview. If for some reason counsel did permit the interview, it is likely to be under controlled circumstances that would make any real probing on your part extremely difficult. So you opt for formal discovery, but which device? You could send an interrogatory asking defendant if he saw the sign, but this method carries a number of limitations. You cannot view the defendant while he answers and, therefore, cannot judge his credibility. Defendant has total control of his response, including its specificity or lack thereof, and you cannot pursue his answer with clarifying follow-up questions. (The turn-around time between filing your request for an interrogatory and receiving a response that you could then follow up might be a matter of months.) When you finally receive defendant's response, he may have objected to your question or provided a legally inadequate reply (one that is conclusory or non-responsive). You would then have to pursue a sometimes lengthy process of compelling compliance in the trial court. Further, even if compelled, defendant's next response may be little better (e.g., incomplete), which will require you again to go into court. In all probability, you technically would have to repeat this cycle several times, with accompanying delay, in pursuing this single response. Finally, by focusing defendant on the significance of the road sign, you may have tipped him off and permitted him a lengthy time period in which to fashion a response. Requests for admission, which generally are served near the end of discovery in regard to non-contentious factual information and the authentication of potential exhibits, suffer drawbacks similar to interrogatories. Also what would you ask defendant to admit? That he never saw the road sign? This would hardly be non-contentious. So, by process of elimination, your best choice is a deposition (assuming the issue warrants the expense—of course, in a case such as the rear-end collision, you would likely have planned to take defendant's deposition in any event).

QUESTION 5
What problems do you anticipate?

You've worked through choosing a means for information-gathering and have decided on a deposition. This choice will, in turn, present a whole new range of potential practical or strategic situations. At this point, we will focus on four specific situations. They are not the only four that could arise, or necessarily the most significant. They are selected because they represent a variety of situations you might encounter: (1) The court reporter may cancel out at the last moment; (2) the defendant/deponent may not appear; (3) defense counsel may disrupt the deposition; (4) legal objections may impede your attempt to "set up" impeachment. The first three are self-explanatory, the fourth not so. Accordingly, we will analyze this last possible problem of legal objection in depth.

Based on what you now know, it is not unlikely that at his deposition the defendant will testify as follows:

Plaintiff's Attorney: And where were you driving?
Defendant: I was going to work. It was a different route than I've taken before—or since.
Plaintiff's Attorney: Can you recall what occurred in the few moments before the collision?
Defendant: Sure. I saw this "SLOW DOWN CONSTRUCTION" sign, and started to brake.

At that point you may decide that, if the case is tried, you would like to take the position with the jury that, if the defendant had really seen the sign, it would be improbable that he would leave this information out of his original statement. Accordingly, you will begin to seek information at the deposition that could serve as a predicate for trial cross-examination and closing argument in support of this desired position. (You may wish to review the discussion under Area Five of planning and taking a deposition.)

Thus, at the **deposition,** you would ask about the timing and circumstances of defendant's statement to the police. At **trial,** you would use this information to cross-examine: "When you gave your statement, things were fresh in your mind?" In **closing argu-**

ment, you would use the information from cross-examination: "Defendant certainly had the ability to give the most accurate information—that day, soon after the accident, when he told you the incident was fresh in his mind, and time and self-interest had not had the opportunity to distort his memory. Yet, nowhere in his statement does he mention the sign."

Likewise, at the **deposition,** you would ask about defendant's desire to cooperate with the police, the officer's patience in taking his statement, and so on. At **trial** you would again use this information to cross-examine: "You wanted to give the police complete information? . . . You wanted to tell everything that was important? . . . You even told them what you were playing on your tape deck moments before the accident?" And, in **closing argument,** you would use the information from cross-examination: "And he had the opportunity to tell his whole story. He told you how he wanted to tell the police everything that was important. He told you how patient the officer was in taking his statement. We can see that, because he even told the officer what was playing on his tape deck. A little insignificant detail in a statement filled with details. No. Defendant had plenty of time to tell his story and made every effort to make a complete one. Yet, nowhere in his statement does he mention the sign."

Finally, at the **deposition,** you would delve into the police investigation of the scene; the fact that police were talking to both parties and to witnesses; defendant's concern that he could be "mistakenly" cited and blamed. At **trial,** you would once more use this information to cross-examine: "You knew the police were trying to determine whom to cite when they took your statement at the scene of the accident? . . . You didn't want to be cited, did you? . . . You wanted to make it clear that it was not your fault? . . . You wanted to impress the police that you were driving safely?" In **closing argument,** you would use these final pieces of information from cross-examination: "And, boy, did he have a motive to tell everything that could make him look careful in the eyes of the officers! He told you that he knew the police were interviewing him, the plaintiff, and witnesses on the scene. He told you he knew the police were trying to decide whom to cite for the accident. He told you that he didn't want it to be him. Well, with his fresh memory, and not being rushed in making his statement, wouldn't he mention something that would make it more likely he was being careful? Wouldn't he mention seeing the sign? That is, *if* he saw the sign. Yet, nowhere in his statement does he mention the sign."

Just when you are feeling confident about this strategy, you are confronted with some disturbing information. Your investigator has found out that construction was completed, and the sign taken down, within ten hours after the accident. In fact, the sign was there only that one day.

You now face a problem if you try to use information generated by the deposition/cross-examination you have been planning to convince the jury that defendant must not have seen the sign. Understandably, the jury will wonder how defendant would have known about the sign if he had not actually seen it on the one day it was standing. You have an idea, however. You want to develop information from which you will be able to argue to the jury that the idea of seeing the sign came to the defendant only *after* he saw the police report. This information, coupled with the type of cross-examination discussed above, will also provide the basis for a line of impeachment that goes far beyond this single factual allegation about the sign: (1) that defendant is embellishing his story; (2) that from the fact that defendant engaged in such embellishment, the factfinder should infer that he has a motive to distort the truth; and (3) that that motive is based on an awareness of his own culpability in the automobile collision and a desire to avoid the consequences of that culpability. (Of course, plaintiff may contend that seeing the report jogged his memory of the sign for the first time, but you could still point out to a jury the unlikelihood of this in light of the circumstances and detail of his initial statement.) In planning how you will obtain this information in the deposition, however, you can anticipate a troubling scenario for which you must also plan:

Plaintiff's Attorney: You met with your attorney prior to this deposition?

Defendant: Yes.

Plaintiff's Attorney: Your attorney showed you Plaintiff's Exhibit 6, the initial police report, didn't she?

Defendant's Attorney: Objection. I will instruct my client not to answer that question based on the attorney-client privilege.

QUESTION 6
How will you meet such problems?

Let's begin with the fourth concern, the objection, and then move to the other three potential problems.

The legal objection. At this point, you don't know if counsel will object on the basis of the attorney-client privilege. But what if she does? You may be able to convince her to abandon the objection, yet, at the

same time, you must be aware that counsel may hold fast to her position and you may need to invoke the power of the trial court with a motion to compel. Accordingly, you want to begin to build a "record" that will tend to undercut this objection of attorney-client privilege. So imagine that counsel claims the privilege, thereby barring your access to the information you desire.

You could begin by trying to convince opposing counsel that the privilege does not apply, while at the same time building a record by stating on the record, for example, "Counsel, you must have misunderstood me. I am not asking for any *communications,* only for what was physically done. That is not privileged." Counsel, however, may not be convinced: "It is clearly a communication. In effect, you're asking 'Did your attorney advise you to review the police report?' " Or she may believe you won't go through the time and expense to bring a motion to compel this helpful, but not vital, piece of information, especially since the objection lies in the extremely sensitive area of attorney-client privilege. If she takes this position, you can then change your questioning in a way that weakens the objection, making the record such that counsel may become aware that she will not appear in a good light with the court if you are forced to make a motion to compel. For instance, you might reword your question as follows: "Since you gave your statement to the police, you've seen the police report, haven't you?" (Notice that the way you pose the question now does not mention counsel, nor does it seek information as to exactly where or when defendant saw the report.)

Now, focus on how you could deal with the other three concerns that we anticipated could arise:

The reporter canceling. This is a matter for preventive medicine. You could reduce the chances of a reporter canceling by obtaining the name of a reporter from an attorney you respect who has personally found the reporter reliable. (Of course, even the most reliable people can get the flu. Depositions can be rescheduled.)

The absent deponent. If you subpoena the defendant to his deposition, rather than just serving a Notice on a Party to Appear, you can invoke the power of the court if he fails to show up. This is likely to serve both as a substantial deterrent to his not appearing in the first place and provide a ready tool to utilize the court's power to ensure a definite appearance on his part at a subsequent deposition in the event of an initial failure to attend.

The offensive opponent. There are three basic principles for dealing with the obnoxious or disruptive attorney in a deposition. One: Stay calm. Do not get diverted from your objectives—ask the questions you must and delve into the areas you intended (even if these attempts are repeatedly met by unreasonable objections). Two: Make your "record." Consider that you will have to go to the trial court. Three: Do not respond in kind. Be professional and reasonable. The trial court will review the transcript. Make certain the equities are clear.

QUESTION 7
If you can't solve the problems, what will you do?

Imagine that the first three problems did not materialize but the fourth did: Opposing counsel is adamantly holding to her objection of attorney-client privilege.

None of your strategies has convinced her to change her position. You even reworded the question, but counsel is still not willing to abandon her objection. In fact, she states on the record: "The only place he would have reasonably seen that report was from me. Your question still asks my client to reveal what is implicitly an attorney-client communication."

What will you do? You can bring a motion to compel if you determine it is worth the time and resources. You may, after all, already be bringing a motion to compel, and raising this issue only means adding another paragraph to your papers. If you decide to seek court enforcement, you should draft a motion emphasizing both the relevance of this information ("the whole case is a credibility contest between plaintiff and defendant, and this strikes at the core of defendant's credibility") and citing your record, which demonstrates that you are only asking if defendant has seen the report, not inquiring into any privileged communications. What if the court denies your motion? You can still do your "set-up" impeachment on cross-examination and argue the appropriate inferences to the jury; but dealing with the "how did he know about the sign?" problem may not be easy.

QUESTION 8
What ethical constraints do you face in attempting to achieve your objectives?

As long as opposing counsel had a reasonable, good faith basis for her position, she was ethically entitled to maintain her objection. Similarly, you were enti-

tled to oppose her objections and argue your position to the court as long as you were in reasonable good faith. ABA Rules 3.3(a)(3), 3.4(d). Terminating and walking out of a deposition you are conducting will not generally run afoul of ethical rules unless it is done as a deliberate delay tactic,[7] ABA Rule 3.2, or to embarrass or harass the deponent, ABA Rule 4.4. Once at trial, you may argue your position to the jury as long as you do not make representations of facts that are not properly in evidence. ABA Rule 3.4(e). Thus, you could argue, "You may ask from what source could defendant have suddenly come up with this road sign, which he didn't mention in his careful, detailed statement, if he hadn't actually seen it? That's an easy one. Isn't it likely he subsequently saw the police report?"

E. PLANNING QUESTIONS

You have considered various factors important in preparing for discovery, and the rationale for each. Following is a series of general questions; you may want to refer to them and expand on them in planning your discovery.

 I. *Objectives*
    1. What possible objectives can you achieve through discovery?
    2. Which ones will motivate your discovery efforts in the present case?
    3. What is your "basic task"?
 II. *Preparation*
    1. What background preparation must you do in order to plan for discovery in this case?
    2. What will you look at? Who will you talk to?
 III. *Content Planning*
    A. *Obtaining Information*
        1. What areas do you want to focus on for discovery?
           a. What guidance do you find in the elements of plaintiff's legal theory? The elements of defendant's affirmative defenses?
           b. What guidance do you find in plaintiff's and defendant's factual theories?

---

7. Although, if there was no good reason for terminating, the court might well grant the opponent's protective order barring a subsequent deposition should you try to reschedule after walking out.

2. Think about the areas you have chosen to focus on:
   a. What information do you want in each of these above areas?
      (1) What is the relationship of this information to your case theory?
      (2) Which sources (receptacles) might contain the above information?
      (3) Who (or what entity) might have control over such sources?
      (4) What information will you seek that bears on (a) motions (b) evidentiary foundations?
   b. Do you want an opportunity to "create" information? What information?
      (1) How would this information fit into your case theory?
      (2) Who can create it (e.g., some expert)?
   c. What possible sources could contain and/or have control over information you would like?
      (1) What types of information are these sources likely to have?
      (2) How would this information fit into your case theory?
   d. What, if any, information could your adversary, or a third person with influence on your adversary (e.g., the complaining witness in a criminal case), have that would make your adversary want to change his or her position (settle the case, dismiss it) rather than turn over the information?
   e. How can you tie this sensitive information to your case theory so you can justify requesting it?
3. What are the legal standards for discovery in your jurisdiction?
4. What is the relationship of the concept of a case theory to these standards?
5. How specifically do each of your discovery requests meet such standards?

B. *Reassessment and Reevaluation (After Receipt of Discovery)*
   1. What information did you obtain in discovery?
   2. How does this information affect your case theory?
   3. How does it affect your representational strategy?
   4. What other information will you now seek through formal and informal fact-gathering?

IV. *Performance Planning*
   A. *Technical Skills*
      1. Looking at the information you want, how will you frame your request so that the opposition cannot reasonably claim to have misunderstood what you were seeking?
      2. How will you make a record so that it will clearly support (a) a motion to compel; (b) an appeal?
      3. What part does your case theory play in making a good record?
      4. What objections to discovery could (theoretically) be raised by your adversary?
         a. Do any seem to apply here?
         b. What is their legal basis?
         c. Can you frame your requests so as to avoid or weaken such objections?
         d. Would you bring a motion to compel this discovery?
            (1) What will be your position?
            (2) What will be your opponent's?
            (3) Will you try to negotiate to settle your disagreement?
            (4) What role does the cost and your time play in your decision whether to bring such a motion?
      5. If served with a discovery request:
         a. How much information will you provide in your response?
         b. Will you object to any requests?
         c. Upon what legal basis?
         d. When will you seek a protective order?
         e. What will be your position if your adversary tries to compel your compliance in a motion to the court?
   B. *Nuts-and-Bolts Matters*
      1. What are the local procedures regarding discovery?
      2. How specifically will these procedures affect your request?

3. What types of discovery devices are available to you?
   a. Which seem appropriate to your case?
   b. How will you use such devices?
   c. Will you employ these devices before, during, or after informal discovery?
   d. How will you sequence these formal discovery devices relative to one another?

C. *Ethical Considerations*
1. Will you limit the amount and scope of information you will request to what is "reasonable"?
   a. How do you determine what is "reasonable"?
   b. Does it matter whether your opponent's client has fewer resources than your client?
2. What is your duty regarding responses to your opponent's discovery requests?
   a. As an advocate, shouldn't you try to keep information that is harmful to your position from your adversary if possible? At the least, shouldn't you provide as little information as you can justify under the law?
   b. Why can't you raise any objection that has a plausible legal basis?
   c. If your opponent did not frame a request with precision so (technically) it does not ask for what the opponent really wants, can you follow the technical meaning even though you know what was really intended? Are there practical reasons not to do this?
   d. Is delay always bad?
      (1) What if delay is in your client's interest? Is in both parties' real interests?
      (2) Even if delay in the particular case is not bad, may you use the discovery process as a tool to effectuate this goal (as opposed to, e.g., moving for a continuance)?
3. Considering advice regarding destruction of documents:
   a. What will you tell the client if:
      (1) no complaint has been filed, but the suit is in the offing?
      (2) a complaint has been filed?
      (3) the destruction would have taken place anyway during the normal course of business?
   b. Even if not unethical, how do you anticipate your opponent would use such destruction if the case goes to trial?

APPENDIX. SAMPLE CRIMINAL DISCOVERY MOTION*

HARRY C. SWINGS
1201 Market Street
Jamner, Major 98455
Telephone: (206) 999-8999

SUPERIOR COURT OF MAJOR
JAMNER COUNTY

| STATE OF MAJOR,
Plaintiff,

vs.

ALAN HENRY KRUB aka
MART FIRS,
Defendant. | No. CR 76-0106 ESE

Motion for Discovery and Inspection
(with Memorandum of Authorities) |

*This is a representative sample taken from an actual criminal discovery motion. It is not, however, intended to be a perfect model. There are many different formats one could use to present a discovery motion.

TO THE HONORABLE EDWARD S. ELLIS, Judge of the Superior Court of Major for Jamner County:

The defendant, by his counsel, requests this Court pursuant to case law and the Due Process Clauses of the Fifth and Fourteenth Amendments to the Constitution of the State of Major to order the District Attorney to produce and permit the defendant to inspect, copy, or photograph each of the following, which are now known to be or are in the possession of the government or any of its agents or which through due diligence would become known from the investigating officer, or witnesses or persons having knowledge of this case:

1. All tangible objects obtained during the investigation in this case, including:

a. All tangible objects obtained from defendant's person or effects.

b. Tangible objects obtained from the person, effects or vehicle driven by defendant, or any home, apartment, or motel room rented by defendant.

2. All books, paper, documents, or tangible objects the government plans to offer in evidence in this case.

3. Books, paper, documents, or tangible objects upon which the government relied in returning the indictment against the defendant, or which the government plans to offer in evidence in this case.

4. All property in the possession of the government or its agents or seized by the government or its agents belonging to or alleged by the government to belong to defendant.

5. All fingerprint impressions, blood samples, clothing, hair, fiber, or other materials obtained by whatever means or process from the scene of the offense and whether such fingerprint impressions, blood samples, clothing, hair, fiber or other materials were those of defendant, or were those of some other person or persons known or unknown.

6. All comparisons of blood, fingerprints, clothing, hair, fiber, or other materials made in connection with this case, particularly including:

a. Original photographs of any latent fingerprints obtained in the investigation of this case, together with the time, place, and manner in which the latent fingerprint was developed and photographed.

b. Copies of all enlarged photographs or other reproductions of the latent fingerprint used for purposes of comparison, including both marked and unmarked copies of any enlargement or reproduction from which unique identification was accomplished.

c. Complete report of the identification procedure employed, including notation of all points of identification which were isolated and used for comparison.

d. Copies of all original and/or enlarged photographs of inked fingerprints used for comparison with latent fingerprint pictures.

7. The written report of any chemical analysis of the alleged plant material seized, prepared by the government or any of its agents or anyone at its direction, together with descriptions, test results, test dates, and determinations as to the nature or weight of said substance.

8. All results or reports of physical or mental examination (e.g., handwriting, fingerprints, drug analyses).

9. All statements, confessions, or admissions made by defendant, whether written or oral, subsequently reduced to writing, or summarized in officers' reports, or copies thereof, within the possession, custody, or control of the government, the existence of which is known or by the exercise of due diligence may become known to the attorneys for the government. This request includes statements made to witnesses other than police officers at any time prior to or subsequent to defendant's arrest, including the precise

words attributed to defendant which caused government agents to conclude that defendant was "associated" with other co-defendants.

10. All documents, instruments, forms, or statements of any kind signed or purported to have been signed by the defendant.

11. All statements of co-conspirators, whether written or oral, subsequently reduced to writing, or summarized in officers' reports, or copies within the possession, custody, or control of the government, the existence of which is known or by the exercise of due diligence may become known to the attorneys for the government.

12. All names and addresses of persons who have knowledge pertaining to this case, or who have been interviewed by the government or their agents in connection with this case.

13. All FBI and local arrest and conviction records of all persons in Paragraph 12 the government plans to call as witnesses.

14. Written statements of all persons in Paragraph 12 whom the government does not plan to call as witnesses.

15. The transcript of testimony of all persons who testified before the Grand Jury in this case.

16. The name, identity, and whereabouts of any informer who gave information leading to the arrest of defendant, and whether the informant was paid by the government for such information.

17. All materials now known to the government, or which may become known, or which through due diligence may be learned from the investigating officers or the witnesses or persons having knowledge of this case, which is exculpatory in nature or favorable material or which might serve to mitigate punishment, and including any evidence impeaching or contradicting testimony of government witnesses or instructions to government witnesses not to speak with or discuss the facts of the case with defense counsel.

18. Any information pertaining to misconduct or bad acts attributable to the informant or any government witness.

19. Information pertaining to consideration or promises of consideration given to any witnesses.

20. Information pertaining to the number of times that any witness who is not an agent of the State of Major has testified for the government before a tribunal, or any other body.

21. Information pertaining to any current or potential prosecution of any witness to be called by the government.

22. All information pertaining to personnel files on any witness to be called by the government, including whether or not such files exist, where they are, and how they are identified.

23. Provide the same records and information set out in items 18-22 with respect to each non-witness declarant whose statements are to be offered in evidence.

24. State whether the government obtained any information or evidence relating to this case by means of electronic listening devices, wire taps, or any form of electronic surveillance. State the circumstances under which such surveillance or eavesdropping was conducted. Provide a copy of any written transcript prepared from the eavesdropping, and an opportunity to listen to and copy electronically all such recordings.

25. State whether the government obtained any information or evidence relating to this case, or the defendant, by means of searches or seizures. For each search and seizure:

a. List the names of the law enforcement agencies and officers participating in the search or seizure, or contributing information leading to the search and seizure.

b. List the places searched or seized, the dates, and the items or information obtained.

c. Provide the name of any informant used to establish probable cause who might reasonably provide information bearing upon the guilt or innocence, or sentencing.

d. List the names of any law enforcement agencies or officers to whom the results of any search or seizure were forwarded, disclosed, or made available.

26. Provide defense counsel with a statement describing in detail the methods and procedures used to identify the defendant and/or co-participants as the perpetrators of the offenses alleged in the indictment.

a. The names and addresses of all persons to whom photographs were exhibited for the purpose of identification, and when and where these displays took place.

b. Copies of all photographs exhibited for the purpose of identification in connection with this case.

c. The names and addresses of those persons who identified the defendant and/or any known co-participant from these photographs as a perpetrator of this offense, and those who were unable to identify these persons.

MEMORANDUM OF POINTS AND AUTHORITIES IN SUPPORT OF MOTION FOR DISCOVERY AND INSPECTION

"In our adversary system for determining guilt or innocence, it is rarely justifiable for the prosecution to have exclusive access to the storehouse of relevant facts. . . . [I]t is especially important that the defense, the judge and the jury should have the assurance that the doors that may lead to truth have been unlocked." *State v. Darby,* 205 Maj. 2d 274, 281 (1963).

"Courts of this state have consistently exercised their discretionary powers to provide defense-discovery in criminal cases broadly, consistently ordering discovery of the tangible evidence and information in possession of the government and police which could 'reasonably be used in, or lead to the development of, a defense at trial,' *State v. Karme,* 100 Maj. App. 3d 420, 422 (1975)." *Kincade v. Superior Court,* 169 Maj. App. 3d 333, 337 (1979).

Under *State v. Darby, supra,* and *Kincade v. Superior Court, supra,* all the requested information is properly discoverable.

Respectfully submitted,

_____

Harry C. Swings
Attorney for defendant
1201 Market Street
Jamner, Major 98455
Telephone: (206) 999-8999

CRIMINAL PROBLEM: STATE v. HARD

PROBLEM 57

Defense Attorney: Seeking Discovery from the Government

Ed Hard finally obtained bail. A wealthy relative provided the cash premium and even threw a nice little party to celebrate Ed's release. You know, however, that unless you can obtain ultimate vindication for Ed or some lesser objective as the goal of your representational strategy there is little cause for celebration. So back to work. Fact-finding in the context of your tentative case theory is now your dominant concern. You want to learn more about the prosecution's case, including its strengths and weaknesses, and to discover evidence that you may want to present should you choose to present a case. While organizing your approach to witness interviews, you are simultaneously planning a formal discovery motion in order to obtain all the information that is in the possession of the government.

For this problem, assume that the *only* documents that you have received from the case file at this point are the police reports.

PREPARATION

READ: (1) Pretrial Case File Entries 4, 75; (2) Chapters VII and VIII. Now think about and answer the following questions:

1. The prosecution has obtained a great deal of information. You must carefully plan a discovery request in order to gain access to this information.

   a. What information will you seek in light of your theory of the case? Why?

   b. Why is it reasonable to think that the prosecution may have this information?

   c. Do you want this information *before* you do any witness interviews? Why?

      1) If so, are there practical problems with delaying the interviews? Explain.

      2) How will you resolve this dilemma?

      3) Does your answer depend upon the length of the delay? The particular witness? Anything else?

2. Should you request information from the investigating police agencies as well as the prosecutor? Why or why not?

3. What is the legal basis for a position that discovery may be addressed to investigating police as well as the prosecution?

4. Suppose FBI agents have been involved in this state court case.

   a. Do you anticipate problems requesting the state court to order FBI agents to provide you with the fruits of their investigation?

b. Do you have any ideas (including legal theories) about how you will deal with these problems?

5. The prosecutor may offer to provide you with "open file" (informal) discovery.

   a. Are there any problems if in following this procedure you make no record of what you sought or received? Explain.

   b. Discuss how you would avoid such problems.

6. What is the nature of the prosecution's duties under *Branty v. State,* 201 Maj. 2d 86 (1962), and *State v. Augie,* 228 Maj. 2d 118 (1968)? (See Case File Entry 75.)

7. What is the relationship between the nature of your discovery request at the trial level, and the application of *Branty/Augie* principles on appeal?

ASSIGNMENT FOR CLASS

1. Outside of class, plan your discovery requests. Be able to explain how each request is likely to lead to information relevant to your case theory. Write a short memorandum summarizing your planning, preparation, and analysis, and give a copy to your supervisor.

2. In class, be prepared to discuss discovery planning for the defense of Ed Hard, including the specific information that you would seek in a discovery motion.*

CIVIL PROBLEMS: SUMMERS v. HARD

PROBLEM 58 _____
Plaintiffs' and Defendants' Attorneys: Discovery Planning

Summers v. Hard progressed through theorizing, informal interviewing, pleading, and response. Plaintiffs and defendants have even had extensive discussions concerning arbitrating or mediating the case. But, alas, no agreement was reached. Settlement also was rejected since the facts are not entirely evident. Therefore, it appears that the parties will proceed with the litigation process (or a similar representational strategy).

The next stage of the litigation process involves formal discovery. It is important to plan what discovery devices will be used, to whom they will be directed, and what items, things, and facts need to be discovered. Discovery planning is particularly important since many courts require that each party submit a discovery plan in order to control the discovery process.

---

*Your instructor may also require that you draft a formal request for discovery (see, e.g., Appendix II at Page 214), including a statement explaining how *each* of your requests fulfills the legal standard expressed in *Kincade v. Superior Court,* 169 Maj. App. 3d 333 (1979) (see page 217). In this event, the prosecution will be given special instructions that deal with complying with or resisting your discovery requests.

PREPARATION

READ: (1) Pretrial Case File Entries 1-39, 59, 60, 63, 82, 90; (2) Chapter VII; (3) Fed. R. Civ. P. 26-37. Now think about and answer the following questions:

1. What are your representational strategies?

2. Explain how discovery will help you achieve your representational strategies.

3. List the discovery devices available.

4. Discuss the advantages and disadvantages of each discovery device.

5. Can you use all the discovery devices as much as you want? Explain.

6. How will you decide which devices to use?

7. How will you decide what information you need? What will you consult?

8. Which discovery devices will you use to obtain the information you described?

9. Will you use the discovery devices in any particular sequence? Explain.

10. Do you anticipate any objections by your opponents?

    a. What, if any, objections do you anticipate?

    b. What response will you have? Why?

11. Using Federal Rule of Civil Procedure 26(f), what are the critical aspects of your discovery plan as to:

    a. Issues you want to explore in discovery?

    b. Devices you will use?

    c. Sequence of devices?

ASSIGNMENT FOR CLASS

1. Outside of class, prepare a written discovery plan. Your plan should detail the devices you will use and what items, things, and facts you need to discover. You should also describe any anticipated objections in obtaining the described items. Give your senior partner a copy of your proposed discovery plan.

2. In class, be prepared to discuss your discovery plan.

PROBLEM 59 _____
Plaintiffs' and Defendants' Attorneys: The Discovery Conference

Summers v. Hard has progressed through theorizing, informal interviewing, pleading, and response. The parties are proceeding with the litigation process and are planning formal discovery.

Any party or the court may request a discovery conference. (The discovery conference referred to is specified in Federal Rule of Civil Procedure 26(f).) Discovery conferences institutionalize, through court order, discovery planning in terms of the issues, permissible discovery, and scheduling, and attempt to resolve anticipated discovery problems. The court has requested a discovery conference.

PREPARATION

READ: (1) Pretrial Case File Entries 1-39, 59-61, 63, 82, 90; (2) Chapter VII; (3) Fed. R. Civ. P. 26-37 and 45. Now think about and answer the following questions:

1. Federal Rule of Civil Procedure 26(f) provides that a discovery conference is discretionary.

    a. What factors would influence your decision to request a discovery conference? Explain.

    b. How will the discovery conference affect your representational strategies?

2. Discuss the advantages and disadvantages to plaintiffs in having a discovery conference.

3. Discuss the advantages and disadvantages to defendants in having a discovery conference.

4. If you were a judge, would you on your own motion order the attorneys in *Summers v. Hard* to a discovery conference? Explain.

5. Suppose you decide that you want a discovery conference. Federal Rule of Civil Procedure 26(f) (1)-(4) sets forth the topics that must be addressed: statement of the issues; a proposed plan and schedule for discovery; proposed limitations; proposed orders. For each of these topics:

    a. List your position.

    b. Predict your opponent's position.

    c. Analyze the differences between your statement of the issue and your opponent's.

    d. Analyze the differences between what you will request as to your discovery plan and schedule and your opponent's request.

    e. Analyze the differences between what limitations on discovery you and your opponent will request.

    f. Analyze the differences between what proposed discovery orders you and your opponent will request.

6. Federal Rule of Civil Procedure 26(f) provides that "each party and his attorney are under a duty to participate in *good faith* in the framing of a discovery plan if a plan is proposed by the attorney for any party [emphasis added]." What do you think is the meaning of good faith?

ASSIGNMENT FOR CLASS*

1. Outside of class, attorneys for plaintiffs and defendants prepare a memorandum discussing the points listed in Federal Rule of Civil Procedure 26(f) (1)-(4). Provide copies to the court and all respective attorneys.

2. In class, meet with the judge in a discovery conference to discuss the memoranda.

PROBLEM 60

Plaintiffs' and Defendants' Attorneys: Written Discovery Requests
(Interrogatories; Requests for Documents; Subpoenas; Requests for Admission)

Summers v. Hard has progressed through theorizing, informal interviewing, pleading, and response. The parties are proceeding with the litigation process and formal discovery.

  You have drafted a discovery plan for *Summers v. Hard* that sets forth the discovery you need to complete. It is time to commence written discovery. Plaintiffs' and defendants' attorneys have prepared a list of written discovery requests that should be drafted. Since discovery appears to be extensive, you will have to be careful in selecting which written discovery to pursue.†

PREPARATION

READ: (1) Pretrial Case File Entries 1-39, 59, 60, 63, 82, 90; (2) Chapter VII; (3) Fed. R. Civ. P. 26-37 and 45.

Plaintiffs' Written Discovery Requests

Interrogatories

1. *Interrogatories to Defendant M.C. Davola:* Outline the areas you would ask interrogatories on and draft no more than ten interrogatories.

2. *Interrogatories to Defendant Mary Apple:* Outline the areas you would ask interrogatories on and draft no more than ten interrogatories.

3. *Interrogatories to Defendant Tom Donaldson:* Outline the areas you would ask interrogatories on and draft no more than ten interrogatories.

---

  *Your instructor may suggest that, instead of your writing a memorandum, the procedures set forth in Rule 26(f) be followed. In that case, your instructor may select either plaintiffs' or defendants' attorney to submit a motion to which the other party responds. After the exchange of the motion and response, the parties should meet and attempt to resolve their differences before meeting with the judge at the discovery conference.

  †Your instructor may select one of the discovery requests included in the following list for you to draft.

4. *Interrogatories to Defendant Ed Hard:* Outline the areas you would ask interrogatories on and draft no more than ten interrogatories.

Requests for Documents

5. *Requests for Documents, Things, and Entry Upon Land for Inspection Addressed to Defendants M.C. Davola, Mary Apple, and Tom Donaldson:* Outline the documents and things you would want and draft no more than ten requests.

6. *Requests for Documents and Things Addressed to Defendant Ed Hard:* Outline the documents and things you would want and draft no more than ten requests.

Subpoena Duces Tecum

7. *Subpoena Duces Tecum Addressed to Non-Parties:* Identify who the non-parties are and draft one subpoena, identifying precisely the items to be produced.

Requests for Admission

8. *Request for Admission Addressed to Defendant M.C. Davola:* Outline the areas you would ask admissions on and draft no more than ten requests for admission.

9. *Request for Admission Addressed to Defendant Mary Apple:* Outline the areas you would ask admissions on and draft no more than ten requests for admission.

10. *Request for Admission Addressed to Defendant Tom Donaldson:* Outline what areas you would ask admissions on and draft no more than ten requests for admission.

11. *Request for Admission Addressed to Defendant Ed Hard:* Outline the areas you would ask admissions on and draft no more than ten requests for admission.

Defendant Davola's Written Discovery Requests

Interrogatories

1. *Interrogatories to Plaintiff Deborah Summers:* Outline the areas you would ask interrogatories on and draft no more than ten interrogatories.

2. *Interrogatories to Plaintiff Gretchen Summers:* Outline the areas you would ask interrogatories on and draft no more than ten interrogatories.

3. *Interrogatories to Plaintiff Hans Summers:* Outline the areas you would ask interrogatories on and draft no more than ten interrogatories.

4. *Interrogatories to Defendant Ed Hard:* Outline the areas you would ask interrogatories on and draft no more than ten interrogatories.

5. *Interrogatories to Plaintiff Ronny Summers:* Outline the areas you would ask interrogatories on and draft no more than ten interrogatories.

6. *Interrogatories to Plaintiff Amanda Summers:* Outline the areas you would ask interrogatories on and draft no more than ten interrogatories.

Requests for Documents

7. *Requests for Documents and Things Addressed to Plaintiffs Deborah Summers, Ronny Summers, and Amanda Summers:* Outline the documents and things you would want and draft no more than ten requests.

8. *Requests for Documents and Things Addressed to Plaintiffs Gretchen and Hans Summers:* Outline the documents and things you would want and draft no more than ten requests.

9. *Requests for Documents and Things Addressed to Defendant Ed Hard:* Outline the documents and things you would want and draft no more than ten requests.

Subpoena Duces Tecum

10. *Subpoena Duces Tecum Addressed to Non-Parties:* Identify who the non-parties are and draft one subpoena, identifying precisely the items to be produced.

Requests for Admission

11. *Request for Admission Addressed to Plaintiff Deborah Summers:* Outline the areas you would ask admissions on and draft no more than ten requests for admission.

12. *Request for Admission Addressed to Plaintiffs Gretchen and Hans Summers:* Outline the areas you would ask admissions on and draft no more than ten requests for admission.

13. *Request for Admission Addressed to Plaintiffs Ronny and Amanda Summers:* Outline the areas you would ask admissions on and draft no more than ten requests for admission.

14. *Request for Admission Addressed to Defendant Ed Hard:* Outline the areas you would ask admissions on and draft no more than ten requests for admission.

Defendant Ed Hard's Written Discovery Requests

Interrogatories

1. *Interrogatories to Defendant M.C. Davola:* Outline the areas you would ask interrogatories on and draft no more than ten interrogatories.

2. *Interrogatories to Defendant Mary Apple:* Outline the areas you would ask interrogatories on and draft no more than ten interrogatories.

3. *Interrogatories to Defendant Tom Donaldson:* Outline the areas you would ask interrogatories on and draft no more than ten interrogatories.

4. *Interrogatories to Plaintiff Deborah Summers:* Outline the areas you would ask interrogatories on and draft no more than ten interrogatories.

5. *Interrogatories to Plaintiff Gretchen Summers:* Outline the areas you would ask interrogatories on and draft no more than ten interrogatories.

6. *Interrogatories to Plaintiff Hans Summers:* Outline the areas you would ask interrogatories on and draft no more than ten interrogatories.

7. *Interrogatories to Plaintiff Ronny Summers:* Outline the areas you would ask interrogatories on and draft no more than ten interrogatories.

8. *Interrogatories to Plaintiff Amanda Summers:* Outline the areas you would ask interrogatories on and draft no more than ten interrogatories.

Requests for Documents

9. *Requests for Documents, Things, and Entry Upon Land for Inspection Addressed to Defendants M.C. Davola, Mary Apple, and Tom Donaldson:* Outline the documents and things you would want and draft no more than ten requests.

10. *Requests for Documents and Things Addressed to Plaintiffs Deborah Summers, Ronny Summers, and Amanda Summers:* Outline the documents and things you would want and draft no more than ten requests.

11. *Requests for Documents and Things Addressed to Plaintiffs Gretchen and Hans Summers:* Outline the documents and things you would want and draft no more than ten requests.

Subpoena Duces Tecum

12. *Subpoena Duces Tecum Addressed to Non-Parties:* Identify who the non-parties are and draft one subpoena, identifying precisely the items to be produced.

Requests for Admission

13. *Request for Admission Addressed to Defendant M.C. Davola:* Outline the areas you would ask admissions on and draft no more than ten requests for admission.

14. *Request for Admission Addressed to Defendant Mary Apple:* Outline the areas you would ask admissions on and draft no more than ten requests for admission.

15. *Request for Admission Addressed to Defendant Tom Donaldson:* Outline the areas you would ask admissions on and draft no more than ten requests for admission.

16. *Request for Admission Addressed to Plaintiff Deborah Summers:* Outline the areas you would ask admissions on and draft no more than ten requests for admission.

17. *Request for Admission Addressed to Plaintiffs Gretchen and Hans Summers:* Outline the areas you would ask admissions on and draft no more than ten requests for admission.

18. *Request for Admission Addressed to Plaintiffs Ronny and Amanda Summers:* Outline the areas you would ask admissions on and draft no more than ten requests for admission.

ASSIGNMENT FOR CLASS

1. Outside of class, draft the discovery request assigned to you. Give your senior partner a copy of your discovery request.

2. In class, be prepared to discuss your written discovery request.

PROBLEM 61 _____

Plaintiffs' Attorney: Preparing a Client for a Deposition
(Deborah Summers)

Summers v. Hard has progressed through theorizing, informal interviewing, pleading, and response. Attorneys for plaintiffs and defendants are proceeding with formal discovery.

As Deborah's attorney, you received a notice from defendants pursuant to Federal Rule of Civil Procedure 30(b)(1) to take the oral deposition of your client Deborah Summers on November 1, 198X + 1. It will be necessary for you to prepare Deborah for her deposition.

PREPARATION

READ: (1) Pretrial Case File Entries 1-41, 47, 48, 51, 55, 59-61, 63, 64, 82, 90; (2) Chapter VII; (3) Fed. R. Civ. P. 26, 29-32, 37. Now think about and answer the following questions:

1. Should you prepare Deborah for her deposition or just let her be "natural"? Explain.

2. Will you provide Deborah with information about a deposition before meeting with her? A letter? Documents? Photographs? Explain.

   a. Can defendants' attorneys ask Deborah about the information, documents, etc. you provided them to prepare for the deposition? Explain.

   b. If the information was privileged before deposition preparation, is that privilege now waived? Explain.

3. Discuss how you will explain the deposition process to Deborah.

4. Will you have Deborah bring anything to the meeting in which you prepare her for the deposition (e.g., notes, photographs)?

5. Will you prepare Deborah for using a diagram of the Unicorn Tavern at the deposition? Why?

6. Suppose that Deborah tells you that she is planning to withhold information about her personal life from opposing counsel at the deposition.

   a. What are your ethical obligations (to your client, your adversary, yourself)?

   b. Explain what you will do.

ASSIGNMENT FOR CLASS

1. Outside of class, prepare written questions as your deposition preparation. Hand in your written deposition preparation to your senior partner.

2. In class, prepare your client, Deborah Summers, for her deposition.

PROBLEM 62 _____

Attorney for Defendant Davola: Preparing a Client for a Deposition
(Mary Apple)

Plaintiffs and defendants are proceeding with the litigation process and formal discovery.

As Mary Apple's attorney, you received a notice from plaintiffs pursuant to Federal Rule of Civil Procedure 30(b)(1) to take the oral deposition of one of your clients, Mary Apple, on October 16, 198X + 1.

PREPARATION

READ: (1) Pretrial Case File Entries 1-39, 44, 59-61, 63, 82, 90; (2) Chapter VII; (3) Fed. R. Civ. P. 26, 29-32, 37. Now think about and answer the following questions:

1. Should you prepare Mary Apple for her deposition or just let her be "natural"? Explain.

2. Will you provide Mary Apple with information about the deposition before meeting with her? (A letter? Documents? Photographs?) Explain.

3. Discuss how you will explain the deposition process to Mary Apple.

4. Will you have Apple bring anything to the meeting with you in which you prepare her for the deposition (e.g., notes, photographs)?

5. Will you prepare Mary for using a diagram of the Unicorn Tavern at the deposition? Why?

6. Suppose that Mary Apple tells you: "I am indebted to Mr. Davola and the salary raise he recently gave me. I think this lawsuit stinks." What, if anything, will you say to Apple? Why?

ASSIGNMENT FOR CLASS

1. Outside of class, prepare written questions as your deposition preparation. Hand in your written deposition preparation to your senior partner.

2. In class, prepare your client, Mary Apple, for her deposition.

PROBLEM 63

Attorney for Defendant Hard: Preparing a Lay Witness for a Deposition
(John Gooding)

Plaintiffs and defendants are proceeding with formal discovery.

John Gooding has telephoned you, defendant Hard's attorney, regarding the subpoena he received for a deposition by plaintiffs' attorney on October 15, 198X + 1. He wants to know whether you want to see him before the deposition. You tell him of course you want to see him and arrange an appointment.

PREPARATION

READ: (1) Pretrial Case File Entries 1-39, 45, 59-61, 63, 82, 90; (2) Chapter VII; (3) Fed. R. Civ. P. 26, 29-32, 37. Now think about and answer the following questions:

1. Is preparing John Gooding identical to preparing a client for a deposition? If not, how does it differ?

2. Will you send anything to John Gooding about the deposition process before meeting with him? Explain what you would send.

3. What are your objectives in preparing John Gooding for his deposition?

4. Is it advisable to go through the questioning process with John Gooding as if it were a "real" deposition? Explain.

5. Will you prepare John Gooding for using a diagram of the Gull Gas Station at the deposition? Explain how you would.

6. Suppose John Gooding tells you: "Just tell me what to do and say. I want to help Ed."

   a. What are your ethical obligations (to your client, your adversary, the deponent, yourself)?

   b. Explain what you will do.

ASSIGNMENT FOR CLASS

1. Outside of class, prepare written questions as your deposition preparation. Give your written questions to your senior partner.

2. In class, prepare John Gooding for his deposition.

PROBLEM 64

Attorney for Defendant Davola: Preparing an Expert Witness for a Deposition
(Dr. Thomas Monday, Economist)

Plaintiffs' and defendants' attorneys have agreed that all experts who will testify at trial can be deposed without a court order. Defendant Davola hired an expert witness to present the valuation of Bruno Summers' life and refute the opinion of plaintiffs' economist, Dr. Bruce Hann. The deposition of defendant's economist has been scheduled to be taken at the law office of plaintiffs' attorney at 9:00 A.M. on October 5, 198X + 1.

PREPARATION

READ: (1) Pretrial Case File Entries 1-39, 42, 43, 52, 54, 59-61, 63, 82, 90; (2) Chapter VII; (3) Fed. R. Civ. P. 26, 29-32, 37. Now think about and answer the following questions:

1. Is there anything you should do before meeting with Dr. Monday?

2. Will you provide Dr. Monday with anything that explains a deposition before your meeting? Explain.

3. Are there documents or things that Dr. Monday should bring or not bring to the meeting with you? Explain.

4. What will you tell your expert about bringing things to the deposition (such as his notes and worksheets)?

5. Suppose that Dr. Monday tells you that he can testify only with notes.

    a. Should he bring notes to the deposition?

    b. His file?

6. Will you go through the questioning process as if it were a real deposition? Explain.

7. What will you advise as to objections?

    a. Can you anticipate what objections you may assert? Explain.

    b. Should you tell your economist to refuse to answer objectionable questions?

8. Suppose Dr. Monday has a habit of dressing in blue jeans and blue work shirts when he is not officially working at his employment. Should you tell him how to dress for the deposition? Why or why not?

9. Should you tell Dr. Monday specfic words or phrases to use in answering questions at the deposition?

10. List the specific differences between preparing an expert witness for deposition and preparing a lay witness client.

ASSIGNMENT FOR CLASS

1. Outside of class, prepare written questions as your deposition preparation. Hand in your written deposition preparation to your senior partner.

2. In class, prepare your economist, Dr. Thomas Monday, for his deposition.

PROBLEM 65

Plaintiffs' Attorney: Taking the Deposition of an Adverse Witness
(Rebecca Karr)

You are proceeding with formal discovery. As you may recall, Rebecca Karr is a friend of Ed Hard's. She was at the Unicorn Tavern with Ed on August 20 and September 3, 198X.

You sent a subpoena to take the deposition of Rebecca Karr. The deposition is scheduled for October 16, 198X + 1 at 9:00 A.M. at your office. Attorneys for defendants Davola and Hard will be attending the deposition. They may examine the deponent if time permits.

PREPARATION

READ: (1) Pretrial Case File Entries 1-39, 59-61, 63, 82, 90; (2) Chapter VII; (3) Fed. R. Civ. P. 26, 29-32, 37. Now think about and answer the following questions:

1. Specifically, how will you prepare for taking the deposition of Rebecca Karr?

2. Why send Rebecca Karr a subpoena to take her deposition?

3. Suppose that Ed Hard wants to attend the deposition and appears at your office with Rebecca Karr.

   a. What will you do or say? Why?

   b. What do you anticipate would be Ed Hard's attorney's response to your position? Why?

4. What are your objectives in deposing this witness?

5. What topics will you cover in the deposition?

   a. Will you follow a particular sequence in the topics you will cover in the deposition?

   b. Why?

6. Rebecca Karr was the person who told Ed Hard that Bruno Summers was a neo-Nazi survivalist.

   a. Will you ask Rebecca Karr about this topic? Explain.

   b. You would like to have the court rule that any evidence that Bruno Summers was a neo-Nazi survivalist is inadmissible. Are there any questions that you can ask Ms. Karr that will help you make the neo-Nazi information inadmissible? Explain.

   c. If you question her about this topic, what specific questions will you ask?

7. Suppose that you ask Rebecca Karr about the August 20, 198X incident between Hard and Summers, and Ms. Karr states: "I do not remember." What will you do?

8. Is it ethical for defendant Hard's attorney to tell Rebecca Karr not to answer a clearly objectionable question? Explain.

9. Defendants can examine the deponent.

    a. Should Hard examine Rebecca Karr? Why or why not?

    b. Should Davola examine Rebecca Karr? Why or why not?

10. Suppose that Hard's attorney decides to examine Rebecca Karr at the deposition.

    a. What topics should Hard select?

    b. Why?

11. Suppose that right after the deposition Rebecca Karr relocates 3,000 miles from the jurisdiction in which *Summers v. Hard* is pending.

    a. Can any of the parties use Rebecca Karr's deposition if Ms. Karr did not read or sign the deposition?

    b. If Ms. Karr read and signed the deposition, are there other objections that any attorneys could raise against using the deposition at trial? Explain what they could be and how they might be avoided.

ASSIGNMENT FOR CLASS*

1. Outside of class:

    a. **Plaintiffs' attorney:** Prepare written questions that you intend to ask in the deposition.

    b. **Attorneys for defendants Hard and Davola:** Prepare a written outline of what you think will be covered in the deposition. (**Attorney for defendant Hard:** If you have not already done so, prepare Rebecca Karr for her deposition.)

    c. **Both plaintiffs' and defendants' attorneys:** Hand in your written preparation of the deposition to your senior partner.

2. In class:

    a. **Plaintiffs' attorney:** Conduct the deposition of Rebecca Karr.

    b. **Attorneys for defendants Hard and Davola:** Attend the deposition, and, if desired, examine Rebecca Karr.

PROBLEM 66
Plaintiffs' Attorney: Taking the Deposition of an Adverse Party
(Tom Donaldson)

Plaintiffs' attorney sent a notice to take the deposition of Tom Donaldson.

Plaintiffs' attorney served written interrogatories on Tom Donaldson. In response to an interrogatory requesting information about Ed Hard's appearance, demeanor, or drinking the night of September 3, 198X,

---

*Your instructor may select which attorneys will examine the deponent and the topics to be covered in the deposition.

Donaldson refused to answer the interrogatories, claiming that to answer would incriminate him. Plaintiffs' attorney has decided to depose Donaldson instead of compelling answers to the interrogatories.

Defendant Davola's attorney, representing Donaldson, has prepared Donaldson for this deposition. The deposition is scheduled for October 1, 198X + 1 at 9:00 A.M. at the law office of plaintiffs' attorney. Attorneys for defendants Hard and Davola will be attending the deposition. They may examine the deponent if time permits.

PREPARATION

READ: (1) Pretrial Case File Entries 1-39, 44, 59-61, 63, 82, 90; (2) Chapter VII; (3) Fed. R. Civ. P. 26, 29-32, 37. Now think about and answer the following questions:

1. As plaintiffs' attorney, what are your objectives in deposing Tom Donaldson?

2. What topics will you examine? Explain.

3. Suppose defendant Davola's counsel (or defendant Hard's counsel) begins the deposition stating: "Let us adopt the standard stipulations, counsel." How should you respond?

4. Suppose that a few days before this deposition is scheduled you learn that Tom Donaldson made a rough diagram of the scene at the Unicorn Tavern. You would like to see the diagram and question him about it.

    a. How will you obtain the sketch to use at the deposition?

    b. Why do you want the sketch?

    c. What will you do?

5. Suppose that you ask Mr. Donaldson: "Tell me about Ed Hard's appearance on the night of September 3, 198X." Donaldson states: "I refuse to answer on the grounds it may incriminate me."

    a. What is the basis for Donaldson's refusal?

    b. What options do you have if Donaldson continues to refuse to answer questions on the topic of Ed Hard's drinking, demeanor, or appearance?

    c. What will you do? Why?

6. Suppose that at the end of the deposition Mr. Donaldson states, "I was very nervous and I think I may want to change some answers that may not be correct."

    a. Can Mr. Donaldson change his answers?

    b. As plaintiffs' attorney, what would you say or do?

7. Suppose that Mr. Donaldson changes some critical answers that are material to the issues.

    a. List all the things plaintiffs can do.

    b. What do you advise doing? Explain why.

8. Should defendants examine the deponent? Explain.

9. Can defendants use leading questions in examining this deponent? Why?

ASSIGNMENT FOR CLASS*

1. Outside of class:

   a. **Plaintiffs' attorney:** Prepare written questions that you intend to ask in the deposition.

   b. **Attorneys for defendants Davola and Hard:** Prepare a written outline of what you think will be covered in the deposition. (**Attorney for Defendant Davola:** If you have not already done so, prepare Tom Donaldson for his deposition.)

   c. **Both plaintiffs' and defendants' attorneys:** Hand in your written preparation of the deposition to your senior partner.

2. In class:

   a. **Plaintiffs' attorney:** Conduct the deposition of Tom Donaldson.

   b. **Attorneys for defendants Davola and Hard:** Attend the deposition, and, if desired, examine Tom Donaldson.

PROBLEM 67

Plaintiffs' Attorney: Taking the Deposition of an Adverse Witness
(John Gooding)

You believe that John Gooding will be a key witness for Ed Hard. He is a good friend of Ed's and was with Ed on August 26 when Bruno Summers allegedly threatened Ed Hard. He was also at the Unicorn Tavern on August 20 and September 3, 198X.

You have sent a notice to take the deposition of John Gooding. The deposition is scheduled for October 1, 198X + 1 at 9:00 A.M. at your law office. Attorneys for defendants Davola and Hard will be attending the deposition. They may examine the deponent if time permits.

PREPARATION

READ: (1) Pretrial Case File Entries 1-39, 59, 60, 63, 82, 90; (2) Chapter VII; (3) Fed. R. Civ. P. 26, 29-32, 37. Now think about and answer the following questions:

1. As plaintiffs' attorney, what are your objectives in deposing John Gooding?

2. What topics will you examine? Explain.

   a. What sequence will you examine?

   b. Why?

---

*Your instructor may select which attorneys will examine the deponent and the topics to be covered in the deposition.

---

3. Will you use a diagram of the Gull Gas Station in questioning John Gooding? Why or why not?

4. Suppose that you ask John Gooding about his knowledge of the characters and reputations of Bruno Summers and Ed Hard. John Gooding responds: "Ed Hard is a beautiful human being. He's a kind and gentle friend. Bruno Summers was a violent man, with an uncontrollable temper." Will you ask any additional questions on this topic? Why or why not?

5. Suppose that defendant Hard's attorney chooses to examine the deponent and begins the deposition stating, "Although the shooting incident took place over a year ago, Mr. Gooding is still very upset. Mr. Gooding may have to take frequent recesses because of his emotions. I hope you will understand and show him the utmost courtesy and respect for his feelings." What response, if any, will you as plaintiffs' attorney have? Why?

6. Is it ethical for defendant Hard's attorney to tell John Gooding not to answer a clearly objectionable question? Explain. What should you as plaintiffs' counsel do?

7. Defendants can examine the deponent:

   a. Should defendant Hard's attorney examine John Gooding? Why or why not?

   b. Should Davola's attorney examine John Gooding? Why or why not?

8. Suppose that Davola's attorney examines John Gooding at the deposition.

   a. What topics should Davola's attorney select?

   b. Why?

   c. Should Davola's attorney inquire into Gooding's knowledge of the characters and reputations of Bruno Summers and Ed Hard?

9. Suppose that attorneys for defendants Hard and Davola use leading questions in examining John Gooding.

   a. Can they? Explain.

   b. What, if anything, should you as plaintiffs' attorney say or do? Why?

10. Suppose that during the deposition John Gooding wants to correct one of his answers. Can he?

11. Suppose that the deposition is sent to John Gooding, but it is returned unopened, indicating John Gooding did not read nor sign it.

    a. List all the things that plaintiffs can do.

    b. What do you advise doing? Explain why.

ASSIGNMENT FOR CLASS*

1. Outside of class:

   a. **Plaintiffs' attorney:** Prepare written questions that you intend to ask in the deposition.

   b. **Attorneys for defendants Hard and Davola:** Prepare a written outline of what you think will be covered in the deposition. (**Attorney for defendant Hard:** If you have not already done so, prepare John Gooding for his deposition.)

   c. **Both plaintiffs' and defendants' attorneys:** Hand in your written preparation of the deposition to your senior partner.

2. In class:

   a. **Plaintiffs' attorney:** Conduct the deposition of John Gooding.

   b. **Attorneys for defendants Hard and Davola:** Attend the deposition, and, if desired, examine John Gooding.

PROBLEM 68

Attorney for Defendant Hard: Taking the Deposition of an Adverse Party
(Deborah Summers)

Summers v. Hard has progressed through theorizing, informal interviewing, pleading, and response. Attorneys for plaintiffs and defendants are in the midst of the litigation process and formal discovery.

Defendant Ed Hard's attorney sent a notice to take the deposition of Deborah Summers. The deposition is scheduled for November 1, 198X + 1 at 9:00 A.M. at the law office of Hard's attorney. Attorneys for plaintiffs and Davola will be attending the deposition. They may examine the deponent if time permits.

PREPARATION

READ: (1) Pretrial Case File Entries 1-39, 40, 41, 48, 59-61, 63, 82, 87, 90; (2) Chapter VII; (3) Fed. R. Civ. P. 26, 29-32, 37. Now think about and answer the following questions:

1. What are your objectives in deposing Deborah Summers?

2. What topics will you examine? Explain.

3. Suppose that plaintiffs' counsel begins the deposition stating: "Let us adopt the standard stipulations, counsel." How should you as defendant Hard's counsel respond?

4. Are there documents or things that you would like to question Deborah Summers about?

   a. What are they?

---

*Your instructor may select which attorneys will examine the deponent and the topics to be covered in the deposition.

---

b. If there are, how will these documents be included in the deposition?

5. Suppose that you ask Deborah Summers if she has a boyfriend. Deborah's attorney answers: "She refuses to answer."

a. Why are you interested in this information?

b. Have you posed an objectionable question? Explain.

c. List all the ways that you could obtain the information if plaintiffs' attorney continues to instruct Deborah to refuse to answer the question.

6. Suppose that at the deposition you, defendant Hard's attorney, have asked Ms. Summers: "Did you ever experience emotional problems before?" Deborah responds: "No." You have information that indicates that Deborah Summers prior to this lawsuit has seen a psychologist.

a. Should you tell Deborah that you have written documents that she has seen a psychologist? Explain.

b. What will you do if Deborah's attorney requests to see the documents?

c. What action, if any, should Deborah's attorney take after Deborah responds? Why?

7. Suppose that during the deposition Ms. Summers states: "You just want to make me sound like a liar." What action, if any, will you take? Why?

8. Do you anticipate that plaintiffs' counsel will examine the deponent? Explain.

9. If plaintiffs examine Deborah at the deposition, can they use leading questions in examining her?

ASSIGNMENT FOR CLASS*

1. Outside of class:

a. **Attorney for defendant Hard:** Prepare written questions that you intend to ask in the deposition.

b. **Attorneys for plaintiffs and defendant Davola:** Prepare a written outline of what you think will be covered in the deposition. (**Plaintiffs' attorney:** If you have not already done so, prepare Deborah Summers for her deposition.)

c. **Both plaintiffs' and defendants' attorneys:** Hand in your written preparation of this deposition to your senior partner.

2. In class:

a. **Attorney for defendant Hard:** Conduct the deposition of Deborah Summers.

b. **Attorneys for plaintiffs and defendant Davola:** Attend the deposition and, if desired, examine Deborah Summers.

---

*Your instructor may select which attorneys will examine the deponent and the topics to be covered in the deposition.

PROBLEM 69

Attorney for Defendant Hard: Taking the Deposition of an Adverse Party
(Gretchen Summers)

Gretchen Summers, Bruno's mother, can be a key witness for plaintiffs as to damages and Bruno's reputation for violence. She has taken care of Bruno's children and presently has custody of Amanda and Ronny. She also might be knowledgeable about Bruno's neo-Nazi activities.

You sent a notice to take the deposition of Gretchen Summers. The deposition is scheduled for November 2, 198X + 1 at 9:00 A.M. at your law office. Attorneys for plaintiffs and defendant Davola will be attending the deposition. They may examine if time permits.

PREPARATION

READ: (1) Pretrial Case File Entries 1-39, 48, 59-61, 63, 82, 90; (2) Chapter VII; (3) Fed. R. Civ. P. 26, 29-32, 37. Now think about and answer the following questions:

1. Specifically, how will you prepare for this deposition? Explain.

2. What are your objectives in deposing Gretchen Summers?

3. What topics will you cover in the deposition?

    a. Will you follow a particular sequence?

    b. Why?

4. Suppose that Hans and Deborah Summers appear at your office with Gretchen and their attorney and want to attend the deposition. What will you do? Why?

5. How will you begin the deposition? Why?

6. Will you use documents in the deposition? If so:

    a. Which documents?

    b. Why will you use those documents?

    c. How will you ensure that the documents are part of the deposition?

7. Suppose that you ask Gretchen Summers: "Your son, Bruno, was a member of a neo-Nazi survivalist group. What do you know about his participation in that group?" Gretchen Summers responds: "None of your business."

    a. What, if anything, can you as Hard's attorney do or say?

    b. Do you anticipate that plaintiffs' counsel will say or do anything? Explain.

8. Suppose that you ask Gretchen Summers: "Mrs. Summers, can you please tell us if you received money from Bruno Summers?" Mrs. Summers responds: "None of your business."

    a. What, if anything, can you as Hard's attorney do or say?

    b. Do you anticipate that plaintiffs' counsel will say or do anything? Explain.

9. Suppose that Gretchen Summers, in response to almost all questions you ask, states: "I do not remember." What will you do?

10. Suppose that you ask Gretchen Summers: "Would you like to settle the *Summers v. Hard* lawsuit?" Plaintiffs' counsel objects and instructs Mrs. Summers to not answer the question.

   a. Is plaintiffs' counsel correct to object? Upon what grounds?

   b. What, if anything, should you as Hard's counsel say or do? Why?

11. Do you anticipate that plaintiffs' counsel will examine Gretchen Summers? Why or why not?

ASSIGNMENT FOR CLASS*

1. Outside of class:

   a. **Attorney for defendant Hard:** Prepare written questions that you intend to ask in the deposition.

   b. **Attorneys for plaintiffs and defendant Davola:** Prepare a written outline of what you think will be covered in the deposition. (**Plaintiffs' attorney:** If you have not already done so, prepare Gretchen Summers for her deposition.)

   c. **Both plaintiffs' and defendants' attorneys:** Hand in your written preparation of this deposition to your senior partner.

2. In class:

   a. **Attorney for defendant Hard:** Conduct the deposition of Gretchen Summers.

   b. **Attorneys for plaintiffs and defendant Davola:** Attend the deposition and, if desired, examine Gretchen Summers.

PROBLEM 70

Attorney for Defendant Hard: Taking the Deposition of a Neutral Witness
(Roberta Montbank)

You sent a notice to take the deposition of Ms. Roberta Montbank. The deposition is scheduled for November 1, 198X + 1 at 9:00 A.M. at the law office of defendant Hard's attorney. Attorneys for plaintiffs and defendant Davola will be attending the deposition. They may examine the deponent if time permits.

The deposition may be critical to establish Ed Hard's defenses. A little history of this witness is important.

Ms. Montbank, 78 years of age, was a patron at the Unicorn Tavern on the night Bruno Summers was shot. The police listed Robin Luntlebunk as a witness, but no statement was taken from her until November 3, 198X (after the criminal case was dismissed). The police claim they could

---

*Your instructor may select which attorneys will examine the deponent and the topics to be covered in the deposition.

not locate Ms. Montbank because they were given the name Robin Luntlebunk instead of Roberta Montbank.

Plaintiffs sent written interrogatories to defendant Davola on May 15, 198X + 1. Attorney for defendant Hard learned from those interrogatories that the EKKO Insurance Company interviewed and received a signed statement under oath from Ms. Roberta Montbank on October 26, 198X. Ms. Montbank declined to give either plaintiffs' attorney or Ed Hard's attorney a copy of her statement. Plaintiffs' written request for the document has been the subject of an unsuccessful plaintiffs' motion to compel Davola to produce the Montbank statement. The court tentatively ruled the statement work product.*

PREPARATION

READ: (1) Pretrial Case File Entries 1-39, 46, 57, 59-61, 63, 82, 90; (2) Chapter VII; (3) Fed. R. Civ. P. 26, 29-32, 37. Now think about and answer the following questions:

1. What are your objectives in deposing Roberta Montbank?

2. What topics will you examine? Explain.

    a. Will you follow a particular sequence?

    b. Why?

3. Roberta Montbank gave a statement on November 3, 198X to the police concerning the September 3, 198X shooting of Bruno Summers.

    a. Will you question her about why she gave the police the statement two months after the incident? Why or why not?

    b. If you question Ms. Montbank about her statement, what specific questions will you ask? Why?

4. Suppose that you use a diagram of the Unicorn Tavern when examining Roberta Montbank. Roberta Montbank places herself at the table near the entrance of the Tavern.

    a. What, if anything, should you say or do? Why?

    b. What, if anything, should plaintiffs' attorney say or do? Why?

    c. What, if anything, should Davola's attorney say or do? Why?

5. Are there documents or things that you, defendant Hard's attorney, would like to question Ms. Montbank about at the deposition?

    a. What are they?

    b. If there are, how will these documents be available for this deposition?

6. Suppose plaintiffs' counsel begins the deposition stating: "Let us adopt the standard stipulation, counsel, waiver of signatures, etcetera." How should you respond? Why?

7. Is it ethical for either plaintiffs' attorney or any of defendants' attorneys to contact Roberta Montbank prior to her deposition? Explain.

---

*This ruling is for purposes of this problem only. See the motion, Problem 97.

8. Suppose that in response to your (defendant Hard's attorney's) question, "Were you at the Unicorn Tavern the evening of September 3, 198X?," Ms. Montbank replies: "I live at the Stillwater Retirement Home." What if anything should you say or do? Why?

9. Suppose that after 45 minutes of the deposition Roberta Montbank states that she is too tired to proceed and asks, "Can we continue this after my afternoon nap?" What should you do?

10. Do you think plaintiffs' counsel should examine Ms. Montbank? Why or why not?

    a. If you were plaintiffs' counsel, what topics would you select? Why?

    b. Can plaintiffs' attorney use leading questions? Why or why not?

11. Can either defendant Hard's attorney or Davola's counsel use leading questions in examining Roberta Montbank? Why or why not?

12. If you were defendant Davola's attorney, would you examine Ms. Montbank? Why or why not?

    a. What topics would you select? Why?

    b. Can you use leading questions? Why or why not?

13. Suppose Ms. Montbank dies right after the deposition.

    a. Can any of the parties use the deposition if Ms. Montbank did not sign it?

    b. If Ms. Montbank read and signed the deposition, are there objections that any of the attorneys could raise against using the deposition at trial? Explain what they could be and how they could be avoided.

ASSIGNMENT FOR CLASS**

1. Outside of class:

    a. **Attorney for defendant Hard:** Prepare written questions that you intend to ask at the deposition.

    b. **Attorneys for plaintiffs and defendant Davola:** Prepare a written outline of what you think will be covered in the deposition.

    c. **Both plaintiffs' and defendants' attorneys:** Hand in your preparation of this deposition to your senior partner.

2. In class:

    a. **Attorney for defendant Hard:** Conduct the deposition of Roberta Montbank.

    b. **Attorneys for plaintiffs and defendant Davola:** Attend the deposition, and if desired, examine Ms. Roberta Montbank.

**Your instructor may select which attorneys will examine the deponent and the topics to be covered in the deposition.

PROBLEM 71

Attorney for Defendant Davola:
Taking the Deposition of a Neutral
Witness
(Bert Kain)

Bert Kain was a patron at the Unicorn Tavern on both August 20 and September 3, 198X. You have heard that he spoke to plaintiffs' attorney, but he has not answered your telephone calls.

You sent a notice to take the deposition of Bert Kain. The deposition is scheduled for November 2, 198X + 1 at 9:00 A.M. at your law office. Attorneys for plaintiffs and defendant Hard will be attending the deposition. They may examine the deponent if time permits.

PREPARATION

READ: (1) Pretrial Case File Entries 1-39, 59-61, 63, 82, 90; (2) Chapter VII; (3) Fed. R. Civ. P. 26, 29-32, 37. Now think about and answer the following questions:

1. Suppose that Bert Kain begins the deposition stating, "I have to miss a day's work because of this deposition. Who is going to pay me for my loss of work, travel and lunch?"

    a. How should defendants' counsel respond?

    b. How should plaintiffs' counsel respond?

2. Specifically, how will you, defendant Davola's attorney, prepare for this deposition?

3. What are your objectives in deposing Bert Kain?

    a. If you were defendant Hard's attorney?

    b. If you were plaintiffs' attorney?

4. What topics will you cover in the deposition?

    a. Will you follow a particular sequence?

    b. Why?

5. Should you have sent a subpoena to Bert Kain instead of a notice to take his deposition? Explain.

6. Suppose that defendants Mary Apple and Tom Donaldson appear at Bert Kain's deposition. You, Davola's attorney, want them to attend the deposition.

    a. How do you think plaintiffs' attorney will respond? Why?

    b. How do you think defendant Hard's attorney will respond? Why?

    c. Is there any way that plaintiffs or defendant Hard could preclude Apple and Donaldson from attending? Explain.

7. Bert Kain may be a witness helpful to plaintiffs or defendants. What can you or Hard's attorney as defense counsel say or do at the deposition to maintain friendly relations with Bert Kain?

8. Which attorneys, if any, can use leading questions in examining Bert Kain?

   a. You? Why?

   b. Hard's attorney? Why?

   c. Plaintiffs' attorney? Why?

9. Bert Kain said he overheard Mary Apple state: "I shouldn't have served them." When you, Davola's attorney, examine Bert Kain about this statement:

   a. What are your objectives in terms of your case theory?

   b. If Davola wants the statement to be inadmissible at trial, what questions can you as Davola's attorney ask Bert Kain to help Davola keep the statement out of evidence?

10. Suppose that at the deposition Bert Kain states, "I can't remember if I heard Mary Apple on August 20th or September 3, 198X say 'I shouldn't have served them.' "

    a. Should you question Kain further on this topic? Explain.

    b. Should you try to refresh Bert Kain's memory? Why or why not?

    c. If examining Bert Kain, should plaintiffs' attorney probe this topic and try to refresh Kain's memory? Explain.

    d. If either you or plaintiffs' attorney wants Bert Kain's memory to be refreshed, what should you or plaintiffs' attorney say or do?

11. Suppose that at the deposition one of defendants' counsel asked Bert Kain: "I understand you met with plaintiffs' attorney before *Summers v. Hard* was filed. Tell me what you told their attorney."

    a. Is it ethical for defendants' counsel to ask such a question? Explain.

    b. If plaintiffs want to object, is there any appropriate objection that plaintiffs' attorney could make? Explain.

    c. What arguments can defendant's counsel make in response to plaintiffs' objections? Explain.

12. Do you (Davola's attorney) think plaintiffs' attorney should examine the deponent? Explain.

ASSIGNMENT FOR CLASS*

1. Outside of class:

   a. **Attorney for defendant Davola:** Prepare written questions that you intend to ask at the deposition.

   b. **Attorneys for plaintiffs and defendant Hard:** Prepare a written outline of what you think will be covered in the deposition.

---

*Your instructor may select which attorneys will examine the deponent and the topics to be covered in the deposition.

   c. **Both plaintiffs' and defendants' counsel:** Hand in you preparation of this deposition to your senior partner.

2. In class:

   a. **Attorney for defendant Davola:** Conduct the deposition of Bert Kain.

   b. **Attorneys for plaintiffs and defendant Hard:** Attend the deposition, and, if desired, examine Bert Kain.

PROBLEM 72

Plaintiffs' Attorney: Taking the Deposition of an Adverse Expert Witness
(Dr. Hollis Lufkin, Defendant Davola's Psychiatrist)

The parties have proceeded with the litigation process and formal discovery. Plaintiffs' and defendants' attorneys agreed that all experts who will testify at trial can be deposed without court order. In addition, plaintiffs' and defendants' attorneys have voluntarily provided each other with copies of the reports submitted by their expert witnesses. The plaintiffs' attorney has learned through answers to interrogatories that defendant Davola's psychiatrist, Dr. Hollis Lufkin, will testify that a reasonable person could not have predicted a shooting between Ed Hard and Bruno Summers at the Unicorn Tavern. Plaintiffs' counsel sent a subpoena to take the deposition for Dr. Lufkin.

   The deposition is scheduled for October 5, 198X + 1 at 9:00 A.M. at Dr. Lufkin's office. Attorneys for defendants Davola and Hard will be attending the deposition. They may examine the deponent if time permits.

   Preparation to take a deposition and preparation of the deponent for a deposition are important. Attorney for plaintiffs, in order to prepare to take an adverse expert witness's deposition it is usually advisable to consult with an expert to educate yourself about the specialty. You have retained Dr. David Bowmun, a clinical psychologist, who believes "it is likely the altercation and shooting between Bruno Summers and Ed Hard could have been anticipated by the bartender and waitress at the Unicorn Tavern." Dr. Bowmun is available to consult with plaintiffs' attorney.

PREPARATION

READ: (1) Pretrial Case File Entries 1-39, 50, 53, 59-61, 63, 64, 82, 90; (2) Chapter VII; (3) Fed. R. Civ. P. 26, 29-32, 37. Now think about and answer the following questions:

1. How will you prepare for taking the deposition of Dr. Lufkin?

2. What are your objectives in deposing Dr. Lufkin?

3. Are there documents or things that you want Dr. Lufkin to bring to the deposition?

   a. What are they?

   b. If there are, how will these documents be available for this deposition?

4. Suppose that you subpoenaed Dr. Lufkin's file and records in the *Summers v. Hard* case. Dr. Lufkin refused to bring her file to the deposition. She brought only her report to the deposition. She did not bring any of the documents or materials that defendant Davola's counsel sent her.

   a. Discuss what objections defendant Davola's attorney and Dr. Lufkin can legitimately rely upon.

   b. What *can* you do?

   c. What *will* you do?

5. One should usually begin an expert witness deposition by inquiring into the expert witness's background and education to determine whether the expert is qualified to testify at trial, whether additional or different experts are needed to compete favorably with the opposing counsel's expert, and generally to educate oneself as to the persuasiveness of the expert's opinion. What specific background and education areas will you question Dr. Lufkin about as to her qualifications?

6. Tactically, can you imagine a situation in which you may not want to develop Dr. Lufkin's background and education at the deposition? Explain.

7. What substantive topics will you question Dr. Lufkin about?

   a. Why?

   b. Will the deposition topics be arranged in a particular sequence? Explain.

8. Dr. Lufkin's opinion that a reasonable person could not have predicted a shooting between Ed Hard and Bruno Summers at the Unicorn Tavern is not helpful to your case theory.

   a. What questions will you ask Dr. Lufkin to keep her opinion from being admissible in evidence?

   b. What questions will you ask Dr. Lufkin to weaken the impact of her opinion if the court rules her opinion is admissible?

9. Discuss the advantages and disadvantages of using a hypothetical question.

10. Will you ask Dr. Lufkin a hypothetical question at the deposition? Explain.

11. Suppose you want to use a hypothetical question. Construct one for Dr. Lufkin.

12. Suppose that Dr. Lufkin tells you that she can testify only from her notes.

   a. Can you make the notes part of the deposition record?

   b. Do you want to make the notes part of the deposition? Explain.

13. Suppose that defendant Davola's attorney advises Dr. Lufkin to refuse to answer questions about conversations she had with Davola's attorney before she was officially hired.

a. What is the basis for the objection of Davola's attorney?

b. What can you do?

14. Do you think that defendant Hard's attorney should examine Dr. Lufkin at this deposition? Why or why not?

15. Dr. Lufkin has a habit of dressing in long, flowing, brightly colored robes, with lots of jewelry. Davola's attorney believes Lufkin will come to the deposition dressed in her "robes." If you were defendant Davola's attorney, what, if anything, should you do? Why?

ASSIGNMENT FOR CLASS*

1. Outside of class:

   a. **Plaintiffs' attorney:** Prepare written questions that you intend to ask at the deposition. (You may also want to meet with your expert, Dr. David Bowmun, a psychologist, in order to prepare for the deposition of Dr. Lufkin.)

   b. **Defendants' attorneys:** Prepare a written outline of what you think will be asked in the deposition. (**Attorney for defendant Davola:** If you have not already done so, meet with your expert witness, Dr. Lufkin, to prepare her for the deposition.)

   c. **Plaintiffs' and defendants' attorneys:** Hand in your written preparation of the deposition to your senior partner.

2. In class:

   a. **Plaintiffs' attorney:** Depose defendant Davola's psychiatrist, Dr. Lufkin.

   b. **Defendants' attorneys:** Attend the deposition and, if desired, examine the expert at the deposition.

PROBLEM 73

Defendants' Attorneys: Taking the Deposition of an Adverse Expert Witness
(Dr. Bruce Hann, Plaintiffs' Economist)

Plaintiffs' and defendants' attorneys have agreed that all experts who will testify at trial can be deposed without court order. In addition, plaintiffs' and defendants' attorneys have voluntarily provided each other with copies of the reports submitted by their expert witnesses. Defendants' attorneys scheduled a deposition of plaintiffs' economist, Dr. Bruce Hann, for November 3, 198X+1 at 9:00 A.M. at the law office of defendant Davola's attorney. Attorneys for both defendants and for plaintiffs will be attending the deposition.

Preparation to take a deposition and preparation of the deponent for a deposition are important. In order to prepare to take an adverse expert

---

*Your instructor may select which attorneys will examine the deponent and the topics to be covered in the deposition.

witness's deposition it is usually advisable to consult with an expert to educate yourself about the specialty. Defendants have retained Dr. Thomas Monday, an economist who believes: "The economic loss for the wrongful death of Bruno Summers is substantially less than the amount calculated by plaintiffs' economist, Dr. Bruce Hann." Dr. Monday is available to consult with defendants' attorneys.

PREPARATION

READ: (1) Pretrial Case File Entries 1-43, 47, 48, 52, 54, 59-61, 63, 82, 90; (2) Chapter VII; (3) Fed. R. Civ. P. 26, 29-32, 37. Now think about and answer the following questions:

1. How will you prepare for taking the deposition of Dr. Hann?

2. Does your preparation differ from preparing to take the deposition of a lay witness? If so, explain how it differs.

3. What are your objectives in deposing Dr. Hann?

4. Are there documents or things that you want Dr. Hann to bring to the deposition?

   a. What are they?

   b. If there are, how will these documents be available for the deposition?

5. Suppose that you subpoenaed Dr. Hann's file and records in the *Summers v. Hard* case. The economist arrives at the deposition without his file.

   a. Discuss what objections plaintiffs' attorney and Dr. Hann can legitimately rely on if they state they refuse to allow you, defendants' attorneys, access to Dr. Hann's file.

   b. What *can* you do?

   c. What *will* you do?

6. What substantive topics will you question Dr. Hann about?

   a. Will the deposition topics be arranged in any particular sequence?

   b. Why?

7. You should usually begin an expert witness deposition by inquiring into the expert's background and education to determine whether the expert is qualified to testify at trial, whether additional or different experts are needed to compete favorably with opposing counsels' expert, and generally to educate yourself as to the persuasiveness of the expert's opinion. What specific background and education areas will you question Dr. Hann about as to his qualifications?

8. Tactically, can you imagine any situation in which you may not want to develop an expert's background and education at a deposition? Explain.

9. Dr. Hann will in all likelihood state his opinion that the death of Bruno Summers has resulted in economic loss to plaintiffs of over $300,000.

a. What questions, if any, would you ask Dr. Hann about his opinion?

b. What questions, if any, can you ask him that would weaken his opinion?

c. Do you want to weaken his opinion at the deposition? Explain.

10. Generally, discuss the advantages and disadvantages of using a hypothetical question in a deposition..

11. Will you ask Dr. Hann any hypothetical questions at the deposition? Why or why not?

12. Suppose that you want to use a hypothetical question. Construct one for Dr. Hann.

13. Are there questions that Dr. Hann may refuse to answer? If so, what do you anticipate they will be?

14. Should plaintiffs' attorney examine Dr. Hann? Why or why not?

ASSIGNMENT FOR CLASS*

1. Outside of class:

   a. **Attorneys for defendants:** Prepare written questions that you intend to ask in the deposition. (You may also want to consult with your expert, Dr. Monday, to help you to prepare for Dr. Hann's deposition.)

   b. **Plaintiffs' attorney:** Prepare Dr. Hann (if you have not already done so) for his deposition. Prepare a written outline of what you think will be covered in the deposition.

   c. **Both plaintiffs' and defendants' counsel:** Hand in your written preparation questions for the deposition to your senior partner.

2. In class:

   a. **Attorneys for defendants Davola and Hard:** Prepare to take the deposition of Dr. Hann.

   b. **Plaintiffs' attorney:** Attend the deposition and, if desired, examine the expert at the deposition.

PROBLEM 74 _____

Attorney for Defendant Hard: Taking the Deposition of an Adverse Expert Witness
(Dr. Brett Day, Plaintiffs' Medical Expert)

Plaintiffs' and defendants' attorneys have agreed that all experts who will testify at trial can be deposed without a court order. In addition, the plaintiffs' attorney has voluntarily provided defendants with copies of the hospital records of Bruno Summers. Defendant Hard's attorney sent a subpoena to take the deposition of one of plaintiffs' medical experts, Dr.

---

*Your instructor may select which attorneys will examine the deponent and the topics to be covered in the deposition.

Brett Day. The deposition is scheduled for November 4, 198X + 1 at 9:00 A.M. at the law office of defendant Hard's attorney. Attorneys for plaintiffs and defendant Davola will be attending the deposition. They may examine the deponent if time permits.

PREPARATION

READ: (1) Pretrial Case File Entries 1-41, 51, 55, 59-61, 63, 64, 82, 90; (2) Chapter VII; (3) Fed. R. Civ. P. 26, 29-32, 37. Now think about and answer the following questions:

1. What specific documents and things will you examine in order to prepare for the deposition of Dr. Day? Why?

2. Are there documents or things that you want to examine Dr. Day about at the deposition?

   a. What are they?

   b. Are there any documents you do not have but need to obtain? If there are, how will you obtain these documents prior to the deposition?

3. What are your objectives in deposing Dr. Brett Day?

4. Suppose that at the deposition (but before Dr. Day is sworn) Dr. Day states, "My minimum fee is $500 for testifying at a deposition; $700 if I read and sign the deposition."

   a. What will you say or do? Why?

   b. What will plaintiffs' attorney say or do? Why?

5. Suppose that at the beginning of the deposition Dr. Day states, "I am 'on call' at Mercy Hospital and will have to leave the deposition in one hour."

   a. What, if anything, will you say or do?

   b. Why?

6. What substantive topics will you question the doctor on?

   a. Will the deposition topics be arranged in a particular sequence?

   b. Why?

7. There are advantages and disadvantages in using a hypothetical question.

   a. Why would you ask Dr. Day a hypothetical question at the deposition?

   b. Why would you avoid asking a hypothetical question at the deposition?

8. Suppose that you want to ask a hypothetical question. Construct a hypothetical question for Dr. Day.

9. You should usually begin the deposition of a medical expert by inquiring into the doctor's background and education to determine whether the expert is qualified to testify at trial, whether additional or different experts are needed to compete favorably with the

opposing counsel's expert, and generally to educate yourself as to the persuasiveness of the expert's opinion.

    a.   Would you question Dr. Day as to his background and education? Why or why not?

    b.   If you would inquire into Dr. Day's background, what specific background and education areas will you question Dr. Day about as to his qualifications?

10.   Tactically, can you imagine a situation in which you may not want to develop Dr. Day's background and education at the deposition? Explain.

11.   Dr. Day heard Bruno Summers state: "I should have left when I saw him."

    a.   Would questioning Dr. Day about this statement help or hurt your theory of the case? Explain.

    b.   Would it help or hurt Davola's theory of his case? Explain.

    c.   Would it help or hurt plaintiffs' theory of their case? Explain.

    d.   Suppose you want the statement admitted into evidence at trial. What questions could you ask Dr. Day to help you admit the statement in evidence at trial?

12.   The death certificate states that the cause of death for Bruno Summers was respiratory distress secondary to pneumonia.

    a.   Would you question Dr. Day about this topic? Do you think defendant Davola's attorney would? Why or why not?

    b.   Do you think plaintiffs' attorney would want to question Dr. Day about this topic at the deposition? Why or why not?

13.   Suppose you question Dr. Day as to conversations he had with plaintiffs. Dr. Day is advised by plaintiffs' attorney to refuse to answer.

    a.   What is the basis for plaintiffs' objection?

    b.   What *can* you do?

    c.   What *will* you do?

14.   Will you ask Dr. Day how many medical malpractice actions he has been named in? Why or why not?

15.   Do you think plaintiffs' attorney should examine Dr. Day at this deposition? Explain.

ASSIGNMENT FOR CLASS*

1. Outside of class:

    a.   **Attorney for defendant Hard:** Prepare written questions that you intend to ask at the deposition.

---

*Your instructor may select which attorneys will examine the deponent and the topics to be covered in the deposition.

---

b.   **Attorneys for plaintiffs and defendant Davola:** Prepare a written outline of what you think will be asked in the deposition.

c.   **Both plaintiffs' and defendants' attorneys:** Hand in your written preparation of the deposition to your senior partner.

2.   In class:

a.   **Attorney for defendant Hard:** Depose Dr. Brett Day.

b.   **Attorneys for plaintiffs and defendant Davola:** Attend the deposition and, if desired, examine Dr. Day at the deposition.

VIII
Pretrial Motions

Question 4.   How will you achieve your objectives?
Question 5.   What problems do you anticipate?
Question 6.   How will you meet such problems?
Question 7.   If you can't solve the problems, what will you do?
Question 8.   What ethical concerns do you face in attempting to achieve your objectives?

E.   PLANNING QUESTIONS

APPENDIX I: CRIMINAL MOTION CHECKLIST

APPENDIX II: SAMPLE CIVIL MOTION

CRIMINAL PROBLEMS: *State v. Hard*

CIVIL PROBLEMS: *Summers v. Hard*

A. INTRODUCTION

A motion is a request to the court to exercise its legal or equitable power in your favor. Motions can take many forms. As your case progresses, you will file many types of pretrial and trial motions—evidentiary motions at the beginning of trial that are heard without the presence of the jury (in limine), motions during trial, post-trial motions. They can include an oral request for a five-minute continuance, an emergency motion for bail or a temporary restraining order, a thirty-page motion for summary judgment, or a motion to suppress evidence accompanied by a full evidentiary hearing that resembles a mini-trial.

In this chapter, we focus on formal, written pretrial motions, although what we say applies to any motion, in any form. To aid you in drafting a motion, as an appendix to this chapter (see page 274) we have included a model civil motion with a full set of supporting papers, including affidavits, points and authorities, and a sample order. While a model, it is still likely (with some variation) to reflect the format required in the jurisdiction where you will practice.

Motions can accomplish a range of objectives. The basic objective of any motion is circumscribed by its particular subject matter (e.g., the objective of a motion to reduce bail is to obtain a reduction of bail). Motions can also be thought of as having certain sub-objectives: (1) to provide information (at a hearing on a motion to suppress evidence, the police may testify that your client "did not look nervous" and "was cooperative"); (2) to gain respect from the court (providing your motion work is of high quality and not frivolous); (3) to put pressure on your opponent; and (4) to aid in negotiation (assuming your motion adds some potential risk to your opponent's case). (These last two sub-objectives may well be tactics in a representational strategy that is geared to eventual settlement.)

B. PREPARING TO DEVELOP AND EXECUTE A MOTION

As was the case with discovery, preparation for making a motion involves both the assimilation of various factual, legal, and procedural information and an understanding of the relationship of this skills performance to case theory. When dealing with motions, however, a further understanding of theory is re-quired. This involves knowing how to develop a strategic concept directly analogous in form and function to the case theory—the motion theory (or MT).

1. Accumulating Information and Developing an Organizational Structure

You must be able to recognize and develop motions that are appropriate to supporting your representational strategy. In order to do this, you must accumulate factual information (e.g., client information concerning possible emergency needs, case facts) and legal information (e.g., by developing a review list of typical motions in your area from experience, discussions with other attorneys, advance sheets, law reviews, and custom and usage in court). You also should know the procedural requirements for filing and presenting motions. From reading local court rules and discussing procedural concerns with court clerks and other attorneys, you can learn the procedures for proof of service, orders shortening time, declarations and exhibits, and subpoenaing police witnesses to an evidentiary hearing. Additionally, you should plan the presentation of your motion so it will be persuasive. This may involve talking to other attorneys about your opponent so you can anticipate his or her likely counterstrategy (compare this to learning your opponent's negotiating behavior when planning for negotiation), and finding out how your judge approaches motions in general and the type of motion you are bringing in particular. For this purpose, you may want to actually watch the judge address motions in another case. Finally, you need to know the form that your motion must take. You can determine this by looking at motions other attorneys have filed or by reviewing local court rules. While individual jurisdictions may vary, the basic form for a motion is somewhat uniform. This form is discussed later at page 263 and is illustrated by the sample civil discovery motion (Appendix II) at page 274.

If you anticipate bringing more than one motion, you will need an overall motion plan. This is analogous to the discovery plan discussed in Chapter VII. This plan will include a list of all the motions you will raise, an indication of whether each motion will require declarations or an evidentiary hearing (and, if so, a list of necessary witnesses) and a time line tracking when the various stages of your motions must be accomplished. This time line might include the dates when you will file each motion, argue that motion to the court, and any evidence-taking will occur. Your plan should keep in mind local court rules (e.g., all pretrial motions must be brought at a single hearing) and procedural rules and case law regarding waiver (e.g., a demurrer to a criminal complaint must be filed *before* a plea is made to the complaint or objection by demurrer is waived; a motion to contest improper service of process of a civil complaint is waived once an answer is filed).

2. The Relationship Between Case Theory and Motion Making

The sole purpose of a particular motion may be to help your case theory by obtaining information for your factual theory ("story"), or by keeping out information helpful to your opponent's theory. Or the issues underlying a motion may directly parallel issues in the case. For example, suppose you brought a motion to keep a crucial document out of evidence on the ground that its method of preparation was too unreliable to permit the document to qualify as a business record. If successful, this would support an attack on the persuasive (and perhaps even factual) sufficiency of the opposing party's case. However, the court denies your motion. You might still cross-examine the custodian of those records before the factfinder, bringing out this same information concerning unreliability in order to convince the factfinder not to give the document any weight in its deliberations. As was the intent of the original motion, this cross-examination would be aimed at supporting an attack on the persuasive sufficiency of the opponent's factual theory. Furthermore, you must be careful that the factual thrust of your motion is *consistent* with the story in your case theory. Otherwise, you could impeach your own case, undercut your credibility with the court, and perhaps even raise the specter of perjury. As an illustration, imagine making a motion to obtain money for experts and, in support of the motion, you submit your client's declaration of indigency. Imagine the potential consequences of then trying to claim at trial that the client wasn't so poor that he needed to steal. Or suppose that as prosecutor you argue at trial that defendant "knowingly" possessed stolen tires found in his trunk after claiming at a defense suppression motion that the defendant had sought police assistance to open his trunk because it was jammed.

3. Developing a Motion Theory (MT)

The content of a motion, and the gathering and presenting of the information that comprises the factual aspects of the motion, are all guided by a strategic theory analogous to the case theory. Like its case theory counterpart, this motion theory (MT) is a plan developed out of an ends-means analysis directed at achieving overall objectives. The ends of the case theory are to achieve the client's overall objectives in the case. The ends of the MT are to achieve success in the mini-case that is termed a "motion." The motion may also resolve your case (e.g., a successful suppression motion of vital prosecution evidence, a successful summary judgment motion). Specifically, the MT is comprised of a motion legal theory (MLT) and a motion factual theory (MFT). These are directly analogous to the legal theory and factual theory that make up the case theory. In fact, just as the legal and factual theories interact so each both suggests and limits the other, the MLT and MFT are likewise interrelated.

a. Plaintiff's Motion Legal Theory (MLT)

The MLT of the moving party parallels the plaintiff's legal theory in the case theory. But unlike the case theory and its underlying legal theory, a single motion will often be based on several MLTs: A motion to suppress evidence may be based on no probable cause to support the search warrant, overly broad description of the thing to be seized, and insufficient information establishing the credibility of an informant. Asserting various motion factual theories (MFTs) will not present a problem if the respective theories present consistent "stories."

When offering an MLT, the moving party is making an assertion that it can establish, within applicable burdens of proof, every element (factor, standard) of the substantive law that underlies the motion. As an example, imagine that police receive a report from a citizen that, two weeks before, the citizen had personally seen a baggie of marijuana in the defendant's living room. Based on this information, police search defendant's apartment for marijuana and find some contraband. Defense counsel wants to bring a suppression motion. What, however, will be counsel's motion legal theory? From research, counsel determines that the government may not conduct a search and seizure without "probable cause." In this search and seizure context, probable cause can be defined as: "A reasonable person would be strongly suspicious of four factors—(1) a particular thing (2) related to a crime (3) is in a particular place (4) at a particular time." If the search is conducted *with* a warrant, the burden to attack the legality of the search generally rests on the defendant to show the police lacked probable cause to search. If the search is conducted *without* a warrant, the burden falls on the government to justify the search as conducted with probable cause. Looking at the facts of his case, counsel would likely raise an MLT focusing on the fourth factor in the probable cause standard—"at a particular time." (Because a baggie was in the apartment two weeks ago does not reasonably mean marijuana will be there now.) Therefore, if the search was conducted with a warrant, and the burden thus falls on the defendant, the defendant's complete MLT would be an assertion that "there is no probable cause because one of the four factors is lacking (i.e., the factor relating to 'at this time')." If the search was without a warrant, and the burden therefore falls on the prosecution, the defendant's MLT would be "the prosecution cannot establish each of the four factors of probable cause."

How does the party bringing a motion actually develop its MLT? We suggest two processes that have worked for us and for our colleagues (although there are undoubtedly many more such techniques). Of course, as is often the case with such processes, the two processes may take place simultaneously. The first process we have termed "searching for possible MLTs"; the second, "fulfilling needs."

In the first process, "searching for possible MLTs," you start with the information you know about the case and try to determine which motions (if any) are indicated by that information. This process can be carried out in a number of ways. From your experience, discussions with other attorneys, treatises, court rules, and statutes, you can compile a list of existing MLTs that are appropriate to your area of practice. This list will appear as a list of motions since motions are generally named after their underlying MLT (motion to change venue due to prejudicial publicity, motion to obtain court funds to pay for an expert necessary to an indigent's defense, motion to quash process for failure to fulfill requirements of service by mail, and so on). Having such a list, you may be able to identify tentative MLTs by going back and forth and comparing your list with the information you know about the case, and comparing the information you know about the case with the list. For an example of such a list, see the Criminal Motion Checklist (Appendix I) at page 272.

There are other ways to search for possible MLTs. Combinations of facts that comprise the information in your case may suggest an idea for a motion. Recall the analogous method in pleadings that we called factual theorizing. We used the method in pleading to develop "cutting-edge" legal theories. Here, this method will not necessarily lead to "cutting-edge" MLTs, but rather may merely focus you on a nice,

safe "old-shoe" theory. For example, police may have talked to your client and obtained some incriminating statement. These facts suggest that you consider some MLT involving suppression of a confession. Or your domestic client may be physically abused by her spouse. These facts trigger the idea of a restraining order. With your "idea," you can then look for authority to help you support and refine your idea (e.g., when looking for authority to suppress the statements to the police, you will begin to develop more precise, refined legal grounds for your position: "The statements were illegally obtained because they were prompted by confronting defendant with illegally seized evidence"). If you do not find clear supporting authority, you may then need to be creative and use analogy, ideas from law reviews, and so forth to develop a cutting-edge MLT to support your idea.

The second process, "fulfilling needs," is a process grounded in ends-means analysis. Here, you begin with the needs in your case, and then look for motions to fulfill those needs. You will have perceived "needs" throughout the case. From our experience, these needs will roughly fall into one or more of what we call "control categories":

- Control of *information* (keeping your adversary's information out of evidence (suppression motion, motion to preclude use of subsequent repairs), obtaining information for your case theory (motion to compel discovery), getting your information into evidence (motion to let expert show jury the videotape that formed the basis of expert's opinion), and giving information (presenting the court or your opponent with a favorable image of your client or your client's cause through a motion for bail))
- Control of the *final outcome* (motions to resolve the case (motion to dismiss, summary judgment, directed verdict, judgment n.o.v.); a motion to control information may also resolve the case (a suppression motion may deny the prosecution the information it needs to support its factual theory))
- Control of the *procedure* (motion for change of venue, motion regarding rules for trial (motion to preclude mentioning of certain matters in voir dire or opening argument, motion for particular procedure for jury selection))
- Control of the *participants* (motion to compel party to appear at deposition, motion for a material witness warrant to stop a party from leaving the jurisdiction, motion for order restraining one party from personally contacting the other)

Starting with your perceived need, you then work

backwards (ends-means) to look for authority for an MLT that can aid you in achieving this need. This authority may be on your list of typical motions (see page 272). You may, however, have to look beyond your list and "create" a non-standard motion from a synthesis of existing authority and analogy. This creative approach to motions is again analogous to pleading where we developed cutting-edge claims, parties, and relief. In this regard, imagine you want a psychiatrist to interview your criminal client under sodium amytol. The problem is your client is in jail, and the jail has no facility for such an interview. Your "need" falls under the "control of information" category. Specifically, you need to obtain the information your client might give under the drug-induced interview, but no existing motion of which you are aware is available to achieve this end. So you begin to create. But, remember, even your created motion must be based on a legal theory that the court can rely on and consider. (In fact, virtually all presentations to the court have legal and factual theories.) You know that your client has a Sixth Amendment right to counsel and a Fifth Amendment right to put on a defense. You know that in various cases courts have found experts to be a necessary part of the attorney-client relationship and that statutes implicitly recognize the importance of experts by providing funds for indigents to obtain experts where the court finds appropriate. Mixing all these fragments together with your need still in mind, you might create "A Motion for Temporary Release (to Ensure Defendant's Fifth and Sixth Amendment Rights to a Fair Trial)." This would be your motion to remove your client to some hospital for the interview on the grounds that it is the only way to obtain information that must necessarily be obtained if you are to function as an effective Sixth Amendment counsel and your client is to realize his rights under the due process clause of the Fifth Amendment to bring forth a defense.

At still other times, your need may instead lead you to put an existing motion to creative use. Imagine a criminal case in which your client is a co-defendant. Early in the case, you have determined that a plea bargain is the most likely outcome and that you have a need falling under the "control of information" category to establish for the prosecutor (court, probation officer, investigating police officer) that your client's culpability is less than that of his co-defendants. With this need in mind, information emphasizing your client's peripheral role and relatively lower culpability in the matter could be brought out in such standard motions as a motion for release on personal recognizance or bail reduction, or motion to dismiss a complaint at a preliminary hearing for lack of cause.

Let's apply all of these processes by developing an MLT for a case example. Imagine a robbery case where the defendant was stopped by the police based on a general description by the victim (including the type and color of the perpetrator's vest), and subsequently was identified by the victim at the scene. You represent the defendant and, because of some shadowy memory from law school criminal procedure, your intuitive sense that there is something wrong with the way the identification was conducted, and a recognition that this event was a crucial evidentiary juncture in the case, you sense that some motion may be indicated. But what will be your MLT?

Start searching for possible MLTs and look back and forth between the facts and your list of typical motions. The "Motion to Suppress an Identification" on your list comports with the "idea" you had while reviewing the information that something might be wrong with the identification procedure. With the focused research made possible by this first level of analysis will now come more refinement. Your research has revealed that identifications can be suppressed on a number of grounds ("taint" from an illegal search, witness is otherwise incompetent, the identification procedure was unduly suggestive, no attorney present at a post-indictment line-up). Which applies to this case? Back to your facts as now known, and the "unduly suggestive identification" tentatively seems to be the most appropriate source for an MLT. Note that a "fulfilling needs" approach would have yielded the same result. You know that without the victim's in-court identification, the prosecution will not have sufficient information to go to the jury on the element of identification and, thereby, succumb to your attack on factual sufficiency. (See page 21). Accordingly, your need would be to control information to the extent of keeping this vital information out of evidence. A suppression motion can fulfill this need. The hearing on the motion also can provide you with a general assessment of the credibility of the victim and information for impeachment. On the other hand, you tactically should consider that it may give the victim "practice" against your cross-examination, so that your cross-examination may be less effective during actual trial.

In this example, your tentative MLT would roughly be that the in-court identification should be suppressed because it was the result of a suggestive identification procedure, violative of due process. The elements of this MLT would be that you can establish that (1) the government used identification procedures (2) that were so suggestive (3) as to lead to a reasonable likelihood of irreparable misidentification.

b. The MLT of the Responding Party

So much for a moving party's MLT, but what about that of a responding party? The formation of a responding party's MLT exactly parallels the development of the defense legal theory discussed in Chapter II.

A responding party can attack the proponent's MLT for legality ("The proponent of this motion claims his client was denied the right to an attorney in the grand jury room, but there is no such right") and procedural insufficiency ("This motion was not filed within required time limits"; "This is not the proper court to hear this motion"). Or a responding party can attack the proponent's motion factual theory (MFT) for persuasive sufficiency ("There is simply not much evidence that the officer did anything but treat the defendant with respect when he questioned him, let alone coerced the statement") and for something akin to factual sufficiency ("It is simply hard for me to believe that the 70-minute delay in letting counsel see his client in the jail can constitute a total denial of effective counsel in this case"). Moreover, it can raise what is, in effect, an affirmative defense—for example, in opposing a motion to compel discovery, a party might argue, "The moving party is not entitled to what would otherwise be discoverable information in this case since my client can rely on the patient-psychiatrist privilege (which in this situation is an affirmative defense to the motion for production) to resist this motion." Analogously, in the case of a defense suppression motion, as already discussed, once it is established that there was no warrant and the burden of justifying the search thereby shifts to the government, the government, if it is not to lose the motion, must in effect establish the affirmative defense that every factor that constitutes probable cause is met.

c. The Motion Factual Theory (MFT)

Like the factual theory underlying the case theory, the "story" that comprises the MFT will initially be conceived from both the information you have and that which you reasonably believe you can subsequently obtain. When collected, this information will generally be presented to the court through the testimony at an evidentiary hearing, a declaration, or an offer of proof. Similar to the factual theory, the MFT must be both factually sufficient and persuasive or, to look at it another way, be able to withstand attacks upon factual and persuasive sufficiency by your opponent.

In the context of an MFT, we are using factual sufficiency as a rough analogy to how that term is used when discussing the case theory. Unlike the situation with the case theory, lack of factual sufficiency in your MFT will not subject you to a formal motion to dismiss. Rather, the court will likely just find your motion to lack merit, and deny it and any request to put on an evidentiary hearing. This is not a desirable result. You will have wasted your client's money, potentially injured your overall credibility in the case, and lost even the opportunity for achieving possible sub-objectives (put witnesses on the stand and test their credibility, find out further information).

Even if the court finds your MFT to be factually sufficient to raise a genuine question in the court's mind, you must still persuade the court to rule in your favor. Just as the factual theory must, the MFT must fulfill the concerns of "quantity" and "quality" discussed in the context of case theory (see pages 24-25). As to the latter concern, this means that the "story" underlying the MFT must make sense. Accordingly, it must comport with human experience as did the story of Bossie the cow (see page 25). Also, when developing an MFT, the story should tie into the underlying legal rationale (gleaned directly from cases, common sense, implications in the doctrine, treatises) that supports the MLT. The judge deciding a motion will be mindful of making a legal decision, although factual findings may be determinative of the issue. To the extent you can focus the judge on values that transcend the individual case by linking your story to underlying policy rationales in the law that is embodied in the MLT, the court is likely to take your position far more seriously.

Back to the robbery case and your proposed motion to suppress the identification. In your proposed motion, you probably will be able to amass (through your fact-gathering) sufficient information as to each element of the legal theory so as to credibly raise this motion: (1) The government used identification procedures (the police conducted a show-up of the suspect on the street), (2) the procedures were suggestive (defendant was by himself, handcuffed, in front of a police car, flanked by police), and (3) the procedures were likely to lead to irreparable misidentification (victim did not get a long look at the robber, gave only a general description). So much for sufficiency. Now, how are you going to make all this persuasive within applicable burdens of proof?

The court is not going to be eager to throw out the prosecution's case (which would be the result of granting the motion). Your story, therefore, should try to present its component information in such a way that, comporting with common sense, the information is tied to the underlying policy rationale that justifies such an MLT in the first place. In the present case, the underlying rationale involves our concern that suggestive identification procedures could result in the conviction of innocent people (likewise, illegal search and seizure motions are founded on the underlying aversion to the image of a police state in which police could rummage through our private lives at will; motions to compel discovery ultimately reach back to a notion that disputes in our adversary system are best resolved when all parties have full and complete information). With this in mind, your story might be as follows:

> "My client is accused of robbery. His real crime is wearing a red down vest. Anyone among the tens of thousands of men in this city who are my client's size would be facing trial today if they too had been wearing a red vest while walking in the area where my client was stopped.
>
> "Let's go back to the evening of May 2nd and see how this identification happened. The victim, upset from being robbed, is taken over to see if he can identify a man whom he must believe the police strongly suspect is the robber—otherwise, why are they going to all the trouble to drive him over? When he gets there, what does he see? A full line-up? No. A single man. My client. Handcuffed. Standing in front of a police car, flanked by officers Garrity and Roan. They might as well have put a neon sign over him—'This is the man. This is the man.' And the victim. This man who got but a brief glance at the robber; this man who could give only a general description of his assailant. What does he see besides the finger of the police department pointing at my client? A common, innocuous piece of clothing. A red down vest. A red down vest which confirms in his mind everything the conduct of this show-up identification procedure is screaming to him. 'That's the man,' he shouts. What a surprise. This identification procedure was not just reasonably likely to lead to irreparable misidentification. It was all but certain to lead to a misidentification."

The MFT of the responding party to a motion will be developed to support that party's MLT. Since these responsive MLTs correspond to defense legal theories, it should afford no surprise that defendant's MFTs are developed in a manner analogous to the development of defense factual theories discussed in Chapter II.

C. PLANNING THE CONTENT OF A MOTION

1. A Suggested Approach: Information-Gathering and Information-Presenting

The content of the written motion will be almost a literal embodiment of the motion theory (MT). Development of a motion, like all aspects of litigation, however, takes place in a dynamic context. It involves information-gathering activities (e.g., interviews, discovery) that provide information from which the MFT can be constructed (and tentative MLTs sorted through) and information-presenting activities (e.g., witness testimony at an evidentiary hearing) that provide this same information to the decisionmaker. Thus, we have a two-part approach to employ when planning the content of motion making, one that reflects both the information-gathering and information-presenting aspects of this performance skill.

The two-part approach consists of five questions that focus on gathering and evaluating information for your motion theory, and four questions that focus on presenting this information to a decisionmaker. The first part of the approach is, not surprisingly, similar to the information-gathering approaches applied in interviewing and discovery, except that the process is guided by the motion theory rather than the case theory. As to the second part, which focuses on presentation, notice how Question 8 anticipates the reaction of the opposing party. This adversary perspective was placed in this part of the approach because presentation will almost always take place in an adversary context.

Part 1: Information-Gathering (gather and analyze)

1. What tentative motion theories are indicated by the information you are presently aware of?
2. What further information will you seek in light of such tentative motion theories?
3. What information did you obtain?
4. What is the significance of the information you obtained? (Does it support, revise, undermine your tentative motion theories?)
5. What further information will you now look for? Where?

Part 2: Information-Presenting (analyze and decide what to present)

6. What motion theory is indicated by existing information?

7. What information will you present (in this particular skills performance) in light of your motion theory?

8. What reaction to this information do you anticipate from the opposing party?

9. How will you anticipate or respond to this reaction?

BASIC TASK: Identify, find supporting information for, and plainly communicate appropriate motion theories.

---

2. *Applying the Approach*

Imagine that you are still representing the defendant in the robbery case. You have tentatively decided to bring a motion to suppress the identification based on suggestive identification procedures. You have just learned that a passerby who witnessed the on-the-scene identification has been located. You have made an appointment with this witness and now must plan for the content of the interview to obtain information for your motion.

Begin applying Part 1 of the approach:

QUESTION 1
What tentative motion theories are indicated by the information you are presently aware of?

You have obtained information that indicates that your client was identified as a robbery suspect in an on-the-scene show-up. Based on existing information, you have decided to bring a motion to suppress the identification on due process grounds. Specifically your MT is that, as the result of a police identification procedure that was unduly suggestive, it is reasonably likely that an irreparable misidentification may have occurred.

QUESTION 2
What further information will you seek in light of such tentative motion theories?

If you are going to file a motion to suppress the identification, you want information that you can incor-

porate into an MFT that supports an MLT centering on the concept of an unduly suggestive identification process. Thus, you will seek anything from which a reasonable factfinder/judge (because a judge will hear the evidence and decide the motion) would infer that the identification procedure was set up or conducted in such a way that, from the nature of the procedure itself, a viewer would effectively be told that "this is the man" (e.g., the defendant was handcuffed, police guns were trained on him). Of course, as always, you also want to know information that might weaken your MFT.

QUESTION 3
What information did you obtain?

Imagine you asked the witness to describe the show-up and she said: "These two big cops were holding up this little guy between them. He was handcuffed and the spotlights from the squad cars were focused on his face."

QUESTION 4
What is the significance of the information you obtained?

The information from the witness is logically probative. It supports your MT, providing detail for a "story" that characterizes the procedure as unfairly focusing on the defendant ("Could anyone have viewed this scene without getting the clear message that the police not only thought that this was the man, but also that he was an extremely dangerous man?"). It seems clearly admissible as relevant to an MLT focusing on "suggestiveness." But what about credibility?

QUESTION 5
What further information will you now look for?

Now you will need information to support the witness's credibility. You need to know both about the witness's ability to perceive (distance from show-up, time watched, lighting, eyeglasses) and the witness's general credibility (background, prior experiences with law enforcement that could be a source of bias). You also need to try to corroborate the witness's story (in-

---

formation in police reports, interviews with the arresting officers).

Credibility is important because you eventually will be in court putting on an evidentiary hearing in support of your motion to suppress the identification. This will be, in effect, a mini-trial in which the court will judge witness credibility. In fact, such hearings used to be conducted at trial but, to avoid delay in which the jury would be excused during what could be an extensive hearing, the motions and hearings were removed to the pretrial stage.

———————

Although we have been discussing a motion in a criminal case, our previous method of analysis would apply equally to one in the civil context. Recall the automobile accident in the pleadings (Chapter VI, page 156). Imagine that you are the plaintiff's counsel and plan to bring a motion for summary judgment on the issue of liability. Specifically, you will seek summary judgment on your claim of negligence per se (driving while intoxicated in violation of a state statute). Your MLT tracks the local procedural rule for summary judgment—"That there is no genuine issue on any material fact and that the moving party is entitled to judgment as a matter of law." (This local rule is in accord with Fed. R. Civ. P. 56(c).) Your MFT is, at present, based on a police report stating that the defendant had a .25 breathalyzer. Under statute in this jurisdiction, evidence of a 1.5 breathalyzer establishes an irrebuttable presumption of intoxication in criminal cases, and you plan to ask the court in your motion to take judicial notice of both this statute and the driving-while-intoxicated statute. Coupled with the .25 breathalyzer, you like your chances for winning the motion.

What further information will you seek? You may want to serve defendant with a request for admission regarding the authenticity of the police report. (The reason that we are concerned about admissibility is that for exhibits to be considered for summary judgment they must be admissible at trial.) Assume now that you serve such a request and defendant acknowledges its authenticity. What is the significance of this information? You can now seek admission of the authenticated report under the public records exception to the hearsay rule, Fed. R. Civ. P. 803(a)(8). But all may not be so simple. First, the court may find that without foundational details about both the actual testing procedures and the preparation and calibration of the machine that was used for defendant's breathalyzer (which are not in the report), the hearsay information in the report about a .25 reading is too lacking in "trustworthiness" to be admitted. Fed. R. Civ. P. 803(a)(8)(c). Second, the court could hold

that, even if the report is admitted, the statutory presumption of intoxication does not apply to civil cases. What further information will you now look for? You could obtain the affidavit of the officer who administered the breathalyzer. The affidavit would state the officer's expert qualifications, the procedures for the breathalyzer, the results, and his opinion as to the meaning of those results (if he is qualified). You could also depose defendant and ask him about his drinking on the day of the accident. You really don't have much to lose by this strategy. If he acknowledges his drinking, you can attach his deposition to your motion. If he denies it, you may not be able to successfully bring your motion because now his intoxication is a matter of "factual dispute" (unless the breathalyzer reading is undisputed and the presumption applies); however, he would have opposed your motion with an affidavit raising this factual denial of intoxication anyway. And it may be more difficult for him to maintain such a denial under probing examination in a deposition, than when calmly assisting the drafting of his declaration in his attorney's office.

Now let's proceed in our criminal matter with Part 2 of the approach, information-presenting. You are about to call the passerby as your witness. You must, therefore, decide what information you will present in her testimony.

QUESTION 6
What motion theory is indicated by existing information?

The interview with the eyewitness merely confirmed your first analyses. This motion will characterize the show-up as an unduly suggestive identification procedure, violative of due process.

QUESTION 7
What information will you present (in this particular skills performance) in light of your motion theory?

You will want to present information establishing "undue suggestiveness":

- defendant was only person being shown to the victim
- he was held up between two large policemen
- he was handcuffed
- the spotlight of a squad car was focused on his face

QUESTION 8
What reaction to this information do you anticipate from the opposing party?

The prosecutor will have read your motion and planned a response. Two attacks on your witness's information, each ultimately cutting at the persuasive sufficiency of your overall motion, seem possible. First, she may attack the witness's credibility (information showing lack of neutrality, perceptual problems, and so on). Second, she may also attack the logical probativeness of the information, basically arguing that, even if the witness is believed, her information cannot support defendant's MLT: "Unless this court is prepared to rule contrary to all authority that single person show-ups on the street are impermissible, it is hard to imagine—given the propriety of such a procedure—how else it should be done. The fact that the suspect is restrained does not make this suggestive. An eyewitness expects that; he or she knows that this person is a *suspect*. Why else is someone being brought over to see if an identification can be made? The spotlight is here so a person can see clearly enough to make a fair identification. In fact, without this lighting, defense counsel would be asserting that the victim couldn't have clearly seen the man he was identifying and was only responding to the identification procedure." In this example, however, the prosecution would not seem to have a plausible attack on the admissibility of the witness's information.

QUESTION 9
How will you anticipate or respond to this reaction?

Attacks on credibility could be anticipated and cut off in the witness's direct examination at the suppression hearing. For example, you might set the stage for the witness's credibility by asking the witness:

- Do you know the defendant? Had you ever seen him before that night?

- Do you have any strong feelings about the police?

- How far away from the show-up were you standing?

- For how long?

Attacks on logical probativeness could be met by pointing out the probative value of the information in your written brief. But some attorneys we know would counsel you to consider filing a "bare-bones" brief out of concern that you might otherwise "coach" the opposition's witnesses, focusing their attention on the type of facts that they could then supply in the hearing to the detriment of your position. Or you could present in argument to the court all the ways the procedure could have been conducted so as to be less suggestive, thereby making the defendant appear more like a "citizen suspect" than the "man who did it": "Was it really necessary to handcuff him? Did he have to be *both* handcuffed and held by *two* police like public enemy number one? Couldn't they have had him stand under a street light, rather than literally placing him 'in the spotlight' "?

D. PLANNING THE PERFORMANCE OF A MOTION

You are representing a criminal defendant who has been accused of embezzling from his business. Your client was given *Miranda* warnings, agreed to talk to the police, and subsequently admitted to "temporarily borrowing some company funds." He made this admission only after being confronted with the statement of a therapeutic counselor he had been seeing in which the counselor allegedly told the police that the client had admitted such diversion of funds in a therapy session. You decide to bring a motion to suppress defendant's statement based on the somewhat unique, but plausible, grounds that the admission was "tainted" by governmental use of privileged information and that the use of such privileged information is "coercive." You face two hurdles. First, although the therapist-patient privilege applies in your jurisdiction to criminal cases where defendant does not put his mental state in issue, case law has applied the privilege only to licensed psychiatrists and psychologists, never considering its application to one with a counseling degree. Second, even if privilege applies, does governmental use of this information violate the Fourth, Fifth, or Fourteenth Amendments? In this illustration, we will deal *only* with the first issue, whether the communication was privileged. How will you proceed? You need a plan.[1]

---

1. Note that this issue could as easily arise in a civil context. For example, in Appendix II at page 274 there is a motion for a protective order in the case of *Summers v. Proust* resisting the production of counseling records on the grounds that counseling records are confidential. This related, but somewhat different, issue should provide an interesting study for you. Once again, these general

You could plan for this complex situation by using the eight-question performance planning approach we have developed in earlier chapters. In doing so, you might seek theoretical and practical insight from the following references: A.G. Amsterdam, *Trial Manual for the Defense of Criminal Cases* (4th ed. 1984); W.L. Bennett & M.S. Feldman, *Reconstructing Reality in the Courtroom* (1981); The Bureau of National Affairs, Inc., *Civil Trial Manual*, ch. 41 (1986); The Bureau of National Affairs, Inc., *Criminal Practice Manual*, ch. 51 (1987); R.S. Haydock, D.F. Herr, and J.W. Stempel, *Fundamentals of Pretrial Litigation* (1985); I.F. Lane, *Goldstein Trial Techniques*, ch. 7 (3d ed. 1984); C.A. Wright and A.R. Miller, *Federal Practice and Procedure* (1987). Now the approach:

QUESTION 1
What is the range of possible practical/strategic considerations and situations that could arise in making a motion?

Based on our experience, we include fourteen areas, each of which suggests a range of possible considerations or situations that could arise within the area. We also provide some pointers within each.

Area One
Deciding which, of all the motions you could theoretically present, you will bring before the court

What is the potential benefit of the motion you are thinking of bringing? Will it take time from working on other aspects of the case or raise costs to the client that are disproportionate to any potential benefits that could be achieved by the motion? Looking at the motion in conjunction with other motions you are bringing, what is the risk that the court will think that you are "shotgunning," that is, just bringing motions because they can be brought without any sense that you believe they raise genuine issues in the case? Is there a risk that the particular motion is of such marginal merit that by mere association it will diminish the credibility of other more deserving motions that you are also raising?

Initially, you must recognize that your credibility

with the court is crucial. The judge has broad discretion and in most decisions she will be upheld on appeal unless the ruling is clearly an abuse of discretion. In exercising discretion, she will be influenced by how you legally and factually back up any motion you may bring. If she believes that you merely have gone through a form book and raised every motion listed, she is not as likely to focus on the merits of the individual motions and will instead be likely to discount your entire presentation.

In determining which motions to raise and how you will raise them (e.g., will you attempt a full evidentiary hearing with witnesses flown in from all over the country?), you must, as discussed in Chapter I, consider your time and the available resources. Accordingly, you will generally bring those motions that are needed to preserve what you see as legitimate issues on appeal; those that are instrumental in filling particular "needs"; and those that are reasonably calculated to give you a particular benefit (gain of information, a helpful procedural ruling).

Area Two
Communicating your motion to the court

Will the motion be written? If so, will it take a form analogous to an extensive appellate brief, or be a simple statement of your position, or be a simple statement to be supplemented later in the process by further points and authorities? Would you ever make a motion by telephone? When? Is there any time an ex parte motion might be appropriate?

Trial courts are generally very busy. Trial judges will not usually have much time to read your motion or do background research (though some trial judges do have law clerks who do some research for them). Accordingly, your motions should tend to be to the point, short, and clear. On the other hand, if you have an issue of first impression (or you are in front of a judge who enjoys delving into the law and its theory), your motion might more closely resemble an appellate presentation with extensive case and policy analysis.

Area Three
Supporting the factual allegations in your motion

Will you require a full evidentiary hearing? Will you include with your motion an offer of proof, witness declarations, documents?

---

types of motion situations where one party seeks information, the second party refuses to answer or files for a protective order, and the first party files a motion to compel are common in civil practice.

This Area embraces much of this illustration concerning the criminal defendant and the patient-therapist privilege. Note that motions that require an evidentiary basis sometimes will be submitted on a transcript or report (preliminary hearing, police report) as the factual basis for the motion. This is usually done when the parties agree on the facts, but dispute the result of applying the law.

Area Four
Determining what is to be included in your motion

What formal parts must be included (heading, statement of facts, proof of service)? How much detail will you provide concerning your factual position if there is going to be an evidentiary hearing (i.e., is there a concern about "coaching" adversary witnesses)? Will you attach any documents (declarations, exhibits)?

Although the precise form required for a motion will vary with the particular motion and jurisdiction, and while you must always check local court rules regarding proper paper size, typeface, spacing, indexes, and so on, the elements that make up a motion are fairly standard. (See the sample civil motion at pages 274-290 for illustrations of these elements.)

1. *Heading and Caption.* The name of the court to which you are addressing the motion appears as the heading at the top of the first page of the motion. The caption is placed just below this heading and is made up of several parts. On the left side of the page, the names of the parties are listed. On the right side the case number, which will be assigned by the court clerk, appears. Directly under the case number, the name of the document being filed appears (e.g., Motion for Protective Order; Declaration of B.Y. Davis in Support of Defendant Proust's Motion for a Protective Order). See page 275. Note, however, that in some jurisdictions, in addition to this information or as an alternative, the attorney lists on the first page of the motion *all* the documents that are being presented to the court.

2. *Notice of Motion.* This establishes the date, time, and courtroom for the hearing on the motion and also states the nature of the motion. See page 274.

3. *Motion.* The motion itself again describes the nature of the request. It also includes a statement of the record on which the motion will be based, and may include a summary statement of the grounds for the motion. See page 275.

4. *Statement of Case.* A statement of the procedural history. It is generally rather summary, but may be a crucial section if the issue is grounded in the proce-

dural history of the case (e.g., a double jeopardy motion). See page 284.

5. *Statement of Facts.* This should include a brief statement of the overall facts in the case and should then primarily focus on the facts underlying the motion. A statement of facts should not be argumentative and therefore should not state conclusions. Yet, it is nevertheless a piece of advocacy and should be organized in such a way as to be persuasive in support of your position on the motion. In constructing this statement, you may use only facts supported in the existing case record (to which you should specifically refer) or in the attachments filed with the motion. See page 284.

6. *Memorandum of Points and Authorities.* A citation of applicable legal authorities and the arguments therefrom as based on your statement of the factual record. See "Memorandum of Law in Support of Defendant Proust's Motion for Protective Order" at pages 284-289.

7. *Conclusion.* A brief summary of the remedy you are seeking from the court and the basic rationale for that request. See page 289.

8. *Attachments.* These are the documents upon which you are making your factual claims—affidavits, declarations, documents, offers of proof, excerpts from transcripts. (Note that if the transcript or any other document is already part of the case record, technically you do not have to include it in your motion. Nonetheless, you may still want to include it for the court's convenience, for emphasis, or for some other tactical consideration.) Each attachment should be identified as an exhibit and given a separate designation (e.g., Exhibit A, Exhibit B, etc.). See, e.g., page 276. However, keep in mind that many courts will not permit you, as the attorney, to assert such facts in an affidavit or declaration since it would be likely to put you in the unethical position of being a witness in a case where you are the attorney. Rather, many courts view an attorney declaration as more properly a vehicle for recounting the procedural posture of the case and the exhibits that are being attached to the motion ("I am submitting in support of this motion Exhibit A, the declaration of Dr. Frances, the treating psychologist").

9. *Proposed Order.* Some jurisdictions require that you include a copy of the written order (if any) you are seeking from the court. Even if not required, you may wish to include such an order to expedite matters if the court rules in your favor. See page 283.

10. *Proof of Service.* This will generally appear on an approved court form. It will establish the proof of service of a copy of your motion papers—by personal service or by mail—on all persons entitled to such service (generally, opposing counsel). See page 290.

While the pieces that constitute a motion are somewhat uniform, the order of those pieces is not. Many lawyers would organize a motion in the sequence suggested above. However, as the sample civil motion illustrates, there are other possibilities. Thus in the sample motion the Statement of the Case and the Statement of Facts are contained as subheadings within the Memorandum of Points and Authorities (page 284). The exhibits follow the motion, but precede the Memorandum. Such a structure is certainly acceptable. Unless there is a particular court rule that governs, your actual construction of the motion should be guided by local custom and the effectiveness of presentation.

Area Five
Making your written motion persuasive

Will you use a more or less formal style? What imagery (if any) will you use? To what extent will your approach be affected by what you know about the judge or your opponent? Will your motion anticipate your adversary's position? Will it anticipate the likely concerns of the court?

This Area has been discussed in the development of an MFT (see page 257). It is also analyzed within this hypothetical (see pages 267-271).

Area Six
Dealing with opposing legal authority

Is it ever ethical to omit such authority? If so, is it tactically wise to do so in your case? If you choose to meet the adverse authority and question its reasoning, attack your opponent's interpretation, or distinguish the adverse authority, will you do so in the main body of your motion or in a footnote?

This issue has both an ethical and a practical aspect. Ethically, you must cite *all* controlling authority in your jurisdiction on an issue even if your opponent does not. ABA Model Rule 3.3(a)(3). Practically, you risk losing the respect of the court in this and future cases if you leave out an important case adverse to your position. If you do, the court will either question your thoroughness and competence or your integrity. Neither option seems desirable. Also, think what your opponent will do if you leave out such authority when you file the motion and opposing counsel then files a response to your motion ("It's interesting that in this 15-page brief, just loaded with cases allegedly favoring the plaintiff, the *only* case on the subject plaintiff omits is one that is dispositive in defendant's favor"). Rather, citing the case will give you an opportunity to weaken its impact ("Although *Grodon v. Hayes* may superficially seem somewhat troublesome, it offers no problem for plaintiff's position in this motion since . . .").

Area Seven
Filing the motion

Will you file it with the court clerk? How many copies do you need? What size paper is acceptable? How will you serve a copy of the motion on your opponent (i.e., personal service, mail)? What type of proof of service do you need?

This information (which may vary from jurisdiction to jurisdiction, court to court, and even judge to judge) can generally be located through the sources provided at pages 253-254.

Area Eight
Getting a hearing on the motion

Will you note the motion with the court clerk or have it set in open court by the judge? Is there a minimum number of days' notice that you must give opposing counsel prior to a hearing on the motion? Can this time be shortened by the judge? Under what circumstances and criteria will the court shorten the time? Must all pretrial motions be set for one hearing? If such a single setting is not mandatory, what are the advantages and disadvantages for your position of having the individual motions heard at separate times?

Information regarding how you calendar a motion can be found in the same manner, and from the same general sources, as the information in Area Seven. Whether to calendar all your motions for a single hearing or separately[2] involves a variety of concerns. If all are brought at once, the court may have difficulty focusing on a particular motion. Also, if a very large number of motions are brought together, the court may become impatient or bored and be likely to deal with each on a rather summary level or give some rulings to one side, some to the other so the

---

2. However, you may not have a choice since many courts require all motions to be brought at once for the sake of efficiency.

process will feel fair. (To combat all this, you can try to submit less important motions on the papers and limit your argument and presentation to a few, significant motions.) On the other hand, if you bring the motions separately (assuming that you can), the court may be annoyed that you are dealing with the motions in piecemeal fashion, or may not give you much time because yours is just one motion in the middle of an entire day's motion calendar (i.e., the court will not have set aside a separate block of time for just your motions). Generally, it's a good idea to first check with court personnel to determine the judge's preference. Remember, however, that if you have a choice, the tactical decision is yours to make. Of course, the court's preference in the matter will be a factor that will weigh heavily in that choice.

Area Nine
Making a persuasive oral argument to the court

What aspects of your motion will you emphasize? How, if at all, will your knowledge of the particular judge affect how you present your argument? How will explicit and implicit time limits set by the court affect your presentation? If you have several motions set for one day, how will you assist the court in focusing sufficient attention on the merits of each separate motion? Will you use any rhetorical questions, imagery, personalization of the issues so they are tied to concerns to which the decisionmaker can relate from his or her own experiences, or any other rhetorical devices?

As a general rule, other than a summary presentation of your important points and the established law, you don't repeat in argument what's already in your papers (or, at least, you do not convey the information in the same way). But trial judges are sometimes too busy to have thoroughly read your motion by the time you are about to argue. If you sense this is possible, be prepared to summarize your position in a few sentences ("As you are aware, Your Honor, our basic position . . ."). Then try to focus on what's really in dispute ("We all agree that the police could stop my client's car. The only issue is whether they could continue his detention after he provided a valid license and registration"). *Encourage* the court to ask you questions. No matter what the question is, providing a reasonable answer will enhance the overall credibility of your position. Deal with practical/administrative concerns that may be implicitly at stake in the judge's mind ("Your Honor, granting this one

motion will not result in this court subsequently facing a flood of similar motions. Here we have a unique, clearly circumscribed situation").

Area Ten
Planning an evidentiary hearing

Which witnesses will you bring? How will you ensure their presence (e.g., subpoena)? What information will the witnesses present? How do you plan to deal with your opponent's witnesses?

This "mini-trial" will involve many basic trial skills that are not dealt with extensively in these materials. We do, however, provide some guidance. Parallels can be drawn to examination of witnesses at a deposition. See Chapter VII at pages 203-206. Also, this hypothetical concerning the patient-psychologist privilege involves the attorney in planning to put on an evidentiary hearing with witnesses.

Area Eleven
Making witnesses effective at an evidentiary hearing

How will you bolster the witness's credibility? Are there admissibility problems with which you need to deal? In how much detail will you present the witness's background? Will you prepare the witness for anticipated cross-examination?

Much of this Area also involves basic trial skills. The crux of this Area—admissibility and credibility of a witness's information—is detailed in Chapter V. These issues are also discussed later at page 268.

Area Twelve
Establishing the record

Will your written motion constitute your record? if not, what will you add (e.g., declarations, testimony)? What will you include in your offers of proof? How much detail will you put in the record? Will you renew your motion throughout the case? When?

This Area is a principal focus in the present illustration in that much of the attorney's energies are directed at making offers of proof and creating a record to support counsel's position at trial and on appeal if necessary.

Area Thirteen
Assessing what to do if the court has ruled against you

Will you move for reconsideration or enter the appellate process, either waiting for appeal or bringing some interlocutory writ? Are the time and dollar costs justified in light of likely results? Do you need to make the record stronger and, therefore, to file a detailed offer of proof with a motion for reconsideration? Did the court give you any room to subsequently renew the motion?

If the court ruled against you, prefacing that ruling with "on the record before me . . . ," the possibility of later providing a different or fuller record is open. If the court stated when making its ruling that "At this time, I am not inclined . . . ," the possibility is left open that this position could change with the court's experiences over time.

One additional point: Sometimes when you believe you are right, you must appeal a judge's ruling on a pretrial writ, should the law in your jurisdiction permit. Just knowing that you're willing to put in this work often makes a judge take your position in subsequent motions seriously. (This will be especially true if you receive anything but a summary denial from the court of appeal—e.g., a stay while the issue is being considered, an order to the opposing party to file a response.)

Area Fourteen
Dealing with the judge if an inappropriate remark is made during your presentation

Suppose that a male judge assigned to the law and motion calendar leans over the bench and says to a female attorney, "Ann, it's so nice to see such a nice pretty young lady in my courtroom. And competent too!" Put yourself in this woman's position. Will you tell the judge that his remarks are inappropriate? Insulting? Or will you just smile? Does your response depend on circumstances, such as the age of the judge? Whether the remark was made in open court or in chambers? Suppose that you think you have an advantage in presenting your client's position by having the judge think kindly of you. Will you encourage the judge by being more feminine in your dress?

Imagine that you consider the remark insulting and unethical conduct by a judge. Do your next steps depend on whether you win or lose the motion? If the judge's remark was not made on the record, should you make a record of the judge's conduct with the court reporter or through a declaration? If it was on the record, should you put your position on the record too? What effect will your actions have on the judge's present and future conduct in the case? On your client who is watching all this? On other judges in the court? On your general reputation with other lawyers? Will you try to just talk to the judge in private? If you do, you need to be aware of the ethics of ex parte contact while a case is being heard by a judge. Your adversary might accuse you of trying to influence the merits of the case, and therefore of unethical conduct. Or is it more appropriate to discuss the matter with the bar association first? Suppose that the bar association does not take any action: Would you report the judge to the appropriate judicial committee for misconduct? If you do, you need to consider the ramifications of your action in terms of the reality of your involvement in the subsequent complaint process: Is the judge's remark truly inappropriate in regard to judicial standards of conduct? What will you accomplish by a complaint? Is the judge known for his "sexist" behavior? Will others support your complaint—both male and female? What will it be like for you personally to go through the complaint process? What is the likely response of the judge? Won't he probably say that the remark was simply made to make you feel comfortable in his courtroom and was not meant disrespectfully? What will be the likely response of other judges you will appear before? Are you just overly sensitive? Or are you entitled to being treated as a mature lawyer?

What if you say to the judge, "Thank you, Your Honor for your kind remarks. But in the future, I would like to be referred to as Ms. Ginger." What effect will that have on your case? Suppose that you make this statement after the case is concluded. Would you want to appear before that judge in the future? If you are practicing in a law office, will your statement affect other lawyers in your office?

Now suppose that you are the adversary. Will you tell the judge his conduct is inappropriate? If you believe the judge's attitude is prejudicing you in the motion, will you put the remark on the record? What would you do if you heard that the other lawyer went to see the judge about the judge's inappropriate remark?

QUESTION 2
Which of these practical/strategic situations will you deal with at this point?

You have a wide range of concerns for which you must plan in presenting your Motion to Suppress the

Defendant's Statement in our hypothetical case dealing with the therapist privilege. While focusing on how to support your motion factual theory (Area Three) and on making a strong record (Area Twelve), bringing this motion also involves drafting a persuasive written motion (Area Five), making a persuasive oral argument (Area Nine), organizing an evidentiary hearing (Area Ten), and making your supporting witnesses credible (Area Eleven).

QUESTION 3
What are your objectives in this situation?

You should develop a record that will convince the trial court of your position, preserve the issue for appeal (interlocutory or after trial) if the court denies your motion, and leave you with a persuasive record for the appellate court to consider.

QUESTION 4
How will you achieve your objectives?

You will likely need to do several things. We have focused on three such tasks (although you may well think of others): (1) filing persuasive written papers in support of your motion; (2) requesting an evidentiary hearing; and (3) planning an effective hearing.

First, you must file persuasive written papers in support of your motion. (These will also preserve your record for appeal.) This written motion must present a clearly articulated motion theory. Therefore, you should start thinking about your motion legal theory. In this hypothetical case, you would probably present two related, but distinct, MLTs. We will spend some time developing these two theories, delving into substantive law. Why this substantive focus in the midst of our performance analysis? Because an effective performance requires effective legal theories. There is, moreover, a necessary interrelationship between your ability to analyze substantive law within the context of your strategic objectives, and your ability to translate that analysis to the court through your performance. Now the two theories:

The first would be based on the traditional criteria, gleaned from case law, for making privileged communications in a particular relationship. Basically, these criteria focus on finding that a strong societal interest in fostering the particular relationship exists and that this relationship is not reasonably possible unless the communications that transpire are kept confidential.

The second MLT would start at a different point. Instead of focusing on criteria derived from case law, this second legal theory would begin with an established privilege—the therapist privilege as applied to psychiatrists and psychologists. That being so, the argument would follow that the counselor *is* a "therapist" under the privilege or, at least, should be treated the same as the analogous groups of professionals who already benefit from the privilege. The presentation of this second MLT would be enhanced if you could cite some cases applying this "functional equivalent" analysis in the area of privilege (e.g., if the physician-patient privilege was applied to a midwife in some, preferably your, jurisdiction).

The general thrust that your supporting motion factual theories must take under these two MLTs is fairly clear. The first motion theory (counseling requires confidential communications) will require a "story" something like:

"One of the greatest losses of human resources in our families, schools, and workplaces comes from emotional maladies and their accomplices, drugs and alcohol. In the past few decades, therapy has increasingly provided a countering force to these maladies. Counseling is one of the chief sources of this desperately needed service. Of course, the intimate and totally open interactions upon which the effectiveness of counseling depends would be all but impossible without an unquestioned obligation of confidentiality."

The "story" for the second MLT (a counselor is a therapist) will probably be something like:

"Though some therapists are wedded to a single school of psychology and a single set of techniques, most draw upon a wide range of therapeutic tools, reflecting a number of schools and movements, and draw on these different tools as the situation requires. Counselors are trained to utilize this same eclectic set of methodologies. For the most part, one would see little difference in therapy conducted by a counselor, psychiatrist, or psychologist. They basically deal with the same problems, have the same goals, follow the same process, and utilize most of the same techniques."

You now have two good-sounding MFTs to support the corresponding MLTs, but on what basis can you make the factual assertions that form the basis of your stories? In the suggestive identification motion (see pages 256-257), you developed your MFT from police reports and witness interviews. Where, however, will you obtain the information for this motion?

You cannot perform without information, so let's briefly mix a little content planning into our performance planning. Expert witnesses would seem to be indicated since both these stories seem to be based on expert knowledge (although you could perhaps add to the impact of the motions if you included the declarations of some sympathetic patients of counselors, who describe the significance of confidentiality for them). For this case, therapists would seem to be the category of experts indicated. (Inclusion of psychologists and psychiatrists, as well as counselors, might be a good idea to avoid the appearance of group self-interest. However, it is most important to find experts with whom you can effectively work.) Thus you must find some experts, interview them, find information that supports or helps further modify and develop both your tentative MLTs and supporting MFTs, draft the experts' declarations, and file the declarations with your motions. Good, but what will the actual experts' declarations that you must draft look like? Probably they will resemble a far more expanded version of the following example of a declaration in support of the first MLT (i.e., the traditional case criteria for privilege):

> "Over 45 percent of people who seek therapy seek out a counselor. Counselors deal with family problems, alcohol addiction, recurrent depression. All counselors, as all therapists, commit themselves to ensuring that their clients' secrets will be kept in total confidence.[3] To permit it to be otherwise in the therapeutic setting would undermine the fragile bond of trust that is central to the therapeutic relationship."

The declarations will also contain sufficient information about each expert's education, training, and practice to establish that they are qualified to give expert opinions under Rules of Evidence (e.g., Fed. R. Evid. 702 et seq.). Also, if you have chosen your experts well, this evidentiary foundation will impress the court with the quality of your experts, rendering your presentation more persuasive.

Second, you probably should request an evidentiary hearing. Evidentiary hearings on motions seem far more common in criminal than in civil areas. Whether this reflects the heavy fact/credibility emphasis in many criminal motions or mere custom, we do not know.

If, however, this hypothetical involved a civil motion to compel answers from a counselor who had claimed the therapist privilege at a deposition, the issue would most likely be resolved on the motion papers submitted and arguments of counsel without resort to an evidentiary hearing. The facts that you would refer to in an argument would be contained in the type of affidavit or declaration discussed in Area Four. For an example of a declaration of a psychologist in support of a protective order in a related, but slightly different, motion, refer to Appendix II at page 281.

A full hearing with live witnesses can paint a picture rich in detail and nuance that is unlikely to be conveyed by your papers alone. This is particularly true if your experts are impressive and would thus favorably affect the atmosphere in which the judge rules on your motion. (Of course, there are witnesses who sound better on paper, either because in person they are unprepossessing or because the weaknesses in their position are not obvious until probed by an opponent's cross-examination.) Your request for the hearing will be noted in your papers, and your experts' declarations will be characterized as "offers of proof" as to what their testimony would be if permitted to testify at the hearing. (These offers of proof will also preserve "testimony" for appeal if your request and motion are subsequently denied by the trial court. In such a circumstance, the appellate court will assume, for purposes of its decision, that your experts would have testified consistently with their offers of proof.) In many jurisdictions you may even calendar the hearing with a court clerk, pending the court's decision whether to permit it to proceed.

Third, you must plan an effective evidentiary hearing. This will involve selecting and preparing your witnesses and exhibits, researching possible evidentiary issues, and thinking through oral presentation.

QUESTION 5
What problems do you anticipate?

Three problems come to mind. First, your experts may be very impressive in person, but the court may not want to allocate time for a full evidentiary hearing. Instead, it may choose to exercise its broad discretion in whether to grant a hearing and choose to rely instead on the declarations or offers of proof. In most jurisdictions, the court can consider hearsay (e.g., a declaration) and otherwise inadmissible evidence when ruling on a motion regarding an evidentiary issue (e.g., the existence of the privilege raised here).

---

3. If counselors already assume confidentiality in their work, you might emphasize that fact to let the court know that it may be facing an interesting wrinkle if it denies the privilege—that is, being forced to put counselors in jail for contempt when they refuse to testify against their clients. (Compare newspaper reporters and their sources.)

See, e.g., Fed. R. Evid. 1001(d)(1). Therefore, the Rules of Evidence do not require an evidentiary hearing in this situation. But in a civil summary judgment motion, Fed. R. Civ. P. 56 prohibits consideration of information that is based on inadmissible evidence.

Second, you face some tough undercurrents that will be likely to pull the court away from granting your motion. You are asking the court to extend the reach of a privilege. Courts, however, tend to view privileges as impediments to "the truth," which accordingly should be construed narrowly. Also, you face the court's natural reluctance to suppress clear evidence of criminal conduct. To the extent finding the communication privileged will lead to such a result, the trial court may not want to extend the privilege further than the existing law absolutely requires. This problem becomes acute when the applicable case law makes a genuine issue of whether the patient-therapist privilege extends to those with a master's degree in counseling.

Third, even if you can locate appropriate experts with whom you can work effectively, your client may not have sufficient resources to pay the experts' fees or the cost may be disproportionate to the overall cost or value of the case.

QUESTION 6
How will you meet such problems?

The first problem: the evidentiary hearing. As to this problem, you can focus on convincing the court that this issue is worth its time by characterizing the issue as an important one with broad implications. How? By including expert witness declarations that refer to statistical data and studies, you can establish that the use of counselors as therapists is widespread. Amicus briefs from respected organizations can assure that this issue has impact on a serious, well-organized profession. Statistical studies and data indicating (if possible) that counselors are the therapists of the less affluent will additionally color the issue as one with significant implication. (We are assuming, for this illustration, that counselors' fees are substantially less than those of psychiatrists and psychologists.) After all, if the less affluent rely on counselors for their therapy, yet therapy cannot be effective without the confidentiality, the court's decision may affect whether the less affluent will have access to effective therapy. All of the above should impress upon the court the desirability of being able to hear and question the witnesses.

Next, you can try to convince the court that the hearing on this important issue will take not a minute more than necessary. Here, your motion can include your assurances that the testimony will be presented in an efficient manner. Finally, having endeavored to convince the court that this issue is worth the time of the hearing, and that the hearing will not take that much time, you might also attempt to convince the court that the issue and experts are *interesting* and the court's role will be significant. You might argue:

> "Although on the horizon for nearly a decade, no court has yet fully analyzed this fascinating issue. . . . Dr. Billstone, our main witness, has almost single-handedly changed American therapy."

The promise of challenge and excitement can hold its own lure.

The second problem: overcoming the factors that might make the court reluctant to grant the motion. Initially, the same tactic that you used to convince the court that the issue was of sufficient importance to merit a full evidentiary hearing should also impress the court that the broad significance of the issue at hand outweighs the court's short-run concerns about suppressing crucial evidence in an embezzlement prosecution. Of course, the court can ignore this entire issue by ruling on the second prong of your argument—"This court does not have to reach the issue of privilege because, even if I found a privilege here, using such privileged information to obtain defendant's confession would not run afoul of any constitutional provision."

But what about the court's reticence to expand the privilege beyond the clearly discernible categories of psychologist and psychiatrist? If the court grants the privilege here, will the court hear from social workers next, with fraternity and sorority mothers looming on the horizon? You can deal with these concerns in a couple of ways. To begin with, you can anticipate them, and incorporate your response into your written motion. For example, you might detail the education and certification of counselors by including declarations, handbooks listing certification requirements, and manuals. This would allow you to argue:

> "Counselors are therapists by education and training. Thus they are like psychologists and psychiatrists, and unlike other occupations in which providing therapy may at times be required (e.g., police officers, prison officials, school teachers). The demanding course of study and subsequent stringent certification of these counselors into a recognized therapeutic profession separate them from other professions that

potentially have some therapeutic aspects to their work. Thus, in extending the benefit of privilege to counselors, the court does not risk that the privilege will be expanded beyond the accepted therapeutic community."

You can point out the unfairness of not expanding the privilege in this situation in your oral presentation (assuming that you have convincing data that counselors are the therapists for the less affluent). Playing on the images of the rich and the poor, you could argue:

"Without this privilege, we send a cruel message to our less affluent. We are saying that not only must you live your days toiling under economic strain, but when that strain and other stresses become too much, and you need professional help to guide you through, you can't have it. Only the rich, who can afford to pay the bills of psychiatrists and psychologists, can meet with a therapist they can trust because theirs is a practice the law shields in confidentiality. You poorer folks are permitted no such trust."

The third problem: cost of expert prohibitive. Be creative and conjure up less expensive alternatives. Due to the significance of this issue to their interests, members of some association of counselors may be willing to donate their time. This could also enhance the image of their professionalism and, with it, the credibility of the counselors presenting information before the court. Or some expert may owe you a favor, and you may decide at this time to call in the favor. Whether you will actually call in this chit at this time will be determined by a number of factors—what's at stake overall (death penalty v. $50 fine), the likely significance of this expert to the overall success of the motion, the significance of the motion to the overall success of the case, and so on. Also, courts often have inherent or statutory power to provide funds for experts when needed. This would, of course, require that you bring a separate motion for the funds. Problem 88 (page 310) is an example of such a motion within a motion. (It involves a motion for court funds to pay for an expert to conduct a community attitudes survey in support of a motion to change venue.)

QUESTION 7
If you can't solve the problems, what will you do?

If the court will not let you present live witness testimony at a full evidentiary hearing, you can ensure

that your offers of proof are rich in detail, you can accompany them with effective exhibits (e.g., charts and graphs comparing per capita use of counselors with that for psychiatrists and psychologists; a chart paralleling the functions and techniques of counselors with the other therapy professionals to show their similarity; and so on), and you can provide extensive resumes detailing the credentials and expertise of your witnesses.

If you cannot overcome the court's reluctance to expand the privilege, you will lose your motion at the trial level, but will have created a record that will both preserve your issue and be persuasive in the court of appeals.

You can similarly be resourceful in facing your inability to pay for the live testimony of top experts (whose fees often exceed $500 a day, plus expenses). You may decide to rely on a declaration from some local counselor. Although not likely to be as persuasive as you might desire, this declaration would still preserve the issue for appeal and provide you with something that you can use in the argument to the trial court on your motion.

QUESTION 8
What ethical concerns do you face in attempting to achieve your objectives?

In filing declarations and written offers of proof, it may be tempting to use these documents as vehicles to slip in otherwise inadmissible information or inflammatory material through which you intend to prejudice the court against the other party or counsel. You may even consider doing it, not to gain an unfair tactical advantage, but in the heat of emotion where you have lost perspective as to your professional role. Control yourself. It's unethical. ABA Rule 3.4(e). It's unprofessional. Judges do not like lawyers getting personal with each other and the opposing party, and such action will generally lessen their respect for you, and possibly, your positions. Your opponent will turn it on you ("Counsel's resort to using the court's process as an excuse to viciously attack me and my client, instead of answering the issues at hand, speaks eloquently to the 'strength' of his position on those vital issues"). After all, what do you think of people who are sneaks? Similarly, a totally frivolous summary judgment motion brought only to familiarize the judge with your side of the case, or as a trial balloon to see how your evidence will be perceived, is ethically suspect. ABA Rule 3.1. In fact, if you file in federal court an affidavit in support of a motion for summary judgment and do so in bad faith (e.g., for purposes of delay), the court can assess you for the other side's costs and attorney's fees for the motion and hold you in contempt. Fed. R. Civ. P. 56(g). On the other hand, as long as you construct your record from information that you believe to be truthful, and you are in good faith in believing the information is appropriate to the issue (as opposed to being injected solely to bring prejudicial information before the judge), you will not run afoul of ethical proscriptions.

E. PLANNING QUESTIONS

You have considered the various facets of preparing a motion and the rationale for each. Following is a series of general questions for preparing legal motions. You may want to refer to them, and expand on them, in planning your motions.

I. *Objectives*
   1. What objectives can you accomplish with a motion?
   2. Which of these objectives apply to your case?
   3. How does your motion objective further your representational strategy?
   4. What is your "basic task"?
II. *Preparation*
   1. What preparation will you do when planning to make motions in your case?
   2. What information will you look at? Who will you talk to?
   3. How will you obtain the information?
III. *Content Planning*
   A. *Obtaining Information*
      1. Looking at the various "situations" in your case, which motions are indicated?
      2. What are the typical motions that arise in a case such as yours?
         a. Are any indicated in this case?
         b. Which ones?
      3. Do you have any "needs" (e.g., problems) that a court order could assist?
         a. Which needs?
         b. What specific type of court order would help?
      4. Think of your motion legal theory (MLT):
         a. Which ones are available to support the motion you have chosen?

   b. Which ones appear viable in the present case?
      (1) What are the "elements" of such theories?
      (2) Are there any problems with your legal theories?
      (3) How do you propose to deal with such problems if raised by your opponent or the court?
5. Think of your motion factual theory (MFT):
   a. What is your "story"?
   b. What is the information upon which you intend to base this story?
      (1) Where did (will) you obtain this information?
      (2) How will you present it to the court (e.g., declaration, testimony)?
      (3) Do you anticipate any admissibility problems?
6. Specify the information that you possess so as to meet "sufficiency" concerns as to each element of your legal theory.
7. How will you make your story persuasive?
   a. Will you tie your story to the policy rationale that underlies your legal theory?
   b. Will you try something else or something additional (e.g., vivid imagery)?
8. How do you expect your opponent to respond to your factual theory?
   a. Do you anticipate your opponent putting forth any information of his or her own?
   b. How will you respond?
9. Thinking of your case theory:
   a. What effect will winning your motion have on your case theory?
   b. What effect if you lose?
   c. What will you do if you lose?
   d. Does your motion risk putting you in a position that is inconsistent with your case theory?
   e. If so, can you avoid this consequence and still bring the motion?
B. *Reassessment and Reevaluation*
   1. Whether you won or lost:

a. How did the result of the motion affect your case theory? Your overall representational strategy?

b. What information did you obtain in the motion process?

c. What bearing (if any) does this information have on your case theory? Your representational strategy?

2. If you lost:

a. Will you seek some form of appeal or reconsideration?

b. Will you try to "clean up" the record?

c. Did the court's decision give you room to renew the motion?

d. If so, will you renew it? When?

IV. *Performance Planning*

A. *Technical Skills*

1. How (generally) do you make a "record"?

a. What record would you make to preserve the issue in your motion for appeal?

b. What kind of record would you make to "win"?

2. What points will you emphasize in argument?

a. Which are the strengths of your argument? Weaknesses?

b. How will you deal with the weaknesses?

c. What practical concerns might the court have?

d. How will you address these concerns?

e. What is the key point on which you must persuade the court in order to win?

B. *Nuts-and-Bolts Matters*

1. What are the local rules, procedures, etc., for bringing motions?

2. Who (if anyone) will you subpoena?

3. What procedure must you follow to serve such subpoenas?

4. Will you calendar all your motions for one hearing?

C. *Ethical Considerations*

1. Do you think it proper to bring a motion to gain some tactical advantage unrelated to the object of the motion itself? For example:

a. Does it seem proper to bring a suppression motion (with a plausible legal basis) solely to get discovery?

b. Is this the same problem as seeking the name of a police informant, not because you want the name, but because you hope the prosecution will dismiss the case rather than turn over the name if the court orders it to be revealed?

c. What about bringing a motion to gain leverage for dismissal or settlement because you know the motion will embarrass your adversary?

2. Assuming that you believe the above conduct improper, how would you have the courts control their use of motions for purposes other than those explicitly stated in the motion if the motion were otherwise based on reasonable legal grounds? Does your method for control jeopardize other interests?

APPENDIX I. CRIMINAL MOTION CHECKLIST

The following checklist provides examples of potential motion topics; we believe that such a list can be helpful when brainstorming for possible motions and motion legal theories (MLTs).

Potential Topics for Criminal Pretrial Motions

Diversion
Civil compromise

Venue/change
Bail/own recognizance
Competency hearing
Speedy trial/prearrest delay
Strike prior conviction for unconstitutionality (generally, failure to provide
      counsel or obtain waiver of rights at a guilty plea)
Continuance
Appointment of expert
Discovery
Destruction/loss of evidence
Free transcript
Informant identity
Jeopardy
Request for line-up
Multiple prosecution ("single transaction" or "course of conduct" charged
      as multiple offenses, or existence of previous acquittal or conviction
      arising from same transaction or course of conduct)
Reduce felony to misdemeanor
Review preliminary hearing/indictment for lack of probable cause or pro-
      cedural defects
Severance of counts
Severance of defendants
Suppression of evidence (search & seizure)
- detention ("stop")
- frisk
- search warrant (place, thing, time, hearsay)
- arrest (with/without warrant)
- search incident to arrest
- search of automobiles
- emergency search
- administrative search
- inventory/booking search
- plain view
- consent
- taint

Suppress statement of defendant
- taint
- involuntary statement
- *Mintz* violation

Challenge of judge
- cause
- preemptory

Suppress identification
- suggestive
- failure to provide counsel at line-up

In limine evidence matters (e.g., use of prior uncharged acts, use of prior
      conviction for impeachment, admissibility of novel scientific test)

APPENDIX II. SAMPLE CIVIL MOTION*

SUPERIOR COURT OF MAJOR

JAMNER COUNTY

GRETCHEN SUMMERS,	)	
Plaintiff,	)	
	)	No. 8x-7-43
v.	)	
	)	NOTE FOR CIVIL
MARC PROUST,	)	MOTION CALENDAR
	)	(Clerk's Action
Defendant.	)	Required)

TO: THE CLERK OF THE COURT; and to all parties named below:

PLEASE TAKE NOTICE that an issue of law in this case will be heard on the date below and the Clerk is directed to note this issue on the Civil Motion Calendar.

DATE OF HEARING: Wednesday (Day of Week) March 15, 198X (Calendar Date)

TIME OF HEARING: 9:30 a.m.

PLACE OF HEARING: Before Hon. S. Frankel, W965

NATURE OF MOTION: MOTION FOR PROTECTIVE ORDER

DATED: February 27, 198X . ______________________
Typed Name: B.Y. Davis
Attorney for Defendant Proust
Phone: (206) 421-0280

OTHER PARTIES REQUIRING NOTICE:
Fill In & Check Box If Backside Is Used [ ]

Name: F. C. Townsend	Name:
Address: 1600 Nat'l Bank Bldg. Jamner, Major 96120	Address:
Phone: (206) 825-6245	Phone:
Attorney for: Plaintiff	Attorney for:

*Read this sample civil motion in conjunction with the commentary at pages 263-264, which discusses the basic elements that constitute a motion with reference to specific examples in this motion.

```
 1

 2                    SUPERIOR COURT OF MAJOR

 3                       JAMNER COUNTY

 4   GRETCHEN SUMMERS,              )
                                    )
 5                    Plaintiff,    )    No. 8X-7-43
                                    )
 6   v.                             )
                                    )
 7   MARC PROUST,                   )    MOTION FOR
                                    )    PROTECTIVE ORDER
 8                    Defendant.    )
     _____)

 9

10        Pursuant to Civil Rule 26(c) defendant Marc Proust

11   requests a protective order in the form of the draft

12   "Protective Order" attached to this motion.  This motion

13   is supported by the accompanying Affidavit and

14   Declarations of B.Y. Davis, attorney for defendant,

15   Exhibit A; and affidavit of Dr. Joaquin Johnson,

16   psychologist, Exhibit C; and a Memorandum of Law in

17   Support of This Motion for a Protective Order.

          DATED: February 19, 198X.
18

19                              By _____
                                   B.Y. Davis
20                                 Attorney for Defendant
                                   Marc Proust
21                                 18 Tulip Lane
                                   Jamner, Major 96120
22                                 (206) 421-0280

23

24

25

26

27

28


     MOTION FOR PROTECTIVE ORDER        B.Y. Davis
```

Exhibit A

SUPERIOR COURT OF MAJOR
JAMNER COUNTY

Gretchen Summers,	)	
Plaintiff,	)	No. 8X-7-43
v.	)	DECLARATION BY B.Y. DAVIS
	)	IN SUPPORT OF DEFENDANT
Marc Proust,	)	PROUST'S MOTION FOR A
	)	PROTECTIVE ORDER
Defendant.	)	

B.Y. Davis declares under penalty of perjury that the following information is correct to the best of his knowledge and belief:

1.   I am the attorney for defendant Marc Proust in Summers v. Proust.

2.   Defendant Proust is seeking a Protective Order. The plaintiff, Gretchen Summers, seeks discovery of, among other documents, medical notes and records of Marc Proust's psychological treatment by Dr. Johnson, Ph.D. Mr. Proust refuses to answer interrogatory and request 10(E) which request a copy of or disclosure of the contents of the medical records in Dr. Johnson's possession.

3.   In support of this motion for a protective order, I am submitting Exhibit A, this declaration; Exhibit B, an excerpt of plaintiff's request for discovery and Mr. Proust's response (Question No. 10(E)); Exhibit C, the affidavit of Dr. Joaquin Johnson, Ph.D., and points and authorities.

DATED: February 19, 198X.

_____
B.Y. Davis
Jamner, Major

Declaration of B.Y. Davis   Page - 1   B.Y. Davis

Exhibit B

SUPERIOR COURT OF MAJOR
JAMNER COUNTY

GRETCHEN SUMMERS,   )
)
            Plaintiff,   )   No. 8X-7-43
)
v.   )   PLAINTIFF SUMMERS' FIRST
)   SET OF INTERROGATORIES
MARC PROUST,   )   AND REQUEST FOR DOCUMENTS
)   TO DEFENDANT PROUST
            Defendant.   )
_____)

TO: Defendant Marc Proust and his attorney, B. Y. Davis.

     In accordance with Rules 26, 33, and 34 of the Civil

Rules for Superior Court, please answer the following

interrogatories and requests for production under oath

separately, fully, in the space provided, adding pages if

additional pages are necessary, within twenty (20) days of the

date of service upon you.

     If any part of the following interrogatories or requests

cannot be answered in full, please answer to the extent

possible, specifying the reasons for your inability to answer

fully and stating whatever information or knowledge you have

concerning the unanswered portion.

     These interrogatories and requests for production are

continuing in nature, and you are requested to provide any

information which alters or augments the answers given through

supplemental answers. Supplemental answers should be provided

within a reasonable time following discovery of the additional

information and prior to trial.

Plaintiff Summers' First   Page - 1   Townsend & Seebreeze
Interrogatories   Attorneys for Plaintiff

MATTERS OF GENERAL APPLICATION AND DEFINITIONS

A.   The answer to each interrogatory or request for production shall include such knowledge of the defendant as is within his custody, possession, or control. Such knowledge includes documents in his custody, possession, or control, or those documents under common control, the control of predecessors in interest, consultants, accountants, attorneys, or other agents. When facts set forth in answers or portions of answers are supplied upon information and belief rather than upon actual knowledge, the defendant should specifically describe or identify the source or sources of such information and belief. Should the defendant be unable to answer any interrogatory or portion of an interrogatory by either actual knowledge or upon information and belief, the defendant should describe his efforts to obtain such information.

B.   In response to each interrogatory or request for production, if the defendant does not answer the interrogatory or request for production in whole or in part because the defendant is unable to do so, defendant should identify each person the defendant believes has information regarding the subject of such interrogatory.

C.   If the defendant contends that the answer to any interrogatory or request for production is privileged in whole or in part, or otherwise objects to any part of any interrogatory or request for production, or maintains that an identified document would be excludable from production to the defendants in discovery regardless of its relevance, defendant

Plaintiff Summers' First   Page - 2   Townsend & Seebreeze
Interrogatories   Attorneys for Plaintiff

should state the reasons for each objection or grounds for exclusion and identify each person having knowledge of the factual basis, if any, on which the privilege or other ground is asserted.

D.   For the purpose of these interrogatories and requests for production, the term "document" shall mean any book, pamphlet, periodical, letter, report, memorandum, notation, message, telegram, cable, record, study, working paper, chart, index, tape, correspondence, records of purchase or sale, contracts, agreements, leases, invoices, electronic or other transcriptions or taping of telephone or personal conversations or conferences, or any and all other written, printed, typed, punched, taped, filmed, or graphic matter, or tangible thing, however produced or reproduced.

E.   For the purpose of these interrogatories and requests for production:

1.   The terms "identify" or "identification" when used in reference to an individual person shall mean to state his full name, present address, telephone number, and, if known, his present position and business affiliation.

. . . .

INTERROGATORY 10(E):

Please attach copies or releases for all medical bills, statements, narrative medical reports, hospital records, medical test results, receipts for prescriptions, written documents, notes and other materials concerning your health, injuries or illnesses during the past ten years which have

Plaintiff Summers' First   Page - 3   Townsend & Seebreeze
Interrogatories   Attorneys for Plaintiff

1

been suffered by you prior to the incident which is the

2

subject matter of this lawsuit.

3

ANSWER: Objection. Privileged.

4

DATE: January 1, 198X.

5

6

By: _____

7

Attorney for Plaintiff Summers
F. C. Townsend

8

Townsend & Seebreeze
1600 Nat'l Bank Building

9

Jamner, Major 96120
Telephone No. (206) 825-6245

10

11

12

13

14

15

16

17

18

19

20

21

22

23

24

25

26

27

28

Plaintiff Summers' First   Page - 4   Townsend & Seebreeze
Interrogatories   Attorneys for Plaintiff

Exhibit C

SUPERIOR COURT OF MAJOR
JAMNER COUNTY

GRETCHEN SUMMERS,	)	
Plaintiff,	)	No. 8X-7-43
v.	)	AFFIDAVIT OF DR. JOAQUIN JOHNSON IN SUPPORT OF
MARC PROUST,	)	MOTION FOR PROTECTIVE ORDER
Defendant.	)	

STATE OF MAJOR   )
) ss.
COUNTY OF JAMNER   )

Dr. Joaquin Johnson sworn on oath states:

1.   I am a licensed clinical psychologist in the State of Major.

2.   Marc Proust has been under my care and treatment for approximately three years for treatment of arachnophobia, the unreasonable fear of spiders.

3.   Arachnophobia is a somewhat rare phobia. Arachnophobia develops most frequently from trauma experienced during early childhood, often before the patient has developed cognitive memory to recall the trauma. In Mr. Proust's case, because his initial trauma was so strong, details of the incident are suppressed in his unconscious.

4.   My treatment of Mr. Proust involves close examination of the manifestations of Mr. Proust's condition as well as intense scrutiny of Mr. Proust's family and intimate relationships. Necessarily, such an examination will involve deeply personal revelations. Confidentiality between me, as

Affidavit of Dr. Joaquin Johnson   Page 1   B.Y. Davis
                                                     Attorney

therapist, and my patient, Marc Proust, is absolutely
essential to his effective treatment.

5.   During the course of therapy, Mr. Proust has
confronted several very personal revelations. While his
condition has greatly improved since therapy began, further
treatment is necessary. Disclosure of psychological notes and
evaluations made during the course of his therapy would
severely impair his future treatment, as well as set back his
current progress. Because his initial childhood trauma and
subsequent manifestations are so very personal, successful
treatment necessarily depends on Proust's sense of security
and confidentiality in his communication with me.

_____
Dr. Joaquin Johnson
Ph.D.

SIGNED AND SWORN before me on February 19, 198X.

_____
Notary Public
Jamner, Major

Affidavit of Dr. Joaquin Johnson   Page 2   B.Y. Davis
                                                  Attorney

```
 1                    SUPERIOR COURT OF MAJOR
 2                       JAMNER COUNTY

 3   GRETCHEN SUMMERS,           )
                                 )
 4            Plaintiff,         )    No. 8x-7-43
                                 )
 5   v.                          )    PROTECTIVE ORDER
                                 )
 6   MARC PROUST,                )
                                 )
 7            Defendant.         )
     _____)
```

8   Defendant Marc Proust applied for a Protective Order in

9   the matter of <u>Summers v. Proust</u>. This Court considered the

10   motion, affidavit of Dr. Johnson and Declaration of B.Y.

11   Davis, the Points and Authorities submitted by plaintiff and

12   defendant and the arguments of counsel. It is ordered:

13   Plaintiff Summers is prohibited from discovering the

14   psychological treatment records of the defendant Marc Proust.

15   <u>Additional Provision</u>. Nothing in this Order shall

16   preclude any party from applying to the court for additional

17   or different protective provisions in respect to specific

18   documents if the need should arise during this litigation.

19   DATED: March 16, 198X.

20   _____
                                Judge
21   Presented by:

22   _____
23   B.Y. Davis
     Attorney for Defendant Marc Proust

24   Approved as to Form,
     Notice of Presentation Waived:
25

26   _____
     F.C. Townsend
     Attorney for Plaintiff
27

28

     Protective Order   Page - 1   B.Y. Davis

SUPERIOR COURT OF MAJOR
JAMNER COUNTY

GRETCHEN SUMMERS,   )
)
              Plaintiff,   )   No. 8x-7-43
)
v.   )   MEMORANDUM OF LAW IN
)   SUPPORT OF DEFENDANT
MARC PROUST,   )   PROUST'S MOTION FOR
)   PROTECTIVE ORDER
              Defendant.   )
_____)

STATEMENT OF THE CASE

A complaint alleging negligent operation of a vehicle and resulting personal injury and property damage was filed in the Major Superior Court on November 1, 198X-1 by Plaintiff, Gretchen Summers. Plaintiff's request for a jury trial accompanied her complaint. On December 7, 198X-1, Defendant Marc Proust filed an answer and a counter-claim, also alleging negligence. The parties are currently in the process of discovery. No trial date has yet been set.

STATEMENT OF THE FACTS

This memorandum is in support of defendant Marc Proust's motion for a Protective Order to protect medical records of Proust's psychological treatment from discovery by plaintiff Gretchen Summers in the action of Summers v. Proust.

Summers v. Proust arises from a rear-end collision which occurred on September 12, 198X-1. Summers is claiming personal injury and property damages totaling $25,000, and special damages of $5,600. Proust denies any liability and is counterclaiming for $1,500 property damage.

Memorandum of Law in Support   1   B.Y. Davis
of Motion for Protective Order

1   Plaintiff Summers sent defendant Proust interrogatories

2   and a request for production of documents. Interrogatory no.

3   10(E) requested production of the following items:

4   All medical bills, statements, narrative medical reports,
        hospital records, medical test results, receipts for
5   prescriptions, written documents, notes and other
        materials concerning the defendant's injuries and/or
6   damages as a result of the incident which is the subject
        matter of this lawsuit.

7   A copy of the request is attached as Exhibit B.

8   Defendant Proust has fully complied with this overly broad

9   request, with the exception of notes and evaluations made in

10 the course of Proust's psychological treatment under Dr.

11 Johnson. It should be noted that Proust, totally unrelated to

12 this case, is currently undergoing psychological treatment

13 with Dr. Joaquin Johnson, a licensed psychologist. Proust has

14 been under Dr. Johnson's care for the past three years for

15 treatment of arachnophobia, the unreasonable fear of spiders.

16 (Exhibit C.)

17   Proust seeks to prevent disclosure of these documents on

18 the following grounds: 1) the notes and evaluations are not

19 relevant to the subject matter of the action pursuant to Court

20 Rule 26(b)(1); 2) the notes and evaluations are privileged

21 matter pursuant to Civil Rule 26(b)(1). Alternatively, Proust

22 seeks to prevent disclosure of the notes and to limit the

23 disclosure of the evaluations to an in camera examination

24 pursuant to Civil Rules 26(c)(2) and 26(c)(4).

25 THE NOTES AND EVALUATIONS ARISING OUT OF PSYCHOLOGICAL THERAPY
        ARE PRIVILEGED AND IRRELEVANT TO THE PENDING ACTION.

26   Civil Rule 26(b)(1) provides:

27

28 Memorandum of Law in Support   2   B.Y. Davis
    of Motion for Protective Order

1   Parties may obtain discovery regarding any matter,
     not privileged, which is relevant to the subject
2   matter involved in the pending action. ...

3 A party may not discover privileged matter or matter

4 irrelevant to the action. To ensure that such matters are not

5 disclosed, a party may bring a motion for a Protective Order

6 pursuant to Civil Rule 26(c), which provides:

7   Upon motion by a party or by the person from whom
         discovery is sought, and for good cause shown, the
8   court in which the action is pending ... may make
         any order which justice requires to protect a party
9   or person from annoyance, embarrassment, oppression,
         or undue burden or expense, including one or more of
10   the following: 1) that the discovery not be had; 2)
         that the discovery may be had only on specified
11   terms and conditions, including a designation of the
         time or place ... 4) that certain matters not be
12   inquired into, or that the scope of the discovery be
         limited to certain matters.

13 Thus, the court may order that discovery of certain matters be

14 prohibited, or limited in scope, or both.

15

16   THE NOTES AND EVALUATIONS ARE NOT RELEVANT TO THE ACTION

17   The threshold test for discovery is relevance to the

18 pending action. Civil Rule 26(b)(1) requires that the matter

19 sought to be discovered be relevant to the subject matter of

20 the pending action. Proust's mental condition is not an issue

21 in the action, nor does his mental condition bear on a claimed

22 issue or defense. The documents arising out of psychological

23 therapy simply are not relevant to this action.

24

25

26

27

28 Memorandum of Law in Support   3   B.Y. Davis
   of Motion for Protective Order

THE PSYCHOLOGICAL/PATIENT PRIVILEGE

Once the psychologist/patient privilege attaches, pretrial discovery as to the privileged matter is prohibited. Clark v. Dist. Ct., 668 Maj.2d 3 (1983). Dr. Johnson is a licensed psychologist in the State of Major. His relationship with Proust is a psychologist/patient relationship. Moreover, notes and evaluations arising out of such therapy are protected by this privilege.

Effective diagnosis and treatment require protecting the patient from the embarrassment and humiliation caused by the psychologist's disclosure of information revealed during therapy. Bond v. Dist. Ct., 682 Maj.2d 33, 38 (1984). The affidavit of Dr. Johnson, Exhibit C, illustrates the sensitive nature of Proust's therapy.

> Because his initial childhood trauma and subsequent manifestations are so very personal, successful treatment necessarily depends on Proust's sense of security and confidentiality in his communication with me.

Dr. Johnson emphasizes that Proust's therapy would be severely impaired by disclosure of the notes and evaluations of treatment. Further, current treatment would be undermined by the loss of confidentiality.

The privilege may be waived by the patient. Clark at 8. The patient has waived the privilege when he has "injected his mental condition into the case as a basis of a claim or an affirmative defense." Clark at 10. Proust has not waived the psychologist/patient relationship and the notes and

Memorandum of Law in Support   4   B.Y. Davis
of Motion for Protective Order

evaluations arising out of that relationship are privileged and not discoverable.

ALTERNATIVELY, THE COURT MAY EXAMINE THE EVALUATIONS IN CAMERA

If the court finds that the evaluations are not protected by the psychologist/patient privilege or that the evaluations are relevant to the action, we require an in camera examination of the evaluations by the court.

Civil Rule 26(c) provides:

> Upon motion by a party ... and for good cause shown, the court in which the action is pending ... may take any action which justice requires to protect a party from annoyance, embarrassment, oppression ... including ... (2) that the discovery may be had only on specified terms and conditions, including a designation of the time and place ... (4) that certain matters not be inquired into, or that the scope of the discovery be limited to certain matters. ...

There is sufficient cause to limit the disclosure of the documents. Dr. Johnson's affidavit emphasizes the personal and potentially embarrassing nature of the therapy. Dr. Johnson also warns that disclosure of the documents is likely to severely impair the current psychologist/patient relationship as well as future treatment. By limiting disclosure to an in camera examination of the documents, the dangers arising from complete disclosure are mitigated.

The notes taken during therapy may be misleading because they express the thoughts and observations of Dr. Johnson during treatment. While we request that the evaluations should also be protected, the notes are far less dispositive and are potentially more destructive to Proust's therapy than

Memorandum of Law in Support   5   B.Y. Davis
of Motion for Protective Order

the evaluations. The evaluations provide a more accurate estimate of Proust's mental condition.

Thus, we request that the court examine the evaluations in camera, since a wrongful disclosure of the evaluations would cause unwarranted damage to Proust's therapy that could not be cured on appeal.

CONCLUSION

Court Rule 26 prohibits discovery of privileged matters that are irrelevant to the action. Likewise, the Rule limits discovery when a party is likely to be unduly oppressed or embarrassed. Thus, the Rule enables all relevant matter to be discovered while ensuring that parties will not be discouraged from necessary litigation by the fear that every aspect of their lives will be scrutinized. Since the records of psychological treatment are unrelated to this action, the motion for a Protective Order should be granted.

DATED: February 19, 198x.

                              B.Y. Davis, P.S.

                              _____
                              B.Y. Davis
                              Attorney for Defendant Proust
                              18 Tulip Lane
                              Jamner, Major 96120
                              Telephone No. (206) 421-0280

Memorandum of Law in Support   6   B.Y. Davis
of Motion for Protective Order

SUPERIOR COURT OF MAJOR

JAMNER COUNTY

GRETCHEN SUMMERS,)
)
   Plaintiff,)   NO. 8X-7-43
)
v.   )   DECLARATION OF SERVICE
)   (MAIL)
MARC PROUST,   )
)
   Defendant.)
_____)

I, STEVEN GRIOSS, declare the following:

1. At the time of service I was at least eighteen years of age and not a party to this cause.

2. I served on: F.C. Townsend, Attorney for Plaintiff the following documents: Motion for Protective Order, Memorandum of Points and Authorities, and Declarations.

3. Manner of Service: United States Mail

4. Date of Mailing: 2-19-8X

  Address to which document(s) were mailed:

   1600 National Bank Building

   Jamner, Major 96120

I declare under penalty of perjury that this information is true and correct.

  Date: 2-19-8X

  Place: Jamner, Major

_____

CRIMINAL PROBLEMS: STATE v. HARD

PROBLEM 75

Defense Attorney: Non-Constitutional Pretrial Motion
(Bail Reduction with a Charge of Assault in the First Degree)

Your client, Edward Taylor Hard, remains in county jail on $15,000 bail after being arrested for assault in the first degree as the result of an alleged shooting in a tavern. Since Hard cannot make this bail, you are in the process of preparing a motion to reduce bail. A local "bail project" has done a background report on Hard that you will use for the factual basis for your motion. This report basically confirms what you have learned in your first interview with Hard.

PREPARATION

READ: (1) Pretrial Case File Entries 8, 65; (2) Chapter VIII. Now think about and answer the following questions:

1. What will be the factual basis for your bail motion? Why (in terms of applicable legal standards)?

2. How will you present these facts to the court (e.g., witnesses, declarations, letters)? Why?

3. Synthesizing all the information that you have, what will be your argument for bail reduction?

4. To what amount will you ask that bail be reduced? How did you arrive at this figure?

5. Assuming that the prosecution opposed your motion, what do you expect will be the substance of that opposition?

6. What will be your reply to the prosecutor's opposition?

7. Should you consider asking the judge to place Mr. Hard on his O.R. (own recognizance) instead of money bail? Why or why not?

8. What do you have to lose by making an O.R. request?

ASSIGNMENT FOR CLASS

1. Outside of class, draft the Points and Authorities* (no longer than one typewritten page) for the bail reduction motion and give a copy to your supervisor.

2. In class, be prepared to argue the motion to the court.

---

*These are your legal arguments and citations, and must be based *only* on the cases and statutes in your case file, unless your instructor tells you otherwise.

PROBLEM 76

Prosecutor: Non-Constitutional Pretrial Motion
(Response to Defense Bail Motion)

This morning you charged Edward Taylor Hard with assault in the first degree. (Note: At this point Bruno Summers is still alive.) Bail was set by schedule at $15,000. Late this afternoon, just as you were about to leave for the weekend, you were served with a defense motion to reduce bail. The hearing on the motion, which is factually based on a "bail project" report, is calendared for the morning of the 9th. Time to get to work.

PREPARATION

READ: (1) Pretrial Case File Entries 8, 65; (2) Chapter VIII; (3) Copy of defense motion to reduce bail. Now think about and answer the following questions:

1. Thinking broadly about your position in responding to a motion as a prosecutor:

    a. Is it your obligation to automatically oppose whatever the other side wants?

    b. Are there circumstances when you would not oppose an opponent's position, even though you knew you could be successful? Explain.

2. Now, focusing on the motion to reduce bail:

    a. Why (in general) would you oppose a motion to reduce bail?

    b. Imagine that your representational strategy is to obtain an early guilty plea from defendant. As part of this plea, defendant would be given probation. Could keeping defendant in jail by opposing a bail reduction motion aid this representational strategy? Does this tactic seem fair?

    c. Will you oppose this motion? Why?

    d. Assuming that you will oppose the motion, what is your basic argument?

    e. What will you respond if the court says, "Look, Hard's presumed innocent, why should he sit in jail?"

ASSIGNMENT FOR CLASS

1. Outside of class, draft Points and Authorities* (no longer than one typewritten page) in opposition to defendant's motion to reduce bail, and hand a copy to your supervisor.

2. In class, be prepared to argue your position to the court.

---

*These are your legal arguments and citations, and must be based *only* on the cases and statutes in your case file, unless your instructor tells you otherwise.

PROBLEM 77

Defense Attorney: Non-Constitutional Pretrial Motion
(Bail Reduction with a Charge of First-Degree Murder)

It is the morning of the 8th and you just learned that Bruno Summers has died. Your client, until now charged with assault in the first degree, is likely to face charges of premeditated first-degree murder, in light of the prior antagonism between Hard and Summers.

Tomorrow morning you have a motion to reduce the current $15,000 bail (based on the original assault) set for hearing. You must now rethink the upcoming motion to reduce bail in light of Summers' death. Being realistic, if Hard is charged with first-degree murder (which is all but certain), it will be quite an extraordinary victory if you even can prevent bail from being drastically raised.

PREPARATION

READ: (1) Pretrial Case File Entries 8, 65; (2) Chapter VIII. Now think about and answer the following questions:

1. Hard is going to be charged with murder instead of assault:

   a. Does this change in the case factually affect your position? If so, explain.

   b. Does it legally affect your position? How?

   c. Overall, will it change how you were going to argue your position to the court? Why or why not?

2. Will you change your objective (e.g., seek to limit the range of increase, rather than argue for a reduction)? Specify.

3. Should you ask that your motion be taken "off calendar" in light of the changes in the case? Why or why not?

4. What do you anticipate will be the prosecution's position now? Do you have a response?

5. How will you respond if the judge states, "A $15,000 bail for murder makes life sound too cheap. I'm inclined to raise it to at least $50,000"?

6. Suppose that the judge asks, "Counsel, isn't your client far more likely to flee a murder charge than an assault charge?" How will you respond?

7. Imagine that you are in a jurisdiction with a statute that provides: "No bail shall be set in a case of first-degree murder where the evidence of guilt is great." Assume that Hard is charged with first-degree murder.

   a. What will you argue if the prosecution urges the court to deny Hard *any* bail under this statute?

   b. Could you attack the legality of the statute itself? How?

1) Can you argue that the statute violates the constitutional provision that "excessive bail shall not be required"? Analyze and evaluate.

2) Can you argue that the statute violates due process because the term "great" is too vague a standard under which to deny bail? Analyze and evaluate.

c. If the prosecution invokes this statute, how could you turn this situation into an opportunity for discovery?

ASSIGNMENT FOR CLASS

1. Outside of class, analyze your bail motion in light of the new charges. Write a short memorandum summarizing your planning, preparation, and analysis, and give a copy to your supervisor.

2. In class, brainstorm your position on the bail motion. Be certain to anticipate both the prosecutor's and the court's reaction in formulating your position.

PROBLEM 78 _____

Prosecutor: Non-Constitutional Pretrial Motion
(Discovery of Self-Defense Witnesses)

From the beginning, you were sure that, if Hard went to trial, he would raise self-defense. You would like to be certain of your belief and, further, to know whether he has any witnesses in support of a self-defense claim. Accordingly, you are contemplating filing a discovery request specified as "Request to Provide Notice of Self-Defense Claim and List of Witnesses in Support of Such Claim." In doing so, you realize that counsel for the defendant is certain to raise the Fifth Amendment in opposition to your request.

PREPARATION

READ: (1) Pretrial Case File Entries 4, 71; (2) Chapters VII and VIII. Now think about and answer the following questions:

1. Why do you want this information?

2. In your attempt to get it, you may have to fight all the way to the Supreme Court (and still lose). Is it worth it? Why?

3. What will be your position as to why you are legally entitled to this information?

4. What do you anticipate will be the defendant's position?

5. Look at the classic Fifth Amendment case of *Huvestern v. State,* 261 Maj. 529 (1948) (Case File Entry 71).

   a. How, specifically, will the defense use this case if you bring your motion?

   b. How will you deal with it?

6. Imagine that you find a case in another, non-controlling, jurisdiction that permits the prosecution to request a notice of alibi and a list of alibi witnesses. (See *Wilson v. Superior Court of Nettle,* 256 Nettle App. 3d 917 (1987) (Case File Entry 71).)

   a. Can you use the case in this jurisdiction? How?

   b. How will you present it to the court?

   c. What analysis will the defense use to argue that *Wilson v. Superior Court of Nettle,* supra, should not be followed? Your response?

   d. What analysis will the defense use to distinguish *Wilson?* Your response?

ASSIGNMENT FOR CLASS

1. Outside of class, analyze the legal theory underlying this tentative motion. Write a short memorandum summarizing your planning, preparation, and analysis, and give a copy to your supervisor.

2. In class, be prepared to brainstorm the theory, tactics, and advisability of bringing this prosecution discovery motion.

PROBLEM 79 _____

Defense Attorney: Planning Constitution-Based Pretrial Motions

You have already raised several common law- and statute-based pretrial motions (e.g., discovery* and bail motions). Later, you will bring motions before the trial judge (i.e., in limine) in order to resolve a variety of evidentiary issues. Now is the time to begin to plan constitution-based pretrial motions. Such motions can exclude evidence vital to the prosecution's case, resolve procedural matters in your favor (e.g., change of venue), or incidentally provide you with additional discovery for your case at trial through evidentiary hearings associated with the motions. Motions can also be part of a representational strategy because by putting constant pressure on the prosecution they may lead to a fairer disposition of the case.

PREPARATION

READ: (1) Pretrial Case File Entries 1, 2, 4, 5, 17, 21, 34; (2) Chapter VIII. Now think about and answer the following questions:

1. Reviewing the Motions Checklist (page 272), which motions (that are constitution-based) would you raise in this case?

2. What form should these written motions (which are filed with the court clerk) take?

3. Without doing any research, see how many of the following questions you can answer:

_____
*See Chap. VII, Problem 57.

a. What is the legal basis of each motion?

b. Does this legal basis require a factual showing (e.g., the lack of an arrest warrant becomes an issue only when an arrest takes place in a home, as opposed to in public)?

c. If the legal basis requires a factual showing, how will you make this showing (e.g., witnesses at an evidentiary hearing, declarations)?

d. What will be the prosecutor's response to each such motion?

e. What will be the legal basis of each such response?

f. Which of these motions will result in the suppression of prosecution evidence if successful?

g. Which of these motions will have other consequences? Explain.

ASSIGNMENT FOR CLASS

1. Outside of class, prepare a short memorandum (one page) listing the constitution-based pretrial motions that you will potentially raise. Hand in a copy to your senior partner.

2. In class, be prepared to discuss and justify your selection.

PROBLEM 80

Prosecutor: Planning Responses to Constitution-Based Pretrial Motions
(Suppression Motions)

In litigation you must plan for every eventuality, good or bad. There are potential defense pretrial motions that, if successful, will exclude evidence in your case. It is important that you now assess the consequences of this possibility.

PREPARATION

READ: (1) Pretrial Case File Entries 4-6, 17, 21, 34; (2) Chapter VIII. Now think about and answer the following questions:

1. What evidence in your case provides a potential subject for defense motions to suppress? (Hint: The evidence will have been obtained by some type of police practice.) Why?

2. What is the legal basis for each attempt to suppress evidence?

3. Do an item-by-item analysis of the effect on the presentation of your case theory to the jury if the defense is successful in its motion to suppress each such item (e.g., the gun).

ASSIGNMENT FOR CLASS

1. Outside of class, look individually at each piece of evidence that you analyzed in Question 3, supra, and imagine that it has been

suppressed. Now taking these pieces of evidence one at a time, analyze how you would then proceed with (e.g., alter, restructure) your case in order to achieve your objectives in light of the loss of the particular piece of evidence. Write a short memorandum summarizing your planning, preparation, and analysis, and give a copy to your supervisor.

2. In class, be prepared to discuss your analysis.

PROBLEM 81

Defense Attorney: Constitution-Based Pretrial Motion
(Suppression of Ed Hard's Gun)

The motions to suppress evidence that you plan to bring could include motions to suppress the gun, defendant's statements to Officer Yale and Detective Kelly, and the result of the breathalyzer. At this point, you should focus on the suppression of the gun.*

In order to successfully bring a suppression motion, you must develop the legal basis for the motion. The first step in this endeavor is to develop the chain of relevant events that led to the seizure of the evidence. If you can break the chain by finding illegal or unsupportable government (police) conduct at any link, you can suppress the evidence.

PREPARATION

READ: (1) Pretrial Case File Entries 4, 21, 22, 30, 76, 77; (2) Chapter VIII. Now think about and answer the following questions:

1. Again, the first step in evolving a theory to suppress the gun is to articulate the chain of events that led to its seizure. This chain begins when the police come to Hard's home to arrest him without a warrant, the police tell Hard that they could get a warrant to search his house, etc., etc. (Hint: It's easiest to develop this chain by starting with what you want to suppress (in this example it is the gun) and then trace backwards through the events that led to the seizure.)

   a. List the chain of relevant events that led to the seizure of the gun.

   b. Is there any government conduct at any link in the chain in seizing the gun that you believe may be illegal or unsupportable? Explain.

2. What do you gain at trial if you suppress the gun?

3. Suppose that the gun is suppressed. Does the prosecution have other evidence to present that would prove what the gun would have established?

4. Let's start with a theory for suppression based on the *lack of an arrest warrant:*

---

*Unless your instructor tells you otherwise, your analysis of this problem should be based *solely* on Officer Yale's version of the search described in his report and statement to the prosecutor. (Case File Entries 21, 22.)

a. Suppose that the judge agrees that the police should have had an arrest warrant.

   1) What bearing does that have on the prosecution's right to introduce the gun at trial? Why?

   2) What legal authority would the judge rely on in deciding the police should have had an arrest warrant?

   3) In this case there was no arrest warrant. Imagine, however, that an arrest warrant was issued, but that the magistrate inadvertently failed to sign it, making the warrant invalid. What bearing would *State v. Lex,* 272 Maj. 3d 115 (1984), have on your "taint" analysis under *Solong v. Warden,* 261 Maj. 417 (1948)? (See Case File Entries 76 and 77.)

b. Now suppose (as is likely) that the necessity of an arrest warrant is in dispute.

   1) What will you respond if the prosecutor states, "No warrant was needed. This was an emergency—police were in 'hot pursuit' of an armed and dangerous man"?

   2) Assume that the prosecutor then adds, "Also, the police did not need a warrant because they entered the home with defendant's consent." If the court finds a valid consent, do you have any response to the prosecution's position? Explain.

5. Now let us think further about the *consent issue:*

   a. How can you argue that the consent was not valid?

   b. What is the significance of the conversation at the door where the police said they could obtain a warrant?

   c. What do you expect to be the prosecution's position concerning this conversation?

   d. What is your reply?

   e. Develop an argument to invalidate the "consent," using the concept of "submission to authority." Focus on the initial discussion at the door and the gathering of police at the entrance.

      1) What will be the likely reply of the prosecution?

      2) Your response as defense attorney?

   f. At an evidentiary hearing, how do you think Officer Yale will describe the conduct of the defendant and the police at the door? Why?

   g. Does Hard's intoxication have bearing on the issue of consent? Explain.

   h. Can you argue that there was no consent, valid or otherwise? Explain.

      1) How will you respond if the prosecution argues that the existence of consent should not be determined by what Hard subjectively intended, but rather by what a "reasonable police officer" would believe Hard intended? (Think: What arguments support each position?)

2) How will it affect your argument for suppression and your conduct of the hearing regarding consent if the court accepts the prosecution's position? What if the court accepts the opposite position?

3) What bearing does the prosecution's burden concerning the issue of consent have on all of this?

6. The prosecution will attempt to justify the seizure of the weapon, once the police were inside the house, under the "plain-view" doctrine.

   a. Does *Tex v. Warden*, 17 Major App. 3d 601 (1970), help the prosecution? (See Case File Entry 76.)

   b. Do you have a reply?

7. Now, imagine that the gun had been found in a back room:

   a. Would *Tex v. Warden* help the prosecution if it were presented at the evidentiary hearing that the gun had been found in a back room, rather than the living room as stated in the report? Why or why not? Does your answer "depend"? If so, upon what?

   b. Looking back at your consent analysis, could you have argued that, even if Hard consented, entrance into the back room was beyond the "scope" of consent? Explain.

   c. Suppose that the prosecution argued, "Beyond the 'scope' of consent or not, once police were in the house they had the right to do a self-protective sweep of the house for a weapon pursuant to *Long v. Superior Court*, 93 Major App. 3d 816 (1974)." (See Case File Entry 76.)

      1) Can you distinguish *Long v. Superior Court*?

      2) Can you use *State v. Muncie*, 268 Major 3d 1003 (1983)? How? (See Case File Entry 76.)

      3) Is *State v. Chums*, 201 Major 2d 191 (1962), applicable? Explain. (See Case File Entry 76.)

   d. Now imagine that Hard had backed into the room where the gun was found. Would that constitute a valid (non-verbal) consent? Even if not valid consent, could the prosecution argue that the police were, nevertheless, justified in following Hard into the room? How?

8. Suppose that at the end of the hearing the court states, "I find the seizure of the gun to be illegal, but believe that its discovery would have been 'inevitable' under *Brakes v. Warden*, 254 Maj. App. 2d 216 (1965). Do you have any response to my position, counsel?" What would be your response? (See Case File Entry 76.)

9. Finally, reviewing all of the above, are there any other facts that you would want to know about the seizure of the gun?

   a. Why, in terms of applicable legal theory?

   b. Where would you find such facts?

ASSIGNMENT FOR CLASS

1. Outside of class, **prosecutor and defense attorney** analyze the legal basis of each side's position on the Fourth Amendment-based motion to suppress the gun. Write a short memorandum summarizing your planning, preparation, and analysis and give a copy to your supervisor.

2. In class:

    a. Imagine that Officer Yale testifies at the evidentiary hearing** regarding the defense motion to suppress the gun. **Prosecutor:** Determine the points you would want to bring out in Yale's testimony in order to support your legal position. Be certain to consider how you would want Yale to characterize the relevant events, particularly those that are problematic for you. **Defense attorney:** Determine the points that you would want to bring out in Yale's testimony.

    b. **Prosecutor and defense attorney:** Be prepared to argue your respective positions (to the trial judge) concerning the suppression of the *gun*.

PROBLEM 82

Defense Attorney: Constitution-Based Pretrial Motion
(Evidentiary Hearing: Suppression of Statements to Officer Yale)

You now wish to plan to suppress defendant's false exculpatory statement to Officer Yale ("I was home watching T.V.") that Hard allegedly made when the police came to his home. The court has reserved ruling on your motion to suppress the gun.*

PREPARATION

READ: (1) Pretrial Case File Entries 21, 22, 30, 73, 76, 77; (2) Chapter VIII. Now think about and answer the following questions:

1. If you fail to suppress this statement, how specifically will you deal with it in:

    a. Defendant's testimony?

    b. Closing argument?

2. Focusing on suppression:

    a. What legal theories exist for suppressing the statement?

**Unless your instructor tells you otherwise, you will *not* actually present the testimony of the witness.

*Unless your instructor tells you otherwise, your analysis of this problem should be based *solely* on Officer Yale's version of the search as described in his report and statement to the prosecutor. (Pretrial Case File Entries 21, 22.)

b. What is the basis for each theory?

c. What are the problems with each theory? How will you deal with these problems?

d. What are the strengths of each theory?

e. What other specific factual information would you want to know? Why?

3. Can any of the Fourth Amendment analysis you did for the suppression of the gun help? Explain.

4. Now, let us think in *Mintz* terms. Suppose that you raise the lack of *Mintz* warnings preceding Hard's statement and the court states, "I think *State v. Rhodes*, 256 Maj. App. 3d 154 (1982), is dispositive against you." (Case File Entry 73.)

a. What does the judge mean? Explain.

b. How will you respond to the judge's statement?

5. Does *State v. Rhodes* provide guidance regarding how you must characterize the initial encounter at the door in order to raise the *Mintz* issue? Explain.

6. Suppose that the prosecution cites *State v. Moth*, 100 Maj. App. 3d 593 (1975), to the judge and argues that *Mintz* does not apply because Hard was not in "custody"? Respond. (See Case File Entry 73.)

7. What will you respond if the prosecutor takes the position that since the general inquiry that produced this response was directed at locating the gun in the interest of "public safety," no *Mintz* warnings were required under *State v. Quirk*, 257 Maj. App. 3d 406 (1982)? (See Case File Entry 73.)

ASSIGNMENT FOR CLASS

1. Outside of class, **prosecutor and defense attorney** analyze the legal basis for each side's position regarding the suppression of the statement. Write a short memorandum summarizing your planning, preparation, and analysis, and give a copy to your supervisor.

2. In class:

a. Imagine that Officer Yale is testifying at the evidentiary hearing** regarding the defense motion to suppress the false exculpatory statements (made at the door). **Prosecutor:** Determine the points you would want to bring out in Yale's testimony in order to support your legal position. (See Problem 30 (Interview with Officer Yale), if applicable.) Be certain to consider how you would want Yale to characterize the relevant events, particularly those that are problematic for you.

b. **Defense attorney:** Determine the points you would want to bring out in Yale's testimony at the evidentiary hearing in support of

---

**Unless your instructor tells you otherwise, you will *not* actually put on the testimony of the witness.

the defense motion to suppress the false exculpatory statements (made at the door).

c. **Prosecutor and defense attorney:** Be prepared to argue your respective positions to the trial judge concerning the suppression of the false exculpatory statement.

PROBLEM 83

Defense Attorney: Constitution-Based Pretrial Motion
(Evidentiary Hearing: Suppression of the Statement Given to Detective Kelly)

You should now focus on suppressing Hard's statements to Detective Kelly. Be careful not to confuse: (1) A Fourth Amendment violation which "taints" the statement; (2) an involuntary statement, which violates due process; and (3) a violation of defendant's rights under *Mintz* (failure to give proper warnings, ineffective "waiver").

You recall that, according to the police report, Ed Hard was interviewed by Detective Kelly at 11:00 P.M. at the police station. In that interview, Hard allegedly told Kelly that at approximately 9:00 P.M. Hard and two friends, John Gooding and Rebecca Karr, went to the Unicorn Tavern for a drink. Hard was sitting at the bar, got up, and went to the restroom. As he approached the restroom, Bruno Summers came out of the restroom and confronted him. Hard stated that he was surprised to see Summers and had been unaware of the fact Summers had been in the tavern prior to the confrontation. Hard said, prior to this time, he had not looked around the tavern but had been drinking and conversing with his friends. Hard stated that Summers threatened and shoved him and then reached into his pocket. Hard stated that, in response, in order to protect himself he pulled a .22 caliber revolver from his coat pocket, cocked it, and pointed it at the wall. But the gun accidentally discharged, hitting Bruno Summers.

Kelly confronted Hard with the fact that (1) Hard had to have been aware of Summers in the tavern before meeting him coming out of the restroom, and (2) it would have been impossible to misjudge the aim at such a short distance. The following conversation then occurred:

Hard: I think I'd better get an attorney. Don't you think I'd better get an attorney?

Kelly: If you want an attorney, I can't ask you any further questions.

Hard: Do you think an attorney could help me?

Kelly: That's up to you to decide. Do you want an attorney?

Hard: I want to tell what happened. That guy is a Nazi. Yes, I knew he was there. He deserved what he got. I couldn't continue to be afraid.

Kelly: Do you want an attorney?

Hard: Yes, probably better get one.

PREPARATION

READ: (1) Pretrial Case File Entries 4, 5, 17, 73, 76, 77; (2) Chapter VIII. Now think about and answer the following questions:

1. Develop the chain of events from defendant's arrest to the time Ed Hard made his statement to Detective Kelly.

2. Let us start with the Fourth Amendment analysis. Suppose that the judge finds that the failure to obtain an arrest warrant violated the Fourth Amendment.

   a. What will be your position on "taint" regarding the statement to Kelly? Explain.

   b. What will be the position of the prosecution on "taint"?

   c. As regards the "taint" issue, what points would you want to present in your examination of Detective Kelly at an evidentiary hearing? Why?

   d. What points would you expect the prosecution to present? Why?

3. Now, consider a Fifth Amendment due process analysis:

   a. What is the difference between an involuntary statement which violates due process, and a statement obtained in contravention of *Mintz*?

   b. What bearing does this distinction have in this case?

   c. What bearing does it have on the nature of the testimony that you would want to present at an evidentiary hearing?

   d. Is there a basis for a claim of involuntariness (due process theory) under *State v. Mike,* 277 Maj. App. 2d 1143 (1968), in this case? (See Case File Entry 73.)

      1) What is the factual basis?

      2) What is the legal basis for a claim of involuntariness?

      3) What do you expect to be the prosecution's response?

   e. Would you have problems using the breathalyzer result in this motion and then trying to suppress the same result in another motion (see Problem 86)?

      1) *Tactically* would you have a problem?

      2) *Legally* would you have a problem?

4. Now, for the *Mintz* analysis. (Note that *Mintz* embodies a concept that Fifth Amendment rights are protected by the Sixth Amendment assistance of counsel.)

   a. What legal significance will you argue that the dialogue concerning "needing an attorney" has? Why?

   b. How will you characterize this discussion?

   c. How can the prosecution argue that this was not a request for an attorney?

---

d. What would be your reply as defense attorney?

e. Suppose that the prosecution states, "The statements were 'volunteered.' No further interrogation took place once the defendant started discussing an attorney." How would you respond?

f. Suppose that the prosecutor also states, "Anyway, even if the statements were not volunteered (that is, they were in response to interrogation), by continuing to talk after being told again that he had the right to an attorney if he so chose, Hard waived his right to counsel under *State v. Buttle,* 201 Major App. 3d 393 (1980)." (See Case File Entry 73.) How would you respond?

g. How does Hard's intoxication affect your *Mintz* analysis?

5. You always need a back-up position for the possibility that you may lose your motion.

a. If Ed Hard's statements are admissible in evidence, how will Hard explain them if he testifies?

b. How will you explain the statements to the jury if Hard does not testify?

6. What bearing (if any) would your analysis for suppressing the statement have if Hard were a defendant in a wrongful death case brought by Deborah Summers?

a. Assume that you contend that the statement was not given voluntarily. Could you argue that the statement should be excluded as "unreliable" under Fed. R. Evid. 403 or the due process clause?

b. Generally, can you make the argument that illegality on the part of the police in obtaining evidence "taints" that evidence in a civil proceeding? (See Pretrial Case File Entry 77.) How?

1) What response would you expect if your civil opponent is the State?

2) What response would you expect if your civil opponent is a private citizen such as Deborah Summers?

ASSIGNMENT FOR CLASS

1. Outside of class:

a. Suppose that Detective Kelly is testifying at the evidentiary hearing* regarding the defense motion to suppress the statements made at the police station. **Prosecutor:** Determine the points you would want to bring out in Kelly's testimony in order to support your legal position. Be certain to consider how you would want Kelly to characterize the relevant events, particularly those that are problematic for you. Write a short memorandum summarizing your planning, preparation, and analysis, and give a copy to your supervisor.

---

*Unless your instructor tells you otherwise, you will *not* actually put on the testimony of the witness.

b. **Defense attorney:** Determine the points you would want to bring out in Kelly's testimony, if Kelly testifies at the evidentiary hearing regarding the defense motion to suppress the statements made at the police station. Write a short memorandum summarizing your planning, preparation, and analysis, and give a copy to your supervisor.

2. In class, **prosecutor and defense attorney,** be prepared to argue your respective positions (to the trial judge) concerning the suppression of the statement.

PROBLEM 84

Defense Attorney: Constitution-Based Pretrial Motion
(Suppressing Statement in Alcohol Influence Report)

You were reviewing the Alcohol Influence Report that Officer Yale filled out when administering the breathalyzer to Ed Hard. In doing so, you noticed that Hard allegedly said "Shot a man" in response to the question "Are you ill?" You are considering adding this statement to the evidence you seek to exclude through your suppression motion.

PREPARATION

READ: (1) Pretrial Case File Entries 4, 5, 73, 76, 77; (2) Chapter VIII. Now think about and answer the following questions:

1. Do you care if this statement gets into evidence (does it hurt or help)?

   a. If not, is it worth adding to your suppression motion?

   b. Are there tactical reasons not to add it? Reasons to add it?

2. If Officer Yale does not testify, can the prosecution bring the statement into evidence? How?

3. Assess the strengths and weaknesses of the following theories for suppression of the statement ("shot a man"):

   a. Hard's initial arrest was illegal (being without an arrest warrant or valid consent) and that illegality "taints" the current statement.

   b. Hard was too intoxicated to "voluntarily" give the statement, thereby violating due process.

   c. The statement is "tainted" by Kelly's prior violation of Hard's right under *Mintz* (i.e., failure to give proper *Mintz* warnings, ineffective waiver).

   d. Even if there was no prior *Mintz* violation, the statement is not admissible because Yale failed to renew the *Mintz* warnings.

   e. Kelly told Yale in front of Hard not to "conduct any further questioning." This misled Hard and, with reasonable effect, told him that any conversation with Yale was not "questioning" and, therefore, was not meant to be used in court.

ASSIGNMENT FOR CLASS

1. Outside of class, analyze the various legal theories under which you would seek suppression. Write a short memorandum summarizing your planning, preparation, and analysis, and give a copy to your supervisor.

2. In class, be prepared to discuss (1) the reasons why you would or would not seek to suppress this statement and (2) the theory or theories you would use if you did seek suppression.

PROBLEM 85

Prosecutor: Constitution-Based Pretrial Motion
(Assessing Loss to Case If Breathalyzer Results Are Suppressed)

The defense attorney will probably attempt to exclude the result of the breathalyzer. You recall that Officer Yale administered a breathalyzer test to Ed Hard at approximately 12:05 P.M. Ed Hard had a .16 reading.

Think about the role that the breathalyzer test result plays in the case. Then try to anticipate the position defense counsel will likely take to prevent its use.

PREPARATION

READ: (1) Pretrial Case File Entries 4, 5, 12, 13, 21, 73, 76, 77; (2) Chapters I, II, and VIII. Now think about and answer the following questions:

1. How will you use the breathalyzer test result in your case?

2. Respond to a "relevance" objection to the admission of the breathalyzer test result.

3. What would be the loss to your case if the breathalyzer test result is suppressed? Explain.

4. The defense could theoretically suppress any breathalyzer result.

   a. List all the grounds upon which breathalyzer test results could be suppressed.

   b. Explain which grounds apply to this case and why.

ASSIGNMENT FOR CLASS

1. Outside of class, analyze the role of Hard's breathalyzer result in your case and how you will deal with the result if it is suppressed. Write a short memorandum summarizing your planning, preparation, and analysis, and give a copy to your supervisor.

2. In class, be prepared to discuss how you would deal with suppression of the breathalyzer test.

PROBLEM 86

Prosecutor: Constitution-Based Pretrial Motion
(Opposing Suppression of the Breathalyzer Results)

The defense has a number of potential, although not necessarily successful, grounds upon which to attack the admission of the breathalyzer test result: (1) "taint" from an initially illegal arrest; (2) failure to obtain a search warrant for the breath sample; (3) no probable cause to seize the breath sample, regardless of the legality of the initial arrest or the necessity of a warrant; and (4) failure to follow administrative procedures.

PREPARATION

READ: (1) Pretrial Case File Entries 4, 5, 21, 68, 76, 77; (2) Chapter VIII. Now think about and answer the following questions:

1. If Hard's arrest is found to be illegal, how can you avoid a successful "taint" argument?

2. Is a search warrant required in order to "seize" a breath sample?

3. Consider the no probable cause argument:

   a. What is "probable cause"?

   b. What does the probable cause standard have to do with whether or not the police could seize the breath sample?

   c. What information did police have to "reasonably believe" Hard was intoxicated?

      1) Was any of this information arguably "tainted" by illegal police conduct? Explain.

      2) If some of the information was tainted by illegal police conduct, what will you do?

      3) Suppose that defense counsel argues, "Even if the police had reason to believe Hard was intoxicated, they had no right to seize the breath sample, because evidence of his intoxication is not evidence of a crime. Hard is charged with murder, not being drunk in public. What the police were really trying to do was preempt a diminished capacity defense, not obtain evidence for their own case." Respond.

4. Now let's consider the argument based upon failure to follow administrative procedures. An administrative regulation in the Major code (not available in your case file) specifies that the breathalyzer operator must warm up the machine until the thermometer indicates 47-53° C.

   a. Suppose that Officer Yale warmed up the machine and the thermometer indicated 46°. Can the defense suppress the results because of Officer Yale's conduct? Upon what grounds?

   b. Does the failure to follow these administrative procedures make the seizure illegal under the Fourth Amendment? Under grounds of a lack of foundation for evidentiary reliability? Respond to both of these grounds.

c. Suppose that lack of foundation for evidentiary reliability is urged by the defense. Can you argue that the motion is not an appropriate pretrial motion?

d. If the defense attacks the breathalyzer on these administrative procedure grounds, would you expect the defense to also request an evidentiary hearing and call witnesses? Why or why not? If so, whom would you expect them to call?

e. Would you call any witnesses? Why or why not?

5. Now imagine that the police threw away the ampoule containing the defendant's breath sample before the defense had a chance to inspect it.

a. How will you respond if the defense files a motion to dismiss the murder case, citing *State v. Brant,* 105 Maj. App. 3d 621 (1975)? (See Case File Entry 68.)

b. Explain how it would affect your position in Question 5(a) if: (1) Destruction of ampoules was a routine procedure in the police department; (2) destruction of ampoules was not guided by any routine (sometimes the ampoules are preserved, sometimes not); (3) destruction of ampoules was the result of the individual officer's negligent failure to follow specific departmental guidelines requiring preservation.

c. At a hearing on a motion to suppress the breathalyzer result, would you present your own evidence? Why?

d. If you would present evidence, detail the source and nature of the evidence.

ASSIGNMENT FOR CLASS

1. Outside of class, plan your legal and tactical response to each of the various attacks on the admissibility of the breathalyzer result. Write a short memorandum summarizing your planning, preparation, and analysis, and give a copy to your supervisor.

2. In class, be prepared to discuss the basis of the above analysis.

PROBLEM 87

Defense Attorney: Constitution-Based Pretrial Motion
(Planning a Change of Venue Motion)

The case *State v. Hard* has received a great deal of publicity in the local community, much of it unfavorable to your client's position. You therefore want to plan and prepare a motion for a change of venue to be presented to the court.

PREPARATION

READ: (1) Pretrial Case File Entries 1, 2, 66; (2) Chapter VIII. Now think about and answer the following questions:

1. What is the legal basis (including applicable legal standards) for a venue motion, and what can a motion to change venue accomplish?

2. What factors affect whether or not to bring a change of venue motion?

3. After considering all the factors, do you want a change of venue in Hard's case? Why or why not?

4. If you want a change of venue, to what venue do you want the trial relocated?

5. Can you include your choice for relocation in your motion? Explain.

6. What type of facts make it more or less likely that such a motion will be granted?

7. List and assess the strengths and weaknesses of your position for advocating a change of venue.

8. How will you deal with the weaknesses in your position?

9. Do you possess facts that support your position? Which ones?

10. Are there facts that are harmful to your position? Specify. How do you propose to deal with them?

11. Will you seek other facts?

    a. Which facts?

    b. Where will you look?

12. How will you present your facts to the court (e.g., witnesses, documents, exhibits)?

13. What will be the general theory of your argument for your motion for change of venue?

    a. What response do you expect from the prosecution?

    b. What will be your reply to the prosecutor's argument?

14. What areas do you anticipate the judge will probe when you argue the motion in court? How will you respond?

15. Suppose that the judge asks, "Wouldn't a less drastic alternative to your concerns than a change of venue suffice—such as a continuance and/or wide latitude in voir dire in the area of pretrial publicity?" How will you respond?

16. Suppose that the judge asks, "I don't understand; it's the victim, not your client, who's the neo-Nazi. Why should I change venue?" How will you respond?

ASSIGNMENT FOR CLASS

1. Outside class, analyze your legal position on the change of venue motion. Write a short memorandum summarizing your planning, preparation, and analysis, and give a copy to your supervisor.

2. In class, be prepared to discuss your position on a motion to change venue.

PROBLEM 88

Defense Attorney: Constitution-Based Pretrial Motion
(Motion for Money for a Survey to Support a Change of Venue)

You want to do a survey of community attitudes toward defendant's case in order to support your motion for a change of venue. The problem is that your client has insufficient funds to pay for the survey.* Accordingly, you should consider filing a motion requesting money to do the survey.

PREPARATION

READ: (1) Pretrial Case File Entries 1, 2, 66, 69; (2) Chapter VIII. Now think about and answer the following questions:

1. Why should the court order that you be given money to do this survey?

2. Does the fact that you are a privately retained attorney, as opposed to an appointed attorney, affect your position?

3. What is the legal basis for your request?

4. What is the equitable (fairness) basis?

5. Is it important to assess and present equitable factors in a legal motion? Why?

6. Why is the survey relevant to your change of venue motion? Is it crucial to the motion?

7. Assess the strength of your venue motion *without* the survey. What bearing does this assessment have on your position?

8. How will you respond if the court says:

   a. "I don't see the relevance of this survey. Its bearing is marginal at most regarding the decision on a change of venue"?

   b. "I don't care about the 'community.' I care about this jury panel"?

   c. What do the above two statements tell you about how you must draft your declaration in support of your motion?

---

*Assume that Hard can now establish indigency.

ASSIGNMENT FOR CLASS

1. Outside of class, write the Points and Authorities (only)** for the motion for money to do the survey and give a copy to your supervisor. Limit yourself to no more than two typewritten pages.

2. In class, be prepared to discuss the analysis in your Points and Authorities.

PROBLEM 89 _____

Prosecutor: Constitution-Based Pretrial Motion
(Response to Motion for a Survey to Support a Change of Venue)

You came back to your office after lunch and with the day's mail was a copy of "Defendant's Motion for Money to Conduct a Survey in Support of a Motion for Change of Venue." You must now analyze the motion and prepare a response.

PREPARATION

READ: (1) Pretrial Case File Entries 1, 2, 66, 69; (2) Chapter VIII; (3) Copy of defense motion for money for survey to support change of venue.

ASSIGNMENT FOR CLASS

1. Outside of class, write the Points and Authorities (only)* opposing the defendant's motion and give a copy to your supervisor. Limit yourself to no more than two typewritten pages.

2. In class, be prepared to discuss the analysis in your Points and Authorities.

PROBLEM 90 _____

Defense Attorney and Prosecutor: Constitution-Based Pretrial Motion
(Argument on the Motion for Money to Support a Change of Venue)

Now is the time to appear before the court to present your respective positions regarding the defendant's motion for money to do a survey.

PREPARATION

READ: (1) Pretrial Case File Entries 1, 2, 66, 69; (2) Chapter VIII; (3) Copies of defense and prosecution motions for money for survey to

---

**These are your legal arguments and citations, and must be based *only* on the cases in your case file, unless your instructor tells you otherwise.

*These are your legal arguments and citations, and must be based *only* upon the cases in your Case File.

support change of venue. Now think about and answer the following questions:

1. How will you prepare for the argument?

2. Explain the strengths and weaknesses of your position.

3. How will you deal with the weaknesses of your position?

4. What points do you want to present to the court? Why?

5. Are there points you must (or, at least, should) concede? Which ones? Why?

6. How will you concede a point and still maintain your position?

7. What areas of your position do you anticipate the court will probe? Why?

8. How will you respond to the specific questions you anticipate in these areas?

ASSIGNMENT FOR CLASS

1. Outside of class, plan how you would argue your position on the motion to the judge. Write a short memorandum summarizing your planning, preparation, and analysis, and give a copy to your supervisor.

2. In class, be prepared to actually argue your position.

CIVIL PROBLEMS: SUMMERS v. HARD

PROBLEM 91

Attorneys for Defendant Hard and Plaintiffs: Defendant Hard's Motion to Strike and Plaintiffs' Response
(Scandalous Matter)

Plaintiffs' complaint in *Summers v. Hard* was filed on November 1, 198X. Attorneys for plaintiffs and defendants interviewed their respective clients and witnesses and obtained the criminal file, *State v. Hard,* from the prosecutor's office. (Before serving an answer to the complaint, the parties and court agreed that all motions would be timely if filed by December 15, 198X.) Defendants served answers to the complaint on November 8, 198X. It is now December 15, 198X, and attorney for defendant Hard plans to file a motion to strike Paragraph 14 in plaintiffs' complaint:

Plaintiffs repeat and reallege paragraphs 1 through 12, and for a third claim herein allege that the above described incident was proximately caused by the willful, violent and negligent acts of defendant EDWARD T. HARD, an ex-felon in that by unlawfully possessing and concealing a pistol, having been convicted of crimes of violence, to wit, rape, he failed to conform his conduct to that which is prescribed by law for persons convicted of such violent crimes in that defendant failed reasonably to avoid confrontation with Bruno Summers; provoked such confrontation; and that defendant failed to use reasonable care in handling the pistol that wounded Bruno Summers.

PREPARATION

READ: (1) Pretrial Case File Entries 1-39, 59-61, 63, 86; (2) Chapter VIII; (3) Fed. R. Civ. P. 5-12.

In preparing and arguing motions, you should prepare both your own and your adversary's position. Therefore, answer the following questions by assuming the role of either plaintiff or defendant attorney (as indicated).

Assume the role of defendant Hard's attorney (Questions 1-7):

1. List all the objectives defendant Hard may have for filing a motion to strike Paragraph 14 of plaintiffs' complaint. (Explain how your representational strategy is affected.)

2. Instead of filing a motion to strike, could Hard's attorney raise the same issue by other means?

    a. What other ways could Hard raise the issue that he is not an ex-felon, was not guilty of rape, nor possesses a violent disposition?

    b. What are the advantages of using other sources?

    c. What are the disadvantages?

3. Defendant Hard is the moving party by filing a motion to strike.

    a. List the advantages of being the moving party.

    b. List the disadvantages of being the moving party.

4. What factors in Federal Rule of Civil Procedure 12(f) support Hard's motion to strike Paragraph 14?

    a. What burden of proof standard should the court use in granting/denying Hard's motion to strike (e.g., preponderance, reasonable doubt)? Why?

    b. For defendant Hard to sustain his burden of proof, what does he have to prove?

5. What arguments should Hard's attorney present?

    a. Legal arguments?

    b. Factual arguments?

6. In order to present your factual position:

    a. Procedurally, can you file documents or affidavits to support your motion or response? Explain.

    b. What documents, if any, will you file? Why?

    c. If you file affidavits, who will be the affiants?

    d. What facts will you include in the affidavits? Why?

    e. Are there evidentiary problems that you may encounter in presenting documents or affidavits to support your motion? Explain.

    f. Are there ethical problems that you may encounter if you include your affidavit as Ed Hard's attorney? Explain.

---

7. Suppose that as Hard's attorney you are aware of documents that indicate that Ed Hard was arrested and charged with a number of serious crimes.

    a. Ethically, can you file a motion to strike? Explain.

    b. Why would you want to file a motion to strike if Hard is an ex-felon?

Now assume the role of plaintiffs' attorney (Questions 8-11):

8. Even though defendant Hard is the moving party for a motion to strike, plaintiffs could file a similar motion. Tactically, should plaintiffs file a cross-motion to strike part of Paragraph 6 in Hard's answer (Bruno Summers was a member of a violent neo-Nazi survivalist group that advocated violence and racial hatred)? Explain how your representational strategy might be affected.

9. What response would you present as plaintiffs' attorney in opposing the motion to strike?

    a. Legal arguments?

    b. Factual arguments?

10. Suppose that plaintiffs' attorney does not have "document proof" that Hard is an ex-felon, but based the allegations about Hard on Hard's general unsavory reputation in the community. Ethically, should Paragraph 14 be struck from the complaint? Explain.

11. Suppose that after hearing arguments from defendant Hard and plaintiffs on the motion, the court suggests that it is "leaning toward" ruling that Paragraph 14 be struck from plaintiffs' complaint. What further arguments could plaintiffs propose? Why?

Now assume the role of a judge (Question 12):

12. Suppose that you were the judge hearing an argument for sanctions against defendant Hard.

    a. Present all the factors that you would consider support an award of sanctions against Hard.

    b. Present all the factors that you would consider negate an award of sanctions against Hard.

ASSIGNMENT FOR CLASS*

1. Outside of class:

    a. **Attorney for defendant Hard:** Prepare a written motion or a written outline of a motion to strike Paragraph 14 of plaintiffs' complaint. If you believe that you should not proceed with a motion, draft a memorandum to your senior partner explaining your reasons for not proceeding.

    b. **Plaintiffs' attorney:** Prepare a written response or a written outline of a response to defendant Hard's motion to strike. If you believe you should not proceed with a response to defendant's

---

*Your instructor will select which assignment you will do and will inform you as to the filing and scheduling of the argument.

motion, draft a memorandum to your senior partner explaining your reasons for not proceeding.

c. **Plaintiffs' and defendant's attorneys:** Give your senior partner a copy of your motion, response, or memorandum.

2. In class, argue or discuss your written motion, response, or memorandum.

PROBLEM 92

Defendants' and Plaintiffs' Attorneys: Defendants' Motion to Dismiss and Plaintiffs' Response
(Mental Distress)

It is now December 15, 198X. (The *Summers v. Hard* time frame is contained in Problem 91.) Attorneys for defendants Hard and Davola plan to file a motion to dismiss plaintiffs' sixth claim for relief as described in plaintiffs' complaint:

> Plaintiffs repeat and reallege paragraphs 1-14 and for a sixth claim, herein allege that by reason of the aforesaid acts, failure, or omission to act, by the said defendants, plaintiffs DEBORAH, AMANDA, RONNY, HANS and GRETCHEN SUMMERS have individually suffered severe negligent and intentional mental distress, resulting in serious mental injuries that would be expected of reasonable, normally constituted persons in the position of the respective plaintiffs.

PREPARATION

READ: (1) Pretrial Case File Entries 1-41, 51, 53, 59-61, 63, 90; (2) Chapter VIII; (3) Fed. R. Civ. P. 5-12.

In preparing and arguing motions, you should prepare both your own and your adversary's position. Therefore, answer the questions by assuming the role of either plaintiff or defendant attorney (as indicated).

Assume the role of attorneys for defendants Hard and Davola (Questions 1-6):

1. List all the objectives defendants Hard and Davola may have for filing a motion to dismiss plaintiffs' sixth claim for relief.

2. Instead of filing a motion to dismiss, defendants' attorneys could raise the same issue by other motions (motions to strike, judgment on the pleadings, summary judgment, directed verdict). Compare and contrast the motions.

a. Explain the advantages (if any) in filing any of the other motions.

b. What are the disadvantages (if any)?

c. Tactically, would you file all the motions you could if you were defendants' attorneys? Why or why not?

3. Suppose that defendants file a motion for summary judgment, requesting judgment as a matter of law on plaintiffs' sixth claim:

a. How does summary judgment differ from a motion to dismiss? Explain.

b. Does the burden of proof differ? Explain.

c. Would your legal argument be the same?

d. Would your factual argument be the same? Explain.

4. What arguments should defendants' attorneys present?

   a. Legal arguments?

   b. Factual arguments?

5. Suppose that defendants' attorneys are aware of a court of appeals case, *Sayer v. Stress,* 277 Maj. App. 2d 826 (1968), which recognizes a claim for negligent and intentional emotional distress without requiring objective physical injuries. Ethically, can defendants' attorneys file a motion to dismiss? Explain.

   a. If defendants' attorneys file their motion to dismiss, should they include the appellate case, *Sayer v. Stress,* in their brief?

   b. Suppose that plaintiffs' attorney does not cite the appellate case, *Sayer v. Stress,* in the brief in opposition to defendants' motion. Do defendants have an ethical duty to tell the court about the case? Explain.

6. Suppose that after hearing arguments from defendants and plaintiffs on the motion, the court suggests that it is "leaning toward" ruling against defendants in light of the appellate case, *Sayer v. Stress.* What further arguments could defendants propose? Why?

Now assume that you are plaintiffs' attorney (Questions 7-8):

7. You could possibly file a motion to dismiss the affirmative defense of assumption of risk. Tactically, in terms of a representational strategy, should plaintiffs file a cross-motion to dismiss defendants' affirmative defense of assumption of risk? Explain.

8. As to defendants' motion to dismiss, what response will you present in opposing the motion?

   a. Legal arguments?

   b. Factual arguments?

Now assume the role of a judge (Questions 9-10):

9. Suppose that you are the judge hearing defendants' motion to dismiss:

   a. What factors would you consider in granting/denying the motion?

   b. Are there any factors that you listed that are more controlling than others? Why or why not?

   c. What burden of proof would you apply in granting/denying defendants' motion to dismiss? (e.g., preponderance, reasonable doubt)? Why?

   d. For defendants to sustain their burden of proof, what do they have to prove?

10. Suppose that you are the judge and ruled against defendants.

    a. Would you award sanctions against defendants? Explain the legal and factual basis for your decision.

    b. If you awarded sanctions, what sanctions would you award?

ASSIGNMENT FOR CLASS*

1. Outside of class:

    a. **Attorneys for defendants Hard and Davola:** Prepare a written motion to dismiss or a written outline of a motion. If you believe that you should not proceed with a motion, draft a memorandum to your senior partner explaining your reasons for not proceeding.

    b. **Plaintiffs' attorney:** Prepare a written response or a written outline of a response to defendants Davola and Hard's motion to dismiss. If you believe that you should not proceed with a response to defendants' motion, draft a memorandum to your senior partner explaining your reasons for not proceeding.

    c. **Plaintiffs' and defendants' attorneys:** Give your senior partner a copy of your motion, outline, response, or memorandum.

2. In class, argue or discuss your written motion, outline, response, or memorandum.

PROBLEM 93 _____

Defendants' and Plaintiffs' Attorneys: Defendants' Motion for Summary Judgment and Plaintiffs' Response
(Mental Distress)

Plaintiffs' complaint in *Summers v. Hard* was filed on November 1, 198X. Plaintiffs and defendants sent written interrogatories, requests for documents, requests for admission, and completed depositions. It is now December 15, 198X + 1. Discovery in *Summers v. Hard* is completed and a trial date has been set.

Defendants' attorneys believe the sixth claim for relief for intentional and negligent emotional distress asserted by plaintiffs Deborah, Amanda, Ronny, Gretchen, and Hans Summers is particularly vulnerable for summary judgment. Attorneys for defendants Hard and Davola plan to file a motion for summary judgment.

PREPARATION

READ: (1) Pretrial Case File Entries 1-41, 51, 55-56, 59-61, 63, 64, 90; (2) Chapter VIII; (3) Fed. R. Civ. Proc. 5-7; 11-12; 56.

    In preparing and arguing motions, you should prepare both your own and your adversary's position. Therefore, answer the questions by assuming the role of either plaintiff or defendant attorney (as indicated).

---

*Your instructor will select which assignment to do and the filing and argument schedule.

Assume the role of attorneys for defendants Hard and Davola (Questions 1-8):

1. What are defendants' objectives in filing this motion for summary judgment?

2. Instead of filing a summary judgment motion:

   a. What other motions could you use to dismiss the Summers' emotional distress claim?

   b. What are the advantages of the other motions?

   c. What are the disadvantages?

3. Defendants are the moving party by filing a summary judgment motion.

   a. List the advantages of being the moving party.

   b. List the disadvantages of being the moving party.

4. The moving party, in this case the defendant, has the burden of proof on a summary judgment motion.

   a. What burden of proof standard should the court use in granting/denying summary judgment (e.g., preponderance, reasonable doubt)? Why?

   b. For defendants to carry their burden of proof, what do they have to prove as the emotional distress claim?

5. Compare the legal and factual basis for requesting summary judgment for Deborah Summers' claim and that of Amanda, Ronny, Gretchen, and Hans Summers. Should all the emotional distress claims be dismissed? Explain.

6. What arguments should defendants present in support of their motion for summary judgment?

   a. Legal arguments?

   b. Factual arguments?

7. In order to present your factual position for summary judgment:

   a. What, if any, documents will you file? Why?

   b. Whose affidavits, if any, will you file?

   c. What facts will you include in the affidavits? Why?

   d. Are there evidentiary problems that you may encounter in filing the affidavits? Explain.

   e. Are there ethical problems that you may encounter if you include an affidavit as the attorney? Explain.

8. Suppose that you are aware of facts that may be in dispute (e.g., whether Deborah Summers suffered objective symptoms accompanying her mental distress). Can you ethically file a summary judgment motion in order to educate the court as to the weakness in plaintiffs' evidence? Discuss.

Now assume the role of plaintiffs' attorney (Questions 9-12):

9. Even though defendants are moving for summary judgment, plaintiffs can also. Tactically, should plaintiffs file a cross-motion for summary judgment? Explain.

10. If the defendants have not met their burden of proof, does that mean plaintiffs should not respond? Explain.

11. What response will the Summers' attorney make to oppose summary judgment?

    a. Legal arguments?

    b. Factual arguments?

12. In order to present your factual position responding to summary judgment:

    a. What, if any, documents will you file? Why?

    b. Whose affidavits, if any, will you file?

    c. What facts will you include in the affidavits? Why?

    d. Are there evidentiary problems that you may encounter in filing the affidavits? Explain.

    e. Are there ethical problems that you may encounter if you include an affidavit as the attorney? Explain.

Now assume the role of judge (Question 13):

13. Suppose that as the judge you denied defendants' summary judgment motion. Would you award any costs, attorney fees, or sanctions against the defendants? Explain the legal and factual basis for your decision.

ASSIGNMENT FOR CLASS*

1. Outside of class:

    a. **Defendants' attorneys:** Prepare a written motion for summary judgment.

    b. **Plaintiffs' attorney:** Prepare a response to the motion.

    c. **Plaintiffs' and defendants' attorneys:** Hand in a copy of your motion or response to your senior partner.

2. In class, plaintiffs and defendants argue or discuss the motion.

---

*Your instructor will inform you as to the filing and argument schedule.

PROBLEM 94

Attorneys for Plaintiffs and Defendant Davola: Plaintiffs' Motion for Partial Summary Judgment and Defendant Davola's Response
(Liability)

It is now December 15, 198X+1. Discovery in *Summers v. Hard* is completed and a trial date has been set. Plaintiffs' attorney believes that Davola's liability for the death of Bruno Summers is particularly vulnerable for summary judgment. Attorney for plaintiffs plans to file a motion for partial summary judgment on the issue of liability.

PREPARATION

READ: (1) Pretrial Case File Entries 1-43, 50-57, 59-61, 63, 64, 90; (2) Chapter VIII; (3) Fed. R. Civ. P. 5-7; 11-12; 56.

In preparing and arguing motions, you should prepare both your own and your adversary's position. Therefore, answer the questions by assuming the role of either plaintiff or defendant attorney (as indicated).

Assume the role of plaintiffs' attorney (Questions 1-7):

1. What are plaintiffs' objectives in filing this motion for summary judgment?

2. Instead of filing a summary judgment motion:

    a. What other motions could you use to obtain partial judgment on the issue of Davola's liability?

    b. What are the advantages of the other motions?

    c. What are the disadvantages?

3. Plaintiffs are the moving party by filing this summary judgment motion.

    a. List the advantages of being the moving party.

    b. List the disadvantages of being the moving party.

4. The moving party, in this instance plaintiffs, has the burden of proof on the summary judgment motion.

    a. What burden of proof standard should the court use in granting/ denying summary judgment (e.g., preponderance, reasonable doubt)? Why?

    b. For plaintiffs to carry their burden of proof, what do they have to prove as to Davola's liability?

5. What arguments should plaintiffs present?

    a. Legal arguments?

    b. Factual arguments?

6. In order to present your factual position for summary judgment:

    a. What, if any, documents will you file? Why?

b. Whose affidavits, if any, will you file?

   c. What facts will you include in the affidavits? Why?

   d. Are there evidentiary problems that you may encounter in filing the affidavits? Explain.

   e. Are there ethical problems that you may encounter if you include your affidavit as the attorney? Explain.

7. Suppose that you are aware of facts that may be in dispute (e.g., whether Davola's employees could foresee the shooting of Bruno Summers). Can you ethically file a summary judgment motion in order to educate the court as to this issue and the weaknesses in defendant's evidence? Discuss.

Now assume the role of defendant Davola's attorney (Questions 8-11):

8. Even though plaintiffs are moving for summary judgment, defendant Davola can also. Tactically, should defendant Davola file a cross-motion for summary judgment? Explain.

9. If plaintiffs have not met their burden of proof on the motion, does that mean defendant should not respond? Explain.

10. What response will you make to oppose summary judgment?

   a. Legal arguments?

   b. Factual arguments?

11. In order to present your factual position responding to summary judgment:

   a. What, if any, documents will you file? Why?

   b. Whose affidavits, if any, will you file?

   c. What facts will you include in the affidavits? Why?

   d. Are there evidentiary problems that you may encounter in filing the affidavits? Explain.

   e. Are there ethical problems that you may encounter if you include an affidavit as the attorney? Explain.

Now assume the role of judge (Question 12):

12. Suppose that, as the judge, you deny plaintiffs' summary judgment motion. Would you award any costs, attorney fees, or sanctions? Explain the legal and factual basis for your decision.

ASSIGNMENT FOR CLASS*

1. Outside of class:

   a. **Plaintiffs' attorney:** Write a motion for summary judgment.

   b. **Defendant Davola's attorney:** Write a response to the motion for summary judgment.

---

*Your instructor will inform you as to the filing and argument schedule.

c. **Attorneys for plaintiffs and Defendant Davola:** Hand in a copy of your motion or response to your senior partner.

2. In class, attorneys for plaintiffs and defendant Davola, argue or discuss the motion.

PROBLEM 95 _____
Plaintiffs' Attorney: Planning Discovery Motions

Plaintiffs' complaint in *Summers v. Hard* was filed on November 1, 198X. Defendants responded to the complaint on November 8, 198X. Extensive discovery by both plaintiffs and defendants has been conducted. Plaintiffs sent interrogatories, requests for documents, and requests for admissions to defendants from June through September 198X + 1. Depositions were conducted in October and the beginning of November 198X + 1. Defendants refused to respond to plaintiffs' interrogatories, requests for documents, and questions at one of the depositions. Plaintiffs' and defendants' counsel met but were unable to resolve the matter satisfactorily.

It is now November 15, 198X + 1 (plaintiffs and defendants have agreed that all motions will be considered timely when filed). Plaintiffs are *thinking about* filing motions to compel discovery. Specifically, plaintiffs requested the following items and defendants responded:

1. PLAINTIFFS' REQUEST TO PRODUCE DOCUMENTS DIRECTED TO DAVOLA DEFENDANTS: REQUEST NO. 4. Witness statement of Roberta Montbank, taken approximately three weeks after the shooting of Bruno Summers.
Answer: Work Product.

2. PLAINTIFFS' REQUEST TO PRODUCE DOCUMENTS DIRECTED TO DAVOLA DEFENDANTS: REQUEST NO. 18. Time sheets and payroll records for all persons who are presently and were employed at the Unicorn Tavern prior to the shooting.
Answer: Irrelevant and burdensome.

3. PLAINTIFFS' FIRST SET OF INTERROGATORIES DIRECTED TO DEFENDANT HARD: INTERROGATORIES NOS. 30-32.
Interrogatory No. 30: Have you contacted any person or persons, who are or may be classified as an expert witness, whether they are going to testify or not, in regard to the intoxication of Edward Hard on the evening of September 3, 198X?
Answer: Work Product.

Interrogatory No. 31: If your answer to Interrogatory No. 30 was at all affirmative, please set forth the name of the person or persons, present residential and/or business address, and telephone number.
Answer: Work Product.

Interrogatory No. 32: If the answer to Interrogatory No. 30 is in the affirmative, do you have any statements or written reports from the person or persons?
Answer: Work Product.

4. PLAINTIFFS' DEPOSITION OF TOM DONALDSON ON
   OCTOBER 1, 198X + 1, PAGE 10, LINES 1-8:

```
 1    Q:   Can you describe the appearance of Ed Hard on
 2         the night of September 3, 198X?
 3
 4    A:   I refuse to answer that question on the
 5         ground it may incriminate me.
 6
 7    . . .
 8
 9    Q:   Can you describe his demeanor?
10
11    A:   I refuse to answer that question on the
12         ground it may incriminate me.
13
14    Q:   Are you refusing to answer all questions as to
15         Ed Hard's appearance, demeanor, and actions
16         the night of September 3, 198X?
17
18    A:   Yes.
```

PREPARATION

READ: (1) Pretrial Case File Entries 1-43, 46, 50-57, 59-61, 63, 82, 90;
(2) Chapter VIII; (3) Fed. R. Civ. P. 11-12, 26-37.

Plaintiffs' attorney should answer the following questions concerning
the items that plaintiffs requested and defendants refused to allow
discovery.

1. What is your burden of proof to successfully obtain the information
   you seek in a motion to compel discovery? (Beyond a reasonable
   doubt you need the information, preponderance of evidence, and so
   on.) Explain.

2. Generally, state your objectives, in terms of your representational
   strategy, in filing a motion to compel discovery.

3. What are your objectives in terms of your case theory in requesting:

   a. Roberta Montbank's statement?

   b. Time sheets and payroll records from persons employed at the
      Unicorn Tavern?

   c. Expert witnesses consulted by Ed Hard's attorney?

   d. Tom Donaldson's opinion concerning Ed Hard's appearance,
      demeanor, and actions the evening of September 3, 198X?

4. As to the four items demanded by plaintiffs:

   a. Are any of defendants' refusals justified?

   b. On what grounds?

5. If you do not need the responses, but still believe that you are entitled
   to the response, are there any other considerations in proceeding with
   a motion for compelling discovery?

a. List all other reasons.

b. Evaluate whether it is ethical to proceed based on the reasons you listed.

6. If you file motions to compel discovery:

a. Are you entitled to sanctions against defendants? Explain.

b. Will you request sanctions against defendants? Explain.

c. Are you entitled to attorney fees? Explain.

7. Are there alternatives that you could explore to obtain the information you seek other than by filing motions to compel discovery?

a. What other alternatives are available?

b. What are the advantages of these alternatives?

c. What are the disadvantages of these alternatives?

8. Technically, what legal papers do you have to file for a motion to compel?

ASSIGNMENT FOR CLASS

1. Outside of class, prepare (as plaintiffs' attorney) a memorandum explaining as to the four items requested, what action you would take and why. Hand in a copy to your senior partner.

2. In class, be prepared to discuss your memorandum.

PROBLEM 96

Defendants' Attorneys: Planning Discovery Motions

Summers v. Hard has progressed. (See Problem 95 for particulars.) It is now November 15, 198X+1 (plaintiffs and defendants have agreed that all motions will be considered timely when filed). Defendants are *thinking about* whether to compel discovery. Specifically, defendants requested the following items and plaintiffs responded:

1. DEFENDANTS' FIRST SET OF INTERROGATORIES AND REQUEST TO PRODUCE DOCUMENTS DIRECTED TO GRETCHEN AND HANS SUMMERS: REQUEST NOS. 15-17.

Q 15: Did Bruno Summers give you any money during the past five years, 198X−5 through 198X?

A: Irrelevant, burdensome, vague, overbroad, and privileged.

Q 16: If your answer to Interrogatory No. 15 was at all affirmative, list for each year:
(a) The amount of money.
(b) When the money was given.
(c) Whether the money was for a specific occasion or item.
(d) To whom the money was given.
(e) Attach copies of your income tax returns for the past five years, 198X−5 through 198X.

A: See answer to Interrogatory No. 15; privileged.

Q 17: At any time did Bruno Summers claim either or both of you as dependents on his income tax returns?

A: Privileged.

2. DEFENDANT HARD—FIRST SET OF INTERROGATORIES AND MOTION TO PRODUCE DOCUMENTS DIRECTED TO DEBORAH MILLER-SUMMERS: REQUEST NOS. 22-23.

Q 22: Have you ever had or suffered from any mental condition, emotional disease, or illness from birth through and including the present?

A: Burdensome, vague, overbroad, privileged, irrelevant.

Q 23: If your answer to Interrogatory No. 22 was at all affirmative, list for each disease, illness, or mental condition:

(a) The year of occurrence.

(b) The treatment.

(c) Medications prescribed or taken.

(d) Doctors consulted or treating the condition.

(e) Hospitals, institutions, clinics involved with the diagnosis and/or treatment of the mental condition—their names, telephone numbers, addresses, and years involved.

A: See answer to Interrogatory No. 22

Also, plaintiffs requested (motion to produce) income tax returns for defendants Davola and Hard for the past seven years (198X – 7 to 198X). Defendants Davola and Hard do not want to provide their tax returns. They would like to seek a protective order.

PREPARATION

READ: (1) Pretrial Case File Entries 1-43, 47-48, 50-57, 59-61, 63, 82, 90; (2) Chapter VIII; (3) Fed. R. Civ. P. 11-12; 26-37.

Defendants' attorneys should answer the following questions concerning the items defendants requested and plaintiffs refused to provide.

1. What is your burden of proof to successfully obtain the information you seek in a motion to compel discovery (beyond a reasonable doubt you need the information, preponderance of evidence, and so on)? Explain.

2. Generally, state your objectives in filing a motion to compel discovery.

3. What are your objectives in terms of your case theory in requesting:

   a. Money that Bruno Summers gave Gretchen and Hans Summers?

   b. Information about Deborah Summers' mental state and treatment from birth through the present?

4. As to the items demanded by defendants:

   a. Are any of plaintiffs' refusals justified?

   b. On what grounds?

5. If you do not need the responses, but still believe you are entitled to the responses, are there any other considerations in proceeding with a motion for compelling discovery?

a. List all other reasons.

b. Evaluate whether it is ethical to proceed based on the reasons you listed.

6. Defendants would like to request a protective order concerning plaintiffs' request for Davola's and Hard's income tax returns.

a. Generally, what standards do courts use to grant protective orders?

b. Explain legally and factually why a court should grant defendants' request for a protective order.

7. If you file motions to compel discovery:

a. Are you entitled to sanctions against plaintiffs? Explain.

b. Will you request sanctions against plaintiffs? Explain.

c. Are you entitled to attorneys' fees? Explain.

8. Are there alternatives that you could explore to obtain the information you seek other than by filing motions to compel discovery?

a. What other alternatives are available?

b. What are the advantages of these alternatives?

c. What are the disadvantages of these alternatives?

9. Technically, what legal papers do you have to file for:

a. A motion to compel?

b. A protective order?

ASSIGNMENT FOR CLASS

1. Outside of class, defendants' attorneys, prepare a memorandum explaining what, if any, action you would take and why. Hand in a copy to your senior partner.

2. In class, be prepared to discuss your memorandum.

PROBLEM 97 _____

Plaintiffs' Attorney and Defendant Davola's EKKO Attorney: Plaintiffs' Motion to Compel Production of Documents and Defendant Davola's Response*
(Roberta Montbank's Witness Statement)

Before filing a complaint for wrongful death, plaintiffs obtained the prosecutor's file in *State v. Hard*, which contained the police witness statements from Deborah Summers, Tom Donaldson, and Officers Yale and West. The police also listed Robin Luntlebunk as a witness, but no statement was taken from her until November 3, 198X (after the criminal

_____
*Davola is represented by a private attorney and the EKKO Insurance Company. For the purpose of this problem, the EKKO Insurance Company is handling the entire motion.

case was dismissed). The police claim that they could not locate Ms. Montbank because they were given the name Robin Luntlebunk instead of Roberta Montbank. Plaintiffs' complaint, *Summers v. Hard*, was filed on November 1, 198X. Defendants responded to the complaint on November 8, 198X.

Plaintiffs sent written interrogatories to defendant Davola on May 15, 198X + 1. In response to plaintiffs' written interrogatories, plaintiffs learned that the EKKO Insurance Company interviewed and received a signed statement under oath from Roberta Montbank on October 26, 198X. Ms. Montbank, 78 years of age, was a patron at the Unicorn Tavern on the night Bruno Summers was shot.

Plaintiffs contacted Ms. Montbank on June 1, 198X + 1. They asked her for the statement she gave to EKKO. Ms. Montbank declined to give it to plaintiffs' attorney. Ms. Montbank explained that she was still a patron at the Unicorn Tavern and did not want to anger Mr. Davola.

Plaintiffs sent defendant Davola a written request for documents on July 15, 198X + 1, requesting the witness statement of Roberta Montbank. Defendant Davola refused to produce the statement. Defendant Davola responded:

> PLAINTIFFS' REQUEST TO PRODUCE DOCUMENTS DIRECTED TO DEFENDANT DAVOLA: REQUEST NO. 4.
> Witness statement of Roberta Montbank, taken by EKKO Insurance Company on behalf of defendant Davola shortly before *Summers v. Hard* was commenced on November 1, 198X.
> *Answer:* Work Product.

After receiving defendant Davola's response, plaintiffs' attorney met with defendant Davola's attorney on August 12, 198X + 1, but they were unable to resolve the matter. The plaintiffs' attorney plans to file a motion to compel Davola to produce the Montbank statement. Defendant Davola's attorney will resist plaintiffs' motion.

PREPARATION

READ: (1) Pretrial Case File Entries 1-39, 46, 50, 53, 57, 59-61, 63, 82, 90; (2) Chapter VIII; (3) Fed. R. Civ. P. 11-12; 26-37.

In preparing and arguing motions, you should prepare both your own and your adversary's position. Therefore answer the questions by assuming the role of either plaintiffs' attorney or defendant Davola's attorney (as indicated).

Assume the role of plaintiffs' attorney (Questions 1-7):

1. What are your objectives in terms of your case theory in compelling production of Roberta Montbank's statement?

2. Are there alternatives that you could explore to obtain the information you seek other than by filing a motion to compel discovery?

   a. What alternatives are available?

   b. What are the advantages of these alternatives?

   c. What are the disadvantages of these alternatives?

3. What arguments can plaintiffs present to refute Davola's assertion that Montbank's statement is "work product"?

a. Legal arguments?

b. Factual arguments?

4. Even if the court rules that the Montbank statement is Davola's work product, you may still be able to obtain the statement since work product is a qualified privilege. You will have to show (factually) that plaintiffs have substantial need of the materials to prepare their case and that they are unable without undue hardship to obtain the substantial equivalent of the materials by other means. In order to make a factual presentation:

a. What documents, if any, will you file? Why?

b. If you file affidavits, whose affidavits will you file?

c. What facts will you include in the affidavits?

d. Are there evidentiary problems that you may encounter in filing the documents or affidavits? Explain.

d. Are there ethical problems that you may encounter if you include your affidavit as the attorney? Explain.

5. The police took a statement from Roberta Montbank on November 3, 198X. What effect does the availability of this statement have on your argument that you have "substantial need" of the Montbank statement prepared by EKKO Insurance Company?

6. Suppose that in addition to the police statement, Ms. Montbank is available for a deposition.

a. What effect would that have if the deposition were scheduled in December 198X?

b. What effect would that have if the deposition were scheduled for November 198X + 1?

7. Are you entitled to sanctions if you succeed on this motion? Explain.

Assume the role of defendant Davola's attorney (Questions 8-13):

8. What are your objectives in refusing to provide plaintiffs' attorney with the statement you have from Roberta Montbank in terms of:

a. Your case theory?

b. Other reasons?

9. Federal Rule of Civil Procedure 26(b) provides: "In ordering discovery of such materials [prepared in anticipation of litigation] when the required showing has been made, the court *shall* protect against disclosure of the mental impressions, conclusions, opinions, or legal theories of an attorney or other representative of a party concerning the litigation." (Emphasis added.) What arguments can you present to show that the Montbank statement is absolutely privileged?

a. Legal arguments?

b. Factual arguments?

10. If the court rules that the Montbank statement is work product, plaintiffs nevertheless may still be able to obtain it if they show

substantial need of the materials to prepare their case and that they are unable without undue hardship to obtain the substantial equivalent of the materials by other means. (Refer to answers to Question 4 that set forth plaintiffs' factual presentation of these issues.) How will you refute plaintiffs' "substantial need" and "undue hardship" factual presentation?

   a. What documents, if any, will you file? Why?

   b. If you file affidavits, whose affidavits will you file?

   c. What facts will you include in the affidavits?

   d. Are there evidentiary problems that you may encounter in filing the documents or affidavits? Explain.

11. You are *contemplating* filing your affidavit as the attorney to support this motion.

   a. What purposes would your attorney affidavit serve?

   b. Would you refer to any documents in your affidavit? Explain.

   c. What, if any, facts would you include in your affidavit? Why?

   d. Are there any ethical problems that you *may* encounter if you include your affidavit as the attorney? Explain.

12. Suppose that plaintiffs' attorney interviewed Ms. Montbank on December 1, 198X. What arguments can you make to refute plaintiffs':

   a. "Substantial need" argument?

   b. "Undue hardship" argument?

13. If the judge grants plaintiffs' motion, what will you do? Why?

ASSIGNMENT FOR CLASS**

1. Outside of class:

   a. **Plaintiffs' attorney:** Prepare a written motion or a written outline of a motion to compel production of documents on Request No. 4. If you believe you should not proceed with a motion compelling discovery, draft a memorandum to your senior partner explaining your reasons for not proceeding.

   b. **Attorney for defendant Davola:** Prepare a written response or a written outline of a response to plaintiffs' motion to compel production of documents on Request No. 4.

   c. **Attorneys for plaintiffs and defendant Davola:** Give your senior partner a copy of your motion, outline, response, or memorandum.

2. In class: argue or discuss your written motion, memorandum, or response.

**Your instructor will select which assignment you will do and the filing and argument schedule.

VIII. Pretrial Motions

PROBLEM 98

Attorneys for Plaintiffs and Defendant Donaldson: Plaintiffs' Motion to Compel Response to Deposition Questions and Defendant Donaldson's Response
(Fifth Amendment Privilege)

Summers v. Hard has proceeded through discovery. Plaintiffs sent written interrogatories to defendant Donaldson on June 15, 198X+1. Donaldson's deposition was taken on October 1, 198X+1. At the deposition, plaintiffs' counsel asked Tom Donaldson the following questions:

4. PLAINTIFFS' DEPOSITION OF TOM DONALDSON ON OCTOBER 1, 198X+1, PAGE 10, LINES 1-18:

```
 1    Q:   Can you describe the appearance of Ed Hard on
 2         the night of September 3, 198X?
 3
 4    A:   I refuse to answer that question on the
 5         ground it may incriminate me.
 6
 7    . . .
 8
 9    Q:   Can you describe his demeanor?
10
11    A:   I refuse to answer that question on the
12         ground it may incriminate me.
13
14    Q:   Are you refusing to answer all questions as to
15         Ed Hard's appearance, demeanor, and actions
16         the night of September 3, 198X?
17
18    A:   Yes.
```

After Mr. Donaldson refused to respond at his deposition, the attorneys agreed to finish the deposition and at a later date resolve the matter of Donaldson's refusal to respond.

Subsequently, plaintiffs' attorney and defendant Donaldson's attorney met but were unable to resolve the matter. Plaintiffs' attorney plans to file a motion to compel responses to deposition questions.

The State of Major Alcoholic Beverage (MAB) Commission has never enforced administrative regulations MAB 2.2 and 2.3.

PREPARATION

READ: (1) Pretrial Case File Entries 1-39, 57, 59-61, 63, 82, 90; (2) Chapter VIII; (3) Fed. R. Civ. P. 11-12; 26-37.

In preparing and arguing motions, you should prepare both your own and your adversary's position. Therefore, answer the questions by assuming the role of either plaintiffs' attorney or defendant Donaldson's attorney (as indicated).

Assume the role of plaintiffs' attorney (Questions 1-5):

1. What are your objectives in terms of your case theory in compelling Donaldson to answer the questions asked?

2. Instead of compelling Donaldson to respond to the deposition questions, have you considered obtaining the information from other witnesses who were at the Unicorn Tavern the evening of September 3, 198X (Mary Apple, Bert Kain, Alan Long, John Gooding, Peter Dean, etc.)?

    a. What are the advantages of obtaining the information you seek from witnesses other than Donaldson?

    b. What are the disadvantages?

3. What arguments can plaintiffs present to refute that Donaldson's assertion is based on Fifth Amendment privilege?

    a. Legal arguments?

    b. Factual arguments?

4. The police took a statement from Mr. Donaldson on September 4, 198X. Could plaintiffs successfully argue that Donaldson waived his privilege? Explain.

5. How would you have had Donaldson respond to the questions asked at the deposition if defendant Donaldson was your client?

Assume the role of defendant Donaldson's attorney (Questions 6-9):

6. What are your objectives in terms of your case theory in refusing to answer the deposition questions?

7. What legal arguments will you present concerning Donaldson's Fifth Amendment privilege?

8. In order to present your factual position on the Fifth Amendment issue:

    a. What documents, if any, will you file? Why?

    b. Whose affidavits, if any, will you file? Why?

    c. What facts will you include in the affidavits? Why?

    d. Are there evidentiary problems that you may encounter in filing the affidavits? Explain.

    e. Are there ethical problems that you may encounter if you include your affidavit as the attorney? Explain.

9. Would you compel answers to the deposition questions asked of Donaldson if plaintiffs were your clients? Why?

Now assume the perspective of both plaintiffs' attorney and defendant Donaldson's attorney (Questions 10-14):

10. Suppose that the Major Alcoholic Beverage Commission chairperson made a statement to the news media. Through its leader MAB stated that it will not criminally or civilly charge, and Davola will not dismiss, any employee for conduct arising out of the September 3, 198X shooting of Bruno Summers. What effect would that have on the motion from:

    a. Plaintiffs' perspective?

    b. Defendant Donaldson's perspective?

11. Now suppose that the chairperson of the Major Alcoholic Beverage Commission stated that if evidence was found that any tavern employee or licensee served intoxicating beverages to an already intoxicated person that MAB would institute proceedings against that employee or licensee, pursuant to MAB Administrative Regulation 2.3(b).

12. Suppose that plaintiffs interviewed Mary Apple on October 1, 198X, and Mary Apple was asked and answered the same questions that Donaldson refuses to answer. What effect would that have on the motion from:

    a. Plaintiffs' perspective?

    b. Donaldson's perspective?

13. If plaintiffs succeed on the motion:

    a. What arguments can you make to support an award of costs, attorneys' fees, or sanctions?

    b. What arguments can you make to negate an award of costs, attorneys' fees, or sanctions?

14. Will you request sanctions against your opponent? Explain.

ASSIGNMENT FOR CLASS*

1. Outside of class:

    a. **Plaintiffs' attorney:** Prepare a written motion or a written outline of a motion to compel discovery on the questions posed to Tom Donaldson at his deposition. If you believe that you should not proceed with a motion compelling discovery, draft a memorandum to your senior partner explaining your reasons for not proceeding.

    b. **Attorney for defendant Donaldson:** Prepare a written response or a written outline of a response to plaintiffs' motion to compel answers to questions asked Tom Donaldson at his deposition. If you believe you should not proceed with a response to plaintiffs' motion, draft a memorandum to your senior partner explaining your reasons for not responding.

    c. **Attorneys for plaintiffs and defendant Donaldson:** Hand in your motion, response, outline, or memorandum to your senior partner.

2. In class, be prepared to argue or discuss your written motion, outline, response, or memorandum.

---

*Your instructor will select which assignment you will do and will inform you as to the filing and scheduling of the argument.

PROBLEM 99

Attorneys for Plaintiffs and Defendant Hard: Plaintiffs' Motion to Compel Answers to Interrogatories and Defendant Hard's Response
(Expert Witnesses)

Plaintiffs' complaint in *Summers v. Hard* was filed on November 1, 198X. Defendants responded to the complaint on November 8, 198X. Plaintiffs sent written interrogatories and a request for documents to Ed Hard on June 15, 198X + 1. Plaintiffs requested information about Ed Hard's expert witnesses. Defendant Hard responded on July 15, 198X + 1, refusing to provide information about expert witnesses, claiming the information was protected by the work product privilege. Specifically, the request and response were as follows:

> *Interrogatory No. 30:* Have you contacted any person or persons, who are or may be classified as an expert witness, whether they are going to testify or not, in regard to the intoxication of Edward Hard on the evening of September 3, 198X?
> *Answer:* Work Product.

> *Interrogatory No. 31:* If your answer to Interrogatory No. 30 was at all affirmative, please set forth the name of the person or persons, present residential and/or business address, and telephone number.
> *Answer:* Work Product.

> *Interrogatory No. 32:* If the answer to Interrogatory No. 30 is in the affirmative, do you have any statements or written reports from the person or persons?
> *Answer:* Work Product.

After defendant Hard refused to respond to Interrogatories 30 through 32, counsel for plaintiffs and defendant Hard met, but were unable to resolve the matter.

However, while at the meeting, Ed Hard's attorney stated that he had consulted four expert witnesses. He does not at the present time intend to have any experts testify at trial. He hired and paid a polygrapher who tested Hard as to whether he intentionally killed Bruno Summers. The polygrapher was paid $1,000 for his testing and report. He is not expected to testify at trial. A toxicologist examined the ampoule from the breathalyzer. The toxicologist did not make a written report to Ed Hard's attorney. The toxicologist was paid $300 for her services. Ed Hard was examined by a psychiatrist who is a friend of Ed Hard's attorney. No fee was paid and no written report was submitted. Finally, Ed Hard's attorney paid $500 to an economist to study the file in the *Summers v. Hard* case. No written report was submitted. Ed's attorney is unsure whether he will consult with the economist again.

Plaintiffs' counsel plans to file a motion to compel responses to Interrogatories 30-32. Defendant Hard will resist plaintiffs' motion.

PREPARATION

READ: (1) Pretrial Case File Entries 1-39, 42, 43, 59-61, 63, 82, 90; (2) Chapter VIII; (3) Fed. R. Civ. P. 11-12; 26-37.

In preparing and arguing motions, you should prepare both your own and your adversary's position. Therefore, answer the questions by assuming the role of either plaintiffs' attorney or defendant Hard's attorney (as indicated).

Assume the role of plaintiffs' attorney (Questions 1-3):

1. What are your objectives in compelling Ed Hard to answer interrogatories concerning:

   a. Expert witnesses he has consulted but will not testify?

   b. Expert witnesses who will testify at trial?

2. Are there alternatives that you could explore to obtain the information you seek other than by filing a motion to compel discovery?

   a. What alternatives are available?

   b. What are the advantages of these alternatives?

   c. What are the disadvantages of these alternatives?

3. What legal and factual arguments should you present to refute defendant Hard's assertion of:

   a. Attorney-client privilege?

   b. Work product?

Now assume the role of defendant Hard's attorney (Question 4):

4. What legal and factual arguments will defendant Hard's attorney present in opposing the motion to compel based on:

   a. Attorney-client privilege?

   b. Work product?

Now assume the role of a judge (Questions 5-6):

5. Suppose that you are the judge hearing plaintiffs' motion to compel:

   a. What factors would you consider in deciding this motion?

   b. Are there any factors that you listed that are more controlling than others? Why or why not?

   c. What burden of proof would you apply in granting/denying plaintiffs' motion (e.g., preponderance, reasonable doubt)? Why?

   d. For plaintiffs to sustain their burden of proof, what do they have to prove?

6. Suppose that you were the judge hearing this motion, and you ruled against plaintiffs.

   a. Would you award sanctions against plaintiffs? Why or why not?

   b. If you awarded sanctions, what sanctions would you award?

ASSIGNMENT FOR CLASS*

1. Outside of class:

    a. **Plaintiffs' attorney:** Prepare a written motion or a written outline of a motion to compel responses to Interrogatories Nos. 30 through 32 sent to defendant Ed Hard. If you believe that you should not proceed with a motion compelling discovery, draft a memorandum to your senior partner explaining your reasons for not proceeding.

    b. **Attorney for defendant Hard:** Prepare a written response or a written outline of a response to plaintiffs' motion to compel responses to Interrogatories Nos. 30 through 32 requested of Ed Hard. If you believe that you should not proceed with a response to plaintiffs' motion, draft a memorandum to your senior partner explaining your reasons for not responding.

    c. **Attorneys for plaintiffs and defendant Hard:** Hand in your motion or memorandum to your senior partner.

2. In class, argue or discuss your written motion, response, or memorandum.

PROBLEM 100

Attorneys for Defendant Hard and Plaintiffs: Defendant Hard's Motion to Compel Answers to Interrogatories and Plaintiffs' Response
(Medical History for Deborah Summers)

The attorneys in *Summers v. Hard* are in the process of formal discovery. Defendants sent written interrogatories and a request for documents to plaintiff Deborah Summers on June 15, 198X + 1. Defendants have received copies of Deborah's medical records from the Medical Services and Health Departments in Jamner County and Neva County. On July 15, 198X + 1, Deborah Summers responded to the interrogatories with the exception of two (numbers 22 and 23), which she claimed were burdensome, vague, privileged, and irrelevant.

Counsel for plaintiffs and defendant Hard met, but were unable to resolve the matter. Counsel for Ed Hard plans to file a motion to compel responses to Interrogatories 22 and 23.

The following were defendant's interrogatories and Summers' response.

INTERROGATORIES DIRECTED TO DEBORAH MILLER-SUMMERS: REQUESTS NOS. 22 AND 23.

Q 22: Have you ever had or suffered from any mental condition, emotional disease, or illness from birth through and including the present?

---

*Your instructor will select which assignment you will do and will inform you as to the filing and scheduling of the argument.

A: Burdensome, vague, overbroad, privileged, irrelevant.

Q 23: If your answer to Interrogatory No. 22 was at all affirmative, list for each disease, illness, or mental condition:

   (a) The year of occurrence.

   (b) The treatment.

   (c) Medications prescribed or taken.

   (d) Doctors consulted or treating the condition.

   (e) Hospitals, institutions, clinics involved with the diagnosis and/or treatment of the mental condition—their names, telephone numbers, addresses, and years involved.

A: See answer to Interrogatory No. 22.

PREPARATION

READ: (1) Pretrial Case File Entries 1-41, 51, 55, 56, 59-61, 63, 64, 82, 90; (2) Chapter VIII; (3) Fed. R. Civ. P. 11-12; 26-37.

In preparing and arguing motions, you should prepare both your own and your adversary's position. Therefore, answer the questions by assuming the role of either plaintiffs' attorney or defendant Hard's attorney (as indicated).

Assume the role of defendant Hard's attorney (Questions 1-4):

1. What are your objectives in terms of your case theory in compelling Deborah Summers to answer interrogatories concerning her physical and mental health?

2. Instead of filing a motion to compel responses to the interrogatories, could you obtain the information from other sources?

   a. What are the advantages of obtaining the information you seek from other than Deborah Summers?

   b. What are the disadvantages?

3. What legal and factual arguments can you present to refute Summers' refusal to answer based on the plaintiff's objections?

   a. Vague?

   b. Overbroad?

   c. Privileged?

   d. Burdensome?

   e. Irrelevant?

4. How would you have responded to the discovery request if plaintiffs were your clients? Why?

Now assume the role of plaintiff Deborah Summers' attorney (Questions 5-7):

5. In order to present your factual position on the "burdensome" issue:

   a. Whose affidavits will you file?

   b. What facts will you include in the affidavits? Why?

   c. Are there evidentiary problems that you may encounter in filing the affidavits? Explain.

d. Are there ethical problems that you may encounter if you include your affidavit as the attorney? Explain.

6. What response will you make as Deborah Summers' attorney to justify your position as to:

    a. Irrelevant?

    b. Burdensome?

7. Would you have compelled discovery if defendant were your client? Why?

Now assume the role of judge (Question 8):

8. Suppose that as the judge you deny defendant Hard's motion. Would you award costs, attorney fees, or sanctions against defendant Hard or his attorney? Explain the legal and factual basis for your decision.

ASSIGNMENT FOR CLASS*

1. Outside of class:

    a. **Attorney for defendant Hard:** Prepare a written motion or a written outline of a motion to compel responses to Interrogatories Nos. 22 and 23. If you believe that you should not proceed with a motion compelling discovery, draft a memorandum to your senior partner explaining your reasons for not proceeding.

    b. **Plaintiffs' attorney:** Prepare a written response or outline of a response to defendant Hard's motion to compel answers to Interrogatories Nos. 22 and 23. If you believe that you should not proceed with a response to defendant's motion, draft a memorandum to your senior partner explaining your reasons for not proceeding. Give your senior partner a copy of your response or memorandum.

2. In class, argue or discuss your written motion, response, or memorandum. Hand in your motion, response, or memorandum to your senior partner.

PROBLEM 101

Defendants' and Plaintiffs' Attorneys: Defendants' Motion for a Protective Order and Plaintiffs' Response
(Income Tax Returns)

Plaintiffs' complaint in *Summers v. Hard* was filed on November 1, 198X. Defendants responded to the complaint on November 8, 198X. Plaintiffs sent written interrogatories and requests for production of documents to defendants Hard and Davola on June 15, 198X + 1. Plaintiffs requested defendants' income tax returns for the past seven years.

---

*Your instructor will select which assignment you will do and will inform you as to the filing and scheduling of the argument.

Attorneys for defendants Hard and Davola do not want to give plaintiffs the income tax returns. (Plaintiffs already have a copy of the Unicorn Tavern accountant statement for 198X – 10 to 198X.) Counsel for plaintiffs and defendants met, but were unable to resolve the matter. Attorneys for defendants Hard and Davola plan to file a motion for a protective order concerning plaintiffs' request for documents 28 and 29.

The specific request was as follows:

> REQUEST FOR PRODUCTION OF DOCUMENTS DIRECTED TO DEFENDANTS HARD AND DAVOLA.
>
> *Request 28:* Directed to Defendant Davola—Please attach Defendant M.C. Davola's income tax returns for the past seven years.
>
> *Request 29:* Directed to Defendant Hard—Please attach Defendant Hard's income tax returns for the past seven years.

PREPARATION

READ: (1) Pretrial Case File Entries 1-39, 49, 59-61, 63, 82, 90; (2) Chapter VIII; (3) Fed. R. Civ. P. 11-12; 26-37.

In preparing and arguing motions, you should prepare both your own and your adversary's position. Therefore, answer the questions by assuming the role of either plaintiffs' attorney or defendants' attorneys (as indicated).

Assume the role of attorneys for defendants Davola and Hard (Questions 1-7):

1. Instead of filing a motion for a protective order, defendants could object to plaintiffs' request and wait to see if plaintiffs file a motion to compel.

    a. List the advantages for defendants in filing for a protective order.

    b. List the disadvantages for defendants.

2. In seeking a protective order, what are defendants' objectives:

    a. Generally?

    b. In terms of defendants' case theory?

    c. Are defendants' objectives ethical?

3. Federal Rule of Civil Procedure 26(c)(1-8) describes remedies a court can order in granting a protective order. What remedies should defendants seek? Why?

4. Federal Rule of Civil Procedure 26(c) lists factors a court should consider in granting a protective order (annoyance, embarrassment, oppression, undue burden, expense). Which ones are the *most* convincing for defendants to rely on in their motion? Why?

5. For a motion for a protective order:

    a. What is defendants' burden of proof to obtain a protective order?

    b. Do defendants have to prove plaintiffs' request for income tax returns is not subject to discovery and/or one or more of the factors set forth in Fed. R. Civ. P. 26(c) (annoyance, embarrassment, oppression, undue burden, expense)? Explain.

6. Are defendants entitled to a protective order? Set forth:

   a. Defendants' factual argument.

   b. Defendants' legal arguments.

   c. Remedies requested.

7. In order to present your factual arguments:

   a. What documents, if any, will you file? Why?

   b. Whose affidavits, if any, will you file?

   c. What facts will you include in the affidavits? Why?

   d. Are there evidentiary problems that you may encounter in filing the affidavits? Explain.

   e. Are there ethical problems that you may encounter if you include your affidavit as the attorney? Explain.

Now assume the role of plaintiffs' attorney (Questions 8-11):

8. Instead of requesting defendants' income tax returns, could you obtain the information from other sources? Explain.

9. What response will you present to defendants' motion for a protective order?

   a. Factual arguments?

   b. Legal arguments?

   c. Positions on remedy?

10. Are defendants entitled to sanctions if they win the motion? Explain.

11. Will you request sanctions against your opponent? Explain.

ASSIGNMENT FOR CLASS*

1. Outside of class:

   a. **Defendants' attorneys:** Prepare a written motion or a written outline of a motion for a protective order. If you believe that you should not proceed with a motion, draft a memorandum to your senior partner explaining your reasons for not proceeding.

   b. **Plaintiffs' attorney:** Prepare a written response or a written outline of a response to defendants Davola and Hard's requests for protective orders. If you believe that you should not proceed with a response to defendants' motion, draft a memorandum to your senior partner explaining your reasons for not proceeding.

   c. **Plaintiffs' and defendants' attorneys:** Give your senior partner a copy of your response or memorandum.

2. In class, argue or discuss your motion or memorandum.

---

*Your instructor will select which assignment you will do and will inform you as to the filing and scheduling of the argument.

Attorneys for Defendant Davola and Plaintiffs: Defendant Davola's Motion to Compel Answers to Interrogatories and Request for Documents and Plaintiffs' Response
(Financial Information and Income Tax Returns for Gretchen and Hans Summers)

Summers v. Hard, filed on November 1, 198X, has proceeded through discovery. Defendants sent written interrogatories and a request for documents to plaintiffs Gretchen and Hans Summers on June 15, 198X + 1. Defendant Davola requested financial information and copies of the Summers' income tax returns. Plaintiffs Gretchen and Hans Summers responded on July 15, 198X + 1, refusing to provide the financial information and income tax returns, claiming the requests were irrelevant, burdensome, vague, overbroad and privileged.

After Gretchen and Hans Summers refused to respond to Interrogatories and Request for Documents Nos. 15-17, counsel for plaintiffs and defendant Davola met, but were unable to resolve the matter. Counsel for Davola plans to file a motion to compel plaintiffs' responses to Interrogatories and Request for Documents Nos. 15-17.

Specifically, defendant's request and plaintiffs' response are as follows:

INTERROGATORIES AND REQUEST TO PRODUCE DOCUMENTS DIRECTED TO GRETCHEN AND HANS SUMMERS: REQUEST NOS. 15-17.

Q 15:   Did Bruno Summers give you any money during the past five years, 198X − 5 through 198X?

A: Irrelevant, burdensome, vague, overbroad, and privileged.

Q 16:   If your answer to Interrogatory No. 15 was at all affirmative, list for each year:

   (a) The amount of money.
   (b) When the money was given.
   (c) Whether the money was for a specific occasion or item.
   (d) To whom the money was given.
   (e) Attach copies of your income tax returns for the past five years, 198X − 5 through 198X.

A: See answer to Interrogatory No. 15; privileged.

Q 17:   At any time did Bruno Summers claim either or both of you as dependents on his income tax returns?

A: Privileged.

PREPARATION

READ: (1) Pretrial Case File Entries 1-39, 42, 43, 47-48, 52, 54, 59-61, 63, 82, 90; (2) Chapter VIII; (3) Fed. R. Civ. P. 11-12; 26-37.

In preparing and arguing motions, you should prepare both your own and your adversary's position. Therefore, answer the questions by assuming the role of either plaintiffs' attorney or defendant Davola's attorney (as indicated).

Assume the role of defendant Davola's attorney (Questions 1-6):

1. What are your objectives in terms of your case theory in compelling Gretchen and Hans Summers to answer interrogatories and the requests for documents concerning financial matters between them and Bruno Summers?

2. Instead of filing a motion to compel responses to interrogatories and requests for documents, could you obtain the information from other sources?

    a. What are the advantages of obtaining the information you seek from other than Gretchen and Hans Summers?

    b. What are the disadvantages?

3. How will you refute the Summers' factual argument that it is too "burdensome" to respond to your requests for documents and interrogatories?

4. What legal arguments can you present to refute Summers' refusal to answer based on "privilege"?

5. Suppose that Gretchen and Hans Summers in the complaint alleged a claim that they were dependent upon Bruno Summers for support. Could you argue that the Summers waived any privilege that they are asserting? Explain.

6. Suppose that the Summers responded to Interrogatories 15 through 17 by asserting a Fifth Amendment privilege? Should they be successful? Explain.

Now assume the role of plaintiffs' attorney (Questions 7-8):

7. What legal arguments will you make to justify the plaintiffs' position based upon:

    a. Irrelevance?

    b. Vagueness?

    c. Overbroad?

    d. Privilege?

8. In order to present your factual position that it is too "burdensome" to respond to defendant's Interrogatories 15 to 17:

    a. Will you file affidavits?

    b. Whose affidavits will you file?

    c. What facts will you include in the affidavits? Why?

    d. Are there evidentiary problems that you may encounter in filing the affidavits? Explain.

    e. Are there ethical problems you may encounter if you include your affidavit as the attorney? Explain.

Now assume the role of a judge hearing this motion (Questions 9-10):

9. If defendant's motion is granted, is he entitled to:

    a. Costs?

    b. Attorney fees?

    c. Sanctions?

    Explain the factual and legal basis for your ruling.

10. How much, if anything, will you award for (a) costs; (b) attorney fees; (c) sanctions?

ASSIGNMENT FOR CLASS*

1. Outside of class:

    a. **Attorney for Defendant Davola:** Prepare a written motion or a written outline of a motion to compel responses to documents and interrogatories. If you believe that you should not proceed with a motion compelling discovery, draft a memorandum to your senior partner explaining your reasons for not proceeding.

    b. **Plaintiffs' attorney:** Prepare a written motion or a written outline of a motion to defendant's motion to compel responses to documents and interrogatories. If you believe that you should not proceed with a response to defendant's motion, draft a memorandum to your senior partner explaining your reasons for not proceeding.

    c. **Attorneys for defendant Davola and plaintiffs:** Hand in your motion, response, outline, or memorandum to your senior partner.

2. In class, argue or discuss your written motion, response, outline, or memorandum.

---

*Your instructor will select which assignment you will do and will inform you as to the filing and scheduling of the argument.

IX

Counseling

A. COUNSELING IN THE CONTEXT OF A REPRESENTATIONAL STRATEGY AND COUNSELING OBJECTIVES
B. PREPARATION
C. CONTENT PLANNING: AN APPROACH AND ILLUSTRATIONS
      Question 1.   What is the counseling problem?
      Question 2.   What are your objectives in counseling?
      Question 3.   Should you counsel?
      Question 4.   What should be the extent of your counseling?
      Question 5.   What further information do you need?
      Question 6.   What counseling advice (alternative solutions) is possible in light of your representational strategy?
      Question 7.   Are there any ethical issues that you should consider?
      Question 8.   Based on all the information, what is an appropriate counseling decision?
D. PERFORMANCE PLANNING: AN APPROACH AND ILLUSTRATION
      Question 1.   What are your counseling performance objectives?
      Question 2.   What potential problems might occur during counseling?
      Question 3.   What tactics and techniques can you use to counsel?
      Question 4.   What strategy should you adopt?
      Question 5.   What will you do after counseling? Follow up? Reevaluate?
E. GENERAL PLANNING QUESTIONS

CRIMINAL PROBLEMS: *State v. Hard*
   Problem 103.   Prosecutor: Counseling a Key Witness Who Does Not Want to Testify (Deborah Summers)
   Problem 104.   Prosecutor: Counseling a Witness Whether to Talk to Your Adversary (Peter Dean)
   Problem 105.   Prosecutor: Counseling a Key Witness Who Is Contemplating the Destruction of Potentially Relevant Evidence (Deborah Summers)
   Problem 106.   Prosecutor: Counseling a Key Witness Who Is Threatening to Leave Town (Deborah Summers)
   Problem 107.   Defense Attorney: Counseling the Defendant Concerning Alleged Harassment in Jail
   Problem 108.   Defense Attorney: Counseling the Defendant Concerning a Drinking Problem
   Problem 109.   Defense Attorney: Counseling the Defendant Concerning His Objections to Cross-Examination of Adverse Witness (Deborah Summers)
   Problem 110.   Defense Attorney: Counseling the Defendant Concerning the Use of a Particular Character Witness (John Gooding)
   Problem 111.   Defense Attorney: Counseling the Defendant Concerning Testifying at a Suppression Motion
   Problem 112.   Defense Attorney: Counseling the Defendant Concerning Use of a Witness at a Suppression Motion (Marty Saunders)
   Problem 113.   Defense Attorney: Counseling the Defendant Concerning Consequences of a Change of Venue Motion
   Problem 114.   Defense Attorney: Counseling the Defendant Concerning Evaluation of the Prosecutor's Plea-Bargaining Offer
CIVIL PROBLEMS: *Summers v. Hard*
   Problem 115.   Plaintiffs' Attorney: Counseling Clients Whether to Litigate
   Problem 116.   Plaintiffs' Attorney: Counseling Client to See a Psychologist (Deborah Summers)
   Problem 117.   Plaintiffs' Attorney: Counseling Client Concerning Remarriage (Deborah Summers)
   Problem 118.   Private Attorney for Deborah Summers: Counseling Client in Child Custody Action

---

A. COUNSELING IN THE CONTEXT OF A REPRESENTATIONAL STRATEGY AND COUNSELING OBJECTIVES

Counseling is a major part of a lawyer's work, since an attorney is so often called on to advise a client, witness, or co-counsel in the resolution of a range of problems. As in the performance of other pretrial skills discussed in this book, we emphasize again the necessity of a plan that will guide the preparation, content, and performance of your counseling endeavors. That plan, based on your representational strategy and general counseling objectives, provides the focus for this chapter. Although we concentrate on counseling clients in a litigation context, many of the planning principles are applicable to counseling in other circumstances.

Each counseling endeavor shares the following general objectives:

- Developing and maintaining a good attorney-client relationship
- Advising a client about a particular matter
- Helping a client resolve a particular problem

Our counseling approach, like our performance models for other pretrial skills, employs ends-means thinking. As such, in addition to helping your client resolve a particular problem, an important function of counseling is to help achieve the overall goals of your case as expressed in your representational strategy. Counseling is thus a means to an end, performed in the context of the legal representation of your client; it is not an end in itself.

The profession's view of counseling has changed over time. Initially, it was not a subject that attorneys even discussed. Then, a decade or so ago, the pendulum swung. For some, the attorney began to resemble a therapist in her dealings with clients. Our approach to counseling is to strike a balance between engaging in counseling as a critical element in the maintenance of the attorney-client relationship and the use of counseling as a strategic tool to carry out your representational strategy.

Generally, you will be counseling your client on matters directly relating to those for which you were retained. Counseling might involve decisions whether to litigate, testify before a grand jury, obtain a physical examination, present a defense, settle the dispute, and so on. In non-litigation, counseling may concern tax strategy, or business, estate, or trust planning. However, counseling also may involve matters that are not as clearly related to the matters in which you represent the client (a drug problem, personal dispute with a friend, a decision whether to go on a safari). In this chapter, we present an approach to counseling that governs both those situations directly arising from your representation as well as those situations that are only tangentially related to the representation of your client.

We also intend our approach to serve as an integrated model for counseling in the context of the performance of other pretrial skills, such as interviewing, pleading, negotiation, discovery, and trial. As you are aware, performance of other pretrial skills might involve counseling. For example, if your representational strategy is settlement, you might interview your client to obtain information for the negotiation and then counsel your client as to the advantages or disadvantages of settlement. Or when pleading, you will need to counsel your client as to whether asserting an affirmative defense helps achieve, or is even consistent with, this representational strategy of eventual negotiation. In this regard, as you read this chapter on counseling, think about counseling in conjunction with other pretrial skills, and, in particular, with client interviewing.

Our planning approach is meant to give you a structure and some ideas regarding counseling techniques. The following references provide further development of counseling theories and techniques that might be helpful in the legal context. In particular, we highly recommend D. Binder and S. Price, *Legal Interviewing and Counseling* 135-223 (1977); A. Watson, *The Lawyer in the Interviewing and Counselling Process* (1976); T.L. Shaffer, *Legal Interviewing and Counseling in a Nutshell* (1976); D.E. Rosenthal, *Lawyer and Client: Who's in Charge?* (1974).

B. PREPARATION

Essentially, you will be counseling throughout your attorney-client relationship. For instance, you might be thrust into the lawyer-counselor role during an initial interview (your advice is sought to identify whether there is indeed a legal problem), or after you have established an attorney-client relationship (explaining alternatives to litigation; assessing the settlement offer; discussing "Jerry's drinking problem"). Likewise, the nature of the client's problem may be known before you first meet with the client, and in fact may be the reason for the first meeting (e.g., tax advice, a possible dissolution). Or counseling can occur while you are discussing or engaged in other matters for your client (advice on a new business venture for a client whose will you are drafting).

Generally, preparation for counseling will be much like preparation for client interviewing. Recall that you should obtain, in advance of meeting with your client, factual and legal information about the counseling matter and personal information about the client (see Chapter IV at pages 70-71).

The amount and type of preparation you do prior to counseling will be directly related to the circumstances of when you counsel (before or after an attorney-client relationship is established); the type of counseling problem (the extent of the problem's relationship to the litigation); and the amount of prior knowledge you have as to the issues or the subject matter for which advice is sought. For example, if you have an established attorney-client relationship (i.e., have already interviewed the client, worked on the client's legal matters), you may be conversant with the client's affairs. You will have an appreciation for her personality, legal case, and even some of her personal affairs. Therefore, the amount of time you devote to information-gathering in order to counsel might be less than if you have just met the client. If the counseling matter is directly related to the legal matter upon which you are representing the client (e.g., counseling one client about whether to testify, another whether to purchase the real estate), then information-gathering and legal research will already

have been completed. If you are aware of a matter that potentially may require counseling, even if it is not directly related to the legal matter for which you have been retained, you might ask your client to prepare a written account of the situation, bring appropriate documents to the counseling meeting, and so forth.

When representing a client, you may be consulted about many different issues, some of which present the need for professional or specialized help. Therefore, it is helpful to maintain a comprehensive list of potential referrals that provide community social services—mental health professionals; hospitals; health treatment centers; accountants; applicable governmental agencies; juvenile facilities; and so on.

C. CONTENT PLANNING: AN APPROACH AND ILLUSTRATIONS

> BASIC TASK: Identify the counseling matter, decide the extent of your counseling role, gather sufficient information to advise the client about alternative solutions, and help the client make an informed decision.

Counseling, like client and witness interviewing, requires a plan. When you interview, you do not aimlessly ask questions; instead, your interview, if its purpose is to obtain information, is guided by a plan based on your case theory. Your case theory guides you in exploring subject areas of inquiry for obtaining information. Just as your case theory guides obtaining and presenting information, counseling in a litigation context is guided by your representational strategy and the particular counseling objectives that are applicable to the situation.

Of course, the point at which you can develop a plan will be affected by the varying degrees of knowledge that you might have as to your client and the counseling subject matter. For example, if you do not know anything about the client and cannot anticipate the subject matter that the potential client is consulting you about, you probably will not be able to plan a specific approach to counseling before meeting with your client. Nevertheless, you can still plan a general counseling strategy by thinking about how you would approach each question covered in this section when it arises in your discussion with your client. Your tentative counseling plan will be much like creating a painting. (You gather your ideas together, make a rough sketch, assemble the materials you will need, and then you can begin painting.)

Our approach for planning the content for counseling is based on eight questions. These questions provide a general structure for organizing substantive areas of inquiry and decisionmaking. We use an illustration to show you how the structure works. We are aware that the illustration does not encompass all the potential range of counseling occurrences. However, we use one client to illustrate the range of counseling problems that *can* occur. In this context, we show you how we would approach counseling this fictitious client about filing for a dissolution; about her drinking problem; and about the sale of her house.

Plan

    1.   What is the counseling problem?
    2.   What are your objectives in counseling?

Analysis

    3.   Should you counsel?
    4.   What should be the extent of your counseling?

Replanning

    5.   What further information do you need?

Strategy

    6.   What counseling advice (alternative solutions) is possible in light of your representational strategy?
    7.   Are there any ethical issues that you should consider?
    8.   Based on all the information, what is an appropriate counseling decision?

Imagine that Rocky, a potential client, has made an appointment to see you. You detect a strong smell of alcohol on Rocky's breath. You ask Rocky, "What can I do for you?" Rocky states, "I want to leave my husband."

QUESTION 1
What is the counseling problem?

The situation posed in our hypothetical supposes that this is the first time that you are meeting with Rocky. The information that you have is gleaned directly from the interview itself and your observations. At this information-gathering stage counseling skills combined with interviewing skills are united in the client interview to obtain information.

You need to obtain information that will help you identify the counseling problem. You might immediately think of two potential problems to explore. Your first inclination is to suggest legal advice, such as filing a petition for dissolution. But you should resist the tendency of the "lawyer" in you to put your client's problems into a legal box. At this stage, you need to decide if you know enough about the facts. Is the problem a legal one requiring a legal solution— dissolution? Even if available, is a legal remedy the best solution? Or is the situation better viewed as involving a non-legal problem, requiring (in this instance) marriage counseling? What about other problems that potentially might be the cause for Rocky's statement, such as abuse, lack of financial support, some other factor?

Your second inclination might be to explore the extent and nature of Rocky's drinking problem. But does she in fact have a drinking problem?

Rather than guessing where to begin, you should gather additional information. Since interviewing and counseling are often a simultaneous process, let's concentrate on information-gathering for this counseling matter. Suppose that you ask, "Can you tell me more about your situation?" Rocky responds:

> "My spouse of eight years beat me and the kids last night. He has done this for the past eight years. I am scared he is going to beat us again."

Now we can tentatively identify some potential problems: dissolution; marital counseling; possible assault and battery; child abuse.

Keep in mind that Rocky could request advice on a wide range of subjects—some related to the matter you are retained to handle, some remote, some seemingly purely personal ("Should I go on a safari?"). Also, unlike our potential counseling matter, some problems for counseling do not easily identify themselves. A client may not come in and readily explain her situation as Rocky did: "I am a battered woman; help me." Rather, the "Rocky" that you encounter may not recognize the full scope of potential problems involved ("My husband and I don't get along. He comes home a lot after drinking"). Or she may not be willing to acknowledge the problem ("I understand; I'm real frustrating to be around. . . . That bruise? I bumped into a cabinet door"). Identifying the particular matter for counseling thus may require counseling.

Furthermore, there are other related areas for which your client will need advice. What about the criminal assault on your client and the children? Is the matter one that should be reported to the police? (If so, what is the bearing on the attorney-client privilege if the client does not want to make such a report?) And how does the client's intoxication at this appointment fit into all of this? (Rocky may have indulged to reduce the physical/psychological pain of the beating; perhaps the prospect of a first meeting with a lawyer may have overwhelmed her.)

QUESTION 2
What are your objectives in counseling?

After identifying the problem, you will need a representational strategy and a framework for determining the nature and scope of your counseling advice.

Generally, in counseling there are two interrelated objectives—your client's representational strategy (the ultimate result that your client desires on the matter that you are retained to handle) and your client's short-term counseling objective (resolution of a particular matter that your client is requesting counseling about). In our battered-spouse illustration, you will need to identify your client's short-term objectives, particularly since they may focus your activity in directions that differ somewhat from your representational strategy. For example, obtaining a dissolution is a long-term representational strategy that involves bringing a full-blown legal case. Short-term objectives that require counseling and are directly related to your representational strategy for Rocky and the children may focus on protecting Rocky and her children from further physical harm. As such, you may need to counsel her upon the advisability of locating temporary emergency shelter; securing short-term financial support should she leave home; arranging private therapeutic counseling and some marital counseling; and seeking police protection and a restraining order from the court. (You should note that some attorneys, particularly those associated with a prosecutor's office, maintain that a lawyer has an ethical duty, transcending the duty to maintain client confidences, to report crimes of child abuse and spousal battery to the proper authorities regardless of the client's wishes.) Some of these objectives can be accomplished by filing for a dissolution, others by your counseling advice and referral to appropriate community services.

QUESTION 3
Should you counsel?

Deciding whether to counsel Rocky appears to be an odd question, doesn't it? After all, isn't your advice one of the main services that your client seeks? Recall that in the beginning of this chapter we suggested that most counseling that you will do as a lawyer is directly related to the matters of representation. Thus counseling Rocky as to areas concerning her dissolution or child custody litigation is part of your legal representation. If Rocky seeks your advice as to whether she should testify at a child custody hearing, you are presented with an easy decision whether or not to counsel since Rocky's representational strategy and the counseling matter will be analyzed in the context of the same goal of obtaining custody of her children.

However, let us now shift gears slightly and examine if you should counsel your client about *everything*. Suppose that you represent Rocky in the dissolution and child custody litigation and Rocky tells you, "I have a drinking problem," or you detect that she has a drinking problem.

Now you must determine whether you should counsel Rocky as to her drinking. Of course, you can advise a client on any matter as a fellow human being. However, as an attorney, you will need to decide if the area is a proper one for you to be involved in.

In deciding this question, you can be guided in part by how related to or remote from your representational strategy the particular counseling matter is. Sometimes it is difficult deciding whether to counsel if the counseling matter appears to be unrelated or only tangential to the client's representational strategy or presents seemingly personal or therapeutic issues.

In our illustration concerning Rocky's drinking, you might be tempted to respond, "Rocky, I am here and available to advise you about your dissolution and child custody; everything else is your problem." Your response might be appropriate because the drinking problem is a personal matter. And, after all, you are retained to represent Rocky in the dissolution and child custody dispute; you are not retained to help her with Life. To determine whether counseling is proper, however, you must analyze the effect that the short-term counseling objectives might have upon your representational strategy. Consider asking yourself: "How is my client's dissolution and child custody affected by the short-term counseling matter—Rocky's drinking?" In our hypothetical, Rocky's representational strategy might be affected by evidence of her drinking—that is, such issues as her inability to provide adequate care for the children because of hangovers, poor witness credibility if the case goes to trial, and so on. Therefore, you might decide to counsel your client.

On the other hand, as already noted, if the counseling matter does not remotely affect your client's representational strategy, you might be inclined to not counsel. For example, suppose that you represented Rocky in a consumer contract dispute. Rocky asks you whether she should use her savings to send her son to Europe for the summer. Even though this matter is seemingly totally unrelated, you still need to assess how, if at all, this issue is related to or can affect your representational strategy and your attorney-client relationship. Of course, if a small, clearly unrelated, matter is brought up in the flow of friendly introductory conversation, you might decide to chat about the client's plans to give her son a trip to Europe. Therefore, your judgment call depends on the circumstances of your relationship with your client and the topic at hand.

However, back to our main hypothetical: You decide that counseling Rocky about her drinking problem is appropriate because of the impact this matter might have on your representational strategy.

QUESTION 4
What should be the extent of your counseling?

You have decided to counsel your client. Now you must examine the extent of your involvement.[1] The extent of your counseling involves a choice that falls somewhere along a spectrum ranging from the most intensive type of involvement (e.g., you provide the therapy) to the least intensive type of involvement (e.g., you make a referral to someone else). There are no specific rules that we can tell you to apply that will magically help decide the scope of your involvement along this spectrum. But we can suggest a number of factors to consider: your comfort zone; the effect on your representational strategy; the availability of other counselors (among family and friends, community agencies); the nature of the problem; and your relationship with your client.

Let's begin by examining who you are. Suppose that you are the type of person who enjoys helping people with their problems. You have been told more than once that you have a way with people—and, after all, wasn't it you who broke Uncle Rick of a 30-year smoking habit? But beware: Your personal en-

joyment and what you find comfortable to do as a family member or friend is different from what you should do as a lawyer. Like most attorneys, you probably lack the educational skills and training to engage in therapeutic counseling. Therefore, generally, unless you are specifically trained to be a therapist, as a lawyer you cannot and should not attempt to give Rocky therapeutic advice about her drinking problem. That is beyond your competence and expertise. And even though you may be skilled or trained in a particular therapy such as family counseling, unless specifically retained in that capacity you will probably want to limit your counseling to those things you are trained to do as an attorney—identify issues, and acquire, evaluate, and organize information.

On the other hand, being a lawyer does not mean that you have a license to ignore human needs and remain insensitive to the human condition. As such, if you are not to damage your attorney-client relationship, you will need to recognize and be prepared to respond appropriately in circumstances that range from those when your client just needs someone to talk to, to those where the client might even be on the edge of suicide (although professional aid should then quickly be sought), to those when the client is in need of medical help. But you also need to be aware of the inherent risks in your involvement. You always have to consider that counseling on sensitive issues might strain or confuse your attorney-client relationship and interfere with your representational strategy.

Now let's suppose that you are the type of person who feels uncomfortable in counseling if you have to advise on any matter that does not present a legal issue directly related to the legal case. You might believe that Rocky's drinking is none of your business. Does that mean you can say no to counseling Rocky? As previously discussed, many seemingly peripheral matters may prove to affect your client's legal case. Your personal comfort zone is, therefore, not a legal excuse to avoid counseling, but it will influence the scope of that counseling.

Suppose that you want to limit the extent of your counseling role regarding Rocky's drinking: You wish only to advise Rocky to seek professional help for her drinking problem. Even this limited role has scope decisions. You will need to determine the extent of your role in referral. Will you suggest an appropriate person or agency? Will you set up the appointment? Accompany Rocky to the appointment or send someone from your office? Follow up that Rocky kept the appointment? The extent of your involvement even in this limited counseling role depends on many of the same factors discussed in determining the spectrum of counseling advice.

---

1. In this regard, you might want to review an article that provides an interesting insight into attorney personalities and attorney counseling. See Redmount, "Attorney Personalities and Some Psychological Aspects of Legal Consultation," 109 U. Pa. L. Rev. 972 (1961).

QUESTION 5
What further information do you need?

Now stand back from this focus on Rocky's drinking and look at the full scope of counseling issues in which you may be involved. Specifically, you might be involved in counseling Rocky on any or all of three related issues—battering and child abuse; a drinking problem; and filing for a dissolution. As to all three you probably now have a better understanding of these counseling matters than when you first met Rocky. Now you will be able to identify specific information that you will need before you can advise Rocky about available alternative solutions. This further information may fall under the categories of legal precedent or particular economic, social, and psychological circumstances and factors that exist in Rocky's situation.

As to the battered woman/abuse issue, you should obtain specific information about the incident in order to determine any necessity for immediate action (restraining order, temporary shelter) or for referral to police or some other agency. When did the incident occur? Who was involved? How did it occur? Any evidence of battering? What about past incidents? Previous involvement by police and social agencies?

Information-gathering for Rocky's drinking problem might also involve finding out how long-standing the problem is, about past and present treatment, about Rocky's attitude toward her problem, and how intoxication affects Rocky. Likewise, further information will help clarify your options in considering dissolution and custody issues. For example, suppose that after meeting with Rocky you learn that she and her husband Colby have limited financial assets. That information will affect options and decisions as to how to deal with obtaining a dissolution, or moving out of the house, or child custody. You might need to explore specific aspects of Rocky's finances or ask her to visit an accountant; you might need to research the requirements for public financing of dissolutions and public welfare support for Rocky and the children.

QUESTION 6
What counseling advice (alternative solutions) is possible in light of your representational strategy?

There are usually many solutions available to resolve a problem, each of which might have attendant risks and benefits (deciding whether to settle the case, present a defense, pose for newspaper photographs). Binder and Price (see page 345) suggest that you need to evaluate potential alternative solutions. Our approach is based on Binder and Price, but we apply their views in the context of considering the effect of the interaction between your representational strategy and the client's objectives on the problem before you.

Let's examine two different types of counseling advice. Leaving Rocky for a moment, we will examine a criminal counseling problem that involves accepting or rejecting a plea offer; this problem illustrates how you would structure counseling when the client's objectives in the counseling matter relate directly to your representational strategy.

Suppose that you represent Carol in a first-degree murder prosecution. The prosecutor has offered to allow Carol to plead guilty to second-degree murder and you need to advise Carol about whether to accept the plea bargain. Should she reject the offer or go to trial? You will need to analyze and evaluate the risks and benefits of Carol's acceptance of the prosecutor's offer if your counseling advice is to be of any help. What are the economic, social, and psychological implications of a guilty plea? The probable sentence? You will need to make an educated prediction as to her legal case and her chances at trial. Review the prosecutor's case as to the sufficiency of the evidence. Are there major flaws in the evidence? Are the witnesses credible? What has occurred in similar cases? What is the prosecutor's trial record? What is the probability that Carol will be acquitted? Convicted for less than first-degree murder? Convicted for first-degree murder? As to each of these possible verdicts, what sentences are possible if Carol is found guilty? Although hardly an easy situation for which to offer advice, this counseling situation, like your representational strategy, involves achieving the objective of obtaining the best possible outcome in the case for the client.

Now let us turn to a more problematic situation in which the counseling matter is tangentially related to your representational strategy but the advice you give might harm or hinder your representational strategy.

Imagine that Rocky wants a dissolution and custody of the children. You have commenced litigation. Rocky owns a house in which she and the children presently reside. (Assume for purposes of this illustration that there is no dispute as to Rocky's separate and distinct ownership.) Rocky asks your advice: "I want to sell the house. It just has too many bad memories. What do you think?" Although the two matters are not directly related to one another, potentially decisions as to one could affect the other. Your representational strategy as to the child custody case is to obtain the best result you can for your client—custody of the children and adequate child support. If you advise your client to sell the house for the sake of her emotional well-being, however, that decision may be harmful to your legal position on custody since the house is a positive factor for child custody. It provides a place for the children to live and allows the children to remain in the same school and maintain friendships. Sale of the house may be disruptive to the children. If you advise Rocky to keep the house, on the other hand, she may face a sadness and depression that will affect the quality of her life and her children's.

You need to consider how counseling advice about the house sale can be reconciled with your representational strategy as to the child custody case. In this example, your client's needs in the custody case and in the house sale appear to be divergent (need for stability in the children's life versus moving and finding personal peace yet disrupting the continuity in the children's lives). In dealing with this apparent dilemma, you could apply a process we discuss in Chapter X for reconciling what appear to be divergent positions. This process applies an "interest analysis" to such situations. (See page 397.) Thus, in Rocky's case, by examining the underlying interests that motivate each of the two seemingly divergent matters of house sale and child custody (a home for the children and the stability afforded by a house in the same general neighborhood area; your client's need to start a new life unburdened by constant reminders of the painful past), you might be able to develop alternatives that might further both your client's short-term objectives and your representational strategy. You could advise her to sell the house and use the house sale money to purchase another house in the same general neighborhood.

Sometimes, however, the advice you give for the counseling problem cannot be reconciled with your representational strategy. Suppose that after discussing all these various options and considerations with Rocky, she decides that the house must be sold. The money from the house sale might be totally inadequate to purchase alternative housing in the same neighborhood and rental housing may not be available. The short-term counseling advice and decision might be devastating for your representational strategy in the child custody case. If that occurs, and your client insists on pursuing the short-term objective, your only alternative might be to counsel your client to accept the consequences and then to put forth your best effort to minimize the damage to your representational strategy ("The source of stability that Rocky gives her children is not some home in some neighborhood. It is her loving and strength that provides their stable environment, and as the psychologist's affidavit states, to remain in that house would have been so painful for Rocky as to jeopardize her ability to provide that loving strength"). Or, at some point, you may even consider changing your representational strategy.

QUESTION 7
Are there any ethical issues that you should consider?

You need to consider ethical dilemmas that can occur and how these concerns might affect the content of your counseling. As you've seen with other pretrial skills, you might encounter many ethical issues but clear-cut rules that can provide instant solutions rarely exist. Thus, in this section, we suggest some of the ethical issues that you might grapple with when counseling and urge you to consult applicable professional responsibility rules for direct guidance.

Ethical issues might arise in identifying the counseling problem, in the advice that you give, and the decisionmaking process you employ. For instance, when counseling Rocky, do your professional responsibility obligations require you to report possible child abuse? But what about confidentiality of the information and your ethical obligations to your client? Does the attorney-client privilege exempt you from reporting?

Counseling means that you give your client advice so that your client can make an informed decision. Does that mean you have to tell your client everything? Or can you protect your client from hearing personally damaging information? Your planning has been directed toward helping your client reach an informed decision. However, some clients cannot or will not make a decision because of indecisiveness or even incompetence. Do you make the decision for them? Other clients might make what you consider an incorrect decision. Do you browbeat them until they do what you think is correct? For example, suppose that Carol decides to plead guilty to second-degree murder. You believe she is making a grave mistake, that manslaughter is the worst she faces at trial. Ethically, should you actively argue with Carol to change her decision? Should you threaten Carol that you will withdraw from the case? Does your decision depend on circumstances?

Finally, although you have an obligation to counsel your client, that role does not extend to helping a client make a decision that is illegal, involves committing a crime, or breaches disciplinary rules. But what if someone walks into your office and asks which countries do not have extradition treaties with the United States, or says, "I want to go right up to the line between legal and illegal, not over it, but right up to it"? Clearly, you will need to not only consult professional responsibility rules, but exercise your own judgment when formulating the content of your counseling.

QUESTION 8
Based on all the information, what is an appropriate counseling decision?

Counseling requires helping your client make an informed decision. Already you have identified, organized, developed, and evaluated realistic options that your client should consider, using your client's short-term and long-term objectives (embodied in the representational strategy) as the framework.

After organizing and explaining the benefits and risks of each alternative, you should guide your client toward an informed decision. Your opinion may be sought or you can volunteer it. For example, you can advise Rocky as to the options she has. You can advise her that she should seek professional marital counseling; that she should report the assault to the police; that she move to a protected shelter. But it is Rocky's decision—although you must recognize that your advice will carry great, and usually determinative, weight ("Well, you should know. You're the lawyer"). Of course, if Rocky balks at making the final decision and cannot be prodded (or is incompetent), you must consider your professional responsibility to your client and you might have to take a more active decisionmaking role.

D. PERFORMANCE PLANNING: AN APPROACH AND ILLUSTRATION

A major part of competence in counseling involves prior thought about a range of concerns—how you will communicate counseling advice, what problems you should anticipate or try to avoid, how you will solve these problems if they do occur. A performance strategy evolving from this prior thought will then enable you to provide meaningful advice for your client, since you will have already anticipated potential problems and will be generally prepared to resolve them.

Counseling, much like other aspects of the attorney-client relationship, is influenced by tactical or technique-focused matters. Many of the same concerns that occur in other aspects of pretrial representation, particularly in client interviewing, also manifest themselves in counseling. For instance, you will be concerned with how you give advice. The communication skills you use for interviewing are identical to those for counseling. You also must obtain and provide information and establish a relationship of cooperation and trust. As in interviewing, you will want to encourage client discussion (posing of open-ended questions), listen to your client (reflective and active listening), and generally establish and maintain rapport and empathy with your client.

Potential problem areas that we could discuss cover a wide range from encountering hostile or other nonproductive reactions from your client to adverse influences because of the physical atmosphere in which counseling takes place. Many of these practical/strategic issues are discussed with illustrations in the client and witness interview chapters. In this section, we will concentrate on client reaction in counseling.

Client reaction generally presents a more acute, subtle, and complex problem in counseling than it does in other areas related to client representation because how the lawyer counsels and views her role in counseling can itself affect client reaction and participation in counseling. Therefore, we would like to identify some potential client reactions to counseling and their ramifications for the attorney. We use a hypothetical client, Harvey, as a basis for discussion.

Not surprisingly, the five questions that provide our structured approach for planning your counseling performance strategy find general counterparts in many portions of our eight-question approach to client interviewing.

Plan

1. What are your counseling performance objectives?[2]

Analysis

2. What potential problems might occur during counseling?

Strategy

3. What tactics and techniques can you use to counsel?

---

2. Note that these objectives may be a function of your client's long- and short-term objectives already discussed at page 347, but, as you will see, they are not the same.

4. What strategy should you adopt?
5. What will you do after counseling? Follow up? Reevaluate?

Imagine that you represent Harvey in an eviction action. Harvey is a shy, disheveled young man. He has begun to telephone you once or twice a week to discuss his case and "just chat." You have invited Harvey to your office to counsel and prepare him for his deposition. Let's begin planning how you will counsel Harvey.

QUESTION 1
What are your counseling performance objectives?

When you counsel Harvey you want to prepare him for his deposition. You are particularly concerned that Harvey make a good impression at the deposition; a good impression will surely aid your representational strategy of eventual settlement. Therefore you want to advise him on how to dress, how to answer questions, and generally on how to present himself.

There is, however, another part to your counseling performance objectives. Based on your own observations, you suspect Harvey is becoming personally dependent on you. You wish to transfer this perceived dependency onto someone else and this becomes the secondary objective of your counseling.

Through all this, you also want to continue and maintain a good attorney-client relationship so you can give Harvey the best possible representation in his eviction case.

QUESTION 2
What potential problems might occur during counseling?

Initially, getting Harvey to listen to your advice will not be a problem. In fact, your concern is the opposite: Harvey will welcome the opportunity to discuss deposition preparation with you as yet another step in his dependence on you. (In contrast, other types of clients may become belligerent and may strongly resist your advice. In particular, client hostility more readily occurs when counseling in matters that are personally sensitive, such as excessive drinking or criminal behavior.)

Specifically, Harvey's possible response to your counseling regarding his dress and deportment at the deposition may lead to three problems that you need

to recognize, avoid, or resolve. First, because of his confidence in you, Harvey might abdicate responsibility for solving his problems ("Whatever you think, I'll do it"). Although you want to encourage Harvey to seek and follow your advice on matters that affect your representation, you also want to establish a relationship in which Harvey retains sufficient independence for decisionmaking. Second, your role can become confused: Are you Harvey's lawyer or his friend? You may find yourself giving advice that is guided by a bias of friendship instead of by the neutral criteria of an attorney. Harvey may also suffer under the same delusion and more readily accept your advice because it is perceived as being given in friendship.

Third, you might eventually become involved in matters that are beyond your competence, and may even hurt Harvey by misleading him or giving him incorrect advice. For instance, you suspect that Harvey's dependence on you is the result of more than just loneliness, and might be indicative of emotional problems. Your suspicions are reinforced by his responses to your discussion of his dress at the deposition: "I never know what to wear, my parents never told me. They just criticized whatever I put on. You're not like that. You tell me exactly what to do, and never make me feel bad." If you introduce this subject, however, you will need to be careful to appropriately limit the scope of your involvement; otherwise, you will merely reinforce the dependency. On the other hand, if you ignore this potential problem of Harvey's dependency, you may put his eviction case in jeopardy (e.g., if he starts seeing you as a parent figure and decides to "rebel" at some crucial juncture in the case), as well as exhibit insensitive behavior to a client who needs help.

Of course, you could face equally difficult problems if Harvey were hostile and aggressive, angrily arguing with you over each aspect of the case. Thus, while for purposes of instruction the potential tactics and techniques we discuss in the next section are applied to the shy, withdrawn Harvey, these same approaches apply to counseling all types of clients whether shy, angry, scared, or whatever.

QUESTION 3
What tactics and techniques can you use to counsel?

Tactics and techniques that you use in counseling will depend on your basic approach to counseling as a lawyer. Some attorneys insist, and their clients acquiesce in, attorney-controlled decisionmaking: "I will tell you how this case is going to be run; how you are going to act in court; how you are going to dress. . . ." Such choices are a matter of style or sometimes of necessity because of the personality or abilities of the client. For example, some clients would be petrified by the entire process if their attorneys did not assume the role of "absolute authority" figure. You should be aware that such an approach might present ethical problems because the attorney may be making important case decisions without meaningful consultation with the client. It also is a troublesome approach, one that a client will either embrace or abhor. If you use this approach with Harvey, you might advise Harvey outright: "This is how I would like you to dress for your deposition . . . ."

Or you can approach counseling as a partnership between you and your client. A counseling partnership implies that you are competent to give the advice your client seeks; that you act as an adviser, not decisionmaker; that the client is indeed receptive to receiving advice; and that the client is able to make appropriate decisions on his or her own behalf.

We are partial to the partnership approach if it seems a plausible one given the particular client. Our partiality stems from our desire to work in a collaborative mode with a client.

Let's consider performance techniques that encourage a counseling partnership. For example, consider your professional demeanor—do you encourage client discussion? As in interviewing, you can promote client discussion by posing open-ended questions; by listening to your client (reflective and active listening); and by choosing language that generally establishes and maintains rapport and empathy with your client. Deposition preparation that employs a partnership style might sound like this:

> "Now, let me explain the setting of the deposition. It will take place in Ms. Frank's office. Of course, all the attorneys will be dressed just like they are in court—in business suits. You want to create a good impression. Let's talk about what would be appropriate dress for you as the deponent. What would you like to wear to create a good business-like impression?"

If you then want to explore whether Harvey's dependence on you is indicative of his need for professional mental health counseling, you must carefully choose language that does not upset him but merely suggests your concern. For example, you might state:

> "Harvey, I really enjoy working with you. I especially appreciate your telephone calls keeping me advised as to various things that might affect

your eviction case. But I am also concerned about whether it may also be helpful for you to discuss some of the more personal matters you have brought up with someone who is more helpful and competent to advise you. What do you think?"

The setting for the counseling is also important. Consider the atmosphere in which you provide counseling advice. It can influence Harvey's receptiveness and decisionmaking. For instance, should you meet with Harvey in your office? At Harvey's place of work? At Harvey's home? Or should you meet in a restaurant? Will you advise Harvey by telephone? By letter? Will others be present? Should Harvey's spouse be present?

Let's consider these choices. If you select a formal setting, then Harvey is less likely to confuse the relationship with friendship. Therefore, you might choose to counsel in your office, while you are seated at your desk, since that setting contributes an air of formality. Who will be present? Your legal secretary? A legal worker who can assist by, for example, role-playing someone in the upcoming deposition? The presence of legal office personnel might be a good idea since this will also focus the counseling on the formal aspect of your representation—preparation for Harvey's deposition.

Consider how you will actually organize counseling. Will you meet with Harvey once? Several times? For how long? What will you discuss when you meet? Will each meeting with Harvey have a specific purpose? How will you decide the purpose? If, when you meet with Harvey, only a short amount of time is devoted to exploring whether Harvey should consult others about his more personal problems, it will become more unlikely that your advice will appear to be given as an act of friendship, as distinguished from your professional role.

Will your advice be written or verbal? Will it be effective to send Harvey a letter advising him about his deposition preparation—how to respond to questions, his choice of appropriate dress, the role of a deposition, and so on? Or will you consider sending him a videotape where he can see what you are talking about? Generally, written advice provides a structure for documenting and organizing relevant information for your client. In a letter, whether it is an opinion letter or one specifically describing the deposition, a basic structure can generally be used. You can identify the issue or problem, provide the information that you considered and relied on (legal and non-legal), evaluate the information, and present your opinion as to potential options and the consequences. A letter explaining the deposition process that also includes specific instructions can therefore achieve many of your counseling ends.

But written advice can have disadvantages. It might be given too much weight by a client merely because it is written and seems more official. A letter may also appear too business-like and impersonal and thus be a somewhat alienating device. Or the letter might contain flaws because you did not have all the information. For example, even though an opinion letter may contain a disclaimer as to its inaccuracies, or explanations as to its incompleteness, it may nevertheless be read as authoritative.

As you can imagine, verbal advice also has advantages and disadvantages. Although it can be more informal, it can be disorganized; it is more time-consuming; and the client can more easily forget what you have said or have attended to your remarks in a very selective way.

QUESTION 4
What strategy should you adopt?

You have given considerable thought to how to counsel Harvey and get him prepared, and to how to avoid Harvey becoming too dependent on you, and yet maintain a good cooperative relationship. Based on the past history of Harvey's behavior, and your perception of his personality, you believe that you probably cannot avoid Harvey becoming dependent on you. You have already explained and discussed how you view the attorney-client counseling relationship with Harvey, and he still telephones you to ask you for advice on issues that appear to be unrelated to his eviction case.

One possible performance strategy is to appear and act as business-like as possible in order to "chill" Harvey's dependence on you and transfer his dependency to a mental health professional. By discussing only specific legal issues concerning Harvey's eviction case in order to create a business-like atmosphere, you can be careful to not show empathy or sympathy for Harvey's emotional problems. But consider these questions: How does this strategy affect your attorney-client relationship with Harvey? Is this a humane approach? Will this strategy be the most effective for deposition preparation? What will it do to Harvey personally? Your attorney-client counseling relationship with Harvey can become confused or harmful. In fact, if you ignore Harvey or do not show empathy, he may even be unwilling to follow your advice.

You, therefore, might decide on a less formal and business-like strategy by showing some empathy, referring Harvey to a mental health counselor if appropriate; or you could advise him of your interest in his case, but explain your limited time and competence to help him with matters other than the eviction case; or you could assign a legal worker in your office to deal with Harvey's dependency needs.

QUESTION 5
What will you do after counseling? Follow up? Reevaluate?

You should plan what will happen if you give particular counseling advice. Your tentative plan includes a general discussion of deposition attire and behavior, and an exploration of possible referral to a mental health professional. (After such exploration, you may find that Harvey is just lonely for a friend and that referral is not appropriate. You could then shift to one of the other strategies discussed above.)

Now suppose that Harvey agrees to wear a white shirt and tie and have his hair cut for the deposition. What is your obligation to see that Harvey listens to the advice? Or if Harvey agrees that he has some matters that could be best discussed with a mental health therapist, should you follow up to see that he goes? Send a confirming letter? Telephone? Visit his house? Why or why not?

Or suppose that Harvey fails to follow your advice and disagrees about how he should present himself and his story at the deposition. You then must evaluate your case in light of Harvey's refusal to follow your advice, considering the impact of that refusal on your representational strategy. Or imagine that the need for therapy is extreme and obvious, that Harvey initially acknowledges this need, but then refuses to go for professional mental health counseling. His eviction case then *might* be adversely affected because of his general inability to cope with life and its problems, and your attorney-client relationship might be affected because Harvey might become more and more dependent on you.

By identifying, analyzing, and planning a performance strategy, you might be able to deal successfully with these and other potential problems.

E. GENERAL PLANNING QUESTIONS

You have considered various factors, and the rationales for each, involved in preparing for counseling.

Following is a series of general questions for preparing client counseling. Also consult the planning questions for client and witness interviews in Chapter IV at pages 83-86 and Chapter V at pages 110-112. You may want to refer to them and expand on them in planning counseling.

I. *Context of Representational Strategy and Counseling Objectives*
   1. What is your representational strategy?
   2. Explain the particular objectives for this counseling matter.

II. *Preparation*
   1. How will you prepare for this counseling?
   2. What information do you know or will seek about your client? (Client's personality? Emotional state?)
      a. How will you obtain this information?
      b. From your client? Others? Office staff?
   3. How will information about your client affect your counseling?
      a. Decision to counsel?
      b. Advice that you give?
      c. Client-attorney counseling relationship?
   4. What do you know about the client's counseling problem?
   5. What do you know about the law in the applicable area?
      a. Will you do any preliminary research?
      b. How will your research help you in counseling?
   6. What facts can you obtain prior to meeting with your client?
   7. What other information will you obtain prior to counseling?
      a. How will you obtain this information?
      b. How will this information help you?
   8. Suppose that you cannot obtain any pre-counseling facts? What will you do? Why?

III. *Content Planning*
   1. What is the problem?
      a. Have you and the client identified the counseling matter?
      b. Are you and your client in agreement as to the matter that should be discussed?
      c. If you are not in agreement, what will you do? Why?
   2. What are your counseling objectives?
      a. What are the possible objectives of counseling a client?
      b. What are your specific objectives for this particular counseling matter? (List your short-term objectives.)

c. Are your specific objectives compatible with the representational strategy you have chosen to carry out in the matter you are retained to handle?
d. Can you make your objectives compatible? Explain.
e. If your objectives are not compatible, what advice will you give? Why?

3. Should you counsel?
   a. How related or remote is the particular counseling matter to the matter you are retained to handle?
   b. How will your counseling advice affect the matter you are retained to handle?
   c. Will you counsel your client on the particular matter?

4. What should be the extent of your counseling?
   a. If you are going to counsel your client, what is the nature and scope of your counseling?
   b. Do you want to counsel your client on this matter? Why?
   c. Do you have the education and training to counsel in this matter?

5. What further information do you need?
   a. What legal information do you need for counseling on this matter?
   b. How will you obtain this information?
   c. What non-legal information do you need for counseling on this matter?
   d. How will you obtain this information? (Client? Others?)
   e. What specific information do you want from your client about the counseling matter?

6. What alternative counseling advice is possible?
   a. What information will you give your client? Evaluate for your client?
      (1) Legal information?
      (2) Non-legal information?
   b. How will you evaluate the alternative options?
   c. What information will you include?
   d. Will you predict the outcome of each alternative?
      (1) What legal consequences can you predict?
      (2) What non-legal consequences can you predict? (Economic, social, psychological?)
   e. Are the alternatives compatible with your client's long-term case objectives?
   f. Are the alternatives reconcilable?

g. What advice will you give if the short- and long-term objectives are irreconcilable?

7. Any decisionmaking issues?
  a. What role do you have in decisionmaking?
  b. What role does your client have in decisionmaking?
  c. What will you do if your client refuses to make a decision?
  d. What will you do if your client is incompetent to make a decision?
  e. What will you do if you believe your client will make a clearly erroneous decision?

IV. *Performance Planning*
  A. *Anticipating Issues and Problems*
    1. What practical issues or problems may occur during counseling?
    2. List them. How do you: counsel shy, hostile, belligerent client; explain your role; identify the problems; etc.?
  B. *Defining the Attorney's Counseling Role*
    1. What kind of counseling relationship will you establish with your client? (Partnership? Attorney-controlled?) Why?
    2. How will you establish this relationship?
    3. When will you discuss your role with your client?
  C. *Defining Your Client's Role*
    1. Did you discuss with your client what areas you will advise the client about?
    2. When will you discuss your client's role in counseling? Why?
    3. What are the client's responsibilities in counseling?
      a. Providing information? (What kind of information?)
      b. Listening to advice?
      c. Decisionmaking?
    4. What will you do if the client is not receptive to advice?
    5. What will you do if the client is unable to make an appropriate decision? (If the client is incompetent as opposed to unwilling to make a decision?)
    6. How will you gain your client's trust and confidence to listen to counseling advice?
      a. What methods are (theoretically) available?
      b. Which methods will you use?
      c. Do you anticipate any particular problems in obtaining your client's trust?
      d. How will you deal with such problems?

  D. *Technical Counseling Areas*
    1. What techniques will you employ to ensure that you will counsel effectively?
    2. Are some of these techniques better for some types of clients than others? If so, what type of client are you dealing with? What tactics or techniques will you use?
    3. How will you organize your counseling?
      a. Will you schedule a series of meetings?
      b. Use some other organization?
      c. Agenda?
    4. Will you communicate your opinion in writing?
  E. *Ethical Considerations*
    1. What are your ethical responsibilities as to:
      a. Confidences?
      b. Conflicts of interest?
      c. Diligence and competence?
      d. Lack of client decisionmaking because of incompetence? Refusal to act?
    2. Will you try to change your client's decision if you believe it is wrong?
    3. What if the client insists that you make the decision?
    4. How could these practical or technical issues affect your counseling?
    5. Can you avoid these issues? How?
    6. If you cannot avoid the issue, what alternative solutions are there to resolve the issue?
    7. Which solution should you adopt?
    8. What techniques can you use to carry out the solution?

V. *Reevaluation and Follow-up*
  1. What impact does the client's decision have on your representational strategy?
  2. What information did you obtain that could be used in the matters you are retained in?
  3. If you referred the client for professional help, will you follow up to see if the client went?
  4. Given the counseling problem, do you need further information?

    a. Where will you look for this information?

    b. Are you seeking any of this information to continue to help your client?

5. Evaluating the client:

    a. Can you still represent the client?

      (1) Are there problems?

      (2) If so, how do you propose to deal with such problems?

    b. How will the client be to work with (cooperative relationship)?

      (1) Are there any problems?

      (2) If so, how do you propose to deal with such problems?

CRIMINAL PROBLEMS: STATE v. HARD

PROBLEM 103

Prosecutor: Counseling a Key Witness Who Does Not Want to Testify
(Deborah Summers)

Deborah Summers just dropped by your office in response to your telephone call. In the course of your preparation for trial, you have been drawn time and time again to the serious inconsistencies between Deborah's first and second statements to the police. It was in order to discuss this subject that you asked to see her.

The moment Deborah walked in your office, however, it was clear that she was very upset. When you asked if anything was wrong, she looked at you and for almost a minute said nothing. She then proceeded to tell you that when the case first began, she had been so angry at Ed Hard and filled with hate that she even refused to talk with his investigator. Now she has come to realize that it is herself that she hates. It was jealousy over her that had cost one man his life and would likely cause another his freedom. At this point, she started to cry, stating, "the whole thing is my fault," and began to waver about testifying.

PREPARATION

READ: (1) Pretrial Case File Entries 4, 16, 17, 19, 61; (2) Chapter IX. Now think about and answer the following questions:

1. What will you do now?

2. Will you try to talk to her? If so, what will you say?

3. What if she says (through sobs), "I don't want to talk about it—now or at trial or ever"?

a. Will you tell her that the case cannot logically proceed if she fails to testify and that her husband's killer will walk away?

b. Will you tell her to just go home and get some rest? Why or why not?

4. What are your ethical obligations to your clients (the "People" of the state).

5. Suppose that you are unable to convince Deborah Summers to testify at trial. Discuss what you will do.

6. Will you stall while you get a subpoena and then serve her?

a. If you do serve her, what will you tell her? Why?

b. Will you serve her and tell her:

   1) That the police will drag her in if she does not show up for trial?

   2) That the judge will throw her in jail for contempt if she refuses to testify once on the stand?

   3) That you will charge her with perjury if she lies on the stand?

7. What (realistically) will be the effect on your case if Deborah does not testify as a witness?

a. How would it affect your case theory?

b. How would it affect your representational strategy?

8. Now imagine instead that Deborah's emotional outburst does not come until after you have begun to press her about the inconsistencies between her two statements. How (if at all) would this affect how you would subsequently counsel Deborah?

ASSIGNMENT FOR CLASS

1. Outside of class, plan to deal with this matter. Write a short memorandum summarizing your planning, preparation, and analysis, and give a copy to your supervisor.

2. In class, meet with Deborah Summers about her testifying.

PROBLEM 104

Prosecutor: Counseling a Witness
Whether to Talk to Your Adversary
(Peter Dean)

Peter Dean has telephoned you at your office to tell you that Ed Hard's investigator is at his home and wishes to interview him. Peter Dean wants your advice regarding what to do. You are aware that the guiding rule in such cases is that a witness has the right to talk with any attorney (or agent of the attorney), and no other attorney (or agent) can interfere with this right. On the other hand, a witness has no obligation to talk with anyone, except when testifying in court proceedings.

PREPARATION

READ: (1) Pretrial Case File Entry 61; (2) Chapter IX. Now think about and answer the following questions:

1. Do you want to know what Dean wants to do?

2. Will you ask if the defense investigator knows Dean is calling you, the prosecutor?

3. What if you ask Dean what he wants to do and he says:

    a. "Whatever you think is best"?

    b. "I'll talk, but only if you're here"?

    c. "Let me put the investigator on the telephone, so you can discuss it and see what he wants"?

4. What about telling Dean the substance of the "guiding rule," supra?

    a. Will you emphasize any portion of the "rule"? Which portion?

    b. Does such emphasis comport with what you perceive to be your ethical responsibilities?

5. What do you want to do in this situation? Why?

6. Are there problems that you envision should Dean refuse to talk with the defense investigator? Explain.

7. How would it affect your advice to Dean if there were a statute in your jurisdiction that provided that depositions may be taken of material witnesses who refuse to speak with an attorney (or agent) seeking their interview?

ASSIGNMENT FOR CLASS

1. Outside of class, plan to deal with this matter. Write a short memorandum summarizing your planning, preparation, and analysis, and give a copy to your supervisor.

2. In class, discuss this matter with Peter Dean *on the telephone*.

PROBLEM 105 _____

Prosecutor: Counseling a Key Witness Who Is Contemplating the Destruction of Potentially Relevant Evidence
(Deborah Summers)

It is early in the day, and you are about to leave for a full day of court hearings when Deborah Summers calls. A few weeks ago she balked at testifying against Hard, but you calmed her down and are now proceeding full-steam with your pretrial fact investigation and preparation.

Deborah begins this morning's conversation by assuring you that, although it makes her unhappy, she is still prepared to testify. She then gets to the point of her call. She has been going through Bruno's old things, and among the souvenirs she intends to keep, there is also a great deal of "trash," like old gas station credit card receipts and a picture of Bruno at the neo-Nazi regional conference standing next to "that guy Jack Waters who hangs around the Unicorn sometimes." She was going to throw all these out, but first thought she should let you know.* She then tells you she wants you to come right over. Great. In five minutes you're due in court on a series of suppression motions and can't get out until the noon recess.

PREPARATION

READ: (1) Pretrial Case File Entries 4, 16, 17, 19, 61, 68, 75; (2) Chapter IX. Now think about and answer the following questions:

1. Do you want to ask more about this "trash"? See it? Why or why not?

2. What potential problems do you envision if you sanction the destruction? (See *State v. Brant,* 105 Maj. App. 3d 621 (1975) (Case File Entry 68).)

3. If the destruction were subsequently brought into court as a *Branty v. State* (201 Maj. 2d 86 (1962)) or a *State v. Augie* (228 Maj. 2d 118 (1968)) issue by the defense, what would be your response? (See Case File Entry 75.)

4. What are your ethical obligations?

5. Does it affect your position if Deborah tells you that the receipts are dated August 26, 198X, from the "Gull Gas Station"? Why? Or that Waters is also wearing a uniform like Bruno's in the picture? Why?

6. What if you do not know about Hard's claim that Bruno threatened him at the gas station? What if you do?

ASSIGNMENT FOR CLASS

1. Outside of class, plan to deal with this matter. Write a short memorandum summarizing your planning, preparation, and analysis, and give a copy to your supervisor.

2. In class, discuss this matter with Deborah *on the telephone*.

PROBLEM 106

Prosecutor: Counseling a Key Witness Who Is Threatening to Leave Town
(Deborah Summers)

Deborah Summers has just telephoned you from a pay phone and told you that she is leaving town and will not testify in the Hard case. "This case is tearing me apart. I feel so guilty, so responsible. I think I'm going crazy. You understand; I just have to leave. I just have to."

---

*This is a self-contained problem. The information that Deborah possesses in this problem does not appear in the case file or anywhere else in this book and, unless your instructor tells you otherwise, this information should not be considered in any of your analyses outside of this particular problem.

Too bad—the day was going well. You had just learned that the judge denied all the defense's suppression motions. Well, this is not the first time Deborah has balked at testifying. Earlier in the month she was in your office crying, but somehow you convinced her that it was her duty to testify.

PREPARATION

READ: (1) Pretrial Case File Entries 61, 75; (2) Chapter IX. Now think about and answer the following questions:

1. What will you do? Explain.

    a. Will you use the same appeal to "duty" that convinced her before? Why or why not?

    b. Will you ask her to "come in and talk"?

    c. Will you tell her that you'll go there?

    d. Will you just try to keep her on the telephone? To what end?

        1) If so, what will you say?

        2) Do you have training for dealing with such a situation?

2. Assess (realistically) the impact on your case if you cannot present Deborah as a witness.

3. Even if Deborah does testify, are you obligated under *Branty v. State*, 201 Maj. 2d 86 (1962), and its progeny to relay this conversation to the defense on the grounds that it has a bearing on Deborah's mental state (and, therefore, credibility) as a witness? (See Case File Entry 75.)

ASSIGNMENT FOR CLASS

1. Outside of class, plan to deal with his matter. Write a short memorandum summarizing your planning, preparation, and analysis, and give a copy to your supervisor.

2. In class, discuss this matter with Deborah *on the telephone*.

PROBLEM 107 _____

Defense Attorney: Counseling the Defendant Concerning Alleged Harassment in Jail

You talked to Ed Hard after his arraignment on the murder charge. The judge set bail at $50,000, which equals the equity that Hard's mother and Ed Hard have in their homes. It appears likely that with contributions from friends and one wealthy (somewhat distant) relative, Hard may be able to obtain the $5,000 premium.

When you arrive at the jail, however, Hard will not talk about the case. All he can talk about is some guard who is always "hassling him." You leave the interview room and discuss the matter with the sheriff who supervises jail personnel. The sheriff promises to "check it out." This does not satisfy Hard. He wants you to obtain a court order to restrain the guard from harassing him. Hard also tells you that he will "punch out the guard the next time he hassles me."

PREPARATION

READ: (1) Pretrial Case File Entries 61, 65; (2) Chapter IX. Now think about and answer the following questions:

1. What are your concerns?

2. What are your options?

3. What additional information do you need? Why?

4. Do you have any tentative goals in this matter? Explain.

5. How do you think you have handled the matter so far? Explain.

6. What if Hard demands that you "immediately talk to the judge"? What if he demands that you file a "civil rights lawsuit"?

7. Could you tell him in good faith that if he assaults the guard he will face an additional charge or have his bail raised?

ASSIGNMENT FOR CLASS

1. Outside of class, plan to counsel Hard regarding this matter. Write a short memorandum summarizing your planning, preparation, and analysis, and give a copy to your supervisor.

2. In class, meet with your client, Ed Hard, about this matter.

PROBLEM 108

Defense Attorney: Counseling the Defendant Concerning a Drinking Problem

It is now a few months since criminal charges were filed. As pretrial preparation has proceeded, you have noticed that Hard has appeared intoxicated the last two times you met. According to his friend, John Gooding, Hard has been drinking a great deal since the shooting of Bruno Summers. You are concerned that he will become difficult to work with, make a bad appearance before a court and jury, will be less effective in his testimony, and will reinforce the view that he was drunk on the night of the shooting.

Although you know it will be difficult to discuss Ed's "drinking problem" with Ed, you have decided to meet with him because you no longer can ignore it.

PREPARATION

READ: (1) Pretrial Case File Entries 5, 61; (2) Chapter IX. Now think about and answer the following questions:

1. Discuss what you will do before meeting with Ed Hard. Why?

2. What are your responsibilities in this situation?

3. What is the basis for these responsibilities?

4. What will you say to Ed Hard? Why?

5. Will you suggest that Hard see an alcohol counselor? Enter a de-tox facility? Explain.

6. How would you discuss such a referral with Hard?

7. Suppose that Ed Hard is hostile and does not want to stop drinking: "Look, you're my attorney, not my mother. This is none of your business."

   a. What will you say?

   b. What will you do?

   c. Will you threaten to withdraw from the case if he doesn't stop drinking? Can you ethically consider withdrawal? (See Pretrial Case File Entry 61.)

   d. Are there problems, other than ethical ones, with threatening your client with withdrawal? Explain.

8. Suppose that Ed Hard denies he has been drinking.

   a. What will you say?

   b. Will you tell him that his close friend, John Gooding, told you otherwise?

ASSIGNMENT FOR CLASS

1. Outside of class, analyze how you would deal with this problem. Write a short memorandum summarizing your planning, preparation, and analysis, and give a copy to your supervisor.

2. In class, meet with Ed Hard and try to deal with this problem. (Note: This is likely to be a very difficult and uncomfortable confrontation with your client. Nevertheless, you must carry through to some resolution.)

PROBLEM 109

Defense Attorney: Counseling the Defendant Concerning His Objections to Cross-Examination of Adverse Witness
(Deborah Summers)

You were meeting with Ed Hard to begin to explain the trial process to him. When discussing the cross-examination and impeachment of adverse witnesses at trial, you used Deborah Summers as an example.

"See, Ed, we can bring out facts that will tend to make the jury not believe Deborah. Besides the bias she must feel against the man who shot her husband, Deborah has told two different stories to the police and has refused to even talk to our investigator. We can make her look pretty bad."

When you said this, Hard became visibly upset. Suddenly he said: "Look, I love her and I've caused her enough pain. You're just not going to impeach her with that prior statement and make her look like a liar. I won't let you!" Ed Hard then made it clear that he will insist that you refrain from cross-examining Deborah Summers.

PREPARATION

READ: (1) Pretrial Case File Entry 61; (2) Chapter IX. Now think about and answer the following questions:

1. What are your responsibilities in this situation?

2. What is the basis for these responsibilities?

3. Isn't it Ed Hard's case to have tried as he desires as long as he appreciates the legal consequences of his decisions?

4. Was there something insensitive or tactless about how you gave your example of impeachment?

5. If you had it to do over again, would you phrase your example differently?

6. Assess the consequences on Hard's case if the prior inconsistent statement is not used.

7. What will you now say to Hard? Why?

8. Could you just say, "Look, trial's a long time off—let's not deal with this now"? Why or why not?

   a. Do criminal "speedy trial" provisions have any bearing on your answer?

   b. On the other hand, does it matter for your immediate purposes whether or not trial really is "a long time off"?

9. Imagine that the type of outburst Hard had over Deborah was not atypical, but rather one of an increasing number of instances where Hard has had a sudden emotional outburst, bordering on irrationality:

   a. What (if anything) will you do?

   b. Will you talk to Hard to try to "get at the bottom" of what's troubling him? Why or why not?

      1) If so, how will you broach the subject?

      2) Are you qualified to do this?

      3) What if he says, "You're my lawyer, stick to law. My private life is none of your business"?

      4) Will you try to refer him to a therapist? How?

ASSIGNMENT FOR CLASS

1. Outside of class, plan how you would deal with this problem. Write a short memorandum summarizing your planning, preparation, and analysis, and give a copy to your supervisor.

2. In class, meet with Ed Hard and try to resolve this problem.

PROBLEM 110

Defense Attorney: Counseling the Defendant Concerning the Use of a Particular Character Witness
(John Gooding)

At your client's recommendation you interviewed his friend, John Gooding. Among other reasons, Hard encouraged the interview in the belief that Gooding could provide evidence regarding Bruno Summers' bad reputation for violence. As a result of this interview, you have come to believe that John Gooding's character testimony has too insubstantial a basis to be credible, and may hurt the case if presented. You have told this to Ed Hard but he insists on presenting John Gooding's character testimony.

PREPARATION

READ: (1) Pretrial Case File Entry 61; (2) Chapter IX; (3) Fed. R. Evid. 404, 405, 608. Now think about and answer the following questions:

1. What is your role in this matter? What is the theoretical basis for this role?

2. Is this problem similar to that of Hard not wanting you to impeach Deborah Summers' testimony (see Problem 109) because he thinks she's "suffered enough"?

3. Must you put on any witness Hard wants?

4. What if Hard says, "Listen. It's my case. I'm the one going to prison for life if the jury doesn't buy my case, not you. And I want Gooding"?

5. What if you believe the witness is lying?

6. What if you know the witness is lying?

7. How much should you pressure Hard to accept your view regarding the character testimony? What will you say to him?

8. What will you do if Hard does not relent? Explain.

9. Does it matter that this is a criminal, as opposed to a civil, case?

ASSIGNMENT FOR CLASS

1. Outside of class, plan your discussion with Hard concerning this matter. Write a short memorandum summarizing your planning, preparation, and analysis, and give a copy to your supervisor.

2. In class, meet with Ed Hard to discuss presenting the character testimony of John Gooding.

PROBLEM 111
Defense Attorney: Counseling the Defendant Concerning Testifying at a Suppression Motion

You are preparing for a motion to suppress the gun Hard used to shoot Summers, the statement Hard made to Yale, and the statement Hard gave to Kelly. Your arguments range from attacking the lack of an arrest warrant and the lack of a valid consent to enter Hard's home, to Hard's failure to waive his *Mintz* rights when questioned by Detective Kelly. As you are discussing these motions with Hard he says, "I want to testify at the hearing. Those cops are liars. They kicked in my door and that Kelly *never* gave me any warnings. I know I signed something after I talked to the cops, but I didn't read the fine print on the form because I was so upset."

PREPARATION

READ: (1) Pretrial Case File Entries 21, 30, 61, 67, 72; (2) Chapter IX. Now think about and answer the following questions:

1. Do you want Hard to testify at the hearing?

2. What could you theoretically gain?

3. What are the risks?

4. As a practical matter, are you likely to gain anything?

   a. How can you make Hard credible versus Officers Yale and Kelly at the hearing?

   b. What problems do you face in this regard?

5. Let's think ahead:

   a. Can the prosecution use the defendant's suppression testimony at trial? (See Pretrial Case File Entry 67.)

   b. Even if the prosecution can't use it at trial, will the prosecution get any benefit from the defendant's testimony at the hearing? Explain.

   c. What concerns do you have about cross-examination (e.g., prosecution questions aimed at eliciting *bias* on the part of the defendant)?

   d. Can you limit the scope of cross-examination by the manner of your direct examination? (See Pretrial Case File Entry 67.)

1) How (specifically)?

2) What problems do you envision? (E.g., what arguments might the prosecution make to open up the scope of cross?)

6. Assume you believe that the theory raised by Hard's factual version is not even your strongest theory (in the sense that you have less chance of being successful under it).

a. What right does Hard have to reject your judgment and testify?

b. What right do you have to dissuade him?

c. What if he says:

1) "Can't I tell my story?"

2) "I thought at least *you* believed me"?

ASSIGNMENT FOR CLASS

1. Outside of class, plan how you will deal with this matter. Write a short memorandum summarizing your planning, preparation, and analysis, and give a copy to your supervisor.

2. In class, meet with your client and advise him in this matter. (Assume that you have decided to dissuade him from testifying.)

PROBLEM 112

Defense Attorney: Counseling the Defendant Concerning Use of a Witness at a Suppression Motion
(Marty Saunders)

Your client wants you to call a house guest, Marty Saunders, to testify at an upcoming hearing on your motion to suppress the fatal gun. According to a prior interview, Saunders is prepared to testify that, contrary to the police reports, the officers who searched Hard's home first kicked in Hard's front door.

You assess that Saunders (who is not even mentioned in the police reports) is of average credibility and unlikely to convince a court, even with the burden on the prosecutor, to discount the testimony of several police officers. You also feel that Saunders' testimony bears only on your *second-best* theory, but that it may so offend the court by calling the police liars, that the court will also reject what you perceive as your best theory (which involves the lack of an arrest warrant, the lack of a valid consent to enter Hard's home, and so on).

PREPARATION

READ: (1) Pretrial Case File Entries 21, 30, 61, 72; (2) Chapter IX. Now think about and answer the following questions:

1. What are your objectives in discussing with Hard the matter of Saunders' testifying?

2. What will you tell your client?

3. What if Hard insists that you call Saunders and adds, "I thought we
   wanted the truth to come out"?

   a. Does the client have the final decisions regarding the legal theory
      to be raised?

   b. Isn't that your area of expertise?

   c. Even so, is it still ultimately the client's decision?

4. How much pressure would you put on Hard to get him to see things
   your way?

5. Can you ethically withdraw? (See Model Rule 1.16 at Pretrial Case
   File Entry 61.)

6. If you can withdraw, can you use this as a threat to coerce Hard for
   his "own good"? Should you?

7. If you can't ethically withdraw, can you still intimate that you might
   in order to get Hard to follow your "advice"?

ASSIGNMENT FOR CLASS

1. Outside of class, analyze how you will deal with this matter. Write a
   short memorandum summarizing your planning, preparation, and
   analysis, and give a copy to your supervisor.

2. In class, meet with Ed Hard and advise him in this matter.

PROBLEM 113

Defense Attorney: Counseling the Defendant Concerning Consequences of a Change of Venue Motion

Throughout the pretrial period, your client's case has been getting a great
deal of publicity, much of it adverse. You were discussing this notoriety
with Hard and raised the subject of a possible motion for change of
venue. Hard immediately became enthusiastic about the possibility, and
since then has been continually asking you about the progress of the venue
motion. Meanwhile, you have been in the process of preparing the motion
and developing appropriate documentation.

   Last weekend, however, you started to have serious reservations about
the advisability of such a motion. You realized that if you win, the case
will likely be transferred to the other side of the state where you will be
cut off from your local resources and be unfamiliar with the courts and
judges. Also, though the jury panels on the other side of the state will
likely be uninformed about Hard's case, those panels tend to contain far
more conviction-prone jurors than the ones on your side of the state.
Clearly, you have to consider talking this over with your client.

PREPARATION

READ: (1) Pretrial Case File Entries 1, 2, 61, 66; (2) Chapter IX. Now
think about and answer the following questions:

1. Will you tell Hard about your concerns? *Must* you as an attorney?

2. What if you tell him and he asks, "What should I do?"

3. What do *you* want to do about this motion?

   a. Why?

   b. What bearing does your own preference in this matter have on the action you will take?

4. Do you want to convince Hard to stop pursuing a change of venue?

   a. If so, how will you persuade him?

   b. What will you respond if Hard says, "Look, this motion was your idea. Now you want to back out. Don't you know what you're doing?"

   c. What if Hard says, "No way I want to be tried here. I'll take my chances on the other side of the state"?

5. Should you wait until you see how the judge rules before you raise a problem that may never occur (the court may deny your motion)? Why or why not?

6. Could you say, "Well, Ed, this changes everything. This case is going to cost you a lot more money if I have to go to the other side of the state"? (See Pretrial Case File Entry 61.)

7. Didn't your initial fee arrangement implicitly include this possibility? Explain.

8. Finally, imagine instead that you're a sole practitioner and that trying Hard's case on the other side of the state will be financially disastrous to your practice.

   a. If Hard wants to pursue the change of venue motion, can you properly emphasize the "negative" in such a motion, without also telling him about your economic motives?

   b. Can you threaten to withdraw? (See Pretrial Case File Entry 61.)

   c. Suppose you couch your real concerns in an explanation such as, "I'll be far away from my resources and strengths—like a ball team on the road—and I'm afraid I'll be less effective for you. You might want to get a local attorney there. And, of course, I'll help." Are you just being manipulative and insincere?

      1) If not, explain.

      2) If you are, justify.

ASSIGNMENT FOR CLASS

1. Outside of class, plan how you will deal with this matter. Write a short memorandum summarizing your planning, preparation, and analysis, and give a copy to your supervisor.

2. In class, explain to your supervisor your rationale for discussing or not discussing this matter with Hard.

3. Afterwards, if you decide to discuss it with Hard, do so in class.

PROBLEM 114

Defense Attorney: Counseling the Defendant Concerning Evaluation of the Prosecutor's Plea-Bargaining Offer

You are still preparing for trial and feel confident in spite of the fact that the judge has denied all of your constitution-based pretrial motions. This morning the prosecutor in the Hard case telephoned to discuss some details about marking the exhibits for trial. During the course of the conversation, the subject of a possible settlement arose. You cannot now recall who initially broached the subject, though you are pretty sure it was the prosecution. In any event, you had thought about settlement once or twice during the past month and, though you have never discussed the matter with your client, you figured it couldn't hurt to just talk and listen. At the end of the conversation, the prosecutor said, "You are about to receive an offer that your client can't refuse."

The prosecutor then offered a plea to voluntary manslaughter and agreed to recommend to the court that the defendant serve a year in county jail as a condition of felony probation.* You must now evaluate the offer and then communicate it to Ed Hard. (Note: If your initial representational strategy was to go to trial and obtain a full acquittal (or dismissal of the charges), you would now obviously be contemplating a strategic shift. On the other hand, if your strategy was "I'll force this case to trial unless we get a good offer," then this is just the next phase of your strategy.)

PREPARATION

READ: (1) Pretrial Case File Entries 3-6, 9, 11, 16, 17, 19, 28, 29, 58, 61, 62; (2) Chapter IX. Now think about and answer the following questions:

1. Is this a good offer? Explain.

2. Why would the prosecution offer this deal?

3. Are the prosecutor's motives of significance to you? Why?

4. What will you advise Ed Hard? Why?

5. How will you approach the subject of pleading guilty when Hard has consistently maintained that he acted in self-defense?

6. Is it your role to advise Ed Hard on the deal, or simply to communicate the offer without comment?

7. What if you believe it is a good offer but Ed Hard wants to go to trial? What will you say?

8. How far will you go to persuade Ed Hard (if at all)?

9. What will you do, on the other hand, if you believe it is a poor offer but Ed Hard wants to accept it?

10. Suppose you believe the offer is a good one, but you believe you can win at trial. What will you do?

---

*If you have already performed Problems 129, 130, or 131, your instructor may tell you to use what you were actually offered in any of those exercises rather than the above offer.

11. Suppose you tell Ed Hard the offer, and he states: "I don't know; I'm unsure. . . . You're the lawyer, what should I do?" What will you say? Why?

12. Suppose Ed Hard states: "I'm innocent. I acted in self-defense, but I won't take the risk of a first-degree murder conviction. I want to take the deal." Are there problems with pleading Hard guilty to anything? Explain.

ASSIGNMENT FOR CLASS

1. Outside of class, plan how you will present the prosecution's offer to Hard. Write a short memorandum summarizing your planning, preparation, and analysis, and give a copy to your supervisor.

2. In class, you will counsel Ed Hard regarding the prosecution's offer.

CIVIL PROBLEMS: SUMMERS v. HARD

PROBLEM 115 _____

Plaintiffs' Attorney: Counseling Clients Whether to Litigate

Shortly after you saw Deborah Summers for an initial interview, you met with Gretchen and Hans Summers.

At the meeting with Gretchen and Hans you obtained information about Bruno Summers and Bruno's minor children, Amanda and Ronny. You discussed in general terms the possible claims the Summers family might have to redress Bruno's death. The Summers authorized you to represent them. You have completed your informal discovery— interviewed witnesses, researched the law, and theorized about the possible claims.

You have scheduled an appointment for October 25, 198X to meet with the Summers family to advise them.

PREPARATION

READ: (1) Pretrial Case File Entries 1-35, 40, 41, 47, 48, 51, 55, 59-61, 63, 90; (2) Chapter IX. Now think about and answer the following questions:

1. Differences and similarities in clients may influence your approach and style. Think about the personalities, needs, and desires of the clients—Deborah, Gretchen, and Hans Summers. How will your personality influence your approach and style in your meeting with the Summers family?

2. Will you prepare written material for the meeting with the Summers? For yourself? For your clients? Explain.

3. How will you begin your meeting with the Summers family?

4. Will you explain alternatives to litigation to the Summers family? Why?

5. Suppose Gretchen Summers asks you to predict the success or failure of each alternative, including litigation. Do you have an obligation to give her this information? Explain.

6. Realistically, how will you obtain the knowledge to predict the outcome of litigation?

7. Suppose you are uncertain about the outcome of litigation. Should you proceed with litigation?

8. Will you discuss the non-legal consequences of litigation with the Summers family?

9. In all litigation there are non-legal consequences that occur if litigation is pursued. Explain what these consequences are for Gretchen, Hans, and Deborah Summers.

   a. Economic.

   b. Social.

   c. Psychological.

10. Explain how your clients will be involved in the process of exploring the legal and non-legal consequences of litigation.

11. Suppose Gretchen and Hans Summers tell you, "It is your job to decide if we should litigate." What will you say?

12. Suppose Deborah Summers tells you at the beginning of this counseling session that she has made up her mind to litigate.

    a. What will you say to her if you think it is a good idea to litigate?

    b. What will you say to her if you think it is a bad idea?

13. Do you expect that a decision whether to pursue litigation will be made at the conclusion of this meeting with the Summers?

    a. If so, who will make the decision? Explain.

    b. If a decision to litigate is not made at the conclusion of this meeting, explain how you will proceed with the Summers case.

14. Often attorneys prepare a client opinion letter which outlines and explains the attorney's opinion by analyzing the applicable law and facts. The attorney then explains the course and scope of action recommended. Should you send an opinion letter to the Summers family? Explain.

ASSIGNMENT FOR CLASS

1. Outside of class, prepare a memorandum discussing your objectives in meeting with the Summers family. Give a copy to your senior partner.

2. In class, meet with the Summers family.

3. After class, prepare an opinion letter for the Summers family concerning redress for Bruno Summers' injury and death. Be prepared to explain your representational strategy.

PROBLEM 116

Plaintiffs' Attorney: Counseling Client to See a Psychologist
(Deborah Summers)

You have completed informal discovery in *Summers v. Hard.* You interviewed witnesses, filed a complaint, and received defendants' responses.

One of the claims you assert on behalf of Deborah Summers is that she has suffered emotional distress. It would be helpful to obtain a psychologist's evaluation of Deborah Summers' emotional condition.

Since your initial meeting with Deborah in September 198X, you have suggested that she obtain professional help. But your suggestion was not acted on. You have made an appointment for December 1, 198X, for Deborah Summers to come to your office to discuss this matter.

PREPARATION

READ: (1) Pretrial Case File Entries 1-41, 50, 51, 55, 59-61, 63, 64, 90; (2) Chapter IX. Now think about and answer the following questions:

1. Discuss what you will do before meeting with Deborah.

2. Suppose that Deborah is hostile and does not want to go to a psychologist. How will you obtain her cooperation?

3. Suppose that after repeated attempts during the interview to obtain Deborah's cooperation, she still refuses to go to a psychologist. What will you do?

4. Suppose that Deborah agrees to go to a psychologist but wants you to go with her.

   a. What will you say?

   b. What will you do?

5. Suppose that Deborah agrees to go but refuses to take a bus, does not have a car, and asks for taxi money. What will be your response? Why?

ASSIGNMENT FOR CLASS

1. Prepare a memorandum discussing what, if anything, you will do before meeting with Deborah Summers. Give a copy to your senior partner.

2. In class, meet with Deborah Summers about going to a psychologist.

PROBLEM 117

Plaintiffs' Attorney: Counseling
Client Concerning Remarriage
(Deborah Summers)

Approximately five months have passed since Bruno Summers died. Deborah Summers has consulted you concerning her desire to marry her boyfriend, Gary Korn. Deborah told you:

> "I may have a better chance in the future to obtain custody of the Summers children and make something of my life if I get married and have some money. But I don't want to mess up the *Summers v. Hard* lawsuit. What should I do?"

After Bruno died, Gretchen and Hans invited Deborah and the children to move in with them. Every time you have talked with Deborah, she has been vague about her plans for the future. The last time you talked to Gretchen she expressed concern that Deborah was still living with them. Gretchen said, "Surely, Deborah should think of going to work, moving out on her own, or at least going to her own parents."

Then Gretchen and Hans consulted a lawyer about obtaining custody of Amanda and Ronny. Deborah immediately moved out of the Summers' house and moved in with her parents. The children remained with Gretchen and Hans.

With Deborah's permission, you have discussed the issue of her remarriage with the attorney representing Deborah in the child custody dispute. Her child custody attorney assured you that the child custody matter was settled. (Deborah voluntarily agreed that Hans and Gretchen retain custody of the children.)*

You have scheduled an appointment with Deborah on February 1, 198X + 1 to discuss the issue of her remarriage.

PREPARATION

READ: (1) Pretrial Case File Entries 1-41, 50, 51, 55, 56, 59-61, 63, 64, 87, 90; (2) Chapter IX. Now think about and answer the following questions:

1. Do you have a position as to whether Deborah's remarriage will hurt the *Summers v. Hard* lawsuit?

   a. What is your position based on?

   b. Will you communicate your position to Deborah? Why or why not?

   c. Would Deborah's remarriage affect your representational strategy? Explain.

2. Suppose Deborah states: "I have to get out of my parents' house, get some money to get on my feet." What will you say?

ASSIGNMENT FOR CLASS

1. Outside of class, prepare a written memorandum discussing your

---

*Your instructor will inform you whether to consider the child custody dispute and its effect on *Summers v. Hard*. See Problem 118.

objectives for your meeting with Deborah Summers. Hand in a copy of your memorandum to your senior partner.

2. In class, be prepared to discuss your objectives. Meet with Deborah Summers concerning the issue of her remarriage.

PROBLEM 118 _____

*Private Attorney for Deborah Summers: Counseling Client in Child Custody Action**

Deborah Summers has consulted you** concerning filing a response to the child custody petition filed by Gretchen and Hans Summers. She would like to request temporary and permanent legal custody of Amanda, age 12, and Ronny Summers, age 8, the children of her deceased husband during his prior marriage.

You have had an initial meeting with Deborah. She related the following facts. Since Bruno's first marriage ended in divorce six years ago, Gretchen and Hans Summers, Bruno's parents, have been taking care of Amanda and Ronny Summers. The children's natural mother, an alcoholic, disappeared six years ago. Her whereabouts are still unknown. While the children were with Hans and Gretchen, Bruno paid his parents approximately $250 per month as child support. When Bruno and Deborah were married, the children moved in with them.

Deborah and Bruno were married for ten days when Bruno was shot and died. After Bruno died, Gretchen and Hans invited Deborah and the children to move in with them. Deborah agreed to move in temporarily with Gretchen and Hans. Hans expressed reluctance to take on a long-term commitment to his grandchildren. Gretchen explained to Deborah, "The children will need a firm hand, now that Bruno is gone. Spare the rod, spoil the child."

Two months passed after Bruno's death. Deborah was still unable to formulate plans for the future. Gretchen was growing more irritable every day. Deborah overheard Gretchen tell Hans, "Surely, Deborah should think of going to work and move out on her own, or at least going to live with her own parents."

Gretchen and Hans told her that they intended to keep the children and be designated the legal guardians in order to receive social security payments of approximately $300 per month for Amanda and Ronny. Deborah told Gretchen:

> "I want the children! That's all that Bruno has left me. The children's social security will help me pay the rent on a nice apartment. I may go to work soon, but then again I may not. Of course, if I get remarried, financially I won't have anything to worry about. But I don't think I will remarry for a while. And besides I like the kids."

Gretchen and Hans consulted a lawyer about obtaining custody of Amanda and Ronny. Deborah immediately moved out of the Summers' house and returned to her parents. The children remained with Gretchen and Hans.

---

*Your instructor will inform you whether this problem takes place during the same time period as *Summers v. Hard*.

**Deborah Summers' personal attorney in her child custody case is a different attorney from the one representing the Summers family in *Summers v. Hard*.

Gretchen and Hans filed a petition for legal custody and a motion requesting temporary custody, naming as respondents Deborah and the natural mother.

An evidentiary hearing on the temporary custody is scheduled for next week. The child custody trial has been set for one month later.

You have scheduled a meeting with Deborah on November 15, 198X to discuss the child custody issue with her before responding to the petition.

PREPARATION

READ: (1) Pretrial Case File Entries 1-41, 50, 51, 55, 59-61, 64, 79, 90; (2) Chapter IX. Now think about and answer the following questions:

1. Will you attempt to convince Deborah Summers not to seek child custody? Explain.

2. Suppose Deborah tells you that she wants the children because the social security money the children receive will help her rent a really nice apartment. Would you try to convince her not to seek custody? Explain.

3. In order to prepare for the evidentiary hearing that is scheduled for child custody, your investigator obtained information about Gretchen and Hans Summers and the Summers children, as well as a report from the psychologist that Deborah visited. Will you share any of the information you obtained with Deborah, such as:

    a. The contents of the psychologist's report? Explain.

    b. Gretchen and Hans's treatment of the children? Explain.

    c. Ronny and Amanda's desires as to who will have custody of them? Explain.

ASSIGNMENT FOR CLASS

1. Outside of class, prepare a memorandum discussing your objectives for your meeting with Deborah Summers. Hand in a copy of your memorandum to your senior partner.

2. In class, be prepared to discuss your objectives. Meet with Deborah Summers concerning child custody.

PROBLEM 119

Plaintiffs' Attorney: Counseling Client Concerning Deposition Testimony
(Deborah Summers)

You received a notice on October 1, 198X + 1 from defendants that Hard and Davola want to take a deposition of Deborah Summers on November 1, 198X + 1.

It is now two weeks prior to the deposition being taken. Your preparation of Deborah Summers for her deposition testimony was proceeding well when suddenly she started to cry, said the "whole thing is my fault," and began wavering about appearing at her deposition.

PREPARATION

READ: (1) Pretrial Case File Entries 1-39, 59-61, 63, 82, 90; (2) Chapter IX; (3) Fed. R. Civ. P. 26, 45, and 37. Now think about and answer the following questions:

1. Will you tell her that the case cannot proceed if she fails to appear for her deposition?

2. Will you try to talk with her? If so, what will you say?

3. If she will not talk to you, what can you do?

4. What are your ethical obligations to the other clients?

5. What will occur if Deborah does not appear at her deposition?

    a. After her deposition is noticed?

    b. After she receives a subpoena?

6. Suppose you are unable to convince Deborah Summers to appear at her deposition. Discuss what you will do.

ASSIGNMENT FOR CLASS

1. Outside of class, prepare a memorandum discussing what if anything you can do to prepare for your meeting with Deborah Summers. Give a copy to your senior partner.

2. In class, meet with Deborah Summers.

PROBLEM 120

Plaintiffs' Attorney: Counseling Client Concerning Granddaughter's School Truancy
(Gretchen Summers)

Three months have passed since Bruno's death. A complaint on behalf of the Summers family, Deborah, Gretchen, Hans, Ronny, and Amanda, was filed on November 1, 198X. Defendants responded on November 8, 198X. Gretchen Summers has taken over the care of Amanda, age 12, and Ronny, age 8, the children of Bruno from his prior marriage. The children are currently receiving social security, supplemented by welfare.

Gretchen has been plagued by personal and financial problems and by coping with two children. Since you are her attorney, Gretchen has unburdened some of her distress and inability to cope on your shoulders. She claims that she has no one else to talk to whom she respects. She telephones you at least three times a week. In fact, you have just spoken with her concerning the most recent upset—Amanda's school truancy. You have made an appointment with Gretchen to discuss Amanda's truancy.

PREPARATION

READ: (1) Pretrial Case File Entries 1-39, 61; (2) Chapter IX. Now think about and answer the following questions:

1. Should you have agreed to see Gretchen Summers? Why?

   a. Should you counsel her in this matter?

   b. If so, what should be the extent of your counseling?

2. Discuss what you can do before meeting with Gretchen Summers.

ASSIGNMENT FOR CLASS

1. Outside of class, prepare a memorandum discussing your objectives in meeting with Gretchen Summers. Give a copy to your senior partner.

2. In class, meet with Gretchen Summers.

PROBLEM 121

Plaintiffs' Attorney: Counseling Clients About the Litigation
(Gretchen and Hans Summers)

The *Summers v. Hard* lawsuit has been proceeding as to discovery. Interrogatories and the depositions of all the parties, including those of Gretchen and Hans Summers, have been concluded.

On November 15, 198X + 1, Gretchen and Hans Summers contacted you, their attorney. Your receptionist, who scheduled the appointment, told you that Gretchen Summers said she was distressed by the litigation.

PREPARATION

READ: (1) Pretrial Case File Entries 1-39, 42, 43, 47, 48, 59-61, 63, 90; (2) Chapter IX. Now think about and answer the following questions:

1. Can you prepare before meeting with Gretchen and Hans Summers? Explain.

2. What will you say in response to Gretchen and Hans Summers if they tell you they want to dismiss the lawsuit?

3. Do you think it is a good or bad idea for Gretchen and Hans Summers to dismiss the lawsuit? Why?

4. Are there alternatives available should Gretchen and Hans insist on dismissing the lawsuit? Explain.

5. Ethically, can Gretchen and Hans Summers dismiss the lawsuit? Explain.

6. If you conclude that the lawsuit as to Gretchen and Hans Summers must be dismissed, will you proceed with Deborah Summers? Ronny and Amanda? Explain.

ASSIGNMENT FOR CLASS

1. Outside of class, prepare a short memorandum discussing your objectives in meeting with Gretchen and Hans Summers. Give a copy to your senior partner.

2. In class, meet with Gretchen and Hans Summers.

PROBLEM 122

Plaintiffs' and Defendants' Attorneys: Counseling Clients Concerning Settlement

Pretrial discovery has been completed in *Summers v. Hard.* Plaintiffs' attorney has contacted attorneys for defendants Hard and Davola and suggested a meeting to try to settle the case. Before this meeting between opposing counsel, each attorney has scheduled a meeting for January 15, 198X + 2 with his or her respective client (or clients) to discuss possibilities for settlement.

PREPARATION

READ: (1) Pretrial Case File Entries 1-57, 59-61, 63, 81, 83, 87, 90; (2) Chapter IX. Now think about and answer the following questions:

1. How will you prepare for the meeting with your client?

   a. Will you prepare anything in writing? Explain.

   b. Who will be present during this meeting? Why?

2. Will you suggest a specific amount that you believe is appropriate for settlement? Explain.

3. Will you try to convince your client to authorize you to settle for a specific amount? Why?

4. What points will you present in favor of settlement? Why?

5. What points will you present against settlement? Why?

6. Suppose that your written fee agreement with your client provides on a contingent fee basis that you are entitled to 40 percent of the judgment and reimbursement for reasonable costs. Your client suggests a willingness to settle the case for a reduced amount and that therefore you should also agree to a smaller fee. What will be your position?

7. If settlement was always the focal point of your representational strategy, what role does counseling regarding settlement offers play in this strategy?

ASSIGNMENT FOR CLASS

1. Outside of class, prepare a memorandum discussing your objectives for your meeting with your client(s). Hand in a copy of your memorandum to your senior partner.

2. In class, be prepared to discuss your objectives. Meet with your client(s) concerning the settlement of *Summers v. Hard*.

PROBLEM 123

Attorney for Defendant Hard: Counseling Client Concerning His Objections to Deposition of Adverse Witness
(Deborah Summers)

You were planning to notice the deposition of Deborah Summers. Ed Hard has come to you visibly upset. Suddenly he said: "Look, I love her and I've caused her enough pain. You're just not going to bother her or make her look like a liar. I won't let you!" Ed Hard insists that you refrain from deposing Deborah Summers.

You have made an appointment to talk with Ed Hard at your office tomorrow (September 20, 198X + 1) so you can discuss this matter with him.

PREPARATION

READ: (1) Pretrial Case File Entries 1-39, 45, 59-61, 63, 82, 90; (2) Chapter IX. Now think about and answer the following questions:

1. As Ed Hard's personal attorney, what will you say to him?

2. What would you say to Ed Hard if you were defending him under his SAPO insurance policy?

3. Isn't it Ed Hard's case? Although he is paying you to represent him, can't he proceed as he desires as long as he appreciates the consequences of his decision? Explain.

ASSIGNMENT FOR CLASS

1. Outside of class, prepare a memorandum discussing what, if anything, you can do to prepare for your meeting with Hard. Give a copy to your senior partner.

2. In class, meet with Ed Hard.

PROBLEM 124

Attorney for Defendant Davola: Counseling Client About the Litigation

Plaintiffs filed a complaint naming Ed Hard, Mary Apple, Tom Donaldson, and M.C. Davola as defendants. Defendants responded on November 8, 198X. Discovery has been conducted by both plaintiffs and defendants. M.C. Davola contacts you as his attorney and requests to speak with you concerning a problem he is having. He does not say anything else and sounds too upset to question further over the telephone.

You have scheduled an appointment to see M.C. Davola on November 10, 198X + 1.

PREPARATION

READ: (1) Pretrial Case File Entries 1-39, 44, 49, 59-61, 63, 81, 83, 90; (2) Chapter IX. Now think about and answer the following questions:

1. Can you prepare for your meeting with Mr. Davola? Explain.

2. Suppose one year has passed since filing an answer in the Summers case. Mr. Davola walks into your office and begins berating you for the delay in litigating his case. Discuss how you will respond.

3. Suppose that Mr. Davola blames the Summers case for his fall-off in business at the Unicorn. He wants to sue the Summers family for libel, slander, and loss of business. What will you say? Why?

ASSIGNMENT FOR CLASS

1. Outside of class, prepare a memorandum discussing what, if anything, you can do to prepare for your meeting with Davola. Give a copy to your senior partner.

2. In class, meet with your client M.C. Davola.

PROBLEM 125

Business Attorney for Defendant Davola: Counseling Client Concerning Lease of the Unicorn Tavern *

Since the shooting at the Unicorn Tavern, business declined substantially. Davola attempted to sell the Unicorn Tavern premises but without success. Davola then decided to lease the Unicorn Tavern or its premises. It was common knowledge in the community and among all potential lessees that Bruno Summers was shot by Ed Hard at the Unicorn Tavern on September 3, 198X, and died on September 7, 198X. A criminal case, *State v. Hard,* for first-degree murder was filed and dismissed on October 1, 198X. The Summers family filed a wrongful death case against Ed Hard, Mary Apple, Tom Donaldson, and M.C. Davola on November 1, 198X. **

On December 1, 198X, Davola leased the Unicorn Tavern premises for five years to Eli Cohen. The Davola-Cohen lease contains the following provisions:

1. In consideration of the covenants and agreements set forth in this lease, Lessee agrees to lease the premises located at 5302 North 49th Street, Jamner, Major for commercial purposes to operate a restaurant, Sweet and Sour Cabbage Patch, for the term of five years, commencing on December 1, 198X and

---

*Davola's business attorney represents Davola on all business matters concerning the Unicorn Tavern. (Another attorney is representing Davola in *Summers v. Hard.*)

**Your instructor will inform you whether this problem takes place during the same time period as *Summers v. Hard.*

ending on November 30, 198X + 5. Monthly rental is: ten percent (10%) of the Lessee's net profit, or one thousand two hundred dollars ($1,200) per month, whichever is greater. Rent is payable in advance on the first day of each month during the term of the lease. . . .

12. In the event of default or non-compliance with any terms of this lease by the Lessee, all rent due and owing for the full term of the lease shall be payable by the Lessee. In the event that either party commences an action to enforce this lease, the prevailing party in such action shall be entitled to recover court costs and reasonable attorney's fees.

13. This lease shall not be assigned by Lessee, voluntarily or by operation of law, nor shall the premises or any part be sublet by the Lessee, without the prior written consent of the Lessor, and acceptance in writing by the assignee or sublessee of all the above terms.

Since January 1, 198X + 1, Cohen has operated a restaurant, Sweet and Sour Cabbage Patch, on the premises. During its first year of business, the restaurant has had net losses of $600 per month.

Cohen has notified Davola that he wants to quit his lease, claiming that he cannot afford to operate the restaurant. Mr. Cohen has located a new tenant, Adrian Mustafa, who is willing to lease the premises for $600 per month for the four years remaining on Cohen's lease. Mustafa plans to operate "The Little Egypt," a bookstore-cafe.

Cohen requested that Davola release him from his lease and lease the premises to Mustafa. Davola responded to Cohen:

> "No. I will not accept The Little Egypt as a tenant. I told you and your attorney that it would be difficult to make a restaurant profitable in a year. I went to a lot of trouble to find a tenant and make the premises ready for your restaurant. You'll make a profit if you work at it."

Mr. Cohen's attorney has contacted Davola's business attorney to discuss the "lease situation." Before meeting with Mr. Cohen's attorney, you have scheduled a meeting with M.C. Davola for February 1, 198X + 2 to discuss this matter.

PREPARATION

READ: (1) Pretrial Case File Entries 1-4, 11, 16-22, 31, 36-39, 44, 49, 59-61, 81, 85, 90; (2) Chapter IX. Now think about and answer the following questions:

1. Suppose you suspect that Davola has reasons in addition to those he has expressed for refusing to accept The Little Egypt as a tenant. Do you want to probe for all of Davola's reasons? Why or why not?

2. Will you explain the law to Davola concerning assignments and subleases?

    a. At the beginning of your meeting?

    b. At the end of a full discussion with Davola?

3. Will you make a specific recommendation to Davola as to what he should do with the Davola-Cohen lease?

    a. What will your recommendation be based on? Why?

    b. Suppose that you make a specific recommendation that Davola should consider The Little Egypt as a possible tenant, but Davola refuses to accept your advice. What will you say? Why?

ASSIGNMENT FOR CLASS

1. Outside of class, prepare a memorandum discussing how you will proceed in your meeting with Davola. Hand in a copy of your memorandum to your senior partner.

2. In class, be prepared to discuss your memorandum. Meet with Mr. Davola.

PROBLEM 126

Plaintiffs' and Defendants' Attorneys: Counseling Clients to Accept Settlement

Shortly after the pretrial conference, attorneys for all parties met to negotiate a settlement in *Summers v. Hard.* Although each of the attorneys had discussed settlement possibilities with his or her client(s) before the negotiation, the individual parties did not give the attorneys an ultimate top or bottom line. The attorneys negotiated a settlement as follows:

> *Hard:* payment of $40,000 (the limit of his SAPO insurance policy is $50,000). The $40,000 to be distributed as follows: $5,000 to Deborah Summers; $35,000 to be divided equally between two trusts to be established for Ronny and Amanda.

> *Davola:* payment by EKKO insurance company of $225,000 (the limits of the policy). This amount will be paid to the estate of Bruno Summers.

It is now time to discuss the settlement offer with your client(s) to see if the client(s) will agree to settlement. You have an appointment to meet with your client(s) on February 1, 198X+2.

PREPARATION

READ: (1) Pretrial Case File Entries 1-57, 59-61, 63, 83, 87, 90; (2) Chapter IX; (3) Fed. R. Civ. P. 68.

Answer the following questions from the perspective of your client's (or clients') interests:

1. Generally, what could you do prior to presenting an offer of settlement to your client(s) to ensure that a valid offer of settlement is acceptable?

2. What will be your role during the meeting with your client(s)?

    a. Will you try to convince your client(s) to accept the offer? Explain.

    b. Will you be neutral? Explain.

3. Suppose you do not believe the negotiated settlement is fair, but it seems fair to your client(s). What will you advise?

4. Suppose it is a fair offer, but the reaction of your client(s) is to reject it.

    a. What will you do?

    b. Is your position the same if the offer is pursuant to Federal Rule of Civil Procedure 68?

5. Suppose plaintiffs offered to settle for an amount within the insurance policy limits.

   a. Should Hard settle?

   b. Should Davola settle?

ASSIGNMENT FOR CLASS*

1. Outside of class, prepare a memorandum discussing your objectives in meeting with your client(s). Give a copy to your senior partner.

2. In class, attorneys for plaintiffs Gretchen, Hans, and Deborah Summers and defendants Davola and Hard, meet individually with your respective client(s) to discuss the settlement offer.

---

*For this particular problem, your instructor may advise you to negotiate a settlement and to use your own settlement figures instead of those in this problem.

X

Negotiation

Question 4.   What tactics should you use?

Question 5.   As to each potential tactic, what are the benefits and risks?

Question 6.   What ethical issues should you consider?

Question 7.   Are the tactics realistic and helpful?

Question 8.   What tactics do you anticipate that your adversary might use in negotiation?

Question 9.   How will you respond to your adversary's anticipated tactics?

Question 10.   What is your tentative negotiation strategy?

Question 11.   What follow-up to negotiation should be considered?

A. INTRODUCTION

1. *Defining Negotiation*

Negotiation is a process through which a dispute or problem is resolved. As a lawyer, you are constantly negotiating. Frequently, negotiation takes place in a litigation context. In that regard, you might negotiate to settle an entire dispute or part of a dispute. If the defendant agrees he is responsible and will pay the plaintiff $100,000, the negotiation agreement settles the entire dispute. On the other hand, negotiating with your adversary on a time frame for discovery solves an immediate problem, but does not settle the

ultimate dispute. Negotiation can take place at any time during the progress of a case or throughout a case—with an initial demand letter, after pleading, during discovery, during and after trial, on appeal.

Even when you are engaged in performing other pretrial skills, you might also be negotiating. You are negotiating when you try to convince a witness to be interviewed, when you counsel your client to stop taking drugs, or when you request that your law partner draft the pleading instead of you. Or there may be no dispute at all, and the representation of your client may consist solely of negotiation, as in the case of negotiating language in contracts, putting together business or financial deals, or engaging in collective bargaining.

Negotiation is referred to as alternative dispute resolution. That is because negotiation is an alternative methodology to litigation. It is an alternative, moreover, in more ways than the obvious procedural differences between trial and settlement. Negotiation can offer a broader range of solutions than those typically available at trial. It also offers the potential for a different philosophy of resolution. In litigation there is generally a winner and a loser (judgment for the plaintiff and against the defendant for the sum of $100). Negotiation also has "win" and "lose" solutions, referred to as "zero-sum" negotiation. Zero-sum negotiation describes a situation where one of the parties wins at another party's expense. (Robert agrees to pay Sally $400. Robert will be $400 poorer, Sally will be $400 richer.) But a more typical negotiation result is that both parties can to some extent be "winners," because generally each party gives up something and receives something in return. For example, imagine a child custody case in which both mother and father want custody of the children. The mother also wants the father to remain in the geographical area in order to share responsibility for raising the children. The father wants to relocate. The parties negotiate and agree that the father will have custody of the children during the school year and remain in the geographical area, and the mother will have custody during the summer months. Both parties compromised. Are both winners? Or losers? The mother may believe *she* won the war by having the father agree to remain in the geographic area. The father may believe *he* won the war because he has custody of the children for nine months and his ex-spouse for only three months.

What does it take to function effectively in this process? Negotiation is not an art. Nor is a negotiator a "gifted" person. Rather a negotiator is successful because of the ability to implement planned strategies to achieve client objectives. These objectives might be multifaceted: (1) settling the dispute for the maximum amount for your client; (2) maintaining a good relationship with the opposing party; and (3) obtaining information during the negotiation.

Planning to achieve these objectives, however, will take place in the context of a variety of variables. The types of disputes can differ significantly—business deals, labor-management collective bargaining, prison disputes, international conflicts, settlement of litigation, and so on. Negotiation can arise in different settings—negotiating against a backdrop of litigation, collective bargaining, even, in the extreme case, the threat of terrorist activity. The negotiation philosophy of the participants—the "how to" of successful negotiation—may vary widely. Some commentators and practitioners advocate positional bargaining, a test of power. Positional bargainers formulate their own negotiation positions ("I want a $1.17 an hour pay increase or we'll strike") and those positions become the basis for negotiation discussion. Other negotiation experts, such as Roger Fisher and William Ury, advocate a process of cooperation—principled bargaining. Principled bargaining, as described by Fisher and Ury in their book, *Getting to Yes*, encourages the parties to negotiate on the basis of underlying interests and to seek solutions that are mutually satisfactory. Still other attorneys believe negotiation just requires skillful manipulation of tactics and techniques. The negotiators themselves may have diverse backgrounds and experience—lay persons, not lawyers, may be involved, or third parties, such as mediators or ombudsmen, may be the principal negotiators. The desired remedies may differ from negotiation to negotiation—an apology may suffice in one instance, nothing less than a $100,000 lump sum payment in another. The particular negotiation process can require quick decisionmaking or the process may be protracted, each step and decision arrived at after meeting, consultation, and reassessment.

2. *Negotiation Planning*

Just as in other pretrial skills, there are two levels of planning you need to be aware of when you approach negotiation. The first involves negotiation as it interacts and coordinates with the other pretrial skills in carrying out your representational strategy. This specifically relates to deciding whether, when, and for what to negotiate. The second type of planning involves deciding how you will negotiate.

Although each negotiation situation may differ, there are general principles that can guide planning both the substance of negotiation and the "how to" of the actual negotiation performance. In this chapter we present our approach to negotiation, which consists of three related parts: (1) preparation; (2) planning a substantive negotiation strategy—what you want to attain for your client, and the range of objectives and solutions[1] you propose and are willing to accept for your client; and (3) planning a negotiation performance strategy—the tactics and techniques you

---

1. The terms *goal, objective, position, proposal, solution* describe the end result that you want to achieve in negotiation.

will use during negotiation to obtain your client's objectives.

Our planning approach, we believe, is compatible with differing philosophies and styles of negotiating. Both principled and positional negotiators need to obtain and analyze information, evaluate interests, and formulate proposals. To emphasize this point, we have purposely taken a middle road between these competing and differing negotiation philosophies in the illustration of our approach. As such, we borrow ideas and concepts from other commentators and texts that we then use within our approach, thereby showing you a broad range of negotiation theory and different negotiation practice styles. We have, however, limited the variables in our illustration. The illustration thus somewhat differs in complexity from many real-life negotiation situations. In this regard, it is our intent to give you a framework within which you can subsequently assimilate more complex factors once you have mastered the approach.

This chapter primarily discusses negotiation in the context of civil litigation, although most of the principles are applicable to negotiation in other contexts. The last part of the chapter is devoted to criminal negotiation, discussing parallels to and divergences from the civil process.

We recommend that you also consider the following references: G. Williams, *Legal Negotiation and Settlement* (1983); R. Fisher and W. Ury, *Getting to Yes* (1981); H. Edwards and J. White, *Problems, Readings, and Materials on the Lawyer as a Negotiator* (1977); H. Raiffa, *The Art and Science of Negotiation* (1982); C. Gilligan, *In a Different Voice* (1982).

However, before we begin to describe and apply our approach, you must first decide whether you want to negotiate—a threshold question.

3. Formulating a Representational Strategy: Deciding to Negotiate

More than likely, sometime after your client consults you, your thoughts will focus on the questions, "Should I negotiate?" and "If I negotiate, when?" These questions are part of your representational strategy. Deciding if and when to negotiate will affect both when you will file a pleading and the content of that pleading. For instance, you need to decide if you will plead first and then negotiate. A pleading often indicates the seriousness of your client's intentions and also the strength and extent of a client's claims. If your pleading can be used to persuade, then you will want to plead, then negotiate. But if your pleading is based, for example, on "cutting-edge" legal theories and your opponent may not be persuaded as to the strength of your claim, you might want to negotiate before pleading. Deciding if and when to negotiate will also affect the informal and formal discovery that you plan, including the sequence and type of information you want. For example, if you are defending against a personal injury claim in which you have a relatively weak position on liability, and you desire a quick settlement as part of your representational strategy, you might immediately concentrate on obtaining all the information available on the extent of plaintiff's injuries (interrogatories inquiring into past injuries, court-ordered examination by your expert doctor, discussions with neighbors about plaintiff's activities before and after the injury). Using the resulting information, you can develop and support your position in negotiation with very specific factual references. The more specific you can be in negotiation discussion, the more likely you can persuade your opponent. (For further discussion, see pages 400-401.) But you also must recognize that some client disputes may not be negotiable, at least to the participants. For instance, if a client wants to establish a principle of law, perhaps only a court judgment will meet the client's needs. Or an adversary might have given a take-it-or-leave-it offer, "We will settle only for $10,000."

Let's assume that circumstances, at present, do not indicate a non-negotiable case. Preliminarily, you probably will think about negotiating because you believe it might be the least expensive method to resolve the dispute. While you might make a preliminary decision that you would like to negotiate, the final decision to negotiate will depend on your evaluation of whether negotiation will result in the best solution for your client. You will need to evaluate and compare negotiation with the various benefits and risks of pursuing dispute resolution by litigation, mediation, arbitration, and so on. Accordingly, you must balance such factors as economic costs, client needs, and how successful you believe you might be in negotiation as opposed to other processes. Therefore, before you can actually compare whether your client will be better off pursuing negotiation rather than litigation or other forms of dispute resolution, you first must prepare and plan the substance of your negotiation and performance strategy.

B. PREPARATION

In this section, we discuss both the preparatory steps in formulating negotiation proposals and how you will actually negotiate to achieve them. These steps consist of gathering legal and factual information just as you do for preparing other pretrial performance skills such as case theory development, interviewing, and pleading. However, negotiation preparation will differ because you will be obtaining a broader range of information and analyzing and using the information for a different purpose. Therefore, although in other chapters we have discussed obtaining legal and factual information, we will now reanalyze that information, along with other information that is particularly germane to negotiation. We have found it helpful to divide the information into six categories: client needs and wishes; facts; substantive law; incentives; the adversary's negotiation behavior; and nuts-and-bolts information.

1. Obtaining Information

a. Client's Needs and Wishes

Generally, by the time you negotiate you will know your client's needs and wishes. In negotiation, however, *both* your client's needs and wishes and those of your adversary's client are of importance and should be reflected in the negotiation. After all, it is the clients who must ultimately accept a negotiated settlement. If you know about the other side's needs, you thus might be able to propose solutions that will meet both clients' needs. You also should have a broad perspective of needs and wishes since prior client wishes that appeared inappropriate for litigation—because the process did not offer any remedy through which they could be met, for example, a public apology—may now be legitimate to pursue.

b. Facts

As preparation for negotiating you will need to plan and coordinate informal and formal discovery with negotiation in mind. Even though you are negotiating, you need to obtain and be familiar with the kind of specific factual information that you would use if you were litigating the case (e.g., witness availability, credibility of witnesses, witness stories, potential evidentiary problems and rulings, availability of documents). Such familiarity is important in formulating negotiation proposals and in your discussion of those proposals. To illustrate, suppose that you represent the plaintiff in an automobile rear-end collision. You believe the defendant negligently followed too close to the plaintiff and could not stop. Your substantive negotiation proposal and discussion of that proposal will in large part be based on how strong liability is

in plaintiff's favor. In particular, the distance the defendant was from the plaintiff when he applied his brakes is critical. Your substantive negotiation strategy (what your client requests) could be quite high if you have information that the defendant was driving two feet behind the plaintiff, as opposed to a situation where you have no information from which to establish the distance. Your discussion of that settlement proposal with opposing counsel will also be more persuasive if you can represent that her client was tailgating two feet behind. Only because you obtained this critical fact in formal or informal discovery—that is, the distance maintained by the defendant driver—will you be persuasive in formulating and presenting your negotiation proposal.

On the other hand, your representational strategy might be to try to settle the case, but to litigate the dispute if a reasonable offer is not forthcoming. If you have those dual objectives, negotiation can be approached as an extension of discovery. You will then plan to obtain as much specific information about the dispute as possible during negotiation discussion.

c. Substantive Law

Legal research will have an extensive and sometimes differing focus for negotiation than for other pretrial tasks. Legal research for negotiation requires obtaining substantive legal rules (precedent), legal theories, remedies requested in pleadings, court judgments, jury verdicts, and negotiated settlements. You can use this information in several ways.

First, you can use the "copy-cat" method. As you may recall from pleading, established law served as a model and guide for drafting claims, parties, and relief under the "old-shoe" approach. The copy-cat method can also be used for formulating negotiation proposals and discussions. By evaluating similar pleading relief requests, negotiated settlements, court judgments, or verdicts, you will have a guide for formulating negotiation proposals. Examining cases, you can extract the arguments and discussions that were used to support a particular case theory and adopt those for your negotiation discussion.

Second, the law is a barometer to determine strengths and weaknesses in negotiation strategies. By examining legal precedent you can determine how favorable the precedent is to your legal position. The more it supports your position, the stronger your negotiation proposal could be. For example, imagine that you are representing Betsy, a skier who was injured when the cable of a cable car in which she was riding collapsed. Acquiring information as to jury verdicts in similar litigated cases may help you evaluate and compare the outcome of Betsy's case if it were to be litigated, thus guiding what you should propose in negotiation. If a jury verdict in a similar case was for two million dollars, you might confidently predict that Betsy could, by litigating, obtain a judgment for approximately two million dollars. You might then advocate a position similar to that amount in your negotiation. (The amount you would expect to receive would be less than what you could obtain if the dispute were litigated because you are not subjected to the risk of litigation, litigation costs, or the emotional trauma of a trial.) Legal precedent can also highlight the weaknesses and limitations of the negotiation strategies you might propose and expect. If verdicts are for substantially less than two million dollars, you would probably set your negotiation proposals for less than two million dollars.

d. Incentives

Information about incentives is generally unique to negotiation and counseling. Incentive information refers to the wide range of circumstances that may affect your and your adversary's motivation to resolve the dispute. For ease of analysis, we classify incentive information into two categories, economic and non-economic, although to some extent information classified as non-economic ultimately might also have economic consequences.

Some negotiation theorists use mathematical formulas for determining the effect of some incentives on a particular negotiation. By assigning "values" to each piece of information, these theorists calculate the influence that incentive may have on decisions to negotiate, negotiation proposals, and negotiation performance strategies.

To obtain incentive information, you should think about everything that could possibly affect the dispute and its outcome. This process is identical to brainstorming a case theory. You may need to consult many diverse sources (your client, other attorneys, court personnel, family or friends of your client and of your adversary's client, trade periodicals, and so on).

(1) Non-Economic

Generally, non-economic information could include such things as the emotional stability of the clients (can your client, or your opponent's client, endure a trial?); the impact on your client's relationship with the adversary (does your client want to maintain a continuing working relationship with her adversary?); either client's "need" for a public trial (is the client litigating the case to establish a principle?); and the impact of favorable or adverse publicity on your client or her opponent. The possible jury appeal of a case can be a factor in your approach to negotiation. Will the presentation of plaintiff's case be likely to favorably impress the factfinder because of a sympathetic issue (injured child) or because the performance of a client, or a witness, or one of the attorneys is likely to be unusually effective (or markedly ineffective) in court? If so, that factor might provide a strong incentive for a defendant to settle close to plaintiff's demand because, if the case is litigated, a jury award might result in much higher damages than the amount for which the case can be settled.

Non-economic information can also help you decide such issues as whether to negotiate and for what amount. Imagine that your client Betsy, the injured skier, has told you she cannot endure the emotional trauma of a trial. Yet you need her testimony to be successful before the jury. Negotiation may be your only alternative. This type of information will not only help you decide to negotiate, but will also affect the limits of your negotiation proposals, probably causing you to set them lower so you can more easily persuade your adversary to settle Betsy's case.

(2) Economic

Economic information can help you evaluate the financial impact on your client should he accept your adversary's proposed solution. Will your client be better or worse off if the dispute is settled? Will your adversary's client be benefited by a negotiated settlement? Economic factors related to the litigation can include litigation expenses (discovery costs, court costs, witness fees, evidence preparation, legal fees, collection of judgment, and so on) as well as the tax aspects of judgments. Or economic concerns can stem from the financial position of the parties and their monetary concerns (need for money, time value of money). Other economic factors may be based on your best estimate of the financial outcome of the case (e.g., the likelihood of a favorable outcome and the amount of verdicts for similar cases; customs in the industry and in the geographical area; and the attitudes of court personnel, judge, and jury).

This type of information can be acquired by consulting specialized lawyer periodicals and by talking with other attorneys, court personnel, and your client.

e. Adversary's Negotiation Behavior

Although your adversary's behavior is significant in other areas such as discovery, it tends to be more significant in negotiation. Negotiation, more than the performance of other pretrial skills, is affected by the personalities of the people involved. In negotiation, behavioral characteristics may directly affect the content of the negotiation and the performance strategy for both you and your adversary. By identifying and studying your adversary's behavior before actually negotiating (requesting information from fellow members of the bar, neighbors, community groups), you may be able to predict your adversary's negotiation content and performance strategies—what demands she may make, how she may react to your proposals and performance strategy. Suppose that you learn that the prosecutor recommends that in all convicted drunk-driving cases the court impose a sentence of six weeks of community service. It may be futile in your representation of a client who wants to plead guilty to try to negotiate a plea for no community service. Rather, your plea-bargaining efforts might be best focused on the type of community service and when it can be done. Or you may plan to use a specific performance strategy such as sending your adversary a written offer prior to your negotiation meeting because you have heard that your adversary will respond only to written offers.

Therefore, before you actually negotiate with your adversary, obtain information as to the behavior your adversary exhibits in negotiation. Subsequently, depending on what you learn or what occurs during your negotiation meeting, you may have to revise your plan. Nevertheless, some of the information will be useful to you in preparing negotiation content and performance strategy.

f. Nuts-and-Bolts Information

Just as nuts-and-bolts information affects interviewing, discovery, and counseling, it also influences negotiation performance. You should consider the following: how and where the negotiation will be held (attorney office, conference room, telephone call); the seating arrangements for any meeting (will you face the door, the client, a window, the sun, the clock); when the meeting will take place (time of day, amount of time reserved); who will be present (clients, members of the public, attorneys); and the arrangements for recording the negotiation meeting or settlement agreement (attorney notes, secretary, stenotype, video, audio recorder). Any advance information you obtain in these and similar areas will help you plan a strategy for how to cope with a particular situation when you actually negotiate.

2. Preparing Yourself: A Frame of Mind

Throughout this text, we have stressed the necessity for you to adopt a frame of mind that allows you to respond quickly and creatively. Your frame of mind is critical in being able to plan, analyze, and strategize prior to and during negotiation. Two mental processes that are interrelated and necessary for negotiators are using ends-means thinking and being creative.

a. Ends-Means Thinking

Ends-means thinking is an integral part of negotiation. During your negotiation, everything you do should be directed toward achieving the end result you want to accomplish. Consciously adopting ends-means thinking puts you in a frame of mind to analyze, strategize, and restrategize, based on goals. For instance, when you actually are negotiating you need to instantaneously analyze, react, and respond to proposals and tactics. By adopting a frame of mind where you constantly think about the end result, you are accustoming yourself to automatically think and respond in this manner.

Some commentators have suggested that negotiating is like playing a game. Each is dynamic and consists of many potential strategies guided by ends-means thinking. Examining the strategy for playing a game of checkers graphically illustrates the ends-means frame of mind that you will need for negotiation performance. However, a word of caution. Although planning game strategies and negotiation strategies are similar, they are not identical. Nor are we suggesting that you should negotiate solely to win. Negotiation has more sophisticated objectives than just winning. Negotiation strategies also consider your adversary's (and perhaps other) interests and needs. Nevertheless, the comparison of game and negotiation strategies does illustrate the ends-means frame of mind that the checker player and negotiator share.

A strategy for a game of checkers is straightforward. You want to win. That is your checker goal. In order to win, your checkers are not moved randomly. Rather, you move your checkers according to a plan—a game strategy. The game strategy describes the moves that you plan to make and your opponent's potential responses. Your game strategy is based on the rules of the game and your knowledge or prediction of how your opponent might be expected to play the game. There are a great many possible moves you can make that are consistent with accomplishing your goal of winning. In planning your game strategy, you will develop strategies by analyzing each move you can make and predicting the responses that your opponent could or would in all likelihood make, and their effect on your ultimate goal. You will plan alternative strategies. As you plan (and again as you play), you will ask yourself questions. If I move my checker to this position, what is the likely result for that checker? The rest of my checkers? The result for the move after that? What will be the likely response by my opponent? If my opponent responds in this manner, what are my alternatives? Each time you move a checker you are either moving closer or further from your objective. Each move is calculated to bring you closer, as is each plan and each fresh strategy. Planning your game strategy has required you to adopt a frame of mind that is directed toward achieving an objective, which here, in a checker game, is to win.

Using ends-means thinking for planning how you will negotiate is much like formulating a checker game strategy. Negotiation strategy requires planning the content of your negotiation and how you will achieve your client's objectives. Just as you need the ends-means frame of mind to plan checker game strategy, you will be planning negotiation by concentrating on your goal—achieving your client's objectives. You will plan your moves, which may be offers, counter-offers, or concessions. You will analyze and assess your opponent's responses. As you plan and again when you actually negotiate, you will analyze and restrategize with your objectives as your guide.

b. Creative Thinking

As a negotiator, you must think creatively about information to use, tactics to employ, and solutions to propose.

As a negotiator, you can use different types of information that probably would be inadmissible if presented in a litigation context. In negotiation, you can rely on any information that is helpful as long as you are ethical and do not violate the law. You can be creative in planning novel solutions (such as periodic payments or requiring an apology). For instance, if you know that your adversary's client is fearful of adverse publicity, you can use that information to persuade your adversary to settle by including in your proposal an accommodation that the settlement will be confidential. If a defendant is adamant about not acknowledging fault, you can create a proposal that permits defendant to disclaim liability. You can even negotiate a solution contrary to substantive law. For example, you may represent the defendant in a jurisdiction where substantive law might provide that in a rear-end collision the following driver is presump-

tively negligent. Nevertheless, you can ignore that principle of law in a negotiated resolution. If you can persuade opposing counsel that your client will have immense appeal before a jury, your adversary might consider accepting your settlement proposal even though legal precedent would not support your position at trial. (But keep in mind that in some jurisdictions, when criminal cases are negotiated, filing and plea-bargaining disposition are controlled by state law and discretion by the prosecutor to make deals may be limited.)

As with your settlement proposals, your negotiation performance can also be creative. The tactics you use as a negotiator can be wide-ranging and not constrained by procedural rules, except for professional ethics and criminal sanctions. You can threaten to walk out, picket, strike, advertise your client's position in a newspaper, and so on. Imagine what would occur if while litigating you walk out because you do not like your adversary's opening statement or the judge's ruling.

The more creative and receptive you are to novel ideas, the greater might be the potential for solving the dispute. Therefore, prepare yourself to plan content and performance strategies with this potential for creativity in mind, so you can draw upon it if required when you actually negotiate.

C. PLANNING THE SUBSTANCE OF NEGOTIATION: AN APPROACH AND ILLUSTRATION

It is now time for you to decide what you want to obtain from the negotiation—that is, the content of your negotiation. Or, if you are defending, you will plan how you can minimize your adversary's demand.

Most likely, you have a tentative idea as to your general negotiation objectives. You might want to settle the dispute by obtaining compensation for your client, or you might want to obtain information. But even though your objective might be to settle the dispute and obtain damages, are damages really the best remedy? Should you in negotiating a breach of contract case try to obtain restitution? Specific performance? You will also be concerned with the content of your solution. If damages is the best remedy, what is the appropriate amount? Will you request one million dollars? Two million dollars?

Seldom do you have only one goal that is The Objective or The One Solution for the negotiation. Likewise, seldom will your adversary accept your best or only solution. Therefore, your negotiation will consist of a hierarchical negotiation preference, that is, a range of solutions, a spectrum running from the best result you can obtain to the least appealing, but still acceptable, solution your client will accept.

This hierarchical order is based on your analysis of the types of information we gathered in the section on preparation. Put simply, the more the information supports your client's position, the stronger your position, and the higher you might set your objectives. The less so, the weaker your position. The process of formulating this range of negotiation solutions, moreover, is identical to that of developing a case theory and back-up theories. We saw that as information is discovered and evaluated, weaknesses may appear in your primary case theory making that theory less persuasive (e.g., doubtful credibility of witnesses, inconsistency in evidence to support your case theory, inadmissibility of evidence). Likewise, negotiation solutions may encounter weaknesses. An optimum solution may be less persuasive because a similar case that was negotiated was settled for less than you are demanding in your negotiation, or your client needs an immediate settlement and is willing to "take anything they offer" if it is paid within ten days.

Later on, when we plan performance, you will use the hierarchical order of your negotiation solutions as the basis for your discussions when you actually negotiate. At this time, however, let's begin to focus on developing that hierarchy. To start, whatever the content (i.e., range or hierarchy) of your negotiation, it must be realistic, logical, and persuasive. A solution proposed in negotiation, just like a case theory, is more likely to be persuasive if it is consistent and logical in relation to the information. Imagine that you represent the father in a child custody dispute that is being negotiated. In the abstract, the best solution you could obtain for your client is legal custody of his child. But it might not be persuasive to advocate that position, even though your client wants custody, if he is a traveling salesman and the mother is a well-respected schoolteacher in the community. Your proposed solution, legal custody for the father, is inconsistent with the facts and substantive law factors (a suitable, stable environment being in the child's best interests). Neither law nor facts logically or persuasively support a proposal of legal child custody with the father. (Of course, your client may be adamant that he wants custody and will not consider settling for anything else, or there may be additional information that would support his request.) Instead, a more persuasive, logical position might be for you to concentrate on negotiating extensive visitation for the father.

But what about developing the range of hierarchy? For that we offer a seven-question approach as a guide for determining the substance of what you wish to achieve for your client in negotiation.

Plan

1. What are your negotiation objectives?
2. What method will you use to determine the range of solutions?

Analysis

3. What information should you consider?
4. What is the significance of this information in setting your client's optimum solution?
5. What is the significance of this information to setting the least, but still acceptable, solution?

Strategy

6. Is the tentative range of solutions persuasive and creative?
7. What is the tentative bargaining range?

The following illustration applies our approach to determining the range of money solutions in a not atypical tort damages negotiation.

Suppose that you represent the plaintiff, Betsy Lash, our injured skier. Recall that Betsy fell from a "runaway" cable car when a cable connecting the car in which she was riding broke, and Betsy suffered extensive injuries. You have filed a complaint alleging negligence, claiming the Amber Ski Lodge Corporation failed to maintain the cables on the ski cable cars. Betsy has alleged special damages (medical expenses), $50,000; loss of earnings, $150,000; and a pain-and-suffering claim based on one-third of her damages, $66,000. Attorney fees are a 25 percent contingent fee of the net recovery. You estimate that litigation costs will be approximately $25,000. If Betsy's case is pursued to trial, an additional $10,000 in costs will be incurred. Amber responded, denying liability and pleading Betsy's contributory fault. Amber has an insurance liability policy allowing recovery of $200,000 for each occurrence.

QUESTION 1
What are your negotiation objectives?

As plaintiff's attorney, you want to settle the dispute and obtain the most compensation you can. A secondary objective, particularly if settlement seems unlikely, is specifically to learn more about defendant Amber's defense theory. All you have learned through discovery is that Amber claims Betsy failed to pay attention on the cable car, causing a shift of weight to one side.

QUESTION 2
What method will you use to determine the range of solutions?

There are various ways to determine a range of negotiation. First, you could develop a bargaining range by determining the optimum solution you believe you can request. You would do this by optimistically interpreting all the relevant information you have (e.g., fact, legal precedent). While you are thinking optimistically, however, you may well note flaws in your analysis. Those flaws will begin to suggest that you should also consider less optimistic solutions. A range of solutions will begin to develop from these flaws or weaknesses until you "hit the bottom." Bottom, in a litigation-motivated negotiation generally means, "I'd rather risk everything I could obtain in negotiation and go to trial." To recognize when you hit bottom, you will need to think about the bottom—the least, but still acceptable, solution—in light of the consequences of not settling.

Second, you could reverse the process for selecting your negotiation range. You could construct your range of solutions by concentrating on your bottom solution. What is the least, but still acceptable, solution that your client should and would accept? By looking at the bottom position, you are pessimistically interpreting information (weaknesses in the law or facts, any strong incentives for accepting a settlement). After determining the bottom position, you would then progress upward by rationalizing and distinguishing the weaknesses in your case. You would continue to rationalize the weaknesses as much as you believe possible until you arrive at the "top."

A third method for setting a range of proposed solutions might be to evaluate both the information that supports and then that which weakens your proposals, and develop the parameters of the range as you consider all the information. If a fact is important, it will affect the strength or weakness of your case and your incentive to settle. You would then consider the effect on your solutions. Does it raise or lower your solution? For instance, imagine negotiating a settlement in a will contest in which you are contesting the will of your father because of your be-

lief the testator was incompetent at the time he made the decision to donate 80 percent of his assets to the Feline Care Institute instead of his three surviving children. You have information that two weeks before the will was made his neighbors called the police to complain about your father's "bizarre" behavior—he was seen painting two of his cats with pink paint. But you also have a copy of a report by your father's attending physician that your father was "eccentric" but not mentally incompetent. Painting the cats is a fact that strengthens your case; this means the solutions you propose can be high. The doctor's report weakens your case. In turn the solutions you propose would then be less.

You may find, as we have, that it is really a matter of personal choice as to which method, or combination of methods, you use. The only effect that might occur in choosing one method instead of another is in the sequence of information that you analyze. In our illustration, we analyze the information by determining the optimum solution, the best result you can achieve for Betsy, and then determine the least but still acceptable amount of damages.

QUESTION 3
What information should you consider?

To help you prepare for negotiation, you will now analyze the categories of information you have obtained:

- Betsy's needs and wishes;
- the law applicable to Betsy's case;
- the facts of Betsy's case;
- incentives (economic and non-economic) that Betsy and defendant Amber might have for settlement;
- defendant Amber's needs and interests.

QUESTION 4
What is the significance of this information in setting your client's optimum solution?

To determine what damages you will request, you need to analyze the strengths and weaknesses of Betsy's case. The more logically the information supports Betsy's solutions, the more optimum Betsy's solutions can be.

Client's Needs and Wishes

Suppose Betsy told you:

> "I *want* three million dollars. It would be nice to have a lot of money, and I heard that another skier who was injured got three million dollars. I want the Amber Ski Lodge to apologize for its failure to repair the defective cable that caused the accident. I also have an immediate financial need to pay for my college education."

Should you disregard Betsy's wish? Probably not, since Betsy is ultimately in charge of her case. Betsy's three million dollar wish might be based on Betsy's whim or fancy or on objective information. (Sometimes your client will be pessimistic and will have an unrealistically low expectation.) Of course, you could strategically present your client's wish even if it is in truth a whim without regard to realistic factors. Nevertheless, you certainly do not want to disregard the story about another skier's three million dollar compensation. Perhaps you want to find out more about that other case. And you certainly should consider the amount of money Betsy needs for her education. You also will include the apology as part of the negotiation content so the settlement reflects Betsy's needs and is a settlement that Betsy will accept. You probably will need to evaluate additional information and again discuss the matter with Betsy.

Substantive Law

Suppose that your legal research indicates the following: In a boating accident case, *Fletcher v. Ryan,* the trial judge had instructed the jury that they should consider and weigh the eyewitness testimony in determining percentage of negligence. The jury found plaintiff 40 percent at fault and defendant 60 percent. The appellate court stated, "We find that in determining comparative negligence of the parties, a defendant's negligence in the course of defendant's commercial recreational business creates a rebuttable presumption of *total* liability on the part of defendant in any resulting recreational accident. This presumption can be rebutted only by direct, not circumstantial, evidence."

Your research also uncovered that, in the similar ski case Betsy told you about, a negotiated settlement was reached. However, the settlement was for $300,000, not the three million Betsy told you about. Also, in discussion with other lawyers, you were told that pleading requests in recreational sport cases generally range from $500,000 to two million dollars and jury verdicts range from $250,000 to one million dollars.

How does the law affect Betsy's optimum solution? The law affects the content of Betsy's optimum solution in three ways, as (1) legal precedent supporting Betsy's position; (2) a guideline as to what to propose; and (3) a limitation.

First, if legal precedent supports Betsy's negligence claim, it is realistic for you to request and anticipate a high optimum negotiation settlement because your strong legal position will provide an incentive for Amber to settle. The stronger Betsy's legal case, the more likely it is that you could obtain a similar or better judgment if you litigated, and the greater the risk for Amber to refuse to negotiate and settle. (In other words, you would have a strong legal theory.) As Betsy's attorney you can optimistically, but rationally, interpret *Fletcher v. Ryan* in a manner that supports 100 percent fault by the defendant, Amber. By relying on the *Fletcher* case you could suggest that the 60-40 percent solution is limited to the particular facts in *Fletcher*. Since there is no direct eyewitness to rebut a presumption of total negligence on the part of Amber in Betsy's case, a jury reasonably could find Amber 100 percent at fault.

Second, legal precedent as a guideline provides a potential model as to how to actually determine the type and amount of Betsy's optimum result. What other litigants have pleaded, settled for, or obtained by jury verdict can guide you. For instance, how do you know what Betsy's optimum solution should be? Should Betsy request ten million? Or one million? Legal precedent as a guideline might strongly support an optimum result of one million dollars. You could reasonably base your optimistic determination on any of three precedents: the pleading range ($500,000-two million dollars); the negotiated settlement of the other ski case ($300,000); and the range of jury verdicts ($250,000-one million). Since you are being optimistic, you might decide to look at the higher end requested in pleadings and in jury verdicts and use those precedents as a guideline. But if you request two million dollars based on pleading requests instead of one million based on jury verdicts, you should also be aware that since pleadings are notoriously inaccurate (attorneys usually lack precise knowledge at the pleading stage to realistically predict the amount in controversy), your proposal may be suspect and vulnerable to attack by your opponent.

Third, you must also consider whether substantive law or procedural rules place any limitation on your optimum solution. In particular, this may occur when there are multiple parties involved in the dispute that is being negotiated. As an example, consider the "Mary Carter agreement," also known as the "sliding scale agreement," which has been prohibited by law in some jurisdictions. This agreement, generally applicable in tort cases, occurs where there are multiple parties who may be responsible for the injury, and not all the parties agree to settle. A plaintiff is prohibited from either agreeing to dismiss or not actively pursue litigation against a settling defendant who, in exchange for the settlement, guarantees judgment whether the plaintiff wins or loses. (In the criminal arena, you should be aware that the court will always be involved in giving final approval to any plea bargain.)

Facts

Suppose that Betsy will be a key witness. We analyze such factors as credibility of Betsy as a witness, availability or admissibility of her evidence, and Betsy's presentation of a "sympathetic" story. You believe she will be a very credible witness. Her story is sympathetic and she presents an excellent appearance. In Betsy's case you might place great weight on these credibility indicia because she is the plaintiff. You believe these facts enhance the strength of your case, making it more likely and consistent with an optimistically high result. (In other words, you would have a strong factual theory.) Additionally, you should consider other information such as physical evidence (was the cable broken? were there similar incidents with this equipment?) and other witness information (did anyone see the accident or what Betsy was doing immediately prior to the accident?).

Incentives (Economic and Non-Economic)

You must consider the incentives that could motivate you and your adversary to negotiate a settlement.[2] Generally, the more incentive a client has to settle, the more willing the client might be to settle for less than what might be indicated by other information.

Suppose you predict that, if Betsy's case is litigated, you would obtain a judgment for one million dollars. Betsy has a very strong litigation case—the law and

facts are strongly in her favor. She will make a credible and convincing witness. You therefore believe that Betsy's case is equally as strong as the cases in which one million dollar judgments were awarded. Betsy has an immediate financial need to pay for her college education and trial and judgment are three years away. As for defendant, you have learned that the ski business is capital intensive and highly competitive. Success is dependent on word-of-mouth by satisfied customers. Through the formal discovery process, you have learned that Amber Ski Lodge is new in the ski business, has a cash flow problem, and is concerned with building a clientele.

What do you do with this information that appears to bear on your client's and the defendant's incentives to settle? You should list and evaluate which factors are an incentive or disincentive for settlement for Betsy. You also should explore alternatives that will lessen Betsy's incentives to accept an inappropriate settlement. You also must do the same analysis for Amber, since the more incentives Amber has to settle, the more likely Amber will be willing to settle close to Betsy's optimum solution.

You believe that if Betsy receives a settlement offer, even if it is substantially less than one million dollars, she will want to accept the settlement because of her perceived immediate financial need for her college education. But what is the economic cost of obtaining Betsy's settlement money now? How much less than the one million dollars is an appropriate settlement? Are there alternatives for satisfying Betsy's immediate financial needs? If Betsy's economic need is not a strong incentive because alternatives exist to temporarily meet her college expenses, then Betsy's financial concerns will be a neutral factor in her wanting to settle the case.

To appropriately answer these questions, you might consult with an expert, such as an accountant specializing in economic evaluations, and structure alternative settlement solutions that consider the circumstances of your client. For instance, an accountant might propose a structured time payment schedule purchase of an annuity, investment opportunities, availability of short- or long-term loans, and so on. You will also discuss alternative solutions with Betsy for meeting her financial needs, other than the necessity for a quick, but substantially reduced, settlement (loans, short-term investments). Negotiation thus also partly involves counseling your client.

In addition to Betsy's incentives to settle, you need to understand Amber's incentives to negotiate and settle. That can be best understood by taking off your shoes and putting on Amber's. The facts suggest that, as a new business, dependent on word-of-mouth by

---

2. The effect of incentives on settlement is graphically illustrated in collective bargaining. To illustrate, suppose you represent a labor union in collective bargaining that is seeking a 20 percent wage increase. You know that the union is committed to strike if it does not obtain its demands during collective bargaining. (The union members have voted affirmatively for a strike, there are adequate strike benefits available, the morale of the union is high, the union has a good public image, and the employer will suffer financial hardship if there is a strike.) Those facts (considered, of course, with other variables) might help to justify setting a high optimum parameter, the 20 percent wage increase. Of course, if the employer will not suffer from a strike at all, the strike factor might provide little incentive for the employer to accept the union's 20 percent wage increase in collective bargaining.

satisfied customers, Amber potentially has a great incentive to settle in order to avoid adverse publicity. Amber's incentive to settle will affect its willingness to negotiate and its owner might be more likely to agree to a solution close to Betsy's optimum.

Adversary's Needs

The more your negotiation solutions reflect your adversary's interests and needs, the more likely your adversary may find the solution acceptable. In order to propose solutions that meet your adversary's needs, you clearly need to be familiar with your adversary's needs and interests. Although you could evaluate your adversary's needs when you evaluate your own client's needs, we have analyzed them separately from our client's needs. This ensures that they are properly and extensively considered. Think about what will make your proposed solution acceptable to Amber. Examining your solutions, ask:

- Do these suggested solutions reflect any of Amber's needs or interests?

- Is there a way to express or present Betsy's solutions in a manner that achieves Betsy's objectives and also takes into account Amber's needs?

One of Amber Ski Lodge's primary needs is to preserve the anonymity of any settlement so there will be no adverse publicity. You might consider as part of your proposals a suggestion that the settlement will be confidential. Or you might propose a solution that takes into consideration Amber's cash-flow problems (gradual payments instead of a large lump sum).

You have now analyzed the categories of information that could affect your optimum solution. You can now tentatively set the optimum solution you think you should advocate. It may be higher or request more than any of the precedents that guided you because it represents your optimistic view of what you think is the best you can obtain for Betsy. Or you may decide, upon reflection, that only one position, your client's optimum solution, would be acceptable as a negotiated settlement. However, be aware that almost never will your adversary accept your first and only suggestion or demand of how to settle the dispute, even if it is reasonable and persuasive. In our illustration, there is clearly more than one proposed solution, because as we considered information optimistically, we also noted flaws in our analysis. However, let's suppose that the appropriate optimum solution is one million dollars (the highest jury verdict awarded), which will be a confidential settlement.

QUESTION 5
What is the significance of this information in setting the least, but still acceptable, solution?

Having formulated an optimum solution, you can now consider the least, but still acceptable, solution for your client. The least acceptable solution is the worst possible result that your client should agree to accept as settlement of the dispute. This bottom position defines the boundary where you will tentatively abandon negotiation. The least, but still acceptable, result is the BANTA, the Best Alternative to a Negotiated Agreement, a principle discussed by Fisher and Ury in *Getting to Yes*. Fisher and Ury suggest the least but still acceptable result can be determined by comparing the negotiated settlement with other alternatives (including no settlement). If the bottom is worse than any other alternative, then it is not an acceptable position.

In determining the bottom position, you want to know how far down you should set your lowest objective. The weaker Betsy's case, the less you may be able to attain if you pursue other alternatives. Your adversary may be aware of these weaknesses and be willing to settle only for your bottom position. Therefore, you need a plan to determine your least but still acceptable result. (You may find that when you actually negotiate, this bottom position may be raised or lowered if different information is revealed or your adversary persuasively provides you with a different perspective.)

To determine your client's least but still acceptable solution, you will do the same analysis of information that you used in determining the optimum solution. However, now you are considering (1) how these factors weaken your client's position; (2) how they affect what your client is willing to accept; and (3) the consequences of not settling. The analysis in this section is simply illustrative of our approach, not exhaustive. If we were to do a complete analysis, we would evaluate many more factors than just these.

Weakness in Case

The weakness in your client's case is determined by considering the most pessimistic view of the law, the facts, and the incentives, which, conversely, is also the most optimistic view of your adversary's position.

Your most pessimistic interpretation of the leading case, *Fletcher v. Ryan*, is that potentially Betsy might be 40 percent at fault. You base your view that Betsy could be found comparatively negligent on the possibility that a court could interpret the phrase "direct evidence" in the *Ryan* case as encompassing more than just eyewitness testimony (e.g., "direct" physical evidence). You base your view of the percentage of comparative fault on jury trial verdicts in three cases, all similar to Betsy's, that found plaintiffs 20-40 percent at fault. The most pessimistic legal precedent is that Betsy's settlement may be as minimal as $200,000 if you compare Betsy's case to the boating accident case, *Ryan,* which presented similar circumstances.

Let's review the facts. Although Betsy will be a strong key witness, your expert witness testimony is weak. Betsy also has a strong incentive to settle. She has rejected all other alternatives that would meet her immediate financial needs. She insists she needs the settlement money immediately for her college education.

Reviewing Amber's position in the most optimistic manner, you believe that Amber, although wanting to settle, might not be very anxious to settle except for a minimal amount (Betsy's bottom position). You base your belief on its financial position. At the present time Amber will be unable to pay a lump sum damage award above $200,000 (its insurance coverage for liability) because of the cash-flow problems. You also do not believe Amber has much fear of having to make a public apology as the result of trial, because that is not a remedy that a judge would order.

Acceptability to Client

Now consider whether Betsy would accept the bottom. Would she benefit? You need to determine how important three aspects of Betsy's needs are—the [apolo]gy, her immediate financial need, and the amount [of dam]ages. For instance, if Amber refuses to apologize [or a]dmit responsibility, would Betsy accept a settlement? If a damage settlement were structured to meet Amber's immediate cash-flow difficulties ($250,000), would that be acceptable to Betsy? How much money does Betsy need immediately?

Alternatives

Before "setting the bottom," explore the consequences of walking away from the negotiation. In some instances, either Betsy or Amber might want to accept a negotiated settlement that does not achieve anything either client wants because the alternative—no settlement at all—is less preferable than continuing the dispute.

Ask the questions, "What consequences will Betsy suffer if she does not accept the bottom position?

What, if any, result would be possible to attain by pursuing other alternatives? Will Betsy lose and, if so, how much, by negotiating? Do I feel comfortable advising Betsy to accept the bottom as a solution?" To answer these questions, consider Betsy's alternatives if you do not accept a negotiated settlement.

Betsy can pursue litigation. Consider how likely is it that Betsy will prevail at trial. If you predict that you reasonably may lose at trial, then you might (if your client agrees) settle at any cost. In Betsy's case, losing at trial is not likely. Rather, the litigation risk is that Betsy might be found 40 percent at fault. You believe a judgment may be as low as $250,000. How likely is it that if Betsy prevails at trial, the judge would order Amber to apologize? Not likely, since it is not required by substantive law. If the case is litigated, when would be the soonest Betsy would obtain a judgment? You estimate three years if no appeal, and, if a successful appeal grants Amber a new trial, perhaps as long as seven years. What is the impact on Betsy's financial needs? Her monetary problems can be solved by other means such as financial loans. Evaluating all the factors, weighing the risks, assessing Betsy's needs, you believe "the bottom" you would recommend to Betsy would be a settlement of approximately $250,000, consisting of $200,000 (the limits of the insurance policy) to be paid immediately and $50,000 paid by Amber (structured to meet Amber's needs). Anything less, you will advise Betsy to "walk away."

QUESTION 6
Is the tentative range of solutions persuasive and creative?

In order to be persuasive, the range of solutions should be based on information that rationally supports each proposed solution. In our approach, the proposed solutions are based on our consideration of relevant information.

Your solutions should also be creative, presenting alternative ways to resolve the dispute. Creative and innovative solutions, which present your adversary with alternatives that meet client needs, present a greater likelihood of being considered acceptable.

For example, if Amber has a cash-flow problem and could not afford to pay an immediate lump sum, do your proposals consider Amber's needs creatively? A possible solution that meets Amber's needs might be a delay in paying a lump sum. Does that meet Betsy's needs? It might, if Amber paid sufficient interest. Or perhaps you could suggest that Amber pay all or part of Betsy's college education now as part of the settlement and Betsy would agree to a delay in receiving the remaining amount of the settlement.

We know that Amber wants to avoid adverse publicity. Can you creatively respond to Amber's need? Suppose Betsy's Aunt Shirley owns a local supermarket. Is Aunt Shirley willing to provide free advertising and publicity for Amber Ski Lodge by distributing Amber Ski Lodge circulars? Hanging Amber Ski posters near a ski food display? Subsidizing a free lift ticket contest for Amber? How do you think Amber would react to Betsy's proposals if coupled with Aunt Shirley's free advertising and publicity? Such solutions require familiarity with both clients' needs and interests. These needs have to be planned for and factored in with other considerations when you set Betsy's bargaining range.

QUESTION 7
What is the tentative bargaining range?

Now consider the tentative range between your optimum and bottom solutions. The range is a matter of judgment because you must decide how much each flaw or weakness adversely affects your optimum solution. How important is it that the expert testimony is weak? Does this weakness substantially affect your ability to prove liability? Or is such testimony important to proving liability and might it affect the strength of your case, justifying a lesser objective? How much weight should be given to legal precedent such as jury verdicts? If jury verdicts in the jurisdiction range from one million dollars to $250,000, does that justify a bargaining range from one million to $250,000? Can the range be logically applied to Betsy's case? Should you decide the range by assigning mathematical values to each weakness in Betsy's case that increases her need to settle?

Or is the most important factor for determining Betsy's range the incentive Amber has to settle? The more incentive for Amber to settle (for example, because Amber's attorney believes Amber would lose more by litigating—financial loss, adverse publicity), the more optimistic Betsy could be in setting her top parameter and a range close to that top. Amber, if highly motivated to settle, will probably be willing to accept a solution close to Betsy's top parameter. Likewise, the less incentive there is for Betsy to settle, the more she can hang tough and set a high optimum range. Therefore, your range will be set close to your top parameter.

D. PLANNING A NEGOTIATION PERFORMANCE: AN APPROACH AND ILLUSTRATION

It is now time to examine how you will actually negotiate. Performance depends on many factors: the subject matter of the dispute, the people involved in the negotiation, your personality and philosophy, and the accuracy of your prediction as to your adversary's use of particular tactics.

We have found it helpful to structure a performance strategy by referring to eleven questions. The focus of our approach is to use ends-means thinking: consider your objectives, anticipate and respond to your adversary's performance, and plan a strategy. After planning, consider preparing a written performance plan based on your tentative performance strategies. Then role-play those strategies so you will be familiar with the possible result from your tactical choices.

Planning

1. What are your negotiation performance objectives?
2. How will you discuss negotiation proposals?
3. What kinds of tactics, issues, or problems might occur in any negotiation?
4. What tactics should you use?

Analysis

5. As to each potential tactic, what are the benefits and risks?
6. What ethical issues should you consider?
7. Are the tactics realistic and helpful?
8. What tactics do you anticipate that your adversary might use in negotiation?

Strategy

9. How will you respond to your adversary's anticipated tactics?
10. What is your tentative negotiation strategy?
11. What follow-up to negotiation should be considered?

Imagine that you are Ann Singer, the attorney representing the defendant, Amber Ski Lodge, in the ski accident case. You have been retained by Amber's insurance company as counsel. You are scheduled to meet with plaintiff's counsel next week.

Plaintiff's attorney, J.M. Rush (known as JMR), sent you a demand letter for one million dollars, documented by $50,000 in medical bills and an economic loss report claiming $150,000 in lost income. JMR then telephoned you to see "if we can work out a settlement." Amber is most anxious to settle and has approved a tentative range to $300,000 ($100,000 in excess of the policy limit), if the settlement can be confidential and paid in installments. Amber's insurance company and Amber, however, would like to settle for less than the policy limit of $200,000. You believe there is an excellent chance to prove that Betsy was 40 percent at fault. You have located an eyewitness (thereby satisfying any interpretation of the *Ryan* case) who will testify, "Just before the cable broke I saw Betsy standing up in the cable car and leaning over the side."

Let's begin applying our approach. However, keep in mind as you read our performance strategy that our illustrations are intended to walk a middle road favoring neither a positional nor a principled bargaining philosophy (see page 388). We are providing you only with a coherent structure. Eventually, as you practice, you will have to choose the philosophy, or mix of philosophies, to apply within this structure.

QUESTION 1
What are your negotiation performance objectives?

As Amber's attorney you wish to persuade plaintiff Lash's attorney to settle the dispute within the insurance policy limit and to avoid adverse publicity for Amber Ski Lodge and the emotional strain of a trial for Mr. Amber, the owner. A secondary and complementary objective is to obtain as much evidentiary information from plaintiff's attorney as possible in case the dispute does not settle and you are forced to go to trial. In particular, as Amber's attorney, you want to know how plaintiff intends to refute Betsy's negligence.

QUESTION 2
How will you discuss negotiation proposals?

In formulating a performance strategy you need to consider how you will persuade your adversary to adopt your client's proposed solution. One method of approaching this task is to plan your presentation in the context of information that you have organized into a coherent theory that supports your proposals and distinguishes the weak points. In other words,

just as in all other aspects of your pretrial and trial work, an underlying theory provides the organizational framework for your discussion. We refer to this theory as a negotiation theory. Negotiation theory serves much the same function in negotiation as your case theory does in litigation.[3] When you negotiate, your theory provides the context for your negotiation discussion. Negotiation theory is relevant regardless of differing negotiation philosophies because it provides the basic context for organizing your objectives, interests, and solutions into cohesive and persuasive discussions to support your positions.

Thus your negotiation theory is a synthesis of information—client wishes, law, fact, and incentive information—that logically supports your range of solutions and distinguishes or explains the weaknesses. As such, your range of negotiation solutions and your negotiation theory constitute one interrelated strategy you will use in trying to persuade your adversary. Of course, as we will discuss later, you may have tactical reasons for not revealing some or most of the information supporting your theory.

To illustrate how negotiation theory is used in both criminal and civil negotiation, we present two examples. Although we will detail the parallels and differences between civil and criminal negotiation at the end of this chapter, let's consider briefly the negotiation theory in the criminal context. Imagine that you represent Carol, who has been charged with first-degree premeditated murder of Richard. You are going to meet with the prosecutor to try to negotiate a plea for Carol. Your proposed solutions range from dismissal based on justifiable homicide (self-defense) to willingness to accept a plea for voluntary manslaughter. Carol's optimum solution, dismissal because the killing was justifiable homicide, is based on the following supportive information: Carol has no prior criminal record; the killing took place after Richard threatened to kill Carol; Richard's police record documents prior incidents of brutality toward Carol; Carol's voluntary confession states that she believed when Richard awoke he was going to kill her. But you also have an alternative proposal, a plea to manslaughter, because of two weaknesses in Carol's information: (1) The killing took place six hours after Richard's threat and (2) there are no witnesses to Richard's threat to kill Carol on this occasion.

---

3. Negotiation theory could be seen as analogous to the factual theory and the bargaining range developed for the content of your negotiation could be seen as analogous to the legal theory. Though theoretically justified, we don't believe this view reflects the realities of negotiating or those of the structure we provide.

In presenting Carol's proposal of justifiable homicide, you will present information to persuade the prosecutor to find the killing justifiable and dismiss (or, at least, begin to move far away from first-degree murder). You might argue the killing was justifiable because Carol had a reasonable fear that Richard would act on his threat and kill her. When Richard advanced toward Carol, she fired in self-defense. Firing five shots indicates her unpremeditated, shocked reaction. (Here you will have attempted to deal with an apparent weakness—five shots, after all, are a lot of shots for self-defense.) Carol's prior documented injuries show Richard's brutality and justify her reaction. As mentioned, Carol has no prior criminal record. Incidents of prior brutality by Richard, coupled with Richard's death threat to Carol and Carol's fear of Richard killing her, justified her conduct. The legal theory, policy arguments, and factual information form the basis of Carol's optimum proposal, justifiable homicide. The melding of this information into a coherent whole is your negotiation theory guiding discussion of your proposals.

To illustrate negotiation theory in a civil context, let's examine our hypothetical ski accident. Suppose that Ann, Amber's attorney, wants to persuade Betsy Lash's attorney, JMR, to adopt Amber's optimum proposal, $50,000.

The $50,000 optimum solution represents Ann's most optimistic evaluation of Amber's case. (The $50,000 was derived by calculating 20 percent of Betsy's medical expenses, loss of earnings, and pain and suffering.) Ann optimistically believes that Betsy was 80 percent negligent. She bases her evaluation on four specific pieces of information: (1) An eyewitness who will testify that Betsy was leaning out of the cable car shortly before the accident occurred; (2) Lash's expert witness failed to affirmatively state in his deposition that the cable was defective or in need of repair; (3) legal precedent, a jury verdict award, supports 80 percent contributory negligence (in a similar case involving a boating accident, the jury found plaintiff 80 percent at fault); (4) the insurance company doctor, Dr. Nancy, after examining Betsy, stated in her report that she does not believe Betsy was seriously hurt and might even be malingering.

These four specific pieces of information can be used as a basis to argue Amber's $50,000 optimum proposal:

> "Well, JMR, I think you know the strong and weak points with your case as well as I do. Liability is not clear-cut. In fact, Betsy's case is similar to that boating accident case in Kitsap

County where the jury found plaintiff 80 percent at fault. It is evident that Betsy might be at fault. Eyewitness and expert witness testimony support that position. But even supposing that liability is found against Amber, damages are not strong. As you know from our insurance company doctor's report, Ms. Lash's injuries do not appear serious. Dr. Nancy even states she believes your client is malingering. Now tell me, what does Betsy want?"

QUESTION 3
What kinds of tactics, issues, or problems might occur in any negotiation?

In addition to advocating your proposed solutions in discussions that are guided by your negotiation theory, information can be tactically presented. Tactics are the techniques you will use to persuade your adversary to accept your proposed solution to the dispute. For instance, in initiating the process toward your proposed solution, there are many techniques for commencing negotiation discussions—making an offer, not making an offer; making a high or low offer; communicating in writing or verbally; and verbally tying the offer to other issues. There are ways of communicating the offer, such as "This is our first and last offer," "This offer is available for the next 30 minutes," or "This offer is negotiable." There is also a wide range of tactics to choose from when actually engaging in the interaction of negotiating. Tactics that can help persuade may range from things that superficially appear to be inconsequential nuts-and-bolts matters (seating arrangements for the negotiation meeting), to those that appear to be near the crux of the negotiation (how or when you might make an offer). You need to be aware of the kinds of tactics you can select, how a particular tactic might be used, and whether it will help or create problems in negotiation.

For your use and convenience, we have roughly classified tactics into five areas. These areas present frequent negotiation tactics that you might encounter in any negotiation session. As you can imagine, this grouping is not exhaustive but rather presents some common tactics you can consider (and anticipate) when planning your negotiation performance strategy. Later we will discuss our approach for selecting tactics.

Area One
Interests, offers, counter-offers, concessions

In every negotiation each party must find out what the other party wants. Each side might have a general understanding because of prior contact—a demand letter, a pleading, a telephone discussion, and so on. However, even if both sides have an understanding of the issues to be negotiated, each will need to discuss its objectives with particularity. How and when you and your adversary communicate your respective proposals presents important tactical choices:

1. Should you begin negotiating by discussing interests or by making or responding to a demand? (*Interest:* "I think we have a mutual interest in purchasing and selling this house by December 31st." *Demand:* "My client wants $100,000 for the house.")

2. If you decide to discuss interests, when should you communicate your interests? (Before pleading? After? After discovery is completed? Before filing a summary judgment motion?)

3. Should you make the first demand? ("The price is $100,000.")

4. Will you tie your demand to other issues? ("I'm willing to offer you $100,000, if you pick up the repair bill for the roof.")

5. Should you refrain from making any demand and wait until your adversary makes a demand? ("Tell me what you have in mind as the purchase price.")

6. How do you maintain firmness on a non-negotiable point and still negotiate? ("I'm sorry, but I can't sell for less than $99,000. Let me explain. . . .")

7. Should you make a counter-offer? When? ("I think a fair price is $90,000.") Or will you be patient and wait for a new proposal?

8. If your adversary rejects your offer, should you make concessions? What concessions will you make? Why? ("I can see your point; I'd be willing to come up a bit from $90,000.")

9. Will you make concessions according to or contrary to your negotiation plan? Generally, you will try to adhere to the negotiation proposals you prepared when planning the content of your negotiation. But there are circumstances that could occur that will compel you to alter or abandon your plan. For instance, during the negotiation you might learn from your adversary critical information you did not have, or that you relied on incorrect information to formulate your range of solutions. Either of these circumstances might make your negotiation proposals incomplete, illogical, unreasonable, or inconsistent.

10. If you make the last concession, should you make another? What will you gain? What will you lose?

Area Two
Exchange of information

When you negotiate, you will be making tactical choices about the information that you give and the information you want to receive. These choices will include considering the kind of information you will reveal or seek, how much information you will reveal or seek, and when you will reveal or seek it.

During negotiation, you will be concerned with persuading your adversary to accept your client's solution. To persuade your adversary, you will in all likelihood discuss your negotiation theory—client needs and interests and factual, legal, and incentive information that supports your client's or refutes your adversary's position. You will need to consider tactically how much of your negotiation theory to reveal. Some of the legal, factual, and incentive information may be known by your adversary. Other information may be privileged communication under the attorney-client or work product privilege.

For instance, suppose you are trying to persuade your adversary to settle. An analytical and factually documented discussion specifically relating how witness testimony and documents support your client's position is more persuasive than a general unsupported discussion. Does that mean you should tell your adversary about an eyewitness (who is presently unknown to your adversary) who will testify favorably on your client's behalf? The information could benefit your adversary if the case is litigated. Information that is learned during negotiation is generally inadmissible as evidence at trial. Nevertheless, information such as credibility of witnesses or interpretation of law may help your adversary prepare for trial. On the other hand, you want to be persuasive. You will have to make a tactical choice.

Or perhaps your negotiation objective is to obtain information from your adversary. Tactically, how will you accomplish this objective? Will you tell your adversary confidential information so she will give you information? But what will you do if she doesn't trade information? Will you directly ask questions if she doesn't volunteer information? (Should you ask, "Why do you believe your client has a strong affirmative defense?") The very act of asking questions reveals information. Do you want to show that you do not know the answers to these questions?

Area Three
Pressure tactics

During a negotiation many things can occur that could affect its success. For instance, your adversary might refuse to take your objectives seriously; negotiation could bog down; discussions could focus on tangential issues; your adversary may offer slightly below the amount your client said she would accept; or your adversary might threaten to walk out after you discuss your optimum solution.

You might be able to deal with these or similar situations by using pressure tactics. Pressure tactics include "carrot" or "stick" techniques intended to influence action. Should you use the carrot, that is, provide an incentive? Or should you use the stick, that is, provide a deterrent? For instance, incentive pressure tactics can be used to persuade your adversary to take your client's solutions seriously. ("Ginger, if you agree to this proposed solution, I'm sure John will be agreeable to ship with your company on an exclusive basis.")

Or you might use a deterrent pressure tactic if negotiation becomes unproductive and you want to rejuvenate discussion. You might pressure your adversary by stating, "I will litigate this matter" or "I am walking out" or "This is my best offer" or "I have only one hour to discuss this matter; I'm due in court at 3:00 P.M."

Pressure tactics are useful to focus discussion if your adversary becomes irrational or obnoxious, or if you and your adversary are too far apart. In such cases, you might even want to consider discontinuing negotiation. In a sense, this ability to walk away (perhaps until another day) is your greatest power in negotiation. (It surely may be preferable to abandon negotiation when compromise is resulting only in your making concessions you don't want to make.) Pressure tactics can help you conclude negotiations. You

may want a graceful exit so negotiation may resume at a future date ("I'll think about our discussions . . .") or you can suggest a cooling off period ("Let's get together in two weeks and discuss the matter of damages"). Or you might want to abruptly close the door because you believe a "take it or leave it" tactic may precipitate your adversary into making a better offer in the future.

Your adversary will also be choosing and using pressure tactics to persuade you, focus discussion, end discussions, and so forth. You will need a plan for how you can and will respond if your adversary threatens to walk out, litigate, or even call the press. We discuss this aspect of negotiation later in this illustration.

Area Four
Nuts-and-bolts matters

Nuts-and-bolts matters present tactical opportunities to influence negotiation. The list of nuts-and-bolts matters that can help or hinder your obtaining the client's objectives is lengthy. Typically, you could be concerned with such matters as seating arrangements—will you or will you not face a door (or a client, a window, the sun, a clock); the setting for the negotiations—your office, your adversary's office, the courtroom; the people who will be present—judge, attorneys, clients, third parties; authority to settle—total or limited; timing—possibility of interruptions, time of day for negotiation, amount of time designated for meetings; method for recording the meeting—notes, tape-recording, videotape; and the method for drafting the agreement—one party writes the first draft, both parties draft it together.

You may find yourself negotiating nuts-and-bolts matters before you negotiate the substantive issues in dispute, or you may find when you actually negotiate that many of these nuts-and-bolts issues do not present any particular problems. Nevertheless, you still need to be prepared with a tentative plan to deal with any such issue if it should arise. Otherwise, you might react haphazardly to the issue if it suddenly arises in negotiation and adversely affects your client's objectives.

A nuts-and-bolts matter that frequently is itself the subject of negotiation is the agenda. Typically, the agenda can influence the outcome of negotiation. Some issues are more easily resolved than others or may be disposed of more favorably for one of the clients; consequently, you and your adversary may differ as to which issues or sequence of issues to discuss. For example, before negotiating, do you have a strategic plan as to the issues you want to negotiate and their sequence? Tactically, how will you implement this strategic plan (i.e., agenda)? Assuming you have a strategic plan, tactical implementation might be based on the following type of strategy: Consider the agenda that is most favorable to achieving your result. Anticipate the effect that alternative agendas may have on obtaining your client's objectives. Ask yourself how a different agenda could affect the ultimate result. How much? How little? What will be your reaction to your adversary's position on the agenda? Will you negotiate the agenda? Present options? What points, if any, will you compromise on the agenda? All? Some? None?

Area Five
Tactical games

Some matters that could, from hindsight, predictably influence negotiation may be difficult to anticipate because your adversary might play tactical "games." Some attorney negotiators view negotiation as an opportunity to use tactics that reduce negotiation to a game won by the person who achieves "power" by playing the most clever or disruptive game. As will be discussed, these games differ qualitatively from the types of tactics we have already discussed. You should be aware that this situation could occur and plan a strategy to deal with it. (You should also recognize that such tactical games, if played, might give a negotiator a poor reputation. And ultimately the tactical games may adversely effect the negotiator's ability to be an effective negotiator because of his or her reputation.) For example, you could anticipate many of the tactical choices we have already discussed and their effect on negotiation performance (seating arrangements, table size, the direction you are facing, the scope of your opponent's agency, inquiries such as "Pierre, are you authorized to settle this matter today?"). But could you predict that your adversary would try to affect your ability to negotiate by controlling the room temperature? Suppose that your adversary places you before an open window and cold air is blowing on you. That factor might adversely affect your ability to concentrate. How would you deal with this situation? Ignore the episode? Ask your adversary to close the window? Would you silently close the window? Move? What if your adversary refuses to close the window because, she claims, it is hot in the room? Will you argue? Try to compromise?

QUESTION 4
What tactics should you use?

Suppose that Amber's insurance company tells Ann, "settle this case, but try to keep the settlement as low as possible." Ann, as Amber's attorney, wants to plan how to begin negotiating. Let's examine how Ann can select tactics. Should Ann begin the negotiation discussion? Should Ann discuss mutual interests that Amber and Betsy Lash may share? ("I am willing to discuss your reasons for plaintiff's one million dollar demand.") Is it best to ignore plaintiff's offer of one million dollars? Should Ann respond with an offer? If Ann responds, is that a counter-offer? Should Ann discuss her case theory? Or should Ann use a pressure tactic? ("This is our final and best offer; take it or leave it.")

A few principles can guide Ann. Tactics must be effective for the circumstances and be appropriate to Ann's personality and advocacy style. With these principles in mind, Ann could use the "copy-cat" method. The copy-cat method can be helpful in selecting some suitable tactics and in eliminating others.

To obtain ideas as to the types of tactics to employ, Ann can review the five categories of tactical situations discussed in Question 3. She might first obtain specific guidance by talking with insurance defense attorneys. Generally, attorneys who represent certain types of clients often share similar advocacy styles and tactics. She can also talk to attorneys who have a reputation as effective negotiators and discuss tactics they use. In *Legal Negotiation and Settlement*, Gerald Williams, a researcher in the area of attorney negotiation, suggests that there are characteristic personality and behavior patterns attributable to good attorney negotiators. His research indicates some of the general characteristics that effective negotiators share. Generally, effective negotiators are highly experienced, ethical, honest, trustworthy, careful to observe the customs and courtesies of the bar, realistic, rational, analytical, and thoroughly prepared on the facts and the law of the case; they exercise good judgment about how and when to act with respect to information, are creative, versatile, adaptable, self-controlled, skilled in reading their opponent's cues, perceptive, and also effective trial attorneys. Although effective negotiators do not all use the same tactics, Ann might profit by examining her selection of tactics in light of the list of behavior characteristics effective negotiators share.

But sometimes law, procedure, or custom will provide more than just guidance to an attorney: They may also impose limitations on the use of tactics. Some jurisdictions require court approval before allowing settlement of cases involving minors, incompetents, or class actions. In negotiations with government officials, in a civil or criminal context, there may be institutional or office rules of procedure that dictate the selection of tactics. For instance, the government might have a policy of refusing to negotiate tort liability cases in which plaintiffs assert negligence claims based on the government's use of nerve, chemical, or biological warfare, or have a policy of refusing to plea bargain trespass to military installations, and so on.

Now, let's apply some of these principles and ideas to Ann's selection of tactics. The custom among defense insurance attorneys in the jurisdiction is to make low counter-offers. Ann has a few choices. Suppose we examine two tactics. She can begin with a low counter-offer. "We are willing to settle this case for $50,000. I have the check right here. . . ." Is Ann required by custom to make a very low counter-offer (i.e., she will suffer negative professional peer response if she doesn't)? Or is the custom merely guidance? Often, such unwritten codes of conduct, and the resulting expectations, make negotiation proceed smoothly. Is a low counter-offer strategically appropriate in Amber's situation? Since the counter-offer is rational and based on analytical information and can be explained by the facts and law of the case, it might be a tactic an effective negotiator would use.

Now suppose that Ann is tentatively thinking of beginning negotiation with a pressure tactic: "Either you have Lash accept this offer, or we go to trial." Ann, however, is an easy-going person. Applying pressure when unprovoked is not complementary to Ann's style. Nor will she feel comfortable using a pressure tactic that requires threatening or cajoling Lash's attorney. Ann's personality will probably help eliminate the use of a pressure tactic such as "this is our final and best offer," but some tactical choices might not evoke any preference based on personal style or comfort. These tactical choices might instead depend on the kind of behavior Lash's attorney might use.

Ann, after sifting through all the ideas she has obtained by the copy-cat method, tentatively is considering either of two strategies: beginning negotiation by making a reasonable, but low, counter-offer, or discussing the interests and needs of the clients.

QUESTION 5
As to each potential tactic, what are the benefits and risks?

Let's analyze the benefits if Ann as Amber's attorney begins the negotiation by discussing mutual interests,

rather than by making the counter-offer. (You can then do a similar analysis yourself imagining that she had started instead with the counter-offer.) A benefit to beginning negotiation with a discussion of the interests and needs of the clients is that positions might not harden and it might be more likely that an agreement will be reached. Beginning the negotiation might allow Ann to control the negotiation—discussion may be likely to center around Amber's interests and needs. Lash's attorney may have great respect for Ann if the offer or discussion of interests appears reasonable and will allow Ann to lead the negotiation discussion. These matters raise the issue of *negotiating image*, that is, whether Ann should make the first offer because it might make her appear to be a formidable opponent, one to be taken seriously. Ann, however, should be motivated by her negotiating image only insofar as that image helps her to achieve her client's objectives.

One risk if Ann proceeds with an interest discussion is that she might be informing Lash's attorney of her view of the case. (Of course, if Ann would have done so anyway, this may not be a negative.) If Amber's interests appear irrational, however, the esteem in the eyes of Lash's attorney may quickly vanish and Ann as Amber's attorney will appear weak and ineffectual. Or Lash's attorney, by learning about Amber's interests, might be able to use that discussion to obtain concessions from Ann.

Another difficulty that might occur: If it is customarily expected that Ann will make a counter-offer, but she does not, this might precipitate non-productive behavior in Lash's attorney—anger, bewilderment, and so on. Or Lash's attorney might believe that Ann is playing tactical games—and Lash's attorney could then do the same. For instance, negotiation can get sidetracked into a discussion of Amber's tactical game of refusing to present a counter-offer, thus causing both attorneys to negotiate who will begin the negotiation discussion. Any of these risks could be a negotiating disaster for Ann.

QUESTION 6
What ethical issues should you consider?

Suppose that Ann knows that the eyewitness who claims to have seen Betsy lean out of the cable car just before the accident occurred may not be available for a deposition or trial. Is it ethical for Ann to state the following during negotiation: "We have an eyewitness to the accident who can testify that just prior to Betsy falling out of the cable car, Betsy was standing up and leaning out the side"? Is this ethically all right because she does have a witness who *can*—it's just that the witness *won't*? Still, doesn't she know (and in fact intend) that this statement will be taken to describe a witness who will appear for trial? On the other hand, is it Lash's attorney's responsibility to ask, "Will the witness be available at trial?" In the same vein, when (if ever) must a party volunteer weaknesses in its position during negotiation?

Or suppose that Lash's attorney during negotiation threatens Ann: "If we don't settle this suit today, we will tell the prosecutor to investigate and prosecute your client's safety violations." Does the ethics of this threat of criminal investigation and prosecution depend on whether safety violations exist? The motive of the party? The affiliation of the attorney making the threat? (If the local prosecutor threatens criminal investigation or prosecution unless Amber settles, would this be unethical?)

As a negotiator you are selling a product, "the best deal" you can obtain for your client. To accomplish that goal, you will try to be as convincing as possible. You might exaggerate, belittle, selectively present information, or use incentives or threats to achieve your goal. However, the question nonetheless is what are the ethical boundaries in negotiating conduct? Just as with other pretrial skills, whether conduct is unethical is usually clear only when the most egregious ethical violations occur—dishonesty, fraud, deceit, misrepresentation. Attempting to murder the prosecutor if she does not agree to a suspended sentence is quite different from a civil litigant threatening to report a safety violation to a government official. (Jurisdictions vary on whether one may ethically use the threat of a criminal prosecution in a civil negotiation.)

In addition to consulting professional codes of responsibility and substantive law for guidance and mandates, you could consider whether the negotiation process itself is conducted fairly and achieves a fair result. In this regard, you might refer to Rubin, "A Causerie on Lawyer's Ethics in Negotiation," 35 La. L. Rev. 577 (1975). (Some would question if a "fair result" is of any importance in a negotiation where the parties will never deal with each other again, and would contend that getting the best they can for their client, fair or otherwise, is their only duty under our adversary system.) Generally, the adversary system acts to ensure that fair practices are used by each negotiator. Fair results, although not guaranteed, usually result when both negotiators negotiate sincerely.

The best ethical check and balance will be Ann's desire to maintain a reputation for using ethical practices in the jurisdiction in which she practices. She will thus want to maintain behavior that is fair and not misleading.

Therefore, even though Ann's failure to disclose the unavailability of an eyewitness (if not directly asked) might not be prohibited by professional rules of conduct, or actionable under criminal or civil law, issues of fairness and concern for reputation can define the ethical boundaries of Ann's negotiation performance.

QUESTION 7
Are the tactics realistic and helpful?

Ann tentatively plans to present a counter-offer for $75,000. To persuade Lash's attorney to accept the $75,000 proposal, Ann might want to exert some pressure. Suppose she decides to hint subtly that she is prepared to litigate the dispute. She plans to state:

> "Amber's desire is to provide Ms. Lash with a timely settlement. We believe we have a very strong case showing Betsy was at least 70 percent at fault. Of course, I can litigate this dispute; Mr. Amber, the owner, told me he isn't concerned if we have to litigate."

Is the subtle pressure of "Amber's willingness to litigate" an effective tactic? If the tactic is realistic and believable in relation to the circumstances of the negotiation and Ann's negotiation theory, it will be persuasive.

In this instance, Lash's attorney specifically may not know that Amber wants to avoid adverse publicity. But common sense would suggest that litigation would generate publicity as to safety concerns at the Amber Ski Lodge. Such publicity would most likely have a major adverse financial impact on Amber. Therefore, using a subtle threat of litigation as a pressure tactic might not be realistic and probably would not be effective.

QUESTION 8
What tactics do you anticipate that your adversary might use in negotiation?

Ann has heard from many attorneys that JMR Lawford, Lash's attorney, is generally obnoxious, argumentative, and bluffs as to his real position. Nevertheless, Ann plans to begin negotiation with the following opening remarks:

> "Good to see you, JMR. I'd like to discuss my client's interest in this case. As you can imagine, Amber has no desire to litigate this matter. Am I correct in interpreting from Ms.

Lash's remarks in her deposition that she would like an immediate settlement for financial reasons? As I see this negotiation, we have a mutual interest—arriving at a fair settlement. Correct? Now tell me what Ms. Lash's financial needs are."

Can you put yourself in Ann's place and predict how JMR might respond? If you are able to predict how your adversary might behave, you can tentatively plan which tactics will be most effective to counter your adversary's behavior. If your adversary then uses tactics in the actual negotiation that you thought he would use, you will be able to anticipate his pattern of offers and counter-offers and respond effectively. (You can also assess how close to a final solution of the dispute you might be by comparing what you thought your adversary might demand and what he actually requested, and considering points he might be willing to concede.)

Understanding the "type" of negotiator you will be facing will aid you in anticipating his or her likely tactics. Gerald Williams, in studying behavioral characteristics of attorney negotiators, "type-cast" negotiators based on behavior patterns ranging from the cooperative to the competitive type. The cooperative negotiator is described as being fair, objective, reasonable, logical, and willing to move from established positions. According to Professor Williams, the cooperative negotiator makes realistic opening positions, supports positions with facts, and is forthright. Generally, cooperative negotiators are friendly, trustworthy, and ethical; they are interested in a fair settlement, want to meet the client's needs, like to avoid litigation, and try to establish or maintain a good personal relationship with an opponent.

The competitive negotiator is dominating, competitive, forceful, tough, arrogant, and uncooperative. Generally, the competitive negotiator makes high opening demands, uses threats, is willing to stretch facts in favor of a client's position, sticks to positions, is parsimonious with information about the dispute, and appears to take a gamesmanship approach to negotiation.

Generally, negotiators who share similar behavior characteristics use similar negotiation tactics. Of course, a negotiator may exhibit all, some, or none of the characteristics of a particular type of negotiator. But it is more than likely that at least some of the behavior characteristics will be evident and the attorney will use some negotiation tactics that are characteristic of a behavior type. In fact, researchers have even identified different styles of reasoning and different ways of resolving problems based on gender differences. Should you consider different tactical

choices if you are negotiating with someone of the opposite sex?

Recall that, in preparing for negotiation, Ann obtained information about JMR's negotiation behavior. This preparatory information can help Ann predict and anticipate tactical choices that JMR might make. According to the data, JMR is obnoxious, argumentative, and bluffs his way through negotiation. Ann believes he is a "competitive-type" attorney negotiator. That in itself does not mean he is ineffective, since both cooperative and competitive negotiators can be effective. But JMR's style of bullying others (which on occasion can be a successful technique when confronting a negotiator who allows himself or herself to be intimidated) makes Ann think he might be ineffective. Ineffective competitive negotiators exhibit negative and irritating behavior. They are generally obnoxious, egotistical, hostile, intolerant, argumentative, demanding, bluffing, headstrong, and quarrelsome. This type of behavior would probably be labeled unacceptable and lead to failure in all human endeavors.

Generally, ineffective cooperative negotiators exhibit socially desirable traits (honesty, trustworthiness, courtesy), but lack the attitudes that effective cooperative negotiators have: They are not perceptive, convincing, analytical, realistic, creative, self-controlled, or versatile.

Ann, judging from her understanding of how competitive attorneys negotiate, anticipates that JMR will refuse to discuss their clients' mutual interests and needs; will stay firm on the demand of one million dollars; will be likely to present a counter-offer that is outrageously high and announce the offer as final; and probably will not readily exchange confidential information. Ann also believes JMR is likely to insult her client, try to obtain evidentiary information from her, and use threats as pressure tactics.

Ann is certainly correct to predict that JMR might be hesitant or refuse to reveal information during negotiation. As Amber's attorney, however, she believes that obtaining information is important, particularly if settlement does not appear to be likely.

QUESTION 9
How will you respond to your adversary's anticipated tactics?

Suppose that JMR begins negotiation by responding to Ann as follows:

"Well, Ann, I really do not know why we are here. I've got better things to do. Quite frankly, your client Amber is sitting on a time bomb of safety violations. His stinginess in making repairs amounts to a callous disregard for his customers. Not at all an attractive businessman! If I were you, I wouldn't bother trying to litigate this case. I'll give you my best and last offer. Discounting the *nuisance value* of this case if we have to go to trial, Betsy is willing to settle for $950,000."

How should Ann respond to JMR?

No surprises here—JMR reacted exactly as Ann anticipated. Ann will now need to evaluate which tactics will be most effective in dealing with JMR's anticipated performance in order to eventually achieve her client's objectives. She could use pressure tactics, that is, threaten to litigate. She could offer information as an incentive to obtain information. She could ask direct questions to obtain information, or be equally parsimonious and curtail which information she will discuss.

Ann must assess the benefits and risks of the tactics she might use. For instance, let's look at how she might respond to JMR's lack of information. If she volunteers information to JMR, it is most likely that JMR will not willingly provide information in turn. However, if the information she volunteers is not confidential, then the risks are not great, and her actions just might result in a more cooperative atmosphere. Threats will probably result only in JMR walking out. On the other hand, the risk of asking direct questions is also not great.

Although Ann may correctly predict the tactics that JMR might use, she should also be prepared that JMR, just like a chameleon, might change color and make different tactical choices than his previous behavioral pattern indicated. JMR could begin negotiation by stating:

"Well, Ann, I hope we can cooperatively negotiate a mutually agreeable settlement to this matter. Let me share with you Betsy Lash's financial needs. . . ."

Ann also should be prepared for the presence of team negotiators (one, for example, who plays the role of hardliner, the other easy-going) as yet another strategy for obtaining advantages during negotiation. Note the team of JMR and Dorian during negotiation:

JMR: I just couldn't recommend a settlement on that basis to our client. What do you think, Dorian?

Dorian: Well, I think we could arrive at a settlement close to our original offer. JMR and I will talk it over and be right back."

Deciding that the benefits outweigh the risks, Ann might respond to JMR's opening statement as follows:

"JMR, I sympathize with the number of cases you litigate. But why do you say Amber is an unattractive businessman? Let me share with you the following awards Amber has received for ski safety. Also, [dangling carrot] here are the bills for maintenance on the ski cables. As you can see, he has always had a reputable company on retainer. These bills are pretty substantial. I have many reasons to support my client's case. I am prepared to discuss our clients' interests and financial needs and cooperatively reach a settlement. Shall we begin our discussions?"

QUESTION 10
What is your tentative negotiation strategy?

Ann tentatively has two performance strategies based on two philosophies of negotiation. One is based on the interests and needs of the clients, the other is "positional" (see page 387). Ann feels more comfortable with an interest-based style. On the other hand, a positional approach might be more effective because of the negotiation style of Lash's attorney. In either case, Ann plans to be realistic: She will guardedly exchange confidential information if progress is being made with JMR, but, if there is a lack of meaningful progress, she plans to litigate. Ann will make her final performance strategy decision after meeting with Lash's attorney.

QUESTION 11
What follow-up to negotiation should be considered?

The last part of a negotiation performance concerns thinking about the conclusion to negotiation. Too often, negotiation ends inconclusively because negotiators are tired or disillusioned or even because they are elated. Therefore, let's consider planning based on three potential conclusions to negotiation: (1) You are close to a settlement; (2) no settlement is in sight; and (3) settlement has been generally agreed on. Remember, however, as in all of our discussion of negotiation, the following scenarios simply present ideas for you to consider; they do not present all the variables that are likely to occur.

Close to Settlement

JMR proposes, "Ann, I suggest we split the difference between our proposals. We aren't that far apart." Or JMR might propose, "If you increase those special damages by $5,000, we have a deal."

Such suggestions are typical. Ann must now consider her substantive plan and how she can deal with these proposals tactically. She might suggest, "JMR, let's go back to our last proposals. First, let's examine my last proposal; it is based on the following factors. . . ."

Ann may want to go back to her previous proposal because it was based on specific factors that made her proposal reasonable. JMR's latest suggestions, "splitting the difference" or "adding $5,000" to Ann's proposal, essentially are not reasonable proposals but rather reflect JMR's last-ditch effort to increase what appears to be Ann's last and final offer. But if Ann can return to her proposal, she might be able to persuade JMR that her proposal is rational, fair, and acceptable. Or she might convince JMR to drop his current compromise or propose a better deal: "OK, let's go with a 40-60 split between our proposal or a $2,500 increase and we have a deal."

Of course, Ann might not be able to convince JMR to change his "split the difference" or the "$5,000 increase." A number of different factors may influence JMR to hang tight—a belief that Ann will not walk away from the deal now, skepticism concerning Ann's reasons for rejecting his proposals, JMR's client instructions. In any case, Ann might have to take JMR's offer or formula if there is to be a settlement.

No Settlement

Or consider the second potential situation: Anticipating the possibility that no settlement will be reached, Ann might suggest a cooling-off period:

> "Let's meet again in two weeks. In the meantime, we can talk things over again with our clients. You might want to consider Betsy's need for financial support and my client can consider Amber's cash flow. Perhaps we can think about mutually beneficial proposals and meet again."

JMR might then agree, or suggest that a neutral third party act as a facilitator, or that the clients be present in follow-up negotiations, or that the parties should abandon negotiation altogether.

Settlement Agreed

Finally, consider that the attorneys have agreed on a settlement.

Following the negotiation, generally there are many things left to do (draft the agreement, then sign, file, or distribute it). Agreeing on who will draft the agreement can be an important part of whether the settlement will be finalized or even implemented. Being well aware of this, Ann might plan to keep progress notes of the discussion, thus making it more likely that she will be the drafter. She will want to consider all the things that will need to be completed in order to implement the settlement and plan how these will be accomplished before the negotiation discussions terminate. Who will sign the agreement? Is there a timetable for signature? Does the agreement need to be filed? Who will file it? What will be the format? Is there specific language that must be included or not included?

E. NEGOTIATION IN THE CRIMINAL PROCESS: PARALLELS TO AND CONTRASTS WITH THE CIVIL PROCESS

You have already been provided with a great deal of information about negotiation in a civil litigation context. An appreciation of negotiation in the criminal context (commonly referred to as plea bargaining) requires that you view the material you have already assimilated against a backdrop that will clarify both the similarities and differences between negotiations in the civil and criminal arenas.

1. Parallels

Criminal negotiation is *analogous* to negotiation in the civil arena in most major respects:

1. **In both arenas, you must initially decide whether to negotiate at all.** A prosecutor may have a variety of reasons for not negotiating, although some of the following reasons may seem inappropriate to many, including some prosecutors we know. A prosecutor's office may have a policy not to offer plea bargains in certain types of serious cases, or a particular case may have sparked such strong community feelings that a full public prosecution seems unavoid-

able, or a particular prosecutor may feel that the evidence in his or her case is so "open and shut" (and that there are no time problems in preparing for trial) that he or she might as well go to trial and get a "win" if the defendant will not plead guilty to the charges. A defendant, on the other hand, may have nothing to lose by going to trial (e.g., with any conviction—and a guilty plea is a conviction—the defendant will be deported, will have a probation revoked, or a suspended sentence imposed that is longer than the potential sentence of the current charge). Or the defendant may have everything to lose by not going to trial (e.g., it is imperative to the defendant to clear his or her name). In contrast, the defendant may have nothing to gain by going to trial. For example, the defendant may have no real defense and the trial judge, who will also pronounce sentence, will be angered by the waste of court time and the lack of contrition—especially if the court believes that the defendant presented a false story. Or the range of the sentence (and not a conviction) may be the real issue for the defendant, and counsel's time may therefore be better spent trying to influence the probation report, drafting a sentencing report, or preparing and putting on a sentencing hearing.

2. **In both arenas you must prepare for negotiation.** Preparation will involve reviewing relevant statutes and case law regarding available penalties and sentencing alternatives (e.g., diversion), learning the defendant's and victim's backgrounds, talking to other attorneys (about your adversary, about the sentencing policies of the institution of which your adversary is a member, and about the sentencing judge), and researching community services that could provide the basis for a sentencing alternative (e.g., half-way house, drug therapy program).

3. **In both arenas you must develop a plan for the substance of your negotiation.** In the criminal arena, planning for the content of your negotiation can also begin by your positing a "wish list" (which will likely be "dismissal of all charges" for the defendant, and "plead to all charges and seek the court's mercy" for the prosecution). Like its civil counterpart, this criminal negotiation plan can then be constructed by developing a hierarchy of positions, moving down along your wish list, that reflects an assessment of the potential risks and costs involved if the case is taken through trial, as viewed in the total context of the strengths and weaknesses of the respective case theories. The prosecutor may face risks such as a loss on his or her personal record, or the total escape from justice of a person he or she believes is guilty. A defendant may risk a longer sentence, the death penalty, the stigma of being convicted of a serious charge, increased legal expenses, the loss of a professional opportunity (e.g., when a felony conviction bars one from a profession and the defendant has been offered a misdemeanor plea), deportation, the trauma of having a case hang over one's head, the pressure of trial, the anticipation of trial publicity and the attendant embarrassment for one's family, or loss of a job (e.g., when a conviction will result in incarceration, but work furlough has been offered as part of a plea bargain). The positions that constitute this hierarchy, moreover, can take a variety of forms—charge bargaining, sentence bargaining, or a creative alternative.

As an illustration of these three forms that your positions may take, imagine a defendant has been charged with a house burglary. A conviction carries a sentence of five to twenty years, to be set by the trial judge. You could charge bargain: "My client will plead to a charge of the lesser included offense of second-degree burglary [one to five years] if you dismiss the house burglary." Or "my client will plead to a misdemeanor trespass." You could sentence bargain: "My client will plead to the house burglary charge if you agree, subject to approval of the court [attempting to involve judges in plea bargains is at least generally frowned on and in many jurisdictions is forbidden], that he serve the minimum five years . . . if you recommend a suspended sentence and probation . . . if you don't oppose our request for probation." Or you could seek a creative alternative, which will generally manifest itself as a condition of probation—restitution, treatment program, half-way house, community service, or civil compromise. These forms, of course, are not mutually exclusive. Restitution or a treatment program may be part of a bargain for a suspended sentence. Reduction to second-degree burglary may affect the sentence as well as the charge. (In fact, that may have been the whole point of the deal.) Charge bargaining may include striking of enhancements (extra penalties for using a weapon, prior convictions, and so on). These positions can be developed, moreover, with either "interest" or "position" bargaining approaches underlying their formation:

Defense Attorney: I want my client on probation after a short jail term.

Prosecutor: No way. I want your client in jail, off the streets.

Defense Attorney: Why do you want my client in jail?

Prosecutor: Because I'm sick of all the trouble he causes in this town. In jail, he'll cause no trouble.

Defense Attorney: What if we put him on probation and transfer the probation to another county? That way I'll get my probation and you'll get my client out of town.

Moreover, as in civil negotiations, the relative power of the parties (i.e., the ability to influence other parties to do as you wish) plays a role. For either side in the criminal process, trial is a risk, an unknown. There are so many contingencies at trial—the judge, the jury panel, how witnesses perform, whether the jury begins deliberation on a Friday or the day before a holiday—and the defense needs only one vote to hang the jury. Rarely can either side be sure of the outcome. As a result, cases taken to juries are generally characterized by the litigating attorney with the cautious label "triable," and rarely the confident label "clear winner." Within this context of risk, the prosecutor has two basic sources of power, both related to the element of risk. The prosecutor first can affect the risk through the interplay of three factors: (1) the merits of the plaintiff's position; (2) the prosecutor's skill; and (3) available time and money resources. The stronger the case theory, the better the prosecutor as an attorney, and the more time and money available to spend on the case, the more the risk shifts to the other side. Second, the prosecutor can *insure* the defendant against risk ("plead to the misdemeanor, which carries a six-month penalty, and you are insured that you will not face the ten-year penalty for the felony, which I will drop in exchange for your plea"). With the risk so great at the extremes—six months versus ten years—and the risk of trying even a strong case so difficult to calculate, this insurance policy is likely to be very tempting.

The defense also has two basic sources of power. The first is precisely analogous to the prosecution's ability to affect risk that is discussed above. The second does not come from anything unique to a particular defense or defendant. It derives from the current reality of the criminal justice system wherein neither prosecutors nor courts have sufficient resources for the task of trying all the cases that have been charged. As an institution, the prosecutor's office thus is often faced with the administrative need to negotiate the majority of its cases. This need of the prosecutor puts some power in the hands of the defense. (Although as discussed later, many public defenders feel a similar need.)

4. **In both arenas, you will employ ends-means analysis in relationship to your representational strategy.** For example, in assessing alternative tactics to achieve settlement, should you initiate negotiation or push to trial and wait for your opponent to make the first offer?

5. **In both arenas, you may gain peripheral benefits from the process.** Such benefits may include obtaining information about your opponent and your opponent's case. Rules of Evidence, however, generally bar the use at trial of statements that were made during the negotiation process. See, e.g., Fed. R. Evid. 408.

2. Contrasts

The ways in which criminal negotiation differs from civil bargaining are subtle, being principally attributable to four aspects of the criminal process itself:

1. **You are negotiating in a system where the substantive law is based exclusively on moral values.** Unlike the civil system where the allocation of economic resources between parties as compensation for harm is the central focus, dollars are not at issue in the criminal system. Rather, the criminal system is structured around an inquiry into the culpability of the individual allegedly causing harm. Does the defendant deserve punishment and, if so, how much? As a result, you will have few options (or, at best, a narrow range of options) available for bargaining in all but relatively minor criminal cases. Why? Because in substantive criminal law, intuitive community moral judgments (codified by the legislature) both establish categories bearing a criminal stigma of various magnitudes (robber, rapist, petty thief) and penalties roughly reflecting the relative culpability that the community attaches to each of those categories. In this realm, a rapist is not the same as a petty thief. They are of different categories, which cannot be mixed. They "deserve" different treatment according to some external community moral sense. Thus, while you might bargain a hundred-thousand-dollar civil case down to ten thousand dollars, you won't bargain a rape case for a plea to petty theft where there is credible evidence that the defendant raped the victim and then stole her gloves.

2. **You are negotiating in a system that is procedurally oriented toward protecting the innocent from governmental power.** The central theoretical inquiry in the process is whether the government can prove guilt beyond a reasonable doubt. How does this affect bargaining? This systematic focus on assuming "innocence" on the part of the defendant and requiring proof of "guilt" by the prosecution structurally places you at a point that is the mutually exclusive opposite of your adversary ("My client is innocent" . . . "Your client is guilty" . . . "You can't prove that beyond a reasonable doubt" . . . "Yes, I can"). You and your adversary will thus theoretically begin your bargaining at positions that are as far apart as possible.

3. **You are negotiating in a system where those participating are generally institutional players.** Except in relatively minor cases (where satisfaction of the victim or compassion for the defendant may come

into play), the nature of the prosecutor's office itself may be far more significant in bargaining than the perspective of the individual prosecutor who is handling a case. (Although there are prosecutor's offices where each attorney has complete authority to make his or her deals.) There are a variety of institutional possibilities that will affect negotiations with the prosecution.

The prosecutor's office may have a set of clear guidelines for reduction of charges or "standard deals" (e.g., first-time grand theft = one month in county jail, followed by probation with a suspended felony sentence). Such standardization may be motivated by a desire for administrative streamlining, a concern for equal treatment in the bargaining system, and a desire that plea bargaining reflect institutional policy and not individual discretion. Standardization can also be mandated by statutes that leave little discretion for the prosecutor once charges are filed, or require extensive proof before deviation from statutory standards is permissible. Bargaining in such an office will generally be limited to "take it or leave it" positions mixed with some discussion over the applications of guidelines. Prosecutors neither have clients nor depend on fees. Thus, cost of the trial process to the client or law office, which weighs so heavily in the calculus when negotiating in civil cases, will generally have no bearing in the criminal area. (Analogous situations may also exist when government attorneys are involved in civil actions.) Likewise, the prosecutor technically does not have to consider the emotional stress of trial on a client when negotiating (though, in reality, concern for a victim may be a significant factor in seeking to avoid trial).

Even in an office without standard deals, tacit institutional policies of the office will determine what the defense can offer in a negotiation that will be of value to the prosecution. Does the prosecutor's office have an overwhelming caseload, and so will try to bargain everything? Then, the defense can offer removing a case (which the defense will try to portray as "time-consuming and complex") from the prosecution's caseload in return for a good bargain. Does the office keep won-lost records? Then, the defense can offer to forego a substantial chance for victory (embodied in a good pretrial motion, a plausible case theory, or a good track record at prior trials) or offer to assist the prosecutor (e.g., provide the client's testimony against a co-defendant). Does the office focus its plea bargain determinations on an assessment of the individual defendant? Then, the defense can put together references, defendant's personal background, and future plans, so as to offer a portrayal of defendant's criminal conduct as idiosyncratic and unlikely to be repeated (if he gets, e.g., alcohol counseling). Does

the office focus its plea bargain determinations on the nature of the crime itself? Then, the defense can offer a perspective, say, that the case at hand was not "really" a burglary but instead the result of a lack of judgment in the heat of a scavenger hunt: The defendant was hungry, a little drunk, saw the cake through the kitchen window, and so on.

The prosecution, of course, is not the only institutional player in the system. Judges and most defense attorneys (public defenders) work within bureaucratic institutions. The courts face administrative realities. They do not have sufficient resources to provide jury trials to all those charged with crimes. Thus, while cost is generally not a concern in any one particular case, overall resources in the system are. Most court systems, accordingly, set an atmosphere where pleas are encouraged and jury trials discouraged. If a judge perceives that a party is failing to reasonably bargain, that party may risk subsequent unfavorable rulings and decisions in discretionary areas. The institutional framework of public defender offices will also affect negotiation. In many such offices, direction from institutional leadership, coupled with time and money resource constraints on the office (and the reality of the legal positions of many of the office's clients), may result in an institutional policy strongly favoring plea bargaining in almost every case. In such circumstances, the public defenders and the prosecutors with whom they deal daily will often develop an informal set of routine deals for various types of cases and defendants. In any event, both the public defender and his or her adversary will be well aware of the institutional constraints (as opposed to those inherent in the case theory) that bear on the defender taking a case to trial.

4. **You are negotiating in a system whose process is constitutionally circumscribed.** This has a number of specific ramifications. The defendant who pleads guilty must knowingly and freely waive the constitutional rights he is foregoing (e.g., cross-examination, trial) and must understand the nature and consequences of that to which he is pleading. The prosecutor is bound by promises made in a plea bargain. The prosecution must provide the defendant, prior to plea, with all evidence in the government's possession that is material to guilt or innocence or to penalty.

F. GENERAL PLANNING QUESTIONS

You have considered the various factors, and the rationales for each, essential to preparing for negotiation. Following is a series of general questions for preparing for negotiation.

I. *Preparation*

  A. *Deciding to Negotiate*

    1. Should you negotiate? (List the reasons.)
    2. What are the benefits of negotiation?
    3. What are the benefits of pursuing other dispute resolution? (Mediation? arbitration? litigation?)
    4. What are the risks of negotiation?
    5. What are the risks of pursuing other dispute resolution?
    6. How does negotiation fit into your representational strategy?

  B. *Obtaining Information*

  Client Information

    1. What information do you know or will you seek as to what your client wants?
    2. What does your client need?
    3. Are your client's wishes and needs realistic?
    4. What other information about your client will affect your negotiation?
    5. What information do you know or will you seek as to what your adversary's client wants? Needs?

  Facts About the Dispute

    6. What witnesses, documents, or other information will you need to negotiate?
    7. How and from whom will you obtain this information?

  Substantive Law

    8. What law will you research to plan negotiation (statutes, jury instructions, law reviews, cases, verdicts, settlements)?

  Incentive Information

    9. What non-economic factors will affect negotiation? (For your client, your adversary's client?)
    10. What economic factors will affect negotiation? (For your client, your adversary's client?)
    11. Can any of these incentive factors be quantified? If so, how?
    12. How will you obtain incentive information? (Client, other attorneys, court personnel, etc.)

  Adversary's Negotiation Behavior

    13. How will you obtain this information?
    14. What information did you obtain?
    15. Can you categorize what type of negotiator your adversary might be?

  Nuts-and-Bolts Information

    16. How will you obtain this information?
    17. What information will you obtain?

  C. *Preparing Yourself: A Frame of Mind*

    1. How will you use ends-means thinking?
    2. What specific things have you planned that are creative? (Use of information, proposed solutions, etc.)

II. *Planning the Substance of Negotiation*

    1. Generally, what are your negotiation objectives? (Your representational strategy?)
    2. What method will you use to determine the range of solutions you want to achieve in negotiation? (Optimum, bottom, parameters.)
    3. What information should you consider?
    4. What is the significance of the information to setting your client's optimum solution?
      a. How do your client's needs and wishes affect your client's optimum solution?
      b. How does the law affect your client's optimum solution?
        (1) Do case law or jury instructions support your optimum solution?
        (2) What legal precedent is a guideline for your optimum solution?
        (3) Are there any limitations on your optimum solution?
      c. How do the facts support your client's optimum solution?
      d. How do your client's economic incentives support your client's optimum solution?
      e. Do your client's non-economic incentives affect your client's optimum solution? How?
      f. How do your adversary's economic incentives affect your optimum solution?
      g. How do your adversary's non-economic incentives affect your optimum solution?
    5. What is the significance of the infor-

mation in setting the least, but still acceptable, solution?

    a. What weaknesses are there in your client's case (law, facts, incentives)?

    b. Is the least solution acceptable to your client?

    c. What are the alternatives to a negotiated settlement? Are they acceptable?

6. Is the bargaining range of solutions persuasive and creative?

7. What is your bargaining range?

III. *Planning a Negotiation Strategy*

1. What are your performance objectives? (Will the negotiation be based on interest bargaining? Positional? A combination of both? Some other theory?)

    a. List your interests in settling the dispute.

    b. List your adversary's interests in settling the dispute.

    c. What interests or points do you and your adversary share in common?

2. How will you discuss your negotiation proposals?

3. What kinds of tactics, issues, or problems might occur during negotiation? (Make a list.)

    a. Offers? (Who might make an offer, when, how?)

    b. Counter-offers? (Who might make a counter-offer, when, how?)

    c. Concessions?

    d. Exchange of information? (To what extent will you exchange information?)

    e. What kind of pressure tactics could be used? (Incentives, deterrents.)

    f. What kinds of nuts-and-bolts matters might affect your negotiation? (Make a list.)

    g. If your adversary engages in tactical games, how do you plan to respond? Why?

    h. What ethical issues or problems can occur?

4. What tactics should you use?

    a. Generally, what tactics can you use?

    b. Personally, how do you feel about using the tactic?

    c. What tactics do other attorneys use? Why?

    d. Does law, procedure, or custom limit the use of a particular tactic?

5. As to each potential tactic, what are the benefits and risks?

6. What ethical issues should you consider?

7. Are the tactics realistic and helpful?

8. What tactics do you anticipate that your adversary might use?

9. How will you respond to your adversary's (anticipated) tactics?

10. What is your tentative performance strategy?

11. What follow-up should be considered?

CRIMINAL PROBLEMS: STATE v. HARD

PROBLEM 127

Prosecutor: Negotiation
(Striking a Deal in Exchange for Jack Waters'
Testimony)

Jack Waters, who is currently in the county jail awaiting trial on charges of receiving stolen property, wants to talk to you about the Hard case. Waters has communicated through the police that he has information that will "nail" Hard. Waters, however, has an extensive record and is facing state prison if convicted of the current charges. Therefore, in return for his information and testimony, Waters has indicated that he wants complete immunity for the current charges "because I wouldn't live a month in prison if I snitched on Hard at trial."

PREPARATION

READ: (1) Pretrial Case File Entries 3-6, 9, 11, 16, 17, 19, 28, 58, 61, 62; (2) Chapter X; (3) Fed. R. Evid. 801. Now think about and answer the following questions:

1. Thinking generally, what is the ethical basis for trading Waters for Hard?

2. Now think about the role Waters could play in your case:

   a. How strong is your case without any information Waters may have? Why is this assessment important?

   b. Are there problems with Waters as a witness (1) even without a deal? (2) with a deal? Explain.

   c. Aren't you concerned that Waters would fabricate a story? What will you do about that concern?

   d. Assume that you do get Waters' story. Can you still get the statement into the case even if he subsequently denies he made the statement when he testifies at trial?

      1) How?

      2) Would you want to? Why or why not?

      3) What if he just says, "I don't remember making the statement"?

3. Now think about how you will get Waters' information:

   a. How can you find out if his information is worth anything *before* you make any deal?

   b. What if Waters says, "If I tell you my information, I've got nothing left to bargain with"?

   c. How will you answer his concern about going to prison with the reputation as a "snitch"?

   d. Would you tell him that now that you know he has valuable information:

      1) You will subpoena him and have him held in contempt if he refuses to testify, or charge him with perjury if he does not give incriminating evidence?

      2) You will get information "through the back door" to the judge in his receiving stolen property case that he is being uncooperative?

4. What, other than complete immunity, could you offer Waters in exchange for his testimony?

ASSIGNMENT FOR CLASS

1. Outside of class, plan for your negotiation with Jack Waters. Write a short memorandum summarizing your planning, preparation, and analysis, and give a copy to your supervisor.

2. In class, meet with Waters and negotiate for his testimony.

PROBLEM 128

Prosecutor: Negotiation
(Offer of Deal If Defendant Drops Motions)

The defense has filed a bundle of Constitution-based pretrial motions. Although you believe you would prevail, a first reading of these extensive papers reveals that the defense position is hardly without merit.

These motions, therefore, raise the specter of long hours of work for you, great inconvenience to your witness who may be shuttled back and forth between evidentiary hearings, and the real possibility you could lose the motions and, perhaps, the case with them. Accordingly, you are considering offering the defendant a plea if he pleads *before* the motions are heard.

PREPARATION

READ: (1) Pretrial Case File Entries 3-6, 9, 11, 16, 17, 19, 28, 58, 61, 62; (2) Chapter X. Now think about and answer the following questions:

1. You are basically asking the defense to drop its motions. Is this the proper basis for a deal?

    a. Are you ethically obligated to plea bargain?

    b. If not, why can't you say "bargain now, because there'll be no deal after the motions"?

2. What if you make the offer and the defense counsel says, "This is outrageous. You're trying to coerce my client out of his Fourth, Fifth, and Sixth amendment rights, the violation of which we are seeking to redress in these motions"?

3. What if counsel tells you that he or she will go to the judge?

4. What would you tell the judge if she asked about your offer?

5. Why would the defense accept your offer? Should they? Why?

6. Might the defense have brought these motions as part of a representational strategy aimed at doing just what is happening — pressuring you into negotiation? If you believe so, how will that perception affect your negotiation behavior?

ASSIGNMENT FOR CLASS

1. Outside of class, plan how you will approach offering this deal. Write a short memorandum summarizing your planning, preparation, and analysis, and give a copy to your supervisor.

2. In class, prosecutor and defense counsel meet and engage in negotiations over the prosecution's condition that any plea be resolved prior to a hearing on the pretrial motions.

PROBLEM 129

Defense Attorney: Negotiation
(Plea Bargaining)

The judge has denied *all* your motions. You just bumped into the prosecutor at the courthouse, and the prosecutor suggested that the two of you might explore a settlement together. While you still believe you have a very triable case, as a matter of thoroughness you must give some consideration to the possibility of plea bargaining. (Or such a plea may have been the objective of your representational strategy.)

PREPARATION

READ: (1) Pretrial Case File Entries 3-6, 9, 11, 16, 17, 19, 28, 58, 61, 62; (2) Chapter X. Now think about and answer the following questions:

1. Generally, what would motivate you to seek a deal in any case?

2. Why would you plea bargain the *State v. Hard* case? (I.e., what are your incentives to negotiate?)

3. Why would the prosecution plea bargain the *State v. Hard* case? (I.e., what are the prosecution's incentives to negotiate?)

4. What is the best deal you can reasonably imagine would be offered or agreed upon by the prosecution in *State v. Hard*? (I.e., what do you believe is the upper side of the prosecution's bargaining range from your point of view?)

5. What is the deal, if any, that you would advise Ed Hard to take? Explain the basis for your evaluation (e.g., your negotiation plan for your bargaining range).

6. Generally, should you initiate the plea bargaining, or is it better strategy to wait for the prosecution to make the first gesture? Explain.

7. Suppose that you decide to initiate the plea bargaining process. Think about tactics. Will you begin by making an offer or just suggest that you and the prosecutor sit down and explore the possibility of a settlement? Why?

8. What preparation would you make for plea bargaining discussions with the prosecutor (regardless of how they are initiated)?

9. Explain how your approach to these discussions would differ if the prosecutor's office is one that:

    a. Operates in a court system that holds the resolution of criminal cases by pleas as a high priority.

    b. Has an office policy of seeking to resolve as many cases as possible by plea bargaining.

    c. Keeps "won-lost" records from trials.

    d. Gives different deals to different defendants depending on their individual backgrounds.

e. Treats all similar offenses similarly for plea bargaining purposes, regardless of the individual's background.

10. Under which of the prosecutors' offices listed in Question 9 would you focus on the weakness of their case, or the strengths of yours? Under which would you focus on something else? What?

11. Suppose the prosecutor replies to your suggestion that you mutually explore a settlement by stating: "Why should I plea bargain; I've got Ed Hard on first-degree murder?" How would you respond?

ASSIGNMENT FOR CLASS

1. Outside of class, all defense attorneys meet and discuss the issues raised in this assignment in the context of plea bargaining. (All prosecutors do the same.) Prepare a short memorandum of your discussion. Hand in a copy to your supervisor.

2. In class, *one* of you meet with the representative of the prosecutor's office, and negotiate the case.*

3. Afterwards, evaluate your side's performance.

PROBLEM 130 _____

Prosecutor: Negotiation
(Plea Bargaining: Special Instruction to Prosecutor)

Plea bargaining is an integral part of our criminal justice system, and you have telephoned defense counsel and suggested that the two of you discuss settlement. As you now near the end of the pretrial process, you feel that thoroughness requires that you at least evaluate this option. Of course, even if nothing works out at this time, you can generally try again immediately before (or sometimes actually during) trial.

PREPARATION

READ: (1) Pretrial Case File Entries 3-6, 9, 11, 16, 17, 19, 28, 58, 61, 62; (2) Chapter X. Now think about and answer the following questions:

1. As a practical matter, why would you ever plea bargain a case?

2. How would you respond if someone said, "Prosecution plea bargaining is ethically suspect. Someone is getting better than he or she deserves—unless, of course, you overcharged or the case is weak—and then the case should be dismissed"?

3. What specific considerations go into:

   a. Whether you bargain?

   b. What you bargain for (your bargaining range)?

---

*Your instructor may require *each* of you to meet with a prosecuting attorney.

4. Would you bargain the Hard case?

   a. Why?

   b. What would you bargain for?

ASSIGNMENT FOR CLASS*

1. Outside of class, *all* prosecutors meet and discuss the issues raised in this assignment concerning plea bargaining the Hard case. (Defense attorneys do the same.) Write a short memorandum summarizing your planning, preparation, and analysis, and give a copy to your supervisor.

2. In class, *one* of you meet with the representative for defendant and negotiate the case.**

3. Afterwards, evaluate your side's performance.

PROBLEM 131 ——————————————————————

Defense Attorney: Negotiation
(Plea Bargaining: Special Instruction to Defense Attorney)

You have lost all your Constitution-based pretrial motions. Although you still believe that you have a triable case, you have decided to explore settling the case. Accordingly, you have just called the prosecutor and proposed a meeting to discuss settlement. The prosecutor agreed to the meeting.

PREPARATION

READ: (1) Pretrial Case File Entries 3-6, 9, 11, 16, 17, 19, 28, 58, 61, 62; (2) Chapter X.

Think about and answer the questions that appear in Problem 129.

ASSIGNMENT FOR CLASS†

1. Outside of class, all defense attorneys meet and discuss the issues raised in this assignment in the context of plea bargaining. (All prosecutors do the same.) Prepare a short memorandum of your discussion. Hand in a copy to your supervisor.

2. In class, *one* of you meet with the representative of the prosectuor's office, and negotiate the case.‡

3. Afterwards, evaluate your side's performance.

---

*Prosecutor: Your instructor will provide you with a special instruction.
**Your instructor may require *each* prosecutor to negotiate with a defense attorney.
†Defense attorney: Your instructor will provide you with a special instruction.
‡Your instructor may require *each* of you to meet with a prosecuting attorney.

CIVIL PROBLEMS: SUMMERS v. HARD

PROBLEM 132

Attorneys for Plaintiffs and the Major Gymnastic Club: Negotiation Concerning Bruno Summers' Salary and Other Compensation*

Bruno Summers was employed by the Major Gymnastic Club at a salary of $5.25 per hour, 40 hours a week, as a parking attendant. He worked for the club for one year and nine months, from December 1, 198X − 2 until he died on September 7, 198X. The Summers claim that the Major Gymnastic Club owes Bruno Summers money for past work performed and for vacation and sick leave. The attorney for the Summers family wrote to the Major Gymnastic Club (MGC) concerning the Summers' claim.

The basis of the Summers' claim is as follows:

(1) Bruno was not paid for six days that he worked, from August 28 to September 2, 198X.

(2) Bruno did not take any vacation while employed, nor was he paid for vacation time that he earned. During the first year, vacation accrued at one day per month with a bonus vacation day for working on Christmas day. (Bruno worked Christmas day in 198X − 2 and in 198X − 1). In the second year of employment, vacation accrued at one and one-third days each month. The Summers family claims the Club promised to pay Bruno a bonus vacation day for working on Christmas day, but did not. _[handwritten: 2 extra vacation days]_

(3) The Summers claim paid sick leave, which accrued at one half-day each month. Bruno took four sick days (September 4-7, 198X) but was not paid for them. _[handwritten: 4 sick days]_

(4) The Summers claim six days' salary, 26 days' vacation,** and 10.5 days' sick leave, totaling $1,785.00.

The Major Gymnastic Club responded:

(1) MGC owes Bruno Summers' estate six days' salary.

(2) MGC claims vacation does not accrue until the end of each year, _[handwritten: B.S.]_ therefore Mr. Summers did not earn vacation for January 1, 198X through September 198X. MGC admitted Bruno Summers was employed for the past two Christmas days but does not know of any arrangement to pay "bonus vacation days." The Club owes Bruno only twelve vacation days. _[handwritten: 14 1/3]_

(3) Sick leave is not paid if not taken. When an employee takes sick leave, the employee must return to work for at least one week. _[handwritten: B.S.]_

(4) The Club is willing to pay Bruno Summers' estate a total of $756.00. _[handwritten: 18 days (12 vaca. + 6 work) × $42/day = $756]_

Plaintiffs' attorney has suggested, and the attorney for the Gymnastic Club has agreed, that the attorneys meet and discuss their differences.

PREPARATION

[handwritten: Personnel Manual / EMPLOYMENT RECORD]

READ: (1) Pretrial Case File Entries 1, 2, 9, 36, 37, 47, 48, 59-61, 63, 81, 84, 89, 90; (2) Chapter X.

[handwritten: Employment records]

---

*Your instructor will inform you whether this negotiation occurs during the same time period that the wrongful death case, _Summers v. Hard,_ is being prepared for trial.

**Rounded off from 25.97 days.

Preparing for negotiation requires understanding your own and your adversary's position. Therefore, answer the questions by first assuming the role of plaintiffs' attorney and then the role of the MGC attorney.

1. What are your objectives in this meeting? Explain.

2. The Summers family is demanding $1,785 from the MGC. The MGC has stated that it is only willing to pay $756.

   a. Why are you meeting if both of your positions are known and divergent?

   b. Are there compromises you can reach? Explain.

3. Are there facts that support your position? Explain.

   a. What response do you expect from your opponent?

   b. What is your position if your opponent responds in the way you expect?

4. What role should the law play in your negotiation?

5. Will you use the law to support your position? Explain.

6. What legal arguments do you expect your opponent might respond with?

7. Suppose the Major Gymnastic Club is adamant about its position and refuses to compromise.

   a. List all the alternatives that are available to the Summers' attorney.

   b. Assess the advantages and disadvantages of each alternative.

   c. Select which alternative, if any, you would pursue if you were the Summers' attorney and explain why.

8. Suppose the Summers family refuses to compromise.

   a. List what action, if any, the MGC can take.

   b. Assess the advantages and disadvantages of each alternative.

   c. Select which alternative, if any, you would pursue if you were the MGC attorney and explain why.

9. Will you make the first offer? Why or why not?

10. Do you have a strategy if your opponent refuses to change his or her position? Explain.

ASSIGNMENT FOR CLASS

1. Outside of class, prepare a written negotiation plan for your side in this dispute. If you intend to use supporting documents in the negotiation session, list them. Hand in a copy of your negotiation plan to your senior partner.

2. In class, be prepared to discuss your negotiation plan.

PROBLEM 133

Private Attorneys for Gretchen and Hans Summers and for Deborah Summers: Negotiation Concerning Child Custody Dispute*

Since Bruno's first marriage ended in divorce six years ago, Gretchen and Hans Summers have been taking care of Amanda and Ronny Summers. Their natural mother, an alcoholic, disappeared six years ago. Her whereabouts are still unknown. While the children were with Hans and Gretchen, Bruno paid his parents approximately $250 per month child support. For the past year and up until the time Bruno and Deborah were married, the children spent their weekends with Bruno and Deborah. When Bruno and Deborah were married, the children moved in with them. Gretchen felt a great void in her life. She had cared for Ronny since he was two and Amanda since she was six.

When Bruno died, there was no question in Gretchen's mind that she would once again care for her beloved grandchildren. (Hans, however, expressed reluctance at such a long-term commitment to the grandchildren.) Gretchen was of the opinion that now more than ever, the children would need a firm hand. Gretchen believes that strict discipline molds good character—"spare the rod, spoil the child" is her adage. It was with great surprise, but with compassion, that Deborah accompanied the children to live with Gretchen and Hans.

Two months after Bruno's death, Deborah still did not give any indication that she had any plans for the future. Gretchen grew more irritable every day. Gretchen told Hans, "Surely, Deborah should think of going to work and move out on her own, or at least of going to her own parents." Just as things were beginning to turn a little nasty (financially and emotionally), the social security office telephoned Gretchen and Hans. The office informed them that if they intended to keep the children they could, by being designated the legal guardians, receive social security payments of approximately $300 per month for Amanda and Ronny.

Excited, Gretchen related the news to Deborah. But instead of being happy, Deborah blurted out:

> "I want the children! That's all that Bruno left me. The children's social security will help me pay the rent on a nice apartment. I may go to work soon, but then again I may not. Of course, if I get remarried, I won't have any financial problem to worry about. But I don't think I will for a while. And, besides, I like the kids."

Gretchen and Hans consulted a lawyer about obtaining custody of Amanda and Ronny. They have filed a petition for legal custody and a motion requesting temporary custody, naming as respondents Deborah and the natural mother.

Deborah moved out of the Summers' house. She consulted an attorney and filed a response to the custody petition, requesting that the court award temporary and permanent legal custody to her. An evidentiary hearing on the temporary custody is scheduled for November 1, 198X. The trial has been set for one month later.

---

*The attorneys representing Gretchen and Hans Summers and Deborah Summers in this child custody dispute are not the same attorneys as those in the *Summers v. Hard* case.

Your instructor will inform you whether this negotiation occurs during the same time period that the wrongful death case, *Summers v. Hard,* is being prepared for trial.

The attorney for Gretchen and Hans interviewed Ronny and Amanda to determine the wishes of the children.

Gretchen and Hans contacted their attorney and requested that their attorney meet with Deborah's attorney. They believe that if Deborah's attorney understands the full situation, an evidentiary hearing and the trial may be avoided. The attorneys have agreed to meet at the law offices of Gretchen and Hans Summers' attorney to try to settle the child custody dispute.

PREPARATION

READ: (1) Pretrial Case File Entries 1, 2, 33, 36, 37, 40, 41, 51, 55, 56, 59-61, 64, 79; (2) Chapter X.

Preparing for negotiation requires understanding your own and your adversary's position. Therefore, answer the questions by first assuming the role of Gretchen and Hans Summers' attorney and then the role of Deborah Summers' attorney, or as a specific question indicates.

1. The standard the court will use in deciding legal custody is "the best interests of the children."

    a. Are your client's objectives based on that standard? Explain.

    b. What should your client's objectives be based on?

2. What are the objectives of your opponent's client?

3. What is the basis for your opponent's objectives? Explain (factually and legally).

4. Is your client willing to compromise his or her position? Why?

5. Should the clients be present during the negotiation? Why or why not?

6. Suppose you represent Deborah Summers. She has told you, "I am interested in the children's well-being, but frankly, the social security money is the main reason why I want custody of the kids."

    a. Ethically, should you represent Deborah Summers if she expresses to you that her main interest is the children's money? Explain.

    b. If the attorney for the grandparents asks you, "Isn't Deborah's main reason for wanting custody the children's social security money?," how would you respond? Why?

7. Hans Summers has expressed reluctance in obtaining legal custody of his grandchildren.

    a. Does his position create any problems for his attorney? Explain.

    b. Suppose Hans's reluctance in obtaining legal custody is raised by Deborah's attorney. How would you as Hans's attorney respond? Why?

8. What role should the judge, who will be hearing the child custody petition, have in the negotiation? Explain.

9. Suppose that during your negotiation meeting, you reach an agreement concerning child custody. What steps will you take at the conclusion of your negotiation meeting? Why?

ASSIGNMENT FOR CLASS

1. Outside of class, prepare a negotiation plan as representative for your client(s). If you intend to use supporting documents in the negotiation session, list them. Hand in a copy of your negotiation plan to your senior partner.

2. In class, both attorneys:

    a. Be prepared to discuss your negotiation plan.

    b. Meet and negotiate concerning child custody.

PROBLEM 134

Private Attorneys for Gretchen Summers and Marc Proust: Negotiation Concerning Settlement of an Automobile Accident*

Gretchen Summers was involved in an automobile accident on September 12, 198X – 1, at 3:00 P.M. The day was overcast. Gretchen states that she was proceeding east on Anderson Street. She stopped for a red light at the intersection of South 12th Street and Anderson Street. While she was waiting for the light to change, a car owned by Marc Proust crashed into her car from behind.

Proust claims that the light was green and that Mrs. Summers' car had begun to proceed through the intersection. Proust states he was approximately 35 feet from the Summers car, when, suddenly, the Summers car stopped. He did not see any brake lights. When he realized ~~were brake lights working?~~ the Summers car was not moving, he blew his horn and applied his brakes. Proust claims he could not stop and hit the Summers car.

Gretchen hired an attorney, who was unsuccessful in trying to negotiate settlement with Proust's insurance company, Frostway. Gretchen filed a lawsuit, *Summers v. Proust,* claiming personal injury and property damages totaling $25,000, and special damages of $5,600.

Proust, represented by an attorney on retainer to the Frostway Insurance Company, responded by denying liability and counterclaimed for $1,500 property damage.

Proust's attorney located an eyewitness to the accident, Marjorie Joyce, a respected elementary school teacher. Proust's attorney deposed Ms. Joyce. During her deposition, Ms. Joyce stated:

> "I was standing on the sidewalk on the southwest corner of Anderson Street facing 12th Street. I was waiting for the "walk" sign in order to cross 12th Street. I noticed that the light facing west on Anderson Street had just changed to green when I heard the squealing of brakes, a horn, and then a loud bang, like a car hitting another car. I looked to my left and saw the Summers car had been hit in the rear by the Proust car. I went to the Summers car and asked Mrs. Summers if she was hurt. She didn't think she was. I

---

*The attorneys in this problem do not represent any of the parties in *Summers v. Hard.* Gretchen Summers' attorney is a private practitioner with a general law practice. Marc Proust's attorney is retained by the Frostway Insurance Company.

Your instructor will inform you whether this negotiation occurs during the same time period that the wrongful death case, *Summers v. Hard,* is being prepared for trial.

then gave my name and address to both drivers and proceeded on my way."

Gretchen's attorney also questioned Ms. Joyce. The following is a summary of the cross-examination deposition testimony.

"Yes, I was facing 12th Street and concentrating on the cross-walk sign. I was waiting for the cross-walk light to flash "walk." It all happened so fast that I cannot state positively that the light on Anderson was green when I heard the squealing of brakes. I am also not absolutely positive that the noise I described as a loud bang occurred when the light was already green on Anderson Avenue. It may have been red and just changing. Yes, that is a possibility."

Both Gretchen and Marc Proust respectively testified at their depositions as set forth in the first two paragraphs of this problem.

Discovery has been completed in the case. Gretchen has submitted medical bills for $3,500, a car repair bill for $2,100, and an affidavit from Ms. Willa Shakespire. Gretchen was returning from her first babysitting session with Ms. Shakespire's daughter Lauren when the accident occurred. Ms. Shakespire stated that she would have hired Mrs. Summers for babysitting at $3.50 per hour for sixteen hours a week for the six-month period, September 12, 198X − 1 through March 12, 198X.

Mr. Proust has submitted a car repair bill for $1,500.

The following is a summary of the medical records prepared by Dr. James on behalf of Mrs. Summers.

"Gretchen Summers is 68 years old. She is currently a patient at the Human Consent Hospital clinic. Gretchen has high blood pressure, varicose veins, and is in generally poor health. She has been advised to rest often during the day and not stand for long periods of time. She should avoid stressful situations.

"Ms. Summers came to see me on September 13, 198X − 1. She complained of severe neck pain. X-rays did not indicate objective symptoms of injury. I diagnosed her condition as cervical radiculopathy, commonly referred to as whiplash. I prescribed a collar for her neck, which she wore for six weeks. She also was given medication for pain, parafon forte and 600 mg. motrin, which she took for approximately six months. Physical therapy was prescribed every day for two weeks and then twice a week for six weeks. Although I did not discover clear objective evidence, I believe that Ms. Summers will suffer permanent pain from her injuries."

Proust's attorney submitted a medical report from Dr. Oates, who examined Mrs. Summers for the defense. The following is a summary of Dr. Oates' report.

"I reviewed the medical records and reports by Mrs. Summers' medical doctors and technicians. I examined Mrs. Summers for one hour in April 198X. I did not find any objective evidence of injury. I conclude that Mrs. Summers' injury is minor. It is highly unlikely that there will be any residual effects. Mrs. Summers is a highly stressed individual suffering from high blood pressure, who may be imagining more pain than she suffered because of the highly stressful nature of an automobile accident."

Attorneys for Summers and Proust have agreed to discuss settlement of *Summers v. Proust.*

PREPARATION

READ: (1) Pretrial Case File Entries 29, 61, 64, 78; (2) Chapter X.

Preparing for negotiation requires understanding your own and your adversary's position. Therefore, answer the questions by first assuming the role of Gretchen Summers' attorney and then the role of Marc Proust's attorney.

1. If you were Gretchen Summers' attorney, what preparation would you do prior to meeting with Proust's attorney? Why?

2. If you were Proust's attorney, what information would you seek prior to meeting with Gretchen Summers' attorney? Why?

3. Incentives to settle are the motivating forces that produce settlement.

   a. Assume you are Gretchen Summers' attorney. What incentives are there for you to settle this matter?

   b. Assume that you are the insurance company attorney representing Proust. What incentives are there for you to settle this matter?

   c. Compare the parties' incentives for settlement. Can analysis of these incentives be helpful to you in formulating your negotiation plan? Explain.

4. In formulating a negotiation plan that deals with obtaining a monetary settlement, each attorney has a top and bottom amount that would be acceptable. Assume the role of the respective attorneys.

   a. If you were the attorney for Gretchen Summers, what is the top and bottom sum you would settle for? Explain the basis for your settlement amounts in terms of the facts, law, documents, and medical evaluations.

   b. If you were the attorney for the insurance company defending Marc Proust, what amount would you be willing to settle the case for? Explain the basis for your settlement amounts based on the facts, law, documents, and medical evaluations.

5. Suppose a medical doctor retained by an insurance company, in the course of a medical examination of an adverse party, discovers that the party has a rare and fatal disease. The doctor informs the insurance company attorney of her finding. Does the attorney have a duty to disclose the information:

   a. To the affected party? Why?

   b. To the other attorney if the disease could have affected the accident? Why?

ASSIGNMENT FOR CLASS

1. You are an attorney representing either Mrs. Summers or Mr. Proust. Prepare a negotiation plan. If you intend to use supporting documents in the negotiation session, list them. Hand in a copy of your negotiation plan to your senior partner.

2. In class, both attorneys: Be prepared to discuss your negotiation plan. Be prepared to meet and negotiate the personal injury and property damage claims.

PROBLEM 135

*Attorneys for Defendant Hard and SAPO Insurance Company: Negotiation Concerning Duty to Defend**

Plaintiffs Deborah, Hans, Gretchen, Ronny, and Amanda Summers filed a complaint on November 1, 198X, naming Ed Hard, Mary Apple, Tom Donaldson, and M.C. Davola as defendants. Plaintiffs allege that defendants are responsible for the wrongful death of Bruno Summers. Ed Hard contacted an attorney to represent him in this case, *Summers v. Hard.*

Ed Hard has a homeowner's insurance policy with the SAPO Insurance Company. Ed Hard's attorney contacted the SAPO Insurance Company and requested that SAPO defend Ed Hard in *Summers v. Hard,* a civil lawsuit. SAPO's position is that it does not have a duty to defend Ed Hard because the shooting by Ed Hard was a premeditated, willful act and therefore not covered by the insurance contract. Ed Hard asserts the shooting was not an intentional or willful act and that the insurance company has a duty to defend him.

A meeting between Hard's attorney and the attorney representing SAPO Insurance Company is scheduled. The purpose of the meeting is to try to reach a settlement of this issue. Planning and preparing for the negotiation are critical.

PREPARATION

READ: (1) Pretrial Case File Entries 1-37, 45, 59-61, 63, 83, 90; (2) Chapter X; (3) 28 U.S.C. §2072.

Answer the questions by assuming the role of the attorney you are assigned (unless otherwise required by a question).

1. What are your objectives in this meeting? State them.

2. What are your opponent's objectives in this meeting?

3. Do you have interests at odds with those of your opponent? If so, what are they?

4. Do you and your opponent have similar interests? If so, what are they?

5. Will you present your position in writing? If so, what will it be?

6. What facts will you present to support your position?

7. State the facts that are the weakest for your position.

   a. How can you deal with them?

   b. What response do you expect from your opponent?

8. Will you present legal arguments? If so, what are they?

9. What response do you expect from your opponent? Explain.

10. Does the law support your position? Explain.

---

*Unless your instructor informs you otherwise, this negotiation occurs before an answer is filed in *Summers v. Hard.*

---

11. Are there any compromises you can reach? Explain.

12. In most negotiations, one party is more powerful.

    a. Explain generally what creates "power" in this case.

    b. Is the insurance company more "powerful" than Ed Hard's attorney?

    c. In this case, does it matter who is more powerful?

    d. Is there any way to shift (or maintain) the power balance in your favor?

13. As Hard's attorney, do you have a strategy if the insurance company refuses to change its position? What strategy would you use?

14. Suppose Ed Hard's attorney suggests that if agreement is not reached, Ed Hard will litigate the tort of bad faith breach of contract and seek punitive damages. Is it ethical for Ed Hard's attorney to threaten litigation of the tort of bad faith breach of contract? Explain.

ASSIGNMENT FOR CLASS

1. Outside of class, prepare a negotiation plan as representative for your client. If you intend to use supporting documents in the negotiation session, list them. Hand in a copy of your negotiation plan to your senior partner.

2. In class, be prepared to discuss your negotiation plan. Attorneys for Ed Hard and the SAPO Insurance Company meet and negotiate on the issue of duty to defend under the SAPO Insurance contract.

PROBLEM 136

Attorneys for Defendant Hard and Faye Flim: Negotiation Concerning Payment of a Painting Contract*

Faye Flim lives in a gingerbread Victorian house. Approximately four months ago, a young man, Tom Gulliver, came to her house and gave Ms. Flim a circular that advertised "reasonable rates for experienced interior and exterior painting by E.T. Hard." Ms. Flim telephoned Hard to obtain an estimate. Hard inspected the house for 30 minutes. He gave Ms. Flim a written estimate that he could paint the interior and exterior of Faye Flim's house in 60 days for $7,000.

Ms. Flim asked Hard for references and Hard referred her to two satisfied customers. Approximately three days after Hard's initial estimate, Flim told Hard she wanted him to paint her house. Ms. Flim suggested that they sign "something." Hard came to her house with a handwritten agreement.

---

*The attorney representing Ed Hard also represents him in *Summers v. Hard. Summers v. Hard* is scheduled for trial on April 1, 198X + 2.

Unless your instructor informs you otherwise, this negotiation occurs during pretrial preparation for *Summers v. Hard.*

E.T. Hard agrees to paint Ms. Faye Flim's house at 27 Stcamore [sic] Street beginning April 198X + 1 for $7,000.

After signing the agreement on April 30, 198X + 1, Ms. Flim and Hard verbally agreed that the $7,000 would be paid in two installments. The first installment would be paid after the interior painting was satisfactorily completed; the second, upon satisfactory completion of the exterior painting.

Hard completed painting the interior of the Flim house on May 15th and submitted a bill to Ms. Flim for $2,000. According to Hard, Ms. Flim said she was short on cash and would pay the total amount when he completed the job. When Hard protested, Ms. Flim agreed to pay Hard $700 for the paint.

Hard then hired Tom Gulliver to help paint the exterior of the Flim house. Gulliver spent approximately 150 hours on the exterior painting.

Hard completed all the painting on July 8th, 198X + 1, <u>68</u> days after he had begun. He gave Flim a bill for $6,630, which included $130 interest (12 percent interest per annum).

Ms. Flim refuses to pay Hard. She claims the interior painting is streaky. Paint was splattered on some of the natural woodwork and Hard did not paint the interior door and window trim. As to the exterior painting, there are air bubbles in some areas and the old paint shows through near the front exterior windows. Finally, Flim states that Hard failed to complete the contract in the time specified.

Hard contends that there was nothing wrong with the interior painting. Hard states that, to keep Flim happy, he repainted a wall and removed some paint from the woodwork. Hard does not believe there is anything wrong with the exterior painting. He said: "Flim is crazy. If she doesn't pay me, I am going to scrape the paint off the house and throw black tar on the exterior paint."

Hard contacted the attorney who represents him in *Summers v. Hard*. Hard's attorney contacted Ms. Flim, who referred the matter to her attorney. The attorneys have agreed to meet at the law office of Ed Hard's attorney in order to try to resolve the painting dispute.

PREPARATION

READ: (1) Pretrial Case File Entries 1-3, 11, 37, 61, 80, 81, 89, 90; (2) Chapter X.

Answer the questions by assuming the role of the attorney you are assigned (unless otherwise required by the question):

1. Ed Hard told his attorney that he would like to be present during the negotiation meeting.

   a. If you were Ed Hard's attorney, would you agree?

   b. If you were Faye Flim's attorney, would you agree? No

2. If you were Ed Hard's attorney, what information would you seek:

   a. Prior to meeting with Faye Flim's attorney? Why?

   b. At this meeting? Why?

3. If you were Faye Flim's attorney, what information would you seek:

a. Prior to meeting with Ed Hard's attorney?

b. At this meeting? Why?

4. Incentives to settle are the motivating forces that produce settlement.

a. Assume you are Faye Flim's attorney. What incentives are there for you to settle this matter? Defense costs
Equitable settlement so Hard doesn't hurt Flim

b. Assume you are Ed Hard's attorney. What incentives are there for you to settle this matter?

c. Compare Hard's and Flim's incentives for settlement. Can analysis of these incentives be helpful to you in formulating your negotiation plan? How?

5. Assume that you are Ed Hard's attorney. Suppose that when you agreed to represent Ed, you asked him for bills, receipts, and any documentation concerning his painting claim. He replied that he did not have anything. He has now given you receipts for paint, the wages he paid to Gulliver, and records showing hours employed on the job.

a. Ethically, can you use these documents to substantiate Hard's claim? Why or why not?

b. If Flim's attorney requests receipts or records, should you give them to her attorney? Why or why not?

ASSIGNMENT FOR CLASS

1. Outside of class, prepare a negotiation plan as representative for your client. If you intend to use supporting documents in the negotiation session, list them. Hand in a copy of your negotiation plan to your senior partner.

2. In class, both attorneys: Be prepared to discuss your negotiation plan. Be prepared to meet and negotiate the painting contract dispute.

PROBLEM 137

*Attorneys for Defendant Hard and Jiffy Motors: Negotiation Concerning Van Repairs**

Ed Hard heard a television advertisement by Jiffy Motors for used trucks and vans. He remembers the commercial was something like the following:

> "We will not be undersold! We have the best bargains in town for A-1 used cars and trucks! We are the only place in town that you can rely on for quality at the lowest price! We give you warranties

---

*State v. Hard, a first-degree murder prosecution against Ed Hard for shooting and killing Bruno Summers, was dismissed by the prosecutor in October 198X. The Summers family in November 198X brought a wrongful death case, naming Ed Hard as one of the defendants. Ed Hard's attorney is the one who represents him in *Summers v. Hard.*

Unless your instructor informs you otherwise, this negotiation occurs during pretrial preparation of *Summers v. Hard.*

that can't be beat! Imagine a six-month warranty on a used auto! We guarantee you six months of free service and parts! We also have the best interest rates in town! Now who can beat that? I want to know! If they can, we will match it! Come see us today while the deals last!"

On approximately June 1, 198X, Ed went to Jiffy Motors. Gale Snod, a salesman, approached him. Ed recalls that he told Snod that he had heard the Jiffy Motors ad on television and that he was interested in purchasing a van for his painting business, wanted to spend approximately $5,000, and needed financing. Snod said: "We have some beautiful machines." Snod recommended a three-year-old Fortia van, 198X-3. Its marked price was $8,500. Snod said:

> "This particular van was originally owned by an elderly person
> who rarely drove it. It is in A-1 condition. It only has 10,000 miles.
> If you like it, I can give it to you for $7,000. With a down payment
> of $2,000, financing is for three years at the low rate of 3/4 percent
> interest per month (9 percent per annum)."

Hard said he thought it was a good deal since he saw a similar van advertised in the newspaper "as is" for $7,800. Snod agreed and showed him a newspaper ad for an earlier model that was selling for $8,200. Snod said: "I can close the deal right now and you could drive the van off the lot. We will let you use the dealer's registration." Hard took a test drive, signed the agreement, paid $2,000, and left with the van.

One day in November 198X, the van would not move. Hard had it *5 mos. later* towed to a garage. The mechanic estimated that repairs would be $1,000. It appeared that the transmission was rebuilt after what appeared to be a collision. In the process, a pin was not properly replaced, which caused the automatic transmission to be damaged beyond repair. The mechanic told Hard that as a consequence the van needed a new automatic transmission. The mechanic also told Hard that the van tires appeared in poorer condition than the mileage on the van odometer indicated.

Hard visited Jiffy Motors and spoke with Snod and the owner, Cary Whimple. Both Snod and Whimple said all their autos and vans have a three-month warranty; trucks have a six-month warranty. Snod and Whimple expressed their sorrow for Hard's poor luck. Whimple said: "Sometimes you win, sometimes you lose. Because you are a good customer, I will have my mechanic look at the van."

The Jiffy mechanic found the van transmission had been recently abused, causing it to burn up. The mechanic said: "The transmission condition appears to be caused by driving the van over its maximum speed."

Whimple said they were not responsible. Hard lost his temper and threatened to picket Jiffy Motors until they returned his money. Whimple replied to Hard: "I wouldn't expect anything more from a murderer."

Hard stopped making payments on the van. On December 1, 198X, Hard received a letter advising him that Jiffy Motors would repossess the van in 30 days if Hard failed to make payments.

On December 2, 198X, at 9:00 A.M., Hard appeared on the public street in front of the Jiffy Motors car lot entrance. He began handing leaflets to pedestrians passing in front of Jiffy Motors. He also used a loudspeaker, which repeated the message from the leaflets. The leaflets stated:

I bought a van from Jiffy Motors. Less than five months later it fell apart. Jiffy refuses to fix it. They claim they are not responsible. But remember the Jiffy Motors T.V. advertisement? Six month werrantys [sic]. They are thieves and liars. Hundreds of other Jiffy customers have been defrauded by Jiffy's diceits [sic]. Their cars and trucks are nothing more than yellow tin lemons. You squeeze them and they fall apart.

DO NOT BUY FROM JIFFY MOTORS. THEY ARE FRAUDS AND CHEATS. LET US PUT THEM OUT OF BUSINESS.

> An angry van owner:
>
> E.T. Hard

Both Hard and Whimple contacted their attorneys. Whimple's attorney contacted Hard's attorney in order to discuss Hard's leafletting.

PREPARATION

READ: (1) Pretrial Case File Entries 1-3, 11, 34, 59, 61, 80, 81, 89; (2) Chapter X.

In preparing for negotiations, you must be familiar with both your own and your opponent's positions. Therefore, in answering these questions, first assume the role of Hard's attorney, then assume the role of Jiffy's attorney, unless the questions indicate otherwise.

1. What preparation would you do prior to this meeting? Why?

2. State your objectives (including monetary objectives).

3. The manager of Jiffy Motors, Cary Whimple, has told his attorney that he and his salesman, Gale Snod, would like to be present during the negotiation meeting.

   a. If you were Jiffy Motors' attorney, what would be your response?

   b. If you were Ed Hard's attorney, what would be your response?

   c. As Jiffy Motors' attorney, assess what you will do now and explain why.

4. Incentives to settle are the motivating forces that produce settlement.

   a. Assume you are Hard's attorney. What incentives are there for you to settle this matter?

   b. Assume you are Jiffy Motors' attorney. What incentives are there for you to settle this matter?

   c. Compare Hard's and Jiffy Motor's incentives for settlement. Can analysis of these incentives be helpful to you in formulating your negotiation plan? Explain.

5. Each attorney can present factual and legal arguments in support of his or her position. Answer as if you were the attorney for either Hard or Jiffy Motors:

   a. What factual arguments support your position?

   b. What facts weaken your position? Why?

   c. What will you say in response to the factual arguments set forth by your opponent's attorney?

d. What law supports your position?

e. What law supports your opponent's position? Why?

f. What will you say in response to the legal arguments set forth by your opponent?

6. Suppose Ed Hard's attorney states: "Both Ed and I believe there is strong evidence to support a criminal charge against Jiffy Motors of odometer tampering. I just want you to know that Ed is thinking about referring the matter to the Attorney General if things are not worked out to Ed's satisfaction."

a. Ethically, should Ed Hard's attorney use such a threat in negotiations?

b. If such a threat is made, what responses would you anticipate Jiffy Motors' attorney to respond with?

c. What would be your response to Jiffy?

d. Now assess whether such a threat would be helpful or harmful in obtaining your objectives.

7. Suppose that Jiffy Motors threatens to go to court for a restraining order against Ed Hard's leafletting and loudspeaker.

a. What effect, if any, would the Jiffy Motors case have on *Summers v. Hard?*

b. Suppose that *State v. Hard* was being prosecuted. What effect, if any, would an injunction against Ed Hard have on the criminal prosecution? Criminal defense? Explain.

ASSIGNMENT FOR CLASS

1. Outside of class, you are an attorney representing either Edward Hard or Jiffy Motors. Prepare a written negotiation plan. If you intend to use supporting documents in the negotiation session, list them. Hand in a copy of your negotiation plan to your senior partner.

2. In class, both attorneys: Be prepared to discuss your negotiation plan. Be prepared to meet and negotiate the van repair dispute.

PROBLEM 138 ⎯⎯⎯⎯⎯⎯⎯⎯⎯⎯⎯⎯⎯⎯⎯⎯
*Attorneys for Defendant Davola and Mary Apple: Negotiation Concerning an Employment Dispute**

Mary Apple, a waitress at the Unicorn Tavern, has contacted an attorney concerning an employment dispute. She is the waitress who was at the Unicorn Tavern the night Bruno Summers was shot, September 3, 198X. Approximately two months before the shooting and death of Bruno

---

*The attorney representing M.C. Davola is on retainer to M.C. Davola and handles all business and financial matters relating to the Unicorn Tavern. The attorney representing Mary Apple is a good friend of Mary Apple's family. You are to assume that *Summers v. Hard,* the wrongful death case by the Summers family, is just about to be filed on November 1, 198X unless your instructor informs you otherwise.

Summers, the owner of the Unicorn Tavern, M.C. Davola, promised Mary Apple an increase in her salary from $160 per week to $200 per week, to begin October 1, 198X.

On October 1, 198X, Ms. Apple's salary was not increased. When she confronted Mr. Davola, he said,

> "I didn't promise you a raise. I thought I made it clear that if things were going good, I'd give you an extra dollar an hour. Things are bad, real bad. I'm really hurting in this business since that neo-Nazi got himself killed at the Tavern. I can't afford no extra money."

Ms. Apple said she was shocked by Davola's response. The next day, she confronted Mr. Davola. She told him:

> "I understood you were making a promise and so I remained at the Unicorn because I thought I would receive an increase in wages."

Mr. Davola, responded:

> "If you don't like it clear out. I don't need your kind. You're fired."

Ms. Apple's attorney telephoned Mr. Davola to attempt to settle the misunderstanding. Mr. Davola, however, responded to the attorney's inquiry by stating: "You tell that Apple that she ain't going to get no raise. If she doesn't like it, let her lump it. Get another job."

In response to Apple's attorney's request to talk about the matter in person, Davola said: "Call my attorney if you want to talk. Don't bother me about Apple."

Ms. Apple's attorney telephoned Mr. Davola's attorney. Davola's attorney was very cordial and willing to meet. She will be attending a deposition in another case that is being held on the 56th floor of the same building where the office of Davola's attorney is located. She stated she would stop by after her meeting, which is set for next Thursday and should conclude at approximately 3:00 P.M.

Ms. Apple has been informed about the meeting with Davola's attorney. Her attorney advised her to continue working and to avoid all discussion with Mr. Davola.

PREPARATION

READ: (1) Pretrial Case File Entries 1-4, 28, 31, 36-39, 44, 49, 59-61, 81, 84; (2) Chapter X.

In preparing for negotiation, you must be familiar with both your own and your adversary's positions. Therefore, in answering these questions, first assume the role of Mary Apple's attorney, then assume the role of Davola's attorney, unless the questions indicate otherwise.

1. Generally, how will you prepare for this meeting?

   a. Are there documents that you may want prior to this meeting? Explain.

   b. Is there legal research you should do before the meeting? If so, explain the issues.

2. The negotiation meeting is to take place after Davola's attorney concludes another meeting. The Apple-Davola meeting is scheduled for 3:00 P.M. at the office of Apple's attorney. Assume you are Apple's attorney:

   a. List the advantages for you in the meeting schedule.

   b. List the disadvantages for you in the meeting schedule.

   c. How would you plan to make this schedule advantageous for yourself?

3. According to Mary Apple, part of the difficulty that has arisen appears to be Davola's refusal to implement his promised raise to Apple.

   a. If you were Apple's attorney, what would you discuss at the negotiations?

   b. What response would you expect from Davola's attorney?

4. Davola may have a reasonable position concerning the tavern's current financial position.

   a. If you were Mary Apple's attorney, would you argue against Davola's financial position? Why or why not?

   b. If you would argue against Davola's financial position, what response would you expect from Davola? How would you respond?

   c. Instead of arguing against Davola's financial position, could you accommodate his concerns and still obtain Apple's raise?

5. The law can affect negotiation.

   a. How does the law support Apple's position? Explain.

   b. How does the law support Davola's position? Explain.

   c. Whose arguments are stronger? Why?

   d. What effect should the law have on these negotiations?

6. Suppose Davola's attorney asks Apple's attorney: "How are you being paid?" If you were Davola's attorney:

   a. Explain why you would respond.

   b. Explain why you would not respond.

   c. Suppose you respond. What will you say? Why?

ASSIGNMENT FOR CLASS

1. You are an attorney representing either Ms. Apple or M.C. Davola. Prepare a negotiation plan. If you intend to use supporting documents in the negotiation session, list them. Hand in a copy of your negotiation plan to your senior partner.

2. In class, both attorneys: Be prepared to discuss your negotiation plan. Be prepared to meet and negotiate the employment dispute.

Attorneys for Defendant Davola and Amy Postle: Negotiation Concerning Sale of the Unicorn Tavern*

M.C. Davola, the owner of the Unicorn Tavern, would like to sell the tavern. It has been listed with Bella Rock, a real estate broker, since September 1, 198X. The tavern (2,600 square feet) is priced at $135,000. The building is approximately 22 years old. Ms. Amy Postle is interested in purchasing the tavern.

Ms. Postle is quite familiar with the Unicorn Tavern mainly from conversations Ms. Postle has had with Bella Rock. Bella Rock is a real estate broker with the Red Rug Real Estate firm. She represents Ms. Postle, the purchaser, and Davola, the seller.

Ms. Rock informed Ms. Postle that approximately eight years ago Davola and his wife purchased the Unicorn Tavern for approximately $75,000-$80,000. There is an outstanding mortgage of $63,000 at 8 percent interest that is <u>not</u> assumable. Taxes are presently $1,200 per year. The tavern is owned by the Unicorn Tavern Corporation. Davola is the president of the corporation and owns 95 percent of the stock; his wife owns 5 percent. Davola works part-time as a welder at an automobile body repair shop during the day and works at the tavern two nights a week.

Ms. Rock also mentioned to Ms. Postle that Bruno Summers was shot by Ed Hard at the Unicorn Tavern on September 3, 198X, and died on September 7, 198X. A criminal case, *State v. Hard,* was filed for first-degree murder and dismissed on October 1, 198X. The Summers family filed a wrongful death case against Ed Hard, Mary Apple, Tom Donaldson, and M.C. Davola on November 1, 198X. Defendants responded on November 8, 198X.

Ms. Rock stated that the Unicorn Tavern has been listed for sale for four months. Approximately two months ago, another party made a firm offer. Davola rejected that offer. Ms. Rock said that the terms of the offer were confidential. She then volunteered that she believes the tavern could sell for the asking price, $135,000. Ms. Rock said she knows Davola wants "top dollar." She also knows that Mr. Davola is not keen on financing the sale. He would rather that the buyer obtain conventional financing. Ms. Rock assured Ms. Postle that "M.C. Davola is an earnest seller."

M.C. Davola has obtained the following information from Ms. Rock concerning Ms. Postle. Ms. Postle is presently a bartender at the Raritan Hotel. She is recently divorced and received a lump sum cash settlement in lieu of alimony. Until her divorce, all credit was in her husband's name. Ms. Postle plans to manage the tavern herself.

Ms. Postle's attorney has received the accountant's summary statement regarding the financial position of the tavern. Ms. Postle arranged for a pest inspection of the tavern, which reveals that the tavern needs approximately $2,000 of work to comply with county health and building code requirements. She also had an architectural study done and this

---

*The attorney representing M.C. Davola is on retainer to M.C. Davola and handles all business and financial matters relating to the Unicorn Tavern. The attorney representing Ms. Postle is a private practitioner in general law practice.

Unless your instructor informs you otherwise, this negotiation occurs during pretrial preparation for *Summers v. Hard.*

indicated that essential cosmetic and modernization changes will also be necessary.

Ms. Postle has asked her attorney to negotiate on her behalf. M.C. Davola is also represented in the negotiation by an attorney. The meeting is scheduled for November 15, 198X.

PREPARATION

READ: (1) Pretrial Case File Entries 1-4, 28, 31, 36-39, 44, 49, 60, 61, 81, 88, 89; (2) Chapter X.

In preparing for negotiations, you must be familiar with both your own and your adversary's positions. Therefore, in answering these questions, first assume the role of M.C. Davola's attorney, then assume the role of Amy Postle's attorney, unless the questions indicate otherwise.

1. What are your objectives? Explain

2. Where should this meeting be held? Why?

3. Who should be present during the negotiation meeting? Why?

4. Ms. Rock, the real estate broker, represents both Postle and Davola. As the attorney for either client respectively, how will you ensure that confidential information is not disclosed?

5. Most real estate transactions begin when the prospective buyer makes a written offer.

   a. Would it be advantageous for Postle if she makes a firm written offer prior to this meeting? Explain.

   b. Should Davola insist that Postle make a firm offer prior to this meeting? Why or why not?

6. If you were Postle's attorney, what information would you seek at this meeting? Why?

7. If you were Davola's attorney, what information would you seek at this meeting? Why?

8. Suppose Davola has told his attorney: "I heard through the grapevine that another restaurant with a bar is going to open approximately one block away from the Unicorn." Imagine Postle's attorney asks: "Give me all the data that you and Davola have or believe could affect the profits of the Unicorn Tavern."

   a. Does Davola's attorney have a duty to disclose?

   b. Does Davola have a duty to disclose?

   c. Does Ms. Rock have a duty to disclose (assuming she knows the above information)?

ASSIGNMENT FOR CLASS

1. Outside of class, prepare a negotiation plan as representative for your client. If you intend to use supporting documents in the negotiation session, list them. Hand in a copy of your negotiation plan to your senior partner.

---

2. In class, both attorneys: Be prepared to discuss your negotiation plan. Meet and negotiate the sale of the Unicorn Tavern.

PROBLEM 140

*Attorneys for Defendant Davola and Eli Cohen: Negotiation Concerning Lease of the Unicorn Tavern**

Business declined substantially since the shooting at the Unicorn Tavern in September 198X. Davola attempted to sell the Unicorn Tavern premises, but failed to do so. Davola then decided to lease the Unicorn Tavern or its premises. It was common knowledge in the community and among all potential lessees that Bruno Summers was shot by Ed Hard at the Unicorn Tavern on September 3, 198X and died on September 7, 198X. A criminal case for first-degree murder, *State v. Hard*, was filed and dismissed on October 1, 198X. The Summers family filed a wrongful death case against Ed Hard, Mary Apple, Tom Donaldson, and M.C. Davola on November 1, 198X.

On December 1, 198X, Davola leased the Unicorn Tavern premises for five years to Mr. Eli Cohen, owner of the Sweet and Sour Cabbage Patch restaurant. The Davola-Cohen lease contains the following provisions:

1. In consideration of the covenants and agreements set forth in this lease, Lessee agrees to lease the premises [description] for commercial purposes to operate a restaurant, Sweet and Sour Cabbage Patch, for the term of five years, commencing on December 1, 198X and ending on November 30, 198X + 5. Monthly rental is ten percent (10%) of the Lessee's net profits and one thousand two hundred dollars ($1,200) per month. Rent is payable in advance on the first day of each month during the term of the lease. . . .

12. In the event of default or non-compliance with any terms of this lease by the Lessee, all rent due and owing for the full term of the lease shall be immediately due and payable by the Lessee. In the event that either party commences an action to enforce this lease, the prevailing party in such action shall be entitled to recover court costs and reasonable attorney's fees.

13. This lease shall not be assigned by Lessee, voluntarily or by operation of law, nor shall the premises or any part be sublet by the Lessee, without the prior written consent of the Lessor, and acceptance in writing by the assignee or sublessee of all the above terms.

Since January 1, 198X + 1, Cohen has operated a restaurant, Sweet and Sour Cabbage Patch, on the premises. During the first year of business, the restaurant had net losses of $600 per month.

Cohen notified Davola that he wanted to quit his lease. He claimed that he could not afford to operate the restaurant. Mr. Cohen located a new tenant, Adrian Mustafa, who is willing to lease the premises for $600 per

---

*The attorneys in this problem do not represent any of the parties in *Summers v. Hard*. The attorney representing M.C. Davola is on retainer to M.C. Davola and handles all business and financial matters relating to the Unicorn Tavern. The attorney representing Mr. Cohen is a private practitioner in general law practice.

Unless your instructor informs you otherwise, this negotiation occurs during pretrial preparation for *Summers. v. Hard*.

month for the four years remaining on Cohen's lease. Mustafa plans to operate The Little Egypt, a bookstore-cafe.

Cohen requested that Davola release him from the lease and lease the premises to Mustafa. Davola responded to Cohen:

> "No. I will not accept The Little Egypt as a tenant. I told you and your attorney that it would be difficult to make a restaurant profitable in a year. I went to a lot of trouble to find a tenant and make the premises ready for your restaurant. You'll make a profit if you work at it."

Mr. Cohen's attorney has contacted Davola's attorney to discuss the "lease situation."

PREPARATION

READ: (1) Pretrial Case File Entries 1-4, 28, 31, 36-39, 49, 61, 80, 81, 85, 89; (2) Chapter X.

In preparing for negotiation, you must be familiar with both your own and your adversary's positions. Therefore, in answering these questions, first assume the role of M.C. Davola's attorney, then assume the role of Eli Cohen's attorney, unless the questions indicate otherwise.

1. Generally, how will you prepare for this meeting?

2. Where should this meeting be held? Why?

3. Should both Davola and Cohen be present during the negotiation meeting? Why or why not?

4. If you were Davola's (or Cohen's) attorney, what information would you seek at this meeting? Why?

5. What are Cohen's options if Davola is adamant about refusing to allow a sublease or assignment?

6. What are Davola's options if Cohen is adamant about turning over his lease to Mr. Mustafa?

7. Suppose Davola told his attorney: "I don't want to consent to a sublease or assignment with The Little Egypt because I don't believe a bookstore-cafe will be a successful business."

   a. Does Davola have a right to refuse on that basis?

   b. What action, if any, can Cohen take? Why?

   c. Assess how Davola's statement could affect these negotiations.

ASSIGNMENT FOR CLASS

1. Outside of class, you as an attorney representing either M.C. Davola or Eli Cohen prepare a plan for negotiation. If you intend to use supporting documents in the negotiation session, list them. Hand in a copy of your negotiation plan to your senior partner.

2. In class, both attorneys: Be prepared to discuss your negotiation plan. Meet and negotiate settlement of the lease dispute.

PROBLEM 141

Plaintiffs' and Defendants' Attorneys: Negotiation Between Plaintiffs and Defendants

Bruno Summers was shot by Ed Hard at the Unicorn Tavern on September 3, 198X and died on September 7, 198X. A criminal case for first-degree murder, *State v. Hard,* was brought and subsequently dismissed on October 1, 198X. The Summers family filed a wrongful death and emotional distress case against Ed Hard, Mary Apple, Tom Donaldson, and M.C. Davola on November 1, 198X. Defendants responded on November 8, 198X. Discovery has been completed in *Summers v. Hard.* The trial has been scheduled to begin on April 1, 198X+2. Plaintiffs' attorney has requested a meeting to discuss settlement.

Attorneys for both sides have met with their respective clients prior to this meeting. This settlement discussion is scheduled for January 20, 198X+2 at 9:00 A.M. in the law offices of plaintiffs' attorney.

PREPARATION

READ: (1) Pretrial Case File Entries 1-57, 59-61, 63, 64, 81-83, 86, 87, 90; (2) Chapter X; (3) Fed. R. Civ. P. 16, 68.

In preparing for negotiation, you must be familiar with both your own and your adversary's positions. Therefore, in answering these questions, first assume the role of plaintiffs' attorney. Then assume the role of either defendant Hard or Davola's attorney, unless the questions indicate otherwise.

1. Generally, what preparation will you do prior to this meeting? Why?

2. Plaintiffs' attorney initiated these settlement discussions.

    a. Does that give plaintiffs an advantage? A disadvantage? Explain.

    b. What are the advantages to defendants? Disadvantages? Explain.

3. In your opinion, should this case be settled prior to trial? Why or why not?

4. Suppose defendants' attorneys present a written offer of settlement to plaintiffs.

    a. List the advantages or disadvantages for defendants in presenting the written offer prior to the meeting.

    b. List the advantages of presenting a written offer at the beginning of the meeting.

    c. List the disadvantages in presenting a written offer at the beginning of negotiation discussions.

5. Would it be more beneficial toward reaching a settlement if these settlement discussions were before a judge? A neutral third party? Why or why not?

6. Suppose plaintiffs' attorney wants to discuss plaintiffs' claims separately. List the advantages or disadvantages for the parties.

7. Suppose defendant Hard's attorney, in discussing the *Summers v. Hard* case, tells the plaintiffs' attorney that if the case goes to trial, he is going to "get even" with "that flake" Deborah Summers. He is going to show her prior emotional problems, her juvenile record, and that even before "Bruno's body was cold in the ground" she had a new boyfriend.

   a. Are such threats ethical?

   b. Can defendant Hard's attorney ethically make such a threat if he knows Ed Hard does not want him to cross-examine Deborah?

   c. What response would you have if you were plaintiffs' attorney? Why?

8. Should defendant Hard's insurance company attorney offer the policy limits, $50,000?

   a. What response would you have if you were plaintiffs' attorney? Explain.

   b. What response, if any, would you have if you were Davola's personal attorney?

9. Should defendant Davola's insurance company attorney offer the policy limits?

   a. What response would you have if you were plaintiffs' attorney? Explain.

   b. What response, if any, would you have if you were Hard's personal attorney?

ASSIGNMENT FOR CLASS

1. Outside of class, prepare a written negotiation plan as representative for your client(s). If you intend to use supporting documents in the negotiation discussions, list them. Hand in a copy of your negotiation plan.

2. In class, be prepared to discuss your negotiation plan. Attorneys for defendants and plaintiffs: Conduct settlement discussions in accordance with your clients' instructions.

PROBLEM 142

Plaintiffs' and Defendants' Attorneys: Court-Directed Settlement Conference

Bruno Summers was shot by Ed Hard at the Unicorn Tavern on September 3, 198X and died on September 7, 198X. A criminal case for first-degree murder, *State v. Hard,* was brought and subsequently dismissed on October 1, 198X. The Summers family filed a wrongful death and emotional distress case against Ed Hard, Mary Apple, Tom Donaldson, and M.C. Davola on November 1, 198X. Defendants responded on November 8, 198X. Discovery is completed in *Summers v. Hard.* The trial is scheduled to begin on April 1, 198X + 2. Judge Sapient requested a meeting with attorneys for both sides to discuss settlement.

Attorneys for both sides met with their respective clients prior to this meeting. This settlement discussion is scheduled for January 20, 198X+2, at 9:00 A.M. in Judge Sapient's chambers.

PREPARATION

READ: (1) Pretrial Case File Entries 1-57, 59-61, 63, 64, 81-83, 86, 87, 90; (2) Chapter X; (3) Fed. R. Civ. P. 16, 68.

In preparing for negotiation, you must be familiar with both your own and your adversary's positions. Therefore, in answering these questions, first assume the role of plaintiffs' attorney. Then assume the role of either defendant Hard or Davola's attorney, unless the questions indicate otherwise.

1. Generally, how will you prepare for this meeting? Why?

2. The judge initiated these settlement discussions.

   a. What should be the role for the judge in settlement?

   b. Should the judge actively suggest solutions?

3. Would it be more beneficial toward reaching settlement if these discussions just involved the parties' attorneys? A neutral third party? Why or why not?

4. In your opinion, should this case be settled prior to trial? Why or why not?

5. Where should the judge hold the settlement conference?

   a. In chambers? Explain.

   b. In open court but without a jury present? Explain.

6. Should a court reporter be present at this settlement conference?

7. Should the parties be present? Explain.

8. Suppose the judge suggests that the attorneys discuss each plaintiff's claims separately.

   a. List the advantages or disadvantages for the parties.

   b. What strategy would you adopt? Why?

9. Suppose defendants' attorneys present a written offer of settlement to plaintiffs.

   a. List the advantages or disadvantages for defendants in presenting the written offer prior to the meeting.

   b. List the advantages or disadvantages in presenting a written offer at the beginning of the meeting.

   c. List the advantages or disadvantages in presenting a written offer after the negotiation discussions are completed.

10. Suppose defendant Hard's attorney in discussing the *Summers v. Hard* case suggests that if the case goes to trial, he is going to show that Deborah Summers had prior emotional problems, has a juvenile record, and even before "Bruno's body was cold in the ground" had a new boyfriend.

a. Are each of these statements ethical if Judge Sapient is the trial judge? Explain.

b. What response would you have if you were plaintiffs' attorney? Why?

c. Should you object to Judge Sapient being the same judge for settlement and trial? Explain.

11. Suppose the judge at the settlement conference states: "I am thinking about dismissing the Deborah Summers claim for emotional distress unless you can show me damages."

a. Do you think it is proper for a judge to make this statement at a settlement conference? Explain.

b. As plaintiffs' attorney, how will you respond?

c. As defendants' attorneys, how will you respond?

d. What role would you like the judge to assume in this settlement conference? Why?

12. Suppose the judge states: "I think liability is clear for plaintiffs as to the tavern owner's responsibility for Bruno Summers' death. I would be inclined to grant summary judgment on that issue."

a. How should plaintiffs respond?

b. How should defendants respond?

13. Are there any remedies in this case other than a lump sum money settlement?

a. What are they?

b. Who should raise the issue of alternative remedies?

14. Should defendant Hard's insurance company attorney offer the policy limits, $50,000?

a. What response would you have if you were plaintiffs' attorney? Explain.

b. What response, if any, would you have if you were Davola's personal attorney?

15. Should defendant Davola's insurance company attorney offer the policy limits?

a. What response would you have if you were plaintiffs' attorney? Explain.

b. What response, if any, would you have if you were Hard's personal attorney?

ASSIGNMENT FOR CLASS

1. Outside of class, prepare a negotiation plan as representative for your client(s). If you intend to use supporting documents in the negotiation discussions, list them. Hand in a copy of your negotiation plan to your senior partner.

2. In class, be prepared to discuss your negotiation plan. Attorneys for plaintiffs and defendants: Participate in the court settlement conference.

PROBLEM 143

*Plaintiffs' and Defendants' Attorneys: Drafting a Settlement Agreement**

Luckily, or perhaps because of the artful use of words, the negotiation meeting concluded to all parties' satisfaction. But your work is not over. The agreement should be in writing. Since you have little experience in writing a settlement agreement, you may want some guidance.

PREPARATION

READ: Chapter VI (pages 156-158, 168) and Chapter X. Now think about and answer the following questions:

1. Negotiation may have been complicated and protracted. The terms of the settlement are a reflection and memorandum of the negotiation. Did you keep progress notes of your settlement discussions?

   a. Were there advantages to keeping progress notes in this case? Explain.

   b. Were there disadvantages to keeping progress notes? Explain.

   c. If you made progress notes, how will you use them?

2. Suppose a dispute arises because you believe a certain point was resolved one way and your adversary disagrees. Your notes and your adversary's mental recollection also differ. What will you do? How could you have avoided this problem?

3. Do you want to draft the agreement? Explain.

4. Do you want a written agreement in this case? A letter? A legal document? Explain.

5. Who should draft the agreement? Explain.

6. Who should sign the agreement? Why?

7. Suppose you decide not to draft a written settlement agreement. What could be the consequence?

ASSIGNMENT FOR CLASS

1. Outside of class, agree among yourselves who will prepare the written settlement agreement. Draft an agreement concerning the issues that were agreed upon.

2. In class, be prepared to discuss the settlement agreement.

---

*The agreement should be based on your successful negotiation. If you did not reach agreement, your instructor will provide you with specific terms the parties agreed upon so you can draft an agreement.

XI

Alternative Dispute Resolution

A.   INTRODUCTION

The title of this chapter refers essentially to a myriad of potential methods of alternative dispute resolution, such as summary or "mini-trials"; advisory juries; arbitration, whether mandatory or voluntary; mediation; ombudsmen; and so on. However, a word of caution is in order. This chapter will not tell you "how to" mediate or arbitrate or perform any other alternative method to resolve your client's dispute. Nor is it about how to plan a specific approach to the content of such alternative methods since the types of alternatives vary significantly and their nuances are numerous. There are excellent sources available that can provide a "how to" approach for arbitration and mediation. To name two: S. Goldberg, E. Green, and F. Sander, *Dispute Resolution* (1986); L. Riskin and J. Westbrook, *Dispute Resolution and Lawyers* (1987).

So why include this chapter if it does not provide a "how to" approach? Although the focus of this book is pretrial advocacy, that process is only one among many alternative methods that can be used to resolve problems. We have already discussed negotiation in Chapter IX, including choosing when to litigate and when to negotiate, and we believe that a text about pretrial advocacy would be incomplete without at least some discussion of other alternative dispute methods. Because of their potential importance to solving dis-

putes, you must be conversant with all these processes in order to fully advise your client. Thus, determining whether you should select to go to trial or choose an alternative to litigation to resolve your client's dispute is part of the pretrial process. The fact that our text discusses these remaining alternatives to litigation last is also not an indicator of the lack of importance of these methods. Rather, we believe that before you can appreciate, compare, or determine alternatives, you must first have an understanding of what they are an alternative to—litigation.

This chapter provides a general overview of the alternatives available, including some of the attributes that alternative methods of dispute resolution share. An important element in examining alternatives to litigation is to consider why these methods are alternatives to litigation.

B.   ATTRIBUTES OF ARBITRATION AND MEDIATION

Two of the more publicized alternatives to litigation are arbitration and mediation. We will discuss some of the attributes that characterize these alternative methods.

Arbitration and mediation are well-accepted methods for settling both public and private disputes outside the courtroom. Providing alternative forums to courtroom trial, the two are dissimilar in their approach to decisionmaking. Nevertheless, their overall goals are to settle differences between two or more parties in a way that supplements the trial process and maintains the structure of our society.

Examining the way these processes differ from each other and from trial can give you a perspective as to why one or both of these alternative methods might be useful in resolving your client's dispute. Often these differing factors will signal which process will best serve your client's needs. We have not attempted to list or discuss every attribute; instead, we have included some of the more distinctive features of either process and described them as they generally appear. You should be aware that characteristics may vary depending on the circumstances and jurisdiction.

1. Arbitration

Arbitration is the referral of a dispute to a third person or persons chosen by the parties. The parties agree in advance to abide by this arbitrator's award, which will be issued after a hearing at which both parties have an opportunity to be heard. Generally, the focus of arbitration is on reaching a resolution that will work for both parties rather than on which party is right or wrong, or which party wins or loses.

Arbitration can be mandatory or voluntary. Arbitration is mandatory in some jurisdictions in some civil action disputes. Actions in which mandatory arbitration occurs are those in which the sole relief requested might involve a small monetary amount (such as $10,000 to $25,000), or certain categories of cases, such as medical malpractice or securities regulation.

Most arbitration proceedings are voluntary, agreed to and commenced by the parties according to prior contracts. Statutory provisions in many jurisdictions establish guidelines to aid these agreements. If an arbitration clause in a contract is valid, a court will compel a party to arbitrate if she refuses to do so.

Arbitrators are generally neutral, functioning much like law judges. However, they need not be trained or knowledgeable about the law. Instead, they might have expertise in a particular subject area that is the focus of the dispute (e.g., construction, architecture, labor). Usually, arbitration proceedings involve one to three arbitrators who listen to the demands of the parties and then make an informed decision based on the proceedings and the evidence submitted by the parties. The parties can, but need not, be represented by attorneys. Parties who submit their disputes to an arbitrator agree to be bound by the ideas of justice, fairness, and equity of the arbitrator even if the arbitrator is not learned in the law. An arbitrator need not comply with the accepted rules of law that a court would use; however, an arbitrator cannot violate strong principles of public policy.

Arbitration is characterized by speed, procedural simplicity, and general lack of appealability on the merits. Arbitration proceedings forego several of the normal litigation procedures. Once the arbitrator or hearing panel is chosen (generally by the consent of the parties in voluntary arbitration), there are few delays leading up to the hearing. There is no significant motion practice. Arbitrators usually do not strictly enforce rules of evidence, and normal discovery is unavailable unless the arbitrator agrees to discovery. The arbitration process is like a mini-trial. The parties or their attorneys present evidence, using the same general order that would be followed in litigation: opening, presentation of direct and cross-examination, presentation of exhibits, closing argument. But the presentation is usually more informal and briefer than it would be in a court proceeding. As a result, some characterize arbitration as "cheap litigation."

Even though arbitration awards are subject to review by an appellate court, the grounds for an appeal are extremely limited, except in mandatory arbitration where it is customary to allow a trial de novo. But exercising the right to a trial de novo is often accompanied by severe economic costs if the party requesting the de novo review does not fare better than it did in the arbitration decision. Arbitration decisions are based on both law and facts, but arbitrators are not bound by legal or factual precedent and, thus, it is very difficult to overturn an arbitration award if it is bad. As a general rule, an award can be overturned only if it amounts to manifest injustice or fraud.

2. Mediation

As a dispute resolution method, mediation differs in several respects from arbitration (although when mediation is mandatory, as it is in some jurisdictions, it might share some of the mandatory arbitration characteristics). Generally voluntary, opted for by the parties, mediation is a party-directed problem-solving process. A third-party facilitator, the mediator, helps the parties resolve their conflict and arrive at a decision; unlike an arbitrator, however, the mediator will not make any decision, nor will the mediator mandate a settlement or convince the parties to settle. The decision is formulated by the parties according to their concept of what is just and fair for them. The parties set the terms and conditions of their settlement, again according to their ideas of fairness. Mediation presupposes the parties' willingness to collaborate in their efforts to resolve their dispute. Its strength lies in the parties' stake in being honest and fair and less manipulative in their dealings with each other than might be so in litigation. The structure of the process does not reward or encourage typical litigation tactics. Because the mediator does not determine the final decision, tactics that would be employed to manipulate a factfinder to decide in one party's favor are not necessary for the parties in a mediation (e.g., relying on evidentiary rules to keep damaging information from the factfinder). Further, the process is a private one, thus ensuring confidentiality of the decision if the parties want to shield themselves from publicity.

Confidentiality plays a final significant role in mediation. Anything told a mediator in private session with one party (generally called a "caucus") is strictly confidential. Only with the party's specific authorization can the mediator relay this information to the other party. This provides a valuable tool for settlement since parties are generally unwilling to give their "best" settlement numbers to the opposition ("If I tell them I'd settle for what is my best offer, $50,000, they'll just take that as a point of departure for bargaining and ask for $60,000"). With the confidentiality of mediation, a party can give its best number to the mediator in confidence and then authorize the mediator to "float" a trial offer in a caucus with the other party ("The other party just authorized me to communicate an offer of $42,500"). The other party may then respond ("Well, we're getting closer but it'll take at least $50,000 to settle this one"). The mediator can then go back to the first party with a possible settlement ("Will you give that $50,000 you just told me about in our last caucus to end this case today?"). All the above factors contribute to making mediation a successful method for resolving disputes.

A mediator can, but need not, be a lawyer or trained in the law. The role of lawyers in the mediation process may vary. A lawyer may take the role of the mediator or the lawyer may represent a client during mediation or limit his role to advising a client as to her rights while the client does the actual talking during the mediation proceeding. The attorney's role may be limited to reviewing the final mediation agreement, or the lawyer's role might be one of merely referring a client to mediation. Sometimes, the mediation process might not even involve lawyers at all.

The role of the mediator is fluid. It is determined in large part by the personal style and personality of the mediator. There are, however, some general principles that all mediators abide by. As noted, the mediator does not decide or resolve the case nor does the mediator recommend a decision to the parties. Rather, the mediator is a facilitator and helps the parties reach a reciprocal agreement. Basically, however, it is the mediator's objectivity that directs the parties toward the issues and away from personal animosities. In other words, the mediator's function is to help the parties establish the mutual trust and understanding that will enable them to work out their own resolution. The mediator merely acts to reduce the communication problems of the parties, make them take some objective view of their positions and interests, and maximize the verbal exchange of alternatives. On the other hand, the mediator can make suggestions for the decision-making process. However, the mediator cannot and does not force the parties to a decision, or even to accept her reasoning. Instead, she might help point out to the parties how to balance rival needs, competing economic factors, and differing social preferences.

Likewise, there is no rigid method for how a mediation might be conducted.[1] The mediation process usually consists of several meetings between the parties and the mediator and the meetings generally take place in the mediator's office. There is no set procedure for conducting the mediation meetings. Some mediators are more directive than others. For instance, a mediator might confer with the two parties separately and gain a perspective on their positions. If the mediator meets with each party, she can encourage dialogue by listening to a party's side of the conflict or by asking questions. Sometimes the mediator might factually present the other party's position during this discussion. By this method the mediator is informing the parties of the equities in each party's position. Then, when the parties meet together with the mediator, each party may be prepared to deal with the other's needs. These techniques and others allow the mediator to guide the negotiation with both parties' goals in mind.

Law, evidence, and procedural rules play varying roles in the mediation process and decisionmaking. Depending on the subject matter and the parties, sometimes legal rules may be applied when they make the decision fair; at other times, law may be ignored or used simply as a guideline. Mediation does not encourage the parties to establish and demand an agreement based on substantive law, but rather tries to fashion the parties' agreement according to the par-

---

1. There are some excellent videotapes of the mediation process; one example is Gary Friedman, Scenes from a Mediation (Center for the Development of Mediation in the Law, Mill Valley, California, 1983).

ties' own fairness concepts. For example, the parties to a mediation can choose to ignore legal precedent.

Imagine a dissolution case in which the parties are deciding how to divide their assets. Suppose legal precedent in a community property state provides that the assets be divided equally (according to community property rules). Parties in a mediation can ignore those legal rules or legal precedent and use a different formula or criteria based on the needs of the parties, such as their future prospects for a livelihood. They might look to legal precedent and community property rules as a guide, but they need not follow those rules. For instance, if it seems fairer for the spouse with a high-paying job and continued prospects of a high salary to divide the community assets 25:75 instead of 50:50, then the parties can do so. Or the parties might agree to one spouse continuing to live in the house because of present needs even though this causes an unequal division of the assets. Thus, instead of the law dictating the division, the parties

can formulate their own ideas of fairness and choose the criteria they want to apply in arriving at a fair settlement.

Likewise, evidence and procedure rules designed to control the flow of information at trial are generally not applicable in mediation (except of course as leverage when a party uses the evidence or procedural law in discussion to convince the other party to settle rather than risk losing at trial). Rather, the mediation process encourages the parties to freely express their position and needs in order to arrive at a fair settlement. Procedural rules that control the order and timeliness of decisionmaking in the trial process are unnecessary since the parties in mediation set their own decisionmaking schedule.

A mediation decision, if it is achieved (sometimes the parties are not successful), is most commonly embodied in a written agreement, much like a contract, that is enforceable. Mediation might provide a less costly method for resolution of disputes depending

Attributes of Dispute Resolution: Litigation, Arbitration, and Mediation

Factors	Litigation	Arbitration	Mediation
Legal precedent	essential part of decision	not necessary part of decision	not necessary unless parties rely upon law
Rules of evidence	essential part	followed informally	not necessary part of the process
Discovery	essential by rule	limited	depends upon disclosure by the parties
Expense	can be costly	less costly (because shorter process, less involved)	less costly than *most* litigation
Speed	most cases very slow-moving	can be very fast	fast depending on the parties' timetable
Rules of procedure for presentation of information	essential	more informal than litigation	informal—rules set by the parties
Decisionmaker attributes	neutral, may/may not be technically knowledgeable	party selection of 1-3 arbitrators; combination of neutrals and partisans balanced by party selection	selection by the parties
Role of decisionmaker in the process of resolution	neutral—makes a decision	neutral—but makes a decision	neutral—not a decisionmaker; facilitator who directs and guides the process
Appeal	full scope of the merits	limited (except in mandatory arbitration, trial de novo)	limited grounds

on the time the mediation might take, whether the parties consult lawyers to check their mediation agreement, and so on.

C. PLANNING ALTERNATIVE DISPUTE RESOLUTION

Like all pretrial planning, determining alternatives to litigation requires familiarity with the factual and legal aspects of the dispute, your client's objectives, and the alternative choices and their attributes. In large part, you will be engaging in a process similar to that described in negotiation for deciding when to choose settlement over litigation. You are determining which process will yield the best result for your client in light of your client's needs and objectives.

After reviewing the attributes of arbitration and mediation, you might want to construct a chart that will help you plan which alternatives might be suitable for your client. These methods can be thought of as representing a spectrum of solutions. On one side of the spectrum would be the most formal method—litigation. On the other side, a far less formal process—mediation. We have included an example of a chart listing the general categories you should consider.

Determining which dispute resolution process is best for your client requires planning based on your client's objectives. While you might eventually formulate your own approach to this planning, we offer you one to help you think about and make choices in the area of alternative dispute resolution. We have included our suggested approach, which is based on the following five questions. These questions should be repeated throughout your representation, since the answers they generate will vary at different times in that representation:

1. What is your representational strategy?
2. What are the alternative methods of dispute resolution processes?
3. What are the advantages and disadvantages of each process?
4. Are there any ethical issues you should consider?[2]
5. Based on all the information, what is an appropriate recommendation?

Our brief discussion here provides a starting point for exploring on your own some of the questions that we pose in the discussion problems that follow on arbitration and mediation. We hope that this limited exposure to two alternative dispute resolution processes will encourage you to explore the other alternatives that exist. But more important, we suggest that, as your enthusiasm and mastery of the litigation approach grows, you think about using your creative energies for developing new ways to approach litigation and alternative methods to resolve disputes.

---

2. Some important issues in alternative dispute resolution concern ethical issues. You should recognize that your role in decision-making and in opting for or choosing alternatives to litigation might engender ethical issues. In some alternative processes, your role might be one of adviser, a role as active here as it would be in litigation. You will need to think about, recognize, and plan to deal with potential conflicts that might arise in recommending one process over another, in relationship to a potential loss of a fee, or in being actively involved and potentially representing adverse or conflicting interests. Consultation with professional alternative dispute resolution guidelines and professional codes of conduct and your own sense of fairness and judgment will have to guide your conduct.

CIVIL PROBLEMS: SUMMERS v. HARD

PROBLEM 144

Plaintiffs' and Defendants' Attorneys: Mediation

Plaintiffs and defendants have been pursuing litigation to resolve the wrongful death and emotional distress claims brought by plaintiffs in *Summers v. Hard*. Formal discovery has been completed by the parties. The discovery process has been time-consuming and expensive. However, as new attorneys, your experience with litigation was limited. Now that you have experienced pretrial preparation, you can imagine how time-consuming and costly litigation in the *Summers v. Hard* case will be.

The plaintiffs' attorney has decided to investigate the possibility of mediation. Plaintiffs' attorney telephoned the defendants' attorneys and suggested a meeting to discuss mediation as an alternative.

PREPARATION

READ: (1) Pretrial Case File Entries 1-39, 59-61, 63, 90; (2) Chapters I and XI. Now think about and answer the following questions:

1. Generally, is mediation binding on the parties? Explain the significance of this answer.

2. Is there any application for mediation in the criminal process?

3. In most litigation, there are weak parties and strong parties. Factors that characteristically make a party "weak" or "strong" are diverse (e.g., wealth or poverty of the party; facts or applicable law in the dispute; abilities of the attorney).

   a. What characteristics make a party weak?

   b. Strong?

   c. Describe the strengths and weaknesses of each of the parties in *Summers v. Hard*.

   d. Why would the strong party mediate? Does strength give this party any advantage in the mediation process?

4. In the mediation process what role should a party's lawyer play?

5. What effect is there on the mediation if the process is mandated by court rules? Court order? Contract? By agreement of the parties? Explain.

6. Generally, what are the advantages of using mediation in the *Summers v. Hard* case?

7. Generally, what are the disadvantages of using mediation in the *Summers v. Hard* case?

8. Can mediation work in a litigation situation such as the *Summers v. Hard* case? Explain.

9. In *Summers v. Hard* would mediation benefit:

   a. Plaintiffs? Why?

   b. Defendants? Why?

10. Would you choose mediation to resolve *Summers v. Hard*? Explain.

ASSIGNMENT FOR CLASS

1. Before class, prepare a memorandum discussing court litigation, its principles and operation; then contrast litigation to mediation, its principles and operation.

2. In class, plaintiffs' and defendants' attorneys meet and discuss mediation and its specific use in *Summers v. Hard*.

PROBLEM 145

Plaintiffs' and Defendants' Attorneys: Arbitration

Plaintiffs and defendants have been pursuing litigation to resolve the wrongful death and emotional distress claims brought by plaintiffs in *Summers v. Hard*. Formal discovery has been completed by the parties. The discovery process has been time-consuming and expensive. However, as new attorneys, your experience with litigation was limited. Now you have learned how time-consuming and costly litigation in the *Summers v. Hard* case will be. Perhaps it is time to reexamine the court litigation model of dispute resolution and explore other models such as arbitration and mediation.

Defendants' attorneys have decided to investigate the possibility of arbitration. Defendants' attorneys telephoned plaintiffs' attorney and at the end suggested a meeting to discuss arbitration as an alternative.

PREPARATION

READ: (1) Pretrial Case File Entries 1-39, 59-61, 63, 90; (2) Chapters I and XI. Now think about and answer the following questions:

1. One of the major differences between court litigation and arbitration is that extensive discovery is not permissible in arbitration.

   a. How would you prepare for arbitration in *Summers v. Hard*?

   b. Since discovery is not permissible, how can it be ensured that the truth will be ascertained in arbitration?

2. Does it matter if the arbitration is binding or non-binding? Why?

3. Should there be a right to trial de novo by either party after the arbitration decision? Why or why not?

4. Explain what effect, if any, there may be on arbitration if the process is pursuant to:

   a. Court rules.

   b. Court order.

   c. Contract.

   d. Agreement of the parties. Explain.

5. Should arbitration be required only for cases in which the disputed amount is under $25,000? Explain.

6. Generally, why select arbitration instead of court litigation?

7. What are the advantages of selecting arbitration for the *Summers v. Hard* case?

8. What are the disadvantages of selecting arbitration for the *Summers v. Hard* case?

9. Does arbitration in *Summers v. Hard* benefit:

   a. Plaintiffs? Why?

   b. Defendants? Why?

10. Is arbitration a viable alternative in *Summers v. Hard*? Explain.

ASSIGNMENT FOR CLASS

1. Before class, prepare a memorandum discussing court litigation, its principles and operation; then contrast litigation to arbitration, its principles and operation.

2. In class, plaintiffs' and defendants' attorneys meet and discuss arbitration and its specific use in *Summers v. Hard*.

Pretrial Case Files

CONTENTS

CRIMINAL CASE FILE: State v. Hard   459

CIVIL CASE FILE: Summers v. Hard   563
(Includes Criminal Pretrial Case File, Entries 1-35.)

GENERAL RESEARCH CASE FILE   645

Criminal Case File
State v. Hard

Local Man Shot by Ex-Con Ed Hard

At 9:10 p.m. last night, a jealousy and alcohol-fueled grudge between an ex-convict and a local survivalist leader exploded with a gunshot. A seeming act of vengeance by Edward Hard, a convicted rapist, left the victim, Bruno Summers, lying in the arms of his newlywed wife, Deborah.

Police Investigators say Summers was shot in the chest with a .22 caliber pistol and is presently at Mercy Hospital listed in critical condition.

The investigators also say Hard was arrested at his home less than two hours after the shooting.

The shooting occurred at the Unicorn Tavern located on the corner of 49th and Baltimore in Ruston.

Bert Kain, a witness at the scene, sketched a history of confrontations between Ed Hard, 27, and Bruno Summers, 30. Kain, a regular at the tavern, stated "I knew something was gonna happen. A couple of weeks ago Ed fought with that Bruno (Summers) guy. Afterwards, Ed (Hard) said he was gonna get that guy and he did just that."

Other witnesses to the bloody shooting detail a similar story of escalating violent encounters between Hard and Summers that began two weeks ago. On August 20th, Hard, who is known to have dated Debbie Summers before her recent marriage to Bruno, allegedly attacked Bruno Summers from behind as Bruno and his then fiancee, Debbie, were attempting to leave the Unicorn Tavern.

Mary Apple, a waitress at the Unicorn was a witness to the first clash.

Barroom Shot Proves Fatal

Early this morning Bruno Summers, local survivalist leader, died of gunshot wounds inflicted four days earlier in a senseless shooting at the Unicorn Tavern in Ruston.

The alleged assailant, Edward Hard, has been held in Jamner County jail since the night of the shooting. Originally, Hard was charged with first degree assault, but Prosecuting Attorney O. Long says the charge against Hard will now likely be changed to murder.

Neo-Nazis March for Death Penalty

Spurred by the shooting death of their local leader Bruno Summers, a neo-Nazi Survivalist group known as "Americans for America," paraded to the Jamner County Courthouse shouting demands of the death penalty for Edward Hard, Summer' alleged assailant.

Feature

Market for Murder

Customer:"A bottle of Wild Turkey and a pack of Camels, please."

Clerk:"Yes, Sir. Will that be all today?"

Customer:"Oh, yeah, and a .22."

Clerk:"Very good, Sir."

As of yet, this scene isn't being played out at your Safeway. But if one considers the ease at which anyone can purchase guns, from "Saturday Night Specials" to machine guns, given the laws that are in effect today, the day of "express-lane check-out, nine items or less no waiting" sales of deadly artillery is close at hand.

The underground illegal sales of guns has been and always will be a disturbing fact of life. More disturbing is the cavalier flaunting of regulations by licensed sellers in purveying their deadly trade.

A recent incident in our "All-American" city of Ruston should again focus public attention on the problem of gun sales to those whom society and the law has deemed unfit to own or possess a "piece," criminals and minors.

Edward Hard, a twenty-seven year old convicted rapist, is now awaiting trial in Jamner County jail for the murder of Bruno Summers. Ed Hard is accused of fatally shooting Bruno Summers in the chest at close range with a .22 caliber handgun purchased at a licensed gunshop.

3-PART FEATURE
Honeymoon to Heartbreak: The Debbie Summers Story

The children, eight year-old Ronnie and Amanda, just twelve, play in the room glancing every so often at the woman sadly rocking in Daddy's chair. Ronnie and Amanda wonder whether the laughing lady who Daddy brought home as their new mother will ever return from behind those vacant eyes.

Debbie Summers became the wife of Bruno Summers and the mother of Amanda and Ronnie on August 27, 198X. Debbie became a widow ten days later. Bruno died of a gunshot wound allegedly inflicted in a jealous rage by an old boyfriend of Debbie.

With one quick shot the alleged assailant, Edward Hard, transformed Debbie Summers from a happy newlywed into a bereaved widow. Debbie Summers is now a widowed, single mother of two children she has only barely gotten to know.

Debbie isn't doing a very good job of being a mother. She is depressed and dazed. Her emotional state is a reflection of the nightmare that haunts her, asleep or awake, since she held the bleeding, dying Bruno in her arms that tragic night.

TELEVISION AND RADIO LOG

SEPTEMBER 3:   RADIO

KIPI: (9:10 a.m., Jamner) - 11:03 p.m. - Report of barroom shooting. No description of suspect given. (30 seconds.)

SEPTEMBER 4:   TELEVISION

KENG: (Channel 5, Jamner) - 6:37 a.m. - Report of "survivalist leader" shooting. Hard described as a suspect. (45 seconds.)
5:17 p.m. - On the scene video report from Unicorn. Hard identified as "convicted rapist" suspect. (60 seconds.)

KMMO: (Channel 4, Jamner) - 5:12 p.m. - Report of "Neo-Nazi" leader being shot. Hard's criminal background described. (30 seconds.)

KARO: (Channel 7, Jamner) - 12:11 p.m. - Barroom shooting incident reported. Hard described as "ex-con suspect." (45 seconds.)
5:12 p.m. - same news copy as for 12:11 p.m. report. (45 seconds.)

                               RADIO

KIPI: 6:20 a.m., 7:03 a.m., 8:03 a.m., 9:02 a.m., 11:02 a.m., 12:04 p.m. - Report on Unicorn Tavern shooting. Hard background criminal and personal, briefly sketched. (45 seconds.)

KARO: (7:20 a.m., Jamner) - Every half hour at 17 minutes after the hour and 13 minutes before the hour between 5:47 a.m. and 12:17 p.m., description of shooting incident. Background (very brief) of Summers and Hard (45 seconds).

SEPTEMBER 7:   RADIO

KIPI: 10:02 p.m., 11:03 p.m. - Report of Summers' death.

SEPTEMBER 8:   TELEVISION

    KARO: 12:12 p.m., 6:12 p.m. - Report of death by
                gunshot of Summers. Describe shooting events
                again. (45 seconds.)

    KSTV: (Channel 13, Ruston) - 5:30 p.m. - Report of
                Summers' death. Detective Kelly gives
                background to shooting and death. (60
                seconds.)

    KIPI: 6:20 a.m., 7:03 a.m., 8:03 a.m., 9:02 a.m.,
                12:06 p.m. - Report of Summers' death and
                possible murder charges against "convicted
                felon" Hard. (45 seconds.)

    KARO: Every half hour between 5:01 a.m. and 12:16
                p.m. and at 6:21 p.m. - Report of Summers'
                death and possible murder charges against
                "convicted felon" Hard. (45 seconds.)

SEPTEMBER 9:   RADIO

    KIPI: 12:21 p.m., 6:22 p.m. - Report of charge of
                first degree murder against "convicted felon"
                Hard. (30 seconds.)

    KARO: 12:16 p.m., 5:24 p.m. - Report of murder
                charge filed against Hard. (30 seconds.)

SEPTEMBER 23:   TELEVISION

    KARO: 12:12 p.m. - Live coverage (including
                helicopter use) of Summers' survivalist group
                march on Jamner County Courthouse demanding
                death penalty for Hard. (1 minute 15
                seconds.)

    KSTV: 5:06 p.m., 10:07 p.m. - Report on "death
                penalty" march by survivalist group. Hard
                referenced to. (45 seconds.)

                            RADIO

    KIPI: 1:02 p.m., 2:01 p.m., 3:03 p.m., 4:03 p.m.,
                5:03 p.m., 6:05 p.m. - Report on
                demonstration calling for death penalty for
                Hard. (45 seconds.)

    KARO: 12:13 p.m., 12:43 p.m., 5:15 p.m. - Report of
                march by survivalist group demanding death
                penalty for Hard. (30 seconds.)

SEPTEMBER 30:   TELEVISION

KENG: 5:41 p.m. - Commentary on "gun control."
              References to Summers' death. Hard as
              suspect, and demonstration of September 23.
              (1 minute 15 seconds.)

SUPERIOR COURT OF THE STATE OF MAJOR FOR JAMNER COUNTY

PEOPLE OF STATE OF MAJOR,	)))	
Plaintiff,	))	No. MJR-1000
	))	INFORMATION
v.	))	
EDWARD TAYLOR HARD,	))	
Defendant,	)))	

I, Prosecuting Attorney for Jamner County in the name and by the authority of the State of Major, do accuse Edward Taylor Hard of the crime of <u>murder in the first degree</u>, committed as follows:

That the defendant Edward Taylor Hard, in Jamner County, Major, on or about September 3, 198X, with premeditated intent to cause the death of another person did cause the death of Bruno Summers, a human being, who died on or about September 7, 198X.

Contrary to statute, and against the peace and dignity of the State of Major.

Prosecuting Attorney
By

L. Yates

L. Yates
Senior Deputy Prosecuting
Attorney

JAMNER POLICE DEPARTMENT REPORT   SUSPECT INFORMATION

DATE	TIME	POLICE DEPT.\ UNIT	CASE NO.	FILE NO.	
9/3/8X	2300 hrs	Jamner/ 4	00432150	5000	

BOOKING DATE	TIME	OFFENSE			B.A. NO.
9/4/8X	0130 hrs	Assault 1st degree			13000

NAME (LAST, FIRST, MI)		SEX	RACE	
Hard, Edward Taylor		M	White	

DATE OF BIRTH	STATE\PROVINCE OF BIRTH	HEIGHT	WEIGHT	HAIR	EYES	SKIN TONE
4/11/5X	Major	5'8"	165 lbs	Brn	Brn	Light

SCARS, MARKS, TATTOOS, ETC.	CAUTION-ARMED, DANGEROUS	STATEMENT TAKEN
"Mom" right forearm		Yes

LAST KNOWN ADDRESS-CITY, STATE, ZIP	PHONE	DRIVER LICENSE NO.
1492 West, Ruston, Major	832-2314	HARDTEJ592AL

STATE	EXPIRES	SOCIAL SECURITY NO.	LOCAL NO.	FBI NO.	STATE ID NO.
Major	8X	522-83-2466		12133	M-1912

FINGERPRINT CLASSIFICATION	ALIAS NAME(S)	VEH. LIC. NO.	STATE
	Ed	HIGH	Major

VEHICLE ID NO.	YEAR	MAKE	MODEL	STYLE	COLOR(S)

OCCUPATION	BUSINESS ADDRESS OR SCHOOL
House Painter	1492 West, Ruston, Major 832-2314

MARITAL STATUS\ CHILDREN (NO.)	LIVING WITH	TIME IN COUNTY	UNION AND LOCAL NO.
Single	Self	Life	

INVESTIGATING OFFICER	SERIAL	UNIT	PHONE
Kelly	113	4	625-2000

CRIMINAL RECORD (CONVICTIONS)

Rape   3 Thefts
Auto Theft
2 DWIs

ACTIVE PAROLE OR PROBATION?	PROBATION OFFICER\PHONE
Yes	Smith 383-0620

FACTS OF CRIME (HOW CRIME PLANNED - HOW CARRIED OUT - ETC.) (INDICATE ANY WEAPONS INVOLVED)

Suspect was observed by witness Tom Donaldson shoot victim,
Bruno Summers, on 9/3/8X in Jamner County, Major.

NAMES OF ACCOMPLICES

ADDITIONAL CASE(S) SUSPECTED\CLEARED

ANTICIPATED DATE OF REFERRAL	ANTICIPATED CHARGE
9/6/8X	Assault 2d degree

FURTHER INVESTIGATION NECESSARY -STATE WHETHER PRESENCE REQUIRED   (LINE-UP, EXEMPLAR, ETC)

OBJECTIONS TO RELEASE: YES X NO___   STATE REASONS FOR RECOMMENDATIONS:

Suspect armed with .22 caliber revolver, shot victim without
provocation.

PRELIMINARY APPEARANCE DATE	JUDGE	BOND POSTED, DATE: AMT: CO:
9/4/8X	Roe	

P.R. YES ___ NO X	CONDITIONS:

RETURN DATE	RETURNED ___	EXCUSED ___	NOT RELEASED X BOND SET:$
9/6/8X			

Entry 4: Jamner Police Department Report   469

FOLLOW-UP POLICE REPORT BY DETECTIVE KELLY

1. ## SUSPECT

    EDWARD TAYLOR HARD, 28, 1492 West, Ruston, Major
    832-2314
    5'8", 165 lbs.

    Arrested and booked Inv. Assault.

2. ## PERSONS INTERVIEWED

DEBORAH SUMMERS	1962 NE 6th	433-1112
TOM DONALDSON	1776 Amble, Apt. 3	(B)233-4173 (H)833-5142
MARY APPLE	1984 South 41st	(B)233-4173 (H)394-8621

3. 9/3/8x 2120 hrs.   Detective B. Kelly was contacted at his home by Detective Sergeant Maida and advised of a shooting which took place at the Unicorn Tavern at 5302 No. 49th Street. Victim has been shot once. His condition is unknown at this time.

4. 9/3/8x 2145 hrs.   Detective Kelly arrives at scene and is met by Officer Downing. Downing advises that the shooting took place at the rear of the interior of the tavern. The victim has been removed from the scene and transported by aid unit to Mercy Hospital. The victim is alive. Officer Downing points out the location of the shooting and blood on the wall. This will be photographed later. Victim is Bruno Summers.

5. 9/3/8x 2155 hrs.   Detective Kelly interviews wife of victim, Mrs. Deborah Summers; Mrs. Summers, who says she did not see what actually happened, identifies the man who ran out of the tavern with a gun as Edward Taylor Hard, a former boyfriend, who resides at 1492 West. Mrs. Summers leaves for Mercy Hospital.

6.   9/3/8x   2158 hrs.   Patrol car dispatched to suspect's residence.

7.   9/3/8x   2205 hrs.   The scene is photographed by a police identification technician. Detective Kelly made the following observations which were recorded: a few blood spots on the floor eight feet south of north wall and four feet west of restroom wall. There was also a mark on the north wall approximately five feet six inches from the east restroom wall which was four feet from the floor. Closer examination revealed that this was not a recently made mark.

8.   9/3/8x   2235 hrs.   The scene was secured and Dets. returned to the Homicide Office.

9.   9/3/8x   2245 hrs.   Detectives advised that patrol has arrested suspect Edward Hard at his residence and recovered a handgun. Officer Yale en route to Homicide Office with suspect Hard and the weapon. Patrol Officer West calls from Mercy Hospital where the victim is receiving emergency treatment, is alive but in critical condition. Patrol Officers are interviewing Tom Donaldson, bartender at the Unicorn Tavern. Interview indicates that two weeks ago, on approximately August 20th, suspect and victim had fought and suspect had threatened the victim's life. Tonight, at approximately 2105 hrs. there was a confrontation between the suspect and the victim at the Unicorn Tavern.

10. 9/3/8x   2250 hrs.   Sergeant Maida placed a hold on 911 tape for call received from the Unicorn Tavern.

11. 9/3/8x   2300 hrs.   Suspect has been placed in interview room by Officer Yale. Detective Kelly into interview room with suspect, Edward Taylor Hard. Information for a Suspect Information Report is obtained from Hard. He states that he is a self-employed house painter. Hard is advised of his rights from the standard form. He reads the form out loud and after each entry he is asked if he understands, and he

answers yes to all four admonishments. He also signifies this by placing his initials in the left hand column of the form alongside each entry. He also places a signature in the appropriate box. At this time he signs the written waiver portion. Suspect Hard appeared to be under the influence of something. He had watery red eyes, spoke with slurred speech and had the odor of alcoholic beverage on his breath. Nevertheless, he appeared to understand his rights and to knowingly waive them.

Hard's Statement

Suspect Hard stated that at approximately 9:00 p.m. he and two friends, John Gooding and Rebecca Karr, had gone to the Unicorn Tavern for a drink. He stated that they were sitting at the bar and he got up and went to the restroom. As he approached the restroom, the victim, Bruno Summers, came out of the restroom and confronted him. Suspect Hard indicated that he was surprised to see Summers and had been unaware of the fact that Summers had been in the tavern prior to the confrontation. Suspect Hard said that prior to this time he had not looked around the tavern, but had rather been sitting at the bar drinking and conversing with his friends. Suspect Hard stated that the victim Summers threatened and shoved him and then reached into his pocket. Hard stated that in response, he pulled a .22 caliber revolver from his coat pocket to protect himself, pointed it at the wall and the gun accidentally discharged hitting the victim.

12. 9/3/8x 2330 hrs. Suspect Hard's statement was reduced to writing and signed by the suspect. After giving this initial statement, Detective Kelly confronted Hard with the fact that he had been overheard to make a remark about Summers prior to the shooting, and that Hard must have been aware of the fact that Summers was in the tavern before meeting him coming out of the restroom. Second, Hard was confronted with the fact that the firearm was obviously pointed at victim Summers rather than at the wall for it would have been impossible to misjudge the aim at that short a distance. At this point, suspect Hard stated, "I think I'd better get an attorney. Don't you think I'd better get an attorney?" Det. Kelly stated, "If you want an attorney, I can't ask you any further questions." Suspect Hard then stated, "Do you think an attorney could help me?" Det. answered, "That's up to you to decide. Do you want an attorney?" Hard then responded, "I want to tell you what happened. That guy is a Nazi. Yes I knew he was there. He deserved what he got. I couldn't continue to be afraid." Det. Kelly

Hard's Confession

then again asked, "Do you want an attorney?" Suspect Hard answered, "Yes, probably better get one." No further questions were asked by Det. Kelly.

13. 9/3/8x 2340 hrs.   Suspect Hard was turned over to the custody of Officer Yale with instructions to conduct a breathalyzer test on suspect Hard but to conduct no further questioning concerning the shooting.

14. 9/4/8x 0030 hrs.   Officer West arrives at Homicide Office from Mercy Hospital. Items of evidence gathered by Officer West from the hospital are delivered by Officer West to the evidence room. Evidence items include the victim's clothing and a closed folding buck knife found in the right hand pocket of the victim's jacket. West reports that victim is in critical but stable condition at Mercy Hospital.

15. 9/4/8x 0130 hrs.   Suspect Hard booked for assault in the first degree.

16. 9/4/8x 0910 hrs.   Several phone messages from the media concerning the case. Victim Summers seems to be the self-proclaimed leader of a neo-Nazi survivalist group. Messages related to Information Officer. Neo-Nazi information confirmed by membership card Officer West found in victim's wallet.

17. 9/4/8x 0920 hrs.   Det. to computer terminal. Check gun for stolen registration and any firearm registration to suspect. Firearm registered to Edward Taylor Hard. Also ran suspect and victim in computer system. They check clear in WACIC and NCIC. Both have rap sheets contained in file.

18. 9/4/8x 1100 hrs.   Affidavit of probable cause completed. Met with Senior Deputy Prosecutor Yates and discussed case. He will inform deputy in charge of preliminary appearance calendar of police department objection to release. Yates agrees on potential charge of assault.

---

19. 9/4/8x 1305 hrs.   Appointment with Deborah Summers. Statement obtained from her. On August 20, suspect Hard had assaulted victim in the Unicorn Tavern. Victim struck suspect Hard, chipping tooth and bloodying suspect's lip. Suspect threatened victim. On Sept. 3, witness Summers and victim were in the same tavern, and suspect made a comment about victim. She now states she witnessed suspect shoot victim on September 3rd. She saw no provocation by victim.

20. 9/4/8x 1410 hrs.   Patrol dispatched to Mercy Hospital to recover slug taken from victim's body in surgery.

21. 9/4/8x 1430 hrs.   Officer Harris delivers slug and victim's blood sample to Homicide Office. He packaged, labeled and placed them in evidence.

22. 9/4/8x 1500 hrs.   Lab reports request forms for fingerprints, victim's clothing and firearm completed and submitted to crime lab.

23. 9/5/8x 1000 hrs.   Report delivered to senior deputy Yates and discussed. Further follow-up requested including additional information from bartender and waitress.

24. 9/5/8x 1300 hrs.   Arrived at the Unicorn Tavern. No additional information obtained from Donaldson, bartender. He can add nothing to statement. He recalls other patrons of tavern at time of shooting as:

Bert Kain and Antje Lenz - regular customers, he will have them call.

Robin Lontlebunk - regular customer, address unknown.

Waitress Mary Apple works later shift. Called at home -- no answer.

25. 9/5/8x 1515 hrs.   Returned Homicide Office. Called Mary Apple. She did not see shooting because her back was to suspect and victim. She witnessed August 20 assault by suspect on victim, and statement is the same as Donaldson about this incident. She said that she thought Hard was intoxicated on September 3rd (speech was slurred). She could not remember if either Summers or Hard was intoxicated on August 20th. She recalls Cindy Rigg, patron, was in the tavern on August 20.

26. 9/6/8x 1030 hrs.   Suspect charged Assault. Case cleared.

27. 9/7/8x 0745 hrs.   Sgt. Maida advised Det. Kelly that victim Bruno Summers died 0130 hrs. this day. Autopsy to be conducted at 1100 hrs. Called Senior Deputy Yates and apprised him.

28. 9/7/8x 1130 hrs.   Present at ME's Office for autopsy. Cause of death is gunshot wound.

29. 9/7/8x 1340 hrs.   Met with Senior Deputy Yates. Discussed ME's conclusion. Yates to have filing deputy re-evaluate case for murder charge. Yates requests that a statement be taken from Peter Dean.

30. 9/7/8x 1430 hrs.   Determine from Detective Boren of burglary and theft unit that a potential witness, Jack Waters, may be in County Jail and wants to talk to homicide investigators. He is charged with possession of stolen property 1, bail $20,000.

31. 9/23/8x 1500 hrs.   Arrive at County Jail. Jack Waters brought down to homicide office. He indicates he observed the shooting, has important information, and that he wants immunity in exchange for testimony. Told him this was for the prosecutor to decide.

MAJOR STATE PATROL

610 3rd Avenue, Public Safety Building, 2nd Floor   Jamner , Major   646-1820

CASE NO. 00432150

DATE OF CRIME: 9/3/8X
DATE OF ARREST: 9/3/8X

HOMICIDE

WITNESSES:

Waitress Mary Apple	1984 So. 41st	(B)	233-4173
Dr. Brett Day	Mercy Hospital	(H)	394-8621
Peter Dean	444 Aitken St.	(B)	352-1000
Bartender Tom Donaldson	1776 Amble, Apt. #3	(H)	833-5142
Fred Faye	210 North Arch St. (American Gun Shop)		543-8444
Dr. L.R. Jackson	Medical Examiner's Office *autopsy*		222-1783
Patron Bert Kain	1408 Talbot Way		833-4829
Det. B. Kelly	Police Dept., Homicide Unit		342-1213
Patron Aug 20 Cindy Rigg	10001 Axcell Blvd.		441-3000
Victim's wife Deborah Summers	1962 N.E. 6th		433-1112
H. Treadwell	Crime Laboratory		981-2222
Off. F. West	Police Dept., Unit 220		342-1183
Off. M. Yale	Police Dept., Unit 13		342-1181

Report prepared by: Det. Kelly, J.P.D.

STATE OF MAJOR

MAJOR STATE PATROL

610 3rd Avenue, Public Safety Building, 2nd Floor   Jamner , Major   646-1820

CASE NO. 00432150

TIME: 2150
DATE: 9/3/8X
TYPE OF PREMISES: Tavern

HOMICIDE

EVIDENCE RECORD

Item	Quantity	Description	
1	1	Bruno Summers' T-Shirt	West
2	1	Bruno Summers' Jacket	West
3	1	Bruno Summers' Buck Knife	West
4	1	Neo-Nazi Card	Kelly
5	1	Edward Taylor Hard's .22 caliber revolver, serial #76636	Yale
6	5	One (1) expended and four (4) live rounds	Yale
7	1	Edward Taylor Hard's breathalyzer ampoule	Yale
8	1	.22 caliber slug removed from Bruno Summers by Dr. Brett Day	Harris
9	1	Blood sample	Harris
10	1	Test fired slug	Treadwell
11	1	Clothes - proximity testing	Treadwell

Entry 4: Jamner Police Department Report

JAMNER POLICE DEPARTMENT
ALCOHOL INFLUENCE REPORT

CITATION NUMBER
00432150

STATUS (DRIVER,PED., ETC.)	MIRANDA GIVEN?	DATE\TIME OF ACCIDENT	INCIDENT NUMBER
Other		9/3/8X 2100 hrs	

SUBJECT'S NAME	DOB	HT	WT	SEX	RACE
Edward Hard					

SUBJECT REQUEST LAWYER?	WAS A LAWYER CONTACTED?	IF YES, TIME
No	No	

SUBJECT'S MOUTH CHECKED?	OPERATING MOTOR VEHICLE AT TIME OF STOP\ACCIDENT?
Capped Tooth	No

PHYSICAL DEFECTS?   IF YES, EXPLAIN:
No

IMPAIRED VISION?   IF YES, EXPLAIN:
No

CORRECTIVE LENSES? IF YES, EXPLAIN:	WEARING LENSES AT TIME OF ACCIDENT?
No	

IMPAIRED SPEECH?   IF YES, EXPLAIN:
No

ILL?   IF YES, EXPLAIN:
Yes   "Shot a man."

TAKING MEDICATION?   IF YES, EXPLAIN:
No

MEDICAL WARNING ON LABEL OF DRUG\MEDICATION?	DIABETIC?	TAKE INSULIN?
	No	No

AMOUNT OF LAST DOSE:	TIME OF LAST DOSE:	EPILEPTIC?
		No

INJURED?   IF YES, EXPLAIN:
Yes   lip - stitches out

UNDER CARE OF MEDICAL\DENTAL PROFESSIONAL?   IF YES, EXPLAIN:
Yes   Broken tooth and severed lip

INJURED\INVOLVED IN ANY ACCIDENT(S) IN LAST 24 HOURS?   IF YES, EXPLAIN:
No

HOW MUCH SLEEP IN LAST 24 HOURS?	WITHOUT LOOKING, WHAT TIME IS IT?
5 hrs.	REPLY: 11pm ACTUAL: 0005 hrs.

WHERE GOING AT TIME OF THE STOP\ACCIDENT?	WHERE STARTED:

TIME STARTED:	ANYTHING MECHANICALLY WRONG WITH VEHICLE DRIVING? IF YES, EXPLAIN:

WHAT DRINKING?	WHERE?
Beer	Unicorn Tavern / Home

HOW MUCH?	TIME STARTED:	TIME STOPPED:
"Couple." "Maybe four."	2000 hrs.	2200 hrs.

FEEL AFFECTED?   EXPLAIN:
Yes   "Tired."

DRINKING SINCE STOP\ACCIDENT?	IF YES, EXPLAIN:
Shooting Yes	"Couple beers at home."

OBSERVATIONS - EXPLAIN:

Clothing - mussed, shirt tail out.   Eyes - watery, bloodshot.
Breath - moderate.   Attitude - cooperative.
Speech - slurred.
Color of face - flushed.

Entry 5:   Alcohol Influence Report

UNUSUAL ACTIONS \ STATEMENTS:	PG 2

TEST AREA (DESCRIBE) Level

WALKING AND TURNING (Have subject walk a straight line, in heel-to-toe manner, then turn and walk back in same manner, describe subject's performance - falling, swaying, staggering, etc.)

Swaying

BALANCE (Have subject stand erect with feet together, eyes closed, and head back. Observe subject's balance. Then describe it - falling, swaying, sure, etc.)

Falling

FINGER TO NOSE (Have subject stand erect with eyes closed, head back, and arms extended horizontally to sides. Then, one arm at a time, have subject touch the tip of his\her nose with tip of index finger, draw an arrow from the appropriate box to the point on face touched.)

ALPHABET (Have subject say alphabet. Record the order of the letters, and letters missed or repeated.)

ABCDEFGHIJKLMNOPQQRSTUVWXYZ

PUPILS 1. Under existing lighting, describe subject's pupils - dilated, contracted, normal, etc.

Dilated--slow

2. Flash light in subject's eyes and describe reaction:

OFFICER'S OPINION (of subject's impairment due to use of alcoholic beverage \ drugs):

IMPLIED CONSENT WARNINGS You are being advised of your right to refuse to submit to a sobriety breath test, and of the following additional sanctions: 1) That your refusal will cause your privilege to drive to be revoked or denied; 2) That if you agree to the test, it will be administered at city expense and the results may be used against you in a criminal prosecution; 3) That you may request an additional test, including a blood test to be administered by a qualified person of your choosing and at your expense; 4) That your refusal to take the test may be used against you in any subsequent criminal trial.

After taking these admonitions into consideration, do you agree to take the test? Yes

BREATHALYZER TEST (Check off each step of the chemical test as it is performed.)

[X] 1. Warm up machine until thermometer indicates 47-53 degrees c.

[X] 2. See that nullmeter is centered.

[X] 3. See that comparison ampoule is in place. In left hand holder.

[X] 4. Guage test ampoule and record test ampoule control number.

[X] 5. Insert and connect test ampoule.

[X] 6. Turn selector to "take," flush out, and turn selector to "analyze."

[X] 7. When (piston down) or (red light) comes on, wait 1 1\2 minutes, or until (read) (green light) comes on, then conter meter using balance wheel or knob with light on and selector left in "analyze" position.

[X] 8. Align scale pointer with start line.

[X] 9. Turn selector to "take," take sample. Turn selector to "analyze." Record time sample was taken.

[X] 10. When (piston down) or (red light) comes on, wait 1 1\2 minutes, or until (read) (green light) comes on, then center meter using balance wheel, or knob with light on, and selector left in "analyze" position.

[X] 11. Read answer on scale and record.

[X] 12. Dispose of test ampoule and bubbler.

[X] 13. Turn selector to off position.

WERE THERE ANY RADIO TRANSMISSIONS MADE FROM INSIDE THE TESTING ROOM WHILE THE BREATHALYZER TESTING WAS IN PROGRESS? NO

BREATHALYZER SERIAL NO.: TEST AMPOULE NO.: 123 CHEMICAL TEST RESULT: .16

DATE \ TIME COMPLETED: 9/4/8x 0100 CHARGE: Assault

As a condition of my release, I agree not to drive or return to my vehicle until:

SIGNED: Edward Taylor Hard 9/4/8x 0045

PRIMARY OFFICER 13 SECONDARY OFFICER (WITNESS)

APPLICATION TO TRANSFER PISTOL OR REVOLVER

STATE OF MAJOR
DEPARTMENT OF LICENSING
DIVISION OF PROFESSIONAL LICENSING

DEALER'S TRANSACTION NO.
826497-S

(ALL INFORMATION MUST BE TYPED OR PRINTED IN INK AND MUST BE LEGIBLE AND ACCURATE.)

INSTRUCTIONS TO DEALER	DEALER MUST BE SURE FORM IS COMPLETE IN FULL AND CLEARLY LEGIBLE. ORIGINAL COPY: SEND AT CLOSE OF BUSINESS DAY TO CHIEF OF POLICE OR SHERIFF DUPLICATE COPY: SEND IMMEDIATELY UPON DELIVERY OF WEAPON TO DEPT. OF LICENSING TRIPLICATE COPY: RETAIN FOR SIX (6) YEARS

SECTION A - DESCRIPTION OF FIREARM

WEAPON'S SERIAL NO.	CALIBER	IDENTIFYING NO.	CONDITION (NEW, USED)	BARREL LENGTH
76636	.22	N/A	Used	

MANUFACTURER AND IMPORTER	NCIC	TYPE OF ACTION (AUTO. REV.)	MODEL (NO. OR NAME)
H&R Arms Company		Revolver	

FORM INITIATED - DATE, TIME	NO DEALER SHALL TRANSFER A PISTOL OR REVOLVER TO THE APPLICANT
8/22/8X 1:30 PM	(BUYER) UNTIL THE STATUTORY TIME REQUIREMENT SHALL HAVE ELAPSED.

SECTION B - STATEMENT OF BUYER

SEX	DATE OF BIRTH	COLOR OF EYES	WEIGHT	HEIGHT	RACE OR COLOR
M	4/11/3X	BROWN	165	5'8"	WHITE

BUYER'S NAME LAST	FIRST	MI	OCCUPATION
HARD	EDWARD	T.	PAINTER

HOME ADDRESS NUMBER	STREET	RESIDENCE/BUS. PHONE
1492	WEST	832-2314

CITY	STATE	ZIP	COUNTY	PLACE OF BIRTH (CITY, STATE)
RUSTON	MAJOR	98139	TAMNER	RUSTON, MAJOR

U.S. CITIZEN?	NATIVE BORN?	NATURALIZED?	DECLARATION OF INTENT	STATE ALIEN CERT. ISSUED?
YES	YES			

BUYER----IMPORTANT READ CAREFULLY	The following persons are prohibited from receiving a firearm in interstate or foreign commerce under 18 USC chapter 44 and title VII of Public Law 90-351, as amended: fugitives from justice, persons under indictment or who have been convicted of a felony, persons adjudicated as mental defectives or mentally incompetent, or who have been committed to any mental institution, veterans discharged under dishonorable conditions, persons who have renounced U. S. citizenship. I certify that I will abide by these restrictions.

BUYER'S SIGNATURE	BUYER'S INITIALS
Edward Taylor Hard	ETH

CONCEALED WEAPON PERMIT NO. (IF APPLICABLE)

MAJOR STATE DRIVER LICENSE OR STATE ID NO. OR RESIDENCY METHOD. (I HAVE BEEN A RESIDENT OF THE STATE OF MAJOR FOR THE PREVIOUS CONSECUTIVE 90 DAYS AT THE FOLLOWING RESIDENCE(S)).

HARD*TEJ59*ZAL

SECTION C - STATEMENT OF DEALER

I certify that I hold Major State Dealers License Number ___14777___ and Federal Firearms License Number ___97820___ and that the above described buyer is personally known to me or has presented clear and satisfactory evidence of his identity and that the above description correctly describes the firearm to be transferred. On the basis of (1) the statements in Section B and (2) the information in State Law and the current list of Published Ordinances, it is my belief that the person named in B is lawfully entitled to purchase a firearm.

DATE WEAPON DELIVERED	TIME	NO DEALER SHALL TRANSFER A PISTOL OR REVOLVER TO THE APPLICANT UNTIL
8/27/8X	1:30 PM	STATUTORY TIME REQUIREMENT SHALL HAVE ELAPSED.

DEALER'S SIGNATURE	DEALER'S TITLE	DEALER'S PHONE NO.
Fred Faye	Owner	543-8444

DEALER'S STORE NAME	ADDRESS	CITY	ZIP
American Gun Shop	210 North Arch Street, Neva		98105

SEND THIS ORIGINAL TO LOCAL POLICE CHIEF OF SHERIFF UNDER WHOSE JURISDICTION YOUR DEALERSHIP IS LOCATED.

Edward Taylor Hard
1492 West
Ruston, Major 98139
(206) 832-2314

First / Point

1501

19-2\1250

August 27 19 *8x*

PAY TO
THE ORDER OF *American Gun Shop* $ *239 00/100*

Two hundred thirty nine and ~ 00/100 DOLLARS

JAMNER-FIRST NATIONAL BANK
Ruston Branch

Edward Taylor Hard

1860000841 84778 184 1601

THE AMERICAN GUN SHOP
210 NORTH ARCH ST.

DATE *8-27-8X*

ID *HARDATET54+7M*

DEPARTMENT OF THE TREASURY
BUREAU OF ALCOHOL, TOBACCO AND FIREARMS

FIREARMS TRANSACTION RECORD PART I - INTRA-STATE OVER-THE-COUNTER	TRANSFEROR'S TRANSACTION NO. *82649M-S*

NOTE: Prepare in original only. All entries other than signatures must be typed or clearly printed in ink. All signatures on this form must be in ink.

SECTION A - MUST BE COMPLETED PERSONALLY BY TRANSFEREE (BUYER)

TRANSFEREE'S (Buyer's) NAME (Last, First, MI) *HARD, EDWARD T.*	HEIGHT *5'8"*	WEIGHT *165*	RACE *WHITE*

RESIDENCE ADDRESS *1492 WEST RUSTON, MAJOR*	DATE OF BIRTH *4/11/5X*	PLACE OF BIRTH *RUSTON*

CERTIFICATION OF TRANSFEREE (Buyer) - An untruthful answer may subject you to criminal prosecution. Each question must be answered with a "yes" or a "no" inserted in the box at the right of the question.

Are you under indictment or information in any court for a crime punishable by imprisonment for a term exceeding one year? A formal accusation of a crime made by a prosecuting attorney, as distinguished from an indictment presented by a grand jury.	*NO*	
		Are you a fugitive from justice? *NO*
		Are you an unlawful user of, or addicted to, a drug(s)? *NO*
Have you been convicted in any court of a crime punishable by imprisonment for a term exceeding one year? (Note- the actual sentence given by the judge does not matter - a yes answer is necessary if the judge could have given a sentence of more than one year. Also, a "yes" answer is required if a conviction has been discharged, set aside, or dismissed pursuant to an expungement or rehabilitation statute. However, a crime punishable by imprisonment for a term exceeding one year does not include a conviction which has been set aside under the Federal Youth Corrections Act.)	*NO*	Have you ever been adjudicated mentally deficient or institutionalized? *NO*
		Discharged from the Armed Forces under dishonorable conditions? *NO*
		Are you a person who, having been a citizen of the U.S., has renounced U.S. citizenship? *NO*

I hereby certify that the answers to the above are true and correct. I understand that a person who answers "Yes" to any of the above questions is prohibited from purchasing and\or possessing a firearm, except as otherwise provided by Federal law. I also understand that the making of any false oral or written statement or the exhibiting of any false or misrepresented identification with respect to this transaction is punishable as a felony.

TRANSFEREE'S SIGNATURE *Edward Taylor Hard*	DATE *8/22/8X*

SECTION B - TO BE COMPLETED BY TRANSFEROR (SELLER)

THIS PERSON DESCRIBED IN SECTION A IS KNOWN TO ME OR HAS IDENTIFIED HIMSELF TO ME IN THE FOLLOWING MANNER:

TYPE OF IDENTIFICATION *Drivers License*	NUMBER ON IDENTIFICATION *NARD*TEJ59*2AL*

On the basis of (1) the statements in Section A; (2) the verification of identity noted in Section B; and (3) the information in the current list of Published Ordinances, it is my belief that it is not lawful for me to sell, deliver or otherwise dispose of the firearm described below to the person identified in Section A.

TYPE *Revolver*	MODEL *S+W Ctge*	CALIBER OR GAUGE *22*	SERIAL NO. *76636*

MANUFACTURER *H+R Arms Company*			

TRADE\CORPORATION NAME AND ADDRESS OF TRANSFEROR *American Ginn Shop, 210 N Arch St, Neva*	FIREARMS LICENSE NO. *97820*

TRANSFEROR'S (seller's) SIGNATURE *Fred Faye*	TRANSFEROR'S TITLE *Owner*	TRANSACTION DATE *8/22/8X*

AFT F 4473 (5300.9) PART 1 (11-81) PREVIOUS EDITIONS ARE OBSOLETE

OFFICE OF THE PROSECUTING ATTORNEY

Jamner County Courthouse
950 Ruston Avenue South
Ruston, Major 98404

(206) 584-2000

O. Long
Prosecuting Attorney

Dr. L.R. Jackson
Chief Medical Examiner
ATTN: Ms. P. Kim
Jamner County Medical Examiner
300 10th Avenue
Ruston, Major 98402

Deceased: Bruno E. Summers

Date of Death: September 7, 198X

Defendant: Edward Taylor Hard

Dear Dr. Jackson:

Because this death involves a possible homicide, we request that you assign a high priority to your examination report. As soon as possible, please send two copies of your report to:

Filing Unit Coordinator
Criminal Division
Jamner County Prosecuting Attorney

If you will return this letter with your report, we can expedite adding it to the criminal investigation file.

Thank you for your cooperation.

For J.B. Burns, Jamner County Prosecuting Attorney:

O. Long
Filing Unit Coordinator

Jamner County
Medical Examiner Division
Autopsy Report

L.R. Jackson, M.D.   J.T. Weal, M.D.
Chief Medical Examiner   Medical Examiner

                                     Dorian Ray Flannery
                                     Assistant Medical
                                     Examiner
                                     M.E. Case 84-543

Date and Time of Examination
7 September 198X at 2045 hours

EXTERNAL EXAMINATION:

IDENTIFICATION:

The body is identified by M.E. number on the right upper leg, as
well as a hospital identification band on the left wrist which
gives the name as "Bruno Summers."

CLOTHING:

The following clothing and therapeutic paraphernalia is initially
present:

1.   A blue and white hospital grown.
2.   A pair of white, jockey style undershorts.

The following therapeutic paraphernalia are present:

1.   An oro-tracheal tube and bite bar are taped in place.
2.   Two adhesive EKG pads are present on the right shoulder, and
      one each on the left shoulder, right subcostal region and
      left side of the abdomen.
3.   Eight sutures close a 10 cm carved incision line 2 cm
      inferior to the right anterior costochondral line.
4.   Intravenous catheters are taped in place in the left
      antecubital fossa, right upper arm.
5.   A chest tube is inserted between ribs 6 and 7, 2 cm medial
      to the posterior axillary line.

Before cleaning, the hands are examined. There is no visible evidence of gunshot residue. The fingernails have up to a 2 mm. overhang and are neatly trimmed and clean.

GENERAL DESCRIPTION:

With the clothing removed and the body cleaned, it is that of a well developed, normally nourished white man who appears to be in his late twenties to early thirties, and whose listed age is 30 years. The length is 6 feet 2 inches and weight as received is 210 pounds. The body is well preserved and has not been embalmed. Slight lividity is present dorsally and blanches with pressure.

The body is cold and has been refrigerated.

The scalp is covered by brown hair which measures up to approximately 3 inches when straightened. The face is clean shaven except for a fine, 1/8 inch stubble over the upper lip and a small amount of course brown hair over the lower chin. The external ears are normally formed and located. The irides are brown, corneae dull and conjunctivae pale. The skeleton of the nose is intact. No foreign material is present in the nares. The lips and tongue are intact. The teeth are natural and in good condition. An oro-tracheal tube is in place. The neck is symmetrical and trachea in the midline. The chest is normally formed. The abdomen is flat and soft and is the site of injuries to be described. No massae are palpable. The external genitalia are circumcised, adult male. The arms are symmetrical and normally formed. Intravenous catheters are present as previously described. The legs are symmetrical and normally formed. The back is straight and symmetrical.

Identifying marks include the following:

a.   A 1/4 inch depressed scar over the right frontal region.
b.   An irregular, 3/4 x 1/4 inch scar over the extensor aspect of the right forearm.
c.   A 3/4 x 1/4 inch scar over the extensor aspect of the right wrist.
d.   Pale striae over the anterior axillary fold bilaterally.
e.   A 1 x 1/4 inch vertical scar over the antero-medial aspect of the left thigh.
f.   Irregular to ovid scars measuring from 1/4 to 1 inch in diameter over the anterior knees and tibia.
g.   A 3/4 x 1/2 inch ovid scar over the left medial malleolus.

h.   A 1/2 x 1/4 inch ovid scar over the midline of the posterior
     neck.

Intravenous catheters are in place in the left antecubital fossa
and medial aspect of the right upper arm.   Three recent needle
punctures are also present in the right antecubital fossa.   Over
the medial aspect of the antecubital fossa there is a 5/8 x 1/2
inch hypertrophic, mottled hypo- and hyperpigmented scar.
Although not typical, this may represent a needle track and will
be examined microscopically.

EXTERNAL EVIDENCE OF INJURY:

1.   Gunshot Wound.

EXTERNAL WOUND: entrance wound is not visible, probably masked
by previously described suture line.

PATH OF BULLET: The bullet perforated the anterior abdominal
chest wall in the right upper quadrant close to the midline.   It
then passed into the anterior aspect of the right lobe of the
liver.   The site of entry in the liver is marked by 3 sutures.   A
1/4 inch tunnel proceeds through substance of liver to an exit
opening 3/8 inch wide.   It then pierced the diaphragm in the 6th
intercostal space in the mid axillary line.   The bullet entered
the anterior basal segment of the right lower lobe of the lung.
It then exited the lung and glanced off the inferior surface of
the 7th rib.   The 7th rib is inferiorly and interiorly grooved.
The bullet came to rest in the chest wall, embedded in the
interior/superior aspect of the 8th rib in the posterior axillary
line.   There is approx. 50 cc of blood in the right costophrenic
recess and 150 cc blood in the peritoneal cavity.

RECOVERY OF BULLET: A distorted copper jacket and lead bullet
were recovered from the 8th rib as noted above, by the hospital
surgery team.

COURSE OF BULLET: Relative to erect body, the bullet passed from
center to right, front to back at an angle of approx. 45°, and
roughly horizontal until striking 7th rib.   Bullet then passed
from above to below, very slightly from right towards center.

2.   Over the anterolateral aspect of the right upper leg there
is a cutaneous defect.   This is at a point 32 1/2 inches above
the heel.   It consists of a 1/2 x 1/4 inch ovid defect with the
long axis vertical. There is drying of the edges but no
significant abrasion is noted.   Incision of this area reveals a

minimal amount of hemorrhage at the borders of the lesion. There
is no deep hemorrhage or track leading from the wound.

The injuries are numbered for orientation only. The number does
not imply temporal sequence. The description of the injuries
will not be repeated under the Internal Examination.

INTERNAL EXAMINATION:

BODY CAVITIES:

There is blood in the cavities as previously described. Fibrous
adhesions are present between the diaphragm and dome of the right
lobe of the liver. The MEDIASTINUM is unremarkable. The organs
are anatomically disposed.

ORGAN SYSTEMS:

CARDIOVASCULAR SYSTEM:

The HEART weighs 330 grams and has its normal shape. The
PERICARDIUM is smooth and glistening. The CORONARY ARTERIES
arise and are distributed in the usual manner with right
dominance. They show no atherosclerosis. The ENDOCARDIUM is
smooth and glistening and the CARDIAC VALVES intent and
unremarkable. The MYOCARDIUM is reddish-brown and firm and shows
no focal lesions. The aorta follows its usual course and shows
no atherosclerosis. The GREAT VESSELS of venous return are
unremarkable.

RESPIRATORY SYSTEM:

The LARYNX, TRACHEA and BRONCHI are unremarkable. The RIGHT and
LEFT LUNGS weigh 540 and 410 grams respectively. The RIGHT is
the site of the previously described injury. The lungs are firm,
subcrepitant and the PLEURA has a diffuse petechial surface.
There are multiple blebs over the apices. Cut surfaces are
moist. With digital pressure the RIGHT exudes a modest amount of
blood, the LEFT a minimal amount of blood. The terminal air
spaces showed dense consolidation in both lungs.

URINARY SYSTEM:

The KIDNEYS weigh 130 grams each. They have their normal shape
and the capsules strip with ease revealing smooth external
surfaces. Cut surfaces show the usual architecture. The PELVES
and URETERS are unremarkable. The BLADDER contains 5 ml. of
urine. Its mucosa is unremarkable.

INTERNAL GENITALIA:

The PROSTATE and TESTES are unremarkable.

LYMPHO-RETICULAR SYSTEM:

The SPLEEN weighs 80 grams. Its capsule is intent and the
parenchyma showed marked acute congestion. The THYMUS is
involuted. The LYMPH NODES where noted are unremarkable.

GASTRO-INTENSINAL TRACT:

The ESOPHAGUS is unremarkable. The STOMACH mucosa is intact and
continuous with an unremarkable duodenum. The SMALL and LARGE
INTESTINES are unremarkable. The APPENDIX is present.

HEPATO-BILIARY SYSTEM:

The LIVER weighs 1380 grams. It is the site of the previously
described injuries. Elsewhere the capsule is intent and the
organ maintains its usual shape. Cut surfaces show the usual
lobular architecture. The GALL BLADDER contains 15 ml. of bile.
Its mucosa is unremarkable and the BILE DUCTS normally disposed.

ENDOCRINE SYSTEM:

The PITUITARY, THYROID, ADRENALS and PANCREAS are unremarkable.

MUSCULO-SKELETAL SYSTEM:

The 7th and 8th ribs on the right side have been described
previously. No other fractures are identified. The BONE MARROW
where visualized is unremarkable. The skeletal muscle has its
usual color and texture.

NECK ORGANS:

There is no hemorrhage in the SOFT TISSUES. The CARTILAGINOUS
and BONY structures are intact.

HEAD:

Reflection of the SCALP reveals no hemorrhage. The CALVARIA is
intact. There is no epidural or subdural hemorrhage. The BRAIN
weighs 1360 grams. The LEPTOMENINGES are glistening and
transparent and the GYRI have their usual orientation and
configuration. There is no evidence of herniation. The VESSELS
at the base of the brain are normally disposed and show no
atherosclerosis. Multiple sections reveal the cortical ribbon to
be intact. The usual landmarks are present and unremarkable.
Removal of the DURA from the base of the SKULL reveals no
fractures.

Autopsy Report--M.E. Case 84-543

MICROSCOPIC:

HEART: No pathological diagnosis.

LUNG: Consolidation and atelectasis of RIGHT LUNG.
                   Consolidation of LEFT LUNG. Exudate was
                   fluorescent for antibody to Legionella.

KIDNEY: No pathological diagnosis.

BRAIN: No pathological diagnosis.

SKIN INCISION: Incision with fibrous replacement and dermal
                   sutures near rib cage area.

ARM: Scar.

MAJOR STATE TOXICOLOGY LABORATORY
DEPARTMENT OF LABORATORY MEDICINE
University of Major
Harborview Medical Center
Ruston, Major
Phone (206) 223 - 3536

Page 8

CASE NO. _25076_ DATE RECEIVED _9/3/8X_ DATE COMPLETED _9/7/8X_

SAMPLE IDENTIFICATION _Flannery, Dorian R.   543_

SAMPLE MATERIAL	QUANTITY	CONTAINER	LABELED
BLOOD	9 ml	VG	Yes
URINE	5 ml	SCB	Yes
GASTRIC			
BILE			

SEND REPORT TO: _Jamner County Prosecuting Attorney_

ANALYSIS PERFORMED	RESULTS	COMMENTS
Blood Alcohol _.10_	_0_ gm	
Urine: _Drug Screen_	Gentamicin	
	Cephalothin	
	Nafcillin	

PLEASE REFER TO OUR CASE NUMBER IN ALL FUTURE CORRESPONDENCE REGARDING THIS CASE.

Martha R. Daisy
MAJOR STATE TOXICOLOGIST

PATHOLOGICAL DIAGNOSES:

1.   Gunshot wound of chest:

   a.   Perforations of liver and lung.
   b.   Right hemothorax (50 cc.), and hemoperitoneum (150 cc.).
   c.   Bullet recovered in right chest wall.
   d.   Course of wound: Front to back at 45° angle, center to right, roughly horizontal until striking 7th rib, then downward and very slightly to center.

2.   Bullous emphysema of apices of lungs.

3.   Pneumonia of lungs.

4.   Recent therapy:

   a.   Endotracheal tube.
   b.   Multiple needle punctures and intravenous catheters.
   c.   Incision and sutures right anterior abdomen.
   d.   Sutures right lobe liver.
   e.   Chest tube right lung.
   f.   Antibiotics in body fluids.

OPINION:

The decedent suffered a gunshot wound and was initially stabilized in ER. Pt developed pneumonia. Antibiotics recovered in urine were appropriate for GI surgery, and most causes of pneumonia. Cause of death was respiratory distress secondary to pneumonia.

Dorian Ray Flannery, M.D.
Medical Examiner

L.R. Jackson, M.D.
Chief Medical Examiner
9-14-8X
Date Signed

SUPERIOR COURT OF MAJOR - COUNTY OF JAMNER

STATE OF MAJOR VS. Edward Hard	Plaintiff, Defendant(s)	BAIL STUDY PROJECT CASE NO. 8X-284

Name: Edward Taylor Hard

Current Charge: First Degree Murder

date of Arrest: 9/3/8X   Court Appearance : 9/8/8X

Pvt. Atty: Y X N   Name: F.C. Townsend 14 National Bank Bldg. Jamner

Co - Def : Y   N   Names:

1. PERSONAL INFORMATION

1.1 DOB 4/11/5X   1.2 Age 28   1.3 Race Caucasian   1.4 Sex Male

1.5 Birthplace: City: Neva   State: Major

2. RESIDENCE

2.1 Present Address: 1492 West, Ruston, Major

For (Length of Time): 3 years   Phone: 832-2314

With (Name and Relation): Self

2.2 Previous Address: 428 West 14th Ruston

For (Length of Time): 1 year

With (Name and Relation): Friends - John, Rick

2.3 Area resident for (Length of Time): 23 years

2.4 Relatives in area that keep in close contact with you:

Name	Address	Phone	Relation	How Often Seen
Emma Hard	241 Morning Crt., Neva	282-4297	Mother	Once a month or so
Gloria Hard	same		Sister	

2.5 Where will you go to live if released today: To own home in Ruston.

3. MARITAL STATUS

3.1 Single __X__

Married On: _____

Divorced On: _____

Separated Since: _____

3.2 Spouse's Name: _____

Spouse's Address: _____

3.3 Number of children: _____

4. EMPLOYMENT

4.1 Presently Employed By: **Self**

Employer's Address: **Home**

For (Length of Time) **Two years** As (a) (an): **Painter**

4.2 If Unemployed, How Long: _____

How Supported: _____

4.3 Previously Employed By: **Auto Wrecking and Gas Depot**

Previous Employer's Address: **22 E. 9th Ruston, Major**

For (Length of Time): **One year** As (a) (an): **gas station attendant**

4.4 If Employed, Support Anyone: _____

5. HEALTH

5.1 What Is Your State of Health: **Good**

5.2 Ever Hospitalized for a Mental Disorder: **No** When:

How Long: Where:

6. PREVIOUS ARRESTS

6.1 How Many Times Arrested Before: **5*** Convictions: **2**

What For: Disposition:

1. 3rd degree rape Plead guilty - sentenced to 2 years state prison

2. Taking and riding a motor

vehicle without permission Convicted - sentenced to one year on

probation

Ever On Probation? **yes** Now? **no** Violate? **no**

Ever On Parole? **yes** Now? **no** Violate? **no**

Officer: **Unknown - Think it was Officer Bond**

Address:

Phone:

* Hard made all of his court appearances while on bail for these matters.

7. REFERENCES

7.1 Is there anyone we can call or speak to to verify this information? (Relative, employer, friend, union, landlord, neighbor, religious leader, teacher, credit reference.)

Name	Address	Phone	Relation	Years Known
Rebecca Karr	140 E. 18th	292-2410	Friend	7 years
Emma Hard	241 Morning Crt., Neva	282-4297	Mother	28 years
John Gooding	1487 Waverly Dr., Ruston	835-7787	Friend	13 years

I AGREE TO ALLOW THE INVESTIGATIVE OFFICER TO CALL THE PEOPLE LISTED IN QUESTION 7.1 TO CHECK MY REFERENCES.

Dated 9/3/8x   Defendant's Signature *Edward Taylor Hard*

Page 3 of 3

STATE OF MAJOR DEPARTMENT OF SOCIAL AND HEALTH SERVICES
VITAL RECORDS

CERTIFICATE OF DEATH   146 - 8

LOCAL FILE NUMBER   STATE FILE NO.

1. NAME-FIRST, MIDDLE, LAST				2. SEX	3. DEATH DATE:
Bruno E. Summers				Male	9/7/8X

4. RACE	5. AGE	6. UNDER 1 YEAR	7. UNDER 1 DAY	8. BIRTHDATE	9. COUNTY OF DEATH
White	30	-------	-------	7/16/5X	Jamner

10. CITY, TOWN OR LOCATION OF DEATH	11. PLACE OF DEATH	12. REC'D EMERG. CARE
Jamner, Major	Mercy Hospital	Yes

13. BIRTH STATE (COUNTRY)	14. CITIZEN OF WHAT COUNTRY	15. MARITAL STATUS	16. SPOUSE	17. ARMED FORCES
Major	US	Married	Deborah Miller	Yes

18. SOCIAL SECURITY NUMBER	19. USUAL OCCUPATION	20. KIND OF BUSINESS OR INDUSTRY
535-46-1671	Garage Attendant	Pri. Ath. Club

21. RESIDENCE-NUMBER AND STREET	22. CITY OR LOCATION	23. INSIDE CITY LIMITS?	24. COUNTY	25. STATE
1962 N.E. 6th Street	Ruston	Yes	Jamner	Major

26. FATHER-NAME:FIRST, MIDDLE, LAST	27. MOTHER-NAME: MAIDEN NAME FIRST, MIDDLE, LAST
Hans O. Summers	Gretchen Hess Summers

28. INFORMANT-NAME	29. MAILING ADDRESS

30. BURIAL, CREMATION ETC.	31. DATE	32. CEMETERY/CREMATORY NAME	33. LOCATION CITY\TOWN STATE
Burial	9/10/8X	Golden Pine Cem.	Town, Major

34. FUNERAL DIRECTOR SIGNATURE	35. NAME OF FACILITY	36. ADDRESS OF FACILITY
	Holiday View	825 So. 182nd

TO BE COMPLETED ONLY BY CERTIFYING PHYSICIAN   TO BE COMPLETED ONLY BY EXAMINER OR CORONER

37. TO THE BEST OF MY KNOWLEDGE, DEATH OCCURRED AT THE TIME, DATE AND PLACE AND DUE TO THE CAUSES STATED.	41. ON THE BASIS OF EXAMINATION AND\OR INVESTIGATION IN MY OPINION DEATH OCCURRED AT THE TIME, DATE AND PLACE AND DUE TO THE CAUSES STATED.
Jackson	*P.J. Official*

38. DATE SIGNED	39. HOUR OF DEATH	42. DATE SIGNED	43. HOUR OF DEATH
9/7/8X	1900	9/7/8X	1900

40. NAME AND TITLE OF ATTENDING PHYSICIAN IF OTHER THAN CERTIFIER Dr. Brett Day	44. DATE PRONOUNCED DEAD 9/7/8X	45. HOUR PRONOUNCED DEAD 1900

46. NAME AND ADDRESS OF CERTIFIER-PHYSICIAN, MEDICAL EXAMINER OR CORONER (TYPE OR PRINT)
Mercy Hospital, Jamner, Major

47. A) IMMEDIATE CAUSE ENTER ONLY ONE CAUSE PER LINE FOR (A) (B) AND (C)	INTERVAL BETWEEN ONSET AND DEATH
Respiratory distress secondary to pneumonia	1 day
B) DUE TO OR AS A CONSEQUENCE OF	INTERVAL BETWEEN ONSET AND DEATH
Gunshot wound - anterior abdominal chest wall	4 days
C) DUE TO OR AS A CONSEQUENCE OF	INTERVAL BETWEEN ONSET AND DEATH

48. OTHER SIGNIFICANT CONDITIONS	49. AUTOPSY?	50. REFERRED TO EXAMINER OR CORONER?

51. ACC. SUICIDE, HOM,	52. INJURY DATE	53. HOUR OF INJURY	54. DESCRIBE HOW INJURY OCCURED
Homicide	9/3/8X	2300	Assault

55. INJURY AT WORK? No	56. PLACE OF INJURY (SPECIFY) Unicorn Tavern	57. LOCATION STREET OR BOX NO. CITY\TOWN STATE

58. REGISTRAR SIGNATURE	59. DATE RECEIVED

FOR STATE REGISTRAR	60. ITEM DATE	DOCUMENTARY EVIDENCE	REVIEWED BY	ITEM DATE	DOCUMENTARY EVIDENCE	REVIEWED BY

Entry 9: Death Certificate

NAME						BIRTH DATE		SEX	

NAME HARD, EDWARD T.   BIRTH DATE 4/11/5x   SEX M

ADDRESS 1492 WEST, RUSTON, MAJOR 98139   PHONE 832-2314   DATE 8/22/8x

SPONSOR _____   ADDRESS _____

OCCUPATION HOUSE PAINTER   REFERRED BY _____   ACKN. _____

ESTIMATE _____

GINGIVA _____

OCCLUSION N/A

PERIODONT N/A

ABNORMALITIES _____

X-RAYS T-9 (CHIP)

REMARKS

NAME			HARD, EDWARD T.	ADDRESS	1492 WEST, RUSTON, MAJOR				
DATE	TOOTH		SERVICE RENDERED			TIME	CHARGE	PAID	BALANCE
8/22/8x	9		EMG. PALL TREATMENT, X-RAY,				38.00		
			P/A, CHIPPED TOOTH				8.00		
8/29/8x	9		PORCELAIN TO METAL CROWN PREP				0		
8/30/8x	9		PORCELAIN TO METAL CROWN SEAT,				388.00		
			Dr. Francis Xavier, D.D.S.						

FBI CRIMINAL RECORD

SUBJECT:

Contributor: Identifier	Name State #	Arrested or Received	C - Charge D - Disposition
PD Sacramento, CA	Jack Waters #67390	9-10-8X-8	c-armed robbery d-5 years
PD Ruston, Major	Jack Waters #32976	5-6-8X-2	c-malicious misch. 1st degree d-6 mo. prison
PD Ruston, Major	Jack Waters #19842	3-9-8X-1	c-burglary, 2nd degree d-1 year and probation
PD Ruston, Major	Edward Taylor Hard #12693	4-15-8X-9	c-rape, 3rd degree d-2 years and 3 months
PD Ruston, Major	Edward Taylor Hard #54932	4-15-8X-7	c-DWI d-dismissed
PD Ruston, Major	Edward Taylor Hard #73921	5-19-8X-7	c-DWI d-dismissed
PD Ruston, Major	Edward Taylor Hard #46384	5-19-8X-6	c-taking and riding a motor vehicle without permission d- ---
PD Ruston, Major	Edward Taylor Hard #89732	5-19-8X-2	c-theft, 3rd degree d-dismissed

(continued)

Entry 11: FBI Criminal Record

FBI CRIMINAL RECORD
SUBJECT:

Contributor: Identifier	Name State #	Arrested or Received	C - Charge D - Disposition
PD Ruston, Major	Alan Long #24931	6-2-8X-15	c-forgery-checks d-5 yr. suspended sentence, condition: obtain treatment for alcoholism
PD Ruston, Major	Alan Long #37236	6-2-8X-15	c-embezzlement d-5 year suspended sentence
PD Ruston, Major	Bruno Summers #53862	2-6-8X-5	c-attempted rape, 3rd degree d-probation

✛ MERCY HOSPITAL

JAMNER, MAJOR

To: Defendant Attorney/Plaintiff Attorney

From: Rose Gadfly
        Mercy Hospital
        1567 Broadway
        Jamner, Major

RECORDS
DEPARTMENT

October 1, 198X

Dear Attorneys:

    As per your mutual request, I am enclosing the hospital records of Mr. Bruno Summers. The documents requested include:
1. Emergency Department Records - 1 page
2. Nursing Record - 5 pages.

Sincerely,

Rose Gadfly

Rose Gadfly
Chief Records Clerk
Mercy Hospital

DESCRIBE INJURY (WHEN, WHERE & HOW) OR ILLNESS:

9/3/8X Gunshot Wound (GSW) at close range. Entered chest (abdomen). Shot at approx. 9:00 p.m.

ALLERGIES: N/a

PREV. TETANUS DATE N/a		GIVEN THIS VISIT? NO			HEIGHT 6'4"	WEIGHT 219	LMP —
TIME 22:20	TEMP. /	PULSE 124	RESP. 40 (labored)	BLOOD PRESSURE 40 (unobtained)	I.V.'S Ringers lactate at 5 amps		

MEDICATIONS TAKEN:

None

MEDICATIONS GIVEN:

None

HISTORY & PHYSICAL FINDINGS: 20:20

① This 30 year old ♂ sustained a .22 caliber GSW to his thoracic area. The bullet penetrated the lower chest cavity and may have struck the liver; other abdominal traumas may be found. No bullet exit. ② Pt. conscious and in extreme pain. ③ Respiration labored ④ Pt. says he was in "perfect" health. ⑤ Pt. has alcohol smell on his breath. ⑥ Pt. states, "I should have left when I saw him."

TREATMENT & ORDERS: * surgery Recommended
- Procedure and risks explained to Pt. and he understands and agrees to proceed
- Immediate surgery for removal of bullet ordered

BROUGHT TO HOSP. BY:
Ambulance

DISPOSITION & CONDITION ON DISCHARGE:
Transfer to IC

DIAGNOSTIC IMPRESSION:
GSW Trauma causing thoracic and abdominal distress

NURSE (SIGNATURE)
Betty Frank, R.N.

PHYSICIAN (SIGNATURE)
Dr. Britt Day

ACCOUNT NO. 1717	ADMIT DATE 9/3/8X	ADMIT TIME 22:15
ADMIT DIAGNOSIS GSW OF CHest		RM -BED 201

PATIENT NAME (LAST, FIRST, MI)
Summers, Bruno E

STREET ADDRESS
1962 N.E. 6th

CITY, STATE Ruston, Major	ZIP 98139	PHONE 433-1112

RELIGION — PHYSICIAN —

DIET 3	COND. 3	AGE 30	SEX M	BIRTH DATE 7/16/5X

NEAREST RELATIVE
Mrs. Deborah Summers

STREET ADDRESS
same

CITY, STATE, ZIP same	PHONE same

GUARANTOR NAME Hans Summers	PHONE 756-3530

EMPLOYER & CITY
Retired

EMERGENCY ROOM
REPORT
MERCY HOSPITAL

DATE	TIME	PROBLEM	PATIENT PROGRESS NOTES
9/4/8X	00:45	NEW TRANSFER	Pt., WHITE MALE 30 YEAR OLD,
			TRANSFERRED FROM ER
			GSW + POST-SURGERY (N.F.)
		P#1	PLEASE SEE DOCTOR'S SUMMARY (INCL.)
			FOR APPROPRIATE DETAILS OF ER AND
		VS / R	SURGERY REPORT
		BP HR / 18	MEDS - none ENT - norm (N.F.)
		40/? 110	NO VOLUME OVERLOAD - IV OF RINGERS
			LACTATE CONTINUED (5 amps X opm)
9/4/8X	04:30	P #1	GSW
			1. VS's RETURNING TO NORMAL
			2. BLOOD VOLUME REPLACING ADEQUATELY
		VS / R 20	
		BP HR / 80	3. Pt.'s ARTERIAL BLOOD GASES
		80/40	IMPROVING
			PCO2 = 31
			(N.F.) PO2 of 50 WITH 90% SATURATION

PATIENT NAME:	NURSING CARE RECORD
ADDRESS: PHYSICIAN: ADMIT DATE: ADMIT TIME:	Mercy Hospital Jamner, Major

---

Entry 12: Hospital Records of Bruno Summers

DATE	TIME	PROBLEM	PATIENT PROGRESS NOTES
9-4	10:36	P-1	VS = $\frac{HR}{30}$ $\frac{BP}{140/80}$ $\frac{R}{norm}$ $\frac{T}{99°F}$
			① Pt. complains of pain
			② Pt. neuro = alert, 0×3
			③ Renal = clear, >150 cc/hr
			A/P ① NO PAINKILLERS ALLOWED AT THIS TIME TO STABILIZE RESPIRATION
			② PT. IS LOOKING BETTER
			③ NO VOLUME OVERLOAD. LASIX 40 mg. IV ×2 FOR URINE <150 cc/hr
9/4/82	17:10	P#1	
		VS HR/50	BP/130/80 R/LABORED T/99°F TO NORM
			T^m 38.7 I/O ^{6}200/3700
			LOOKS GREAT c/o EXTREME DIS- COMFORT/PAIN
			Pt. NEURO- ORIENTED x 3, FOLLOWS COMMANDS & COOPERATIVE
			Pt. PULM - CLEAR UPPER BS↓ BS SOFT
			ABG 7.46/38/89 40% M.ASK Ø SPUTUM
			CXR = NO VOLUME OVERLOAD GI -
			ABD-SOFT BS⊕ TUBEFEEDS c ^{250}/cc/hr 1/2 STRENGTH
			RENAL - >200 cc/hr CLEAR
			* NO LASIX NOW
			A/P OVERALL, LOOKS GREAT

PATIENT NAME:
ADDRESS:
PHYSICIAN:
ADMIT DATE:
ADMIT TIME:

NURSING CARE RECORD
Mercy Hospital
Jamner, Major

DATE	TIME	PROBLEM	PATIENT PROGRESS NOTES
9/5/8X	00:30	P#1	MEMO-28 (N.F.)
		VS BP HR T R LABORED	C/O STILL IN PAIN
		139/10 24 98°F	
			T IS SPIKING
9/5	11:45	VS BP HR T R LABORED	PE C/O EXTREME PAIN IN CHEST
		120/60 28 102°	X x-RAY SHOWS RE-EXPANDED LUNG
		(N.F.)	HEMOTHORAX REDUCED TO INSIGN SIZE
			P NEURO - ALERT, OX3, DISTRACTED B/ PAIN
			COV - NSR 5 ECTOPY
	(R.B.)		RENAL - OL LASIX PO URINE <200 cc/hr
			METABOLIC - 142/2.6 /178 T.B - 6.1
			97/35 <15 HCT 31
	A/P		OVERALL DOING WELL, T PROBLEM
			STILL SHOWING EVIDENCE OF
			DISTRESS
			? VOLUME EXCESS, WILL FORCE DISTRESS
9/6/8X	00:30	P#1	VS BP 100/50 HR/30 R/LABORED T/101°F
		(N.F.)	* INCREASING (30→40 mg/hr) SEROSANG
			DRAIN FROM DRAIN TUBES (THORACIC)
			NOTIFIED DR. DAY
			(N.F.)

PATIENT NAME:
ADDRESS:
PHYSICIAN:
ADMIT DATE:
ADMIT TIME:

NURSING CARE RECORD
Mercy Hospital
Jamner, Major

DATE	TIME	PROBLEM	PATIENT PROGRESS NOTES
9/6/8X	07:00	P#1	VS/BP 110/50 HR/30 R/LABORED T/100°F
			SOME INCREASING CONSOLIDATION IN RIGHT LOWER LOBE
			-EXTENDS TO RIGHT MIDDLE TUBE
			ETIOLOGY- UNKNOWN AT THIS TIME
		A/P	① PRELIMINARY DIAGNOSIS OF PNEMONITES (P#2)
			② WORK-UP OF SPUTUM & B CULTURES IMMEDIATELY
			③ CEPHALOTHIN -1 g 4th GENTAMICIN
	B.D.		④ CULTURE OF SEROSANG DRAIN NOW
			VS/BP 100/50 HR/32 R/20 LABORED T/105°F
9/7/8X	23:35	N.F.	* T SPIKE
		Pt #1 P#2	P. NEURO- LETHARGIC, ORIENT POOR X2
			DEMON TOXICITY
			-X-RAY REVEALS CONSOLIDATION IN RIGHT LUNG
			-MIDDLE LOBE ENTIRELY INVOLVED
			-RIGHT UPPER- INVOLVED
			-SAME IN LEFT LOWER
	B.D.		IAB- SPUTUM & 6 CULTURES ARE Ø GROWTH IN 24 HRS.
			[NEXT PG.]

PATIENT NAME:
ADDRESS:
PHYSICIAN:
ADMIT DATE:
ADMIT TIME:

NURSING CARE RECORD
Mercy Hospital
Jamner, Major

DATE	TIME	PROBLEM	PATIENT PROGRESS NOTES
9/6/8X	23:35	P#1	A/P
		P#2	※ DIFFER DIAG — STAPH PNEMONIA
			① — PROBABLY NOT STRESS LUNG SYN
			② CONSULTATION REQUEST + INFECTIOUS DISEASE CONSULT
			③ NAFCILLIN IV, 2gm q4h IMMEDIATELY
	BD.		④ BLOOD IV. TO STABLE
9/7/8X	08:30	P#1	VS/HR BP/100/40 LABORED T/104°F \n 32
		P#2	Pt. NOT RESPONDING TO MEDS.
		A/P	① CONTINUE MEDS
	BD.		② CONSULT PULMONARY
9/7/8X	19:00	P#1	VS/ BP/N/A HR/N/A R/N/A T/n/A
		P#2	A/P
			— Pt EXPIRED
			— AUTOPSY ORDERED N.F.
	BD.		

	NURSING CARE RECORD
PATIENT NAME:	Mercy Hospital
ADDRESS:	Jamner, Major
PHYSICIAN:	
ADMIT DATE:	
ADMIT TIME:	

Elizabeth Lift, Ph.D.
Licensed   Psychologist
1422   Columbia Plaza
Jamner,   Major

October 6, 198X

Dear Counselor:

This is to confirm our appointment for 10:00 a.m., next Tuesday in my office. As I told your associate over the telephone, I have previously been involved in developing surveys of community attitudes and analyzing these surveys under the z-test for proportionality for change of venue motions.

I have enclosed a sample survey with explanation.   Looking forward to our meeting.

Sincerely,

Elizabeth F Lift

Elizabeth F. Lift, Ph.D.
Licensed Psychologist

CHANGE OF VENUE MOTION SURVEY

Your answers will be used solely in a survey for a change of venue motion and for no other purpose.

1. Are you a registered voter in _____ county?
   (if not, thank the person for their trouble and go on to the next person on your list)

2. When was the last time you voted in an election?
   (if more than a year, thank the person for their trouble and go on to the next person on your list)

3. Name:

4. Address:

5. List all places where you have resided for the past 15 years indicating the length of residence at each location.

6. Do you own your own home, rent or share an apartment, or live with parents or other relatives?

7. What is your marital status? Are you presently married, divorced, separated, or have you never been married?

8. How far did you go in school?
   Through grade
   High school graduate
   Vocational/technical
   Business school
   Secretarial
   Community College, incomplete or complete
   4 year college, incomplete or complete
   Post-graduate

9. What kind of work do you do?

10. Which newspapers do you subscribe to?

11. What sections of the newspaper do you read first?

12. What sections of the newspaper do you read most often?

13. Which magazines do you or any one in your household subscribe to?

14. Which of these magazines do you read?

15. List the last three books which you have read.

16. List the last three movies which you have seen in a movie theater.

17. How frequently do you watch national news on TV?

18. How frequently do you watch local news on TV?

19. Have you heard of the (case specific) incident?

20. Would you rate yourself:
    knowledgeable of the incident
    aware of the incident
    vaguely aware of the incident
    never heard of the incident

21. How would you describe the incident:
    defendant intentionally committed the crime
    defendant recklessly committed the crime
    I do not know enough about it to say
    defendant was justified in what he/she did
    defendant did not commit any crime

22. From what you know of the incident, do you think the defendant is guilty or innocent of the crime?

23. Do you have any principles or scruples based on religious or ethical teachings or dogma that would affect your ability to serve as a fair and impartial juror?

24. Would your membership or identification with any political party or your vote for a particular candidate affect your ability to serve as a fair and impartial juror?

25. Have you ever served on a jury other than federal court:
    Civil or criminal
    County
    Common pleas or Municipal court
    Total number of cases

Thank you for your time in answering our questions.

EXPLANATION OF CHANGE OF VENUE MOTION SURVEY

Phone surveys are based on the assumption that people answer truthfully and accurately about their feelings about the incident questioned about. Such surveys are accepted as gaining accurate information if done correctly.

Most jurors are chosen from registered voter lists. Question 1 and 2 are screening devices to determine if the person is a registered voter and thus on the jury lists of the county. Some people think they are registered, but have not voted in the last year and have to re-register in order to vote.

Questions 3 and 4 verify that the survey was done.

Questions 5 through 18 and 25 can be used to establish relationships between these items and extreme prejudice against the defendant. Ninety percent of the persons questioned might have a college degree while in the general population only thirty percent have such a degree. If one found that all non-college degree people questioned are prejudiced against the defendant (and this group was representative of the population), then counsel could move for a change of venue because seventy percent of the population in the venue are prejudiced against the defendant.

Questions 19 through 22 establish the knowledge the person believes they have of the incident and whether they have already made a decision as to defendant's guilt. Ranges of responses are provided so that the person's feelings can be accurately measured.

Questions 23 and 24 are to find the religious and political climate and whether this climate will affect the defendant.

NEO-NAZI SURVIVALIST ORGANIZATION

BRUNO SUMMERS

---

is a member in good standing

RUSTON CHAPTER

PRESIDENT

STATE OF MAJOR

MAJOR STATE PATROL

610 3rd Avenue, Public Safety Building, 2nd Floor   Jamner , Major   646-1820

CRIME LABORATORY REPORT

Agency: Jamner Police Department   **Laboratory   No.:** 222-3000

Suspect: Hard, Edward   **Agency   Case   No.:** 00432150
Victim: Summers, Bruno

Officer: Detective Kelly

EVIDENCE EXAMINED:

W-1:   One T-shirt

Y-5:   One S and W .22 caliber revolver bearing serial number 76636

Y-6:   One spent cartridge case and four live rounds

H-8:   One spent bullet

RESULTS OF EXAMINATION:

The firearm (Y-5) was examined, test fired, and found to be in operable condition. Trigger pull pressure required to discharge the weapon was measured at 4.2 pounds. Both trigger pulls are within normal range for this firearm.

The revolver (Y-5) was test fired using ammunition of the same make as those in Y-6. It was determined that the spent bullet (H-8) had been discharged by the revolver (Y-5).

Results of proximity testing indicates the muzzle of the revolver was approximately 18 to 36 inches away from the shirt (W-1) at the time of discharge, assuming no intermediate target.

_____   9/9/8X
Signature   Date

Entry 15:   Crime Laboratory Report   521

DEPARTMENT OF PUBLIC SAFETY - JAMNER, MAJOR | STATEMENT

Victim ___ Date 9/3/8X Time 2300 hrs.

Witness X

Case No. 0 0 4 3 2 1 5 0

Taken by _____ Serial _____

Statement of Thomas Donaldson Age _____

Alias _____

Address 1776 Amble, Apt. 3 Zip _____ Phone 833-5142

Date of Birth _____ at _____

Occupation & Employer Bartender, Unicorn Tavern Bus. Phone 233-4173

    This is a true and correct statement which is voluntarily given by me to Officer Rule, #1441. I am employed as a bartender at the Unicorn Tavern, which is located at 5302 N. 49th. The owner of the tavern is M.C. Davola.

    On approximately August 20 of this year, I was on duty in the tavern at approximately 11:00 p.m. At this time, Bruno Summers and his fiancee, Debbie, were sitting at a table. Bruno was a regular customer at the Unicorn. I know that Bruno is the leader of some sort of survivalist group, but he rarely causes any trouble in the tavern. Bruno and Debbie had been in the Unicorn for about two hours and had had several rounds of drinks. I caught a glimpse of a man, who I later recognized as Ed Hard, a "semi-regular" customer at the Unicorn, go to their table. Ed had several drinks and was acting loud and obnoxious. He also staggered slightly. I do not believe Ed Hard was intoxicated. Ed sat down at the table, and I could hear him talking to Debbie. I saw Bruno and Debbie get up to leave when Ed jumped Bruno from behind. They fought, and Ed got knocked to the floor. Ed had a split lip and a chipped tooth. I told them both to leave the tavern.

    Tonight, Ed came into the tavern at about 8 o'clock with two other people. The three of them sat at the bar, and I served them several rounds of drinks. At one point, I overheard Ed make a remark to his friend, "That Nazi had better not come near me again."

    At about 9:00 p.m., Bruno and Debbie came into the Unicorn and went to a table nearer the back.

    I was busy working at the bar when I heard a noise in the back. I heard a gunshot and saw Bruno fall to the floor. Ed immediately left the tavern.

    I immediately called 911 and reported the shooting. Others gathered around Bruno, who was laying on the floor.

PAGE 1 OF 2

DEPARTMENT OF PUBLIC SAFETY - JAMNER, MAJOR | STATEMENT

Victim ___ Date 9/3/8X Time 2300 hrs.

Witness X

Case No.

0 0 4 3 2 1 5 0

Taken by _____ Serial _____

Statement of Thomas Donaldson Age _____

Alias _____

Address 1776 Amble, Apt. 3 Zip _____ Phone 833-5142

Date of Birth _____ at _____

Occupation & Employer Bartender, Unicorn Tavern Bus. Phone 233-4173

After making the call, I went to where Bruno was lying and waited for the aid car to arrive.

Thomas Donaldson
Thomas Donaldson

9/3/8X

PAGE 2

OF 2

Jamner Police Department
EXPLANATION OF RIGHTS

INCIDENT NUMBER

UNIT FILE NUMBER

Date 9/3/8x Time 2330 hr. Place HOMICIDE OFFICE

Statement of EDWARD TAYLOR HARD

EXPLANATION OF MY CONSTITUTIONAL RIGHTS

Before questioning and the making of any statement, I, EDWARD TAYLOR HARD
have been advised by DET. B. KELLY of the following rights:

1. I have the right to remain silent;

2. Any statement that I do make, either oral or written, can be used as evidence against
   me in a court of law (I understand that if I am a juvenile my statement may be used against me
   in a criminal prosecution in the event that juvenile court declines jurisdiction in my case);

3. I have the right at this time to an attorney of my own choosing and to have him
   present before and during questioning and the making of any statement;

4. If I cannot afford an attorney, I am entitled to have one appointed for me by a court
   without cost to me and to have him present before and during questioning and the making of any
   statement.

Signature Edward Taylor Hard

WAIVER OF CONSTITUTIONAL RIGHTS

I have read the above explanation of my constitutional rights and I understand them. I
have decided not to exercise these rights at this time. The following statement is made by me
freely and voluntarily and without threats or promises of any kind.

Witnesses Det. J. Bull   Signature Edward Taylor Hard

On Sept. 3, 198x, at about 9:00 pm, I went to the
Unicorn Tavern with two friends. I was just sitting at
the bar talking to them. I got up and
headed towards the restroom. Bruno Summers came
out of the restroom and came up to me. Until
then I did not know he was in the tavern. About
two weeks before, Summers had struck me, broken
my tooth and cut my lip so I needed stitches. Summers
threatened to kill me when he came up to me in the
tavern last night. He pushed me and was reaching into
his pocket. I pulled a gun out of my pocket. It accidentally went off when I pointed it at the wall and hit Summers.

Page 1 of 1

DEPARTMENT OF PUBLIC SAFETY - JAMNER, MAJOR | STATEMENT

Victim ____ Date 9-5-8x Time _____ Case No.

Witness _x_

__ __ __ __ __ __ __

Taken by _____ Serial _____

Statement of Robin Luntlebunk _____ Age _____

Alias _____

Address _____ Zip _____ Phone _____

Date of Birth _____ at _____

Occupation & Employer _____ Bus. Phone _____

can't be found.

B.K. B.K.

PAGE ___

OF ___

DEPARTMENT OF PUBLIC SAFETY - JAMNER, MAJOR | STATEMENT

Victim ___ Date 9-4-8X Time 13:05 hrs.

Witness X

Case No. ___ ___ ___ ___ ___ ___ ___ ___

Taken by _____ Serial _____

Statement of Deborah Summers Age 21 years

Alias _____

Address 1962 NE 6th Zip 98139 Phone 433-1112

Date of Birth 8-8-6X at _____

Occupation & Employer _____ Bus. Phone _____

I am the wife of Mr. Bruno Summers. We were married on August 27th of this year.

About a week before I got married, I was in the Unicorn Tavern with Bruno in the evening. We had been out to dinner and then to the Unicorn for a drink. Ed Hard came into the Unicorn. I had dated Ed before I met Bruno. Ed came over to the table where we were and sat down and ordered a drink. He was drunk, and he said things to me like: "Let's put things right", "We can make it tonight," and "Come home with me." He acted like Bruno wasn't there. Bruno didn't say anything to Ed. He just said, "Come on." to me, and we got up to leave. When we got up, Ed got loud and started yelling at me not to leave.

Bruno put some money on the table for the tab, and we started to leave. Then, Ed just grabbed Bruno around the neck. Bruno wrestled with Ed and then hit him. Ed was knocked to the floor. He had a bloody lip. Ed said that he'd get Bruno the next time. Tom, the bartender, told us all to leave.

On August 22, I was home with Bruno and Peter Dean when the telephone rang. I picked it up and a man who wouldn't iden-tify himself, but who I recognized to be Ed Hard, said, "Tell that Nazi you live with that he's a dead man." Then Bruno took the telephone and after a few minutes hung up. Bruno then said: "Slime-head. You know what Slime-head said? I am going to kill you if you marry Deborah." Bruno then said, "Not if I can help it."

Yesterday, September 3, at approximately 9:00p.m., Bruno, a friend, Peter Dean, and I went to the Unicorn.

PAGE 1 OF 2

Entry 19: Deborah Summers' Statement   529

Victim ___   Date 9-4-8X   Time 13:05 hrs.

Witness X___   Case No.

                                                      __ __ __ __ __ __ __

Taken by _____   Serial _____

Statement of Deborah Summers _____   Age 21 years _____

Alias _____

Address 1962 NE 6th _____   Zip 98139   Phone 433-1112

Date of Birth 8-8-6X _____   at _____

Occupation & Employer _____   Bus. Phone _____

When we went in, we saw Ed sitting at the bar and talking real loud. I told Bruno we should leave, but Bruno said it was O.K. and we could sit down away from him. We sat down, and Bruno ordered a round of drinks. At first, I didn't think Ed saw us, but then I saw him look around and say, "Look at who's back." He then turned to the man next to him at the bar, whispered something and they both laughed.

About five minutes after we entered the Unicorn, Bruno got up and went to the restroom, which is in the back of the Unicorn. A couple minutes later, I saw Ed go toward the restroom. When Bruno came out, Ed walked up to Bruno, and they were talking to each other. Bruno was pointing at Ed with his finger. All of a sudden, Ed pulled a gun out of his pocket and shot Bruno. Bruno fell to the floor holding his chest. Ed then ran out of the tavern.

I started screaming. I saw Bruno had blood on his chest. Medical aid arrived and then the police. I talked to the police and then went to Mercy Hospital where Bruno is now.

I have read the above statement, and it is a true and voluntary statement made by me, and I will testify to it in a court of law.

9-4-8X

Deborah Summers
Deborah Summers

PAGE $\frac{2}{2}$

OF __

DEPARTMENT OF PUBLIC SAFETY - JAMNER, MAJOR   STATEMENT

Victim ___ Date _____ Time _____   Case No.

Witness _X_   __ __ __ __ __ __ __ __

Taken by _____ Serial _____

Statement of Officer F. West _____ Age _____

Alias _____

Address Police Dept., Unit 220 _____ Zip _____ Phone 342-1183 ____

Date of Birth _____ at _____

Occupation & Employer Police Officer, Jamner Co. Bus. Phone _____

_____On 9/3/8X at 2120 hrs., I was working car 2-X-4 when PD
radio advised there was a shooting at the Unicorn Tavern at
5302 N. 49th Street. I responded from about 5th and Union.
On arrival at approximately 2125 hrs., I ran into the tavern
and found a group of people around a white male, about 30
years of age, lying on his back in the rear of the tavern.
I called for a medic unit and also advised radio that the
victim had been shot in the chest. I stayed with the victim,
who was moaning, until the medic personnel arrived.
_____I followed the aid car to Mercy Hospital where victim
was taken to the emergency unit and into surgery. The victim
was alive upon arrival at Mercy Hospital. I obtained the
victim's clothing from Nurse Frank. I then transported the
victim's clothing to the Evidence Room where I turned it over
to Officer Smith for placement into evidence. Nurse Frank
found a folded buck knife in the victim's jacket and gave it
to me with the victim's clothing. The clothing was turned
over to the Evidence Room at 0030 hrs. on 9/4/8X.

                                        Officer F. West
9/4/8X   Officer F. West

                                                          PAGE ___

                                                          OF ___

Entry 20: Officer F. West's Statement   531

DEPARTMENT OF PUBLIC SAFETY

STATEMENT

Victim ___ Date _____ Time _____   Case No.

Witness X   __ __ __ __ __ __ __

Taken by _____ Serial _____

Statement of Officer M. Yale   Age _____

Alias _____

Address Police Dept., Unit 13   Zip _____ Phone _____

Date of Birth _____ at _____

Occupation & Employer Police Officer, Jamner Co. Bus. Phone _____

    On 9/3/8X at approximately 2210 hrs., I was working 4-R-5 with Officer DiJulio. At that time, we responded to 1492 West to apprehend suspect Edward Taylor Hard. According to Homicide Detective, Hard had been observed shooting victim.

    Arrived at suspect's residence at 2230 hrs. Officer DiJulio covered rear door. I knocked on the door. When suspect Hard opened the door, I explained that a shooting had taken place at the Unicorn Tavern and he had been identified as the shooter. I indicated that he should tell us where the gun was and that if it was in the house, let us get it.

    Suspect Hard asked officers what would happen if he denied the officers into the house. I informed him that we felt that we had enough probable cause to obtain a search warrant and that officers would stand guard around the house until it was obtained. Two other patrol cars had already arrived at the scene at this time, and officers gathered near the door.

    At this point, suspect Hard stated he's been home watching TV and drinking beer and made a motion to show officers the living room. He then retreated into the house. Once inside the house, I looked in the living room and saw the television on and a six-pack of beer on the table. Suspect was placed under arrest and advised of his rights.

    I approached the coffee table which had three empty beer cans and three unopened ones. Near the table on the floor in plain view was a .22 caliber revolver. I took the revolver into custody. There were four live rounds and one expended round in the chamber. I initialed the revolver and later delivered the evidence to the property room.

PAGE 1

OF 2

Entry 21: Officer M. Yale's Statement   533

Victim ___ Date _____ Time _____

Witness X__

Case No. __ __ _____ __

Taken by _____ Serial _____

Statement of Officer Yale   Age _____

Alias _____

Address Police Dept., Unit 13 _____ Zip _____ Phone _____

Date of Birth _____ at _____

Occupation & Employer Police Officer, Jamner Co. Bus. Phone _____

_____ Suspect Hard was taken to the Homicide Office where he was placed in an interview room.

_____ At 2340 hrs., after being questioned by detectives I took custody of suspect and conducted a breathalyzer test. Suspect's reading was .16. There was a strong odor of intoxicants about him. His eyes were red and watery, and his speech was slurred. End of Statement.

9/4/8X

Officer M. Yale

PAGE ___

OF ___

TRANSCRIPT OF INTERVIEW OF OFFICER YALE BY DEPUTY PROSECUTOR

9/11/8X

Deputy Prosecutor ["DP"]:   I know you've already talked this over with Detective Kelly, but why don't you tell me again about how you got the gun in that Hard case.

Officer Yale ["Y"]:   You want it on tape? I've never had a D.A. interview me on tape before.

DP: It's O.K. I work a little different than some, but I find taping helps get ready for defense suppression motions, and I've never had any trouble from having taped.

Y: O.K., if that's how you work . . . . About 2210 I was on patrol with DiJulio. We got a call that there had been a shooting at the Unicorn and that this guy, Ed Hard, was the suspect.

DP: Uh huh.

Y: Well, the dispatcher gave us Hard's address and told us to pick him up.

DP: What did you do then?

Y: Went over there. Oh yeah . . . I called for back-up. This was a man with a gun we were dealing with, and I didn't want anyone to get hurt.

DP: Sure.

Y: Anyway, me and DiJulio went over to the address we were given. A one story house. I pulled in the drive . . .

DP: Had your back-up come yet?

Y: No. So, DiJulio went around the back door just in case he saw us and was going to try and run, and I walked up on the front porch, stepped to the side of the door -- and waited for the back-up.

DP: How long did they take?

Y: 30-35 seconds.

DP: Who arrived?

Y: Two marked cars.

DP: So with yours, there were three marked units?

Y: Yeah.

DP: Who joined you?

Y: Monroe, Banks, Blake and Sonns.

DP: All in uniform?

Y: All of us were.

DP: Any weapons out?

Y: Banks had an automatic shotgun. The rest of us had our
     holsters unsnapped. We were dealing with a shooting . . . .

DP: I know. What did you do next?

Y: I told Blake to join DiJulio in the back. Just in case.
     And told Monroe, Banks, and Sonns to join me at the front
     door.

DP: Go on.

Y: Well we positioned ourselves on both sides of the door, and
     I knocked -- announcing that we were police officers.

DP: Did anyone answer?

Y: Not right away. So I knocked again -- and about five
     seconds later this guy comes to the door.

DP: What happened then?

Y: I asked if he was Ed Hard and he asked why did I want to
     know. So, I told him about the shooting at the Unicorn, and
     Hard being a suspect -- and he said he was Hard but he'd
     been home watching TV and drinking beer.

DP: I'm looking at your report of 9/4 and some of the sequences
     of events seem slightly different than you're telling me
     now.

Y: Well, things happened fast at that door. All in a real
     short time.

DP: OK. What happened after he told you he was Ed Hard?

Y: I told him to step outside slowly, which he did, placed him
     spread-eagle against the house and pat searched him for
     weapons.

DP: Did you find any?

Y: No. Then I cuffed him, told him he was under arrest for the shooting and cuffed him.

DP: Did you get a description of the shooter from the dispatcher?

Y: Yeah. And he fit it.

DP: OK. What then?

Y: I wanted to find the gun. So I told the suspect we wanted the gun and that he should tell us where it was.

DP: Did he?

Y: Not at first. He said, "What if I don't want you guys in my house?" So I told him that if he wanted to play that game, we've got more than enough for a warrant and that I'd take him to jail, then go to the judge for the warrant while the rest of the officers guarded his house.

DP: What did he say?

Y: Nothing. He just looked at all of us for a while, shrugged his shoulders, pointed towards his living room with his shoulder, and slowly started to step inside.

DP: You followed him?

Y: Sure. He was telling us that the gun was in the living room.

DP: Did he say that?

Y: Not with words. But it was clear. He was telling us that the gun was in the living room and that we could look.

DP: So, you looked?

Y: You bet. We wanted that gun.

DP: And you found it?

Y: Yeah. We took Hard in the living room and there on the floor between a coffee table and the couch was the gun.

DP: And this was in the living room?

Y: Right in plain view in the area Hard gave us permission to search.

DP: Good. And this was the gun with the four live rounds which
     you took into custody?

Y: Yes. The murder weapon.

Curriculum Vitae

DR. BRETT DAY
1870 S. Tacoma Way
Ruston, Major
(206) 756-7849

Personal: Age: 55; Divorced, 2 children - 30 and
                     25 years old; Health: excellent.

Undergraduate: University of Washington, Bachelor of
                     Science Degree, Basic Medical Science
                     (198X-37 through -34).

Medical School: University of Washington School of
                     Medicine, 4 years; Degree: M.D. (198X-
                     34 through -30).

Internship: U.S. Public Health Services, San
                     Francisco, CA.

Residency: 4 years at Swedish Hospital, Seattle, in
                     general surgery.

                     Thoracic residency fellowship at St.
                     Mary's Hospital in Minneapolis,
                     Minnesota.

Board Certified: American College of Surgeons in General
                     Surgery.

                     Board eligible for certification in
                     thoracic surgery, but not certified.

Practice: General surgery for 20 years.
                     Associated with Mercy Hospital, Flower
                     Hospital and Sunnyview Nursing Home.

Military: Navy for 2 years, rank of Captain.

Professional Associations and Affiliations:

                     Jamner County Medical Society
                     American Lung Association of Major,
                     President local chapter.

Community Services:

Heart Association of Major: President,
local chapter.

Jamner County Memorial Division American
Heart Association: Director of Heart
Association Fund Drive, 198X-6.

Curriculum Vitae

DR. L. R. JACKSON
430 S.W. Fawcett
Jamner, Major
(206) 242-3190

Personal: Age: 44; Married, 1 child - 15 years
                     old; Health: Excellent

Undergraduate: University of North Dakota,
                     Bachelor of Science Degree, Biology,
                     198X-10.

Medical School: Guadalupe, Mexico,
                     4 years; Degree: M.D.

Internship: U.S. Public Health Services, Presonton,
                     Wyoming.

Residency: 4 years at St. Steven's Hospital,
                     Duluth, Minnesota, in Pathology.

Board Certified: American College of Forensic
                     Pathologists.

Practice: Forensic Pathologist for 16 years.
                     Pierce County Medical Examiner's Office.

Professional   American Society of Clinical
Associations and   Pathologists; College of American
Affiliations: Pathologists.

CURRICULUM VITAE

Elizabeth F. Lift

PERSONAL DATA

    Address: Department of Psychology
                       University of Major
                       Jamner, Major
                       (206) 543-7184 or (206) 543-2650 (messages)

    Born: October 16, 198X-44; Los Angeles,
                       California

    Married: Geoffrey R. Lift

EDUCATION

    B.A., with highest honors in Mathematics and Psychology,
        U.C.L.A., 198X-22.
    M.A., Psychology, Major University, 198X-21.
    Ph.D., Psychology, Major University, 198X-18.

TEACHING EXPERIENCE

Permanent

        Assistant, Associate, Full Professor, University of
        Major, 198X-15 to present.
        Assistant Professor, New School for Social Research,
            Graduate Faculty, 198X-18 to 198X-15.

Visiting

        National Judicial College, University of Nevada,
            198X-14 to 198X-13.
        Harvard University, Seminar on Law and Psychology,
            198X-13 to 198X-12.

HONORS AND AWARDS

Honorary Degrees

        Doctor of Science, Miami University (Ohio), 198X-6.

Honor Societies

        Pi Mu Epsilon, National Mathematics Honorary,
            elected 198X-23;
        Mortar Board, National Senior Women's Honorary,
            elected 198X-23.

Grants and Contracts

National Science Foundation, 198X-8 to 198X-5. (Jury Behavior)

PROFESSIONAL MEMBERSHIPS

American Psychological Association (Fellow - Div. 3, 35, 41; President, Law & Psych Division, - Div. 41, 198X-3).

OTHER PROFESSIONAL EXPERIENCE

Member, Editorial Board:

Law and Human Behavior, 198X-8 to present.
Law and Society Review, 198X-6 to present.

PUBLICATIONS

Books

Bourne, L. E., Dominowski, R. L., Lift, E. F., & Healy, A., Cognitive Processes. Englewood Cliffs: Prentice-Hall, 198X-3.

Lift, E. F., Hypnosis: Cool Tricks To Play On People At Parties. Rockin Rob Productions, 198X-2.

Articles and Chapters

Lift, E. F., The Eyewitness on Trial. In B. D. Sales & A. Elwork (Eds.) With Liberty and Justice for All. Englewood Cliffs, N.J.: Prentice-Hall, in press.

Lift, E. F. Statistics and the Change of Venue Motion, Journal of Clever Lawyers. Renton, WA: Rockin Rob Productions, 198X-2.

CURRICULUM VITAE

Dr. T.A. Loopman
5698 SE Ryan
Jamner, Major

PERSONAL DATA

Born - April 24, 198X-71, Jamner, Major.
Married, two children.

EDUCATION

B.S., University of Major (Pharmacy, 198X-49).
M.S., University of Buffalo (Pharmacology, 198X-47).
Ph.D., University of Buffalo (Pharmacology and Physiology, 198X-45).
M.D., Yale University, Medical School (198X-42).

POSITIONS

Professor of Pharmacology and Toxicology - School of Medicine, Jamner State, 198X-12 to present.
Research Affiliate - Regional Primate Center, University of Major, 198X-20 to present.
Professor of Pharmacology and State Toxicologist - School of Medicine, University of Major, 198X-31 to 198X-12.

SOCIETIES

American Association for the Advancement of Science.
Society of Toxicology.
Western Pharmacology Society.

COMMITTEES AND BOARDS

President - Western Pharmacology Society, 198X-19 to 198X-18.
President - Society of Toxicology, 198X-19 to 198X-18.
National Safety Council Committee on Tests for Intoxication, 198X-37 to present.

PUBLICATIONS

Loopman, T. A., "A Study of the Rate of Metabolism of Ethyl Alcohol," Quart. J. Studies Alcohol 11: 527-537 (198X-38).
Loopman, T. A., "Pharmacology of Alcoholism," Western Medicine 7: Supplement 3, 5-7 (198X-22).
Loopman, T. A., "Acute and Prolonged Toxicity Tests," Journal of the Association of Official Analytical Chemists 58: 4, 645-649 (198X-13).
Loopman, T. A., "Suggestibility and the Person Under the Influence," Journal of Clever Lawyers 9: 2-9 (198X-2).

Curriculum Vitae

Mr. James Raven
4909 Laurel Place
Ruston, Major
(206) 756-3936

Personal: Age 46; Divorced, no children; Health:
                 excellent

Undergraduate: University of Iowa, Bachelor of Arts Degree,
                 Criminal Psychology

Military: U.S. Army 4 years, 198X-29 to 198X-25. Rank
                 of Sergeant. Trained at Army's Polygraph
                 School at Fort Gordon, Georgia. Accredited
                 by the American Polygraph Association.

Employment: Boston Police Department, 20 years, 198X-20
                 to 198X. Chief Polygraph Examiner for 8
                 years.
                 Scientific Security, Inc., Boston,
                 Massachusetts, 198X to present.

Professional   American Polygraph Association
Associations   Northwest Polygraph Examiner's Association
and
Affiliations:

Publications: "Truth or Fancy?," Vol. 16 Journal of the
                 American Polygraph Association, 416-24
                 (198X).

                 "Truth or Consequence?," Vol. 14 Journal of
                 the American Polygraph Association, 320-29
                 (198X-2).

                 "Believe It or Not," Vol. 3 Journal of
                 Forensic Behavior, 214-24 (198X-10).

UNICORN TAVERN

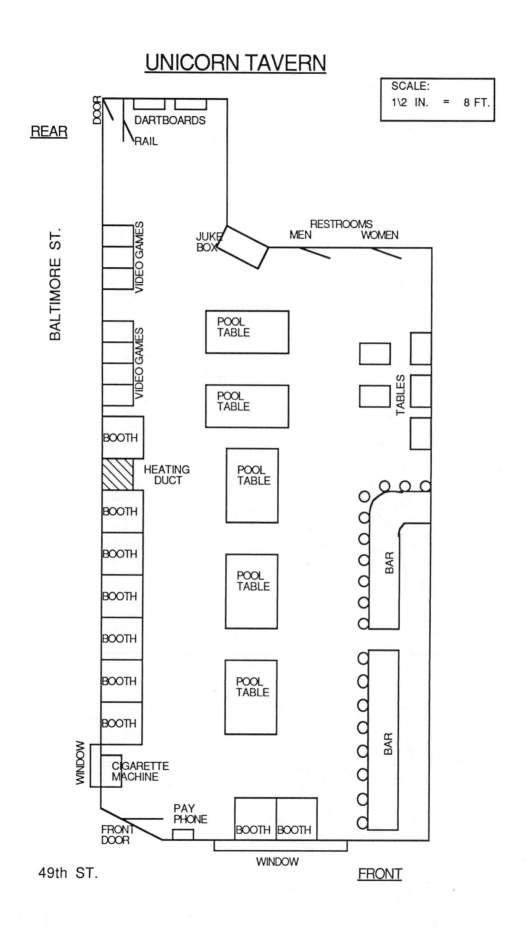

SCALE:
1\2 IN. = 8 FT.

REAR

DOOR

DARTBOARDS

RAIL

BALTIMORE ST.

VIDEO GAMES

VIDEO GAMES

BOOTH

HEATING
DUCT

BOOTH

BOOTH

BOOTH

BOOTH

BOOTH

BOOTH

WINDOW

CIGARETTE
MACHINE

FRONT
DOOR

PAY
PHONE

49th ST.

JUKE
BOX

RESTROOMS
MEN   WOMEN

POOL
TABLE

POOL
TABLE

POOL
TABLE

POOL
TABLE

POOL
TABLE

TABLES

BAR

BAR

BOOTH BOOTH

WINDOW

FRONT

GULL GAS STATION

SCALE:
1\2 IN. = 8 FT.

TRAFFIC LIGHT

+

PEDESTRIAN
LIGHTS

CROSSWALK

CROSSWALK

PINE ST.

ENTRANCE \ EXIT

N

W   E

S

ENTRANCE \ EXIT

SOUTH 12th ST.

DUMPSTER

SIGN
POLE

POLE

POLE

POLE

POLE

DOOR

ENTRANCE \ EXIT

WINDOW

CASH
REGISTER

CROSSWALK

PEDESTRIAN
LIGHTS

+

TRAFFIC LIGHT

CROSSWALK

ANDERSON ST.

DIAGRAM OF EDWARD TAYLOR HARD'S HOME AT THE TIME OF THE SEARCH

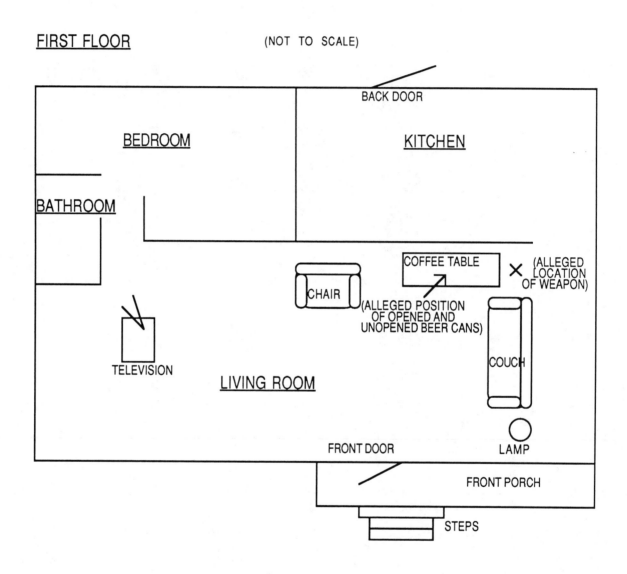

FIRST FLOOR   (NOT TO SCALE)

BACK DOOR

BEDROOM

KITCHEN

BATHROOM

COFFEE TABLE

CHAIR

X (ALLEGED LOCATION OF WEAPON)

(ALLEGED POSITION OF OPENED AND UNOPENED BEER CANS)

TELEVISION

LIVING ROOM

COUCH

FRONT DOOR

LAMP

FRONT PORCH

STEPS

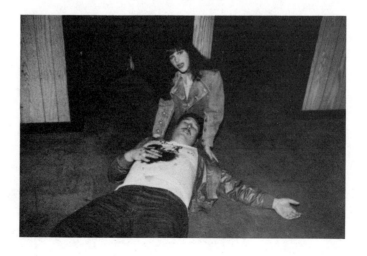

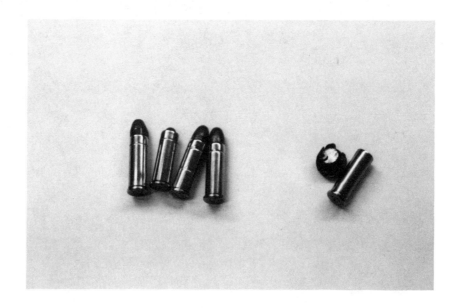

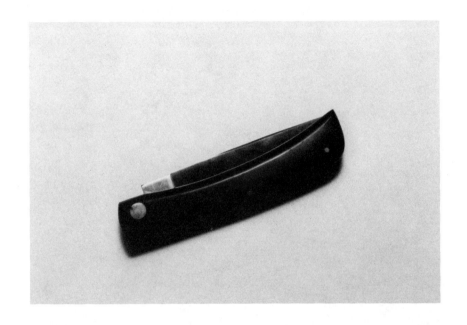

Civil Case File
Summers v. Hard

IN THE SUPERIOR COURT OF THE STATE OF MAJOR

IN AND FOR THE COUNTY OF JAMNER

GRETCHEN and HANS SUMMERS,
and as guardians for
AMANDA and RONNY SUMMERS; and
DEBORAH SUMMERS, individually,
 	
        Plaintiffs,
 	
vs.
 	
EDWARD TAYLOR HARD; M.C. DAVOLA
and JANE DOE DAVOLA, his wife;
TOM DONALDSON; MARY APPLE; and
JOHN DOE and MARY DOE, his wife,
and the DOE CORPORATION, d/b/a
THE UNICORN TAVERN,
 	
        Defendants.
	No. 8X 01234 9
	
	SUMMONS[*]

TO THE DEFENDANTS: A lawsuit has been started against you in the above-entitled court by the above-named plaintiffs. Plaintiffs' claim is stated in the written Complaint, a copy of which is served upon you with this Summons.

In order to defend against this lawsuit, you must respond to the Complaint by stating your defense in writing, and serve a copy upon the person signing this Summons within twenty (20) days after the service of this Summons, excluding the day of service, or a default judgment may be entered against you without notice. A default judgment is one where Plaintiffs are entitled to what they ask for because you have not responded. If you serve a notice of appearance on the undersigned person you are entitled notice before a default judgment may be entered.

---

[*]Review for critique purposes only. This document is not intended as a model summons.

You may demand that the Plaintiffs file this lawsuit with the court. If you do so, the demand must be in writing and must be served upon the person signing this Summons. Within fourteen (14) days after you serve the demand, the Plaintiffs' must file this lawsuit with the court, or the service on you of this Summons and Complaint will be void.

If you wish to seek the advice of an attorney in this matter, you should do so promptly so that your written response, if any, may be served on time.

This Summons issued pursuant to Rule 4 of the Superior Court Civil Rules of the State of Major.

DATED this ___/___ day of _____November_____, 198x.

By: _____F. C. Fank_____
Attorney for Plaintiffs
F. C. Fank

IN THE SUPERIOR COURT OF THE STATE OF MAJOR

IN AND FOR THE COUNTY OF JAMNER

GRETCHEN and HANS SUMMERS individually and as Administrators, Personal Representatives of the Estate of BRUNO SUMMERS, deceased, and as guardians for AMANDA and RONNY SUMMERS; and DEBORAH SUMMERS, individually,	No. 8X 01234 9 COMPLAINT FOR DAMAGES*
Plaintiffs,	
vs.	
EDWARD TAYLOR HARD; M.C. DAVOLA and JANE DOE DAVOLA, his wife; TOM DONALDSON; MARY APPLE; and JOHN DOE and MARY DOE, his wife, and the DOE CORPORATION, d/b/a THE UNICORN TAVERN,	
Defendants.	

COMES NOW the plaintiffs herein and for cuases of action allege and complain:

1.   Plaintiffs GRETCHEN and HANS SUMMERS are the personal representatives and the duly appointed, qualified, and acting Administrators of the estate of BRUNO SUMMERS, deceased, who died on or about September 7, 198x.

2.   Plaintiffs GRETCHEN and HANS SUMMERS are also the duly appointed guardians for the minors, AMANDA and RONNY SUMMERS. Plaintiffs bring this action for the benefit of decedant's estate, and for the benefit of themselves individually, decedant's surviving wife, DEBORAH, and minor children, AMANDA and RONNY.

*Review for critique purposes only. This document is not intended as a model complaint.

3.   DEBORAH SUMMERS, surviving wife of BRUNO SUMMERS brings this action pursuant to paragraph 2 and individually and on behalf of herself.

4.   Plaintiffs DEBORAH SUMMERS, the widow of BRUNO SUMMERS, AMANDA and RONNY SUMMERS, the minor children of BRUNO SUMMERS, and HANS and GRETCHEN SUMMERS, parents of BRUNO SUMMERS, are residents of Jamner, Major.

5.   Defendant EDWARD T. HARD is a resident of Jamner, Major.

6.   Defendants M.C. DAVOLA and JANE DOE DAVOLA, his wife, are residents of Jamner, Major.

7.   Defendant TOM DONALDSON is a resident of Jamner, Major.

8.   Defendant MARY APPLE is a resident of Jamner, Major.

9.   Defendant DOE CORPORATION is a coporation duly incorporated under the laws of Major, and with M.C. DAVOLA and JANE DOE DAVOLA, his wife, or with JOHN DOE and MARY DOE, is doing business in Jamner, Major as the Unicorn Tavern.

10.   Defendants M.C. DAVOLA, MARY APPLE, and TOM DONALDSON are lawful employees of the Unicorn Tavern and/or of M.C. DAVOLA and/or of DOE CORPORATION and/or of JOHN and MARY DOE.

11.   On or about the 7th day of September, 198x, at the Unicorn Tavern, 5302 N. 49th, Jamner, Major, decedent BRUNO SUMMERS was and did subsequently died by a handgun negligently, willfully, wontonly and recklessly discharged by EDWARD T. HARD.

12.   The herein above-described prior incident was proximately caused by the negligent acts of TOM DONALDSON, MARY APPLE, and M.C. DAVOLA in that they unlawfully failed to use

reasonable care in serving liquor to EDWARD T. HARD on September 3, 198x; failed to protect BRUNO SUMMERS from foreseeable injury at the hands of EDWARD T. HARD.

13. Plaintiffs repeat and reallege each and every allegation contained herein in paragraphs 1 through 12, and for a second claim herein allege that the prior above-described incident was proximately caused by the willful, wanton, malicious and reckless acts of defendants TOM DONALDSON, MARY APPLE, and M.C. DAVOLA in that they unlawfully failed to observe reasonable care in serving liquor to EDWARD T. HARD on September 3, 198x; failed adequately to protect BRUNO SUMMERS from foreseeable injury at the hands of EDWARD T. HARD; and failed to perform the duties imposed by the lawful and duly promulgated laws, regulations, and codes of the State of Major.

14. Plaintiffs repeat and reallege each and every allegation contained herein in paragraphs 1 through 12, and for a third claim herein allege that the above-described incident was proximately caused by the willful, violent and negligent acts of defendant EDWARD T. HARD, an ex-felon, in that by unlawfully possessing and concealing a pistol, having been convicted of crimes of violence, to wit, rape, he knowingly failed to conform his conduct to that which is prescribed by law, for persons convicted of such violent crimes in that defendant failed reasonably to avoid confrontation with BRUNO SUMMERS; provoked such confrontation; and in that defendant failed to use reasonable care in handling the pistol that wounded BRUNO SUMMERS.

15. Plaintiffs repeat and reallege each and every allegation contained herein in paragraphs 1 through 14, and for a fourth claim herein allege that the above-described indicent was proximately caused by the willful, wanton, malicious, and reckless acts of defendant EDWARD T. HARD.

16. Plaintiffs repeat and reallege each and every allegation contained herein in paragraphs 1 through 14, and for a fifth claim, herein allege that the prior above-described shooting and killing was proximately caused by the negligent, willful, wonton, malicious and reckless acts of defendant M.C. DAVOLA, in that defendant failed reasonably to protect a patron, plaintiffs' decedant, BRUNO SUMMERS, from foreseeable harm at the hands of EDWARD T. HARD, by failing to instruct employees of the Unicorn Tavern to take precautions to prevent violent confrontations between defendant EDWARD T. HARD and plaintiffs' decedant BRUNO SUMMERS.

17. Plaintiffs repeat and reallege each and every allegation contained herein in paragraphs 1-14, and for a sixth claim, herein allege that by reason of the aforesaid acts, failure or omission to act, by the said defend nts, plaintiffs DEBORAH, HANS and GRETCHEN SUMMERS have individually suffered severe negligent and intentional mental distress.

18. At the time of his death, plaintiffs' decedant, who was age 30, had a life expectency of sixty years. Decedent was a devoted husband and father, constantly interested in the welfare of his wife and children. He was in excellent physical heatlh, worked hard and regularly, and devoted his earnings to the care,

support and maintenance of his wife and children. By reason of
the death of plaintiffs' decedant, plaintiffs' decedant's
surviving parents, spouse and minor children have been deprived
of support, comfort, society, counsel, and services, all to their
damage in amounts to be determined at trial.

19. By reason of the injury and death of plaintiffs'
decedant, BRUNO SUMMERS, his estate has become liable for funeral
expenses in an amount to be determined at trial.

20. By reason of the death of decedent, decedent's estate
has been deprived of accumulations to the estate during his life,
in an amount to be determined at trial.

21. Plaintiffs DEBORAH SUMMERS, individually, and AMANDA
and RONNY SUMMERS, the minor children of the deceased, and
plaintiffs HANS and GRETCHEN SUMMERS repeat and reallege each and
every allegation contained herein in paragraphs 1 - 19.

WHEREFORE, PLAINTIFFS GRETCHEN and HANS SUMMERS,
INDIVIDUALLY and as PERSONAL REPRESENTATIVES, and as
ADMINISTRATORS OF THE ESTATE OF BRUNO SUMMERS, and as GUARDIANS
AD LITEM of AMANDA and RONNY SUMMERS, the minor children of
plaintiffs' decedant, BRUNO SUMMERS; and DEBORAH SUMMERS as the
surviving spouse of BRUNO SUMMERS, and individually, PRAY
JUDGMENT for the damages heretofore described, and for such other
sums as the COURT deems proper by was of exemplary or punitive

damages, for costs of suit, attorneys fees', and for such other relief as the COURT deems proper in the premises, in an amount to be determined at trial.

Respectfully Submitted,

F. C. Fank
_____

Attorney for Plaintiffs

F. C. Fank

DATED: This __/__ day of November, in the year, 198x

IN THE SUPERIOR COURT OF THE STATE OF MAJOR

IN AND FOR THE COUNTY OF JAMNER

GRETCHEN and HANS SUMMERS individually and as Administrators, Personal Representatives of the Estate of BRUNO SUMMERS, deceased, and as guardians for AMANDA and RONNY SUMMERS; and DEBORAH SUMMERS, individually,))))))))	No. 8X 01234 9 ANSWER BY ED HARD*

GRETCHEN and HANS SUMMERS
individually and as Administrators, Personal Representatives
of the Estate of BRUNO SUMMERS,
deceased, and as guardians for
AMANDA and RONNY SUMMERS; and
DEBORAH SUMMERS, individually,   )

                Plaintiffs,   )

vs.   )

EDWARD TAYLOR HARD; M.C. DAVOLA
and JANE DOE DAVOLA, his wife;
TOM DONALDSON; MARY APPLE; and
JOHN DOE and MARY DOE, his wife,
and the DOE CORPORATION, d/b/a
THE UNICORN TAVERN,   )

                Defendants.   )

No. 8X 01234 9

ANSWER BY ED HARD*

COMES NOW the defendent, EDWARD T. HARD, by a   through his attorney, D.G. CASE, and answers:

1.   Defendent ED HARD has insufficient informat   with which to form a belief as to the truth or falsity of par   aphs 1-10, 12, 13, 16, 17, 18, 20 and 21 and therefore denys   same.

2.   Defendent HARD admits in paragraph 11 th   Bruno Summers died, but denies each and every other alleg   on in that paragraph.

3.   Defendent HARD denies the allegation   n paragraphs 14 and 15.

4.   Paragraph 14 of the complaint is inflamatory, prejudicial and scandalous and included to prejudice defendent HARD.

---

*Review for critique purposes only. This document is not intended as a model answer.

Defendant requests that it be strikned from the complaint forthwith.

FIRST AFFIRMATIVE DEFENSE

5.   Bruno Summers' injuries as duly set forth and alleged in the complaint were accidantal in that the gun discharged accidentelly and subsequently injured Bruno Summers.   Such conduct was reasonable.

SECOND AFFIRMATIVE DEFENSE

6.   Defendant Hard alleges as a second affirmative defense that Bruno Summers proximately caused his own injuries in failing to avoid a confrontation, failure to use reasonable care, by voluntary intoxication, and failing to leave the tavern, he assumed the risks and hazards.   By reason of his conduct, Bruno Summers caused and provoked his own injuries.   Such negligent conduct must be imputed to plaintiffs by reason of State of Major statutes.

THIRD AFFIRMATIVE DEFENSE

7.   Plaintiffs' damages if any, were solely and proximately caused by and contributed to by the actions of third parties.

8.   By way of reservation of rights, without waiver, EDWARD HARD specifically reserve the right to amend its answer and claims herein by way of adding additional parties, affirmative defenses, cross-claims, and third-party claims as additional investigation, discovery or circumstances warrant.

PRAYER FOR RELIEF

WHEREFORE Defendant EDWARD TAYLOR HARD respectfully prays for the following heretofor described relief:

1.   That paragraph 14 of plaintiffs complaint be striken
immediatley;

2.   That plaintiffs complaint against EDWARD TAYLOR HARD be
dismissed with prejudice;

3.   That defendent HARD be awarded costa and attorneys fees and
other relief as the court deems fit.

DATED this _8_ day of November, 198x.

Edward Taylor Hard
EDWARD TAYLOR HARD

D. G. Case
D. G. CASE

77 4th Ave. S.E.

Ruston, Major 94802

(206) 877-4777

Attorney for Defendent

IN THE SUPERIOR COURT OF THE STATE OF MAJOR

IN AND FOR THE COUNTY OF JAMNER

GRETCHEN and HANS SUMMERS individually and as Adminis-trators, Personal Representatives of the Estate of BRUNO SUMMERS, deceased, and as guardians for AMANDA and RONNY SUMMERS; and DEBORAH SUMMERS, individually, Plaintiffs, vs. EDWARD TAYLOR HARD; M.C. DAVOLA and JANE DOE DAVOLA, his wife; TOM DONALDSON; MARY APPLE; and JOHN DOE and MARY DOE, his wife, and the DOE CORPORATION, d/b/a THE UNICORN TAVERN, Defendants.	No. 8X 01234 9 ANSWER by DAVOLA, DONALDSON & APPLE*

COMES NOW the defendants DAVOLA, DONALDSON and APPLE, by way of answer to plaintiffs complaint, by and through their attorney answer as follows:

1.   With regard to paragraphs 1 through 5, 14, 15, 17, 18, and 20 defendants are without knowledge or information to form a belief as to the truth of the allegations as to admit or deny themn, and therefore deny the same.

2.   With regard to paragraphs 6 through 10, defendants admit the allegations contained therein.

3.   With regard to paragraphs 11 through 13, 16, and 21 of the complaint, defendants specifically deny each and every allegation contained therein, as though fully set forth in full.

BY WAY OF FURTHER ANSWER, defendants state as though fully set forth in full:

4.   The plaintiffs have failed to state a claim upon which relief can be granted under Rule 12(b)(6) as stated in paragraphs

---

*Review for critique purposes only. This document is not intended as a model answer.

2, 11, 13, 15, 16, and 21 and defendants move that those claims be dismissed.

BY THE WAY OF FURTHER ANSWER AND AS A FIRST AFFIRMATIVE DEFENSE, defendants allege:

5.   At the time and place alleged in plaintiffs' complaint, the deceased, Bruno Summers, acted carelessly and negligently. That he by his own negligence, contributed proximately and negligently to his own alleged injuries.

6.   Plaintiffs were intoxicated when they arrived at the Unicorn Tavern, September 3rd, 198x. By remaining on the premises with knowledge aforethought of Ed Hard's presence both Deborah and Bruno Summers voluntarily assumed the risk of later events and harm.

THIRD AFFIRMATIVE DEFENSE AND BY WAY OF A CROSS-CLAIM AGAINST EDWARD HARD

7.   Defendant Ed Hard's shooting and killing of Bruno Summers constituted an independent superseding event not reasonably foreseeable by defendants.

WHEREFORE, DEFENDANTS DAVOLA, DONALDSON AND APPLE, PRAY THAT

Plaintiff's complaint as set forth in paragraph 4 of the answer be dismissed, and that plaintiffs take nothing by his action and that defendants be awarded costs and all other relief that the court finds is equitable and just.

D. L. Hass
D. L. Hass
Attorney for Defendants

JAMNER COUNTY HEALTH DEPARTMENT
Community Health Care Delivery System

NAME Summers, Deborah M.

ADDRESS 1962 N.E. 6th

CITY, TOWN Ruston, Major 98139

PHONE (206) 433-1112

EMPLOYER\OCCUPATION
NONE

NEXT OF KIN Hans Summers

ADDRESS 1200 Maple Ave.

CITY, TOWN Ruston, Major 98465

PHONE (206) 784-2076

RESPONSIBLE PARTY Myself

ADDRESS Same as above.

CITY, TOWN Same as above.

PHONE Same as above.

CURRENT PHYSICIAN NONE

PHONE

ALLERGIES None.

MEDICATIONS NONE

BIRTHDATE 8 8 6X AGE 21

SS# 534-46-1672

ETHNIC White

MARITAL STATUS Married

FINANCIAL DATA

FAMILY SIZE 4

INCOME \ MO NONE

FEE CODE

INSURANCE COVERAGE &#

MEDICARE

MEDICAID

PCMB

OTHER

Where would you have gone if clinic not available?
Don't Know

Referred to clinic by
friend

* *

CONSENT FOR TREATMENT\AUTHORIZATION FOR RELEASE OF INFORMATION

Having voluntarily presented myself at Jamner County Clinic, I acknowledge awareness of the fact that evaluation and treatment to be received may be administered by a physician or a mid-level practitioner. I consent to and authorize evaluation and treatment that may be advisable or necessary in the judgment of the physician or the mid-level practitioner. I also authorize release of this record for insurance or medical follow-up purposes.

Martha Lindsey
_____
Witness

Sept. 5, 198x
_____
Date

Deborah Summers
_____
Signature

INACTIVE PATIENT REGISTRATION \ MEDICAL RECORD

JAMNER COUNTY HEALTH DEPARTMENT
CLINIC PROGRESS NOTES

NAME _Summers, Deborah M._   CLINIC # ___2___

DATE	PROB # V\S	NOTE (SOAP) *c/o Body Aches and Anxiety*
9/5/8X		S: 21-year-old white female who has no current
	wt 110	family physician. Pt. reports that two days ago
	BP 140/80	her husband, Bruno, was critically shot in a
	T 98⁴	barroom altercation. Pt. states that she feels
		she cannot handle the stress caused by witnessing
		the shooting. She feels like she is "going
		crazy." She also indicates that she "hurts" all
		over her body. She does not state the exact
		location or nature of these "hurts." Pt. has
		no history of mental problems. Pt. states that
		she does not use drugs.
		O: Anxious young female in distress. Heart
		rate is regular. Abdomen is regular. Throat
		is clear. Lungs are clear.
		A: 21-year-old female appears to be suffering
		from acute situational anxiety symptoms brought
		on by the severe shock of seeing her husband shot.
		Situational anxiety symptoms manifest themselves
		in Pt.'s physical ailments (perceived) and psy-
		chological hysteria. Hypertension.
		P: 1. Valium 5 mgs - TID for 30 days
		2. No renew of Valium after 30 days
		3. After 30 days - RTC for possible referral
		to psychiatrist
		Provider's Signature:
		Ed Tissier

PROGRESS NOTES

    Entry 40: Deborah Summers' Medical Records (Jamner County Health Department)

TIME	ROOM
in 9:45 am	201
out 10:00 am	

NEVA COUNTY
MEDICAL SERVICES

CHIEF COMPLAINT:

VITAL SIGNS

TIME:	TEMP.:	P:	R:	BP:

DATE:

10-3-8X

NAME:

Summers, Deborah M.

SEX:	BIRTHDATE:
F	8-8-6X

ADDRESS:

1200 Maple Ave.

CITY:

Ruston

STATE:	ZIP:
Major	98465

PHONE:

756-3436

BROUGHT BY:

Self

WEIGHT:

110

LAST TETANUS:

1973

ALLERGY TO MED.:

None

CURRENT MEDICATIONS:

NURSING ASSESSMENT:

PROBLEMS:

#1 - Anxiety

S: Pt. has been in internal conflict since the shooting death of her husband one month ago. Pt. complains that she has "fallen to pieces" and feels "numb" ever since the shooting. She has been drinking moderately since the occurrence and before but does not smoke. Past med. and surg. histories are negative. Currently, Pt. says she is taking Valium to reduce her anxiety. Valium prescribed by Dr. Risseen of Jamner Co. Health Clinic. Rev. of system negative for body hurts, headaches.

O: Agitated shy female in apparent mild distress and hysterical physical trauma. Pupils are equal and react to light. Her heart is normal without murmurs. Lungs are clear. Abdomen is soft without enlarged organs or tenderness. Pelvic and rectal tympanic membranes are slightly reddened.

A: 21-year-old female with recent severe trauma in life wishes medication to inhibit anxiety. Pt. is a mild hysteric who has a history of hysteric displays. Valium would effectively mitigate Pt.'s physical/emotional trauma. Agitated condition is a reflection of M. Summers' "personality type."

P: 1. No refill of Valium prescription.
   2. Encouraged to quit drinking and watch diet.
   3. FU in 2 weeks suggested.

ORDERS:

DISCHARGE INSTRUCTIONS:

CBC

CHEMISTRY

BLOOD GASES

DISPOSITION	ADMIT	HOME	OW	OTHER	ON
		XX			DISCHARGE

Mild distress

PRIMARY PHYSICIAN		AT		CLINIC
Sherman Croup	Neva Co. Medical			

SPECIALIST		AT		CLINIC
N/A		N/A		

URINALYSIS

N/A	N/A
X-RAY	EKG

ECONOMIC REPORT

The Value of the Economic Loss
Due to the Death of
Mr. Bruno Summers

Prepared by
Bruce D. Hann, Ph.D.
Department of Economics
University of Willow Bay
Ruston, Major 98416

LOST EARNINGS: BRUNO SUMMERS

This report, which presents our estimate of the
economic loss resulting from the death of Bruno Summers, is
divided into four sections. We first present the basic
background data and assumptions used in our analysis. The
second section of this report is our estimate of the income
loss due to Mr. Summers' death. Adjustments to this income
loss are presented in section three. Finally, our
conclusions are presented in section four. Numbers enclosed
in brackets refer to footnotes at the end of the report.

ASSUMPTIONS AND BACKGROUND DATA

Mr. Summers was born in 198X-30. At the time of his
death he was 30 years old. He was a high school graduate.
Mr. Summers entered the Armed Service after high school.
Following his discharge from the Army he alternated periods
of employment and unemployment. At the time of his death he
was employed at the Major Gynmastic Club. Apparently Mr.
Summers was to have received a promotion from his employer
within six months. Mr. Summers had no major health
problems. We are not aware of any unusually risky habits or
hobbies. Therefore, the national norm data will be used for
statistical computations.

At the time of his death Mr. Summers was married. This
was his second marriage. He was divorced from his first
wife. He had two children from his first marriage. While
Mr. Summers and his current wife had no children, we will
assume, based on national norms, that they would have had
one child [1].

Based on United States Life Tables [2] for white males,
Mr. Summers would have lived for an additional 43 years, or
until age 73. We have assumed that he would have remained
in the labor force until the year 198X+35 when he would have
been 65 years of age.

Further, we assumed that Mr. Summers' savings and his
Social Security benefits would have been just sufficient for
retirement purposes.

Over a sustained period of time an individual's wage
and salary income tends to rise at a rate equal to the
individual's growth in productivity (real growth) plus the
rate of inflation. At the same time market interest rates
include both real interest rate and inflation premium
components. Inflation, therefore, increases both the dollar
value of income and the market interest rate by the same

proportional amount. Thus, when income values are discounted the impact of inflation is removed, since both the amounts in the numerator and denominator are adjusted in equal proportion in the same direction.

All calculations in this report are done in real terms since inflationary effects are immaterial. Our estimates, then, are based on real income, productivity growth, and real interest rates.

ESTIMATED INCOME LOSS

To estimate the income loss due to the death of Mr. Summers we first calculated a base income stream. Our calculations assume that Mr. Summers would have remained employed at the Major Gynmastic Club and that he would have obtained the promotion to assistant day manager. Based on his previous work history and his education and training we did not assume any further promotions or occupational changes.

The base income for Mr. Summers was calculated by estimating a gross income stream from 198X for 35 years. To do this we assumed that he would have finished 198X (September through December) at his current rate of pay, $5.25 per hour. We assumed that Mr. Summers would have received his promotion to assistant day manager in April 198X+1. For the years 198X+5 and subsequently for the next 30 years we assumed that his pay rate would have been $8.65 per hour.

This gross income stream was adjusted for productivity and experience effects to calculate Mr. Summers' yearly base income estimates. While his record of earnings growth since the Army has exceeded the national average [3], we did not continue this trend in our calculations. Based on national data for occupational and industrial forecasts we believe that employees in similar circumstances will experience real wage growth equal to average United State growth [4]. Thus, we increased Mr. Summers' gross income stream by 0.68% per year to recognize this increase in real income [5].

As individuals gain experience on the job they become more productive, and hence their incomes rise to reflect this. This pattern of income growth generates an age-earnings profile. We adjusted Mr. Summers' gross income stream based on the average age-earnings profile for a male high school graduate [6].

Our estimate of Mr. Summers' base income stream is presented in Exhibit 1 under the column headed "Base

Income." These estimates assume a forty hour work week and a fifty week work year.

The second step in estimating the income loss was to convert base income to net income. Net income represents the statistically expected income based on normal labor force behavior and actuarial considerations. Base income was adjusted for the probability that Mr. Summers would not be active in the labor market at all times. Labor force participation rates for male high school graduates were used to make this adjustment. The second adjustment to base income recognized the actuarial probability that he would not survive in any given year. This adjustment was made based on mortality rates for white males [7].

Adjusting base income for these two statistical effects generates our estimates of net income. This is shown in Exhibit 1 under the column headed "Net Income."

The present value of the income loss due to the death of Mr. Summers is calculated by taking the present value of the annual net income estimates. We used a real rate of four percent for discounting to present value. These figures are shown in Exhibit 1 under the column headed "Discounted Income."

The present value of Mr. Summers' lost income is $364,681. This represents the amount, which if invested at a four percent real rate of return, would reproduce the stream of net income on an annual basis.

ADJUSTMENTS

Three adjustments to lost income are needed to estimate the economic loss resulting from the death of Mr. Summers. First, the value of his own consumption must be subtracted from the income loss. Second, the value of lost fringe benefits must be added to the income loss estimate. Third, the value of Mr. Summers' contributions to his household must be included in the loss estimate.

The estimate of income lost does not recognize the fact that Mr. Summers would have used some of the income for his own consumption purposes. The amount of income consumed by him would not represent a loss due to his death. The lost income should be reduced by the amount of self consumption.

To estimate self consumption we assumed that the Summers would have had a child in 198X+5 when Mr. Summers would have been 35 years old. We also assumed that the child would have remained in the household until age 18. From standard family consumption tables we then estimated the proportion of family income which would be consumed by Mr. Summers [8]. The present value of this self consumption allowance equals $79,224.

Our income estimates are based on straight time hourly wage rates. However, typically employees receive additional compensation in the form of fringe benefits. These benefits include leave time allowance, private retirement plans, health insurance, supplemental unemployment compensation, and production bonuses. For non-manufacturing employees in the United States fringe benefits average 17.7% and wage and salary payments average 82.3% of total compensation [9]. Based on these averages the value of fringe benefits for Mr. Summers is equal to $78,431.

Mr. Summers would have contributed to the operation of his household by providing services in kind. These lost services, car repair, lawn maintenance, general repairs, have value to the household which must be replaced. We assumed, based on national average time management studies, that he would have contributed three hours per week to household service [10]. This represents 7.5% of his work time. Thus, the present value of services provided, based on a market wage equivalent, is equal to $27,351.

CONCLUSION

The lost economic value due to the death of Mr. Bruno Summers is equal to $391,239. This represents the present value (based on a four percent real discount rate) of his lost income (364,681) minus an allowance for personal consumption (79,224) plus the present value of lost fringe benefits (78,431) and lost services to the household (27,351).

EXHIBIT 1

Income Estimates for Mr. Bruno Summers

Year	Base Income	Net Income	Discounted Income
198X*	$ 3,612	$ 3,581	$ 3,873
198X+1	14,127	14,008	14,568
198X+2	17,300	16,572	16,572
198X+3	19,217	18,408	17,700
198X+4	19,978	19,137	17,693
198X+5**	21,933	21,009	18,677
198X+6	21,725	20,768	17,753
198X+7	21,604	20,652	16,974
198X+8	22,538	21,366	16,886
198X+9	22,227	21,072	16,013
198X+10	21,622	20,499	14,978
198X+11	20,878	19,687	13,832
198X+12	19,909	18,774	12,683
198X+13	22,019	20,112	13,064
198X+14	21,639	19,766	12,346
198X+15	22,175	20,255	12,165
198X+16	22,071	19,954	11,523
198X+17	22,400	20,251	11,245
198X+18	22,936	19,551	10,438
198X+19	23,698	20,203	10,372
198X+20	21,743	18,534	9,149
198X+21	24,390	20,432	9,698
198X+22	22,642	18,968	8,657
198X+23	21,172	14,838	6,511
198X+24	21,881	15,335	6,471
198X+25	20,860	14,619	5,931
198X+26	22,123	15,114	5,896
198X+27	21,518	14,700	5,514
198X+28	21,154	12,300	4,436
198X+29	22,435	13,045	4,524
198X+30	21,691	12,612	4,206
198X+31	20,428	11,429	3,665
198X+32	21,397	11,970	3,691
198X+33	21,241	11,883	3,523
198X+34	21,656	12,116	3,454
TOTAL		$593,520	$364,681

* September to December at $5.25 per hour base rate

** January to April at $5.25 per hour base rate;
April to December at $8.65 per hour base rate

FOOTNOTES

[1.]   United States Department of Commerce, Bureau of the
Census, Marital Status and Living Arrangements: March 198X-
1, Current Population Reports, Series P-20, No. 380 and
Population Profile of the U.S.; 198X-2, Current Population
Reports, Series P-20, No. 378, Government Printing Office,
Washington D.C.

[2.]   United States Department of Health and Human Services,
Public Health Service, Monthly Vital Statistics Report,
1980, "Advance Report of Final Mortality Statistics, 1980,"
National Center for Health Statistics, Volume 32, No. 4,
(PHS) 83-1120, August, 198X, Hyattsville, Md.

[3.]   From 198X-7 to 198X the average annual growth in Mr.
Summers' hourly pay was 18.4%. During this same period the
average annual rate of inflation was 7.7%. Thus Mr.
Summers' real hourly wage grew by 10.7% per year on average.

[4.]   United States Department of Commerce, Bureau of
Industrial Economics, 198X U.S. Industrial Outlook,
Government Printing Office, Washington, D.C.

[5.]   President's Council of Economic Advisors, Economic
Report of the President, Table B-39, Government Printing
Office, Washington, D.C., 198X.

[6.]   United States Department of Commerce, Bureau of the
Census, Lifetime Earnings Estimates for Men and Women in the
United States: 198X-5, Current Income Reports, Series P-60,
No. 139, Government Printing Office, Washington, D.C.

[7.]   Labor force participation rates based on the source
cited in [6] and mortality estimates based on the source
cited in [2].

[8.]   United States Department of Labor, Bureau of Labor
Statistics, Handbook of Labor Statistics, Bulletin 1905,
Table 141, Government Printing Office, Washington, D.C.

[9.]   Ibid., Table 112.

[10.] Peter Watson, The Value of Time, D.C. Heath,
Lexington, Ma., 198X-10; F.S. Chapin, Human Activity
Patterns in the City, John Wiley, New York, N.Y., 198X-10;
C. Sharp, The Economics of Time, John Wiley, New York, N.Y.,
198X-2.

ECONOMIC REPORT

Critique   of   Plaintiffs'   Economic   Report

Prepared   by

Thomas   Monday,   Ph.D.
Professor,   Department   of   Economics
University   of   Santa   Laura

Economic Report of Dr. Thomas Monday, Defendants' Economist

I have been retained as an economist to help prepare the defendants representing Edward Taylor Hard and M.C. Davola, to take the deposition of Dr. Hann and to examine Dr. Hann at trial. The following is my critique of Dr. Hann's report concerning the value of Bruno Summers' lost earnings.

In my opinion Bruno Summers' earning capability was much lower than that stated in Dr. Hann's report. I believe that Bruno Summers' life earnings are worth less than $300,000.

I agree with Dr. Hann that the ratio to calculate the present value of Bruno's lost earnings is:

$$\frac{\text{VALUE OF LOST INCOME}}{\text{DISCOUNT FACTOR}} = \text{Present Value of Bruno's lost earnings}$$

I differ, however, from Dr. Hann in my mathematical computation of total lost earnings.

I have examined four factors used by Dr. Hann:

I.   Real Interest Rate Used in the Discount Factor
II. Length of Bruno's Life and Work Life
III. Growth in Bruno Summers' Work Productivity
IV. Basic assumptions - number of children, employed spouse etc.

It is my opinion that Dr. Hann, when he used these four factors, made some incorrect assumptions.

I.   REAL INTEREST RATE USED IN THE DISCOUNT FACTOR

I would increase the real interest rate used in the discount factor of the denominator. Increasing the interest rate is the most significant way to lower the total lost earning award. The plaintiff's economist, Dr. Hann, has used 4% as the interest rate. I conclude that 4% is an unrealistic interest rate and that 5% or 6% should be used. A 5% or 6% interest rate more accurately reflects the risk of actually realizing Bruno's total life income.

I would also decrease the value in the numerator of the lost income. The number of years Bruno is in the work force, multiplied by the yearly wage amount, plus an industry growth factor, individual productivity growth factor, and an inflation factor equals the total lost income figure in the numerator.

II. LENGTH OF BRUNO SUMMERS' LIFE AND WORK

I would decrease Bruno's last income figure by decreasing the total number of years Bruno was in the work force. The result of a decrease in total years in the work force is a decrease in total lost earnings. The plaintiff's economist, Dr. Hann, has used a thirty year work life for Bruno. I would show that a person like Bruno, would leave the work force after twenty-five years and not work up to the maximum age of 65 years old. I would show this decrease in Bruno's work life by examining:

A.   Bruno's Ability to Stay in the Work Force

Bruno may involuntarily leave the work force due to illness; accident; inability to find employment; lay off or death.

I would contend that the plaintiff's economist's calculations did not consider involuntary absences from the work force.

I would assert that Dr. Hann should adjust Bruno's total years in the work force for a greater amount of unemployment. The result would be to lower the total years Bruno would be in the work force, thus lowering Bruno's total lost earnings.

B.   Bruno's Age of Retirement

1.   Dr. Hann's calculations did not consider voluntary absences from the work force. Dr. Hann assumed an age of 65 for Bruno's retirement. Dr. Hann's assumptions of age 65 for Bruno's retirement are based upon:

a.   the worker remaining in the blue collar work force until mandatory retirement;

b.   statistics of people who entered the work force 40 years ago and are leaving now.

I would show that the assumptions underlying a choice of age 65 for Bruno's retirement are unrealistic. Bruno may voluntarily leave the work force at any time.

2.   I could even justify an age of 59 that Bruno would be out of the work force based on

Bruno's erratic employment record and Bruno's potential for unemployment.

3. The current trend is a lowering in age of "out of work force" to age 63.

4. I would also show a decrease in Bruno's life by factors that will shorten Bruno's life. A shorter life results in fewer years in the work force, therefore lowering total earnings.

   a. Bruno's Health

      If Bruno smokes, a High Risk Mortality Table should be used. I would assert that Dr. Hann's calculations are not correct because a Normal Mortality Table was used.

   b. Bruno's Hobbies

      Bruno's survivalist and neo-Nazi activities are high risk hobbies. They involve the use of guns and knives for protection and survival. This increases the possibility of a premature death for Bruno. Dr. Hann has estimated Bruno's length of life to extend to age 73 (43 more years).

      I would show that because of Bruno's participation in these high risk activities, Bruno's life would not continue to age 73 and would be reduced significantly. This results in a decrease in total lost earnings.

III. GROWTH IN BRUNO SUMMERS' WORK PRODUCTIVITY

I would also decrease the lost income figure by:

A. Decreasing the industry growth potential factor and eliminating the individual productivity factor. Dr. Hann has used an industry growth rate of 10% and an individual productivity growth rate of .68%.

   1. I would show that the parking garage industry has little growth potential.

   2. I would also indicate that Bruno's productivity would not increase over time.

3. Changing these two factors, however, would result in only a small difference. (The defendants may not want to question the use of the 10% and .68% growth rates.)

B. Not Increasing Bruno's wage from $5.65 per hour to $8.25 per hour.

1. Dr. Hann has increased Bruno's wage after Bruno completed six months employment at the Gymnastic Club. This increase was to reflect Bruno's promotion to garage manager. I would attempt to show that Bruno lacked the ability to be promoted to garage manager. Thus, Bruno's lack of ability results in $5.65 being the maximum wage that Bruno could earn.

2. I suggest that additional factors be examined to show that Bruno's productivity and therefore his wage rate would increase little over Bruno's work life:

   a) Bruno's education.

   b) Bruno's ability to learn on the job.

   c) The likelihood or probability that Bruno would become manager or even stay at this job ("Best that could be hoped for").

   d) Bruno's past work history (length at each job, type of absences, etc. "Bad track record").

3. Dr. Hann's report and information defendants gave me did not indicate whether Bruno is a member of a union. If he is a union member, his productivity growth would increase at an established rate (automatic raises over his work life).

IV. BASIC ASSUMPTIONS

Dr. Hann calculated total loss of earnings by relying on assumptions as to the real interest rate, growth in Bruno's work productivity, and length of Bruno's work life. I would correct the assumptions Dr. Hann made in adjusting total lost earnings. The adjustments I would make are to include three additional factors:

-- Value of Bruno's Own Consumption;
-- Compensation in the Form of Fringe Benefits;

-- Lost Value of Bruno's Services.

A.   Value of Bruno's Own Consumption

I looked at two underlying factors that Dr. Hann assumed about the value of Bruno's consumption. These factors are: the possibility that Bruno will have one more child, and the possibility Deborah will enter the work force. The value of Bruno's own consumption must be subtracted from the income loss.

1.   The Possibility Bruno Will Have One More Child

Dr. Hann has assumed that Bruno will conform to the statistics of a person in his age bracket and have one more child. Bruno's personal consumption would not increase if he would have had another child. This results in a lower number subtracted from total lost income. I would assert that it is unlikely Bruno would want or have another child because he has not cared for his two children from his first marriage for six years. If I assume Bruno will have no more children, Bruno's personal consumption would go up because no income would be used to support a child. An increase in personal consumption reduces Bruno's total net lost earnings. An example of an increase in self-consumption is that Bruno would participate more in activities that do not involve children: drinking; hobbies; etc.

2.   The Possibility Deborah Will Enter the Work Force

Dr. Hann has assumed that Deborah will not enter the work force. I believe this is unrealistic due to the trend that women work away from the home. An increase in Bruno and Deborah's total income increases Bruno's consumption. This is because an increase in total disposable income for Bruno increases the amount he can spend on himself. However, Bruno's increase in consumption is taken against only his income, reducing his total lost earnings. Bruno can increase his consumption since there is more total income. I would also show that Deborah will enter the work force after her marriage to Bruno. An illustration of how this factor, Deborah entering the work force, would reduce Bruno's lost earnings is as follows:

<u>Bruno alone earns wages</u>

Bruno's total wages =	$150,000
Bruno's total consumption =	25,000
NET TOTAL WAGES	$125,000

<u>Bruno and Deborah earn wages</u>

Bruno's total wages =	$150,000
Bruno's total consumption =	50,000
NET TOTAL WAGES	$100,000

B. <u>Compensation in the Form of Fringe Benefits</u>

An amount equal to fringe benefits received is added to Bruno's total lost income. Fringe benefits include health insurance, leave time, allowances, etc. Dr. Hann has assumed that Bruno received a "typical package" of fringe benefits. It is possible that Bruno received little or no fringe benefits. It would be incorrect to add an amount into total lost earnings for fringe benefits if none were received.

C. <u>Lost Value of Bruno's Services</u>

An amount for the value of Bruno's services around the house (services in kind) is added to Bruno's total lost earnings. Dr. Hann has assumed that there is some value to the work Bruno did around the house, <u>i.e.</u>, fixed leaky faucets. Defendants could show Bruno "never lifted a finger around the house." If Bruno never provided these services, it would be incorrect to add an amount for them into total lost earnings.

<u>CONCLUSION</u>

Based on my assumptions, defendants can show that Bruno Summers' earning capability was much lower than that stated in Dr. Hann's report.

Dr. Hann's ratio to calculate the present value of Bruno's earnings:

[35yrs x ($8.65/hr x 2080 hrs)] x [10% + .68% + 10%]
                    (industry (individual (inflation)
                    growth) productivity
                           growth)
———————————————————————————————————— = $391,239
Discount Factor (Using 4% Real Interest Rate)

The result of Dr. Hann's ratio is a present value of Bruno's lost earnings of $391,239.

My ratio using the changed assumptions is:

[25 yrs x ($5.65/hr x 2080 hrs)] x [7%(industry) + 10%(inflation)]
———
Discount Factor (Using 6% Real Interest Rate)

The result of my ratio is a present value of Bruno's lost earnings of less than $300,000.

Submitted by,

Thomas Monday, PH.D.

Thomas Monday, Ph.D.

EKKO INSURANCE

SAFEPLAN POLICY
for
APARTMENTS, MOTELS, OFFICES, SERVICES and MERCANTILES

TABLE OF CONTENTS*

1

*Pages not applicable to the *Summers v. Hard* lawsuit are not included.

EKKO   HOME OFFICE: 4888 BROOKLYN AVE. N.E., JAMNER, MAJOR 98455

(A stock insurance company herein called the company)

SAFEPLAN   SP   20112235
                                                            POLICY

NAME OF THE INSURED and MAILING ADDRESS   POLICY PERIOD

UNICORN TAVERN   from 01-12-8X   to   01-12-8X+1
5302 NO. 49th STREET
RUSTON, MAJOR   98212   Beginning and ending (12:01 A.M. at the
                                        mailing address of the Insured)

                                                    REPLACES

BUSINESS OF THE NAMED INSURED IS: THE NAMED INSURED IS:

SALE OF ALCOHOLIC BEVERAGES   SOLE PROPRIETORSHIP

INSURANCE IS PROVIDED FOR THE INSURED WITH RESPECT TO THE DESCRIBED PREMISES AND COVERAGES SHOWN

| LOC | DESCRIBED PREMISES |

1   5302 NO. 49th STREET
         RUSTON, MAJOR   98212

Sec	COVERAGE	Loc	Bldg.	Limit of Liability
I	ALL RISK COVERAGE			
I	B-BUSINESS PERSONAL PROPERTY	1	01	$5,900
	LOSS OF INCOME			ALL ACTUAL LOSS SUSTAINED, NOT EXCEEDING 12 CONSECUTIVE MONTHS
II	BUSINESS LIABILITY			ALL $300,000 EACH OCCURRENCE
	PREMISES MEDICAL PAYMENTS			ALL $1,000 EACH PERSON / $10,000 EACH OCCURRENCE
III	EXTERIOR BUILDING GLASS			REPLACEMENT COST

| POLICY FORMS AND ENDORSEMENTS: | ANNUAL PREMIUM $3,500.00

CF - 932 07 - 80   CF - 969   1 - 83   TOTAL ANNUAL PREMIUM $3,500.00

Countersignature *B Johnson*   *1/12/8X*
                                        Date   JOHNSON INS. AGENCY   Agent
City or Town   Issue Date 02 - 05 - 8X

THIS PAGE AND THE ATTACHMENTS ARE YOUR COMPLETE NEW INSURANCE
POLICY. WE APPRECIATE THE OPPORTUNITY TO SERVE YOUR INSURANCE   AGENT NO. 43 - 0488
NEEDS. PLEASE SEE OR CALL YOUR INDEPENDENT AGENT FOR INFORMATION
ON THIS OR OTHER TYPES OF PROTECTION.   OP - 852 7\81 PRINTED IN U.S.A.

2

SECTION I—PROPERTY COVERAGES

COVERAGE A—BUILDINGS

This policy covers the replacement cost of the building(s) at the premises described in the Declarations for which a limit of liability is shown.

COVERAGE B—BUSINESS PERSONAL PROPERTY

This policy covers replacement cost of the Business Personal Property owned by the insured, usual to the occupancy of the insured, at the premises, or within 100 feet of the premises, described in the Declarations for which a limit of liability is shown, including:

1. The personal property of others, but not that of an employee, in the care, custody or control of the insured for business purposes while in or on the premises described in the Declarations, or within 100 feet of such premises. Such insurance shall apply without regard to the insured's legal liability.
2. The business personal property of the insured and the property of others in the care, custody or control of the insured for not more than $1,000 for all losses arising out of any one occurrence while such property is in due course of transit, or otherwise temporarily away from the described premises.
3. PERSONAL PROPERTY AT NEWLY ACQUIRED LOCATIONS:
   This policy also covers the business personal property of the insured for not exceeding $10,000 while at premises owned, leased or operated by the insured, other than those described in the Declarations, but this coverage shall cease thirty (30) days from the date of acquisition of such premises or on the date values at such locations are reported to the Company or on the expiration date of the policy, whichever occurs first.
4. Tenant's improvements and betterments, meaning the insured's use interest in fixtures, alterations, installations or additions comprising a part of the building occupied but not owned by the insured and made or acquired at the expense of the insured, exclusive of rent paid by the insured, but which are not legally subject to removal by the insured.
5. ACCOUNTS RECEIVABLE:
   This policy covers loss of or damage to accounts receivable and shall be adjusted on the value of:
   (a) All sums due the insured from customers, provided the insured is unable to effect collection thereof as the direct result of loss of or damage to records of accounts receivable;
   (b) Interest charges on any loan to offset impaired collections pending repayment of such sums made uncollectible by such loss or damage;

(c) Collection expense in excess of normal collection cost and made necessary because of such loss or damage;
(d) Other expenses, when reasonably incurred by the insured in re-establishing records of accounts receivable following such loss or damage.

EXCLUSIONS. In addition to exclusions listed under SECTION I—PERILS AND EXCLUSIONS, Accounts Receivable are not covered for loss or damage due:
(a) to loss due to bookkeeping, accounting or billing errors or omissions;
(b) to loss due to alteration, falsification, manipulation, concealment, destruction or disposal of records of accounts receivable committed to conceal the wrongful giving, taking, obtaining or withholding of money, securities or other property but only to the extent of such wrongful giving, taking, obtaining or withholding;
(c) to loss due to electrical or magnetic injury, disturbance or erasure of electronic recordings, except by lightning.

6. MONEY AND SECURITIES:
   This policy covers money and securities used in the conduct of the insured's business for an amount not exceeding $1,000 per occurrence, as follows:
   (a) On Premises: While in or on the premises described in the Declarations, or within a bank or savings institution; and
   (b) Off Premises: While enroute to or from such described premises, bank or savings institution, or within the living quarters of the custodian of such funds.

The insured shall keep records of all the insured property in such manner that the Company can accurately determine therefrom the amount of loss.

The limit of the Company's liability for loss shall not exceed:
(a) what it would cost at the time of loss to replace the property with other of like kind and quality, or
(b) the actual cash value thereof at the time of loss provided, however, at the option of the insured, payment of the cost of replacing securities may be determined by the market value at the time of such settlement.

Dishonest or fraudulent acts or a series of similar or related acts of any person acting alone or in collusion with others during the policy period shall be deemed to be one occurrence for the purpose of applying the deductible and the limit of liability.

3

COVERAGE C—LOSS OF INCOME

This policy covers the actual business loss sustained by the insured and the expenses necessarily incurred to resume normal business operations resulting from the interruption of business or the untenantability of the premises when the building or the personal property, at a location shown in the Declarations, is damaged as a direct result of an insured peril. The actual business loss sustained by the insured shall not exceed:

1. the reduction in gross earnings, less charges and expenses which do not necessarily continue during the interruption of business; and
2. the reduction in rents, less charges and expenses which do not necessarily continue during the period of untenantability.

The actual business loss sustained shall not include charges and expenses which do not necessarily continue during the interruption of business or during the untenantability of the premises.

Loss of income shall be payable for only such length of time as would be required to resume normal business operations but not exceeding such length of time as would be required to rebuild, repair or replace such part of the building or personal property as has been damaged or destroyed as a direct result of an insured peril. Such loss shall not exceed twelve consecutive months from the date of loss and shall not be limited by the expiration date of this policy. The insured is required to resume normal business operations as promptly as possible and shall use all available means to eliminate any unnecessary delay.

The term "normal business operations" of the insured means the condition that would have existed had no loss occurred.

RESUMPTION OF OPERATIONS: It is a condition of this insurance that if the insured could reduce the loss resulting from the interruption of business:

1. by complete or partial resumption of operation of the property herein described, whether damaged or not; or
2. by making use of merchandise or other property at the locations described herein or elsewhere; or
3. by making use of stock at the locations described herein or elsewhere

such reduction shall be taken into account in arriving at the amount of loss hereunder.

LIMITATIONS: The Company shall not be liable for any increase of loss which may be occasioned by:

1. interference at the described premises by strikers or other persons with rebuilding, repairing or replacing the property or with the resumption or continuation of business; or
2. the suspension, lapse or cancellation of any lease, license, contract or order unless such suspension, lapse or cancellation results directly from the interruption of business, and then the Company shall be liable for only such loss as affects the insured's earnings during, and limited to, the period of indemnity covered under this policy.

SECTION I—PERILS AND EXCLUSIONS (NAMED PERIL)

When Named Peril Coverage is designated in the Declarations for Section I, the section titled Perils and Exclusions (Named Peril) is applicable.

PERILS INSURED

This policy insured against all direct loss, subject to all the provisions contained herein, for loss caused by:

1. Fire.
2. Lightning.
3. Windstorm or Hail.
4. Explosion, including direct loss resulting from the explosion of accumulated gases or unconsumed fuel within the firebox (or combustion chamber) of any fired vessel or within the flues or passages which conduct the gases of combustion therefrom.
5. Smoke, meaning sudden and accidental damage from smoke, other than smoke from agricultural smudging or industrial operations.
6. Aircraft or Vehicles, meaning only direct loss resulting from actual physical contact of an aircraft or a vehicle with the property covered or with the building(s) containing the property covered, except that loss by aircraft includes direct loss by object falling therefrom.
7. Riot. Riot Attending a Strike or Civil Commotion, including direct loss by acts of striking employees of the owner or tenant(s) of the building(s) while occupied by said striking employees and shall also include direct loss from pillage and looting occurring during and at the immediate place of a riot attending a strike or civil commotion.
8. Vandalism or Malicious Mischief, meaning only the willful and malicious damage to or destruction of the property covered.
9. Sprinkler Leakage, meaning leakage or discharge of water or other substance from within an automatic sprinkler, or direct loss caused by collapse or fall of a tank forming a part of such system.

4

EXCLUSIONS

The Company shall not be liable for loss:

1. occasioned directly or indirectly by enforcement of any ordinance or law regulating the construction, repair or demolition of buildings or structures;
2. caused by or resulting from power, heating or cooling failure, unless such failure results from physical damage to power, heating or cooling equipment situated on premises where the property covered is located, caused by perils not otherwise excluded;
3. caused by any electrical injury or disturbance of electrical appliances, devices, fixtures, or wiring caused by electrical currents artificially generated unless fire as insured against ensues and then this Company shall be liable for only loss caused by the ensuing fire.
4. caused by, resulting from, contributed to, or aggravated by any of the following:

(a) earth movement, including but not ted to earthquake, landslide, mudflow, eart king, earth rising or shifting;
(b) flood, surface water, waves, tidal wate tidal waves, overflow of streams or other b s of water, or spray from any of the forego all whether driven by wind or not;
(c) water which backs up through sewers or ns;
(d) water below the surface of the ground inc ng that which exerts pressure on or flows, se or leaks through sidewalks, driveways, founda s, walls, basement or other floors, or through d ·, windows or any other openings in such walks, driveways, foundations, walls or floors
(e) delay or loss of market
unless fire or explosion as insured against ensues, then this Company shall be liable for only loss caus by the ensuing fire or explosion.

SECTION I—DEDUCTIBLE

This deductible clause does not apply to coverage as provided for Loss of Income.

For loss by theft, the sum of $250 shall be deducted from the amount of loss to property in any one occurrence. For loss other than loss by theft, the sum deducted will be $100.

The aggregate amount of this deductible in any one occurrence shall not exceed $1,000.

SECTION II—BUSINESS LIABILITY AND PREMISES MEDICAL PAYMENTS

PERSONS INSURED

Each of the following is an **insured** under this insurance to the extent set forth below:

1. The **named insured** and, if an individual, the spouse of such **named insured** if a resident of the same household.
2. If the **named insured** is designated in the Declarations as:
   (a) partnership or joint venture, the partnership or joint venture so designated and any partner or member thereof but only with respect to his liability as such;
   (b) other than an individual, partnership or joint venture the organization so designated and any executive officer, director or stockholder thereof while acting within the scope of his duties as such.

3. Any person or organization while acting as real estate manager for the **named insured.**
4. Any employee of the **named insured** while acting within the scope of his duties as such.
5. Any entity which the **insured** acquires or forms, and over which the **insured** maintains financial control through ownership of more than 50% of its capital stock or assets. This coverage for such entities will expire 90 days after the acquisition or formation of such entity.

INSURING AGREEMENTS

1. BUSINESS LIABILITY
   The Company will pay on behalf of the **insured** all sums which the **insured** shall become legally obligated to pay as damages because of **bodily injury, property**

5

damage, **personal injury** or **advertising injury** caused by an **occurrence** to which this insurance applies.

2. STOP-GAP EMPLOYER'S LIABILITY

The company will pay for the legal liability of the **insured** for such **bodily injury** of any employee of the **insured** who sustains an injury which arises out of and in the course of the **insured's** employment, provided such employee is reported and declared under the workers' compensation fund of the State(s) of Montana, Nevada, Ohio, Utah, Major, and West Virginia.

3. PREMISES MEDICAL PAYMENTS

The Company will pay to or for each person who sustains **bodily injury** caused by accident all reasonable **medical expense** incurred within one year from the date of the accident on account of such **bodily injury,** provided such **bodily injury** arises out of (a) a condition in the **insured premises** or (b) operations with respect to which the **named insured** is afforded coverage for bodily injury liability under this policy.

RIGHT AND DUTY TO DEFEND

The Company shall have the right and duty to defend any claim or suit against the **insured** seeking damages payable under this policy, even though the allegations of the suit may be groundless, false or fraudulent. The Company may make such investigations and settlements of any claim or suit as it deems expedient. The Company is not obligated to pay any claim or judgment or to defend any suit after the applicable limit of the Company's liability has been exhausted by payment of judgments or settlements.

SUPPLEMENTARY PAYMENTS

The Company will pay, in addition to the applicable limit of liability:

1. all expenses incurred by the Company, all costs taxed against the **insured** in any **suit** defended by the Company and all interest on the entire amount of any judgment therein which accrues after entry of the judgment and before the Company has paid or tendered or deposited in court that part of the judgment which does not exceed the limit of the Company's liability thereon;

2. premium on appeal bonds required in any such **suit,** premiums on bonds to release attachments in any such **suit** for an amount not in excess of the applicable limit of liability of this policy, and the cost of bail bonds required of the **insured** because of accident or traffic law violation arising out of the use of any vehicle to which this policy applies, not to exceed $250 per bail bond, but the Company shall have no obligation to apply for or furnish any such bonds;

3. expenses incurred by the **insured** for first aid to others at the time of an accident, for **bodily injury** to which this policy applies;

4. reasonable expenses incurred by the **insured** at the Company's request in assisting the Company in the investigation or defense of any claim or **suit,** including actual loss of earnings not to exceed $50 per day.

EXCLUSIONS

Under Insuring Agreement 1 Business Liability:

This insurance does not cover:

1. **bodily injury** or **property damage** included within the **war hazard** with respect to liability assumed by the **insured** under any contract or agreement or expenses of first aid under the Supplementary Payments provision;

2. any obligation for which the **insured** or any carrier as his insurer may be held liable under any workers' compensation, unemployment compensation or disability benefits law, or under any similar law;

3. with respect to employee injuries:

    (a) **bodily injury** to any employee of the **insured** arising out of and in the course of his employment by the **insured** for which the **insured** may be held liable as an employer or in any other capacity; or

    (b) any obligation of the **insured** to indemnify or contribute with another because of damages arising out of the **bodily injury;** or

    (c) **bodily injury** sustained by the spouse, child, parent, brother, or sister of an employee of the **insured** as a consequence of **bodily injury** to such employee arising out of and in the course of his employment by the **insured.**

This exclusion applies to all claims and suits by any person or organization for damages because of such **bodily injury** including damages for care and loss of services.

This exclusion does not apply to liability assumed by the **insured** under a contract.

4. **property damage** (a) to property owned or transported by the **insured;** (b) to personal property rented to the **insured;** (c) to property under **bailment** to the insured (except injury to or destruction of such property arising out of the use of elevators or escalators or to liability assumed under sidetrack agreements); (d) to that particular part of any property (i) upon which operations are being performed by or on behalf of the **insured,** or (ii) out of which such injury or destruction arises; (e) to premises alienated by the **named insured** arising out of such premises or any part thereof; (f) to the **named insured's products** arising out of such products or any part of such products; (g) with respect to the **completed operations hazard** to work performed by or on behalf of the **named insured** arising out of such work or any portion thereof, or out of such materials, parts or equipment furnished in connection therewith;

6

5. damages claimed for the withdrawal, inspection, repair, replacement or loss of use of the **named insured's products** or work completed by or for the **named insured** or of any property of which such products or work form a part if such products, work or property are withdrawn from the market or from use because of any known or suspected defect or deficiency therein;

6. **bodily injury or property damage** arising out of the ownership, maintenance, operation, use, loading or unloading of any **mobile equipment** while being used in any prearranged or organized racing speed or demolition contest or in any stunting activity or in practice of preparation for any such contest or activity;

7. loss of use of tangible property which has not been physically injured or destroyed resulting from
   (a) a delay in or lack of performance by or on behalf of the **named insured** of any contract or agreement, or
   (b) the failure of the **named insured's products** or work performed by or on behalf of the **named insured** to meet the level of performance, quality, fitness or durability warranted or represented by the **named insured**
   but this exclusion does not apply to loss of use of other tangible property resulting from the sudden and accidental physical injury to or destruction of the **named insured's products** or work performed by or on behalf of the **named insured** after such products or work have been put to use by any person or organization other than an **insured**;

8. liability or injury arising out of or in connection with domestic activities of any **insured** which are not connected with the business of any **insured**;

9. **bodily injury** or **property damage** arising out of the ownership, maintenance, operation, use, loading or unloading of:
   (a) any **automobile** or aircraft owned or operated by or rented or loaned to any **insured**; or
   (b) any other **automobile** or aircraft operated by any person in the course of his employment by any **insured.**
   This exclusion does not apply to the parking of an **automobile** on premises owned by, rented to or controlled by the **named insured or the ways immediately adjoining,** if **such automobile** is not owned by or rented or loaned to any **insured.**

10. [alcoholic beverages liability deleted]

11. **bodily injury** to (a) another employee of the **named insured** arising out of or in the course of his employment or (b) the **named insured** or, if the **named insured** is a partnership or joint venture, any partner or member thereof;

12. liability for **personal injury** assumed by the **insured** under any contract or agreement;

13. **personal injury** arising out of the willful violation of a penal statute or ordinance committed by or with the knowledge or consent of any **insured;**

14. **personal injury** arising out of a publication o̶ ̶ ̶ter- ance described in item (b) of the Definitions ̶ ̶ ̶ ̶er- sonal injury:
   (a) if the first injurious publication or uttera̶ ̶ ̶ of the same or similar material by or on beh̶ ̶ ̶ ̶f the named insured was made prior to the ̶ ̶ ̶ ̶ ̶ tive date of this insurance; or
   (b) concerning any organization or business e̶ ̶ prise or its **products** or services made by o̶ the direction of any **insured** with knowledg̶ the falsity thereof.

15. **personal injury** arising out of the legal, accountir̶ advertising or medical occupations, or any activiti̶ related to, associated with, or made possible by th̶ **insured's** professional knowledge of these occup̶ tions. This exclusion does not apply to veterinarians̶ optometrists or dentists;

16. **advertising injury** arising out of:
   (a) failure of performance of contract, but this exclusion does not apply to the unauthorized appropriation of ideas based upon alleged breach of implied contract; or
   (b) infringement of trademark, service mark or trade name, other than titles or slogans;
   (c) incorrect description or mistake in advertised price of goods, products or services sold, offered for sale or advertised;

17. **advertising injury** for any **insured** in the business of advertising, broadcasting, publishing or telecasting;

18. **bodily injury** or **property damage** due to rendering of or failure to render any professional service, including but not limited to:
   (a) legal, accounting, advertising, engineering, drafting, architectural, and
   (b) medical, dental, pharmacological, cosmetic, hearing aid, optical, or ear piercing services.
   This exclusion does not apply to Incidental Medical Malpractice Injury. Incidental Medical Malpractice Injury means injury arising out of the rendering of or failure to render the following services, if the **insured** or any **insured's** indemnitee is not engaged in the business or occupation of providing any of these services:
   (a) medical, surgical, dental, X-ray or nursing service or treatment or the furnishing of food or beverages in connection therewith; or
   (b) the furnishing or dispensing of drugs or medical, dental or surgical supplies or appliances.

19. any claim made against the **insured** for loss of revenue, caused by the loss of use of data processing records, during restoration of such data processing records, resulting from the **named insured's** negligence, failure to perform, or products. This exclusion applies only to **insureds** engaged in the business of providing data processing services for others;

20. **bodily injury** or **property damage** caused by the dumping, discharge or escape of irritants, pollutants or contaminants. This exclusion does not apply if the discharge is sudden and accidental.

7

Under Insuring Agreement 2 Stop-Gap Employers' Liability:

This insurance does not cover:

1. any premium, assessment, penalty, fine, benefits, liability, or other obligation imposed by the Federal Employer's Liability Act, Jones Act, or any workers' compensation, unemployment compensation or disability benefits law, or under any similar law;
2. **bodily injury** suffered or caused by any person knowingly employed by the **insured** in violation of any law as to age, or under the age of 14 years regardless of any such law;
3. aircraft operation or the performance of any duty in connection with aircraft while in flight;
4. any claim for **bodily injury** with respect to which the **insured** is deprived of any defense or defenses or is otherwise subject to penalty because of default in premium payment, or any other failure to comply with the provisions of any workers' compensation law;
5. any liability assumed by the **insured** under any contract or agreement;
6. any injury sustained because of any act committed intentionally by or at the direction of the **named insured** and, if the **named insured** is a corporation or partnership, by an executive officer, director, stockholder or partner thereof.

Exclusions 1 and 6 above shall not exclude coverage for the legal liability of the **insured,** other than benefits or compensation provided for under any workers' compensation act, resulting from the deliberate intentional act of an employee or agent (other than an executive officer, director, stockholder or partner) to produce injury or death to another employee when such act is committed within the scope of employment.

Under Insuring Agreement 3 Premises Medical Payments:

This insurance does not cover:

1. **bodily injury** if excluded by Exclusions, Under Insuring Agreement 1;
2. **bodily injury**
   (a) included within the **completed operation hazard** or the products **hazard;**
   (b) arising out of operations performed for the **named insured** by independent contractors other than (i) maintenance and repair of the **insured premises** or (ii) structural alterations at such premises which do not involve changing the size of or moving buildings or other structures;
   (c) included within the **war hazard;**
3. **bodily injury**
   (a) to the **named insured,** any partner therein, any tenant or other person regularly residing on the **insured premises** or any employee of any of the foregoing if the **bodily injury** arises out of and in the course of his employment therewith;
   (b) to any other tenant if the **bodily injury** occurs on that part of the **insured premises** rented from the

named insured or to any employee of such a tenant if the **bodily injury** occurs on the tenant's part of the **insured premises** and arises out of and in the course of his employment for the tenant;
   (c) to any person while engaged in maintenance and repair of the **insured premises** or alteration, demolition or new construction at such premises;
   (d) to any person if any benefits for such **bodily injury** are payable or required to be provided under any workers' compensation, unemployment compensation or disability benefits law, or under any similar law;
   (e) to any person practicing, instructing or participating in any physical training, sport, athletic activity or contest;
4. any **medical expenses** for services by the **named insured,** any employee thereof or any person or organization under contract to the **named insured** to provide such services.

LIMITS OF LIABILITY

For the purpose of determining the limit of the company's liability, all **bodily injury, property damage, personal injury** and **advertising injury** arising out of continuous or repeated exposure to substantially the same general conditions shall be considered as arising out of one **occurrence.**

Regardless of the number of **insureds** under this policy the Company's liability is limited as follows:

1. The limit of liability expressed in the Declarations as applicable to "each **occurrence**" is the total limit of the Company's liability under the **bodily injury, property damage, personal injury** and **advertising injury** liability coverages combined for all damages as the result of any one **occurrence** provided:
   (a) with respect to all damages included within the (i) **completed operations hazard** and the (ii) **products hazard,** or arising out of **advertising injury,** such limit of liability shall be the total limit of the Company's liability during each annual policy period as the result of one or more than one **occurrence;**
   (b) with respect to all damages arising out of **property damage** (other than the **completed operations hazard,** or the **products hazard**) such limit of liability shall be the total limit of the Company's liability during each annual policy period as the result of one or more than one **occurrence,** but said limit of liability shall apply separately to each project with respect to operations being performed away from premises owned by or rented to the **insured.**
2. The limit of liability for Premises Medical Payments Coverage stated in the Declarations as applicable to "each person" is the limit of the Company's liability for all **medical expense** for **bodily injury** to any one person as the result of any one accident but subject to the

8

above provision respecting "each person," the total liability of the Company under Premises Medical Payments Coverage for all **medical expense** for **bodily injury** to two or more persons as the result of any one accident shall not exceed the limit of liability stated in the Declarations as applicable to "each accident."

DEFINITIONS

When used in this policy (including endorsements forming a part hereof):

"advertising injury" means injury which arises out of one or more of the following offenses committed in the course of the **named insured's** advertising activities:

(a) libel, slander or defamation;
(b) any infringement of copyright, title or slogan;
(c) piracy or unfair competition;
(d) idea misappropriation under implied contract;
(e) invasion of right of privacy;

"automobile" means a land motor vehicle, trailer or semi-trailer designed for travel on public roads (including any machinery or apparatus attached thereto), but does not include **mobile equipment;**

"bailment" means a delivery of personal property by any person to the **insured** for some purpose beneficial to either the **insured** or such person or both under a contract, express or implied, for the **insured** to carry out such purpose and to redeliver such property or otherwise dispose of it as provided;

"bodily injury" means bodily injury, sickness or disease sustained by any person which occurs during the policy period, including death at any time resulting therefrom;

"completed operations hazard" includes **bodily injury** and **property damage** arising out of operations or reliance upon a representation or warranty made at any time with respect thereto, but only if the **bodily injury** or **property damage** occurs after such operations have been completed or abandoned and occurs away from premises owned by or rented to the **named insured.** "Operations" include materials, parts or equipment furnished in connection therewith. Operations shall be deemed completed at the earliest of the following times:

(a) when all operations to be performed by or on behalf of the **named insured** under the contract have been completed;
(b) when all operations to be performed by or on behalf of the **named insured** at the site of the operations have been completed; or
(c) when the portion of the work out of which the injury or damage arises has been put to its intended use by any person or organization other than another contractor or subcontractor engaged in performing operations for a principal as a part of the same project.

Operations which may require further service or maintenance work, or correction, repair or replacement because of any defect or deficiency, but which are otherwise complete, shall be deemed completed.

The **completed operations hazard** does not include **bodily injury** or **property damage** arising out of

(a) operations in connection with the transportation of property, unless the **bodily injury** or **property damage** arises out of a condition in or on a vehicle created by the loading or unloading thereof;
(b) the existence of tools, uninstalled equipment or abandoned or unused materials;

"insured" means any person or organization qualifying as an insured in the "Persons Insured" provision of the applicable insurance coverage. The insurance afforded applies separately to each insured against whom claim is made or **suit** is brought, except with respect to the limits of the Company's liability;

"insured premises" means all premises owned by or rented to the **named insured** with respect to which the **named insured** is afforded coverage for **bodily injury** liability under this policy, and includes the ways immediately adjoining on land;

"medical expense" means expenses for necessary medical, surgical, X-ray and dental services, including prosthetic devices, and necessary ambulance, hospital, professional nursing and funeral services;

"mobile equipment" means a land vehicle (including any machinery or apparatus attached thereto), whether or not self-propelled, (a) not subject to motor vehicle registration, or (b) maintained for use exclusively on premises owned by or rented to the **named insured,** including the ways immediately adjoining or (c) designed for use principally off public roads, or (d) designed or maintained for the sole purpose of affording mobility to equipment of the following types forming an integral part of or permanently attached to such vehicle: power cranes, shovels, loaders, diggers and drills; concrete mixers (other than the mix-in-transit type); graders, scrapers, rollers and other road construction or repair equipment; air-compressors, pumps and generators, including spraying, welding and building cleaning equipment; and geophysical exploration and well servicing equipment;

"named insured" means the person or organization named in the Declarations of this policy;

"named insured's products" means goods or products manufactured, sold, handled or distributed by the **named insured** or by others trading under his name, including any container thereof (other than a vehicle), but **"named insured's products"** shall not include a vending machine or any property other than such container, rented to or located for use of others but not sold;

"non-owned private passenger automobile" means a four-wheel, self-propelled vehicle which is not owned, leased,

9

hired or borrowed by the **named insured** and which is one of the following types:

(a) a private passenger vehicle, such as a sedan, station wagon or jeep-type vehicle;

(b) a pick-up or panel truck not used primarily in the occupation, business or profession of the owner;

(c) a utility automobile designed for personal use as a camper or motor home or for family recreational purposes but a utility automobile does not include any such automobile used primarily

    (1) in the occupation, profession or business of the owner or

    (2) for the transportation of passengers;

"**occurrence**" means:

(a) an event including continuous or repeated exposure to conditions, which results in **bodily injury** or **property damage,** or

(b) with respect to **personal injury** or **advertising injury,** the commission of an offense or a series of similar or related offenses

which is neither expected or intended from the standpoint of the **insured. Occurrence** also includes any intentional act by or at the direction of the **insured** which results in **bodily injury,** if such injury arises solely from the use of reasonable force for the purpose of protecting persons or property;

"**personal injury**" means injury which arises out of one or more of the following offenses committed in the conduct of the **named insured's** business:

(a) false arrest, detention or imprisonment, or malicious prosecution;

(b) the publication or utterance of a libel or slander or of other defamatory or disparaging material, or a publication or utterance in violation of an individual's right of privacy, except publications or utterances in the course of or related to advertising, broadcasting or telecasting activities conducted by or on behalf of the **named insured;**

(c) wrongful entry or eviction, or other invasion of the right of private occupancy;

"**policy territory**" means anywhere in the world, provided, however, that (a) resulting claims are asserted within the United States of America, its possessions, or Canada, and (b) it shall apply to **suits** and judgments for damages resulting therefrom only if **suit** is commenced in a court in the United States of America, its possessions or in Canada;

"**products hazard**" includes **bodily injury** and **property damage** arising out of the **named insured's products** or reliance upon a representation or warranty made at any time with respect thereto, but only if the **bodily injury** or **property damage** occurs away from premises owned by or rented to the **named insured** and after physical possession of such products has been relinquished to others;

"**property damage**" means (a) physical injury to or destruction of tangible property which occurs during the policy period, including the loss of use thereof at any time resulting therefrom, or (b) loss of use of tangible property which has not been physically injured or destroyed provided such loss of use is caused by an **occurrence** during the policy period;

"**suit**" includes an arbitration proceeding to which the **insured** is required to submit or to which the **insured** has submitted with the Company's consent;

"**war hazard**" includes all **bodily injury** and **property damage** due to war, whether or not declared: civil war, insurrection, rebellion or revolution or to any act or condition incident to any of the foregoing.

GENERAL CONDITIONS

CONDITIONS APPLICABLE TO SECTIONS I & II

1. **Action Against Company**

No action shall lie against the Company unless there shall have been full compliance with all of the terms of this policy nor until the amount of the **insured's** obligation to pay shall have been finally determined either by judgment against the **insured** after actual trial or by written agreement of the **insured,** the claimant and the Company.

Any person or organization or the legal representative thereof who has secured such judgment or written agreement shall thereafter be entitled to recover under this policy to the extent of the insurance afforded by this policy. No person or organization shall have any right under this policy to join the Company as a party in any action against the **insured** to determine the **insured's** liability, nor shall the Company be impleaded by the **insured** or his legal representative. Bankruptcy or insolvency of the **insured** or of the **insured's** estate shall not relieve the Company of any of its obligations hereunder.

2. **Insured's Duties in the Event of Occurrence, Claim or Suit**

(a) In the event of an **occurrence,** written notice containing particulars sufficient to identify the **insured** and also reasonably obtainable information with respect to the time, place and circumstances

10

thereof and the names and addresses of the **insured** and of available witnesses shall be given by or for the **insured** to the Company or any of its authorized agents as soon as practicable.

(b) If claim is made or **suit** is brought against the **insured,** the **insured** shall immediately forward to the Company every demand, notice, summons or other process received by him or his representative.

(c) The **insured** shall cooperate with the Company and, upon the Company's request, assist in making settlements, in the conduct of **suits** and in enforcing any right of contribution or indemnity against any person or organization who may be liable to the **insured** because of injury or damage with respect to which insurance is afforded under this policy; and the **insured** shall attend hearings and trials and assist in securing and giving evidence and obtaining the attendance of witnesses. The **insured** shall not, except at his own cost, voluntarily make any payment, assume any obligation or incur any expense other than for first aid to others at the time of the accident.

3. **Other Insurance**

If, applicable to the loss, there is any valid and collectible insurance, whether on a primary, excess or contingent basis, available to the **insured** (in this or any other carrier), there shall be no insurance afforded hereunder as respects such loss; except that if the applicable limit of liability of this policy is in excess of the appli-

cable limit of liability provided by the other insurance, this policy shall afford excess insurance over and above such other insurance in an amount sufficient to afford the **insured** a combined limit of liability equal to the applicable limit of liability afforded by this policy. Insurance under this policy shall not be construed to be concurrent or contributing with any other insurance which is available to the **insured.**

4. **Nuclear Exclusion**

This policy does not apply.

5. **Medical Reports: Proof and Payment of Claim (Applicable to Premises Medical Payments)**

As soon as practicable the injured person or someone on his behalf shall give to the Company written proof of claim, under oath if required, and shall, after each request from the Company, execute authorization to enable the Company to obtain medical reports and copies of records. The injured person shall submit to physical examination by physicians selected by the Company when and as often as the Company may reasonably require. The Company may pay the injured person or any person or organization rendering the services and the payment shall reduce the amount payable hereunder for such injury. Payment hereunder shall not constitute an admission of liability of any person or, except hereunder, of the Company.

This policy has been signed for the Company by its president and secretary and shall not be valid unless countersigned by an authorized representative of the Company.

W.D. Hammersley
_____
W.D. Hammersley, SECRETARY

J.W. Gannon
_____
J.W. Gannon, PRESIDENT

11

HOMEOWNERS POLICY—SPECIAL FORM

SAPO INSURANCE COMPANY OF AMERICA

Home Office: 5081 Macintosh St. N., Jamner, Major 98462

(a stock insurance company)

READY REFERENCE TO YOUR HOMEOWNERS POLICY

Table of Contents*

1

---

*Pages not applicable to the *Summers v. Hard* lawsuit are not included.

BILL CODE	AGENT NO. 90312	COMM.	RATE	AMOUNT	RATE	AMOUNT
FIRE TERR.						

SAPO

insurance company
HOMEOWNERS DAILY REPORT
POLICY NUMBER

	L	AMOUNT	
	O	LOSS DATE	
INT.	DATE	S	TYPE
R		S	AMOUNT
U		E	LOSS DATE
C		S	TYPE

RENEWAL OF NUMBER

Named Insured and P.O. Address

EDWARD T. HARD
1492 WEST ST.
RUSTON, MAJOR   98319

Agent and Address

RON WHALLEY, 3001 ALASKA ST., JAMNER

To the extent that coverage in this policy replaces coverage in other policies terminating noon standard time on the inception date of this policy, coverage under this policy shall not become effective until such other coverage has terminated.

1	7/17/8X	7/17/8X+1
Years	Inception	Expiration

The described residence premises covered hereunder is located at the above address unless otherwise stated herein.

SAME   FRAME   JAMNER CO.   CL 2

Insurance is provided only with respect to the following Coverages for which a limit of liability is specified.

Coverages and Limit of Liability	Section I				Section II		
	A. Dwelling	B. Appurtenant Structures	C. Unscheduled Personal Prop.	D. Additional Living	E. Personal Liability Each Occurence		F. Medical Payments to Others
	50,000	5,000	10,000	1,000	50,000	1,000	25,000
Premium	Basic Policy Premium	Theft Extension	Additional Premiums		Total Prepd.	Premium installment	Payable:
	220				220		
	Premium for Scheduled Personal Property						

DEDUCTIBLE-SECTION 1: any loss by perils insured against under Section I of this policy is subject to a deductible.	Deductible applicable only to loss caused by the peril of windstorm or hail (Clause 1)	Deductible applicable to loss caused by other perils (Clause 2)	Deductible not applicable	Special Loss Deductible X Clause $ 100

Special State Provisions: Valuation Clause $	Coinsurance Clause Applies $

Section II--Additional residence premises, if any, located: (No., Street, City, County, State, Zip)

Mortgagee(s)   Name and Address   N/A

Countersignature Date   7/30/8X   Agency at Federal, Major   Agent Ron Whalley

RATING INFORMATION	NO. OF FAMILIES	NOT TOWNHOUSE	TOWNHOUSE	HO - 4 SELF RATING	YEAR OF CONSTRUCTION	ZONE
CONSTRUCTION						
PROTECTION					FIRE DIST. OR TOWN	
PREM. GR. NO.		DEDUCTIBLE				

STATISTICAL REPORTING INFORMATION	PREMIUM: PREPAID	INSTALLMENT	INCEPTION	ANNIVERSARY
Snowmobiles				
Watercraft				
Outboard Motor				
ALL OTHER PREMIUMS				

2

AGREEMENT

We will provide the insurance described in this policy in return for the premium and compliance with all applicable provisions of this policy.

DEFINITIONS

Throughout this policy, "you" and "your" refer to the "named insured" shown in the Declarations and the spouse if a resident of the same household, and "we," "us" and "our" refer to the Company providing this insurance. In addition, certain words and phrases are defined as follows:

1. **"actual cash value"**
   a. When the damage to property is economically repairable, "actual cash value" means the cost of repairing the damage, less reasonable deduction for wear and tear, deterioration and obsolescence.
   b. When the loss or damage to property creates a total loss, "actual cash value" means the market value of property in a used condition equal to that of the destroyed property, if reasonably available on the used market.
   c. Otherwise, "actual cash value" shall mean the market value of new, identical or nearly identical property, less reasonable deduction for wear and tear, deterioration and obsolescence.

2. **"bodily injury"** means:
   a. bodily harm, sickness or disease, including required care, loss of services and death resulting therefrom;
   b. personal injury arising out of one or more of the following offenses:
      (1) false arrest, detention or imprisonment, or malicious prosecution;
      (2) libel, slander or defamation of character; or
      (3) invasion of privacy, wrongful eviction or wrongful entry.

   As used in this paragraph, 2.b. personal injury coverage does not apply to:
      (1) liability assumed by any **insured** under any contract or agreement except any indemnity obligation assumed by the **insured** under a written contract directly relating to the ownership, maintenance or use of the premises;
      (2) injury caused by a violation of a penal law or ordinance committed by or with the knowledge or consent of any **insured;**
      (3) injury sustained by any person as a result of an offense directly or indirectly related to the employment of this person by any **insured;**

      (4) injury arising out of the **business** pursuits of any **insured;** or
      (5) civic or public activities performed for pay by any **insured.**

   Except as stated in paragraph 2.b., **Section II—Exclusions** does not apply to personal injury coverage.

3. **"business"** includes trade, profession or occupation.

4. **"insured"** means you and the following residents of your household:
   a. your relatives;
   b. any other person under the age of 21 who is in the care of any person named above.

   Under Section II, **"insured"** also means:

   c. with respect to animals or watercraft to which this policy applies, any person or organization legally responsible for these animals or watercraft which are owned by you or any person included in 4.a. or 4.b. A person or organization using or having custody of these animals or watercraft in the course of any **business,** or without permission of the owner is not an **insured;**
   d. with respect to any vehicle to which this policy applies:
      (1) any person while engaged in your employment or the employment of any person included in 4.a. or 4.b.; or
      (2) any other person using the vehicle on an **insured location** with an **insured's** permission.

5. **"insured location"** means:
   a. the **residence premises;**
   b. that part of any other premises, other structures and grounds, used by you as a residence and which is shown in the Declarations or which is acquired by you during the policy period for your use as a residence;
   c. any premises used by you in connection with the premises included in 5.a. or 5.b.;
   d. any part of a premises not owned by any **insured** but where any **insured** is temporarily residing;
   e. vacant land owned by or rented to any **insured** other than farm land;

3

f. land owned by or rented to any **insured** on which a one or two family dwelling is being constructed as a residence for any **insured;**

g. individual or family cemetery plots or burial vaults of any **insured;**

h. any part of a premises occasionally rented to any **insured** for other than **business** purposes.

6. **"occurrence"** means an accident, including exposure to conditions which results, during the policy period, in **bodily injury** or **property damage.**

7. **"property damage"** means physical injury to or destruction of tangible property, including loss of use of this property.

8. **"residence employee"** means an employee of any **insured** who performs duties in connection with the maintenance or use of the **residence premises,** including household or domestic services, or who performs duties elsewhere of a similar nature not in connection with the **business** of any **insured.**

9. **"residence premises"** means:
   a. the one or two family dwelling, other structures and grounds; or
   b. that part of any other building
   where you reside and which is shown in the Declarations.

SECTION I—PROPERTY COVERAGE

COVERAGE A—DWELLING

We cover:

1. the dwelling on the **residence premises** shown in the Declarations used principally as a private residence, including structures attached to the dwelling; and

2. materials and supplies located on or adjacent to the **residence premises** for use in the construction, alteration or repair of the dwelling or other structures on the **residence premises.**

SECTION II—LIABILITY COVERAGES

COVERAGE E—PERSONAL LIABILITY

If a claim is made or a suit is brought against any **insured** for damages because of **bodily injury** or **property damage** caused by an **occurrence** to which this coverage applies, we will:

1. pay up to our limit of liability for the damages for which the **insured** is legally liable; and

2. provide a defense at our expense by counsel of our choice even if the allegations are groundless, false or fraudulent. We may make any investigation and settle any claim or suit that we decide is appropriate.

COVERAGE F—MEDICAL PAYMENTS TO OTHERS

We will pay the necessary medical expenses incurred or medically ascertained within three years from the date of an accident causing **bodily injury.** Medical expenses means reasonable charges for medical, surgical, x-ray, dental, ambulance, hospital, professional nursing, prosthetic devices and funeral services. This coverage does not apply to you or regular residents of your household other than **residence employees.** As to others, this coverage applies only:

1. to a person on the **insured location** with the permission of any **insured;** or

2. to a person off the **insured location,** if the **bodily injury:**
   a. arises out of a condition in the **insured location** or the ways immediately adjoining;
   b. is caused by the activities of any **insured;**
   c. is caused by a **residence employee** in the course of the **residence employee's** employment by any **insured;** or
   d. is caused by an animal owned by or in the care of any **insured.**

ADDITIONAL COVERAGES

We cover the following in addition to the limits of liability:

1. **Claim Expenses.** We pay:
   a. expenses incurred by us and costs taxed against any **insured** in any suit we defend;

4

Entry 45: SAPO Insurance Company Policy

b. premiums on bonds required in a suit defended by us, but not for bond amounts greater than the limit of liability for Coverage E. We are not obligated to apply for or furnish any bond;

c. reasonable expenses incurred by any **insured** at our request, including actual loss of earnings (but not loss of other income) up to $50 per day, for assisting us in the investigation or defense of any claim or suit;

d. interest on the entire judgment which accrues after entry of the judgment and before we pay or tender, or deposit in court that part of the judgment which does not exceed the limit of liability that applies.

2. **First Aid Expenses.** We will pay expenses for first aid to others incurred by any **insured** for **bodily injury** covered under this policy. We will not pay for first aid to you or any other **insured**.

3. **Damage to Property of Others.** We will pay on a replacement cost basis up to $500 per **occurrence** for **property damage** to property of others caused by any **insured**.

We will not pay for **property damage**:

a. to the extent of any amount recoverable under Section I of this policy;

b. caused intentionally by any **insured** who is 13 years of age or older;

c. to property owned by or rented to any **insured**, a tenant of any **insured**, or a resident in your household; or

d. arising out of:
   (1) **business** pursuits;
   (2) any act or omission in connection with a premises owned, rented or controlled by any **insured**, other than the **insured location**; or
   (3) the ownership, maintenance, or use of aircraft, watercraft or motor vehicle or any other motorized land conveyances.

4. **Credit Card, Fund Transfer Card, Forgery and Counterfeit Money.**

We will pay up to $1,000 for:

a. the legal obligation of any **insured** to pay because of theft or unauthorized use of credit cards issued to or registered in any **insured's** name.

b. loss resulting from theft or unauthorized use of a fund transfer card used for deposit, withdrawal or transfer of funds, issued to or registered in any **insured's** name.

We do not cover use by a resident of your household, a person who has been entrusted with the credit card or fund transfer card or any person if any **insured** has not complied with all terms and conditions under which the credit card or fund transfer card is issued.

c. loss to any **insured** caused by forgery or alteration of any check or negotiable instrument; and

d. loss to any **insured** through acceptance in good faith of counterfeit United States or Canadian paper currency.

All loss resulting from a series of acts committed by any one person or in which any one person is concerned or implicated is considered to be one loss.

We do not cover loss arising out of **business** pursuits or dishonesty of any **insured**.

Defense:

a. We may make any investigation and settle any claim or suit that we decide is appropriate.

b. If a suit is brought against any **insured** for liability under the Credit Card or Fund Transfer Card Coverage, we will provide a defense at our expense by counsel of our choice.

c. We have the option to defend at our expense any **insured** or any **insured's** bank against any suit for the enforcement of payment under the Forgery Coverage.

SECTION II—EXCLUSIONS

1. **Coverage E—Personal Liability and Coverage F— Medical Payments to Others** do not apply to **bodily injury** or **property damage**:

a. which is expected or intended by any **insured**;

b. arising out of **business** pursuits of any **insured** or the rental or holding for rental of any part of any premises by any **insured**.

This exclusion does not apply to:
   (1) activities which are ordinarily incident to non-**business** pursuits;
   (2) the rental or holding for rental of a residence of yours:

   (a) on an occasional basis for the exclusive use as a residence;
   (b) in part, unless intended for use as a residence by more than two roomers or boarders; or
   (c) in part, as an office, school, studio or private garage;

   (3) employment as clerical office employees, salesmen, collectors, messengers or teachers (including activities of a teacher in inflicting corporal punishment);

c. arising out of the rendering or failing to render professional services;

5

d. arising out of any premises owned or rented to any **insured** which is not an **insured location;**

e. arising out of the ownership, maintenance, use, loading or unloading of:

(1) aircraft. This exclusion does not apply to model aircraft. Any aircraft designed for carrying persons or cargo is not a model aircraft.

(2) (a) motor vehicles or all other motorized land conveyances, including any trailers, owned or operated by or rented or loaned to any **insured;** or

(b) entrustment by any **insured** of a motor vehicle or any other motorized land conveyance to any person.

This exclusion does not apply to:

(a) a trailer not towed by or carried on a motorized land conveyance;

(b) a motorized land conveyance designed for recreational use off public roads, not subject to motor vehicle registration and owned by any **insured,** while on an **insured location;**

(c) a motorized golf cart; or

(d) a motorized land conveyance designed for assisting the handicapped or for the maintenance of an **insured location,** which is:

i. not designed for travel on public roads; and

ii. not subject to motor vehicle registration.

f. caused directly or indirectly by war, including undeclared war, civil war, insurrection, rebellion, revolution, warlike act by a military force or military personnel, destruction or seizure or use for a military purpose, and including any consequence of any of these. Discharge of a nuclear weapon shall be deemed a warlike act even if accidental.

2. **Coverage E—Personal Liability** does not apply to:

a. Liability:

(1) for your share of any loss assessment charged against all members of an association of property owners;

(2) under any contract or agreement in connection with any **business** of any **insured;**

(3) under any other contract or agreement except those contracts directly relating to the maintenance or use of the **insured location** not excluded in (1 or 2) above or elsewhere in this policy;

b. **property damage** to property owned by any **insured;**

c. **property damage** to property rented to, occupied or used by or in the care of any **insured.** This exclusion does not apply to **property damage** caused by fire, smoke, explosion or water;

d. **bodily injury** to any person eligible to receive any benefits required to be provided or voluntarily provided by any **insured** under:

(1) any workers' or workmen's compensation;

(2) non-occupational disability; or

(3) occupational disease law;

e. **bodily injury** or **property damage** for which any **insured** under this policy is also an insured under a nuclear energy liability policy or would be an insured but for its termination upon exhaustion of its limit of liability. A nuclear energy liability policy is a policy issued by Nuclear Energy Liability Insurance Association, Mutual Atomic Energy Liability Underwriters, Nuclear Insurance Association of Canada, or any of their successors;

f. **bodily injury** to you and any **insured** within the meaning of part a. or b. of Definitions, 4. "insured."

3. **Coverage F—Medical Payments to Others** does not apply to bodily injury:

a. to a **residence employee** if it occurs off the **insured location** and does not arise out of or in the course of the **residence employee's** employment by any **insured;**

b. to any person, eligible to receive any benefits required to be provided or voluntarily provided under any workers' or workmen's compensation, non-occupational disability or occupational disease law;

c. from any nuclear reaction, radiation or radioactive contamination, all whether controlled or uncontrolled or however caused, or any consequence of any of these;

d. to any person, other than a **residence employee** of any **insured,** regularly residing on any part of the **insured location.**

SECTION II—CONDITIONS

1. **Limit of Liability.** Regardless of the number of **insureds,** claims made or persons injured, our total liability under Coverage E stated in this policy for all damages resulting from any one **occurrence** shall not exceed the limit of liability for Coverage E stated in the Declarations.

6

Our total liability under Coverage F for all medical expense payable for **bodily injury** to one person as the result of one accident shall not exceed the limit of liability for Coverage F stated in the Declarations.

2. **Severability of Insurance.** This insurance applies separately to each **insured**. This condition shall not increase our limit of liability for any one **occurrence**.

3. **Your Duties After Loss.** In case of an accident or **occurrence**, the **insured** shall perform the following duties that apply. You shall cooperate with us in seeing that these duties are performed:
   a. give written notice to us or our agent as soon as practicable, which sets forth:
      (1) the identity of the policy and **insured**;
      (2) reasonably available information on the time, place and circumstances of the accident or **occurrence**;
      (3) names and addresses of any claimants and available witnesses; and
      (4) in case of loss under the Credit Card or Fund Transfer Card coverage also notify the Credit Card or Fund Transfer Card Company;
   b. forward to us every notice, demand, summons or other process relating to the accident or **occurrence**;
   c. at our request, assist in:
      (1) making settlement;
      (2) the enforcement of any right of contribution or indemnity against any person or organization who may be liable to any **insured**;
      (3) the conduct of suits and attend hearings and trials;
      (4) securing and giving evidence and obtaining the attendance of witnesses;
   d. under the coverage—Damage to the Property of Others—submit to us within 60 days after the loss, a sworn statement of loss and exhibit the damaged property, if within the **insured's** control;
   e. submit within 60 days after the loss, evidence or affidavit supporting a claim under the Credit Card,

Fund Transfer Card, or Forgery and Counterfeit Money coverage, stating the amount and cause of loss;
   f. the **insured** shall not, except at the **insured's** own cost, voluntarily make any payment, assume any obligation or incur any expense other than for first aid to others at the time of the **bodily injury**.

4. **Duties of an Injured Person—Coverage F—Medical Payments to Others.** The injured person or someone acting on behalf of the injured person shall:
   a. give us written proof of claim, under oath if required, as soon as practicable;
   b. execute authorization to allow us to obtain copies of medical reports and records.

   The injured person shall submit to physical examination by a physician selected by us when and as often as we reasonably require.

5. **Payment of Claim—Coverage F—Medical Payments to Others.** Payment under this coverage is not an admission of liability by any **insured** or us.

6. **Suit Against Us.** No action shall be brought against us unless there has been compliance with the policy provisions.

   No one shall have any right to join us as a party to any action against any **insured**. Further, no action with respect to Coverage E shall be brought against us until the obligation of the **insured** has been determined by final judgment or agreement signed by us.

7. **Bankruptcy of any Insured.** Bankruptcy or insolvency of any **insured** shall not relieve us of any of our obligations under this policy.

8. **Other Insurance—Coverage E—Personal Liability.** This insurance is excess over any other valid and collectible insurance except insurance written specifically to cover as excess over the limits of liability that apply in this policy.

SECTION I AND SECTION II—CONDITIONS

1. **Policy Period and Changes.**
   a. The effective time of this policy is 12:01 A.M. Standard Time at the **residence premises**. This policy applies only to loss under Section I, or **bodily injury** or **property damage** under Section II, which occurs during the policy period. This policy may be renewed for successive policy periods if the required premium is paid and accepted by us on or before the expiration of the current policy period.

   The premium will be computed at our then current rate for coverage then offered.
   b. Changes:
      (1) Before the end of any policy period, we may offer to change the coverage provided in this policy. Payment of the premium billed by us for the next policy period will be your acceptance of our offer.
      (2) This policy contains all agreements between

7

you and us. Its terms may not be changed or waived except by endorsement issued by us. If a change requires a premium adjustment, we will adjust the premium as of the effective date of change. Additional or return premium of $3.00 or less will be waived.

2. **Concealment or Fraud.** We do not provide coverage for any **insured** who has:

   a. intentionally concealed or misrepresented any material fact or circumstance; or

   b. made false statements or engaged in fraudulent conduct relating to this insurance.

3. **Liberalization Clause.** If we revise this policy to provide more coverage without additional premium charge, your policy will automatically provide the additional coverage as of the day the revision is effective in your state.

4. **Cancellation.**

   a. You may cancel this policy at any time by returning it to us or by notifying us in writing of the date cancellation is to take effect.

   b. We may cancel this policy only for the reasons stated below by notifying you in writing of the date cancellation takes effect. This cancellation notice may be delivered to you, or mailed to you at your mailing address shown in the Declarations. Proof of mailing shall be sufficient proof of notice.

   (1) When you have not paid the premium, whether payable to us or to our agent or under any finance or credit plan, we may cancel at any time by notifying you at least 20 days before the date cancellation takes effect.

   (2) When this policy has been in effect for less than 60 days and is not a renewal with us, we may cancel for any reason by notifying you at least 31 days before the date cancellation takes effect.

   (3) When this policy has been in effect for 60 days or more, or at any time if it is a renewal with us, we may cancel if there has been a material misrepresentation of fact which if known to us would have caused us not to issue the policy or if the risk has changed substantially since the policy was issued. This can be done by notifying you at least 31 days before the date cancellation takes effect.

   c. When this policy is canceled, the premium for the period from the date of cancellation to the expiration date will be refunded. When you request cancellation, the return premium will be based on our rules for such cancellation. The return premium may be less than a full pro rata refund. When we cancel, the return premium will be pro rata.

   d. If the return premium is not refunded with the notice of cancellation or when this policy is returned to us, we will refund it within a reasonable time after the date cancellation takes effect.

This policy has been signed by the Company by its President and shall be valid when also countersigned by an authorized representative of the Company.

D. Bogel

D. Bogel, PRESIDENT

8

2200 Gorden Arms Building
Ruston, Major
(206) 248-3222

June 1, 198X+1

FILE COPY

Mrs. Roberta Montbank
Stillwater Retirement Home
1812 East 9th Street
Ruston, Major

Dear Mrs. Montbank:

Thank you for personally meeting with plaintiffs' investigator, Mr. Peter Nye last week. Both Peter and I were delighted to meet with you.

We appreciate your efforts to locate the written statement that you gave to defendant's insurance company. We also understand your inability eight months later, to recall the details in your statement. Naturally, we understand your reluctance to have us request or you to directly request a copy of your statement from defendant Davola or his insurance company since you are still a regular patron at the Unicorn Tavern.

If you change your mind about requesting the statement, please telephone us at 248-3222.

Keep well, and we will be speaking with you further.

Sincerely,

F.C. Fank

F.C. Fank
Attorney for plaintiffs

Entry 46: Letter to Roberta Montbank

MAJOR GYMNASTIC CLUB

Personnel   Manual

Preamble

This manual shall contain the rules and regulations governing personnel matters between the MAJOR GYMNASTIC CLUB, hereafter called the COMPANY, and its EMPLOYEES. All agreements as to benefits and company policies are stated and set forth in the manual, except as otherwise provided for in writing.

VACATION / ANNUAL   LEAVE

EMPLOYEES are entitled to annual leave. Annual leave shall accrue at one day (1) per month during the first year of consecutive employment with the company. Thereafter it shall accrue at one and one third (1 1/3) days each calendar month.

An employee may use annual leave after the employee is employed with the COMPANY 365 days.

SICK   LEAVE / PERSONAL   LEAVE

EMPLOYEES shall accrue sick leave at 1/2 day per calendar month. Such leave shall be used for medical purposes. Use of such leave for other than medical purposes requires prior approval of the employee's immediate supervisor.

HOLIDAYS

The COMPANY shall provide its EMPLOYEES nine paid holidays: New Year's Day, Martin Luther King Day, Presidents' Day, Memorial Day, Labor Day, Columbus Day, Armistice Day, Thanksgiving Day, and Christmas Day.

Nothing in this agreement shall contravene the laws of the State of Major.

SUMMARY PAYROLL AND EMPLOYMENT RECORD

Bruno Summers   535-46-1671   MB

MO. \YR.	DAYS	HOLID.	VACATION EAR. TAK.	SICK EAR. TAK.	PAID GROSS	FICA	DISAB. MED.	NET
198X-2 Dec 1-31	25	x-mas	1.0	.5				
198X-2 TOTAL	(25)		1.0	.5				
198X-1 January	24	New Yrs. MLK	1.0	.5				
February	21	Pres.	1.0	.5				
March	22		1.0	.5				
April	22		1.0	.5				
May	22	memor.	1.0	.5				
June	20		1.0	.5				
July	22		1.0	.5				
August	21		1.0	.5				
Sept.	20	Labor	1.0	.5				
October	22	Columbus	1.0	.5				
November	20	Armist. Thanksg.	1.0	.5				
December	24	X-mas	1.33	.5				
198X-1 TOTAL	(260)		12.33	6.0	10,080.00	542.00	1,416.00	8,122.00
198X January	23	New Yrs MLK	1.33	.5				
February	21	Pres.	1.33	.5				
March	23		1.33	.5				
April	23		1.33	.5				
May	24	Memor.	1.33	.5				
June	20		1.33	.5				
July	22		1.33	.5				
August	21		1.33	.5				
Sept.	2							
October								
November								
December								
198X TOTAL	(179)							

Entry 48: Summary Payroll and Employment Record of Bruno Summers

DEWEY, CHEATUM, and KOCH

Certified Public Accountants

D.L. Hass   August 12, 198X
Attorney for M.C. Davola
983 Senator Way
Jamner, Major 98606

Dear Mr. Hass:

In order to comply with your request for an analysis of the
financial position and results of operations of the Unicorn Tavern for
the eight years ending July 31, 198X, it was necessary for me to
prepare compiled financial statements.

A compilation is limited to presenting, in the form of financial
statements, information that is the representation of management. I
have neither audited nor reviewed the compiled financial statements.
Accordingly, I do not express an opinion or any form of assurance on
them.

The following is a pro forma synopsis of the compiled financial
statements of the Unicorn Tavern for the eight years ending July 31,
198X.

UNICORN TAVERN
PRO FORMA STATEMENT OF PROFIT AND LOSS
FOR THE EIGHT YEARS ENDING JULY 31, 198X
(in thousands)

	8X-8	8X-7	8X-6	8X-5	8X-4	8X-3	8X-2	8X-1
SALES	346	333	336	345	330	333	324	294
COST OF SALES	245	236	235	242	234	240	233	212
20% GP	101	97	101	103	96	93	91	82
OPERATING EXPENSE	47	50	53	55	53	57	51	46
GENERAL AND ADMINISTRATION	12	11	11	13	10	10	11	10
PROFIT	42	36	37	35	33	30	29	26
% OF SALES	12	11	11	10	10	9	9	9

Sales show a declining trend over the eight years ending July 31,
198X. As a result, profit as a percentage of sales has declined
slightly but averaged 10.13% over the eight year period.

August 12, 198X

    It has been our pleasure to provide this information for you. If we can be of any further assistance please let us know.

Sincerely,

Lawrence Koch

Lawrence Koch, C.P.A
DEWEY, CHEATUM and KOCH

LK/rt

DEWEY, CHEATUM, and KOCH

Certified Public Accountants

August 13, 198X

UNICORN TAVERN
PRO FORMA STATEMENT OF PROFIT AND LOSS
FOR THE PERIOD AUGUST 1, 198X TO
OCTOBER 15, 198X
(in thousands)

	AUG., 198X	SEPT., 198X	OCT., 198X
SALES	24	20	9
COST OF SALES	17.5	15	7
20% GP	6.8	5.5	2.4
OPERATING EXPENSE	3.7	3.0	1.3
GENERAL AND ADMINISTRATION	.83	.75	.35
PROFIT	2.1	1.8	.8
% OF SALES	8.5	7.8	3.7

LK/rt

DEWEY, CHEATUM, and KOCH

Certified Public Accountants

August 13, 198X

UNICORN TAVERN
PRO FORMA BALANCE SHEET
ENDING JULY 31, 198X

ASSETS
    Current Assets $ 28
    Property and Equipment   215
    Non-current Assets   4

        TOTAL ASSETS $ 247

LIABILITIES
    Current Liabilities $ 21
    Long Term Liabilities   64

        TOTAL LIABILITIES $ 85

OWNER'S EQUITY
    Capital Stock $ 25
    Retained Earnings   137

        TOTAL OWNER'S EQUITY $ 162

        TOTAL LIABILITIES AND
        OWNER'S EQUITY $ 247

The current ratio for Unicorn Tavern at July 31, 198X, is 1.33 showing the ability to service current debt. The debt to equity ratio is .52, which we believe to show little indebtedness compared to the industry.

Sincerely,

LK

Lawrence Koch, C.P.A.
DEWEY, CHEATUM, and KOCH

LK/rt

Curriculum Vitae

Dr. David Bowmun, Ph.D.*
2443 Alder
Ruston, Major 98406
(206) 473-7733

Personal:

57 years old, married, 2 grown children.

Education:

University of Texas, at El Paso
B.S. Degree: Psychology

University of Texas, El Paso
Ph.D.: Clinical Psychology (6 years to earn degree)
Dissertation: "Situation Specific Behavior Relating to Aggression Tendencies."

Internship:

Western State Hospital, Ruston, Major (1 year 198X-20 Supervisor: Dr. G. Campbell).

Employment:

Western State Hospital, Ruston, Major (19 years). Chief Psychologist for past 10 years in charge of a staff of 50 including 10 psychologists, residents and interns. Began as a staff member; after 3 years promoted to deputy chief and then to chief psychologist.

Awards, Honors, Licenses:

Henry Baine Fellowship -- awarded to one Ph.D. candidate at the University of Texas, El Paso for achieving the highest grades in graduate psychology courses.

Teaching Assistant -- University of Texas, El Paso (5 years as Teaching Assistant).

Licensed 19 years as a Clinical Psychologist by the State of Major.**

Certified Clinical Psychologist by the American Board of Examiners in Clinical Psychology.

Invited guest lecturer in the Pacific Coast Small College Guest Lecture Series.

---

*Dr. Bowmun is a behaviorist, a school of psychological theory made famous by B.F. Skinner. Behaviorists believe that under certain circumstances human behavior may be predicted.

**The State of Major follows the same licensing procedure as other jurisdictions.

Publications:

Bowmun, "A Behaviorist's View of Criminal Behavior," 5
Journal of Mental Health 18 (198X-15).

Curriculum Vitae

Dr. Sherman Croup, M.D.
3669 N. Filbert
Jamner, Major 98113

Education

    Undergraduate: Arizona State University
                      Degree: B.S. Biological Sciences,
                      198X-24.

    Medical School: University of Southern California
                      School of Medicine. Degree: M.D.,
                      198X-20.

    Internship and
    Residency: Ruston General Hospital, Ruston,
                      Major. Specialty: family
                      practice and family counseling,
                      198X-20 through 198X-16.

Employment

    Neva County Medical Services Clinic, Ruston, Major
    (198X-9 through present).

    Orange County Practice Clinic, Irvine, California
    (198X-15 through 198X-9).

Associations and Affiliations

    Member: Heart Association of America Local Chapter.

              Family Practice Institute of Ruston (198X-5).

Curriculum Vitae

BRUCE DAVID HANN

OFFICE ADDRESS	HOME ADDRESS
Department of Economics	20 Cedar Street
University of Willow Bay	Ruston, Major 98408
Ruston, Major 98416	(206) 859-2898
(206) 786-8188	

EDUCATION

198X-8
> Indiana University, Bloomington, Indiana Ph.D.
> Economics

198X-10
> Indiana University, Bloomington, Indiana M.A.
> Economics

198X-14
> Antioch College, Yellow Springs, Ohio   B.A.
> Economics

RESEARCH AREAS

> Urban Economics
> Real Estate Economics
> Human Capital Theory
> Labor Economics

EMPLOYMENT HISTORY

198X-4 through present	Associate Professor, Department of Economics, University of Willow Bay
198X-9 through 198X-4	Assistant Professor, Department of Economics, University of Willow Bay
198X-11 through 198X-10	Associate Instructor, Department of Economics, Indiana University
198X-14 through 198X-13	Urban Economist (Peace Corps Volunteer), Department of City Planning, Teheran, Iran
198X-14	Research Assistant, Brookings Institution

PUBLICATIONS AND PRESENTATIONS

"Moderate Rent Controls: A Microeconomic and Public Choice Analysis" (with M. Veseth), <u>American Real Estate and Urban Economics Association Journal</u>, Volume 11, No. 3, Fall, 198X.

"The Influence of School Busing on House Values,"in <u>Research in Real Estate</u>, C.F. Sirmens (Editor), Volume 2, 198X.

"Report on the Northwest: Economic Review" (with D. Goodman), <u>Pacific Northwest Outlook</u>, Piper, Jaffray, & Hopwood, Jamner, MA, October, 198X-2.

"Pacific Northwest Retailing: Economic Review" (with D. Goodman), <u>Pacific Northwest Outlook</u>, Piper, Jaffray, & Hopwood, Jamner, MA, October, 198X-2.

"The Costs of Growth," Major Association of Realtors, Olympia, MA, April, 198X-2.

"Exercises in Intermediate Microeconomics" (with E. Combs), Department of Economics, University of Puget Sound, September, 198X-2.

"A Review of Housing Market Policies and a Suggested Program," Washington Coalition for Affordable Housing, July, 198X-3.

"Methods of Analysis of Unsold Speculative Housing Inventory," Presentation to the Real Estate Research Conference of the Twelfth District Federal Home Loan Bank, 198X-3.

<u>Study to Accompany Bradley's Macroeconomics</u>, Scott, Foresman, Chicago, IL, 198X-4.

"The Apartment Market: An Economic Approach" (with James Hubert), <u>The Cain and Scott Apartment Report</u>, Volume 3, Number 2, Summer, 198X-5.

"The Use of Regression Analysis in Property Value Determination," Presentation to the Society of Real Estate Appraisers Seminar, 198X-6.

"New Influences on Persian Cities: A Case Study of Kerman, Iran" (with R. Frieden),in <u>The Architects' Yearbook</u>, Wiley-Halstead Publishers, 198X-6.

"Education and Equality of Opportunity," Presentation at the Southern Economics Association Meeting, 198X-6.

Introduction to Microeconomics, Indiana University
Continuing Education, Bloomington, Indiana, 198X-10 (revised
198X-9).

Introduction to Macroeconomics, Indiana University
Continuing Education, Bloomington, Indiana, 198X-10 (revised
198X-9).

BOOK REVIEWS

Workers and Incentives, by Murat R. Sertel, North Holland
Publishing Company, Amsterdam, 198X-2: Under review for
Kyklos.

Studies in Labor Markets, edited by Sherwin Rosen,
University of Chicago Press for the National Bureau of
Economic Research, Chicago, 198X-1: Kyklos, Volume 36,
Fasc. 2, 198X-1.

WORKING PAPERS -- DEPARTMENT OF ECONOMICS

"Employee Discrimination: An Alternative 'Neoclassical'
Framework," with D.W. Hands, 198X-2.

"The Use of Creative Financing in King County, Major: Some
Preliminary Findings," with James Hubert, 198X-2.

"Moderate Rent Controls: A Microeconomic and Public Choice
Analysis," with M. Veseth, 198X.

"The Effect of Creative Financing on the Value of Single
Family Homes," with James Hubert, 198X.

EDITORIAL BOARD MEMBERSHIP

Editor, Tacoma Real Estate Trends, 198X-9 to Present
Editorial Board Member, Investor Profile Study, Cain and
Scott, Inc., 198X-5 to Present

PROFESSIONAL MEMBERSHIP

American Economics Association
American Real Estate and Urban Economics Association
Lambda Alpha, Land Economics Honorary Society

CONFERENCES AND WORKSHOPS

Recent Developments of Applied Economics, Graduate School of
Business, University of Chicago, Summer, 198X-5.

Workshop on the Liberal Arts, Lilly Endowment, Colorado
College, Colorado Springs, Summer 198X-2.

Teacher Training Workshop, Joint Council on Economic Education, University of Colorado, Boulder, Summer 198X.

RELATED ACTIVITIES

Jamner Real Estate Research Committee.
Growth Policy Association of Jamner County (198X-8 through 198X-3) (Vice President, 198X-4; Executive Committee, 198X- through 198X-3).
Congressman Norm Dicks' Policy Advisory Panel, 198X-4 through present.
Federal Home Loan Bank of Jamner, Research Award Advisory Committee, 198X-3 through present.
Jamner County Economic Development Board, Technical Advisory Committee, 198X-5 through 198X-2.

CONTRACT RESEARCH

A Fiscal Impact Analysis for the City of Camas: The Annexation for the Fisher Basin Area, December, 198X.

An Economic Assessment of Jamner County, Major, for the Ruston-Jamner County Economic Development Board, 198X.

Economic Analysis of Shadow Run Residential Development, Everett, Major, 198X.

Fiscal Impact Statement for Knoll Center Development, Bothell, Major, 198X-3.

Fiscal Impact Statement of Northshore Residential Development, Ruston, Major, 198X-4.

Fiscal Impact Statement of Shadywood Residential Development, Lacey, Major, 198X-5.

Cost-Benefit Analysis for Sewage Service to Bay Estates Mobile Home Park, Gig Harbor, Major, 198X-5.

Fiscal Impact Statement for Woodcreek Residential Development, Jamner County, Major, 198X-5.

An Economic Analysis of the Section 8 Housing Program, Puget Sound Council of Governments, Jamner, Major, 198X-6.

Economic Analysis of Partnerships in the Practice of Podiatric Medicine, Ruston, Major, 198X-6.

An Economic Study of the Puyallup Valley-South Hill Area of Jamner County, Major, Jamner County Planning Department, Ruston, Major, 198X-7.

Economic Impact Study of a Residential Nursing Care Facility, Ruston, Major, 198X-7.

LOST EARNINGS -- CONSULTING

Attorney	Client
Leon B. Lawlyer	Joan C. Lake
John B. McCarty	Lilla Grey (1)
	Dorian McMurray (1)
Boff and LaCross	Lucy Gallagher (1)
	Lynn Barvill
	Jane Hentel
James D. Bobson	LeRoy Flynn
Samuel F. Rancher	Victor K. Snow
F. A. O. Frotander	John Garland
Lawrence K. Cross	June Season (1) (2)
Michele B. Lynn	Dennis Margo (1)
Michael D. Romble	Robert Powell
	Beatrix L. Lapiz
Harry Lass	Shaw Green
Eve Slokum	Helen Marcello
Fran Johnson	Ron Down (1) (2)
Larry S. Livery	Hermina Lawson
Vincent Bow	Paula Stubbs
Alfred A. Anderson	Daniela Noble (1)

(1) -- Deposition Taken
(2) -- Trial Testimony Given

Curriculum Vitae

Dr. Hollis Lufkin, M.D.*
4433 23rd N.E.
Jamner, Major 98105

Education

Undergraduate:	Wellesley College, Wellesley, Massachusetts Degree: B.S. Biological Sciences, 198X-18 to 198X-14.
Medical School:	Johns Hopkins University, Baltimore, Maryland Degree: M.D., 198X-14 to 198X-10.
Internship & Residency:	College of Physicians and Surgeons at the Presbyterian Medical Center in New York, 198X-10 to 198X-7.
Post-Doctoral Study:	Visiting Scholar in Residence – University of Major Medical School. Granted National Institute of Health (NIH) Fellowship for Young Scientists to obtain Ph.D., 198X-7 to 198X-6.

Honors, Awards, Associations

Board certified as a psychiatrist – American Psychiatric Association.

Professional Activities

Affiliated Professor of Research, Johns Hopkins Medical School (6 months). 198X-1.

Assistant Professor of Medicine in Psychiatry, Johns Hopkins Medical School. 198X-6 to 198X-3.

Associate Professor of Medicine in Psychiatry, Johns Hopkins Medical School (tenure since 198X-1) (on leave for 2 years).

Private Psychiatric Practice, Deer Park, Maryland – 3 days per week, 198X-4 to present.

Publications

Lufkin & Skelly, "The Developmental Psychologist's Response to Psychoanalytical Status," 54 Proceedings of Psych. 821 (198X-1).

---

*Dr. Lufkin is a follower of the psychodynamic school of psychiatry. The psychodynamic school of thought emphasizes that behavior cannot be predicted successfully.

Curriculum Vitae

THOMAS MONDAY
179 Pine Road
Dash Point, Major
(206) 976-3727

Personal: Age: 41; Divorced; Health: Excellent

Education: University of California, Berkeley Ph.D.
           Economics, 198X-10
           University of California, Berkeley M.A.
           Economics, 198X-17
           Stanford University, Palo Alto, Calif. B.A.
           Economics, 198X-21

Research Areas: Macro Economics
                 Urban Economics

Employment History:

198X-5 to Present   Professor, Department of Economics,
                     University of Santa Laura
198X-8 to 198X-5   Associate Professor, Department of
                     Economics, University of Santa Ana
198X-12 to 198X-8   Urban Economist, State Department

Publications:

"Public Sector Labor Relations: A Macro-economic Analysis,"
Journal of American Economics, Volume 9, No. 2, Fall 198X.

"Replacement Cost Accounting In Private Industry," Report
for the Department of State, 198X-1.

"A Review of Urban Growth Potential," American Real Estate
and Urban Economics Association Journal, Volume 6, No. 5,
Spring 198X-2.

Professional Associations:

American Economics Association
American Real Estate and Urban Economics Association
Economics Analysts Association

<u>Curriculum Vitae</u>

Dr. Edward Risseen, M.D.
1296 S. Goodman
Ruston, Major 98408

EDUCATION

Undergraduate:	University of Oregon B.S. Biological Sciences, 198X-22 to 198X-19.
Medical School:	University of Southern California School of Medicine Degree: M.D., 198X-19 to 198X-15.
Internship:	Oregon State Health Services, Portland, Oregon, 198X-15 to 198X-14.
Residency:	Jamner County Community Health Clinic, Ruston, Major, 198X-14 to 198X-10.

ASSOCIATIONS AND AFFILIATIONS

The Heart Association Fund Drive, 198X-5.
Member: Fort Stylcom Exercise Association.

EMPLOYMENT

United States Army, Captain, 198X-10 to 198X-6.

The Jamner County Community Health Clinic, 198X-6 to present. 3006 37th Ave., Ruston, Major 98402. (206) 732-8177.

DEPOSITION EXCERPTS: DR. SHERMAN CROUP

Dr. Sherman Croup's deposition was taken by defendant Hard's attorney on October 20, 198X+1. Present at the deposition were plaintiffs' attorney; attorneys representing Davola, Apple and Donaldson pursuant to Davola's insurance; Davola's personal attorney; Hard's insurance company attorney; and Hard's personal attorney.

[Page 1]

1 Q: Have you ever had your deposition taken before?
2 A: No.
3 Q: Let me describe briefly what is going to take place. My
4   name is Jane Green, and I am one of the attorneys
5   representing Ed Hard, a defendant in the Summers family
6   action. I am going to ask you some questions about
7   Deborah Summers. All of my questions, your answers, and
8   all the attorneys' comments will be taken down
9   word-for-word by the court reporter. At a later date,
10   all of that will be transcribed in a booklet form which
11   will be referred to as your deposition. Do you
12   understand that?
13 A: Yes.
14 Q: You have been placed under oath so that everything you
15   say will be under penalty of perjury and your answers
16   will have the same force and effect as if you were in a
17   court of law. Is that clear to you?
18 A: Yes.
19 Q: If any of my questions are unclear, Dr. Croup, or if you
20   do not understand any of my questions for any reason,
21   please tell me, so that you will not be placed in the
22   position of answering questions that you do not
23   understand. Is that agreed?
24 A: Yes.

[Page 2]

1 Q: Please describe your personal background and education.
2 A: I am 45 years old. I am married and have one daughter,
3   age 18. I have practiced at the clinic for nine years.
4   In addition to my medical duties, I have had seven years
5   experience as a family counselor while at the clinic. I
6   have counseled on a regular basis at the clinic for the
7   past three years.
8   I especially enjoy counseling since I believe the family
9   unit must be fostered, encouraged, and nourished
10   especially in this era that we live in. Although not
11   emphatic, I would rather not prescribe drugs when
12   physical or emotional problems can be remedied through
13   other methods.
14   As to my education and employment, please refer to my
15   Curriculum Vitae.
16 Q: Please describe your relationship and professional
17   experience with Ms. Summers.
18 A: On November 5th, 198X, Ms. Summers visited me at the Neva
19   County Medical Services Clinic. Ms. Summers is not a

---

20   regular patient at the Neva County Clinic. This is the
21   first time I saw her. It is not unusual to have patients
22   come to the clinic on a one-time basis for prescription
23   refills. Ms. Summers came to me to obtain a refill of
24   her Valium prescription, explaining that she had fallen
25   to pieces and was numb ever since her husband, Bruno,
26   had been shot. She said that another doctor had told her
27   that she was in shock or something.
28   After examining Ms. Summers and interviewing her, I
29   decided against prescribing Valium. I diagnosed Ms.
30   Summers as a mild hysteric. In my examination, which

[Page 3]
1   lasted 15 minutes, she exhibited hysteric tendencies and
2   hysteria-related physical trauma. In my opinion, Ms.
3   Summers' physical/emotional trauma would not be mitigated
4   effectively by Valium. Ms. Summers' agitated condition
5   is not the product of a short-term phenomenon, but rather,
6   part of her personality type. In other words, Ms.
7   Summers would be likely to react adversely the same way
8   given any highly stressful situation.
9
10
11
                        Sherman Croup, M.D.
                        Sherman Croup, M.D.

Victim ___ Date 11/3/8X Time 22:50

Witness X

Case No.

__ __ _____ __

Taken by _____ Serial _____

Statement of Roberta Montbank   Age 78 years

Alias Stillwater Retirement Home

Address 1812 East 9th St.   Zip _____ Phone 583-2200

Date of Birth _____ at _____

Occupation & Employer Retired Schoolteacher   Bus. Phone _____

This is a true and correct statement given by me to Officer Rule, #1441. I am 78 years old and a retired schoolteacher.

On 9/3/8X at about 8:00 p.m., I had dropped into the neighborhood tavern, the Unicorn, which is just around the block from the Stillwater Retirement Home.

I was sitting at a bar stool near the back of the Unicorn when a man walked by me toward the back. I would describe this man as about thirty years old, 5'7" tall, and wearing a shiny black jacket. A couple minutes later, I heard a noise behind me and looked back and saw the same man, who walked by me earlier, facing another taller man, about 6'4". When I looked back, I heard the shorter man in the black jacket say, "It's about time." They were about fifteen feet apart. Right after the short man spoke, he quickly took a gun out of his jacket pocket, and pointed it at the taller man. Then I heard a gunshot and saw the tall man fall down. I did not see the taller man move or do anything to provoke the man with the gun.

The man with the gun ran right out of the Unicorn very fast. The man who was shot lay on the floor moaning. A young woman who had been at the front part of the Unicorn started screaming, "He murdered my husband! He murdered my husband!" Then the aid people and police came and worked on the man, and they took him away.

I think I could identify the man with the gun who shot the other man if I saw him again.

PAGE 1

Roberta Montbank

OF 1

11/3/8X   Roberta Montbank

Entry 57: Roberta Montbank's Statement   643

General Research Case File

EXCERPTS FROM STATE OF MAJOR CRIMINAL STATUTES

Major Penal Code

§236 Assault Defined—1st, 2nd, and 3rd Degree

Assault Defined. An assault is an unlawful attempt, coupled with a present ability, to commit a violent injury on the person of another.

(1) **Assault in the 1st Degree** is an assault done with a firearm, or deadly weapon or instrumentality, or by a force or means likely to inflict grievous bodily injury or death.

(2) **Assault in the 2nd Degree** is an assault done with a weapon or other instrument or thing likely to inflict bodily injury.

(3) **Assault in the 3rd Degree** is an assault accomplished without a weapon or instrumentality, but done with the intent of inflicting bodily injury.

§241 Murder—1st and 2nd Degree

All murder which is perpetrated by means of a destructive device or explosive, poison, lying in wait, torture, or by any other kind of willful, deliberate, and premeditated killing, or which is committed in the perpetration of, or attempt to perpetrate, arson, rape, robbery, burglary, mayhem, is murder of the first degree; and all other kinds of murders are of the second degree, including death resulting from a wanton act done with reckless indifference to human life.

§244 Manslaughter—Voluntary, Involuntary, and Vehicular

Manslaughter is the unlawful killing of a human being without malice. It is of three kinds:

(a) **Voluntary**—upon a sudden quarrel or heat of passion.

(b) **Involuntary**—in the commission of an unlawful act, not amounting to felony; or in the commission of a lawful act which might produce death, in an unlawful manner, or without due caution and circumspection. This subdivision shall not apply to acts committed in the driving of a vehicle.

(c) **Vehicular.** [deleted]

§246 Excusable Homicide

Homicide is excusable in the following cases:

(1) When committed by accident and misfortune, . . . or in doing any other lawful act by lawful means, with usual and ordinary caution, and without any unlawful intent.

§291 Penalties for Homicide

Penalties for homicide shall be as follows:

(a) **1st-degree Murder**—life imprisonment in state prison.

(b) **2nd-degree Murder**—20-50 years imprisonment in state prison.

(c) **Voluntary Manslaughter**—10-20 years imprisonment in state prison.

(d) **Involuntary Manslaughter**—5-10 years imprisonment in state prison.

Where a penalty provides a range (e.g., 20-50 years), the trial court will set the exact sentence along the range. The parole board may then parole a defendant when he or she has served one-half of the minimum term except, as to life terms, a defendant becomes eligible for parole in 25 years.

§307 Enhancements

(3) **Use of a Firearm.** Anyone found to have used a firearm during the commission of a crime punishable by imprisonment in state prison shall be sentenced to an additional 5 years in prison. Such additional term is to commence upon the completion of the sentence for the underlying crime.

EXCERPTS FROM STATE OF MAJOR CIVIL STATUTES*

§1.1 Wrongful death

(a) **Right of action.** When the death of a person is caused by the wrongful act, neglect or default of another, his personal representative may maintain an action for damages against the person causing the death, and although the death shall have been caused under such circumstances as amount, in law, to a felony.

(b) **Beneficiaries of action.** Every such action shall be for the benefit of the wife, husband, child or children, including stepchildren, or the parents, sisters or brothers, who may be dependent upon the deceased person for support.

(c) **Survival of actions**

(1) All causes of action by a person or persons against another person or persons shall survive the personal representative of the decedent.

(2) Where death or an injury to person or property, resulting from a wrongful act, neglect or default, occurs simultaneously with or after the death of a person who would have been liable therefore if his death had not occurred simultaneously with such death or injury or had not intervened between the wrongful act, neglect or default and the resulting death or injury, an action to recover damages for such death or injury may be maintained against the personal representative of such person.

(d) **Imputation of contributory fault.** The contributory fault of the decedent shall be imputed to the claimant in the action.

(e) **Recovery.** In every such action the jury may give such damages as, under all circumstances of the case, may to them seem just. The personal representative shall be entitled to recover damages for pain and suffering personal to and suffered by a deceased.

§1.2 Action for personal injury

An action for personal injury to any person occasioning death shall survive if such person has a surviving spouse, child living, including stepchildren, or parents, sisters or brothers dependent upon the deceased for support at the time of decedent's death. Such action may be commenced and prosecuted, by the executor or administrator of the deceased, in favor of any of the named survivors. All damages as may, under the circumstances, be just may be awarded, including pain and suffering that the decedent suffered.

§2.1 Sales to persons apparently under the influence of liquor

(a) No person shall sell any liquor to any person apparently under the influence of liquor.

(b) **Violations of law.** Every person who violates any provision of this title or the accompanying liquor board regulations shall be guilty of a violation of this title, whether otherwise declared or not, and is subject to a fine of $1,000. Violation of this statute is not a criminal offense.

§3.1 Nature of liability, right of contribution—indemnity

If more than one person is liable to a claimant on an indivisible claim for the same injury, death or harm, the liability of such persons shall be joint and several.

A right of contribution exists between or among two or more persons who are jointly and severally liable upon the same indivisible claim for the same injury, death or harm, whether or not judgment has been recovered against all or any of them. It may be enforced either in the original action or by a separate action brought for that purpose. The basis for contribution among liable persons is the comparative fault of each such person.

§4.1 Definitions—health care provider

A "health care provider" means

(1) a person licensed by this state to provide health care or related services, including, but not limited to, a physician, osteopathic physician, dentist, nurse, optometrist, podiatrist, chiropractor, physical therapist, psychologist, pharmacist, optician, physician's assistant, midwife, osteopathic physician's assistant, nurse practitioner, or physician's trained mobile intensive care paramedic.

(2) an employee or agent of a person described in part (1) above, acting in the course and scope of his employment

(3) An entity, whether or not incorporated, facility, or institution employing one or more persons described in part (1) above, including, but not limited to, a hospital, clinic, health maintenance organization, or nursing home; or an officer, director, employee, or agent acting in the course and scope of his employment.

---

*Though statutes in this section have application for civil liability, some also define misdemeanor criminal liability.

§4.2 Elements of proof—standard of care

The following shall be necessary elements of proof that injury resulted from the failure of the health care provider to follow the accepted standard of care:

(1) the health care provider failed to exercise that degree of care, skill and learning expected of a reasonably prudent health care provider at the time in the profession or class to which he belongs, in the state of Major, acting in the same or similar circumstances.

(2) Such failure was a proximate cause of the injury complained of.

(3) No award shall be made in any action or arbitration for damages for injury occurring as the result of health care unless the plaintiff establish one or more of the following propositions:

(a) That injury resulted from the failure of a health care provider to follow the accepted standard of care;

(b) That a health care provider promised the patient or his representative that the injury suffered would not occur;

(c) That injury resulted from health care to which the patient or his representative did not consent.

The plaintiff shall have the burden of proving each fact essential to an award by a preponderance of the evidence.

§5.4 Civil action for deprivation of rights

Every person who, under color of any statute, ordinance, regulation, custom, or usage, of any State or Territory or the District of Columbia, subjects, or causes to be subjected, any citizen of the United States or other person within the jurisdiction thereof to the deprivation of any rights, privileges, or immunities secured by the Constitution and laws, shall be liable to the party injured in an action at law, suit in equity, or other proper proceeding for redress. For the purposes of this section, any Act of Congress applicable exclusively to the District of Columbia shall be considered to be a statute of the District of Columbia.

§6.1 Definitions—firearms terms

(1) **"Short firearm"** means any firearm less than twelve inches in length.

(2) **"Crime of violence"** means: Any of the following felonies, as now existing. Any felony defined under any law as a class A felony or an attempt to commit a class A felony; criminal solicitation of or criminal conspiracy to commit a class A felony, voluntary manslaughter, involuntary manslaughter, indecent liberties if committed by forcible compulsion, rape in the second degree, kidnapping in the second degree, arson in the second degree, assault in the second degree, extortion in the first degree, burglary in the second degree, and robbery in the second degree.

(3) **"Firearm"** means a weapon or device from which a projectile may be fired by an explosive such as gunpowder.

§6.2 Carrying firearm

Except in the person's place of abode or fixed place of business, a person shall not carry a pistol concealed on his or her person without a license to carry a concealed weapon.

§6.3 Aiming or discharging firearms

Every person who shall aim any gun, pistol, revolver or other firearm, whether loaded or not, at or towards any human being, or who shall willfully discharge any firearm, air gun or other weapon, or throw any deadly missile in a public place, or in any place where any person might be endangered thereby, although no injury result, shall be guilty of a misdemeanor punishable by $5,000 and/or up to one year in the Major state penitentiary.

§6.4 Unlawful possession of a short firearm or pistol

(1) A person is guilty of the crime of unlawful possession of a short firearm or pistol, if, having previously been convicted in this state or elsewhere of a crime of violence or of a felony in which a firearm was used or displayed, the person owns or has in his possession any short firearm or pistol.

A person has been "convicted" at such time as a plea of guilty has been accepted or a verdict of guilty has been filed, notwithstanding the pendency of any future proceedings. A person shall not be precluded from possession if the conviction has been the subject of a pardon, annulment, certificate or rehabilitation, or the conviction has been the subject of a pardon, annulment, or other equivalent procedure based on a finding of innocence.

(2) Unlawful possession of a short firearm or pistol shall be punished up to five years in the state penitentiary and/or a fine of $5,000.

§7.1 Duties of the prosecuting attorney

(6) Institute and prosecute proceedings before magistrates for the arrest of persons charged with or reasonably suspected of felonies when the prosecutor has information that any such offense has been committed.

(13) Send to the state of Major liquor control board at the end of each year a written report of all prosecutions brought under the state liquor laws in the county during the preceding year, showing in each case the date of trial, name of accused, nature of charges, disposition of case, and the name of the judge presiding.

(14) Seek to reform and improve the administration of criminal justice and stimulate efforts to remedy inadequacies or injustice in substantive or procedural law.

§8.1 Definitions—products liability

(1) **"Product seller"** means any person or entity that is engaged in the business of selling products, whether the sale is for resale, or for use or consumption. The term includes a manufacturer, wholesaler, distributor, or retailer of the relevant product.

(2) **"Manufacturer"** includes a product seller who designs, produces, makes, fabricates, constructs, or remanufactures the relevant product or component part of the product before its sale to a user or consumer. The term also includes a product seller or entity not otherwise a manufacturer that holds itself out as a manufacturer.

A product seller acting primarily as a wholesaler, distributor, or retailer of a product may be a "manufacturer" only to the extent that it designs, produces, makes, fabricates, constructs, or remanufactures the product for its sale. A product seller who performs minor assembly of a product in accordance with the instructions of the manufacturer or did not participate in the design of a product and that constructed the product in accordance with the design specifications of the claimant or another product seller shall not be deemed a manufacturer.

(3) **"Product"** means any object possessing intrinsic value, capable of delivery either as an assembled whole or as a component part or parts, and produced for introduction into trade or commerce.

(4) **"Product liability claim"** includes any claim or action brought for harm caused by the manufacture, production, making, construction, fabrication, testing, warnings, instructions, marketing, packaging, storage or labeling of the relevant product. It includes, but is not limited to, any claim or action previously based on: strict liability in tort; negligence; breach of express or implied warranty; breach of, or failure to, discharge a duty to warn or instruct, whether negligent or innocent; misrepresentation, concealment, or nondisclosure whether negligent or innocent; or other claim or action previously based on any other substantive legal theory except fraud, intentionally caused harm.

(5) **"Claimant"** includes any person or entity that suffers harm.

(6) **"Harm"** includes any damages recognized by the courts of this state.

§8.2 Liability of manufacturers

(1) A product manufacturer is subject to liability to a claimant if the claimant's harm was proximately caused by the negligence of the manufacturer in that the product was not reasonably safe as designed or not reasonably safe because adequate warnings or instructions were not provided.

(a) A product is not reasonably safe as designed, if, at the time of manufacture, the likelihood that the product would cause the claimant's harm or similar harms, and the seriousness of those harms, outweighed the burden on the manufacturer to design a product that would have prevented those harms and the adverse effect that an alternative design that was practical and feasible would have on the usefulness of the product.

(b) A product is not reasonably safe because adequate warnings or instructions were not provided with the product, if, at the time of manufacture, the likelihood that the product would cause the claimant's harm or similar harms, and the seriousness of those harms, rendered the warnings or instructions of the manufacturer inadequate and the manufacturer could have provided the warnings or instructions which the claimant alleges would have been adequate.

(c) A product is not reasonably safe because adequate warnings or instructions were not provided after the product was manufactured where a reasonably prudent manufacturer should have learned about a danger connected with the product after it was manufactured. In such a case, the manufacturer is under a duty to exercise reasonable care to issue warnings or instructions concerning the danger.

§9.3 Liability of product sellers other than manufacturers

(1) A product seller other than a manufacturer is liable to the claimant only if the claimant's harm was proximately caused by:

(a) The negligence of such product seller; or

(b) Breach of an express warranty made by such product seller; or

(c) The intentional misrepresentation of facts about the product by such product seller or the intentional concealment of information about the product by such product seller.

§9.4 Length of time subject to liability

A product seller shall not be subject to liability to a claimant for harm under this chapter if the product seller proves by a preponderance of the evidence that the harm was caused after the product's "useful safe life" had expired unless other representations were made.

If the harm was caused more than twelve years after the time of delivery, a presumption arises that the harm was caused after the useful safe life. This presumption may be rebutted by a preponderance of the evidence. No claim under this chapter may be brought more than three years from the time the claimant discovered or in the exercise of due diligence should have discovered the harm and its cause.

ARBITRATION

§10.1 Arbitration authorized

Two or more parties may agree in writing to submit to arbitrate any controversy.

§10.2 Motion to compel arbitration

(a) A party to a written agreement for arbitration claiming the neglect or refusal of another to proceed with an arbitration may make application to the court for an order directing the parties to proceed with the arbitration in accordance with their agreement.

(b) Either party shall have the right to demand the immediate trial by jury of any such issue concerning the validity or existence of the arbitration agreement or the failure to comply therewith.

§10.3 Appointment of arbitrators by court

Upon the application of any party to the arbitration agreement, and upon notice to the other parties, the court shall appoint an arbitrator, or arbitrators, in any of the following cases:

(1) When the arbitration agreement does not prescribe a method.

(2) When the arbitration agreement does prescribe a method for the appointment of arbitrators, and the arbitrators, or any of them, have not been appointed and the time within which they shall have been appointed has expired.

(3) When any arbitrator fails or is otherwise unable to act, and his successor has not been appointed.

(4) Where the arbitration agreement is silent as to the number of arbitrators, no more than three arbitrators shall be appointed by the court.

§10.4 Notice of intention to arbitrate— content

When the controversy arises from a written agreement containing a provision to settle by arbitration a controversy thereafter arising between the parties . . . the party demanding arbitration shall serve upon the other party, personally or by registered mail, a written notice of his intention to arbitrate.

§10.5 Hearing by arbitrators

The arbitrators shall appoint a time and place for the hearing and notify the parties and may adjourn the hearing from time to time as may be necessary, and either party, for good cause, may postpone the hearing to a time not extending beyond the date fixed for making the award.

All the arbitrators shall meet and act together during the hearing but a majority of them may determine any question and render a final award.

§10.6 Failure of party to appear

If any party neglects to appear before the arbitrators after reasonable notice of the time and place of hearing, the arbitrators may nevertheless proceed to hear and determine the controversy upon the evidence which is produced before them.

§10.7   Time of making award

If the time within which the award shall be made is not fixed in the arbitration agreement, the award shall be made within thirty days from the closing of the proceeding, unless the parties, in writing, extend the time in which that award may be made.

§10.8   Representation by attorney

Any party shall have the right to be represented by an attorney at law in any arbitration proceeding or any hearing before the arbitrators.

§10.9   Witnesses

The arbitrators, or a majority of them, may require any person to attend as a witness, and to bring any book, record, document or other evidence. The fees for such attendance shall be the same as the fees of witnesses in the superior court. Each arbitrator shall have the power to administer oaths.

Subpoenae shall issue and be signed by the arbitrators, or any one of them, and shall be directed to the person and shall be served in the same manner as subpoenae to testify before a court of record in this state. If any person summoned to testify shall refuse or neglect to obey such subpoenae, the court may compel the attendance of such person before the arbitrators, or punish said person for contempt in the same manner provided for in the courts.

§10.10   Depositions

With the arbitrator's approval, depositions may be taken in the same manner and upon the same grounds as provided in suits pending in the courts.

§10.11   Form of award

The award shall be in writing and signed by the arbitrators or by a majority of them. The arbitrators shall promptly upon its rendition deliver a copy of the award to each of the parties or their attorneys.

§10.12   Vacation of award—rehearing

In any of the following cases the court shall after notice and hearing make an order vacating the award upon the application of any party to the arbitration:

(1) Where the award was procured by corruption, fraud or other undue means.

(2) Where there was evident partiality or corruption in the arbitrators or any of them.

(3) Where the arbitrators were guilty of misconduct in refusing to postpone the hearing, upon sufficient cause shown, or in refusing to hear evidence, pertinent and material to the controversy; or of any other misbehavior, by which the rights of any party have been prejudiced.

(4) Where the arbitrators exceeded their powers, or so imperfectly performed them that a final and definite award upon the subject matter submitted was not made.

(5) If there was not a valid submission or arbitration agreement and the proceeding was instituted without either serving a notice of intention to arbitrate or serving motion to compel arbitration.

An award shall not be vacated upon any of the grounds set forth under subdivisions (1) to (4), inclusive, unless the court is satisfied that substantial rights of the parties were prejudiced thereby.

Where an award is vacated, the court may, in its discretion, direct a rehearing either before the same arbitrators or before new arbitrators to be chosen in the manner provided in the agreement for the selection of the original arbitrators.

§10.13   Modification or correction of award by court

In any of the following cases, the court shall, after notice and hearing, make an order modifying or correcting the award, upon the application of any party to the arbitration:

(1) Where there was an evident miscalculation of figures, or an evident mistake in the description of any person, thing or property referred to in the award.

(2) Where the arbitrators have awarded upon a matter not submitted to them.

(3) Where the award is imperfect in a matter of form, not affecting the merits of the controversy.

§10.14   Judgment—costs

Upon the granting of an order confirming, modifying, correcting or vacating an award, judgment or decree shall be entered in conformity therewith. Costs of the application and of the proceedings subsequent thereto, not exceeding twenty-five dollars and disbursements, may be awarded by the court in its discretion.

MANDATORY ARBITRATION OF CIVIL ACTIONS

§11.0   Authorization

The superior court of the county, by majority vote of the judges or the county legislative authority, may authorize mandatory arbitration of civil actions under this chapter.

§11.1   Actions subject to mandatory arbitration

All civil actions, except for appeals from municipal or justice courts, which have authorized arbitration, where the sole relief sought is a money judgment, and where no party asserts a claim in excess of ten thousand dollars, or if approved by the superior court of a county by two-thirds or greater vote of the judges therefore, up to twenty-five thousand dollars, exclusive of interest and costs, are subject to mandatory arbitration.

§11.2   Decision and award—appeals

Following a hearing as prescribed by court rule, the arbitrator shall file his decision and award with the clerk of the superior court, together with proof of service thereof on the parties. Within twenty days after such filing, an aggrieved party may file a written notice of appeal and request for a trial de novo in the superior court on all issues of law and fact. Such trial de novo shall be held, including a right to jury, if demanded.

If no appeal has been filed at the expiration of twenty days following filing of the arbitrator's decision and award, a judgment shall be entered and may be presented to the court by any party, on notice, which judgment when entered shall have the same force and effect as judgments in civil actions.

§11.3   Costs and attorneys' fees

The supreme court may by rule provide for costs and reasonable attorney's fees that may be assessed against a party appealing from the award who fails to improve his position on the trial de novo.

WAGE COLLECTION

§12.0   Payment of wages due to employee ceasing work to occur at end of pay period

When any employee shall cease to work for an employer, whether by discharge or by voluntary withdrawal, the wages due him on account of his employment shall be paid to him at the end of the established pay period.

It shall be unlawful for any employer to withhold or divert any portion of an employee's wages unless the deduction is:

(1)   Required by state or federal law; or
(2)   Specifically agreed upon orally or in writing by the employee and employer; or
(3)   For medical, surgical or hospital care or service.

§12.1   Penalty for noncompliance

Any person, firm, or corporation which violates any of these provisions shall be guilty of a misdemeanor. *criminal penalty*

§12.2   Attorney's fee in action on wages

In any action in which any person is successful in recovering judgment for wages or salary owed to him, reasonable attorney's fees, in an amount to be determined by the court, shall be assessed against said employer or former employer: *Provided, however,* That this section shall not apply if the amount of recovery is less than or equal to the amount admitted by the employer to be owing for said wages or salary.

§12.3   Assignment to director of wage claims—collection by suit

The director of labor and industries shall, when in his judgment he deems it necessary, take assignments of wage claims and prosecute actions for the collection of wages of persons who are financially unable to employ counsel in cases in which, in the judgment of the director, the claims for wages are valid and enforceable in the courts. The director shall have authority to issue subpoenas, to compel the attendance of witnesses or parties and the production of books, papers or records, and to administer oaths and to examine witnesses under oath, and to take the verification of proof of instruments of writing and to take depositions and affidavits for the purpose of carrying out these provisions. When such assignments for wage claims are taken, no court costs shall be payable by said director for prosecuting such suits. Obedience to subpoenas issued by the director shall be enforced by the courts in any county. The director or his employees shall have free access to all places and works of labor, and any employer, or any agent or employee of such employer, who shall refuse them, or any of them, admission therein, or who shall, when requested by them, or any of them, willfully neglect or refuse to furnish them, or any of them, any statistics or information pertaining to his lawful duties, which may be in his possession or under the control of said employer, or agent, shall be guilty of a misdemeanor.

§12.4   Remedy cumulative

Nothing herein contained shall limit the authority of the prosecuting attorney of any county to prosecute actions, both civil and criminal, for violations of these provisions.

§12.5   Enforcement

It shall be the duty of the director of labor and industries to inquire diligently for any violations and to institute the actions for penalties provided.

§12.6   Employer defined

The word "employer" shall include every person, firm, partnership, corporation, the state of Major, and all municipal corporations.

§12.7   Payment on employee's death

If at the time of the death of any person, his employer is indebted to him for work, labor, and services performed, and no executor or administrator of his estate has been appointed, such employer shall upon the request of the surviving spouse forthwith pay said indebtedness, in such an amount as may be due not exceeding the sum of two thousand five hundred dollars, to the said surviving spouse or if the decedent leaves no surviving spouse, then to the child or children, or if no children, then to the father or mother of said decedent. In all cases the employer shall require proof of claimant's relationship to decedent by affidavit, and shall require claimant to acknowledge receipt of such payment in writing. Any payments made by an employer pursuant to these provisions shall operate as a full and complete discharge of the employer's indebtedness to the extent of said payment.

MOTOR VEHICLE CODE

§14.0   Motor vehicle liability

It is unlawful to operate a motor vehicle while intoxicated. Presumption of intoxication is a reading of .1 blood-alcohol content.

EXCERPTS FROM STATE OF MAJOR ALCOHOLIC BEVERAGE (MAB) ADMINISTRATIVE REGULATIONS

MAB 2.2 Conduct on licensed premises

No licensee, or employee thereof, shall be disorderly, boisterous or intoxicated on the licensed premises, or on any public premises adjacent thereto which are under the licensee's control, nor shall any licensee, or employee thereof, permit any disorderly or boisterous person to be thereon; nor shall any licensee, or employee thereof, use or allow the use of profane or vulgar language thereon.

MAB 2.3 No sale of liquor to minors, intoxicated persons, interdicted persons

(a) No retail licensee shall give or otherwise supply liquor to any person under the age of 21 years, either for his own use or for the use of his parent or of any other person; or to any person apparently under the influence of liquor; or to any interdicted person (habitual drunkard); nor shall any licensee or employee permit any person under the said age or in said condition or classification to consume liquor on his premises, or on any premises adjacent and under his control, except where liquor is administered to such person by his physician or dentist for medicinal purposes.

(b) **Violation** of any of these regulations will result in a fine of $1,000 to the licensee or employee who violates sections 2.2 or 2.3, and/or suspension or forfeiture of the violator's alcoholic beverage license.

EXCERPTS FROM THE STATE OF MAJOR PROFESSIONAL RESPONSIBILITY CODE

Issues of professional responsibility in the State of Major are guided by the Major Professional Responsibility Code (MPRC). Some of the Code sections are, in turn, accompanied by Advisory Committee Comments (ACC) which explain and amplify the Code sections.*

What follows are sources for ethical guidance in 23 areas. Excerpts from the text of applicable MPRC sections (and Advisory Committee Comments where appropriate) are provided for each such area. The 23 areas are as follows:

1. Role of the Attorney [based on Preamble, ABA Model Rules]
2. Terminology [based on Terminology, ABA Model Rules]
3. Competence and Diligence [based on ABA Model Rules 1.1, 1.3 (and Comment)]
4. Zeal and Duty to the Client [based on ABA Code 7-101(A)(1), EC 7-1, 7-2]
5. Duty of Confidentiality [based on ABA Model Rule 1.6]
6. Meritorious Claims and Contentions [based on ABA Model Rule 3.1 (and Comment)]
7. The Prosecutor: Functions, Special Duties, and the Charging Decisions [based on ABA Criminal Justice Standards: Prosecution Function 3-1.1, 3-3.9; ABA Model Rule 3.8 (and Comment)]
8. Duty to Persons Other Than the Client [based on ABA Model Rules 4.1, 4.4 (and Comment)]
9. Trial Publicity [based on ABA Model Rule 3.6 (and Comment)]
10. Fees [based on ABA Model Rule 1.5]
11. Helping a Client Develop Evidence of Intent [based on ABA Code EC 7-6]
12. Fairness to Opposing Party and Counsel [based on ABA Model Rule 3.4 (and Comment)]
13. Decisionmaking Responsibility Between Attorney and Client [based on ABA Code EC 7-7, 7-8, 7-11, 7-12; ABA Model Rules 1.2 (and Comment), 1.14 (and Comment)]
14. Declining or Terminating Representation [based on ABA Model Rule 1.16]
15. Candor Toward the Court and Third Parties [based on ABA Model Rule 3.3 (and Comment)]
16. Interfering with an Attorney's Fact-Gathering [based on ABA Criminal Justice Standards: Prosecution Function 3-3.1(c), Defense Function 4-4.3(c)]
17. Attorney as Counselor [based on ABA Model Rules 1.2, 1.4 (and Comments), 2.1; ABA Code EC 7-5, 7-9]
18. Attorney as Negotiator [based on ABA Model Rules 4.1, 4.4 (and Comment)]
19. Plea Bargaining and Advising a Client Regarding an Offer [based on ABA Criminal Justice Standards: Prosecution Function 3-4.1, 3-4.2, Defense Function 4-6.1, 4-6.2]
20. Reporting Professional Misconduct [based on ABA Model Rule 8.3]
21. Misconduct [based on ABA Model Rule 8.4 (and Comment)]
22. Witness Fees [based on ABA Code DR7-109(c), EC7-28]
23. Conflict of Interest [based on ABA Model Rule 1.6]

MPRC 1: Role of the Attorney

Preamble: A Lawyer's Responsibilities

A lawyer is a representative of clients, an officer of the legal system and a public citizen having special responsibility for the quality of justice.

As a representative of clients, a lawyer performs various functions. As adviser, a lawyer provides a client with an informed understanding of the client's legal rights and obligations and explains their practical implications. As advocate, a lawyer zealously asserts the client's position under the rules of the adversary system. As negotiator, a lawyer seeks a result advantageous to the client but consistent with requirements of honest dealing with others. As intermediary between clients a lawyer seeks to reconcile their divergent interests, acting as an adviser and, to a limited extent, as a spokesman for each client. A lawyer acts as evaluator by examining a client's legal affairs and reporting about them to the client or to others.

In all professional functions a lawyer should be competent, prompt and diligent. A lawyer should maintain communication with a client concerning the representation. A lawyer should keep in confidence information relating to representation of a client except so far as disclosure is required or permitted by the Professional Responsibility Code.

---

*The MPRC and Advisory Committee Comments are fictitious, but have been compiled from excerpts from the ABA Model Rules, the ABA Code, and the ABA Criminal Justice Standards.

A lawyer's conduct should conform to the requirements of the law, both in professional service to clients and in the lawyer's business and personal affairs. A lawyer should use the law's procedures only for legitimate purposes and not to harass or intimidate others. A lawyer should demonstrate respect for the legal system and for those who serve it, including judges, other lawyers and public officials. While it is a lawyer's duty, when necessary, to challenge the rectitude of official action, it is also a lawyer's duty to uphold legal process.

As a public citizen, a lawyer should seek improvement of the law, the administration of justice and the quality of service rendered by the legal profession. As a member of a learned profession, a lawyer should cultivate knowledge of the law beyond its use for clients, employ that knowledge in reform of the law and work to strengthen legal education. A lawyer should be mindful of deficiencies in the administration of justice and the fact that the poor, and sometimes persons who are not poor, cannot afford adequate legal assistance, and should therefore devote professional time and civic influence in their behalf. A lawyer should aid the legal profession in pursuing these objectives and should help the bar regulate itself in the public interest.

Many of a lawyer's professional responsibilities are prescribed in the Professional Responsibility Code, as well as in substantive and procedural law. However, a lawyer is also guided by personal conscience and the approbation of professional peers. A lawyer should strive to attain the highest level of skill, to improve the law and the legal profession and to exemplify the legal profession's ideals of public service.

A lawyer's responsibilities as a representative of clients, an officer of the legal system and a public citizen are usually harmonious. Thus, when an opposing party is well represented, a lawyer can be a zealous advocate on behalf of a client and at the same time assume that justice is being done. So also, a lawyer can be sure that preserving client confidences ordinarily serves the public interest because people are more likely to seek legal advice, and thereby heed their legal obligations, when they know their communication will be private.

In the nature of law practice, however, conflicting responsibilities are encountered. Virtually all difficult ethical problems arise from conflict between a lawyer's responsibilities to clients, to the legal system and to the lawyer's own interest in remaining an upright person while earning a satisfactory living. The Code prescribes terms for resolving such conflicts. Within the framework of this Code many difficult issues of professional discretion can arise. Such issues must be resolved through the exercise of sensitive professional and moral judgment guided by the basic principles underlying the Code.

The legal profession is largely self-governing. Although other professions also have been granted powers of self-government, the legal profession is unique in this respect because of the close relationship between the profession and the processes of government and law enforcement. This connection is manifested in the fact that ultimate authority over the legal profession is vested largely in the courts.

To the extent that lawyers meet the obligations of their professional calling, the occasion for government regulation is obviated. Self-regulation also helps maintain the legal profession's independence from government domination. An independent legal profession is an important force in preserving government under law, for abuse of legal authority is more readily challenged by a profession whose members are not dependent on government for the right to practice.

The legal profession's relative autonomy carries with it special responsibilities of self-government. The profession has a responsibility to assure that its regulations are conceived in the public interest and not in furtherance of parochial or self-interested concerns of the bar. Every lawyer is responsible for observance of the Professional Responsibility Code. A lawyer should also aid in securing its observance by other lawyers. Neglect of these responsibilities compromises the independence of the profession and the public interest which it serves.

Lawyers play a vital role in the preservation of society. The fulfillment of this role requires an understanding by lawyers of their relationship to our legal system. The Professional Responsibility Code, when properly applied, serves to define that relationship.

MPRC 2: Terminology

"Belief" or "Believes" denotes that the person involved naturally supposed the fact in question to be true. A person's belief may be inferred from circumstances.

"Consult" or "Consultation" denotes communication of information reasonably sufficient to permit the client to appreciate the significance of the matter in question.

"Firm" or "Law firm" denotes a lawyer or lawyers in a private firm, lawyers employed in the legal department of a corporation or other organization and lawyers employed in a legal services organization.

"Fraud" or "Fraudulent" denotes conduct having a

purpose to deceive and not merely negligent misrepresentation or failure to apprise another of relevant information.

"Knowingly," "Known," or "Knows" denotes actual knowledge of the fact in question. A person's knowledge may be inferred from circumstances.

"Partner" denotes a member of a partnership and a shareholder in a law firm organized as a professional corporation.

"Reasonable" or "Reasonably" when used in relation to conduct by a lawyer denotes the conduct of a reasonably prudent and competent lawyer.

"Reasonable belief" or "Reasonably believes" when used in reference to a lawyer denotes that the lawyer believes the matter in question and that the circumstances are such that the belief is reasonable.

"Reasonably should know" when used in reference to a lawyer denotes that a lawyer of reasonable prudence and competence would ascertain the matter in question.

"Substantial" when used in reference to degree or extent denotes a material matter of clear and weighty importance.

MPRC 3: Competence and Diligence

A. Competence

A lawyer shall provide competent representation to a client. Competent representation requires the legal knowledge, skill thoroughness and preparation reasonably necessary for the representation.

B. Diligence

A lawyer shall act with reasonable diligence and promptness in representing a client.

Advisory Committee Comment

ACC 3-1 A lawyer should pursue a matter on behalf of a client despite opposition, obstruction or personal inconvenience to the lawyer, and may take whatever lawful and ethical measures are required to vindicate a client's cause or endeavor. A lawyer should act with commitment and dedication to the interests of the client and with zeal in advocacy upon the client's behalf. However, a lawyer is not bound to press for every advantage that might be realized for a client. A lawyer has professional discretion in determining the means by which a matter should be pursued. A lawyer's workload should be controlled so that each matter can be handled adequately.

MPRC 4: Zeal and Duty to the Client

A lawyer shall not intentionally fail to seek the lawful objectives of his client through reasonably available means permitted by law. A lawyer does not violate this Code, however, by acceding to reasonable requests of opposing counsel which do not prejudice the rights of his client by being punctual in fulfilling all professional commitments, by avoiding offensive tactics, or by treating with courtesy and consideration all persons involved in the legal process.

Advisory Committee Comment

ACC 4-1 The duty of a lawyer, both to his client and to the legal system, is to represent his client zealously within the bounds of the law, which includes this Code. The professional responsibility of a lawyer derives from his membership in a profession which has the duty of assisting members of the public to secure and protect available legal rights and benefits. In our government of laws and not of men, each member of our society is entitled to have his conduct judged and regulated in accordance with the law; to seek any lawful objective through legally permissible means; and to present for adjudication any lawful claim, issue, or defense.

ACC 4-2 The advocate has a duty to use legal procedure for the fullest benefit of the client's cause, but also a duty not to abuse legal procedure. The law, both procedural and substantive, establishes the limits within which an advocate may proceed. However, the law is not always clear and never is static. Accordingly, in determining the proper scope of advocacy, account must be taken of the law's ambiguities and potential for change.

The bounds of the law in a given case are often difficult to ascertain. The language of legislative enactments and judicial opinions may be uncertain as applied to varying factual situations. The limits and specific meaning of apparently relevant law may be made doubtful by changing or developing constitutional interpretations, inadequately expressed statutes or judicial opinions, and changing public and judicial attitudes. Certainty of law ranges from well-settled rules through areas of conflicting authority to areas without precedent.

MPRC 5: Duty of Confidentiality

A. A lawyer shall not reveal information relating to representation of a client unless the client consents after consultation, except for disclosures that are impliedly authorized in order to carry out the representation, and except as stated in paragraph (B).

B. A lawyer may reveal such information to the extent the lawyer reasonably believes necessary:

1. To prevent the client from committing a criminal act that the lawyer believes is likely to result in imminent death or substantial bodily harm; or

2. To establish a claim or defense on behalf of the lawyer in a controversy between the lawyer and the client, to establish a defense to a criminal charge or civil claim against the lawyer based upon conduct in which the client was involved, or to respond to allegations in any proceeding concerning the lawyer's representation of the client.

MPRC 6: Meritorious Claims and Contentions

A lawyer shall not bring or defend a proceeding, or assert or controvert an issue therein, unless there is a basis for doing so that is not frivolous, and which includes a good faith argument for an extension, modification or reversal of existing law. A lawyer for the defendant in a criminal proceeding, or the respondent in a proceeding that could result in incarceration, may nevertheless so defend the proceeding as to require that every element of the case be established.

Advisory Committee Comment

ACC 6-1 The filing of an action or defense or similar action taken for a client is not frivolous merely because the facts have not first been fully substantiated or because the lawyer expects to develop vital evidence only by discovery. Such action is not frivolous even though the lawyer believes that the client's position ultimately will not prevail. The action is frivolous, however, if the client desires to have the action taken primarily for the purpose of harassing or maliciously injuring a person or if the lawyer is unable either to make a good faith argument on the merits of the action taken or to support the action taken by a good faith argument for an extension, modification or reversal of existing law.

MPRC 7: The Prosecutor: Functions, Special Duties, and the Charging Decision

A. The Function of the Prosecutor

1. The office of prosecutor is charged with responsibility for prosecutions in its jurisdiction.

2. The prosecutor is both an administrator of justice and an advocate. The prosecutor must exercise sound discretion in the performance of his or her functions.

3. The responsibility of a public prosecutor differs from that of the usual advocate; his duty is to seek justice, not merely to convict. This special duty exists because:

(a) the prosecutor represents the sovereign and therefore should use restraint in the discretionary exercise of governmental powers, such as in the selection of cases to prosecute;

(b) during trial the prosecutor is not only an advocate but he also may make decisions normally made by an individual client, and those affecting the public interest should be fair to all; and

(c) in our system of criminal justice the accused is to be given the benefit of all reasonable doubts.

B. Special Duties

The prosecutor in a criminal case shall:

1. Make reasonable efforts to assure that the accused has been advised of the right to, and the procedure for obtaining, counsel and has been given reasonable opportunity to obtain counsel;

2. Not seek to obtain from an unrepresented accused a waiver of important pretrial rights, such as the right to a preliminary hearing;

3. Recognize that, with respect to evidence and witnesses, the prosecutor has responsibilities different from those of a lawyer in private practice: the prosecutor should make timely disclosure to the defense of available evidence known to him that tends to negate the guilt of the accused, mitigate the degree of the offense, or reduce the punishment. Further, a prosecutor should not intentionally avoid pursuit of evidence merely because he believes it will damage the prosecutor's case or aid the accused; and

4. Exercise reasonable care to prevent investigators, law enforcement personnel, employees or other persons assisting or associated with the prosecutor in a criminal case from making an extra-judicial statement that the prosecutor would be prohibited from making.

C. The Charging Decision

The prosecutor in a criminal case shall refrain from prosecuting a charge that the prosecutor knows is not supported by probable cause.

Advisory Committee Comment

ACC 7-1 Discretion in the Charging Decision
(a) It is unprofessional conduct for a prosecutor to institute, or cause to be instituted, or to permit the continued dependency of criminal charges when it is known that the

charges are not supported by probable cause. A prosecutor should not institute, cause to be instituted, or permit the continued pendency of criminal charges in the absence of sufficient admissible evidence to support a conviction.

(b) The prosecutor is not obliged to present all charges which the evidence might support. The prosecutor may in some circumstances and for good cause consistent with the public interest decline to prosecute, notwithstanding that sufficient evidence may exist which would support a conviction. Illustrative of the factors which the prosecutor may properly consider in exercising his or her discretion are:

    (i) the prosecutor's reasonable doubt that the accused is in fact guilty;

    (ii) the extent of the harm caused by the offense;

    (iii) the disproportion of the authorized punishment in relation to the particular offense or the offender;

    (iv) possible improper motives of a complainant;

    (v) reluctance of the victim to testify;

    (vi) cooperation of the accused in the apprehension or conviction of others; and

    (vii) availability and likelihood of prosecution by another jurisdiction.

(c) In making the decision to prosecute, the prosecutor should give no weight to the personal or political advantages or disadvantages which might be involved or to a desire to enhance his or her record of convictions.

(d) In cases which involve a serious threat to the community, the prosecutor should not be deterred from prosecution by the fact that in the jurisdiction juries have tended to acquit persons accused of the particular kind of act in question.

(e) The prosecutor should not bring or seek charges greater in number or degree than can reasonably be supported with evidence at trial.

MPRC 8: Duty to Persons Other Than the Client

A. Truthfulness in Statements to Others

In the course of representing a client a lawyer shall not knowingly:

(1) Make a false statement of material fact or law to a third person; or

(2) Fail to disclose a material fact to a third person when disclosure is necessary to avoid assisting a criminal or fraudulent act by a client, unless disclosure is prohibited by confidentiality.

B. Respect for Rights of Third Persons

In representing a client, a lawyer shall not use means that have no substantial purpose other than to embarrass, delay or burden a third person, or use methods of obtaining evidence that violate the legal rights of such a person.

Advisory Committee Comment

ACC 8-1 Responsibility to a client requires a lawyer to subordinate the interest of others to those of the client, but that responsibility does not imply that a lawyer may disregard the rights of third persons. It is impractical to catalogue all such rights, but they include legal restrictions on methods of obtaining evidence from third persons.

MPRC 9: Trial Publicity

(a) A lawyer shall not make an extra-judicial statement that a reasonable person would expect to be disseminated by means of public communication if the lawyer knows or reasonably should know that it will have a substantial likelihood of materially prejudicing an adjudicative proceeding.

(b) A statement referred to in paragraph (a) ordinarily is likely to have such an effect when it refers to a civil matter triable to a jury, a criminal matter, or any other proceeding that could result in incarceration, and the statement relates to:

    (1) the character, credibility, reputation or criminal record of a party, suspect in a criminal investigation or witness, or the identity of a witness, or the expected testimony of a party or witness;

    (2) in a criminal case or proceeding that could result in incarceration, the possibility of a plea of guilty to the offense or the existence or content of any confession, admissions, or statement given by a defendant or suspect or that person's refusal or failure to make a statement;

    (3) the performance or result of any examination or test or the refusal or failure of a person to submit to an examination or test, or the identity or nature of physical evidence expected to be presented;

    (4) any opinion as to the guilt or innocence of a defendant or suspect in a criminal case or proceeding that could result in incarceration;

    (5) information the lawyer knows or reasonably should know is likely to be inadmissible as evidence in a trial and would if disclosed create a substantial risk of prejudicing an impartial trial; or

    (6) the fact that a defendant has been charged with a crime, unless there is included therein a statement explaining that the charge is merely an accusation and that the defendant is presumed innocent until and unless proven guilty.

(c) Notwithstanding paragraph (a) and (b)(1-6), a lawyer involved in the investigation or litigation of a matter may state without elaboration:

    (1) the general nature of the claim or defenses;

    (2) the information contained in a public record;

(3) that an investigation of the matter is in progress, including the general scope of the investigation, the offense or claim or defense involved and, except when prohibited by law, the identity of the persons involved;

(4) the scheduling or result of any step in litigation;

(5) a request for assistance in obtaining evidence and information necessary thereto;

(6) a warning of danger concerning the behavior of a person involved, when there is reason to believe that there exists the likelihood of substantial harm to an individual or to the public interest; and

(7) in a criminal case:

(i) the identity, residence, occupation and family status of the accused;

(ii) if the accused has not been apprehended, information necessary to aid in apprehension of that person;

(iii) the fact, time and place of arrest; and

(iv) the identity of investigating and arresting officers or agencies and the length of the investigation.

Advisory Committee Comment

ACC 9-1   It is difficult to strike a balance between protecting the right to a fair trial and safeguarding the right of free expression. Preserving the right to trial necessarily entails some curtailment of the information that may be disseminated about a party prior to trial, particularly where trial by jury is involved. If there were no such limits, the result would be the practical nullification of the protective effect of the rules of forensic decorum and the exclusionary rules of evidence. On the other hand, there are vital social interests served by the free dissemination of information about events having legal consequences and about legal proceedings themselves. The public has a right to know about threats to its safety and measures aimed at assuring its security. It also has a legitimate interest in the conduct of judicial proceedings, particularly in matters of general public concern. Furthermore, the subject matter of legal proceedings is often of direct significance in debate and deliberation over questions of public policy.

MPRC 10:   Fees

A.   A lawyer's fee shall be reasonable. The factors to be considered in determining the reasonableness of a fee include the following:

(1) The time and labor required, the novelty and difficulty of the questions involved, and the skill requisite to perform the legal service properly;

(2) The likelihood, if apparent to the client, that the acceptance of the particular employment will preclude other employment by the lawyer;

(3) The fee customarily charged in the locality for similar legal services;

(4) The amount involved and the results obtained;

(5) The time limitations imposed by the client or by the circumstances;

(6) The nature and length of professional relationship with the client;

(7) The experience, reputation, and availability of the lawyer or lawyers performing the services; and

(8) Whether the fee is fixed or contingent.

B.   When the lawyer has not regularly represented the client, the basis or rate of the fee shall be communicated to the client, preferably in writing, before or within a reasonable time after commencing the representation.

C.   A fee may be contingent on the outcome of the matter for which the service is rendered, except in a matter in which a contingent fee is prohibited by paragraph (D) or other law. A contingent fee agreement shall be in writing and shall state the method by which the fee is to be determined, including the percentage or percentages that shall accrue to the lawyer in the event of settlement, trial or appeal, litigation and other expenses to be deducted from the recovery, and whether such expenses are to be deducted before or after the contingent fee is calculated. Upon conclusion of a contingent fee matter, the lawyer shall provide the client with a written statement stating the outcome of the matter and, if there is a recovery, showing the remittance to the client and the method of its determination.

D.   A lawyer shall not enter into an arrangement for, charge, or collect:

(1) any fee in a domestic relations matter, the payment or amount of which is contingent upon the securing of a divorce or upon the amount of alimony or support, or property settlement in lieu thereof; or

(2) a contingent fee for representing a defendant in a criminal case.

E.   A division of fee between lawyers who are not in the same firm may be made only if:

(1) the division is in proportion to the services performed by each lawyer or, by written agreement with the client, each lawyer assumes joint responsibility for the representation;

(2) the client is advised of and does not object to the participation of all the lawyers involved; and

(3) the total fee is reasonable.

MPRC 11: Helping a Client Develop Evidence of Intent

Whether the proposed action of a lawyer is within the bounds of the law may be a perplexing question when his or her client is contemplating a course of conduct having legal consequences that vary according to the client's intent, motive, or desire at the time of the action. Often a lawyer is asked to assist his or her client in developing evidence relevant to the state of mind of the client at a particular time. He or she may properly assist his or her client in the development and preservation of evidence of existing motive, intent, or desire; obviously, he or she may not do anything furthering the creation or preservation of false evidence. In many cases a lawyer may not be certain as to the state of mind of his or her client, and in those situations he or she should resolve reasonable doubts in favor of the client.

MPRC 12: Fairness to Opposing Party and Counsel

A lawyer shall not:

A. Unlawfully obstruct another party's access to evidence or unlawfully alter, destroy or conceal a document or other material having potential evidentiary value. A lawyer shall not counsel or assist another person to do any such act;

B. Falsify evidence, counsel or assist a witness to testify falsely, or offer an inducement to a witness that is prohibited by law;

C. Knowingly disobey an obligation under the rules of a tribunal except for an open refusal based on an assertion that no valid obligation exists;

D. In pretrial procedure, make a frivolous discovery request or fail to make a reasonably diligent effort to comply with a legally proper discovery request by an opposing party;

E. In trial, allude to any matter that the lawyer does not reasonably believe is relevant or that will not be supported by admissible evidence, assert personal knowledge of facts in issue except when testifying as a witness, or state a personal opinion as to the justness of a cause, the credibility of a witness, the culpability of a civil litigant or the guilt or innocence of an accused; or

F. Request a person other than a client to refrain from voluntarily giving relevant information to another party unless:

    (1) the person is a relative or an employee or other agent of a client; and

    (2) the lawyer reasonably believes that the person's interests will not be adversely affected by refraining from giving such information.

Advisory Committee Comment

ACC 12-1 The procedure of the adversary system contemplates that the evidence in a case is to be marshalled competitively by the contending parties. Fair competition in the adversary system is secured by prohibitions against destruction or concealment of evidence, improperly influencing witnesses, obstructive tactics in discovery procedure, and the like.

Documents and other items of evidence are often essential to establish a claim or defense. Subject to evidentiary privileges, the right of an opposing party, including the government, to obtain evidence through discovery or subpoena is an important procedural right. The exercise of that right can be frustrated if relevant material is altered, concealed or destroyed. Applicable law in this jurisdiction makes it an offense to destroy material for the purpose of impairing its availability in a pending proceeding or one whose commencement can be foreseen. Falsifying evidence is also generally a criminal offense. Paragraph A (MPRC 12) applies to evidentiary material generally, including computerized information.

With regard to Paragraph B (MPRC 12), it is not improper to pay a witness's expenses or to compensate an expert witness on terms permitted by law. The common law rule in this jurisdiction is that it is improper to pay an occurrence witness any fee for testifying and that it is improper to pay an expert witness a contingent fee.

Paragraph F (MPRC 12) permits a lawyer to advise employees of a client to refrain from giving information to another party, for the employees may identify their interests with those of the client.

MPRC 13: Decisionmaking Responsibility Between Attorney and Client

A. In certain areas of legal representation not affecting the merits of the cause or substantially prejudicing the rights of a client, a lawyer is entitled to make decisions on his or her own. But otherwise the authority to make decisions is exclusively that of the client and, if made within the framework of the law, such decisions are binding on his or her lawyer. As typical examples in civil cases, it is for the client to decide whether he or she will accept a settlement offer or whether to waive his or her right to plead an affirmative defense. A defense lawyer in a criminal case has the duty to advise his or her client fully on whether a particular plea to a charge appears to be desirable, whether to waive a jury, as to the prospects of success on appeal, and whether taking the stand is advisable;

but it is for the client to decide what plea should be entered, whether to waive the right to a jury trial, whether an appeal should be taken, and whether or not to take the stand.

B. A lawyer should exert his or her best efforts to ensure that decisions of his or her client are made only after the client has been informed of relevant considerations. A lawyer ought to initiate this decision-making process if the client does not do so. Advice of a lawyer to his or her client need not be confined to purely legal considerations. A lawyer should advise his or her client of the possible effect of each legal alternative. A lawyer should bring to bear upon this decisionmaking process the fullness of his or her experience as well as an objective viewpoint. In assisting his or her client to reach a proper decision, it is often desirable for a lawyer to point out those factors which may lead to a decision that is morally just as well as legally permissible. He or she may emphasize the possibility of harsh consequences that might result from assertion of legally permissible positions. In the final analysis, however, the lawyer should always remember that the decision whether to forego legally available objectives or methods because of non-legal factors is ultimately for the client and not for himself or herself. In the event that the client in a non-adjudicatory matter insists upon a course of conduct that is contrary to the judgment and advice of the lawyer but not prohibited by this Code, the lawyer may withdraw from the employment.

C. The responsibilities of a lawyer may vary according to the intelligence, experience, mental condition or age of a client, the obligation of a public officer, or the nature of a particular proceeding. Examples include the representation of an illiterate or an incompetent, service as a public prosecutor or other government lawyer, and appearances before administrative and legislative bodies.

D. Any mental or physical condition of a client that renders the client incapable of making a considered judgment on his or her own behalf casts additional responsibilities upon his or her lawyer. Where an incompetent is acting through a guardian or other legal representative, a lawyer must look to such representative for those decisions which are normally the prerogative of the client to make. If a client under disability has no legal representative, his or her lawyer may be compelled in court proceedings to make decisions on behalf of the client. If the client is capable of understanding the matter in question or of contributing to the advancement of his or her interests, regardless of whether he or she is legally disqualified from performing certain acts, the lawyer should ob-

tain from him or her all possible aid. If the disability of a client and the lack of a legal representative compel the lawyer to make decisions for the client, the lawyer should consider all circumstances then prevailing and act with care to safeguard and advance the interests of his or her client. But obviously a lawyer cannot perform any act or make any decision which the law requires his or her client to perform or make, either acting for himself or herself if competent, or by a duly constituted representative if legally incompetent.

Advisory Committee Comment

ACC 13-1   Both lawyer and client have authority and responsibility in the objectives and means of representation. The client has ultimate authority to determine the purposes to be served by legal representation, within the limits imposed by law and the lawyer's professional obligations. Within those limits, a client also has a right to consult with the lawyer about the means to be used in pursuing those objectives. At the same time, a lawyer is not required to pursue objectives or employ means simply because a client may wish that the lawyer do so. A clear distinction between objectives and means sometimes cannot be drawn, and in many cases the client-lawyer relationship partakes of a joint undertaking. In questions of means, the lawyer should assume responsibility for technical and legal tactical issues, but should defer to the client regarding such questions as the expense to be incurred and concern for third persons who might be adversely affected. Substantive law plays a part in defining the lawyer's scope of authority in litigation.

ACC 13-2   When a client's ability to make adequately considered decisions in connection with the representation is impaired, whether because of minority, mental disability or for some other reason, the lawyer shall, as far as reasonably possible, maintain a normal client-lawyer relationship with the client.

ACC 13-3   A lawyer may seek the appointment of a guardian or take other protective action with respect to a client, only when the lawyer reasonably believes that the client cannot adequately act in the client's own interest.

ACC 13-4   The normal client-lawyer relationship is based on the assumption that the client, when properly advised and assisted, is capable of making decisions about important matters. When the client is a minor or suffers from a mental disorder or disability, however, maintaining the ordinary client-lawyer relationship may not be possible in all respects. In particular, an incapacitated person may have no power to make legally binding decisions. Nevertheless, a client lacking legal competence often has the ability to understand, deliberate upon, and reach conclusions about matters affecting the client's own well-being. Furthermore, to an increasing extent the law recognizes intermediate degrees of incompetence. For example, children as young as five or six years of age, and certainly those of ten or twelve, are regarded as having opinions that are entitled to weight in legal proceedings concerning their custody. So, also, it is recognized that some persons of advanced age can be quite capable of handling routine financial matters while needing special legal protection concerning major transactions.

The fact that a client suffers a disability does not diminish the lawyer's obligation to treat the client with attention and respect. If the person has no guardian or legal representative, the lawyer often must act as de facto guardian. Even if the person does have a legal representative, the lawyer should as far as possible accord the represented person the status of client, particularly in maintaining communication.

MPRC 14: Declining or Terminating Representation

A. Except as stated in paragraph (C), a lawyer shall not represent a client or, where representation has commenced, shall withdraw from the representation of a client if:

(1) The representation will result in violation of the rules of professional conduct or other law;

(2) The lawyer's physical or mental condition materially impairs the lawyer's ability to represent the client; or

(3) The lawyer is discharged.

B. Except as stated in paragraph (C), a lawyer may withdraw from representing a client if withdrawal can be accomplished without material adverse effect on the interests of the client, or if:

(1) The client persists in a course of action involving the lawyer's services that the lawyer reasonably believes is criminal or fraudulent;

(2) The client has used the lawyer's services to perpetrate a crime or fraud;

(3) A client insists upon pursuing an objective that the lawyer considers repugnant or imprudent;

(4) The client fails substantially to fulfill an obligation to the lawyer regarding the lawyer's services and has been given reasonable warning that the lawyer will withdraw unless the obligation is fulfilled;

(5) The representation will result in an unreasonable financial burden on the lawyer or has been rendered unreasonably difficult by the client; or

(6) Other good cause for withdrawal exists.

C. When ordered to do so by a tribunal, a lawyer shall continue representation notwithstanding good cause for terminating the representation.

D. Upon termination of representation, a lawyer shall take steps to the extent reasonably practicable to protect a client's interests, such as giving reasonable notice to the client, allowing time for employment of other counsel, surrendering papers and property to which the client is entitled and refunding any advance payment of fee that has not been earned. The lawyer may retain papers relating to the client to the extent permitted by other law.

MPRC 15: Candor Toward the Court and Third Parties

A. A lawyer shall not knowingly:

(1) Make a false statement of material fact or law to a tribunal;

(2) Fail to disclose a material fact to a tribunal when disclosure is necessary to avoid assisting a criminal or fraudulent act by the client;

(3) Fail to disclose to the tribunal legal authority in the controlling jurisdiction known to the lawyer to be directly adverse to the position of the client and not disclosed by opposing counsel; or

(4) Offer evidence that the lawyer knows to be false. If a lawyer has offered material evidence and comes to know of its falsity, the lawyer shall take reasonable remedial measures.

B. The duties stated in paragraph (A) continue to the conclusion of the proceeding, and apply even if compliance requires disclosure of information otherwise protected by lawyer-client confidentiality.

C. A lawyer may refuse to offer evidence that the lawyer reasonably believes is false.

D. In an ex parte proceeding, a lawyer shall inform the tribunal of all material facts known to the lawyer which will enable the tribunal to make an informed decision, whether or not the facts are adverse.

Advisory Committee Comment

ACC 15-1 Whether paragraph B applies to information obtained from a criminal client is a matter of state and federal Constitutional law.

MPRC 16: Interfering with an Attorney's Fact-Gathering

An attorney should not discourage or obstruct communication between prospective witnesses and opposing counsel. It is unethical conduct for an attorney to advise any person or cause any person to be advised to decline to give to the opposing party information which such person has the right to give.

MPRC 17: Attorney as Counselor

A. Scope of Representation

1. A lawyer shall not counsel a client to engage or assist a client in conduct that the lawyer knows is criminal or fraudulent, but a lawyer may discuss the legal consequences of any proposed course of conduct with a client and may counsel or assist a client to make a good faith effort to determine the validity, scope, meaning or application of the law.

2. When a lawyer knows that a client expects assistance not permitted by the rules of professional conduct or other law, the lawyer shall consult with the client regarding the relevant limitations on the lawyer's conduct.

B. Communication

1. A lawyer shall keep a client reasonably informed about the status of a matter and promptly comply with reasonable requests for information.

2. A lawyer shall explain a matter to the extent reasonably necessary to permit the client to make informed decisions regarding the representation.

C. Adviser

In representing a client, a lawyer shall exercise independent professional judgment and render candid advice. In rendering advice, a lawyer may refer not only to law but to other considerations, such as moral, economic, social and political factors, that may be relevant to the client's situation.

Advisory Committee Comment

ACC 17-1 The client should have sufficient information to participate intelligently in decisions concerning the objectives of the representation and the means by which they are to be pursued, to the extent the client is willing and able to do so. For example, a lawyer negotiating on behalf of a client should provide the client with facts relevant to the matter, inform the client of communications from another party and take other reasonable steps that permit the client to make a decision regarding a serious offer from another party. A lawyer who receives from opposing counsel an offer of settlement in a civil controversy or a proffered plea bargain in a criminal case should promptly inform the client of its substance unless prior discussions with the client have left it clear that the proposal will be unacceptable. Even when a client delegates authority to the lawyer, the client should be kept advised of the status of the matter.

Adequacy of communication depends in part on the kind of advice involved. For example, in negotiations where there is time to explain a proposal, the lawyer should review all important provisions with the client before proceeding to an agreement. In litigation a lawyer should explain the general strategy and prospects of success and ordinarily should consult with the client on tactics that might injure or coerce others. On the other hand, a lawyer ordinarily cannot be expected to describe trial or negotiation strategy in detail. The guiding principle is that the lawyer should fulfill reasonable client expectations for information consistent with the duty to act in the client's best interests, and the client's overall requirements as to the character of representation.

ACC 17-2 Where the bounds of law are uncertain, the action of a lawyer may depend on whether he or she is serving as advocate or adviser. A lawyer may serve simultaneously as both advocate and adviser, but the two roles are essentially different.

ACC 17-3 A lawyer as adviser furthers the interest of his or her client by giving his or her professional opinion as to what he or she believes would likely be the ultimate decision of the courts on the matter at hand and by informing his or her client of the practical effect of such decision. He or she may continue in the representation of his or her client even though his or her client has elected to pursue a course of conduct contrary to the advice of the lawyer so long as he or she does not thereby knowingly assist the client to engage in illegal conduct or to take a frivolous legal position. A lawyer should never encourage or aid his or her client to commit criminal acts or counsel his or her client on how to violate the law and avoid punishment therefor.

ACC 17-4 In the exercise of his or her professional judgment on those decisions which are for his or her determination in the handling of a legal matter, a lawyer should always act in a manner consistent with the best interests of his or her client. However, when an action in the best interest of the client seems to be unjust to the lawyer, he or she may ask the client for permission to forego such action.

See also MPRC 13: Decisionmaking Responsibility, supra.

MPRC 18: Attorney as Negotiator

See MPRC 8: Duty to Persons Other Than the Client, supra.

MPRC 19: Plea Bargaining and Advising a Client Regarding an Offer

A. Prosecution Availability for Plea Discussions

(1) The prosecutor should make known a general policy or willingness to consult with defense counsel concerning disposition of charges by plea.

(2) It is unprofessional conduct for a prosecutor to engage in plea·discussion directly with an accused who is represented by counsel, except with counsel's approval. Where the defendant has properly waived counsel, the prosecuting attorney may engage in plea discussions with the defendant, although ordinarily a verbatim record of such discussions should be made and preserved.

(3) It is unprofessional conduct for a prosecutor knowingly to make false statements or representations in the course of plea discussions with defense counsel or the accused.

B. Fulfillment of Plea Discussions

(1) It is unprofessional conduct for a prosecutor to make any promise or commitment concerning the sentence which will be imposed. A prosecutor may properly advise the defense what position will be taken concerning disposition.

(2) It is unprofessional conduct for a prosecutor to imply a greater power to influence the disposition of a case than is actually possessed.

(3) It is unprofessional conduct for a prosecutor to fail to comply with a plea agreement, unless a defendant fails to comply with a plea agreement or other extenuating circumstances are present.

C. Defense Duty to Explore Disposition Without Trial

(1) Whenever the nature and circumstances of the case permit, the lawyer for the accused should explore the possibility of an early diversion of the case from the criminal process through the use of other community agencies.

(2) A lawyer may engage in plea discussions with the prosecutor, although ordinarily the client's consent to engage in such discussions should be obtained in advance. Under no circumstances would a lawyer recommend to a defendant acceptance of a plea of guilty unless a full investigation and study of the case has been completed, including an analysis of controlling law and the evidence likely to be introduced at trial.

D. Defense Conduct of Discussions

(1) In conducting discussions with the prosecutor the lawyer should keep the accused advised of developments at all times and all proposals made by the prosecutor should be communicated promptly to the accused.

(2) It is unprofessional conduct for a lawyer knowingly to make false statements concerning the evidence in the course of plea discussions with the prosecutor.

See also MPRC 13: Decisionmaking Responsibility, supra; MPRC 17: Attorney as Counselor, supra, and comment; MPRC 8: Duty to Persons Other Than the Client, supra.

MPRC 20: Reporting Professional Misconduct

A. A lawyer having knowledge that another lawyer has committed a violation of the Rules of Professional Conduct that raises a substantial question as to that lawyer's honesty, trustworthiness or fitness as a lawyer in other respects, shall inform the appropriate professional authority.

B. A lawyer having knowledge that a judge has committed a violation of applicable rules of judicial conduct that raises a substantial question as to the judge's fitness for office shall inform the appropriate authority.

C. This rule does not require disclosure of information otherwise protected by MPRC 5.

Advisory Committee Comment

ACC 20-1 Self-regulation of the legal professional requires that members of the profession initiate disciplinary investigation when they know of a violation of this Code. Lawyers have a similar obligation with respect to judicial misconduct. An apparently isolated violation may indicate a pattern of misconduct that only a disciplinary investigation can uncover. Reporting a violation is especially important where the victim is unlikely to discover the offense.

A report about misconduct is not required where it would involve violation of lawyer-client confidentiality. However, a lawyer should encourage a client to consent to disclosure where prosecution would not substantially prejudice the client's interests.

If a lawyer were obliged to report every violation of the Code, the failure to report any violation would itself be a professional offense. Such a requirement existed in many jurisdictions but proved to be unenforceable. This Code limits the reporting obligation to those offenses that a self-regulating profession must vigorously endeavor to prevent. A measure of judgment is, therefore, required in complying with the provisions of this Code. The term "substantial" refers to the seriousness of the possible offense and not the quantum of evidence of which the lawyer is aware. A report should be made to the bar disciplinary agency unless some other agency, such as a peer review agency, is more appropriate in the circumstances. Similar considerations apply to the reporting of judicial misconduct.

The duty to report professional misconduct does not apply to a lawyer retained to represent a lawyer whose professional conduct is in question. Such a situation is governed by the rules applicable to the client-lawyer relationship.

MPRC 21: Misconduct

It is professional misconduct for a lawyer to:

A. Violate or attempt to violate the rules of professional conduct, knowingly assist or induce another to do so, or do so through the acts of another;

B. Commit a criminal act that reflects adversely on the lawyer's honesty, trustworthiness or fitness as a lawyer in other respects;

C. Engage in conduct involving dishonesty, fraud, deceit or misrepresentation;

D. Engage in conduct that is prejudicial to the administration of justice;

E. State or imply an ability to influence improperly a government agency or official; or

F. Knowingly assist a judge or judicial officer in conduct that is a violation of applicable rules of judicial conduct or other law.

Advisory Committee Comment

ACC 21-1 Many kinds of illegal conduct reflect adversely on fitness to practice law, such as offenses involving fraud and the offense of willful failure to file an income tax return. However, some kinds of offense carry no such implication. Traditionally, the distinction was drawn in terms of offenses involving "moral turpitude." That concept can be construed to include offenses concerning some matters of personal morality, such as adultery and comparable offenses, that have no specific connection to fitness for the practice of law. Although a lawyer is personally answerable to the entire criminal law, a lawyer should be professionally answerable only for offenses that indicate lack of those characteristics relevant to law practice. Offenses involving violence, dishonesty, or breach of trust, or serious interference with the administration of justice are in that category. A pattern of repeated offenses, even ones of minor significance when considered separately, can indicate indifference to legal obligation.

Lawyers holding public office assume legal responsibilities going beyond those of other citizens. A lawyer's abuse of public office can suggest an inability to fulfill the professional role of attorney. The same is true of abuse of positions of private trust such as trustee, executor, administrator, guardian, agent and officer, director or manager of a corporation or other organization.

MPRC 22: Witness Fees

A lawyer shall not pay, offer to pay, or acquiesce in the payment of compensation to a witness contingent upon the content of his testimony or the outcome of the case. But a lawyer may advance, guarantee, or acquiesce in the payment of:

(1) Expenses reasonably incurred by a witness in attending or testifying.

(2) Reasonable compensation to a witness for his loss of time in attending or testifying.

(3) A reasonable fee for the professional services of an expert witness.

Advisory Committee Comment

ACC 22-1 Witnesses should always testify truthfully and should be free from any financial inducements that might tempt them to do otherwise. A lawyer should not pay or agree to pay a non-expert witness an amount in excess of reimbursement for expenses and financial loss incident to his being a witness; however, a lawyer may pay or agree to pay an expert witness a reasonable fee for his services as an expert. But in no event should a lawyer pay or agree to pay a contingent fee to any witness. A lawyer should exercise reasonable diligence to see that his client and lay associates conform to these standards. See also ACC 12-1.

MPRC 23: Conflict of Interest

(a) A lawyer shall not represent a client if the representation of that client will be directly adverse to another client, unless:

(1) The lawyer reasonably believes the representation will not adversely affect the relationship with the other client; and

(2) Each client consents after consultation.

(b) A lawyer shall not represent a client if the representation of that client may be materially limited by the lawyer's responsibilities to another client or to a third person, or by the lawyer's own interests, unless:

(1) The lawyer reasonably believes the representation will not be adversely affected; and

(2) The client consents after consultation. When representation of multiple clients in a single matter is undertaken, the consultation shall include explanation of the implications of the common representation and the advantages and risks involved.

STATE OF MAJOR CRIMINAL JURY INSTRUCTIONS

Jury Instruction No. 1

Assault—Defined

Defendant is charged in [Count _____ of] the complaint, with the commission of the crime of assault.

[The crime of] [An] assault is an unlawful attempt, coupled with a present ability, to commit a wrongful act by means of physical force upon the person of another.

In order to prove the commission of the crime of assault, each of the following elements must be proved:

1. That an attempt was made to commit a wrongful act by means of physical force upon the person of another.
2. That such attempt was unlawful, and
3. That at the time of such attempt, the person who made the attempt had the present ability to commit such act.

To constitute an assault, it is not necessary that any actual injury be inflicted, but if an injury is inflicted, it may be considered in connection with other evidence in determining whether an assault was committed and, if so, the nature of the assault.

Jury Instruction No. 2

Assault in the First Degree

Defendant is charged in [Count _____ of] the complaint, with the commission of the crime of assault in the first degree.

Every person who commits an assault upon the person of another [with a deadly weapon or instrument] **[or]** [by means of force likely to produce great bodily injury] **[or]** [with a firearm] is guilty of assault in the first degree.

In order to prove the commission of such crime, each of the following elements must be proved:

1. That a person was assaulted, and
2. That the assault was committed [by the use of a deadly weapon or instrument] **[or]** [by means of force likely to produce great bodily injury] **[or]** [with a firearm].

As used in this instruction, a deadly weapon is any object, instrument, or weapon which is used in such a manner as to be capable of producing, and likely to produce, death or great bodily injury.

As used in this instruction, great bodily injury refers to significant or substantial bodily injury or damage; it does not refer to trivial or insignificant injury or moderate harm.

As used in this instruction, firearm includes a _____.

Actual bodily injury is not a necessary element of the crime. If such bodily injury is inflicted, its nature and extent are to be considered in connection with all the evidence in determining whether the means used and the manner in which it was used were such that they were likely to produce great bodily injury.

Jury Instruction No. 3

Insulting Words—Not Justification for Assault

No words of abuse, insult or reproach addressed to a person or uttered concerning him, howsoever insulting or objectionable the words may be, if unaccompanied by any threat or apparent threat of great bodily injury or any assault upon the person or any trespass against lands or goods, will justify him in an assault [with a deadly weapon] **[or]** [by any means of force likely to produce great bodily injury], and the provocation only of such words will not constitute a defense to a charge of having committed an assault.

Jury Instruction No. 4

Deliberate and Premeditated Murder

All murder which is perpetrated by any kind of willful, deliberate and premeditated killing with express malice aforethought is murder of the first degree.

The word "willful," as used in this instruction, means intentional.

The word "deliberate" means formed or arrived at or determined upon as a result of careful thought and weighing of considerations for and against the proposed course of action. The word "premeditated" means considered beforehand.

If you find that the killing was preceded and accompanied by a clear, deliberate intent on the part of the defendant to kill, which was the result of deliberation and premeditation, so that it must have been formed upon preexisting reflection and not under a sudden heat of passion or other condition precluding the idea of deliberation, it is murder of the first degree.

The law does not undertake to measure in units of time the length of the period during which the thought must be pondered before it can ripen into an intent to kill which is truly deliberate and premeditated. The time will vary with different individuals and under varying circumstances.

The true test is not the duration of time, but rather the extent of reflection. A cold, calculated judgment and decision may be arrived at in a short period of time, but a mere unconsidered and rash impulse, even though it includes an intent to kill, is not such deliberation and premeditation as will fix an unlawful killing as murder of the first degree.

To constitute a deliberate and premeditated killing, the slayer must weigh and consider the question of killing and the reasons for and against such a choice and, having in mind the consequences, he decides to and does kill.

Jury Instruction No. 5

First-Degree Felony-Murder

The unlawful killing of a human being, whether intentional, unintentional or accidental, which occurs as a result of the commission of or attempt to commit the crime of [robbery, burglary, rape, arson] and where there was in the mind of the perpetrator the specific intent to commit such crime, is murder in the first degree.

The specific intent to commit [robbery, burglary, rape, arson] and the commission or attempt to commit such crime must be proved beyond a reasonable doubt.

Jury Instruction No. 6

Unpremeditated Murder of the Second Degree

Murder of the second degree is [also] the unlawful killing of a human being with malice aforethought when there is manifested an intention unlawfully to kill a human being but the evidence is insufficient to establish deliberation and premeditation.

Jury Instruction No. 7

Second-Degree Murder—Killing Resulting from Unlawful Act Dangerous to Life

Murder of the second degree is [also] the unlawful killing of a human being as the direct causal result of an intentional act, [involving a high degree of probability that it will result in death, which act is done for a base, antisocial purpose and with wanton disregard for human life.] [or] [the natural consequences of which are dangerous to life, which act was deliberately performed by a person who knows that his conduct endangers the life of another and who acts with conscious disregard for human life.]

When the killing is the direct result of such an act, it is not necessary to establish that the defendant intended that his act would result in the death of a human being.

Jury Instruction No. 8

Second-Degree Felony-Murder

The unlawful killing of a human being, whether intentional, unintentional or accidental, which occurs as a direct causal result of the commission of or attempt to commit a felony inherently dangerous to human life, namely, the crime of [list crime other than one of those enumerated for first-degree felony-murder] and where there was in the mind of the perpetrator the specific intent to commit such crime, is murder of the second degree.

The specific intent to commit _____ and the commission of or attempt to commit such crime must be proved beyond a reasonable doubt.

Jury Instruction No. 9

Voluntary Manslaughter—Defined

Defendant is charged in [Count _____ of] the complaint with the commission of the crime of voluntary manslaughter.

The crime of voluntary manslaughter is the unlawful killing of a human being without malice aforethought when there is an intent to kill.

There is no malice aforethought if the killing occurred upon a sudden quarrel or heat of passion.

In order to prove the commission of the crime of voluntary manslaughter, each of the following elements must be proved:

1. That a human being was killed,
2. That the killing was unlawful, and
3. That the killing was done with the intent to kill.

Jury Instruction No. 10

Sudden Quarrel or Heat of Passion and Provocation Explained

To reduce an intentional felonious homicide from the offense of murder to manslaughter upon the ground of sudden quarrel or heat of passion, the provocation must be of such character and degree as naturally would excite and arouse such passion, and the assailant must act under the smart of that sudden quarrel or heat of passion.

The heat of passion which will reduce a homicide to manslaughter must be such a passion as naturally would be aroused in the mind of an ordinarily reasonable person in the same circumstances. A defendant is not permitted to set up his own standard of conduct and to justify or excuse himself because his passions were aroused unless the circumstances in which he was placed and the facts that confronted him were such as also would have aroused the passion of the ordinarily reasonable man faced with the same situation. The question to be answered is whether or not, at the time of the killing, the reason of the accused was obscured or disturbed by passion to such an extent as would cause the ordinarily reasonable person of average disposition to act rashly and without deliberation and reflection, and from such passion rather than from judgment.

If there was provocation, but of a nature not normally sufficient to arouse passion, or if sufficient time elapsed between provocation and the fatal blow for passion to subside and reason to return, and if an unlawful killing of a human being followed such provocation and had all the elements of murder, as it has been defined in these instructions, the mere fact of slight or remote provocation will not reduce the offense to manslaughter.

Jury Instruction No. 11

Involuntary Manslaughter—Defined

Defendant is charged in [Count _____ of] the Complaint, with the commission of the crime of involuntary manslaughter.

Involuntary manslaughter is the unlawful killing of a human being without malice aforethought and without an intent to kill.

In order to prove the commission of the crime of involuntary manslaughter, each of the following elements must be proved:

1. That a human being was killed, and
2. That the killing was unlawful.

A killing is unlawful within the meaning of this instruction if it occurred:

1. During the commission of a misdemeanor which is inherently dangerous to human life, namely, the offense(s) of _____; or
2. In the commission of an act ordinarily lawful which involves a high degree of risk of death or great bodily harm, without due caution and circumspection.

Jury Instruction No. 12

Homicide—Proximate Cause—Definition

To constitute [murder] **[or]** [manslaughter] **[or]** [negligent homicide], there must be a causal connection between the death of a human being and the criminal conduct of a defendant so that the act [done] **[or]** [omitted] was a proximate cause of the resulting death.

The term "proximate cause" means a cause which, in a direct sequence, unbroken by any new independent cause, produces the death, and without which the death would not have happened.

There may be more than one proximate cause of a death.

Jury Instruction No. 13

Homicide—Effect of Improper Treatment

Where the original injury is a proximate cause of the death, the fact that the immediate cause of death was the medical or surgical treatment administered or that such treatment was a factor contributing to the cause of death will not relieve the person who inflicted the original injury from responsibility.

Where, however, the original injury is not a proximate cause of the death and the death was proximately caused by such medical or surgical treatment or some other cause, then the defendant is not guilty of an unlawful homicide.

Jury Instruction No. 14

Burden of Proof—Presumption of Innocence—Reasonable Doubt

The defendant has entered a plea of not guilty. That plea puts in issue every element of the crime charged. The state is the plaintiff and has the burden of proving each element of the crime beyond a reasonable doubt.

A defendant is presumed innocent. This presumption continues throughout the entire trial unless you find it has been overcome by the evidence beyond a reasonable doubt.

A reasonable doubt is one for which a reason exists and may arise from the evidence or lack of evidence. It is such a doubt as would exist in the mind of a reasonable person after fully, fairly and carefully considering all of the evidence or lack of evidence. If, after such consideration, you have an abiding belief in the truth of the charge, you are satisfied beyond a reasonable doubt.

Jury Instruction No. 15

Self-Defense Against Assault

It is lawful for a person who is being assaulted to defend himself from attack if, as a reasonable person, he has grounds for believing and does believe that bodily injury is about to be inflicted upon him. In doing so he may use all force and means which he believes to be reasonably necessary and which would appear to a reasonable person, in the same or similar circumstances, to be necessary to prevent the injury which appears to be imminent.

Jury Instruction No. 16

Justifiable Homicide—Defense of Self and Others

It is a defense to a charge of [murder] [or] [manslaughter] that the homicide was justifiable as defined in this instruction.

Homicide is justifiable when committed in the lawful defense of [the slayer] [the slayer's [husband] [wife] [parent] [child] [brother] [sister]] [any person in the slayer's presence or company] when the slayer reasonably believes that the person slain intends to inflict death or great bodily harm and there is imminent danger of such harm being accomplished.

The slayer may employ such force and means as a reasonably prudent person would use under the same or similar conditions as they appeared to the slayer at the time.

Jury Instruction No. 17

Self-Defense by an Aggressor

The right of self-defense is not immediately available to a person who was originally an assailant, but such person must really and in good faith endeavor to decline further combat and fairly and clearly inform his adversary of his desire for peace and that he has abandoned the contest. After such steps have been taken, if his opponent continues the fight, the rights of the person who was the original assailant, with respect to self-defense, are then the same as the rights of any person assailed by another.

Jury Instruction No. 18

Self-Defense—Actual Danger Not Necessary

Actual danger is not necessary to justify self-defense. If one is confronted by the appearance of danger which arouses in his mind, as a reasonable person, an honest conviction and fear that he is about to suffer bodily injury, and if a reasonable person in a like situation, seeing and knowing the same facts, would be justified in believing himself in like danger, and if the person so confronted acts in self-defense upon such appearances and from such fear and honest conviction, his right of self-defense is the same whether such danger is real or merely apparent.

Jury Instruction No. 19

Insanity at Time of Offense—Definition

In addition to the plea of not guilty, the defendant has entered a plea of insanity existing at the time of the act charged.

Insanity existing at the time of the commission of the act charged is a defense.

For a defendant to be found not guilty by reason of insanity you must find that, as a result of mental disease or defect, the defendant's mind was affected to such an extent that the defendant was unable to perceive the nature and quality of the acts with which the defendant is charged or was unable to tell right from wrong with reference to the particular acts with which defendant is charged.

Jury Instruction No. 20

Duress—Defense

Duress is a defense to a criminal charge if the defendant participated in the crime under compulsion by threat or use of force which created an apprehension in the mind of the defendant that in case of refusal [the defendant] **[or]** [another person] would be liable to immediate death or immediate grievous bodily harm; and if such apprehension by the defendant was reasonable and if the defendant would not have participated in the crime except for the duress involved.

The defense of duress is not available if the defendant intentionally or recklessly placed himself or herself in a situation in which it was probable that he or she would be subject to duress.

Jury Instruction No. 21

Intoxication—Defense

No act committed by a person while in a state of voluntary intoxication is less criminal by reason of that condition, but whenever the actual existence of any particular mental state is a necessary element to constitute a particular kind or degree of crime, the fact of intoxication may be taken into consideration in determining such mental state.

Jury Instruction No. 22

Voluntary Intoxication—When Relevant to Specific Intent

In the crime of _____ of which the defendant is accused [in Count _____ of the complaint], a necessary element is the existence in the mind of the defendant of the [specific intent to _____] **[or]** [mental state of _____].

If the evidence shows that the defendant was intoxicated at the time of the alleged offense, the jury should consider his state of intoxication in determining if defendant had such [specific intent] **[or]** [mental state].

If from all the evidence you have a reasonable doubt whether defendant formed such [specific intent] **[or]** [mental state], you must give the defendant the benefit of that doubt and find that he did not have such [specific intent] **[or]** [mental state].

Jury Instruction No. 23

Involuntary Intoxication—Consideration

Intoxication is involuntary when it is produced in a person without his willing and knowing use of intoxicating liquor, drugs or other substance and without his willing assumption of the risk of possible intoxication.

Proof of the involuntary intoxication of a defendant should be considered in determining whether the defendant had the necessary [criminal intent] **[or]** [mental state] at the time the crime is alleged to have been committed.

STATE OF MAJOR CIVIL JURY INSTRUCTIONS

Jury Instruction No. 1

Negligence

Negligence is the failure to exercise ordinary care. It is the doing of some act which a reasonably careful person would not do under the same or similar circumstances or the failure to do something which a reasonably careful person would have done under the same or similar circumstances.

Jury Instruction No. 2

Negligence Per Se

The violation, if you find any, of a statute or a regulation is negligence as a matter of law. Such negligence has the same effect as any other act of negligence.

The violation of a regulation is actionable negligence only if its violation was a proximate cause of the injury in question.

Jury Instruction No. 3

Duty of Tavern Owner

The keeper of an establishment where intoxicating liquors are dispensed, while not an insurer of the safety of his patrons, owes the duty to his patrons to exercise reasonable care and vigilance to protect them from reasonably foreseeable injury, mistreatment or annoyance at the hands of other patrons.

If you find from the evidence that the defendant, his agents and/or employees knew or should have known the possibility of injury, mistreatment or annoyance by other guests, then it was his duty to exercise reasonable care, vigilance and prudence to protect his patrons from injury from the acts of the defendant.

Jury Instruction No. 4

Emotional Distress

A person who through intentional or reckless action causes severe emotional distress to another is liable if his or her actions are outrageous. The duty is owed:

(a) Only to the direct victim of the outrageous conduct, or a person who has a close relationship with the victim,
(b) Was present at the time of the conduct, and
(c) Was foreseeably endangered by the conduct.

The emotional suffering, to be compensable, must be manifested by objective symptoms. It is not necessary that there be any physical impact or the threat of an immediate physical invasion of the plaintiff's personal security.

Finally, the plaintiff's mental distress must be the reaction of a normally constituted reasonable person.

Jury Instruction No. 5

Intoxication

A person who becomes intoxicated voluntarily is held to the same standard of care as one who is not so affected. Whether a person is intoxicated at the time of an occurrence may be considered by the jury, together with all the other facts and circumstances, in determining whether that person was negligent.

Jury Instruction No. 6

Affirmative Defense

The defendant has the burden of proving the following affirmative defenses claimed by the defendant:

A. Contributory Negligence

Contributory negligence is negligence on the part of a person claiming injury or damage which is a proximate cause of the injury or damage complained of.

If you find contributory negligence, you must determine the degree of such negligence, expressed as a percentage, attributable to the person claiming such injury or damage. The court will reduce the amount of any damages you find to have been sustained by a party who was contributorily negligent by the percentage of such contributory negligence.

B. Self-Defense

You may find that the defendant acted as a reasonably prudent person under the circumstances that existed when the deceased was killed and reasonably believed that killing the decedent was necessary to protect the defendant's own life or to ward off great bodily harm; if so, the defendant's act was excusable and justifiable so as to bar recovery for the plaintiffs. The defendant may employ such force and means as a reasonably prudent person would use under the same or similar conditions as they appeared to the defendant at the time.

If you find from your consideration of all the evidence that this affirmative defense has been proved, your verdict should be for the defendant.

Jury Instruction No. 7

Principal and Agency

The defendants are sued as principal and agent. The defendant _____

_____ is the principal and the defendants _____
are the agents.

A.   An agent is a person employed under an express or implied agreement to perform services for another called the principal, and who is subject to the principal's control or right to control the manner and means or performing the services. The agency agreement may be oral or in writing.

B.   One of the questions for you to determine is whether the agents were acting within the scope of authority.

An agent is acting within the scope of authority if the agent is engaged in the performance of duties which were expressly or impliedly assigned to the agent by the principal or which were expressly or impliedly required by the contract of employment. Likewise, an agent is acting within the scope of authority if the agent is engaged in the furtherance of the principal's interests.

If you find the defendant agents are liable, then you must find that the principal is also liable. However, if you do not find that the agents are liable, then the principal is not liable.

Jury Instruction No. 8

Burden of Proof

The plaintiffs have the burden of proving each of the following propositions:

First, that the defendants acted, or failed to act, in one of the ways claimed by the plaintiffs and that in so acting or failing to act, the defendants were negligent;

Second, that the plaintiffs were injured;

Third, that the negligence of the defendants was a proximate cause of the injury to the plaintiffs;

Fourth, the amount of money which will compensate the plaintiffs.

The defendants have the burden of proving both of the following propositions:

First, that the plaintiffs acted, or failed to act, in one of the ways claimed by the defendants, and that in so acting or failing to act, the plaintiffs were negligent;

Second, that the negligence of the plaintiffs was a proximate cause of the plaintiffs' own injuries and was therefore contributory negligence.

When a party has the burden of proof on any proposition, the proposition must be proved by a "preponderance" of the evidence, or if the expression "if you find" is used, it means that you must be persuaded, considering all the evidence in the case bearing on the question, that the proposition on which that party has the burden of proof is more probably true than not true.

Jury Instruction No. 9

Proximate Cause

The term "proximate cause" means a cause, which in a direct sequence, unbroken by any new independent cause, produces the injury complained of and without such, injury would not have happened.

There may be one or more proximate causes of an injury.

Jury Instruction No. 10

Independent Intervening Cause

If you find that a person was negligent but that the sole proximate cause of the alleged injury was a later independent intervening cause that a person, in the exercise of ordinary care, could not reasonably have anticipated as likely to happen, the person's original negligence is superseded by the intervening cause and is not a proximate cause of the alleged injury.

If in the exercise of ordinary care, however, a person should reasonably have anticipated the intervening cause, that independent intervening cause does not supersede the person's original negligence and that original negligence can still be considered a proximate cause of the alleged injury.

It is not necessary that the sequence of events or the particular resultant injury be foreseeable. It is only necessary that the resultant injury fall within the general field of danger which a person should reasonably have anticipated.

Jury Instruction No. 11

Expert Opinion

A witness who has special training, education or experience in a particular science, profession or calling may be allowed to express an opinion in addition to giving testimony as to facts. You are not bound, however, by such an opinion. In determining the credibility and weight to be given such opinion evidence, you may consider, among other things, the education, training, experience, knowledge and ability of that witness, the reasons given for the opinion, the sources of the witness's information, together with the factors already given you for evaluating the testimony of any other witnesses.

Jury Instruction No. 12

Damages - For Wrongful Death

The State of Major permits an award of damages for a survival action, and for an alleged wrongful death.

The following factors should be considered to measure damages in a survival action:

1. The reasonable value of the deceased's lost earnings.
2. Medical and hospital expenses which were reasonably and necessarily incurred by the deceased's estate because of his injuries.
3. Any pain and suffering that the deceased experienced before his death. There are no fixed standards by which to measure pain or suffering. Rather, you must be governed by your judgment, the evidence in the case, and these instructions.

The following factors should be considered to measure damages for wrongful death.

1. Pecuniary loss. In determining "pecuniary loss" you should consider what benefits of pecuniary value, including money, goods and services the

decedent would have contributed to the widow and children had the decedent lived.

2. What decedent could reasonably have been expected to contribute to the survivor in the way of support, love, affection, care, services, companionship, society and consortium.

3. What the decedent could reasonably have been expected to contribute to his children in the way of support, love, care, guidance, training, instruction and protection.

4. What the decedent could reasonably have been expected to contribute to his dependent mother and father in the way of support, love, care, guidance, training, instruction and protection.

5. Medical, hospital, and funeral expenses which were reasonably and necessarily incurred by the deceased's estate because of his injuries and death (if not claimed in a survival action).

In determining damages you should consider: the decedent's age, health, life expectancy, occupation and habits of industry, sobriety and thrift.

(a) According to mortality tables, the average expectancy of life of a male aged 30 years is 71.25 years. This one factor is not controlling, but should be considered in connection with all the other evidence bearing on the same question, such as that pertaining to the health, habits and activity of the person whose life expectancy is in question.

You should also consider the decedent's earning capacity, and in this connection you should consider the actual earnings prior to death, and what earnings might reasonably have been expected in the future, together with the amount which you find the decedent customarily contributed to his spouse and children, and what contribution might reasonably have been expected in the future.

(b) The burden of proving damages rests upon the plaintiffs and you must determine whether pecuniary loss has been proved by a preponderance of the evidence. You should not base damages upon speculation, guess, conjecture, grief or sorrow of or for the survivors.

GLOSSARY FOR MEDICAL SUMMARY AND CLINIC REPORTS

A

A—assessment.

Antecubital fossa—the longitudinal depression in front of the elbow.

Anterior—situated at or directed toward the front; opposite of posterior.

Anterolateral—situated before and to one side.

Anteromedial—situated in front and on median line.

Apices—plural of apex, the top of a conical part.

Aspect—that part of a surface viewed from a particular direction.

Atelectasis—see *Consolidation*.

Atherosclerosis—a condition characterized by the degeneration and hardening of the walls of the arteries and sometimes the valves of the heart.

Axillary—pertaining to the axilla, or armpit.

B

Basal—situated near a base.

"Blanches with pressure"—color disappears when that area of the body is touched.

Bleb—a bulla or skin vesicle filled with fluid.

B/P—blood pressure.

Bruit—abnormal sound or murmur.

Bullous emphysema—air-filled blisters on the surface of the lungs with air present in the connective tissue.

C

Calvaria—domelike skull cap of the cranium.

Carotid—principal artery of the neck.

Cartilaginous—consisting of cartilage.

Catheter—see *Intravenous catheters*.

Cephalothin—semisynthetic antibiotic administered intravenously or intramuscularly.

Cervical radiculopathy—there are three levels of whiplash injury. Minor whiplash is Cervical Muscular Discomfort; intermediate level: Cervical Radiculopathy; major whiplash injury: Cervical Sponylosis with nerve root or spinal cord compression. Modern treatment consists of two tablets of Parafon Forte by mouth four times a day, and 600 mg Motrin by mouth every four hours.

Chest tube—tube inserted into pulmonary, pleural to reexpand a collapsed lung.

C/O—complains of.

Conjunctivae—delicate mucous membrane lining the eyelids and covering the eyeballs.

Consolidation—solidification.

Consolidation and atelectasis—solidification into a firm thick mass marked with an absence of gas from the lungs due to a failure of resorption of gas in the lungs alveoli (air sacs).

Cornea—the clear, transparent anterior covering of the eye.

Cortex—the outer layer of an organ or part.

Costochondral—pertaining to a rib and its cartilage.

Costophrenic recess—the indentation where rib and diaphragm meet.

Cutaneous—pertaining to the skin.

D

Dependent Personality Disorder—a psychiatric term used to describe people who are unable to make everyday decisions on their own. Dominant behavioral characteristics are dependency and submissiveness. Feelings of helplessness, low self-confidence, and fear of abandonment are common. This disorder is diagnosed more frequently in females than males.

Dermal—pertaining to the skin.

Diazepam—useful in the symptomatic relief of tension and anxiety states resulting from stressful circumstances or whenever somatic complaints are concomitant with emotional factors. Useful in psycho-neurotic states manifested by tension, anxiety, apprehension, fatigue, depressive symptoms of agitation. Also marketed under the tradename Valium.

Dorsal—pertaining to the back.

Duodenum—the first division of the small intestine, about ten inches long, plays an important role in digestion of food.

Dura—the fibrous membrane forming the outer envelope of the brain and spinal cord.

E

EKG (electrocardiogram) pads—sensor pads attached to the body and used to monitor the heartbeat.

Emphysema—see *Bullous emphysema*.

Endocardium—the membrane lining the chambers of the heart and covering the cusps of the various valves.

Endocrine—applies to organs whose function is to secrete into the blood or lymph a substance that has a specific effect on another organ or part.

Endotracheal tube—hose-like device inserted into the air passage (wind pipe) extending from the larynx to the lungs.

Epidural—external to the dura.

Etiology—the science dealing with the causes of disease.

Extensor—a muscle which tends to straighten a limb when contracted.

Exudate was . . . legionella—fluid which escapes from immune system as antibodies sent to combat legionella (a genus of bacteria).

F

Fibrous adhesions—connective tissue that develops when an injured area begins to heal.

Fibrous replacement—localized overgrowth of fibrous tissue.

Flurazepam Hydrochloride—hypnotic agent useful in all types of insomnia characterized by difficulty in falling asleep, frequent nocturnal awakenings, and/or early morning awakenings. Can be used effectively in patients with recurring insomnia or poor sleeping habits, and in acute medical situations requiring restful sleep.

Possible Adverse Reactions—Dizziness, drowsiness, lightheadedness, staggering, and falling have occurred in elderly or debilitated persons. Severe sedation, lethargy, disorientation, and coma probably indicative of drug intolerance or overdosage have been reported.

Frontal—pertaining to the forehead.

FU—follow up.

G

Gentamicin—antibiotic used in treating infections of the central nervous system, GI tract, urinary tract, respiratory tract, bone, skin, and soft tissue.

GI tract—gastrointestinal system.

Gyri (plural of gyrus)—the prominent rounded elevations that form the cerebral hemisphere.

H

Hematocrit—the percentage of the volume of a blood sample occupied by erythrocytes.

Hematology specimen—blood sample.

Hemoglobin—the oxygen-carrying primary protein pigment of the blood.

Hemoperitoneum—effused blood in the peritoneal cavity.

Hemorrhage—bleeding, the escape of blood from a ruptured vessel.

Hemostasis—the arrest of the escape of blood by either natural (clot formation) or artificial (compression) means.

Hemothorax—a collection of blood in the pleural (chest) cavity.

Hepatobiliary—liver and bile systems.

Herniation—an abnormal protrusion of an organ or other body structure through a defect or natural opening.

Hypertrophic mottled hypo- and hyperpigmented scar—overgrown scar tissue with some areas that are white and some that are deeply colored.

I

Inferior—situated below or directed downward; reference to the lower surface of an organ or other structure.

Intercostal—situated between the ribs.

Interior—situated inside.

Intravenous catheters—tubes used in administering drugs/solutions directed into the veins.

Involute—to regress; to change to an earlier or more primitive condition.

Irides (plural of Iris)—iris, the colored membrane behind the eye's cornea.

L

Leptomeninges (plural of leptomeninx)—the two most delicate membranes beneath the dura enveloping the brain and spinal cord.

Lesion—any wound or damage to a tissue.

Lividity—the quality of being livid, discolored, black and blue.

Lymphatic—a vessel conveying lymph; one of the system of absorbent vessels that drain the lymph from various body tissues and return it to the blood stream.

Lymphoreticular system—net of lymphatic tissue.

M

Malleolus—a rounded bone process on either side of the ankle joint.

Massae (plural of massa)—lumps.

Medial—pertaining to the middle.

Mediastinum—a median septum or partition between two parts of an organ or cavity.

Mononeuritis—lesions without inflammation but degenerative in nerve roots or peripheral nerves. May be caused by: mechanical stress, vascular disorder, microorganisms, toxic agents, metabolic disorder, malignancy. Treatment: Mild cases may recover without treatment; more severe cases need physical therapy and splints. Some cases require surgery, including neurolysis or transplant.

Motrin—a nonsteroidal anti-inflammatory analgesic that reduces joint swelling, pain, and duration of morning stiffness. It is available in 300, 400, and 600 mg tablets for oral administration.

Mucosa—mucus membrane.

Myocardium—the muscular middle layer of the heart.

N

Nafcillin—semisynthetic antibiotic used in treating bacterial infections.

Nares (plural of Naris)—nostril openings.

O

O—objective diagnosis.

Oro-tracheal tube—a breathing tube inserted into the mouth and down into the trachea.

Ovoid—egg-shaped.

P

P—prescription or plan.

Palpable—perceptible by touch.

Parafon Forte—provides symptomatic relief of pain, stiffness, and limitation of motion associated with most musculo-skeletal disorders through relaxation of muscle spasm by chlorzoxazone, an effective and well-tolerated centrally acting agent. Analgesia by acetaminophen, a nonsalicylate analgesic, is useful in skeletal muscle pain.

Parenchyma—the essential or functional elements or specific cells of an organ, as distinguished from its framework.

Pelves—plural of pelvis; basin-shaped ring of bone at the posterior extremity of the trunk, supporting the spinal column and resting upon the lower extremities.

Pericardium—the fibrous membrane enclosing the heart.

Peritoneal cavity—the space between the two tissue layers of the peritoneum (abdominal cavity).

Petechial—characterized by purplish red spots, indicates hemorrhaging.

Pleura—membrane enclosing the lungs.

Pneumonia—inflammation of the lung due to infection.

Posterior—pertaining to the back.

Post-traumatic Stress Disorder—psychiatric term for describing characteristic symptoms that develop following a psychologically distressing event that is outside the range of usual human experience. Examples of this type of event are natural disasters, military combat, witnessing another person being seriously injured or killed by accident or physical violence. Symptoms include avoidance of situations, thoughts, or activities associated with the event; feeling detached from others; difficulty sleeping; recurrent nightmares; depression. Symptoms must persist longer than one month to be diagnosed under this disorder. The disorder is more severe when the stress-inducing event was of human design.

Pt—patient.

R

Renal—pertaining to the kidney.

Respiratory Distress Syndrome—filling of the gas exchanging units of the lung with protein-rich fluid. This leads to severe reduction in oxygenation of blood passing through the lung.

S

S—subjective diagnosis.

Serosanguineous drainage—systematic withdrawal of a fluid compound of serum and blood from a wound, sore, or cavity.

Staphylococcal—a genus of an infectious bacteria.

Striae—streaks or lines.

Subcostal region—area below a rib or ribs.

Subcrepitant—characterized by faint crackling or rattling sounds.

Subdural—beneath the dura.

Superior—situated or directed above.

Sutures—stitches.

T

Thoracic—pertaining to the chest.

Thymus—a ductless gland-like body situated in the anterior mediastinal cavity which reaches its maximum development during the early years of child-hood.

TID—three times daily (dosage rate).

Trachea—the air passage extending from the throat to the lungs.

Tympanic membranes—a thin, oval membrane that stretches across the ear canal separating the middle ear from the outer ear.

U

Ureter—fibromuscular tube that conveys the urine from the kidneys to the bladder.

V

Valium—see *Parafon Forte*.

W

Whiplash—see *Cervical radiculopathy*.

CRIMINAL RESEARCH MEMORANDA

Research Memorandum #65: Bail

Strack v. Burns, 143 Maj. App. 2d 401 (1958): "The traditional right to freedom before convictions both permits an unhampered preparation of a defense and serves to prevent the infliction of punishment prior to conviction. Without this right to bail, the presumption of innocence would lose its meaning. . . . The right to release before trial is conditioned upon the accused giving adequate assurance that he will stand trial and submit to sentence if found guilty. The purpose of bail is to provide this assurance. Bail set at a figure higher than an amount reasonably calculated to fulfill this purpose is 'excessive' under the 8th Amendment of our Constitution. . . ."

Milburn v. State, 272 Maj. 3d 272 (1984): "Petitioner has been charged with kidnapping the son of a respected civil official for ransom. The case has received a great deal of publicity and engendered a substantial amount of community hostility against the crime and the accused. The Petitioner has pled not guilty, and is thereby cloaked in the presumption of innocence. . . . At the hearing on bail, the trial court set bail at one million dollars, stating, 'The community wouldn't tolerate less.' For Petitioner, a million dollar bail is the equivalent of no bail. . . . Petitioner argues that the trial court applied the wrong standard for bail and didn't consider relevant factors such as Petitioner's ties to the community and prior record of appearing in court. While Petitioner concedes that the nature of the crime as well as any prior criminal record may be considered insomuch as these factors bear upon the likelihood of Petitioner's appearance for trial and possible sentencing, *Strack v. Burns,* 143 Maj. App. 2d 401 (1958), he contends that the bearing of these factors upon the general community attitude is not relevant. We agree. Bail is to assure a defendant's appearance, not to assuage the moral mood of the community. *Strack v. Burns,* supra. We remand with instructions that the trial court consider Petitioner's (1) community ties; (2) prior record of appearances; (3) present crime; and (4) prior criminal record inasmuch as these factors bear upon the likelihood of Petitioner's appearance at trial."

Major Const., Art. 8: ". . . and no excessive bail shall be set or required."

Major Penal Code §1019: "Every person charged with an offense may be bailed by sufficient sureties, or placed upon his own recognizance [O.R.] if the court sees fit. The amount of bail in each case shall be determined by the Court in its discretion and may from time to time be increased or decreased as circumstances may justify."

Research Memorandum #66: Change of Venue

State v. Murst, 205 Maj. 2d 12 (1962): "Appellant claims he was denied a 'fair trial' because jurors learned about his prior convictions through various newscasts and that venue should have been transferred. While the Constitution requires 'impartial, indifferent jurors' (cit. omitted), they do not have to be totally ignorant of the facts of the case or free from preconceived notions of guilt. All that is required is that these jurors be able and willing to lay aside their impressions and opinions and render a verdict based upon the evidence. No doubt, where a majority of jurors say they think the defendant guilty, we may therefrom presume some community-wide bias. In the present case, however, we have neither such inferred, nor actual bias, in the jury panel. Accordingly, we cannot say that there is a 'reasonable probability that the defendant cannot get a fair trial in this venue' (cit. omitted)."

State v. Makil, 144 Maj. App. 2d 27 (1958): "Appellant's motion for a change of venue, or, in the alternative, a continuance, due to pretrial publicity (which had begun the day before trial) was denied by the trial court. Certainly, outside influences can so infiltrate a community at large as to render the existence of community prejudice against the defendant highly probable. In this case the trial court plainly shielded the defendant from such potential prejudice by (1) admonishing the jurors not to read anything about the case, or listen to TV or radio; (2) allowing defense counsel considerable latitude on voir dire."

Creole v. Warden, 260 Maj. App. 3d 211 (1982): "This is yet another appeal from the trial court's denial of a motion for a continuance or a transfer of venue. Defendant, a public official tried for bribery, received a great deal of media attention as would be expected. Wherever and whenever such a case is set for trial, there will always be publicity. That is simply a fact of modern life, where media and the public follow such cases as they do soap operas. The only question then is 'Can the defendant get a fair trial?' "

State v. Yutz, 255 Maj. App. 2d 517 (1966): "In support of Appellant's claim that prejudicial publicity denied him an 'impartial jury' under the 6th Amendment, and a 'fair trial' under the 5th Amendment, appellant cites to the nature of the pretrial publicity, the voir dire of the panel as a whole, and the voir dire of those who were seated on the jury. Initially we note that the trial court accorded defense great latitude in voir dire, and it is this Court's experience that such thorough jury selection is generally effective in rooting out bias. More significantly, we will only reverse the trial court in a decision denying a transfer if there is 'manifest error,' *State v. Eves*, 207 Maj. 2d 412 (1962). There is no such error in the record before us."

Research Memorandum #67: Suppression Hearing Testimony

L.C. Proof, "Can a Defendant Take the Stand After *Havie*?," 26 Jamner L. Rev. 306, 314 (1982): "Evidentiary rules and constitutional principles have criss-crossed in *State v. Havie*, 269 Maj. 3d 342 (1983). For several years prior to *Havie*, courts have allowed otherwise suppressed evidence, forbidden to be used in the State's case in chief by the exclusionary rule, to be brought in for impeachment. Trumpeting that 'a criminal defendant may not use the exclusionary rule as a shield against perjury,' *Cleader v. State*, 198 Maj. 2d 315 (1961), courts have permitted illegally seized evidence, *Cleader v. State*, supra, and illegally obtained statements, *Fitz v. Warden*, 199 Maj. 2d 523 (1961), to be brought in to impeach a testifying defendant. Recently, the courts have similarly allowed a 'Seeman' statement[102] to be used for impeachment. *Moris v. State*, 17 Maj. App. 3d 621 (1970).

"In an unrelated line of cases, our courts have held that criminal defendants who take the stand waive their right against self-incrimination as to all appropriate cross-examination, *Brune v. State*, 200 Maj. 2d 34 (1962), which under accepted evidentiary rules includes 'all areas reasonably indicated by the direct examination.' *Sprunie v. State*, 143 Maj. App. 2d 751 (1958). Herein is where the *Havie* criss-cross takes place.

"In *Havie*, the trial court had suppressed certain narcotics paraphernalia which had been found upon the defendant in what the court found to be an illegal search. Defendant Havie took the stand at trial and denied involvement with the drug conspiracy with which he was charged, but made no mention of the paraphernalia. On cross-examination the prosecutor examined defendant about his knowledge of the methods of drug dealers and users, leading up to, 'You know about the kind of paraphernalia that's used, don't you? You know about carburetors? You know about . . . ? Etc.' His denial of special knowledge about a device known as a 'carburetor' was followed by a court ruling that the suppressed evidence could be used for impeachment. While the cross-examination arguably was proper under evidentiary rules, permitting the prosecution to set up admission of suppressed evidence by its cross-examination is problematic. After *Havie*, a defendant on direct examination may be careful not to make a general denial of any knowledge of narcotics or otherwise invite subsequent impeachment with suppressed evidence. Yet the latitude given the cross-examiner under evidentiary rules is so great that this defendant can never take the stand to deny the elements of the charged offense without knowing that somehow the prosecution can set up impeachment with the suppressed evidence on cross-examination."

Research Memorandum #68: Destruction of Evidence

State v. Brant, 105 Maj. App. 3d 621 (1975): "Appellant has been convicted of 'offering to furnish narcotics,' Major Penal Code section 1136 (1961), based solely upon the testimony of an undercover police officer concerning her conversation with the defendant. At trial, defendant denied making any such offer. That conversation was secretly recorded, but the tape was lost prior to the time that defense counsel could inspect it. We, of course, do not know what the tape would reveal. The government's negligence has precluded this possibility. All we know is that the appellant was denied what may have been a crucial piece of evidence in his case. The government simply must not destroy evidence where there is a reasonable possibility that it may be material and favorable to the defendant's case, unless the government has made earnest efforts to promulgate a system to insure preservation of evidence and good faith efforts to follow that system. Since the latter was not done here, and the 'reasonable possibility' standard was clearly met, we have no alternative but to reverse and order dismissal."

---

102. In *Seeman v. State*, 201 Maj. 2d 137 (1962), the court recognized the dilemma a defendant faces when considering testifying at a suppression hearing. 'In order to vindicate his 4th Amendments rights at the hearing, defendant risks giving up 5th Amendment rights at trial if the prosecution can use his testimony from the suppression hearing in the case in chief.' *Seeman v. State*, supra, 201 Maj. 2d at 151. Accordingly the *Seeman* court developed a prophylactic rule whereby defendant's testimony at a suppression hearing may not be used in the State's case in chief."

Wrile v. Warden, 110 Maj. App. 3d 832 (1975): "The prosecution has a duty not only to disclose favorable evidence to the accused, but to preserve evidence prior to a request for discovery."

Research Memorandum #69: Equal Protection and Right of Indigent to Offset Economic Imbalance

State v. Grift, 204 Maj. 2d 617 (1962): "We have decided that an indigent defendant cannot be denied a free transcript for an appeal. For surely there can be no equal justice when the kind of trial or appeal a man gets depends upon the amount of money he has."

Concurring opinion: "Of course a State need not equalize economic conditions. A man of means may be able to retain an expensive, able attorney a poor man could not afford. Those are contingencies of life which are hardly within the power, let alone duty, of the State to correct or cushion."

Lester v. Mack, 212 Maj. 2d 592 (1963): "Petitioner seeks a free verbatim transcript of his trial so his appointed attorney can review it for possible ground for a habeas corpus petition. In our decision, we are guided by certain principles and procedures. First, the principles. The principle established by *State v. Grift,* 204 Maj. 2d 617 (1962), does not guarantee indigents the same treatment afforded wealthy defendants: Rather, it is only necessary that they be given equivalent and fundamentally fair treatment. Equal Protection does then require that indigents have an adequate opportunity to present their claims fairly within the adversarial system. An affluent society ought not be miserly in support of justice, for economy is not an objective of the system. Accordingly, '[d]estitute defendants must be given as adequate review of their claims as defendants who have money enough to pay for transcripts.' *State v. Grift,* supra, 204 Maj. 2d at 624. Now, the procedures. Once the defendant (as here) has made a showing of 'colorable need' for the full transcript, the State then has the burden of showing that other alternatives would provide adequate appellate review."

Lester v. Black, 101 Maj. App. 3d 287 (1975): "To interpose any financial consideration between an indigent prisoner of the state and his exercise of a state right to sue for his liberty, is to deny that prisoner the equality of protection of the law. Here, however, petitioner seeks a full transcript at state expense by merely whispering 'habeas corpus' as if that had some talismanic quality. There is simply no showing of any need, colorable or otherwise. Petitioner cannot expect the expenditure of state funds to assuage his curiosity or provide him with some light reading."

State v. Duggan, 111 Maj. App. 3d 977 (1976): "Indigent appellant seeks an appointed attorney on appeal. The right to an attorney at trial is established (cits. omitted). Here, *State v. Grift,* 204 Maj. 2d 617 (1962), controls. The appointment of appellate counsel is ordered."

State v. Main, 169 Maj. App. 3d 713 (1979): "Believing that *State v. Grift,* 204 Maj. 2d 617 (1962), applies only to felony cases, the court below has denied preparation of a free transcript in this misdemeanor appeal. While the lower court's interpretation of *Grift* is wrong and we herein so rule, that is not the end of the inquiry. Other alternatives to a full transcript may be available (e.g., an agreed statement of facts, a full narrative from the trial judge's minutes, selected relevant portions of the full transcript). Of course, a full transcript is required when it is necessary for as 'effective' an appeal as would be available to a wealthy defendant."

State v. Britt, 202 Maj. App. 3d 367 (1980): "We view the *Grift* principles as requiring that the State, as a matter of equal protection, provide indigent defendants with the basic tools of an adequate defense or appeal, when those tools are available for a price to other defendants. In fairness we must say that the outer limits of this principle are not clear, yet they clearly encompass the request in this case for a free transcript of defendant's first trial where a second trial must be prepared after there was a mistrial in the first."

State v. Andrews, 280 Maj. App. 2d 117 (1969): "Indigent defendant asks for money for experts and investigators under Major Penal Code section 40(1) (1962)—the "Costs for Experts" statute. Defendant has a constitutional right to an attorney (cits. omitted). The right includes the right to use any experts that will assist counsel in preparing a defense (cits. omitted). Contrary to the contentions of the government, the fact that friends and family have retained counsel for adult defendant does not bar defendant from access to these indigent funds. The contribution of family and friends is only one factor in assessing defendant's 'ability to pay.' "

Research Memorandum #70: Felony-Murder and "Merger"

State v. Iman, 198 Maj. 2d 214 (1960): "Appellant was convicted of felony-murder based upon a death occurring during an assault with a deadly weapon. At trial Appellant tried to present evidence that he did not have the requisite 'malice' for murder due to his ingestion of alcohol and medication. The trial court ruled such evidence irrelevant inasmuch as the felony-murder rule itself imputes malice. Appellant's counsel thereupon objected to the use of the felony-murder rule in a case such as defendant's. We agree with defendant's trial counsel. The net effect of the imputation of malice by the felony-murder rule is to eliminate the possibility of finding unlawful killings resulting from the commission of a felony to be manslaughter, rather than murder. Applying the doctrine to a case such as the present one would mean that intentional killings with deadly weapons would always be murders, never manslaughter, since all such killings include *in fact* an assault with a deadly weapon. This kind of bootstrapping finds support in neither logic nor law. We, therefore, hold that a felony-murder instruction should not be given when it is based upon a felony which is an integral part of the homicide and which the evidence produced by the prosecution shows to be an offense included *in fact* within the offense charged."

Concurring, Davis, J.: "I agree with the majority, save that they have made their reasoning too obscure. This jurisdiction has spent decades refining the distinctions between intentional killings which we call 'murder' and those which, because there exists that elusive quality in the mind of the perpetrator known as 'heat of passion,' we call the far less serious offense of 'manslaughter.' Now, probably no one outside of a law professor could conceive of an intentional killing that is not carried out by some form of felonious assault (guns, mailing poison, etc.). So all intentional killings could be charged as felony-murder if this underlying assault could be used as the underlying felony. With me so far? Good. The problem is that 'heat of passion' has no place in the analytic framework of felony-murder (take my word for it.) It won't reduce felony-murder to manslaughter. So all intentional killings would be murder, even if there were heat of passion, if the underlying assault could be used to charge felony-murder. And if that's the case, why have we spent decades developing the law of 'manslaughter'?"

Kern v. Superior Court, 93 Maj. App. 3d 41 (1974): "Cases decided after *State v. Iman,* 198 Maj. 2d 214 (1960), demonstrate the unwillingness of the courts to expand the *Iman* holding—the so-called 'merger rule'—much beyond the *Iman* facts. In *State v. Vipman,* 270 Maj. App. 2d 714 (1967), defendant entered a home to kill his victim. A felony-murder conviction based upon burglary was upheld as the *Vipman* court distinguished *Iman* on the grounds that

an assault in one's home, one's inner sanctum, is far more likely to have fatal results than one in public such as *Iman.* In *State v. Bruto,* 277 Maj. App. 2d 57 (1968), the court refused to accept an argument that the 'merger rule' should apply to robbery because robbery is basically an 'assaultive' crime. The *Bruto* court held that, unlike the assault in *Iman,* in the case of a robbery there is an 'independent felonious purpose' for committing the assault (i.e., to wrongfully acquire money or property belonging to another). 'One who embarks upon a course of conduct directed at achieving such felonious purpose falls directly within the prohibition of the felony-murder statute.' *State v. Bruto, supra,* 277 Maj. App. 2d at 59."

Research Memorandum #71: Fifth Amendment

Fifth Amendment (general)—

Huvestern v. State, 261 Maj. 529 (1948): "The Fifth Amendment prevents compelled self-incrimination. In this case Mr. Huvestern, a grand jury witness, has refused to answer certain inquiries put to him on the stand while claiming protection of this privilege. In assessing his claim we are mindful that 'the privilege extends not only to disclosures which would in themselves support a conviction, but also to those which would furnish a link in the chain of evidence needed to prosecute the claimant for a crime.' *State v. Rodrege,* 260 Maj. 114, 119 (1947)."

Fifth Amendment and prosecution request for notice of alibi and list of alibi witnesses—

Wilson v. Superior Court of Nettle, 256 Nettle App. 3d 917 (1987): "Petitioner contends that the trial court's order under a Notice of Alibi statute, which requires that he provide the prosecution with notice if he intends to raise an alibi and a list of names and addresses of alibi witnesses, violates his right against compelled self-incrimination. We disagree. Trials are filled with situations which 'compel' a defendant to risk incrimination. A strong prosecution case may force a defendant to put on witnesses and/ or take the stand. This may, in turn, result in incriminating cross-examination and lead to incriminating rebuttal testimony. Such natural compulsions from our adversary system do not, however, offend the 5th Amendment. The pressures from a pretrial order to provide a notice of alibi and alibi witness, such as here, are not different. The order does not force Petitioner to either choose an alibi defense or prevent him from later abandoning it. The reality of the prosecution's case, not the pretrial order, will determine that. At most, the order only compels Petitioner to disclose this information at an earlier point than he intended. Nothing in the 5th Amendment privilege entitles a defendant as a matter of constitutional right to await the end of the State's case before announcing the nature of his defense. Moreover, without such an order the prosecution could surely get a continuance to investigate Petitioner's alibi witnesses once they took the stand. Such an order thus both avoids a delay of the trial and protects the State from having an all too easily manufactured alibi sprung upon them at trial."

Dissent. Lift, J.; Hoist, J.: "Our Constitution has given a criminal accused certain advantages over his powerful government accuser. Today, the majority takes one of those advantages away; for, contrary to the majority's fiat, the 'right to await the end of the State's case before announcing the nature of his defense' is the essence of the 5th Amendment. That amendment allows the defendant to stand mute and require the government to 'Prove it!' at every juncture without his aid. Without the court order here, defendant could listen to the prosecution case, determine that the prosecution cannot carry its burden, and decide not to put on a case. With the court order, petitioner could have made the same decision yet still have been compelled to give names and addresses of witnesses who could provide a 'link in the chain of evidence needed to prosecute [him].' *Huvestern v. State,* 261 Maj. 529 (1948)."

Wilts v. Warden, 269 Nettle 3d 1193 (1983): "Due process requires that when an order under the Notice of Alibi Act is made, the prosecution *must* be likewise required to provide reciprocal discovery regarding alibi rebuttal witnesses to the defendant."

Research Memorandum #72: "Knock-Notice"

State v. Cocs, 269 Maj. 3d 209 (1983): "Police, armed with arrest and search warrants, came to defendant's home to arrest her for possession and sale of crack. An informant, upon whose information the warrants had been obtained, had told police that a large quantity of this illegal substance would be found in defendant-Appellant's home. Upon their arrival, police looked through the front window and saw Appellant beginning to smoke something they reasonably believed was crack. They thereupon forced in Appellant's front door, took Appellant into custody,

and searched the home. It is upon the failure of the police to comply with knock-notice requirements that this appeal rests. The law is clear. Unless otherwise excused, police may not force in a door or window of a home to search or arrest unless they first announce their presence, identify themselves as police, announce their purpose, and request admittance. Failure to comply with these requirements will result in our finding the ensuing search and seizure 'unreasonable' under the Fourth Amendment. In this case, the government concedes non-compliance, but alleges grounds which it asserts excuses compliance. We find these grounds insufficient. The government does not allege that there was a risk of defendant's escape if a quick entrance was not made. *State v. Boote,* 142 Maj. App. 2d 1013 (1957). It does assert danger to police from defendant, but this danger is not based upon any known specific violent propensities of the defendant, but upon the general dangers of drug dealers. Our Supreme Court has recently held that to base non-compliance upon the general category of crime (such as drug trafficking here) would undermine knock-notice. See *Cams v. State,* 93 Maj. 301 (1974). Finally, the government's position that evidence would be destroyed (*Warden v. Evram,* 254 Maj. App. 2d 519 (1965)) unless police acted quickly is likewise without merit. Police had information that a large quantity of crack was secreted in defendant's home. The minuscule amount which could have been smoked while police followed knock-notice procedures cannot justify their actions here."

Dissent. Crabb, J.: "Compliance with knock-notice was excused here. Police had the right to enter to protect the defendant, who though a criminal is still a citizen, from the potentially lethal effect of crack."

State v. Solix, 201 Maj. App. 3d 401, 407 (1980): "Accordingly, the policies underlying knock-notice—(1) protection of the privacy of the individual in his or her home; (2) protection of innocent persons on the premises; (3) avoidance of violent confrontations between occupants and individuals entering without proper notice; (4) protection of police who might be injured by a startled or fearful homeowner—do *not* apply when police have probable cause to believe the 'occupant' is a burglar busy at his trade."

Research Memorandum #73: Police Interrogation

State v. Mintz, 201 Maj. 2d 1 (1962): "Having reviewed the variety of physical and psychological techniques police have used to elicit confessions from suspects, and having analyzed the deleterious effect of these techniques upon the 5th Amendment rights of these suspects, we pronounce the following rules. . . . Statements given without the full constitutional warnings and recitation of rights [which are identical to those in *Miranda*] are inadmissible when such statements are made during interrogation while the suspect is in custody or otherwise deprived of his freedom in a significant way. These warnings provide the opportunity to bring in an attorney who can combat the pressures on a defendant's 5th Amendment rights which are inherent in this situation. A defendant may, of course, waive these rights if done knowingly and intelligently, without threat or trick. Waiver will not be presumed, however, from a suspect's mere silence in face of the recitation of rights and warnings. Once a suspect indicates in any manner that he wants an attorney, all questioning must cease. Further, a suspect may 'cut off' questioning at any time. On the other hand, statements which are volunteered, and therefore not the product of questioning, do not involve any 5th Amendment concerns."

State v. Rhodes, 256 Maj. App. 3d 154 (1982):
"*Mintz* applies to 'interrogations' involving express questioning or its functional equivalent. We define this 'functional equivalent' as 'words or actions on the part of police that police should know are reasonably likely to elicit an incriminating response.' "

State v. Moth, 100 Maj. App. 3d 593 (1975):
"Appellant gave a confession when questioned at the police station without first being given *Mintz* warnings. Appellant, a parolee, had voluntarily come down to the station in response to a phone call from a detective who was investigating a series of burglaries. When he arrived at the station, he was told that he was not under arrest and was free to go at any time. Under these circumstances, Appellant was neither in custody nor in the coercive atmosphere envisioned by *Mintz*. As such, the *Mintz* warnings are not required."

State v. Quirk, 257 Maj. App. 3d 406 (1982):
"Police arrested the Appellant, who was a suspect in a shooting, in a public supermarket. At the time of the arrest, the suspect wore an empty shoulder holster. Fearing he had ditched the gun in the market, police asked, 'where's the gun?,' without first giving *Mintz* warnings. Nevertheless, we refuse to suppress the weapon which was located in the produce section, relying upon what we will term a 'public safety' exception to *Mintz*. The police motive in questioning was public safety and not obtaining incriminating evidence, and time was of the essence."

Eddy v. Warden, 170 Maj. App. 3d 274 (1979):
"In the case before us, police began questioning Petitioner shortly after his arrest. When Petitioner requested an attorney, the police followed the dictates of *Mintz* and ceased their interrogation. However, they came back a few hours later and resumed questioning. This they could not lawfully do. Once a defendant has requested an attorney, police may not again initiate questioning. While a defendant may initiate further discussions with the police, the mere fact that he may respond to renewed police questioning is not sufficient evidence of a valid waiver of counsel on his part."

State v. Fark, 157 Maj. App. 3d 142 (1977):
"We have two issues before us. Appellant, a juvenile, confessed to police after the officers denied his request to see his probation officer. Is the request for a probation officer equivalent to a request for an attorney? If not, is a juvenile capable of waiving the right to counsel without advice? As to the first issue, our answer is 'no.' In no way does a probation officer stand in a position that can in any way be equated with that of counsel envisioned in *Mintz*. As to the second, our answer is 'yes.' While age is a factor, an alleged waiver by a juvenile must be assessed as would be the waiver of an adult, i.e., by looking at the 'totality of circumstances' to determine if it was made knowingly and voluntarily. In this regard, the court must evaluate the defendant's age, experience, background, and intelligence, and assess whether he has the capacity to understand the warnings given him, the nature of the 5th Amendment rights, and the consequences of waiving these rights."

State v. Thoms, 220 Maj. App. 2d 927 (1963):
"While appellant's request for an attorney was somewhat equivocal, here the police did not try to 'clarify' the request, but rather tried to talk the defendant out of having an attorney. That violated *Mintz*."

State v. Monk, 280 Maj. App. 2d 57 (1969): "In the *Thoms* case, defendants' question 'Do you think we need an attorney?' was viewed by the court as 'ambiguous, but capable of being construed as a request for counsel' (cit. omitted). We take a similar view of the statement in the case before us—'Well, maybe I should talk to my attorney.' When Detective Crimms ignored that statement and instead continued to discuss the case the police had against Monk, Monk's subsequent confession was obtained in violation of *Mintz*."

State v. Buttle, 201 Maj. App. 3d 393 (1980):
"Defendant, a graduate of the 11th grade, was given her *Mintz* warnings off a form, told police she understood her rights, and confessed. She now argues that

her confession should not have been admitted at her trial because she never made an explicit waiver of her rights. We disagree. While *mere* silence cannot constitute a waiver under *Mintz,* an explicit statement of waiver is not necessary. Rather, we must look to the 'totality of the circumstances.' Here, silence *coupled with* an understanding of the *Mintz* rights and a subsequent course of conduct indicative of a waiver is sufficient to find a valid waiver."

Wyke v. Warden, 268 Maj. App. 2d 113 (1966): "Once defendant waived his *Mintz* rights before taking the polygraph, police were free to question him without renewing the warnings."

State v. Mike, 277 Maj. App. 2d 1143 (1968): "We deal here with a confession which violates due process in that it was involuntary. When appellant was questioned and confessed he was in the intensive care unit of the hospital, there were tubes in his nose, an 'IV' in his arm, and he was on strong drugs. Such a situation is not conducive to the exercise of a rational intellect and free will. The confession was not the product of 'free and rational choice.' *State v. Gerber,* 230 Maj. 1212 (1940)."

State v. Cult, 151 Maj. App. 3d 727 (1976): "Appellant claims his confession, given to police while in the hospital, was involuntary due to the fact he was on demerol and scopalomine at the time. He cites us to *State v. Mike,* 277 Maj. App. 2d 1143 (1968), and *State v. Gerber,* 230 Maj. 1212 (1940). We first note that there is no expert testimony in the record regarding the effect of these drugs on the 'exercise of a rational intellect and free will.' *State v. Mike,* supra. We do not rest on our decision here, however. Rather we deny appellant's claim based upon the fact that there is nothing in the record before us establishing that he was on these drugs at the time he was questioned in the hospital."

State v. Peters, 147 Maj. App. 3d 59 (1976): "Appellant, a 13-year-old juvenile, attacks his confession as constitutionally involuntary. In this area of law, the prosecution must establish voluntariness 'beyond a reasonable doubt.' Further, one's 'will can be overborne' (cit. omitted) by (1) physical or psychological coercion; (2) drugs; (3) insanity. In these latter two categories, a defendant may be incapable of making a free and rational choice, although this incapacity is not the fault of the police. Here, during Appellant's questioning he was vomiting, had the dry heaves, and almost fell out of his chair. He had consumed nine beers shortly before his arrest, and when arrested had an empty beer bottle in his hand. Under these circumstances, the government has failed to carry its burden that the confession was voluntary."

Research Memorandum #74: Prosecution Discovery and the Work Product Privilege

Nibbles v. State, 202 Maj. 2d 791 (1962): "Appellant's investigator took the stand to rebut the testimony of a key prosecution witness she had interviewed. When the prosecutor's question on cross-examination as to whether she had taken notes of the interview was answered in the affirmative, the prosecution moved, and the court ordered, that the notes be turned over for the prosecution's inspection. Whereupon, counsel for the defendant raised the Work Product Privilege as a bar to such submission. Initially, we note that the Work Product Privilege applies to criminal as well as civil litigation. This privilege protects certain materials prepared by an attorney. At its core, the work product doctrine shelters the mental processes of the attorney, providing a privileged area within which he can analyze and prepare his client's case. But the doctrine is an intensely practical one, grounded in the realities of litigation in our adversary system. One of those realities is that attorneys often must rely on the assistance of investigators and other agents in the compilation of materials in preparation for trial. It is therefore necessary that the doctrine protect material prepared by agents for the attorney as well as those prepared by the attorney himself. . . . The privilege derived from the work product doctrine is, however, not absolute. Like other qualified privileges, it may be waived. Here respondent sought to adduce the testimony of the investigator and contrast her recollection of the contested statements with that of the prosecution's witnesses. Appellant, by electing to present the investigator as a witness, waived the privilege with respect to matters covered in her testimony."

Research Memorandum #75: Prosecution's Duty to Provide Defendant with Exculpatory Evidence

Branty v. State, 201 Maj. 2d 86 (1962): "Appellant and a co-defendant were charged and convicted of first-degree murder, and sentenced to death. At his trial, which had been severed from that of his co-defendant, appellant had conceded participation in the fatal robbery and therefore liability under felony-murder principles. Appellant had, however, unsuccessfully sought to avoid the death penalty by relying upon his unsupported testimony that his co-defendant, and not him, had committed the actual killing. Several weeks after his conviction it was discovered that the prosecution had in its possession a statement of the co-defendant admitting to the killing. Appellant's trial counsel had requested all extrajudicial statements of the co-defendant. While some statements had been shown to her, this crucial one was never provided. This suppression provides the factual basis for the constitutional issue raised today.

"We have already held that both the deliberate use of perjured testimony and intentional suppression of favorable testimony by the prosecution violates principles of due process. The State argues that where, as in the present case, the suppression was unintentional, no due process violation can occur. We disagree. The basis of our previous holdings in this area was not to punish society for the misdeeds of the prosecution, but avoid an unfair trial to an accused. Accordingly, we hold that suppression by the prosecution of evidence favorable to an accused upon request violates due process where the evidence is material to either guilt or to punishment, irrespective of the good or bad faith of the prosecution. Appellant is entitled to a new trial on the issue of punishment."

State v. Augle, 228 Maj. 2d 118 (1968): "This duty to provide exculpatory evidence under *Branty* focuses upon 'materiality.' We, herein, further refine *Branty* by articulating three categories of evidence upon which the prosecutor's *Branty* duty could focus and the respective standards of materiality which accompany each category:

(1) perjured testimony that the prosecutor knew or should have known of will always be considered material;

(2) suppressed information following a specific request for information, such as in *Branty,* will be material if the suppressed information might have affected the outcome of the trial;

(3) suppressed information following no request for exculpatory information or a general request such as 'all *Branty* evidence' (which we find equivalent to no request) will be found material if the omitted evidence creates a reasonable doubt that did not otherwise exist such that its exculpatory nature would be obvious to the prosecution."

Research Memorandum #76: Search and Seizure

State v. Purgis, 269 Maj. 3d 511 (1983): "An arrest in a home encroaches on many of the same interests as would a search of that same home. Cognizant of the value our Constitution places on the security of one's home from government intrusion,

we hold that all arrests of defendants in their homes require arrest warrants, unless consent is obtained, or true exigency exists (e.g., specific evidence demonstrating a risk of flight, destruction of evidence, danger to police or the community, etc.). We find no such exigencies to excuse the police from obtaining a warrant to arrest the murder suspect in this case."

State v. West, 269 Maj. 3d 523 (1983): "Because of the sanctity of the home, the circumstances in which the need for an arrest warrant can be excused for 'exigency' should be few in number and carefully delineated. No such exigency exists here where police have made a warrantless nighttime entry into the defendant's home to arrest him for driving while intoxicated, a misdemeanor."

State v. Lex, 272 Maj. 3d 115 (1984): "The purpose of the exclusionary rule in this state has always been to deter illegal police conduct, not to protect the 'integrity' of the courts by denying the use of ill-gotten evidence. That being so, there seems little to gain in suppressing the products of a search warrant under which police acted believing in reasonable good faith it was valid. The case would be different if the police initially applying for the warrant had intentionally or recklessly provided the issuing magistrate with false information, or if no 'reasonable' police officer could have believed that there was 'probable cause' to support the search."

State v. Shenk, 143 Maj. App. 2d 75 (1959): "The only issue in a consent search is whether the consent was 'voluntary' under the 'totality of circumstances.' The burden is on the prosecution to demonstrate that the consent was not the product of coercion, express or implied."

State v. Brempo, 198 Maj. 2d 703 (1961): "Here police told defendant's 66-year-old grandmother that they had a warrant to search the house. As a result, the grandmother 'consented' to the police entry. In fact, no evidence that any such warrant existed was ever produced. The government now seeks to justify the search of defendant's home, which led to discovery of the murder weapon, as consensual. However, where law enforcement claims authority to search a home under a warrant, where they announce to the occupant that the occupant has no right to resist, such a situation is filled with coercion—albeit colorably lawful coercion. Where there is coercion, there cannot be consent."

State v. Ham, 270 Maj. App. 2d 112 (1967): "In response to the police request to search appellant's car, he asked if they had a warrant. Officer Biff responded, 'I can get one,' and appellant replied 'OK. You can search.' We find no legal infirmity in a consent following the threat to get a warrant."

State v. Bozi, 271 Maj. App. 2d 777 (1967): "We find the consent to search the First Avenue apartment valid. While police did say they would attempt to get a warrant if Appellant did not consent, it is significant to us that Appellant was not in custody, there was no discourtesy, abuse, threat, ruse, or force, and police did not say, 'You might as well consent, we can get a warrant quickly.' "

Rust v. Warden, 277 Maj. App. 2d 23 (1968): "Petitioner attacks his alleged consent to search the trunk of his car on two grounds. First, he claims that the police statement that they 'would' get a warrant if he refused to consent runs afoul of *State v. Brempo,* 198 Maj. 2d 703 (1961). We disagree. This case is plainly distinguishable from the 'claim of authority' in *Brempo.* Second, he claims he did not have the capacity to consent. While the record indicates that he was 'upset and quite nervous' when arrested, by the time of giving his consent to search at the police station he had 'calmed down so as to reasonably appear rational' and thus was capable of understanding the decision to consent."

State v. Hart, 200 Maj. 2d 951 (1962): "Where, as here, 4-5 police officers came to appellant's home at 1:45 A.M., dragged him out of bed, and made his wife leave the room, there is no free and specific consent, but rather a mere 'submission to authority.' . . . Further, the nighttime entry into Appellant's home in violation of 'knock-notice' requirements itself involves an illegal assertion of authority by police, thereby tainting any consent which follows."

Tex v. Warden, 17 Maj. App. 3d 601 (1970): "Seeing the heroin in defendant's glove compartment when defendant opened the compartment to remove his car registration allowed the officer to make a 'plain view' seizure of the contraband without benefit of a warrant. The only requirements for such a plain view seizure are (1) the officer was standing in a place she had a legal right to be when she saw the article in question; (2) there was 'probable cause' to associate the item with criminal activity."

A. Sneld, "A Discourse On 'Probable Cause,' " 6 Jamner Law Rev. 312, 313 (1974): "The concept of 'Probable Cause' runs throughout our criminal procedure, with some confusion regarding the difference between Probable Cause to search as opposed to arrest. In both instances, the standard refers to whether a 'reasonable man' must be 'strongly suspicious.' The

difference lies in what this man must be suspicious of. In a search, the 'reasonable man' must be strongly suspicious that a particular thing associated with criminal activity is in a particular place at a particular time. In the area of arrest, the suspicion focuses on whether a particular person is associated with a particular crime."

Long v. Superior Court, 93 Maj. App. 3d 816 (1974): "Police entered defendant's car to search for weapons; when they stopped her car on 'reasonable suspicion' of a traffic violation, she could produce no license or registration, and they saw a large hunting knife on the floor. In the course of this cursory, self-protective search of the passenger compartment, police discovered the baggie of marijuana which is the subject of this writ. Our Supreme Court has already approved temporary detentions of persons and autos when there is 'reasonable suspicion' of criminal activity, *State v. Sykes,* 202 Maj. 2d 121 (1962), and has also approved the pat-down (i.e., 'frisk') of persons so detained for weapons when there is reason to believe the safety of the detaining officer or others is involved. Extending this 'pat-down' rationale to self-protective searches for weapons of the passenger compartments of automobiles which have been temporarily detained seems eminently reasonable to us. Accordingly, we find the officers' conduct lawful, and deny the writ."

State v. Chums, 201 Maj. 2d 191 (1962): "Police arrested defendant in his home and subsequently searched the entire home, finding numerous incriminating items of evidence. The government now seeks to justify the search as 'incident to arrest.' We cannot accept their characterization. Our Constitution requires that all searches be conducted only upon probable cause and with a warrant. The warrant is only to be dispensed with under 'closely circumscribed exigencies' (cit. omitted). An arrest involves such exigencies since the suspect may try to assault the arresting officer or to destroy evidence. These risks, however, plainly justify only the search of the area within the suspect's immediate control or 'wing span.' "

State v. Muncie, 268 Maj. 3d 1003 (1983): "After a murder, police searched the suspect's apartment without a warrant. The Court of Appeals upheld the search finding the need for a warrant obviated by what it called 'the murder scene exception.' We reverse. All agree there was ample 'probable cause.' Yet a warrant can be excused only for true exigency, expressed in closely circumscribed exceptions (*State v. Chums,* 201 Maj. 2d 191 (1962)), not general categories such as 'murder scene' as was attempted here."

Brakes v. Warden, 254 Maj. App. 2d 216 (1965): "Here an illegal search of Petitioner's apartment produced information which led to the buried body. Normally, we would order the evidence suppressed and require a new trial. However, the government opposes suppression, claiming that 'routine police procedures' would have led to discovery of the body without aid of the illegally seized evidence. We agree that the government should have a hearing where it will have the burden to establish a 'reasonable probability' that the body would have been discovered without aid of the illegality and that, therefore, the discovery was 'inevitable.' This comports with other jurisdictions which have considered this issue and held that when the illegal police act merely contributes to the discovery of evidence which would have been acquired lawfully through 'routine police practices,' there is no taint from the illegality (cit. omitted)."

Research Memorandum #77: "Taint" Cases

Solong v. Warden, 261 Maj. 417 (1948): "The State must not be permitted to profit from its own misconduct. Accordingly, all products of illegal 4th Amendment activity, whether direct or indirect, tangible or intangible, must be suppressed as the 'fruit of the poisonous tree.' In the case before us, a Petitioner seeks suppression of a confession which followed an arrest which all parties agree was patently illegal. The confession, however, took place several days after defendant's release following her arrest when she voluntarily returned to the police station to talk to Detective Meyers. Under these circumstances, the relationship between the initial illegality and the eventual confession had become so attenuated so as to dissipate the taint. Appeal denied."

Trucker v. Warden, 253 Maj. App. 2d 1017 (1965): "Defendant was arrested without any cause whatsoever and taken to the station for questioning, whereupon a confession followed immediately upon administration of the *Mintz* warnings [which parallel the *Miranda* warnings]. The State confesses the blatant illegality of this 'dragnet arrest,' but contends that the *Mintz* warnings purge the taint of the initial illegality. We disagree. While the *Mintz* warnings may obviate the 5th Amendment concerns the *Mintz* court dealt with, the warnings do not automatically purge the confession before us from the taint of the 4th Amendment violation (i.e., the arrest) we deal with here. See gen. *Solong v. Warden,* 261 Maj. 416 (1948). While administration of the *Mintz* warnings is one factor to consider in deciding whether an ensuing confession has been purged of the taint of an illegal arrest, we must also consider (1) the time between arrest and confession; (2) the purpose and flagrancy of the official police misconduct; and (3) the nature of the intervening circumstances from arrest to confession. . . . Considering all these factors in the case before us, we find the taint of the arrest has not been purged, and accordingly order the confession suppressed."

CIVIL RESEARCH MEMORANDA

Research Memorandum #78: Automobile Negligence

Fox v. City of Benton, 143 Maj. App. 2d 20 (1958): "Modern cases involving rear-end collisions hold that the doctrine of last clear chance is not applicable where the following driver, using 'reasonable prudence,' is unable to react in time to prevent the collision.

"The City of Benton trial court correctly held that the last clear chance doctrine was found to be not applicable where the plaintiff driver unexpectedly stopped at a flashing yellow light and the defendant bus driver noticed the plaintiff, from a distance of 90 feet, and applied his brakes, but nevertheless collided into the rear-end of plaintiff's car.

"Where the defendant driver does, however, have the last clear chance to avoid the accident by swerving, honking, or braking from a great enough distance, the doctrine is applicable."

Simmons v. Lakewood, 271 Maj. App. 2d 19 (1967): "This is a case involving an intersection collision between a passenger car and truck where the truck driver saw the car 45 feet from the intersection. We hold that the last clear chance doctrine is applicable where the truck driver could have, but failed to, brake or swerve in time to avoid the collision.

"Major law provides that in cases involving rear-end collisions, the rebuttable presumption of negligence is primarily on the following driver. The 'driver of a motor vehicle shall not follow another vehicle more closely than is reasonable and prudent, having due regard for the speed of such vehicle and the traffic upon and the condition of the highway,' Major Code sec. 46.00."

Johnson v. Nelson, 256 Maj. App. 3d 100 (1982): "The presumption of negligence was rebutted by defendant in a rear-end collision where plaintiff unexpectedly stopped her vehicle to allow other vehicles access to an arterial. The following driver can rebut a presumption of negligence by claiming that an emergency or unusual condition exists. If a car in front stops suddenly and without warning at a place where a sudden stop was not to be anticipated, the jury can be instructed that defendant was not following too closely. The plaintiff must give some notice of the intention to stop if there is a reasonable opportunity to do so. Nevertheless, the following driver must reasonably anticipate an emergency situation that can result from ordinary traffic conditions. The defendant pick-up truck, which had been travelling legally at 40 m.p.h., ran into the back of the plaintiff. Defendant claimed that plaintiff failed to sufficiently signal or warn the following driver, and had defective brake lights.

"It is a case of first impression regarding whether alleged defective brake lights create a presumption of negligence in a rear-end collision. Generally, the owner or operator of a motor vehicle does not have an absolute duty to insure the safety of herself or other users of the road from the condition of her vehicle. The owner operator, however, must use reasonable care to see that the vehicle's condition is safe and in proper working order, and is chargeable with the knowledge that a reasonable inspection would disclose. The State of Major imposes statutory requirements regarding certain aspects of motor vehicles, such as brakes, which must meet certain minimum standards.

"A factor in determining potential negligence regarding defective equipment is the causal relation between the defect and the injury. The injuries incurred must be proximately caused by the defective condition of the vehicle, otherwise a plaintiff cannot claim that the defective condition causally contributed to the accident.

"But we need not decide the issue of defective brake lights since we find that defendant was not negligent. In this case, defendant, faced with an emergency situation, was unable to react in time to avoid the collision."

Wichman v. United Disposal, Inc., 284 Maj. 3d 817 (1987): "We reverse judgment of the Superior Court of Callam County. This case involves a rear-end collision where defendant truck driver, United Disposal, Inc., negligently tried to pass Wichman, the plaintiff, but could not because of the traffic congestion. Consequently, defendant hit the plaintiff. Defendant United Disposal relies upon *Taylor v. Ganas*, 269 Maj. 3d 1492 (1983). In that case the following driver struck plaintiff's disabled vehicle on a bridge. In *Taylor*, plaintiff's car was either stopped or slowly moving but in either case plaintiff failed to use brake lights or other warning signal. Plaintiff was found 75% negligent and defendant 25% negligent.

"The facts here are distinguishable. Defendant United Disposal admitted that when he tried to pass plaintiff's car, that plaintiff either slowed down or was almost stopped. Plaintiff's inoperational brake lights did not causally contribute to the mishap. Judgment reversed. Case remanded to the Superior Court of Callam County for retrial."

Research Memorandum #79: Child Custody

Minkon v. Ford, 260 Maj. 3d 10 (1982): "The maternal grandparents requested legal custody or in the alternative, visitation of their daughter's minor children over the objection of the father and new stepmother (the natural mother was deceased). We conclude that forcing either custody or visitation over parental objection would not be in the best interest of the children. The paramount factor in determining visitation and custody rights of minor children is the best interest of the children. In determining best interests, Major courts consider:

(a) The wishes of the parents;
(b) The wishes of the child;
(c) The interaction and relationship of the child with parent or parents, siblings, friends, and any other person who may significantly affect the child's best interests;
(d) The child's adjustment (or disruption) to home, school, and community;
(e) The emotional and physical health of all individuals involved; and
(f) Violence or potential child abuse.

"We unanimously find that since the children were with their natural father and there was no evidence of child abuse, the status quo, custody with the father and mother, should be maintained.

"We now consider the issue of visitation for the grandparents. The controlling rule of law is that if there is only one remaining parent (no adoption by stepparent), the grandparents should have visitation rights. We hold that a grandparent not granted custody is generally entitled to reasonable visitation unless this is not in the best interest of the child. In addition, visitation rights for any person may be ordered if in the best interests of the child.

"In this case, we are reluctant to force visitation against the wishes of the custodial party, the father. Disharmony is not in the best interest of the child. Ordinarily, a parent's obligation to allow grandparent visitation is moral, not legal. Judicial enforcement might harm parental authority. Nevertheless, on balance, this case involves a natural grandparent. We are persuaded to allow the grandparents reasonable visitation."

Crocker v. Crocker, 195 Maj. 2d 236 (1960): "Parties may negotiate an agreement awarding custody of minor children unless the agreement is contrary to the best interests of the children. A court will incorporate the agreement into a decree (dissolution cases) or in the case of child custody into an order. But the court is not bound by the terms of the agreement. State of Major courts have the equitable power to intercede if the agreement is not in the best interests of the child. The power of the court to modify the agreement or decree continues throughout the minority of the child."

Research Memorandum #80: Consumer Actions

Brauscher v. Hollydick, 284 Maj. 3d 14 (1987): "Hollydick purchased a 1987 Lyon stationwagon from Brauscher Auto Deals. Hollydick asserts that the stationwagon is a 'lemon' and has not been mechanically operative since he bought it. He claims a breach of warranties.

"Any affirmation of fact or promise will create an express warranty. The statement, 'This car has never been in a wreck,' created an express warranty. A seller does not have to use the term 'warrant' or 'guarantee.'

"An affirmation merely of the value of the goods, seller's opinion, or commendation does not create a warranty. Therefore, terms such as 'A-1,' 'mechanically perfect,' 'good quality,' 'last a lifetime,' 'perfect condition,' do not give rise to a warranty. They are the seller's opinion or commendation, and are not a warranty. Likewise, laudatory comments about a product can be merely 'puffing.'

"The test to decide if statements are warranties was suggested by the Major Supreme Court in *Warkentine v. Cohen,* 198 Maj. 2d 500 (1961). 'Did the seller assume to assert a fact of which buyer was ignorant, or merely express judgment on something as to which each would have an opinion?'

"In this instance, Brauscher, the seller stated, 'This car has been driven only 10,000 miles and has been garaged for the past year while the old man was in Hawaii.' The statement created an express warranty, because it became part of the basis of the bargain.

"In addition to an express warranty, plaintiff Hollydick claims that the seller may be liable under an implied warranty of merchantability. We are in accord. The Uniform Major Commercial Code provides in part:

(a) goods must pass without objection under the contract description, and
(b) be fit for the ordinary purpose for which such goods are used.

If Hollydick, the buyer, can show that the goods were not merchantable when sold, he may recover if he can show actual damage.

"A seller may only disclaim the implied warranty of

merchantability through specific terms, 'AS IS.' In this case, since the car was not sold, 'AS IS,' the plaintiff, Hollydick, might also have a claim for breach of implied warranty of merchantability."

Aristocratic Foods v. Consumer Action, 284 Maj. 3d 122 (1987): "A nonprofit group, Consumer Action, picketed and leafleted Aristocratic Foods. The consumer group claimed that Aristocratic Foods sells dairy products which are tainted and misrepresents the packaging date on dairy product labels. Aristocratic Foods has requested a preliminary and permanent injunction against the leafleting claiming the leaflets are misleading and interfere with customer access to its store.

"The Supreme Court in the State of Major has recognized that handbilling in front of a business may be the only manner to reach the intended audience. A municipality may, however, impose reasonable time and manner restrictions on the use of sidewalks. A governmental entity may not, however, premise these restrictions on the content of the speech nor may it assess the tastefulness of the handbills, as long as any information is being disseminated. But if the speech is untruthful, that speech, commercial or otherwise, will not be protected. Then a governmental entity may regulate the speech even if it is not provably false, but merely deceptive and misleading.

"We cannot help but comment that in this case such leafleting is protected speech, and not subject to regulation. Leafleting should not interfere with access to the store. It should be restricted to the parking lot and sidewalks and should not block the doors. Likewise, use of a loudspeaker system is protected and only when it is a clear public nuisance is it to be enjoined. An injunction would be issued in the rarest of cases. We are satisfied by the affidavits submitted by Consumer Action that the doors to the store have never been blocked by the leafleters. The movant, Aristocratic Foods, has also failed to prove irreparable harm. The mere assertion that profits declined by 5% per week since the consumer leafleting began can be caused by many factors, the poor economy, or other market factors. Aristocratic must make a more convincing case showing that Consumer Action's leafleting caused a significant loss of sales per week. Application for a preliminary injunction is denied without prejudice."

Random v. Quint, 285 Maj. 3d 130 (1988): "Defamation requires communication to a third person. If communication is only to the injured person, no action for defamation arises.

"The alleged defamation must hold the plaintiff up to hatred, ridicule, or contempt, or cause him to be shunned or avoided. The term 'crook,' as heard by others, has been held to be sufficient grounds to give rise to an action for defamation. Publication can be shown by the report of a rumor, if the other elements of defamation are met. Generally, the plaintiff must show actual damages for slander. One of the major exceptions is imputation of crime, even if it is made clear that plaintiff was not to be prosecuted.

"Mr. Random claims that he was defamed when Ms. Quint said the words, 'I know your kind, anyone prosecuted for murder can't be trusted.' Two months prior to the statement, Random was arrested for murder, but subsequently charges were dropped. Since truth is an absolute defense, and plaintiff has shown *no injury,* we dismiss."

Major Rev. Code §46.37.500 (1987): "It is unlawful for any person to sell, disconnect, turn back, or reset the odometer of any motor vehicle with the intent or knowledge that the odometer has been turned back if that person fails to notify the buyer, prior to the time of sale, that the odometer has been turned back or that he has reason to believe that the odometer has been turned back.

"Any person found in violation of this statute is guilty of a misdemeanor and shall, upon conviction, be sentenced to three months in jail and/or a fine of $300.

"In any suit brought by the purchaser of a motor vehicle against the seller of such vehicle, the purchaser shall be entitled to recover three times the amount of actual damages sustained or $1,500, whichever is greater, and in the case of a successful recovery of damages, the costs of the action as well as reasonable attorney fees."

Research Memorandum #81: Contracts; Interference with Business Relationships

Black v. Whyte, 283 Maj. 3d 129 (1987): "In a breach of contract action, conversation about warranties was properly admissible as parol evidence because it clarified and did not vary or contradict the written terms of the contract. Verbal statements concerning a written agreement are also admissible if the writing is incomplete, is an impartial memorandum, or not a full integration of the terms. 'All ambiguities in the contract must be construed in favor of the defending party,' Major Restatement of Contracts 2d, section 22 (1986).

"The elements required for existence of an enforceable contract include: (1) that the parties are capable of contracting; (2) the parties are consenting; (3) the contract is for a lawful object; and (4) there is sufficient consideration. Further, parties to a contract do not have to deal with every contingency in order to have a valid contract."

Brucher v. Oldycke, 283 Maj. 3d 817 (1987): "Plaintiff brought an action to recover compensatory and punitive damages from a telephone company that had omitted her name from telephone directories, operator lists, and disrupted her telephone service.

"Interference with at-will relationships is now a recognized tort in most jurisdictions. It may be called inducing refusal to deal, interference with reasonable expectancy or with business relationships or, most frequently, interference with prospective economic advantage.

"Interference with at-will relationships includes five basic elements: (1) existing business relationship or expectancy—no contract is required; (2) knowledge by the interferer of the relationship or expectancy; (3) intentional act of interference; (4) proof that the interference caused the injury; and (5) damage to the plaintiff.

"A business relationship between the plaintiff and a third party must be proven by the plaintiff with some degree of specificity. The plaintiff must show future profit is a realistic expectation and not wishful thinking. The plaintiff, however, need not prove a guaranteed relationship; a prospective relationship is sufficient.

"Intent of the interferer is also an essential element of interference with at-will relations. The interferer must have intentionally interfered with the business relationship or expectancy of plaintiff and a third party.

"Some courts require malice as the intention. Malice is defined in the legal sense: the intent to do harm without justification. Malice does not require spite or ill-will.

"In the alternative, if no improper motive can be established, a court can look to the defendant's means of interference. If the means were tortious in themselves, the means were improper.

"See *Esta Trail Tours, Inc. v. Cotton*, 281 Maj. 3d 7 (1986). In *Esta Trail Tours*, the manager of a bus station carried out a campaign calculated to discourage prospective fares from using plaintiff's cabs. The manager damaged plaintiff's cabs and tore plaintiff's advertisements from telephone books in booths in the area. The court held that the defendant tortiously interfered with plaintiff's taxi cab business. Plaintiff was not required to prove that defendant was motivated by a desire to secure a business advantage over plaintiff. The tortious conduct of defendant was sufficient to prove improper means.

"But in this instance, we find that the plaintiff has not sufficiently proven with reasonable probability a business relationship between herself and a third party which would be consummated had her name been in the directory. Plaintiff could not prove that a caller was unable to reach plaintiff and consequently took her business elsewhere."

Research Memorandum #82: Discovery

1. Privileges

Bottom Corp. v. Major, 271 Maj. 3d 100 (1986): "This case addresses important questions concerning the scope of the attorney-client privilege and the applicability of the work product doctrine in proceedings to enforce tax summonses.

"Bottom Corporation sells widgets. In January 1986, the corporation discovered that its subsidiary made payments to foreign government officials in order to secure government business. General counsel conducted an internal investigation, sending questionnaires and interviewing corporate officers and employees. In March 1986, the Major Tax Department demanded production of:

all files relative to the investigation conducted under the supervision of counsel to identify payments to employees of foreign governments and any political contributions made by the company or any of its affiliates since January 1, 1971.

The records should include but not be limited to written questionnaires sent to managers of the Company's foreign affiliates, and memoranda or notes of the interviews conducted with officers and employees of the company and its subsidiaries.

"The company declined to produce the documents specified, claiming they were protected from disclosure by the attorney-client privilege and constituted the work product of attorneys prepared in anticipation of litigation. On August 31, the Major Tax Department filed a petition seeking enforcement of its summons. The trial court ordered the corporation to produce the documents. The Court of Appeals affirmed. We reverse.

"Federal Rule of Evidence 501 provides:

the privilege of a witness . . . shall be governed by the principles of the common law as they may be interpreted by courts in light of reason and experience.

The attorney-client privilege is the oldest of the privileges for confidential communications known to the common law. Its purpose is to encourage full and frank communication between attorneys and their clients, thereby promoting broader public interest in the observance of law and administration of justice. The privilege recognizes that sound legal advice or advocacy serves public ends and that such advice or advocacy depends upon the lawyer being fully informed by the client.

"We hold that the communications by Bottom Corporation employees to counsel are covered by the attorney-client privilege as to the responses to the questionnaires and any notes reflecting responses to interview questions.

"The summons reaches further, however, to notes and memoranda of interviews, which go beyond recording responses to questions. This raises the work product privilege. The Tax Department asserts that it has made a sufficient showing of necessity to overcome the work product doctrine protections. The Tax Department relies on the following language in the leading case, *Sickman v. Sayler,* 198 Maj. 2d 503 (1961):

> We do not mean to say that all written materials obtained or prepared by an adversary's counsel with an eye toward litigation are necessarily free from discovery in all cases. Where relevant and nonprivileged facts remain hidden in an attorney's file and where production of those facts is essential to the preparation of one's case, discovery may properly be had. And production might be justified where the witnesses are no longer available or may be reached only with difficulty.

"The above-quoted language from *Sickman,* however, did not apply to oral statements made by witnesses whether presently in the form of the attorney's mental impressions or memoranda. As to such material, the *Sickman* court did 'not believe that any showing of necessity can be made under the circumstances of this case so to justify production.' Forcing an attorney to disclose notes and memoranda of a witness's oral statements is particularly disfavored because it tends to reveal the attorney's mental processes.

"Rule 26 accords special protection to work product revealing the attorney's mental processes. The Rule permits disclosure of documents and tangible things constituting attorney work product upon a showing of substantial need and inability to obtain the equivalent without undue hardship. Rule 26 goes on to state:

> [I]n ordering discovery of such materials when the required showing has been made, the court shall protect against disclosure of the mental impressions, conclusions, opinions or legal theories of an attorney or other representative of a party concerning the litigation.

Although this language does not specifically refer to memoranda based on oral statements of witnesses, the *Sickman* court stressed the danger that compelled disclosure of such memoranda would reveal the attorney's mental processes. Some courts have concluded that *no* showing of necessity can overcome protection of work product which is based on oral statements from witnesses.

"We do not decide the issue at this time. It is clear that the wrong standard was applied by the trial court when it concluded that the Government had made a sufficient showing of necessity to overcome the protections of the work product doctrine, articulated by the first part of 26(b)(3). The notes and memoranda sought by the Government here are work product based on oral statements. If they reveal communications, they are, in this case, protected by the attorney-client privilege. To the extent they do not reveal communications, they reveal the attorneys' mental processes in evaluating the communications. As Rule 26 and *Sickman* make clear, such work product cannot be disclosed simply on a showing of substantial need and inability to obtain the equivalent without undue hardship.

"While we are not prepared at this juncture to say that such material is always protected by the work-product rule, we think a far stronger showing of necessity and unavailability by other means than was made by the Government or applied by the trial judge in this case would be necessary to compel disclosure."

Jude v. Harvey, 284 Maj. 3d 500 (1987): "This lawsuit arose from a car collision on a state highway near Judith Lake, Major, on March 15, 1982. Ms. Jude was traveling west when suddenly her car was surrounded by a dense cloud of smoke, causing her to collide with the car ahead. Ms. Jude claims the cloud of smoke and the ensuing collision were caused by Mr. Harvey's negligence in burning grain stubble in an adjacent field.

"At the time of the incident, Mr. Harvey had a liability insurance policy issued by Michael Insurance Company. Under the terms of this policy, Michael was obligated to defend Mr. Harvey against all insured claims. This contractual duty allowed Michael to select and retain an attorney to represent the insured and required the insured to cooperate in his defense.

"Two days after the accident, an investigator and adjuster for Michael contacted Mr. Harvey and tape-recorded his statement relating to the accident. The tape was subsequently transcribed. Several months later Ms. Jude filed a personal injury action against Harvey. Thereafter Mr. Harvey's deposition was taken, at which time he testified about the existence of the statement.

"Counsel for Jude requested a copy of the transcript of Mr. Harvey's statement. Defense counsel objected, claiming attorney-client privilege and work product. Jude requested an order compelling production. The trial court denied the order. The Court of Appeals reversed. The specific issue at hand is whether an insured's statement to his insurance carrier is protected from discovery by State of Major Rule of Civil Procedure 26(b)(3).

"Many federal and state courts have struggled over the proper interpretation of 26(b)(3), commonly referred to as the work product rule. The test for determining whether such work product is discoverable is whether the documents are prepared in anticipation of litigation and, if so, whether the party seeking discovery can show substantial need and that the party is unable without undue hardship to obtain the substantial equivalent of the materials by other means.

"It is difficult in this context to determine whether a document was prepared in anticipation of litigation since an insurance company's ordinary course of business entails litigation. The requirement of having an attorney involved in the case before documents prepared by an insurance carrier are protected is a conclusory determination of the issue and is contrary to the plain language of the rule. On the other hand, broad protection for all investigations conducted by an insurer is likewise an unsatisfactory answer to the problem. Should such a general rule be adopted, it is not hard to imagine insurers mechanically forming their practices so as to make all documents appear to be prepared in 'anticipation of litigation.' We believe the better approach to the problem is to look to the specific parties involved and the expectation of those parties.

"This case involves statements by a defendant. An insured is contractually obligated to cooperate with the insurance company. Such an obligation clearly creates a reasonable expectation that the content of statements made by the insured will not be revealed to the opposing party.

"The insurer on the other hand has a contractual obligation to act as the insured's agent and secure an attorney. The insured cannot choose the attorney but can expect the agent to transmit the statement to the attorney selected. Without an expectation of confidentiality, an insured may be hesitant to disclose everything known. Such nondisclosure could hinder representation by the selected attorney and the expectation is that statements made by the insured will be held in confidence. Without such protection, the in-

sured would bear many of the burdens of the insurance contract without reaping the benefits. The contractual obligation between insured and insurer mandates extension of this protection to statements made by an insured to his insurance company. Such an extension comports with the policy of maintaining certain restraints on bad faith, irrelevant and privileged inquiries and helps to ensure the just and fair resolution of disputes. Therefore, we hold that a statement made by an insured to an insurer following an automobile accident is protected from discovery under Fed. R. Civ. P. 26(b)(3).

"The question then remains whether respondents have shown substantial need. The determination of this issue is vested in the sound discretion of the trial judge, who should look at the facts and circumstances of each case in arriving at an ultimate conclusion. To justify disclosure, a party must show the importance of the information to the preparation of his case and the difficulty the party will face in obtaining substantially equivalent information from other sources if production is denied.

"The clearest case for ordering production is when crucial information is in the exclusive control of the opposing party. The substantial need standard is not met if the discovering party merely wants to be sure nothing has been overlooked or hopes to unearth damaging admissions. Several courts have held that statements contemporaneous with the occurrence may in some instances be unique and cannot be duplicated by later interviews or depositions, *Dougall v. Dunn,* 269 Maj. 3d 117 (1983). In general there is no justification for discovery of the statement of a person contained in work product materials, when the person is available for deposition. Whether a statement is contemporaneous and unique is a question of fact.

"In light of all these considerations, we are unable to see any error in the trial court's determination that Jude had 'substantial need' of Harvey's statement. Although the statement was taken two days after the accident, the passage of time alone is insufficient to allow discovery. Ms. Jude has failed to show any other extenuating circumstances justifying disclosure. The more important fact is that the statement in question is that of the defendant. The defendant is not unavailable; it was in his deposition that the conflict arose. There is no claim that he has no present recollection of the events in question. The primary reason for Ms. Jude wanting the statement in this instance, as we see it, is impeachment. General impeachment, alone, is insufficient to show substantial need. Since Jude made no other argument as to her substantial needs, we hold that Jude has failed to show a substantial need for the statement. We reverse the Court of Appeals and reinstate the ruling of the trial court upholding the work product privilege."

Dissent. Figment, J.: "I would affirm the Court of Appeals decision finding the statement of the insured to his insurance company is not protected by either the attorney-client privilege, or the work product immunity rule, Fed. R. Civ. P. 26(b)(3).

"I believe it is incorrect to hold that the initial inquiry or involvement by an insurance company regarding the possibility of a potential claim involving one of its insureds is made in anticipation of litigation. The initial inquiry is a gathering of facts from which the insurance company determines whether there may be a claim and if so whether the claim is covered by the insurance contract. I would hold the initial inquiry is always made in the ordinary course of the insurer's business. Only after the initial discussion of the claim can the insured and the insurance company determine whether the incident is covered and whether litigation can be anticipated. If litigation is anticipated, subsequent statements made by the insured would be protected. This determination accords broad and liberal treatment to the discovery rules and achieves the goal of ensuring mutual knowledge of all relevant facts, *Sickman v. Saylor*, 198 Maj. 2d 503 (1961)."

2. Fifth Amendment Privilege in a Civil Case

Skelly v. Sham, 260 Maj. 3d 777 (1982): "This is an appeal of the trial court ruling granting defendant a default judgment. We reverse and remand.

"Plaintiff Skelly brought a libel proceeding alleging that defendant Sham libeled her in a newspaper article which asserted that 'Darcy Skelly didn't write her last book; she relied on a ghost writer. She is a fraud.' Sham denied the libel. Plaintiff Skelly, when served with interrogatories, refused to answer those interrogatories inquiring whether she had sexual intercourse with a married man other than her husband. State of Major Statutes declare that adultery and fornication are misdemeanors. Skelly claimed the Fifth Amendment. Defendant Sham convinced the trial court that the inquiry was relevant to the issues [discussion of relevancy omitted]. The trial court, after plaintiff's invocation of privilege, struck her answer and allowed default judgment against her.

"Generally, the threat of incrimination must be a genuine and present one and is usually used in civil actions where conduct or testimony giving rise to civil liability also makes up an element of a crime. The general American rule is that the Fifth Amendment privilege may be invoked as long as a mere 'possibility' of prosecution for the crimes suggested by the response exists. A response or document 'tends to incriminate' as long as it might help discover facts that could tie together circumstantial evidence proving the invoker's criminal conduct.

"If a criminal threat is not pending, a sufficient 'penalty' or 'forfeiture' in a civil case may warrant invocation of the privilege. A 'sufficient penalty,' however, is not clearly defined in civil cases. But proceedings instituted for the purpose of declaring the forfeiture of a person's property because of offenses committed by him, although they may be in civil form, are in their nature criminal for Fifth Amendment purposes. However, this concept of 'penalty' should be 'strictly construed' so as to protect the non-invoking party from abuse of the privilege.

"The privilege protects against real dangers and not speculative possibilities. A party or witness must satisfy the court at trial that the claim of privilege is justified and not an abuse of the right.

"The use of the privilege may be asserted at the pretrial or trial stage by a civil litigant. We recognize that pretrial discovery may be deterred by the invocation of the privilege that important information necessary for the presentation of a prima facie case or a defense may be at the center of the discovery attempt which might be obstructed by the exercise of the privilege. But the importance of the privilege to our freedoms is too important to draw a restrictive line between criminal and civil actions. But the exercise of the privilege in a civil case is not absolute. No criminal sanctions can be used, such as contempt, and the usual sanctions for failing to grant discovery are not applicable when discovery is resisted by a good-faith claim of the privilege. (The courts have generally declined to strike a civil lawsuit or responsive answer or permit a default judgment.) Courts, however, have been willing to impose lesser sanctions since pretrial discovery is essential for a private civil litigant to develop a case.

"In the instant case, we are convinced that plaintiff really acted in good faith fearing a criminal prosecution. Although the trial court correctly ordered Skelly to comply with the court order to respond to defendant's interrogatories, the sanction imposed for refusal was improper. Imposition of lesser sanctions would have been proper. A default judgment was unduly harsh. We suggest the trial court consider the availability of broad choices of sanctions when dealing with good-faith exercises of the privilege in civil litigation. Reversed and remanded."

State of Major Bar v. Hawk, 268 Maj. 3d 244 (1983): "The State of Major Bar brought disciplinary charges for professional misconduct against attorney George Hawk, a member of the Bar. Hawk refused to produce demanded financial records and to testify at an administrative hearing on the grounds that the records and/or testimony would incriminate him. The judge correctly balanced the prejudice to the defendant against the probative need for the particular information sought in order to make a fair determination.

"We hold that the self-incrimination clause of the Fifth Amendment applies to lawyers. Exercising one's Fifth Amendment privilege should not be diluted nor penalized by imposing the dishonor of disbarment or the deprivation of livelihood as a penalty for asserting it. But consequences may follow failure to produce information."

3. Discovery of Expert Witness

Sarah v. Davidel, 283 Maj. 3d 144 (1987): "The question on appeal is whether plaintiff must identify each and every doctor, physician, or medical expert plaintiff's counsel retain or specially employ during pretrial investigation and preparation. The courts have been divided on the issue. Court Rule 26(b)(4) governs the scope of discovery concerning experts.

"First we will explore whether discovery of experts informally consulted, but not retained or specially employed, is required by the rule. No provision in Court Rule 26(b)(4) expressly deals with nonwitness experts who are informally consulted by a party in preparation for trial, but not retained or specially employed in anticipation of litigation.

"In our view, the status of each expert must be determined on an ad hoc basis. Several factors should be considered: (1) the manner in which the consultation was initiated; (2) the nature, type, and extent of information or material provided to, or determined by, the expert in connection with his review; (3) the duration and intensity of the consultative relationship; and (4) the terms of the consultation, if any (e.g., payment, confidential data or opinions, etc.). Of course, additional factors bearing on this determination may be examined if relevant.

"The determination of the status of the expert rests, in the first instance, with the party resisting discovery. Should the expert be considered informally consulted, that categorization should be provided in response. The propounding party should then be provided the opportunity of requesting a determination of the expert's status based on an in camera review by the court. Inasmuch as the District Court failed to express its

views on this question, we deem it appropriate to remand rather than attempt to deal with the merits of this issue on appeal. If the expert is considered to have been only informally consulted in anticipation of litigation, discovery is barred.

"Second, we need to determine if plaintiff needs to give defendant discovery of the identities of experts retained or specially employed. Subdivision (b)(4)(B) of Rule 26 specifically deals with nonwitness experts who have been retained or specially employed by a party in anticipation of litigation. Facts or opinions of nonwitness experts retained or specially employed may only be discovered upon a showing of 'exceptional circumstances under which it is impracticable for the party seeking discovery to obtain facts or opinions on the same subject by other means.' Discovery of the identities of the experts, absent a showing of exceptional circumstances, was not expressly precluded by the text of subdivision (b)(4)(B); the District Court found the general provisions of Rule 26(b)(1) controlling. Subdivision (b)(1) provides:

(b) *Scope of Discovery.* Unless otherwise limited by order of the court in accordance with these rules, the scope of discovery is as follows:

(1) *In General.* Parties may obtain discovery regarding any matter, not privileged, which is relevant to the subject matter involved in the pending action, . . . including the . . . identity and location of persons having knowledge of any discoverable matter.

"The advisory committee notes to the rule indicate that the structure of Rule 26 was largely developed around the doctrine of unfairness, designed to prevent a party from building a case by means of his opponent's financial resources, superior diligence, and more aggressive preparation.

"There are several reasons for overruling the District Court. Once the identities of retained or specially employed experts are disclosed, the protective provisions of the rule concerning facts known or opinions held by such experts are subverted. The expert may be contacted or his records obtained and information normally nondiscoverable, under Rule 26(b)(4)(B), revealed. Similarly, although perhaps rarer, the opponent may compel an expert retained or specially employed by an adverse party who does not intend to call that expert, to testify at trial. The possibility also exists that a party may call his opponent to the stand and ask if certain experts were retained in anticipation of trial, but not called as a witness, thereby leaving with the jury an inference that the retaining party is attempting to suppress adverse facts or opinions. We also agree with plaintiff's view that disclosure of the identities of medical consultative experts would inevitably lessen the number of candid opinions available as well as the number of consultants willing to even discuss a potential medical malpractice claim with counsel. . . .

"Lastly, we affirm that the identity, and other collateral information, concerning an expert who is retained or specially employed in anticipation of litigation, but not expected to be called as a witness at trial, is not discoverable except as 'provided in Rule 35(b) or upon a showing of exceptional circumstances under which it is impracticable for the party seeking discovery to obtain facts or opinions on the same subject by other means.' Court Rule 26(b)(4)(B). The party seeking disclosure under Rule 26(b)(4)(B) carries a heavy burden in demonstrating the existence of exceptional circumstances.

"The order of the District Court is vacated and remanded. On remand, the status of the nonwitness experts against whom discovery is sought should be undertaken as a two-step process. First, was the expert informally consulted in anticipation of litigation but not retained or specially employed? If so, no discovery may be had as to the identity or opinions of the expert. Second, if the expert was *not* informally consulted, but retained or specially employed in anticipation of litigation, but not expected to testify at trial, do exceptional circumstances exist justifying disclosure of the expert's identity, opinions or other collateral information?

"Vacated and remanded."

4. Discovery of Expert's Report and Notes

Old City v. Bond, 281 Maj. 3d 77 (1986): "Plaintiff brought suit against defendant aircraft manufacturer for personal injuries as a result of an aircraft crash. Plaintiff requested discovery of three reports compiled by defendant's expert witnesses. Plaintiff delivered allegedly defective aircraft parts to defendant for analysis. Defendant's three experts each compiled a report based on examination of the aircraft parts. Defendant supplied plaintiff with one of the three reports.

"Generally, reports and notes of an expert are not discoverable by the opposing party absent a showing of exceptional circumstances demonstrating an undue hardship. Written reports compiled by expert employees of defendant manufacturer are not discoverable where the reports were prepared in anticipation of litigation. Plaintiff did not assert that the reports were necessary to build plaintiff's own case-in-chief. While plaintiff asserted that the reports were necessary for cross-examination, this was not a sufficient showing of exceptional circumstances. We conclude

that plaintiffs can obtain the substantial equivalent of the reports by other means without undue hardship."

Williams v. Oakes, 283 Maj. 3d 111 (1987): "This case involves a contract action for damages stemming from the collapse of a giant ore excavating machine. The third party defendant filed a motion to compel production of certain documents compiled by the plaintiff's auditors. The auditors had prepared a settlement proposal for plaintiff, estimating the amount of damages due from the collapse. The proposal was advanced as an alternative claim for damages. Defendant sought discovery of all materials used in formulating assumptions and alternate assumptions.

"Defendant may discover all materials used in arriving at assumptions and alternate assumptions, since the settlement offer had become a formal alternative claim for damages. Since the auditors will testify as to why they have selected the particular proposal, defendant should have access to materials which are relevant to the decisions."

5. Discoverability of Income Tax Records

Neddleman v. Knowles, 274 Maj. 3d 112 (1984): "Plaintiff brought an action for wrongful death asserting that defendant acted willfully and maliciously, claiming punitive damages. Plaintiffs requested copies of defendant's income tax returns for the prior two years.

"It is discretionary with a court in which a civil action is pending to require one party to produce a copy of a federal or state tax return for inspection by the adverse party in a discovery proceeding. Absent unusual circumstances, income tax records are not subject to discovery. Where punitive damages are alleged, the wealth of the defendant is pertinent and material to the issue of the case. Pretrial discovery of a defendant's financial condition is not available to a plaintiff who merely seeks compensatory damages. Plaintiff need only allege punitive damages and need not establish a prima facie case to discover tax records."

6. Discovery of Medical Records

Branson v. Superior Court of Jamner County, 269 Maj. 3d 43 (1983): "Plaintiffs filed a petition seeking extraordinary relief challenging the superior court order requiring plaintiffs to respond to defendant's interrogatories. Plaintiffs seek damages for diminution of property value, personal injuries, and emotional disturbance allegedly caused by Jamner County's operation of an airport. They complain of noise, vibrations, air pollution, and smoke, caused by the international airport. Defendants in interrogatories requested complete disclosure of each plaintiff's entire lifetime medical histories.

"The patient/litigant exception to the physician/patient privilege allows only a limited inquiry into the confidences of the physician/patient relationship, compelling disclosure of only those matters directly relevant to the nature of the specific condition the patient has disclosed or tendered in the pleading or answer to discovery inquiries. It is a limited waiver concomitant with the purpose of the exception.

"In this case, the trial court's order requiring unlimited disclosure is impermissibly overbroad. Plaintiffs are not obligated to sacrifice all privacy to seek redress for a specific physical, mental, or emotional injury. Plaintiffs are entitled to retain the confidentiality of all unrelated medical or psychotherapeutic treatment they may have undergone in the past. Plaintiffs may not, however, withhold information which relates to any physical or mental lawsuit. For example, if plaintiff claims that airport operations have damaged his respiratory system, he would be obliged to disclose all medical information relating to his respiratory condition and could not limit discovery simply to those airport-related incidents which have allegedly injured his condition."

Roberts v. Superior Court, 268 Maj. 3d 42 (1983): "We affirm the Superior Court order compelling plaintiff to respond to defendant's interrogatories.

"Plaintiff brought a personal injury action against defendant for personal injuries allegedly caused by an automobile collision. Plaintiff claimed that as a result of the collision she was rendered 'sick, distressed, lame, and disabled.' Defendant requested plaintiff's lifetime medical and psychological history and requested a description of the injuries she claimed to have suffered in the collision. Plaintiff refused to disclose any information about her physical or psychiatric history.

"Since plaintiff alleged vague, *unspecified* injuries, i.e., emotional disturbances, personal injuries, defendant should be able to discover a larger scope of records in order to narrow down *specific injuries* allegedly caused by the accident. Where plaintiff is not specific in identifying the injuries, defendant should not be liable for wholesale injuries without regard to whether injuries were caused by defendant. Plaintiff should not be able to claim damages for unspecified injuries and deny defendant access to information relevant in identifying specific injuries."

7. Use of Witness Deposition

Towndale v. Hefty, 276 Maj. 3d 144 (1985): "Defendant contended that plaintiff's deposition was not admissible because plaintiff was mentally incompetent to testify. At the time of the taking of the deposition, the plaintiff was undergoing hip treatment and had a progressive disease involving the hardening of her arteries.

"The trial court ruled the deposition admissible even though at the time of trial the court excluded plaintiff's oral testimony after examining her competency.

"Generally, a deposition is not admissible into evidence if the presence of the deponent nonparty witness can be attained at the trial, see Court Rule 32. Nevertheless, a deposition can be admissible into evidence at trial if the absence of the deponent at the time of the trial is based upon sufficient grounds. If a deponent is within the jurisdiction and a prescribed distance from the place of the trial but cannot offer competent proof of his inability to attend trial, his deposition is rendered inadmissible. Old age and infirmity, illness, or some other reasonable excuse for his absence are generally sufficient. The general rule, however, is that the deposition of a witness will not be admitted when he has been called and examined at trial or can be examined absent an agreement or waiver.

"Under Major law, a person is competent to testify if, at the time, he understands the oath and can give a correct account of what he has seen and heard. Plaintiff was not competent to testify at trial, but was competent at the time the deposition was taken. The general rule is that a subsequent change in the deponent's competency may render the deposition admissible if, at the taking of the deposition, the competency of the deponent was adequately determined. In this case, the deposition was properly admitted at trial since the competency of the deponent was established in the record of the deposition and by the trial judge at the time it was used."

Lauren v. Michaels, 284 Maj. 3d 164 (1987): "The trial court properly ruled that the deposition of witness Rose was inadmissible.

"A deposition will not be admitted into evidence if the deponent's attendance could have been attained at trial. Proof which raises a reasonable presumption that the witness is outside the jurisdiction or proof of death is all that is needed. When any uncertainty as to the deponent's location exists, however, mere statements by the offeree or a returned subpoena is not enough to allow the deposition to be admitted. Plaintiffs in this case failed to provide objective evidence that witness Rose had left the jurisdiction. Affirmed."

In re Fife, 276 Maj. 3d 222 (1985): "The State Bar found petitioner guilty of violating certain rules governing attorney conduct. Petitioner made a motion to exclude three witness depositions because they were not signed. Petitioner's motion was denied and the depositions were admitted. We reverse. There is no evidence that the witnesses waived signature. The depositions were therefore inadmissible."

8. Sanctions

Straight v. Ike, 280 Maj. 3d 8 (1986): "Appellant appeals the trial court's order granting default judgment against him.

"Respondent Ike sent interrogatories to appellant Straight on September 1, 1984, which Straight represented would be answered by December 1, 1984. Between January 3, 1985 and March 1985 appellant made numerous representations that the interrogatories would be answered. In response to respondent's motion to compel filed in April 1985, the trial court issued an order compelling appellant Straight to answer the interrogatories. Appellant ignored the order. Court Rule 37 enumerates sanctions that are not exclusive but are flexible which may be applied in many varied forms at the court's discretion. The appropriate sanction is determined through analysis of the particular facts of the case grounded in the sound discretion of the trial court.

"A court should consider not only the prejudice to the discovering party but also the necessity to maintain the power of a court order and the deterrent effect of the sanction.

"Sanctions imposed by a court are only somewhat affected by a party's willingness or good faith attempt to comply with the discovery order. These are relevant in mitigating the sanction imposed but will not forego application of a sanction altogether (unless the party cannot be culpable because of circumstances out of his control).

"Under Court Rule 37 a court may deem established, facts which a plaintiff cannot fairly prove because of the defendant's refusal to comply with the court's discovery order. Use of this sanction enables a court to carefully use its order to confront the specific information sought and wrongfully withheld so as to give the responding party due process. Consequently, a party may be deprived of at least one issue. The sanction is not limited, however, to one issue and so the court may find facts dispositive of an entire action and enter summary judgment.

"A court may use Court Rule 37(b)(2)(B) to stop a party from presenting material into evidence that it did not bring in during discovery, or from presenting evidence backing up certain claims or defenses. A court also may issue an order striking out all or any part of a party's pleading if the party (or counsel) refuses to obey a discovery order or willfully fails to appear for the taking of his deposition upon proper notice. This sanction is warranted in such cases as where the defendant fails to answer interrogatories, fails to seek a protective order, or moves for an extension of time after the deadline is reached.

"A court may use preclusion of testimony as a sanction. This sanction can be used when a defendant refuses to answer deposition questions by asserting the self-incrimination privilege. Barring testimony is also appropriate where a party does not disclose a witness in response to a discovery request.

"A court has discretion to dismiss an action for failure to comply with a discovery order. Since this sanction is of last resort, it should be strictly construed by the court and a less drastic but as equally effective remedy should be possibly used. A dismissal is appropriate for deliberate, repeated, or persistent failures to answer interrogatories, for filing incomplete or evasive answers, or for intending to disregard further discovery orders.

"The sanction of default judgment is much the same as a dismissal and since it is an extreme measure, it should be used only as a last resort. This sanction is generally appropriate where a party (or counsel) has acted in bad faith in failing to comply with discovery rules or with court orders enforcing the rules.

"In this instance, the trial court did not abuse its discretion when it struck appellant Straight's answer and granted default judgment for amounts owing. Appellant unreasonably delayed responding and showed a calculated disregard of the Court Rules."

Rudolph v. Fibb, 281 Maj. 3d 53 (1986): "Plaintiff is the surviving spouse, bringing this wrongful death action. She refused to be deposed prior to trial so as not to incriminate herself. Trial court held that it would prohibit plaintiff from testifying if she continued in her refusal to be deposed. The trial court's sanction is proper, even though plaintiff acted in good faith."

Research Memorandum #83: Duty to Defend

Major Insurance Code (1987):

Section 12743: Conflict of Interest Problems Arising from Insurer's Duty to Defend. "A conflict of interest may arise if the insured is sued for an amount in excess of the insurance coverage and the insurer assumes the defense of its insured. To avoid this, the insurer must act in good faith and immediately disclose any conflict that arises. The insurer can then withdraw or make arrangements for appointment of counsel to alleviate the conflict."

Section 826: Insured's Duty Under Liability Policy. "The insured is required to comply with his obligations under the policy. Breach of the insured's duties such as the duty to cooperate in his or her defense may relieve the insurer of the duty to defend. The breach must be material or prejudicial."

Prejudice Insurance Company v. Hanson, 260 Maj. 3d 518 (1982): "The Prejudice Insurance Company refused to defend its insured, Hanson, in an incident involving Hanson and the Wakefield Shipping Company. The insured, covered by a homeowner's policy, brought an action against the yacht policy insurer for recovery of the settlement sum. Insured was awarded the settlement sum, $500,000; punitive damages of $200,000; attorney's fees; and costs. The insurance company has appealed the judgment.

"An insurer has four alternatives when presented with notice of a claim against its insured.

"1. The insurer can elect to defend. Under a standard insurance policy, the insurer has exclusive control over the defense in any action brought against the insured. The insurer may be precluded from asserting the defense of noncoverage or other policy defenses if it assumes the defense and has not obtained a non-waiver agreement or reserved its rights.

"2. The insurer can elect to defend but reserves its right to bring defenses against the insured. A Reservation of Rights is a unilateral offer by the insurer to defend subject to preservation of the insurer's rights to assert policy defenses.

"3. The insurer can elect to defend, but withdraw from the defense before concluding the case. This is only allowed, however, where prejudice to the insured will not result.

"4. The insurer can seek a declaratory judgment in order to determine if it has a duty to defend.

"The State of Major follows the general rule that an insurer's duty to defend is determined from the allegations of the complaint. The test used is whether the facts alleged in the complaint, if proved, would render the insurer liable under the policy. Major courts liberally construe the pleadings, requiring the insurer to defend if there could be *any* interpretation that creates the duty.

"There are four types of allegations in a complaint:

"1. The allegations clearly fall within or outside the scope of the insurance coverage. The insurer has a duty to defend if the facts alleged are within policy coverage. Conversely, the insurer is not under a duty to defend if the facts alleged are outside the policy.

"2. The factual allegations are both covered and not covered under the policy. Where the court cannot separate the claims within and outside the policy coverage, the insurer is under a duty to defend.

"3. The allegations of the complaint are ambiguous or inadequate. If there is an ambiguity or the allegations are inadequate, the insurer may be required to conduct a reasonable investigation.

"4. There is a conflict between the known or ascertainable facts and the facts as alleged in the complaint. The reasonable investigation rule may apply in this situation.

"Thus, the insurer's duty to defend is not always defined by the facts recited in the complaint. The insurer may be required to go beyond the tactical allegations in the complaint and conduct a reasonable investigation into the facts before disclaiming a duty to defend.

"The insurance company's duty arose even though the complaint failed to describe facts which were covered under the policy coverage. Nevertheless, there was a reasonable possibility that facts would arise in the course of the action which would be covered. And, in fact, these facts did arise. Judgment affirmed."

Gloss Insurance v. Dotts, 276 Maj. 3d 32 (1985): "Gloss Insurance Co. (Gloss) issued Harry Dotts a mobile homeowner's liability policy providing personal liability for damages due to bodily injury caused by an 'occurrence.' The policy defines 'occurrence' as:

an *accident,* including injurious exposure to conditions, which results, during the policy term, in bodily injury or property damage.

"The policy excluded from personal liability 'bodily injury or property damage which is either expected or intended from the standpoint of the insured.'

"During early morning hours, Mr. Dotts went to visit his girlfriend. He found his girlfriend with another man, David McKee. Mr. McKee was sitting on the bed. Dotts and his girlfriend agreed David McKee should leave. Mr. Dotts sat down on the bed next to Mr. McKee and asked him if he would leave. Mr. McKee did not respond nor look at Mr. Dotts. To get Mr. McKee's attention, Mr. Dotts began a motion to slap Mr. McKee with his open palm. Mr. McKee started to lean back, and Mr. Dotts instinctively adjusted the motion of his arm and hand. Thus, the contact between Mr. Dotts' hand and Mr. Mc-Kee's face was an open-handed, backhanded slap. The contact did not mark the insured's hand or McKee's face. No other physical contact occurred. Soon, Mr. McKee left the premises, seemingly unaffected by Mr. Dotts' slap. Later that morning, Mr. McKee was taken to a hospital, where he lapsed into a coma. He died five days later without regaining consciousness.

"A county jury convicted Mr. Dotts of involuntary manslaughter and second-degree assault. At the trial, Mr. Dotts testified he did not intend to hurt the deceased and he was not angry with him; Mr. Dotts just wanted to get Mr. McKee's attention.

"James McKee brought a civil suit for damages. Later, Gloss Insurance filed a separate declaratory judgment action seeking a determination it had no duty to defend Mr. Dotts and no duty to pay any judgment. Gloss moved for summary judgment that David McKee's death was not an 'occurrence' covered by the policy. Gloss Insurance Company's motion was granted, and James McKee and Mr. Dotts appeal.

"Appellants maintain coverage exists under an 'occurrence' policy for intentional acts which cause subjectively unintended resultant injuries. Mr. Dotts' policy equates an 'occurrence' with an 'accident.' The longstanding Major rule in accidental death in all cases except products liability is:

> [T]o recover under a policy insuring against death or injury by accidental means, (1) it is not enough that the *result* was unusual, unexpected, or unforeseen, but it must appear that the *means* were accidental; and (2) *accident is never present when a deliberate act is performed, unless some additional unexpected, independent, and unforeseen happening occurs which produces or brings about the result of injury or death.*

"The appellants claim support from *Zinn v. Pride Insurance Co.*, 130 Maj. 2d 921 (1947). In that case, a doctor intentionally made a small incision in the insured's arm to withdraw blood to evaluate treatment of the insured's high blood pressure. The usual precautions for this routine procedure were taken, but the insured nevertheless developed blood poisoning and died from bacteria introduced into the incision. The court found an accident:

> Although the incision which afforded a channel of entry for the germs was intentionally made, the entry of the deadly germs was not normally effected, but was wholly unintentional, unforeseen, and unexpected, and it was the admission of those germs, rather than the intentional act of the doctor, which caused the death. Id. at 923.

In reaching its conclusion, the *Zinn* court articulated the rule which was the majority rule in 1947 as it is today, that 'death is accidental, even though the means are intentional, where the results are unusual, unexpected, or unforeseen.' *Zinn*, at 927.

"But in this case, Dotts intended to slap McKee. His act and the results were foreseeable.

"Having found no material factual issue of whether Mr. McKee's death resulted from the slap, as a matter of law there was no occurrence within the meaning of the insurance policy. We therefore do not address whether the insured's criminal convictions established he subjectively 'expected' or 'intended' to inflict bodily harm on the decedent.

"The judgment of the Superior Court is affirmed."

Reliance Insurance Company v. Randall, 284 Maj. 2d 174 (1987): "The Reliance Insurance Company refused to defend Boe in a negligence action, claiming the action as described in the complaint was not covered by Boe's insurance policy. Plaintiffs obtained a default judgment against Boe for one million ($1,000,000) dollars which was $500,000 in excess of Boe's insurance policy. Boe claimed that the insurance company negligently and in bad faith breached its duty to defend him. Boe claims punitive damages for the company's tortious breach of contract and for his emotional distress because of the company's failure to defend him. Boe assigned his claim against Reliance Insurance Company to plaintiff Randall.

"The trial court ruled that, in determining whether the insurer was guilty of negligence or bad faith in failing to defend the action and to settle for an amount in excess of the policy limits, the jury should consider whether the insurer calculated its potential liability for failure to defend; investigated the potential recoverable damages; concluded what the settlement value of the case would be after the default judgment; initiated or pursued settlement negotiations after the default judgment; or sought to enlist a contribution from its insured commensurate with that portion of the settlement which the insured should contribute.

"Major courts have adopted the bad-faith test in cases involving an insurer's refusal to settle within the policy limits, and would likewise apply the bad-faith test to excess judgment cases where the insurer wrongfully refused to defend because of a denial of coverage and refused to settle within the policy limits during the course of the litigation.

"The duty of a liability insurer to defend its insured is distinct from, and broader than, the duty to indemnify; the policy gives the insurer the right to defend and to control the investigation, handling, and settling of a lawsuit; and the duty to the insured in the exercise of those rights is in the nature of a fiduciary one, requiring the exercise of good faith. The concept of bad faith presupposes that the company is not attempting to exercise skill, judgment, and fidelity on behalf of the insured.

"Damages for an insured's emotional distress, caused by his insurer's bad-faith refusal to defend an action against him, have been allowed on a tort theory, *Great Blue Insurance v. Herron,* 268 Maj. 3d 420 (1983). In *Great Blue Insurance,* an automobile liability insurer initially refused to defend a personal injury action against its insured, claiming noncoverage. The insured then sued the insurer in breach of contract and tort before the personal injury action was tried. The insurer undertook the defense of the action against the insured under a reservation of rights. The *Great Blue Insurance* court held that, although the personal injury action against the insured was still pending, the insured was entitled to recover, in tort, for the insurer's breach of the implied covenant of good faith and fair dealing. Damages were allowed for the following injuries: (1) emotional distress resulting from the insurer's initial refusal to defend, and the uncertainty as to whether it would actually defend the personal injury action; and (2) severe emotional distress intentionally inflicted by the insurer. The court stated that to limit the recovery by the insured and the liability of the insurer to the amount of the policy plus attorney's fees and costs in instances in which the insurer has breached its duty to act fairly and in good faith by failing to defend the insured would, in many instances, preclude recovery by the insured for damages for emotional distress.

"Punitive damages for tortious breach of contract and/or emotional distress is recognized by some courts. Major courts, however, have disallowed all but consequential damages for breach of contract. In Randall's case, the insurance company undertook extensive investigation before refusing to defend and in good faith refused to defend. The company is liable only for consequential damages since it acted in good faith."

Research Memorandum #84: Employment Dispute

Murphy, Contracts §17 (1985):

General Principles of Employment Law in the State of Major. "An employment contract must contain the elements necessary to form a simple contract. These elements include: (1) definitiveness as to parties, nature of services, and compensation, (2) mutuality of obligation, and (3) promises supported by consideration.

"A contract that is not to be performed within one year must comply with the Statute of Frauds.

"Employment contracts with no time provisions, however, are generally considered terminable at will by either party. Employment contracts that are terminable at will may potentially be completed within one year; therefore, they are not subject to the Statute of Frauds. Oral employment contracts which purport to fix a multi-year term also may escape the Statute of Frauds. If either party may repudiate the contract prior to complete performance, the contract may potentially be performed within one year.

"If an employee cannot sustain the burden of showing compliance with the Statute of Frauds, a contract may be implied in law."

Warner v. Texas Pacific R.R., 257 Maj. App. 3d 418 (1982): "An employee seeking to enforce an oral promise of wage increase which is subject to the Statute of Frauds prevailed on the ground of equitable estoppel. The purpose of the Statute of Frauds is to prevent fraud. Nevertheless, an employer cannot use the statute as a shield.

"An employee who has been induced to change position in reliance on an oral promise may seek enforcement through promissory estoppel. Generally, the employee must demonstrate injury or unjust enrichment to the employer. In this instance, the employer benefitted from the employee's unique services. By continually promising a wage increase, plaintiff was induced to forego other employment opportunities at a substantially higher salary. Judgment affirmed."

McFish v. Bait, 257 Maj. App. 3d 16 (1982): "An employer's right of arbitrary discharge is limited. Plaintiff claimed that the McFish Company dismissed her for reporting the restaurant to the Environmental Fish Club for keeping live squid in a nonhumane manner. The trial court refused to extend the common law to recognize an action for tortious breach of contract. Instead the trial court ruled that in this instance, the plaintiff stated a good claim for relief on a number of theories based in contract and on bad faith breach of an implied contract of employment, as being contrary to public policy."

Concurring, JJ. Bickel and Brewsic: "We would follow a minority of jurisdictions which would allow recovery in tort for a wrongful discharge. Several state supreme courts have allowed recovery for malicious or retaliatory termination. In those cases, the plaintiff must demonstrate that the primary reason for termination was retaliation or malice, and such termination is contrary to well established public policy. In this instance, we note that retaliation for report to authorities is violative of well established public policy interest."

Research Memorandum #85: Leases

List v. Drake, 280 Maj. 3d 26 (1986): "Jury verdict in favor of landlord is affirmed. Drake was operating a Thai restaurant, which he claimed was a failing enterprise. He asked the landlord to allow him to assign his ten-year written lease to a man who wanted to operate a laundromat. The landlord refused assignment claiming he felt the laundromat would be unsuccessful.

"A sublease and assignment must be distinguished. If the lessee transfers the entire term and has no reversion, the transfer is an assignment. If, however, a reversion in the estate is retained, the transfer is a sublease. Under a sublease, the tenant-in-chief is liable under the terms of the original lease, and merely receives rent from the sublessee.

"The State of Major has a statutory provision, Maj. Real Property Sec. 140 regarding a landlord's discretion in denying an assignment.

> The rental agreement may restrict the tenant's right to assign the rental agreement in any manner. The tenant's right to sublease the premises may be conditioned on obtaining the landlord's consent, which shall not be unreasonably withheld. No consideration of race, creed, sex, marital status, religion, national origin, or political opinion or affiliation may be relied on by the landlord as reasonable grounds for rejection.

"Leases are generally considered contracts, with implied covenants of reasonableness and fair dealing. We note five factors which a trial court may properly allow the jury to consider in determining reasonableness of the assignment or sublease:

(a) The financial responsibility of the proposed tenant,

(b) suitability of the proposed sub-tenant for the leasehold,

(c) the sub-tenant's needs in excess of the tenant-in-chief,

(d) legality of the proposed use,

(e) nature of the proposed occupancy (retail, manufacturing, etc.).

"Thus, the lessor must only be reasonable in refusing consent. The landlord's refusal should be related to the purposes of the tenancy created. In *Kelly v. Arnold,* 269 Maj. 3d 126 (1983), the landlord's refusal to allow an assignment of the lease was reasonable when the potential assignor had sufficient capital, but not equal business acumen. 'A landlord's decision (based on an objective and documented investigation) that a potential business will not be successful may be

valid grounds to refuse an assignment. The burden is upon the lessee, who in this case failed to prove unreasonableness.'

"We note that if a tenant, over the landlord's objections, subleases and then abandons the property, the landlord should mitigate damages by accepting the sub-tenant and suing the tenant-in-chief for cover damages. A landlord may not reject a suitable sub-lessee and accelerate the lease.

"Generally, however, the landlord may consider the lease terminated and enjoin the tenant or seek damages. But courts generally prefer awarding damages, rather than injunctive relief, if the attempted transfer is a breach of contract.

"In this case, the landlord correctly mitigated his damages by accepting the laundromat as a tenant after the Thai restaurant abandoned its obligations under the lease. The landlord is entitled to the difference in rent and profits that he would have collected from the Thai restaurant offset by his mitigated rent from the MJR laundromat. We note that if the Thai restaurant had assigned against the terms of the lease it would not be a forfeiture, merely grounds for forfeiture. The landlord may, however, waive his rights by continuing to accept rents."

Whitman v. Branson, 280 Maj. 3d 502 (1986): "The tenant, Whitman, brought an action for an injunction to mandate landlord Branson to assign the lease to the Frankel Boutique. The Frankel Boutique claimed to be financially sound, operated quality boutiques, had excellent business experience, and attracted excellent clientele. Whitman claimed that the landlord Branson was unreasonably refusing to consent to an assignment. We note that State of Major courts are split on the effect of a landlord's unreasonable refusal to consent to an assignment. Some courts treat an unreasonable refusal as a breach of the lease by the landlord. *See Fernandez v. Vasquez,* 269 Maj. 3d 1171 (1983). Other courts refuse to treat an unreasonable refusal as a breach, allowing the lessee only damages, *Rock County Savings v. Yost's Inc.,* 268 Maj. 3d 153 (1983). A few Major courts do not place the requirement of reasonableness on the landlord at all, *R. Oil Co. v. Ray's Mobile Homes, Inc.,* 276 Maj. 3d 122 (1985).

"If a landlord's refusal is unreasonable, a lease will be limited to reasonable terms, if a tenant has made a reasonable demand for consent. A tenant is thus not liable for subsequently accruing rents, but runs the risk that a landlord's refusal will later be held reasonable, thus placing the tenant in breach. (If the landlord's denial is later found reasonable, the landlord is entitled to rent and damages.)

"If the landlord unreasonably denied the assignment, a tenant is entitled to a declaratory judgment. A tenant may stay, or abandon the property, and may also be entitled to actual damages. But a tenant may not assign without consent.

"In this instance, the landlord claimed that although the boutique was a successful business, the clientele it attracted brought undesirable people (drug-related) to the neighborhood. We find no evidence to support the landlord's contention. Tenant Whitman was entitled to an injunction and damages for the unreasonable refusal by the landlord Branson to consent to assignment."

Research Memorandum #86: Motion to Strike

Oakes v. City of Fairhope, 200 Maj. 2d 826 (1962): "A motion to strike will be granted if all or part of a pleading is scandalous or irrelevant to the issues of a case. When a word or statement in a pleading casts a derogatory light on someone (usually a party to the action), then the matter is deemed scandalous or indecent and is stricken from the pleading. A court can strike from the pleadings any matter that is immaterial in developing the issues of a case.

"Material in a pleading is often not stricken because of its relevance and truthfulness in relation to the issues of the case even though the material may embarrass or offend the party against whom the pleading is filed, if it is designed to have a useful and necessary effect upon the case's outcome and no prejudice would result to the defendant.

"A motion to strike regarding material in a pleading is usually allowed when an allegation is frivolous, unnecessary, sham, impertinent, or scandalous."

In re Stevens, 144 Maj. 2d 421 (1958): "Statement that father had been previously convicted of carnal abuse of his child under the age of 18 was not scandalous prejudicial matter unnecessarily inserted in the pleadings. Therefore, the trial court was correct in its ruling to not strike because of its relevance to the issue of the abuse of the child. Judgment affirmed."

Thompson v. United States, 143 Maj. 2d 17 (1957): "Action by alleged owner of trust deed and note to quiet owner's title to trust deed and note against the United States. The United States government consequently withheld the deed and note as security for tax purposes. The complaint contained abusive and reproachful language that was not necessary or material to the cause of action.

"The trial judge correctly ordered that the word 'feloniously' be stricken wherever found in the complaint and the plaintiff redraft and file an amended complaint. Judgment affirmed."

Research Memorandum #87: Remarriage

Stuart v. Clark, 260 Maj. 3d 111 (1982): *"Stuart* is an action to recover for the wrongful death of a telephone utility employee who was electrocuted. The Major Superior Court allowed evidence of the surviving spouse's remarriage or prospective remarriage. We find that such admissibility was error. We agree with *Wakefield v. Wakefield,* 1 Maj. 4 (1907), which enunciated the rule:

> The exclusion of such evidence leaves to the understanding and experience of the jury the possibility of remarriage and avoids *excursions into collateral investigations* which, even if allowed, would leave a jury in no better than a speculative position. If we should enter upon an inquiry as to the relative merits of the new husband as a provider, coupled with his age and employment, unavoidably we should embark upon a realm of *speculation*. Adherence to the rule is consistent with the holding that, upon the death of the first husband, there is an *immediate, final, and absolute vesting* in his widow of a claim on that account. (Id. at 14.)"

Dissent. JJ. Fargut and Sleaver: "Since formulation of the rule, times have changed. We are in an era of looking at costs, mitigating damages, and allowing recovery for compensation. We no longer, in this era of litigiousness, can afford windfall plaintiff recoveries. Evidence of remarriage is relevant to the measure of damages and more probative than prejudicial, and this evidence should be admissible because it is a change in the conditions on which the suit is based. Such information should be available to the jury to mitigate damages."

Research Memorandum #88: Sale of Real Estate

Westerly v. Garret Corp., 269 Maj. 3d 1301 (1983): "Generally, mere silence is not a representation. If no representation is made, there can be no fraud or misrepresentation. Accordingly, failure to volunteer information is generally not actionable. Generally, business people acting at arm's length do not have a duty to disclose or volunteer. In this instance, the court noted that a duty to disclose may have arisen, but it was effectively disclaimed by contract provision that the sale was subject to all zoning restrictions. The seller was not obligated to disclose the zoning restrictions. The burden of discovery is placed on the purchaser."

Shockley v. Rider Truck Rental, Inc., 274 Maj. 3d 89 (1984): "The seller by use of rugs or vinyl concealed water damage. If a party takes steps to conceal material facts or averts inquiry, it may be fraudulent concealment. Fraudulent concealment is actionable."

Carr Biscuit Co. v. Moore, 125 Maj. 2d 423 (1943): "Specifically, a duty may arise if a party has a peculiar advantage in obtaining the information and the other person is justified in assuming the nonexistence of the fact. The seller's failure to disclose that the State of Major has taken temporary and permanent easements is actionable, since recordation of the easements had not taken place until after the real estate contract was signed by Carr Biscuit Company."

Gilbey v. Cooper, 143 Maj. App. 2d 119 (1958): "If a person is asked specific questions, failure to answer is not fraudulent unless there is reason to know that his/her opponent will rely on silence. In this instance silence is considered actionable. Purchaser was from out-of-town. He asked during the negotiation, 'This house isn't haunted is it?' The seller didn't answer the question. The seller did not reveal that the house had been the site of multiple murders ten years prior to sale. The purchaser did not learn of these facts until after sale. The jury properly awarded the amount of dimunition in value caused by the stigma of the prior murders, $9,000."

Major Real Property Practice Manual §41 (1986):
Scope of Real Estate Agent's Duty When Representing Both Parties. "Entering into a fiduciary relationship with the purchaser while being the listing broker may only be done with full disclosure and approval of both parties. That duty extends beyond bare written disclosure, and requires the broker to explain all relevant factors.

"A broker acting for both buyer and seller who learns of an encumbrance but fails to make further inquiry breaches the duty of good faith to the buyer and is liable for damages. If the broker acts as a middle man only, exercising no judgment, there is no agency.

"Possible measure of damages has a wide range: forfeiture of compensation; lost benefit of bargain; special damages. Punitive damages are only allowed if fraud, malice, or oppression is proved. Damages will be denied where both parties' interests were actually advanced."

Research Memorandum #89: Unlicensed Contractors and Performance of Contracts

Wahlberg v. Whig, 274 Maj. 3d 921 (1984): "Substantial performance of a construction contract is a question of fact which depends upon: (1) the extent of the defect or nonperformance; (2) the degree to which the defect or nonperformance defeats the purpose of the contract; (3) the ease of construction; and (4) the use or benefit to the owner of the work performed.

"Substantial performance exists when the contracting party fails to render full performance and all defects are considered minor.

"Once substantial performance of a construction contract has been shown, the burden of proof shifts to the owner, who must prove the existence of the defects, and that they are due to faulty workmanship.

"Failure to complete work within the time specified does not constitute a material breach of the contract or preclude substantial performance. The fact that the contract states the date of performance does not, of itself, mean that time is of the essence. Ordinarily, time is not of the essence in a contract. A provision that 'time is of the essence' must be added to a contract for performance to be considered essential to the contract.

"If there is substantial performance, the contractor may receive the contract price and the owner is relegated to having the price reduced by the amount necessary to perfect or complete the work. But if there has not been substantial performance, the owner is entitled to damages and may rescind the contract and require return of the status quo.

"We do not find that the judgment was arbitrary and capricious. Judgment affirmed, costs awarded to respondent."

Landscape Design v. Chiparelli, 276 Maj. 3d 400 (1985): "Landscape Design installed a sprinkler system in homeowner Chiparelli's garden. Chiparelli refused to pay for the system, claiming that it was not the type he verbally agreed upon. Landscape Design has brought this action, claiming breach of contract or in the alternative quantum meruit recovery, and unjust enrichment.

"Quantum meruit permits an action to be brought where there is no contract at all, either expressed or implied in fact. Quantum meruit is not an available remedy for a plaintiff with a legally enforceable contract. Restitutionary relief is allowable only when it would be inequitable or unjust for the defendant to benefit without compensating the plaintiff.

"The amount of quantum meruit recovery should correspond to reasons underlying that recovery. Reasonable value of services rendered is determined largely by the nature of the work and customary rate of pay for such work in the community and at the time the work was performed. To prevail in an action for quantum meruit, the plaintiff must satisfy five elements: (1) there must be enrichment (services were rendered and knowingly, voluntarily, accepted and not given gratuitously); (2) there must be impoverishment; (3) there must be a connection between (1) and (2); (4) there must be an absence of justification or cause for enrichment and impoverishment; and (5) there must be no other remedy at law.

"We find that there was not a valid contract between the parties and allow recovery in quantum meruit. Chiparelli received the services. The amount of Landscape Design's request appeared reasonable for the type of sprinkler installed. We do not find the trial court's judgment excessive. Reversed and remanded."

Marantville v. Weaber, 284 Maj. 3d 111 (1987): "Appellant Marantville, an unlicensed carpenter, submitted a final bill to respondent for $2,405.81. Respondent, Weaber, refused to pay more than $1,800.

"Appellant asserts that respondent would be 'unduly enriched.' The superior court dismissed appellant's claims because appellant is an unlicensed contractor. We reverse. We recognize that if the contractor is an independent business person who engages in the defined activity in his regular course of business, then that person must be registered according to the Major statute in order to force compensation. The State of Major Construction Industries Licensing Act provides:

> The purpose of the Licensing Act is to promote the general welfare of the people of Major by providing for the protection of their lives, property and economic well-being against substandard or hazardous construction, alteration, installation, connection, demolition, or repair work, and by providing protection against the fiscal irresponsibility of persons engaged in construction occupations or trades. To effect this purpose, it is the intent of the legislature that:
> A. examination, licensing, and certification of the occupations and trades within the jurisdiction of the Construction Industries Licensing Act be such as to ensure or encourage the highest quality of performance and to require compliance with approved standards, and be, to the maximum extent possible, uniform in application, procedure, and enforcement;
> B. contractors be required to furnish and maintain evidence of financial responsibility and of integrity so that the public, the laborer, the materialman, the supplier, and other parties will be protected against economic loss.

"We generally hold a strict view that if the legisla-

tive intent behind a licensing statute is to bar unlicensed contractors from maintaining actions for compensation, we will not permit recovery. But several jurisdictions other than the State of Major have held that an unlicensed contractor may maintain an action based upon quantum meruit for the actual expenses involving labor and materials expended on the project that can be proven by clear and convincing evidence. A New York court recently held that a construction company could base a claim on quantum meruit even though the company was not licensed and, therefore, not in compliance with statute and county code provisions. *See Taylor v. Youngs,* 197 New York 2d 535 (1986) (countervailing equitable principles of unjust enrichment must also be considered). We reverse and remand in accordance with our opinion that it would be unequitable to refuse appellant quantum meruit recovery."

Pro Hard

Research Memorandum #90: Wrongful Death; Emotional Distress

Restatement (2nd) of Torts §281, State of Major (1988): "An action based on common law negligence requires that there be a duty, a breach of that duty, and that the breach be the proximate cause of harm."

Meva v. Dalbert, 276 Maj. 3d 60 (1985): "This case raises the issue of liability of a tavern owner for injuries to patrons. In an establishment where intoxicating liquors are sold the tavern owner/operator, while not an insurer of the safety of his patrons, owes a duty to his patrons to exercise reasonable care and vigilance to protect them from foreseeable injury, mistreatment, or annoyance by other patrons. Richard was a patron who had caused a fight earlier in the evening, and was told to leave. Dalbert, an experienced tavern keeper, 'wise in the ways of pugnacious patrons,' instructed the bartender to call the police if Richard returned and to pass those instructions on to the bartender coming on shift. The duty of care was breached by the bartender when she did not call the police or eject Richard, who later returned. Richard subsequently injured plaintiff, Meva, a patron in the tavern.

"Foreseeability of risk of harm to plaintiff was established when Dalbert testified at trial, 'Under the circumstances known to me on the evening in question, and with my experience in the tavern business I guess I could anticipate that Richard might well return to renew his quarrel with Meva.' See Trial Transcript at 128." P won

Dissent. J. Beaver: "I sharply differ from the majority. A duty of reasonable care requires notice of the peril confronting a guest. There was no actual notice to the tavern operator of peril to his guest where the plaintiff's injury was caused by a sudden affray on a busy evening. Absent actual notice, there was no foreseeable risk. I would reverse the judgment."

Nan v. Brady, 280 Maj. 3d 22 (1986): "Brady the tavern owner was not liable to a patron shot by a third person. Nan was a patron at Brady's tavern. Nan was dancing with the assailant Colby's estranged girlfriend. The occurrences were so highly extraordinary or improbable as to be wholly beyond the range of expectability. We hold that the shooting of Nan was not foreseeable and therefore there was no breach of any duty owed by the tavern owner to the patron.

" 'The duty to use care to avoid injury to others arises from the foreseeability of the risk created,' see *Meva v. Dalbert*, 276 Maj. 3d 60 (1985). The foreseeability of risk was not evident where there was a slapping incident between Nan and Colby two weeks before; the estranged girlfriend had advised Brady of her fear that she would be killed by her ex-boyfriend and the girlfriend had requested Brady to call the police if the boyfriend appeared.

"The factors which we considered in determining that the owner Brady did not breach the duty of reasonable care were that the assailant boyfriend appeared calm (although he had been drinking for four hours previously at another bar and was refused service there); Brady had not seen or served the assailant the night of the shooting; Brady had no personal knowledge of when the assailant had threatened the girlfriend, what the threat was, or that he had a propensity to use a gun; the assailant entered through a back door used mainly by daytime deliverymen; and the incident took fifteen to twenty seconds from the time the assailant confronted the plaintiff until the time the plaintiff was shot. Judgment affirmed."

Michaels v. Seawind Tavern, Inc., 280 Maj. 3d 116 (1986): "This case concerns a wrongful death action. Plaintiff's husband was shot while at the Seawind Tavern. The trial court found that the plaintiff's husband's injury was not foreseeable even though three weeks earlier the assailant had been removed from the tavern for carrying a concealed weapon. The court held that the tavern owner and his agent were not required to search the assailant every time he entered the tavern.

"We agree with the factors the Appellate court used in affirming the trial court judgment that the assailant's acts were not foreseeable. The assailant appeared quiet and in full control; he had only two drinks in two hours; his gun was concealed (hidden in a shoulder holster under a leather jacket); and the gun discharged accidentally when the assailant attempted to unload it under the table. Because the assailant did not appear intoxicated, there was no notice (or it was not foreseeable) that the assailant posed a threat to other patrons, see dissent in *Meva v. Dalbert*, 276 Maj. 3d 60 (1985). We reject the notion that liability should be imposed because the tavern served intoxicants to an already intoxicated person. 'His state of sobriety must be judged by the way he appeared to those about him, not by what a blood test later reveals." See *Nock v. Newcity*, 143 Maj. App. 2d 4 (1958).

"Strict liability should not be imposed against one who furnishes liquor to a patron who commits a tort while intoxicated. Here the assailant had a .16 blood-alcohol reading. The common law does not permit liability to attach without a concomitant showing of a violation of an established standard of reasonable care thereby causing foreseeable injury. *Nock v. Newcity*, supra at 917. The defendant's employees did not have notice that they were furnishing liquor to an individual who was intoxicated where he had ordered only two drinks while in the tavern, he was never boisterous, and he appeared quiet and in full control of his faculties."

O'Leary v. Johns, 268 Maj. 3d 576 (1983): "The defendant had a Christmas party and supplied food, refreshments, and alcoholic beverages. Mr. Wolf, a friend of the defendant Johns, attended the party and became intoxicated. Wolf later drove away from the party and struck plaintiff, O'Leary. Plaintiffs asserted the defendants were negligent because they furnished alcohol to Wolf knowing that Wolf was already intoxicated and that Wolf would be unable to safely drive away from the party.

"We reject plaintiff's claim that the furnishing of alcohol to a person already intoxicated was negligence as a matter of law. Plaintiffs relied upon the following statute:

> (a)   No person shall sell any liquor to any person apparently under the influence of liquor.
> (b)   Every person who violates any provision of this title or the accompanying liquor board regulations shall be guilty of a violation of this title, whether otherwise declared or not, and is subject to a fine of $1,000. Violation of this statute is not a criminal offense.

"There is no clear legislative intent to create a right to recover civil damages for those who were engaged in a 'purely social setting.' The expansion of such liability is at this time within the province of the legislature. We choose to not address it at this time."

Fried v. Lice, 269 Maj. 3d 800 (1983): "We affirm the dismissal of plaintiff's claim upon summary judgment. Both the trial and appellate courts correctly rejected plaintiff's argument that liquor furnished to one in violation of a statute imposes civil liability.

"Unless the recipient is obviously intoxicated, in a state of helplessness, or within a special relationship to the supplier, any further expansion of liability as a policy decision should be made by the legislature after full investigation, debate, and examination of the relative merits of both positions.

"The trial court found that Fried 'was not in such a state of helplessness or debauchery as to be deprived of his will power or responsibility for his behavior.' "

Old v. Bacon Inn, 284 Maj. 3d 777 (1987): "We affirm the Appellate ruling that the violation of a Major statute prohibiting the sale of alcohol to minors constitutes negligence per se. In *Old,* a restaurant owner continued to serve seventeen-year-old Richard Old despite the fact that Old was obviously intoxicated. Old drove away from a cocktail lounge and was killed in a one-car accident. The plaintiffs reasoned that since a specific statute makes the furnishing of alcohol to minors a misdemeanor, the unlawful furnishing constituted negligence per se. We agree."

Burger v. Calhoun, 274 Maj. 3d 42 (1984): "Contributory negligence of a decedent can be imputed to the heirs in a wrongful death case. But since the adoption of the comparative fault doctrine in our state, we no longer may need to consider assumption of risk as a necessary defense. The appellate court properly ruled that the jury should have been instructed that it should consider contributory negligence of plaintiff's decedent Burger as being a proximate cause of decedent's injury and death. Decedent Burger was dancing with defendant Calhoun's ex-girlfriend at the time decedent Burger was shot. Defendant Calhoun stated, 'Shove off or I'll shoot you.' The girlfriend told Burger to ignore Calhoun. Calhoun repeated his threat and Burger, not knowing Calhoun had a gun, said 'Bug off, twirp.' Calhoun then shot Burger."

Emotional Distress

Noe v. Flowers, 281 Maj. 3d 400 (1986): "Judgment affirmed for Plaintiffs for emotional distress. Plaintiffs' parents witnessed defendant lifeguard's unsuccessful rescue and revival of Plaintiffs' four-year-old daughter from the lake into which she wandered. Lifeguards were not equipped with a boat or flotation devices. Plaintiffs after the incident suffered from physical and mental injuries: headaches, nervous indigestion, insomnia, and emotional distress.

"We are continually concerned about the genuineness of plaintiffs' emotional distress and the potential scope of defendant's liability. Not all acts give rise to emotional distress. Only acts which if considered by reasonable persons would be outrageous or reckless will be considered as actionable.

"Judicial reluctance to recognize emotional tranquility as deserving legal protection has traditionally been grounded in a variety of policy rationales: (1) the difficulty of quantifying 'intangible' injuries by objective standards, (2) the tenuous proximate cause relationship between defendant's conduct and plaintiff's subjective emotional response, (3) the specter of a flood of fraudulent claims, and (4) unlimited liability for defendants. To address these considerations, the Major courts generally focus on six elements in determining liability:

(1) The bystander's proximity to the accident scene;
(2) The bystander's immediate perception of the accident;
(3) A close relationship between the plaintiff and the primary victim;
(4) Foreseeability of the bystander's presence;
(5) Resulting degree (and manifestation) of injury to the plaintiff;
(6) Degree of outrage or recklessness of the act."

Gun Manufacturer

Martin v. AJB, Inc., 268 Ill. App. 3d 11 (1987): "During January of 1981, Donovan and James Barnes shot and killed Larry Martin. Plaintiffs seek to recover for the injuries suffered by Martin, but not from the Barnes brothers, who have little or no money. Plaintiffs have filed this action against AJB, the manufacturer of the gun used by the Barnes, alleging that the gun was an unreasonably dangerous product and that AJB was therefore strictly liable for the damage caused by the weapon. The trial court found no support for plaintiffs' theory in Major law and dismissed the suit for failure to state a cause of action.

"Plaintiffs' claim, in essence, is that manufacturing and selling handguns to the public is an ultrahazardous activity that gives rise to strict liability for any damage done by the guns.

"Illinois recognizes strict liability under two theories: unreasonably dangerous defective products and ultrahazardous activities. Strict products liability follows the Restatement (Second) of Torts (1965), which imposes strict liability upon one 'who sells any product in a defective condition unreasonably dangerous to the user or consumer or to his property.' Under Illinois law, a product is 'unreasonably dangerous' when it is dangerous to an extent beyond that which would be contemplated by the ordinary consumer who purchases it, with the ordinary knowledge common to the community as to its characteristics.

"Plaintiff has not directly pursued a products liability approach here because the gun involved in the shootings was not defective and posed an obvious danger that required no warning, and thus was not unreasonably dangerous. Judgment affirmed."

Olen v. Richardson Guns, Inc., 269 Md. App. 3d 14 (1983): "Olen was injured when an unnamed assailant shot him in the chest during an armed robbery of the grocery store where he was employed. The weapon used in the crime was a Richardson Revolver Handgun, designed, marketed, assembled, and sold by Richardson Guns, Inc.

"Olen and his wife filed a tort action against Richardson Guns, Inc. in the Circuit Court for Mont County, setting forth several theories for recovery. The first claim was strict liability, plaintiffs claiming the handgun was 'abnormally dangerous.' Claim two, also strict liability, alleged the handgun was defective in its 'marketing, promotion, distribution and design,' rendering it 'unreasonably dangerous.' Claim three rested on a negligence theory. Claim four, for loss of consortium, was due to negligence.

"The trial court dismissed plaintiffs' claims for failure to state a claim for relief. We reverse and remand.

"This court has repeatedly said, 'The common law is not static; its life and heart is its dynamism—its ability to keep pace with the world while constantly searching for just and fair solutions to pressing societal problems.' *Harris v. Board of Educ.*, 295 Md. 442 (1983). Indeed, we have not hesitated to change the common law to permit new actions or remedies where we have concluded that such course was justified.

"In our view, generally to impose strict liability upon the manufacturers or marketers of handguns for gunshot injuries resulting from the misuse of handguns by others would be contrary to Maryland public policy as set forth by the Legislature.

"There is, however, a limited category of handguns which clearly is not sanctioned as a matter of public policy. To impose strict liability upon the manufacturers and marketers of these handguns, in instances of gunshot wounds caused by criminal use, would not be contrary to the policy embodied in the enactments of the General Assembly. This type of handgun, commonly known as a 'Saturday Night Special,' presents particular problems for law enforcement officials. Saturday Night Specials are generally characterized by short barrels, light weight, easy concealability, low cost, use of cheap quality materials, poor manufacture, inaccuracy and unreliability. These characteristics render the Saturday Night Special particularly attractive for criminal use and virtually useless for the legitimate purposes of law enforcement, sport, and protection of persons, property and business.

"The legislative policies of both the United States Congress and the Maryland Assembly reflect the view that Saturday Night Specials comprise a distinct category of handguns that, because of their characteristics, should be treated differently from other handguns. See Gun Control Act of 1965, 82 Federal Code Sect. 291; Maryland Code Sect. 30 (1982).

"Saturday Night Specials are largely unfit for any of the recognized legitimate uses sanctioned by the Maryland gun control legislation. They are too inaccurate, unreliable and poorly made for use by law enforcement personnel, sportsmen, homeowners or businessmen. The chief 'value' a Saturday Night Special handgun has is in criminal activity, because of its easy concealability and low price.

"Moreover, the manufacturer or marketer of a Saturday Night Special knows or ought to know that it is making or selling a product principally to be used in criminal activity. For example, a salesman for Richardson Guns, describing what he terms to be a 'special attribute' of a Richardson handgun, was said to have told a potential handgun retailer, 'If your store is anywhere near a high crime area, these ought to sell real well. This is more assuredly a crime gun.'

"For the above reason, we conclude that it is entirely consistent with public policy to hold the manufacturers and marketers of Saturday Night Special handguns strictly liable to innocent persons who suffer gunshot injuries from the criminal use of their products. In light of the ever-growing number of deaths and injuries due to such handguns being used in criminal activity, the imposition of such liability is warranted by today's circumstances.

"Reversed and remanded in accordance with this opinion. Each party to pay its own costs."